THE CAMBRIDGE HISTORY OF MORAL
PHILOSOPHY

With fifty-four chapters charting the development of moral philosophy in the Western world, this volume examines the key thinkers and texts and their influence on the history of moral thought from the pre-Socratics to the present day. Topics including Epicureanism, humanism, Jewish and Arabic thought, perfectionism, pragmatism, idealism and intuitionism are all explored, as are figures including Aristotle, Boethius, Spinoza, Hobbes, Hume, Kant, Hegel, Mill, Nietzsche, Heidegger, Sartre and Rawls, as well as numerous key ideas and schools of thought. Chapters are written by leading experts in the field, drawing on the latest research to offer rigorous analysis of the canonical figures and movements of this branch of philosophy. The volume provides a comprehensive yet philosophically advanced resource for students and teachers alike as they approach, and refine their understanding of, the central issues in moral thought.

SACHA GOLOB is a Senior Lecturer in Philosophy and the Director of the Centre for Philosophy and the Visual Arts at King's College London. He is the author of *Heidegger on Concepts, Freedom and Normativity* (Cambridge 2014), and of articles on the histories of French and German philosophy and the philosophy of mind.

JENS TIMMERMANN is Professor of Moral Philosophy at the University of St Andrews. He is the co-editor of *Kant's 'Critique of Practical Reason': A Critical Guide* (Cambridge 2010) and of *Immanuel Kant: Groundwork of the Metaphysics of Morals* (Cambridge 2011).

THE CAMBRIDGE
HISTORY OF
MORAL PHILOSOPHY

★

Edited by

SACHA GOLOB

King's College London

JENS TIMMERMANN

University of St Andrews, Scotland

 CAMBRIDGE
UNIVERSITY PRESS

CAMBRIDGE
UNIVERSITY PRESS

Shaftesbury Road, Cambridge CB2 8EA, United Kingdom

One Liberty Plaza, 20th Floor, New York, NY 10006, USA

477 Williamstown Road, Port Melbourne, VIC 3207, Australia

314–321, 3rd Floor, Plot 3, Splendor Forum, Jasola District Centre, New Delhi – 110025, India

103 Penang Road, #05–06/07, Visioncrest Commercial, Singapore 238467

Cambridge University Press is part of Cambridge University Press & Assessment,
a department of the University of Cambridge.

We share the University's mission to contribute to society through the pursuit of
education, learning and research at the highest international levels of excellence.

www.cambridge.org
Information on this title: www.cambridge.org/9781009364034

DOI: 10.1017/9781139519267

First published 2017
First paperback edition 2023

A catalogue record for this publication is available from the British Library

Library of Congress Cataloging-in-Publication data
NAMES: Golob, Sacha, 1981– editor.
TITLE: The Cambridge history of moral philosophy / edited by Sacha Golob,
King's College London, Jens Timmermann, University of St Andrews, Scotland.
DESCRIPTION: New York : Cambridge University Press, 2017. | Includes
bibliographical references and index.
IDENTIFIERS: LCCN 2017012392 | ISBN 9781107033054 (alk. paper)
SUBJECTS: LCSH: Ethics – History.
CLASSIFICATION: LCCBJ71.C36 2017 | DDC 170.9–dc23
LC record available at https://lccn.loc.gov/2017012392

ISBN   978-1-107-03305-4   Hardback
ISBN   978-1-009-36403-4   Paperback

Contents

Contents

Contents

Contents

Contributors

ANNA AKASOY, Department of History, CUNY Graduate Center

STEFANO BACIN, Department of Philosophy, Università di Milano

GREGORY BROWN, Department of Philosophy, University of Houston

SARAH BYERS, Department of Philosophy, Boston College

DESMOND M. CLARKE, Department of Philosophy, University of Cork

JESSE COUENHOVEN, Department of Humanities, Villanova University

STEPHEN DARWALL, Department of Philosophy, Yale University

SABRINA EBBERSMEYER, Philosophy Section, Københavns Universitet

BEN EGGLESTON, Department of Philosophy, University of Kansas

JOHN ERIKSSON, Department of Philosophy, Linguistics and Theory of Science, Göteborgs Universitet

KATRIN FLIKSCHUH, Department of Government, London School of Economics

SEBASTIAN GARDNER, Department of Philosophy, University College London

SACHA GOLOB, Department of Philosophy, King's College London

RUSSELL B. GOODMAN, Department of Philosophy, University of New Mexico

PAUL GUYER, Department of Philosophy, Brown University

EDWARD HARCOURT, Faculty of Philosophy, University of Oxford, and Keble College, Oxford

JAMES A. HARRIS, Department of Philosophy, University of St Andrews

LAWRENCE HATAB, Department of Philosophy, Old Dominion University

TOBIAS HOFFMANN, School of Philosophy, The Catholic University of America

SARAH HUTTON, Department of Philosophy, University of York

BRAD INWOOD, Departments of Classics and Philosophy, Yale University

DUDLEY KNOWLES, Department of Philosophy, University of Glasgow

KATARZYNA DE LAZARI-RADEK, Department of Philosophy, Uniwersytet Łódzki

DAVID LEVY, Department of Philosophy, University of Edinburgh

S.A. LLOYD, School of Philosophy, University of Southern California

A.G. LONG, School of Classics, University of St Andrews

CHRISTOPHER MACLEOD, Department of Politics, Philosophy and Religion, University of Lancaster

R. ZACHARY MANIS, Department of Theology, Southwest Baptist University

JOHN MARENBON, Trinity College, University of Cambridge

TODD MAY, Department of Philosophy and Religion, Clemson University

CHERYL MISAK, Department of Philosophy, University of Toronto

JÖRN MÜLLER, Institute of Philosophy, Julius-Maximilians-Universität Würzburg

STEVEN NADLER, Department of Politics, University of Wisconsin-Madison

PETER NIESEN, Department of Politics, Universität Hamburg

MICHAEL PAKALUK, Busch School of Business and Economics, The Catholic University of America

JEFFREY REIMAN, Department of Philosophy and Religion, American University

SIMON ROBERTSON, Department of Philosophy, Cardiff University

CATHERINE ROWETT, Department of Philosophy, University of East Anglia

TAMAR RUDAVSKY, Department of Philosophy, Ohio State University

FRED RUSH, Department of Philosophy, University of Notre Dame

ALEXANDRINE SCHNIEWIND, Department of Philosophy, Université de Lausanne

LISA SHAPIRO, Department of Philosophy, Simon Fraser University

SUSAN MELD SHELL, Department of Political Science, Boston College

CRAIG SMITH, School of Social and Political Sciences, University of Glasgow

JEAN-LUC SOLÈRE, Department of Philosophy, Boston College / CNRS, PSL Research University, LEM (UMR 8584)

ROBERT STERN, Department of Philosophy, University of Sheffield

PHILIP STRATTON-LAKE, Department of Philosophy, University of Reading

JENS TIMMERMANN, Department of Philosophy, University of St Andrews

VOULA TSOUNA, Department of Philosophy, University of California, Santa Barbara

KATJA MARIA VOGT, Department of Philosophy, Columbia University

JAMES WARREN, Faculty of Classics, University of Cambridge

NICOLAS DE WARREN, Husserl Archives and Pennsylvania State University

ALISTAIR WELCHMAN, Department of Philosophy and Classics, University of Texas at San Antonio

ALLEN WOOD, Department of Philosophy, Indiana University Bloomington

Acknowledgements

Involving well over sixty contributors and referees, this book has been a long time in the making: we would like to express our gratitude to all involved for their patience. Our thanks in particular go to Peter Adamson, Tobias Hoffmann, John Marenbon, Tom Pink and Voula Tsouna for their advice and guidance. Above all, we should like to thank Hilary Gaskin and her colleagues Daniel Brown, Gillian Dadd, Christina Sarigiannidou and Ross Stewart at Cambridge University Press for their support throughout the process, and Virginia Catmur for her heroic copy-editing.

Introduction

SACHA GOLOB AND JENS TIMMERMANN

This book has what might seem an impossible goal: to provide in a single volume a sophisticated analysis of the dominant figures in the development of Western moral thought from the pre-Socratics through to the present day. Chronologically, this spans close to three thousand years. Exegetically, most of the figures involved are already the subjects of a secondary literature running into thousands of publications – in the case of authors such as Plato or Aristotle, of course, it goes far beyond even that. Offering a synoptic treatment of the shifting development of ethical and meta-ethical thought over this time frame is thus difficult, but it is also, we believe, extremely important – and for at least three reasons.

First, and most obviously, the type of focussed analysis offered in this volume provides a natural point of orientation for anyone approaching a given thinker or school for the first time. This applies both to scholars of one period interested in examining how the questions and the debates with which they are familiar are developed, discussed or dismissed in a very different intellectual context, and to those working on contemporary ethics or meta-ethics who want to explore some of the sedimented background that shapes current thinking on these matters. We have sought throughout to ensure that all chapters are accessible without specific prior knowledge of the philosopher's terminology or technical apparatus. Contributors have also flagged, at the end of each chapter, secondary literature especially suitable for further reading: these items are marked with an asterisk.

Second, by offering an overview of each figure or school, the chapters in this volume are able to sustain a form of clarity that is not always possible in much lengthier and more detailed works. In short, there are benefits in operating at all of the possible levels of resolution when doing the history of philosophy, and we believe that the combination of concision and use of the latest research will allow the chapters here to shed new light even on authors whom the reader may know very well.

Third, the scope of the volume fosters an important type of conceptual juxtaposition. In some cases, this juxtaposition is formally recognised, as it tracks patterns of influence so significant that they dictate the agenda: for example, the chapter on Albert, Aquinas and the issue of 'Christian Aristotelianism'. In many other cases, however, the juxtapositions involved occur naturally in the mind of the reader as he or she sees questions, methods and concepts picked up, reformulated and transmuted by different authors. Sometimes this takes the form of cross-period thematic similarities – for example, the complex pattern of similarities and dissimilarities between aspects of Anselm's position and parts of Kant's. Sometimes it takes the form of changes in what one might call the 'standing constraints', the underlying assumptions in a given period on what any adequate moral theory or moral method should look like. A particularly prominent example is the question of how philosophy should interact with revealed religion, an issue central to the discussion of cases ranging from medieval Jewish thought through the Scholasticism of the later middle ages to Bayle, Kant and others. The developments in such constraints that this book chronicles are, of course, in part a result of factors outside of philosophical competence – industrialisation, for example. But by bringing together these authors and schools in a single volume, the hope is to provide a bird's eye view of some of the key conceptual shifts that feed into this type of large-scale change in the moral landscape.

Edited volumes often open with an introduction that provides a series of potted summaries of the various contributions. Given the scale of the present text, that would not be helpful, and we will leave the individual chapters to speak for themselves. It may help, however to make three brief remarks that can serve as background to what follows.

In the opening paragraph of this introduction, we moved fluidly between talk of 'ethics' and talk of 'morals'. This type of shift is particularly visible in contemporary writing. Indeed, it is to a large extent forced by current terminology: even those who see themselves as doing moral philosophy are unlikely to talk about 'meta-morals' rather than 'meta-ethics'. For some of the authors and movements discussed below much the same applies – over half of the contributors state that they will use 'ethics' and 'morals' interchangeably, with the same applying to their cognates. But for others the distinction marks a fundamental difference. Compare, for example, Hegel and the Habermas of texts such as *Justification and Application*. Both agree that there is a philosophical distinction to be drawn between ethics and morals; and they are readable as having opposing views on the explanatory priority of the two. More broadly there is also the further issue, one that arises particularly but not exclusively when ethics and morality are equated, of whether the normative standards discussed in what follows are really best thought of as either moral *or* ethical (rather than, say, ontological). This type of issue is particularly visible in modern thinkers – it is discussed extensively here, for example, in relation both to Marx and to Heidegger. Ultimately, the philosophical theories that follow are attempts to gloss terms like 'morality' and 'ethics', and to trace their boundaries – this introduction can serve only to highlight the issue, and particularly the complex problems, problems of translation in the deepest sense, that arise when one tries to switch between these ideas in a Greek or German Idealist or French post-war context.

The next issue concerns scope. This volume is intended not as a history of moral thought *simpliciter*, but rather of moral thought within the Western tradition. Terms like 'Western' are evidently as contested and problematic as 'moral', but we have attempted to read the category broadly. It thus includes, for example, a study of traditions that existed to some degree in dialogue with the standard Western canon – for example, medieval Islamicate thought. Why is the text limited in this fashion? One immediate reason is simply scope – no global study of moral thought (one which would immediately make the issue of what constitutes the moral even more problematic) could hope to achieve the desired balance between tightness of focus and depth of coverage in a single volume. A second reason is that in concentrating on a single tradition, broadly construed, one in which many of the figures would have read or at least known of many of those who preceded them, the volume is able to track and illustrate the way in which arguments and concepts are appropriated, challenged and transformed by a philosopher and his or her successors. This is an important part of what makes the volume a *history*, rather than simply a chronological list or a study of certain conceptual problems that happened to have been addressed by many different people in many different places – and it would not be possible in a study that encompassed large numbers of authors who lacked this kind of common textual framework.[1]

The final issue concerns the distinctive status of moral philosophy and its interaction with other forms of reflection. Moral philosophy is characterised by the kind of urgency that other branches of philosophy lack. There is a perfectly coherent sense in which questions about the nature of time, the identity of

---

[1] One might agree with this and nevertheless object that the histories, in this sense, of non-Western thinkers have been inexcusably neglected by professional philosophers. We are sympathetic to that view, but rectifying that failing is not the task of the present text.

persons, the possibility of causation or life after death can be postponed; one may even reach the conclusion that they do not permit of definitive universal answers at all. Things are different in moral matters. If we suspend judgement about what to do we will, in effect, have done something already. Moreover, we will have done something about which we do not know whether it was justified. In this sense, action is inevitable in a way in which belief is not. Yet there are rarely any sharp boundaries between moral philosophy and other philosophical and non-philosophical disciplines. Which of the many other areas – epistemology, metaphysics, theology, political philosophy, psychology, education and aesthetics – are principally aligned with moral philosophy, even whether it is perceived as a distinct discipline and, if so, what it is called, largely depends on historical circumstances. One of the aims of this volume is to bring that out, and to show how ethics and morals have been variously aligned with ontology, politics, aesthetics, mathematics and others depending on the particular assumptions and goals of the thinker in question.

As will become clear in what follows, the solutions proposed to the question of how to lead our lives differ vastly. It is, for instance, tempting to assume that the moral status of an action depends on the effects it has on the well-being of the agent, the community, the human race in general or some even broader group of beings – which in turn immediately leads to the question of what well-being consists in. It is also plausible to assume that, as human beings, we ought to obey certain authoritative laws; but then we would also like to know what makes these laws authoritative, whether they are, for instance, imposed upon us by some higher being, by society or by the very nature of these laws. Or maybe we think that agreement among rational agents as such is what makes a good action good (to name but a few of many available options). And there are further problems that a moral philosopher, of whatever persuasion, needs to address. How do we come to apprehend the norms or values that underpin good choices? How do we come to act on them? What, if anything, separates judgement or apprehension from action? Can moral goodness be taught, and if so how? And do any of these answers depend on a notion of freedom of the will that is incompatible with the various determinisms philosophy and theology have to offer? What is more, disagreement about these higher-level as well as concrete moral questions among philosophers and ordinary moral agents may well fuel scepticism as to whether there *are* universal answers after all. For the reasons mentioned above, the challenge then is whether such scepticism is sustainable. The fifty-four chapters united in this volume reflect the diversity and richness of these questions, and of the methods and approaches which have been employed to make sense of them throughout the history of moral philosophy.

Ethics before Socrates

CATHERINE ROWETT

It is sometimes said that no one talked about ethics until Socrates diverted philosophy from its early investigations into nature towards matters of practical value. The popularity of this rather inaccurate claim may be due to Aristotle, or perhaps Cicero.[1] Part of my aim in this chapter is to put the record straight, to investigate what we can find among the Presocratic philosophers that can be construed as ethical, and to note a few small but interesting contributions made by these thinkers to the development of Western moral philosophy. Since the Sophists, who are sometimes counted among the Presocratics, are, for the purposes of this volume, included with Socrates in Chapter 2, our task in this chapter is to focus on ethical thought before the Sophists. That means we shall be covering the period up to the fifth century BCE. Before going further we should also note that most of the work of the Presocratic philosophers is lost, so we must reconstruct their ideas and arguments from a mixture of quotations in later writers and second-hand reports (*testimonia*). I cite the quoted fragments using the standard referencing system from Diels-Kranz.[2]

Obviously, the highly sophisticated challenges to traditional ethics that we find in the Presocratics, the Sophists and Socrates did not emerge out of nothing. When they investigate the notion of 'virtue', *aretê* – so prominent in Greek ethics – Greek philosophers are deploying and scrutinizing a concept that was familiar from ordinary language. 'Virtue' for any society consists in whatever characteristics command admiration and respect, which are the standard target in the society's education and training for young citizens. Just as modern societies privilege certain behaviors and attitudes of mind, so also

---

[1] Probably it was Aristotle (*Parts of Animals* 642a28; *Metaphysics* 987b1–4). See also Cicero *Tusculan Disputations* 5.4.10 and *Academica* 1.5.15.

[2] Diels and Kranz 1951. All subsequent editions and translations have concordances that link to these references.

did the social conditioning of ancient Greek *polis* cultures. These values are then the starting point of their enquiries into ethics.

In archaic Greece, a male child from a good family typically took classes with a grammar teacher and a music teacher, learning to read, copy and sing the works of the poets. He would also learn wrestling and athletics at the gym. Training in body and soul were needed to turn a boy into what a man should be. The psychological part of this training included poetry by Homer and Hesiod, and also the lyric poets, such as Simonides (c. 500 BCE). In Plato's dialogue *Protagoras*, set in about 433 BCE, the characters discuss some lines from a poem by Simonides about how hard it is to be good.[3] Plato's character Protagoras asserts that the mark of a properly educated man is the ability to discuss poetry and to distinguish what is well said from what is not.[4] Such discussions were not primarily literary or aesthetic, as the example in *Protagoras* shows: Protagoras considers whether Simonides' views about virtue and its attainability are consistent. The discussion of poetry was clearly not just a way to entertain friends. It provided an opportunity to engage with the ideas expressed there, in critical thinking and discussion. The poet is taken as a partner in the debate: someone who offers an opinion. The educated man is then expected to explain it, debate it, compare it with rival views in other poems. In studying and discussing the poets, young citizens would learn to think and ask questions, not just habituate themselves to an existing moral code (though there clearly was some of that).[5]

DO THE GODS LIE?

Homer's poems portray many colorful human characters, many of them with failings and character traits unsuitable for emulation. Achilles and Agamemnon squabble because Agamemnon (who still has a wife at home) has commandeered Achilles' favorite war prize (a princess, whose parents and husband Achilles had killed when the Greeks sacked Lyrnessus). That squabble forms the starting point of the Iliad; and things show little improvement in the rest of the poem.[6] Equally, in the Odyssey, the wily Odysseus displays a canny habit of

[3] Plato *Protagoras* 338e–347b. The poem is otherwise lost, apart from the lines that Plato quotes.
[4] *Protagoras* 339a.
[5] On early Greek moral thought, including Homer and Pindar, see McKirahan 1994: 356–63.
[6] Arguably the Trojans appear more admirable, morally, than the Greeks. See Mackie 1996 and Hall 1989, and contrast the nineteenth-century attempt to show otherwise in Gladstone 1858.

lying to avoid trouble. Some Homeric characters are admirable (Penelope for instance); others are not. Rather than presenting these characters as ideal role models, schoolmasters surely must have valued the poems because they dramatize difficult choices in life, and illustrate the need for strength of character, to bear up through trials and misfortunes. There are also similar themes in Greek tragedy – as when Agamemnon must decide whether to sacrifice his daughter[7] and when Antigone opts to bury her traitor brother.[8] Students who read or performed these plays would clearly acquire a vivid understanding of the dilemmas and risks of adult life, and how to face misfortune with dignity.

It was not only the mortals who were portrayed as fickle and false, but also (more problematically, it seems) the gods. Homer's gods engage in deception, protect their favorites, set the odds against one in battle. Arguably such stories offer a salutary lesson for life. There is explanatory value in the idea that fortune is fickle, and that bad luck might be visited upon us by 'the gods'. We could see these motifs as evoking something equivalent to the idea that unfairness is built into the metaphysics of the world. Potentially this represents an ethical assessment of our predicament that we could still endorse even now.

On the other hand, by attributing this unpredictability to the disreputable behavior of the *gods*, the poets exposed themselves to potential criticism. In the sixth century BCE, the philosopher-poet Xenophanes developed a new philosophical notion of the divine as a single, unitary, all-powerful being, with perfect moral standards. In comparison with that ideal god, Xenophanes saw serious deficiencies in those all-too-human gods in Homer and the other poets.[9] In Fragment 11, he writes:

> Everything that's shameful and disgusting among human beings–
> all this, Homer and Hesiod have attributed to the gods!
> Stealing, adulterous affairs, cheating each other.

His implicit argument can be understood as follows: (1) proper gods are perfect, and cannot cheat or be deceived; (2) in Homer and Hesiod, the gods are immoral and easily corrupted; (3) therefore Homer and Hesiod present bad theology. His reasoning seems to draw on the following three ethical assumptions: first, the divine perfections include moral perfection; second, what is offensive among mortals is, or should be, equally offensive among gods, which implies that morality is no mere mortal convention; and third, one can criticize the poets (despite their reputation as the traditional

---

[7] Aeschylus *Agamemnon* 204–27. See Nussbaum 1986.   [8] Sophocles *Antigone*.
[9] Plato *Republic* Book 3 continues the same campaign, a century or more later.

authority concerning theology and morality), because (apparently) reasoning trumps tradition in judging theological and ethical truth.

Besides philosophical poems, Xenophanes wrote after-dinner lyrics, of which two survive complete. In one of these (Fragment 2) Xenophanes remarks on the mistaken values of the *polis*, insofar as it typically bestows great honors on those who win at the Olympic Games. This is silly, he suggests, since athletic ability is of no real value to the athlete's city: no city improves its laws or fattens its coffers by winning in the Olympics. By contrast, real benefits can accrue if the city has a wise person in charge, so that is what should be honored and rewarded. It seems clear that Xenophanes is thinking of his own role as philosopher, and that he considers it a useful one and deserving of honor. The wise man contributes real benefits to the city's political and economic prosperity. Among other things, Xenophanes may well be thinking of the widespread practice of inviting a 'wise man' to draft the constitutions for new colonies, or to revise existing codes of law.[10]

In the other poem (Fragment 1), Xenophanes reflects on proper behavior at drinking parties. He is no puritan: 'It's not impolite to drink as much as you can take, so long as you can still get home without assistance.'[11] On the other hand, he has some ethical advice to give about what kind of stories to tell in the sympotic entertainment: one should not tell of the battles of Titans, Giants and Centaurs, he says, which are just figments of past ages. One should speak rather of historical deeds of valor (or virtue – the scope is unclear), based on actual living memory.[12]

NATURAL LAW AND HUMAN MORALITY

In Heraclitus (c. 500 BCE) we find what looks like a rival to Xenophanes' views on divinity, although much is uncertain, due to the obscurity and brevity of the Heraclitean sayings. Certainly, Homer and Hesiod come in for further attacks. Heraclitus wants Homer beaten and expelled from the poetry contests (along with Archilochus);[13] he challenges Hesiod's reputation as a teacher of 'many things' (referring, perhaps, to the practical advice in *Works and Days*).[14] On the other hand, Heraclitus denies that we can read off

---

[10] Xenophanes fr 2.19 DK. Cf. Aelian *Varia Historia* 3.17 on known philosophers involved in political guidance or legislation (though Xenophanes is not included there).

[11] Xenophanes frr 1.17–18 DK. [12] Xenophanes fr 1.20 DK. [13] Heraclitus fr 42 DK.

[14] Heraclitus fr 57 DK. Cf. fr 40 DK which criticizes Hesiod, Pythagoras, Xenophanes and Hecataeus for achieving polymathy without wisdom.

theological ethical standards from human ones. As regards ethics (*êthos*), he says, 'human life lacks standards, while the divine life has them'.[15] And 'Compared to God, the wisest human resembles an ape, in wisdom, beauty and everything else.'[16] So when he says 'To God, all things are noble and good and just, but human beings have understood some of them to be unjust and others just',[17] it seems that Heraclitus probably means that we cannot discover absolute moral truths by looking at human moral codes. This could imply that there are no absolute moral truths. Alternatively he may mean that, if such truths exist, they are quite unlike morality as we know it. On the other hand some sayings suggest a close dependency connection between divine morality and civic customs: Fragment 114 claims that human customs draw nourishment from a divine law and are to be respected and defended. And in Fragment 53 Heraclitus pithily observes that war (here called 'king') is what divides people into the slaves and the free.

REINCARNATION AND CLEAN HANDS

Particularly characteristic of early philosophy in southern Italy (including the Pythagorean tradition) is an interest in the transmigration of the soul into other bodies (human, animal or plant) after death. These reincarnation theories typically include ethical components. For instance, there may be a way to escape from the cycle of lives, or advance to a higher life, by achieving certain exacting standards of purity and sanctity.

For Pythagoras himself (sixth century BCE) we struggle to reconstruct the doctrines reliably, due to limited and often contaminated evidence, but we have better resources relating to the poet-philosopher Empedocles (fifth century BCE). Empedocles holds that the world is alternately governed by forces of increasing love (drawing things together) and increasing strife (setting things at odds and apart), with intervening periods of unity and division. Alongside this cosmic structure, he has an ethical story about souls (*daimones*) that wander in exile, tormented by strife and longing to return to their divine home under love.[18]

---

[15] Heraclitus fr 78 DK. I have translated *êthos* as 'life' and *gnômai* as 'standards'. Alternatively *gnômai* might mean 'measures', or 'wits', or 'judgement'.

[16] Heraclitus fr 83 DK.   [17] Heraclitus fr 102 DK.

[18] For present purposes we need not settle the controversy over whether Empedocles wrote separate poems about cosmology and ethics. I shall treat the two topics as interrelated, and I adopt 'soul' as a serviceable (but not loaded) term for what Empedocles means by *daimon*.

If this cycle of love and strife is cosmic and automated, what prospect can there be that the soul could voluntarily improve its chances of a rapid return from exile? What scope do we have to combat the inexorable advance of strife?[19] It seems that there must be some room for choice and moral responsibility; for according to the poem's protagonist, pictured as a soul in exile, we are held blameworthy for some offences, and for their dire consequences. There are passages that lament the sin of eating meat,[20] and exhort the listener to avoid killing animals for sacrifice and eating 'each other'.[21] The reason is apparently that the animals due to be killed and eaten are members of one's own family. The argument must be something like this: 'You would be horrified by eating your own child or mother; but you kill and eat some animal, supposing it is not your mother or child; but in fact it is, or might be, just that. So, you should be horrified.' The argument is not spelled out in this way, but is expressed as a myth, and a cry of despair. Nevertheless, it clearly appeals to motifs such as the sanctity of life, and the kinship of all living beings (or the impossibility of knowing which are kin).[22]

In other surviving fragments, Empedocles describes a world in which everyone was gentle and kind, humans and animals lived together, and there were no blood sacrifices.[23] This was apparently a sort of golden age, when Love was Queen.[24] Is this alternative regime something that we can restore by our own moral efforts, or does it just happen automatically when the time is right? The answer is unclear, but either way, it is clearly an ethically superior society, and an ideal that the true followers should long for.

DID DEMOCRITUS ANTICIPATE SOCRATES?

Our search for ethics before Socrates concludes with Democritus (fifth century, contemporary with the Sophists and Socrates). He is famous above all for his atomist physical theory, but we also have a considerable body of material, albeit fragmentary, that relates to ethics.

In approaching Democritus' ethics, there is a risk of falling into one of two problematic patterns of thought. One is to treat the texts as isolated

---

[19] For a more technical (and controversial) exploration of this question see Osborne 2005: 283–308.

[20] Strasbourg Papyrus, Ensemble d (probably identical to fr 139 DK, or repetition of identical lines).

[21] Empedocles frr 136, 137, 138 DK.

[22] For a fuller exploration see Osborne 2007: ch. 3.   [23] Empedocles frr 128, 130.

[24] Empedocles fr 128.3.

moralizing sayings, banal, trivial, with no systematic theory to offer in either ethics or meta-ethics. Another is to allow expectations from later (or indeed contemporary) Greek ethics to color our reading of Democritus' work. For instance, it might be tempting to read motifs from specifically Socratic ethics into Democritus, or to look for motifs from later Greek ethics more generally, e.g. by looking for evidence of 'eudaimonism' – that is, the idea that the ultimate goal of ethical conduct is 'happiness' or *eudaimonia*.[25] Both approaches can be problematic. They encourage us to slide across the surface and miss what is distinctive in Democritus' sayings. Instead I shall try to pick out what is distinctive, by looking carefully at just a few texts. We can then ask, once we have read the texts, whether what we find there looks Socratic in anything more than a shallow sense.[26]

Democritus suggests that we should take as our goal a certain cheerful psychological condition that he calls '*euthumia*' (which I shall translate as 'good spirits').[27] This is clearly a technical term in his writings. The '*thumos*' component of the word seems to refer to the emotions and feelings, which is why I say that it is a psychological condition. The '*eu*' component means 'well' or 'good'. If we understand *euthumia* as a sense of well-being – a subjective attitude or feeling rather than an objective state of one's external affairs – it need not be directly tied to worldly success or external conditions.

Should we equate 'good spirits' with merely feeling good about oneself, whether or not one's inner or outer situation is actually any good? The answer is probably 'no'. Democritus has things to say about what kind of life is worth pursuing, and what one should feel good about: it seems that one needs wisdom and virtue; one should not choose (or be satisfied with) a life of wrongdoing or folly. So it seems that one cannot achieve genuine 'good spirits' by pursuing base pleasures, or feeling content with those. Perhaps he thinks that if one lacks wisdom, one will not actually be able to adopt the correct attitude to fortune and misfortune.

A good life is not, however, primarily one of civic or domestic hyperactivity. On the contrary, Democritus seems to have a rather simpler life in mind, to reduce the risk of misfortune that accompanies public service and

---

[25] See Annas 2002: 169–82. Osborne 2007: 198–201 finds a form of utilitarianism in the material on the death penalty and killing animals.

[26] Note that we have no sources uncontaminated by knowledge of Socrates and later ethical traditions. This affects what material has survived.

[27] For the noun *euthumia* and the verb *euthumeisthai* see Democritus DK 68 A166, A167, A169 (where Cicero gives the technical term in Greek), B3, B4, B189, B258.

ambition. A relatively long extract from Democritus recorded by both Plutarch and Stobaeus advises the reader not to be excessively busy:

> To be in good spirits, you need to avoid doing a lot of things, either at home or in the community; and in choosing what to do, you should avoid things beyond your own capacities and nature. There is nothing else you need to guard against – then if you encounter misfortune and it invites you to consider something beyond what is fitting, you can lay it to rest, and not apply yourself to things beyond your means. For something of a good size is more secure than something of a vast size.[28]

Here we see a pattern of thought that was picked up by Martha Nussbaum, in her motif of 'the fragility of goodness'.[29] Democritus suggests that we should find a way of life that is relatively immune to misfortune, and relatively secure from total disaster and failure. Misfortune may throw us off course; but the reason for that, he suggests, is that it can encourage us to aim for the impossible, in our urgent attempt to preserve what was always going to be too vulnerable to save. We may well lose more in the process of trying to save the grand things that we had. It is better, then, to settle for a moderate life, relatively unambitious, and adopt an attitude of equanimity, that resists the desire to get the biggest things (which are at the same time the most risky).

The text just quoted does not specify exactly what those bigger (but risky) rewards might be. Nor does it say what are the more moderate rewards that are within our power to obtain and keep. The picture is filled out somewhat by another text on the same theme, quoted at length by Stobaeus:

> Good spirits is what people get as a result of a moderate amount of pleasure and a symmetry of life.[30] When things are lacking, or superabundant, that tends to throw one off track, and cause large motions in the soul. But souls that are moved that far are not well settled or in good spirits.
>
> So one should set one's heart on things that are possible, and be content with the things that are available. When it comes to the things that people desire and wonder at, one should hardly remember them and not dwell on them in one's mind. Instead one should regard those whose lives are afflicted with misfortune, thinking upon how sorely they are troubled. That way, what is available to you, and what belongs to you, will appear magnificent and desirable. The soul will not any longer be afflicted with the disease of wanting more ...

---

[28] Democritus DK 68 B3. [29] Nussbaum 1986.
[30] 'Symmetry' is a literal translation of *summetriê*. It might mean a life that is not unbalanced, or avoids having areas of lack and areas of excess.

With a heart in this condition, you will pass your life in better spirits, and will rid yourself of more than a few of life's trials: envy, possessiveness and ill will.[31]

It seems that the 'greater and more risky things' (paraphrase) of the earlier passage, and the 'things that people desire and wonder at' in this passage, are roughly the same. Here they are contrasted with the misfortunes of those who are in trouble. The wise thing to do is to avoid ambitious activity in the public and private sphere, which can lead to vast and impressive achievements that are the envy of ordinary people. The less ambitious things that are merely of a 'good size', and not 'vast' (in the first passage) may be activities reflecting intellectual virtue or moral virtue or both. Like Socrates, Democritus sometimes implies that doing wrong is the result of ignorance,[32] that the wrongdoer is less happy than the one wronged,[33] and that the best policy for achieving secure contentment is to be self-controlled and set one's heart on immaterial goods.[34] Wisdom is also mentioned as the *sine qua non* of the life of good spirits.[35]

There are clearly some similarities between these thoughts and those attributed to Socrates. But we should be careful to notice the differences as well. Democritus is interested in how one can make oneself feel good about one's own moderate success, rather than envying the success of others. We are advised to attend to the misfortunes of others, in order to restore a balance in our perception of what counts as good. This is about one's subjective attitude of acceptance, not about objective success or failure in either one's inner life or one's outer activities. Democritus' interest is in the person's psychological good spirits rather than the objective justice and goodness of their soul.

This seems to me to be different from Socrates, who is concerned with the health of the human soul in a very different sense; because, in Socrates' view, nothing, however painful, can outweigh the objective damage that one does to oneself by committing injustice or avoiding punishment – regardless of whether one feels pained by it or not. Socrates does not suggest that we look at the miseries of others in order to feel good about ourselves. When he talks about the misfortunes of the 'miserable' and their pitiable lives, he means those who have embraced corruption in their lives and in their souls, and he points at them in order to warn us of the incomparable dangers of an evil and corrupted soul, and especially of feeling happy about being in that terrible condition. So whereas, for Democritus, the 'unfortunate' ones are those with very few worldly goods and little power – that is, even fewer and less than one's own – for Socrates, by contrast, the 'unfortunate' ones are those with

[31] Democritus DK 68 B191. [32] Democritus DK 68 B83. [33] Democritus DK 68 B45.
[34] Democritus DK 68 B77, 189, 211, 235, 236, 284, etc. [35] Democritus DK 68 B216.

masses of worldly goods and immense political power. Such tyrants are unfortunate not because they have lost the enviable goods of this world, but because they have lost their moral virtue, and have not grasped the extent of their own misfortune.[36]

If I am right, Democritus thinks that a person is best off if they have a modicum of successful achievements and worldly goods, of a kind that are relatively secure and not subject to loss, or moderate goods whose loss will be relatively painless. He also thinks (rightly, I suspect) that it is easier to be carefree and happy with little than with much, and that one can achieve that sense of well-being effectively by comparing one's life with that of others, noticing how well off one is, by comparison with those who have even less. Although it is probable that among the simple goods that he proposes for a carefree life, immaterial goods such as simple virtue, wisdom and friendship would be good examples – thing that have a low risk of loss – Democritus does not really anticipate Socrates' radical division between inner health and outward goods, which is what leads to the Socratic position, a self-sacrificial preference for virtue over any other rival value.

BIBLIOGRAPHY

An asterisk denotes secondary literature especially suitable for further reading.

Annas, Julia 2002. 'Democritus and Eudaimonism', in Victor Caston and Daniel W. Graham (eds.), *Presocratic Philosophy: Essays in Honour of Alexander Mourelatos* (Aldershot: Ashgate), 169–82.

Diels, Hermann and Walther Kranz (eds.) 1951. *Die Fragmente der Vorsokratiker*, 3 vols. (6th edn, Berlin: Weidmann).

Gladstone, William Ewart 1858. *Studies on Homer and the Homeric Age* (Cambridge University Press).

Hall, Edith 1989. *Inventing the Barbarian* (Oxford University Press).

Mackie, Hilary 1996. *Talking Trojan: Speech and Community in the Iliad* (Oxford: Rowman and Littlefield Publishers).

McKirahan, Richard 1994. *Philosophy before Socrates* (Indianapolis: Hackett).

Nussbaum, Martha C. 1986. *The Fragility of Goodness: Luck and Ethics in Greek Tragedy and Philosophy* (Cambridge University Press).

Osborne, Catherine 2005. 'Sin and Moral Responsibility in Empedocles's Cosmic Cycle', in Apostolos L. Pierris (ed.), *The Empedoclean Κόσμος: Structure, Process and the Question of Cyclicity* (Patras: Institute for Philosophical Research), 283–308.

Osborne, Catherine 2007. *Dumb Beasts and Dead Philosophers: Humanity and the Humane in Ancient Philosophy and Literature* (Oxford University Press).*

---

[36] E.g. the references to the tyrant Archelaus in Socrates' discussion with Polus in Plato's *Gorgias*.

2

Socrates and Sophists

A.G. LONG

The so-called 'sophist' was a new kind of professional intellectual in the fifth-century Greek world. The label 'sophist' (Greek *sophistês*) originally indicated expertise or wisdom, not superficiality or the use of bogus arguments. The sophists had shared philosophical interests, especially in the distinctive features of *human* life: language, virtues and society. They also resembled one another in their itinerant careers, their offer to teach members of the cities they visited, and the intellectual nature of their teaching and writing. But there was no institutional affiliation beyond the agreement or contract between an individual sophist and his pupils, and there was no doctrine to which one was committed by the mere fact of becoming, or studying with, a sophist – except perhaps the view that certain skills or qualities of character can be instilled by teaching. What made the sophists innovators was not only the content of their education but the manner in which it was made available: all that was needed was that the sophist accept the pupil and that the two of them agree on a fee. One key challenge for sophists was relating their own teaching to the education offered through more conventional means, such as myths, poetry and the laws of the state.

Sophists have often been regarded as specialists in rhetoric. The sophists did have a special interest in language, but no less central to the representation of sophists, even in the works of their opponents or critics (on whom we usually have to rely), is the offer to *teach virtue*. When Plato's Socrates compares sophists and orators, he describes sophists as 'those who claim to educate people in virtue' (*Gorgias* 519e). Gorgias, a teacher of rhetoric who is usually treated as a sophist, is said to have ridiculed those who offered to teach virtue (Plato *Meno* 95c), but here he was distancing himself from the sophists, or from other sophists, and striking out on his own. Protagoras and Antiphon are the sophists who will receive most attention in this chapter.

The sophists' offer to teach virtue provoked hostility and opposition, but it provoked a more complex reaction in their junior contemporary

Socrates (469–399 BCE). Socrates set himself against the sophists, most obviously by avoiding any taint of salaried professionalism (his company and time were offered for free) and by *not* claiming to be wise or an expert, at least in the matters in which sophists claimed expertise. Plato experimented with different versions of an alternative 'Socratic' expertise, famously representing Socrates' wisdom as recognition of his own ignorance (*Apology* 20d–23b), but elsewhere suggesting that it consisted in his knowledge of love (*Symposium* 177d–e) or alternatively in his ability to help other people articulate their theories and to give the theories a proper examination or 'reception' (*Theaetetus* 148e–151d, 161b). Unlike the sophists, Socrates did not set down his philosophy in writing, and so we rely exclusively on the accounts of Socrates by others, especially those of his admirers, such as Plato, Xenophon, Aeschines, Antisthenes, Eucleides and Phaedo, who wrote 'Socratic' dialogues. It is worth remembering that the dialogues of Plato and Xenophon, which have survived, were part of a larger attempt to make sense of Socrates' life and thought.

There are, however, important affinities between Socrates and the sophists. In particular, the moral doctrines attributed to Socrates show why it is rational to teach – or, in Socrates' case, spur – others to become virtuous, and to this extent Socrates is the sophists' ally, not their opponent. The fullest surviving account of the relationship between Socrates and sophists, Plato's *Protagoras*, explores similarities as well as differences between them, and shows that aspects of Socrates' moral philosophy, especially his thesis that nobody does wrong willingly, would have been very congenial to sophists. I shall follow Plato's lead in placing the emphasis, when appropriate, on the similarities between Socrates and sophists. But we shall need to be on our guard for cases where Plato is offering his own development or interpretation of sophistic and Socratic thought.

SOPHISTS ON SOCIETY, JUSTICE, AND VIRTUE

Much of the sophists' contribution to moral philosophy is an outgrowth of sociology. Sophists sometimes took part in politics (Protagoras is said to have written laws for the Athenian-led colony at Thurii), and sometimes distanced themselves from contemporary society and politics. From the sophists' own perspective, they had either the right experience or the right detachment with which to discuss society and its conventions and laws.

In Plato's *Protagoras* (337c–d) the sophist Hippias says that he regards his fellow sophists, 'the wisest of the Greeks', as his 'fellow citizens', and then takes aim at the conventions that divide them:

> Gentlemen, I regard you as akin, related, fellow citizens – by nature, not by convention. Like is naturally akin to like, but convention, a tyrant over mankind, brings about by force many things contrary to nature.

Hippias confers shared 'citizenship' only on the wise; what all mankind shares is not citizenship but a despotic master, 'convention', prominently contrasted with 'nature'. The contrast between 'convention' (*nomos*) and 'nature' (*phusis*) was a major theme of fifth-century literature and thought. It is developed much more fully in the fragmentary remains of Antiphon's *On Truth*. The author, 'Antiphon the sophist', as he is described by Xenophon, was a contemporary of Socrates and is identified by some scholars with Antiphon of Rhamnus, an Athenian rhetorician executed for masterminding an oligarchic coup in 411 BCE. The truths offered by Antiphon concern the relationship between conventions and laws (the Greek term *nomos* covers both kinds of constraint) on the one hand and our interests on the other. He outlines the origin of laws and conventions, arguing that they derive from an agreement rather than from nature, and uses their origin to show that the power of convention, formidable though it is, depends on the presence of witnesses who are parties to the agreement. In Antiphon's own words, 'when someone transgresses the laws and conventions, he avoids shame and punishment if he is not noticed by those who agreed to them; otherwise, he does not'. But our 'nature' does not derive from an agreement, and therefore retains its power independently of the presence or absence of external witnesses; so in the absence of witnesses it is most advantageous to be directed by nature, not convention. Usually it is impossible to serve the two masters simultaneously: 'most of what is just according to convention is in conflict with nature'.

We might expect Antiphon to urge his readers to throw off the rule of convention and align themselves with nature. But this is a development of the *nomos/phusis* antithesis that we find in Plato, not in Antiphon himself. Plato was intrigued by countercultural normativity and saw well that it could take contrasting forms. In his dialogue *Gorgias* he sets two countercultural figures against each other: Socrates and Callicles. Socrates argues that injustice is so harmful to our interests that unjust people should seek out the remedy for injustice – punishment. To the astonishment of his interlocutor, Socrates argues that unjust people should haul themselves before a judge and accuse themselves. Callicles for his part has often been regarded as a representative of sophistic thought, but this is unwarranted, not merely because we know nothing about Callicles independently of Plato, but also because Callicles expresses contempt for sophists – or at least for sophists who offered to teach people virtue (*Gorgias* 520a). (Callicles probably has a higher opinion of Gorgias.) Like Antiphon Callicles treats the difference between nature and convention as all-important. Unlike Antiphon, however, Callicles suggests that there is a 'natural' kind of justice, radically different from conventional justice: 'nature herself proclaims that it is just for the better to have more than the inferior, or the more powerful than the weaker' (483c–d). In Callicles' theory nature becomes a legislator: aggressors and conquerors are said to act according to nature's justice and nature's 'law' (483e). An individual of sufficient strength and resourcefulness can, by promoting his own interests, trample convention underfoot. Such an individual would be transferring himself from conventional law and morality to their 'natural' counterparts.

In Antiphon's *On Truth*, on the other hand, it is purely self-interest, not some unconventional justice or law, that requires people to defy convention – and then only if they can do so undetected. Antiphon's own development of the *nomos/phusis* antithesis is thoroughly pessimistic: he silences attempts to reconcile oneself to law and convention. Overcoming convention by force is not envisaged. It might be said that laws protect those who obey them – but, Antiphon counters, laws intervene only *after* the crime has been committed. And, he continues, any attempts to get redress through judicial means will impose harm, moral as well as non-moral, on someone else, namely the witnesses. Calling the witnesses to testify requires them to wrong the defendant (by harming someone who had done *them* no harm) and to incur the defendant's enmity. Antiphon is offering not a call to action but further uncomfortable truths. So too when he talks about the similarity of all mankind, now extending it more indiscriminately than Hippias in Plato's dialogue would later extend citizenship: 'none of us has been marked off as foreign ["barbarian"] or Greek. We all exhale into the air by our mouths and nostrils; we laugh when happy and cry when sad ...' Antiphon's readers are being urged to regard non-Greeks in a different way, but this is so that they will grasp a truth about society, namely that laws and conventions, not nature, have made people 'foreigners in relation to one another'.

Another sophisticated discussion of society is credited to Protagoras, and in this discussion too the power of social conventions and institutions is a central theme. We return now to Plato's dialogue *Protagoras*. Plato is usually thought to have been simply hostile to sophists, but evidently even in Plato's eyes Protagoras was such a significant thinker that it was worth giving a sympathetic account of his teaching. In Plato's dialogue Protagoras delivers a speech – sometimes called his 'Great Speech' – on the distribution and origin of virtue (320c–328d): (1) how many people are virtuous, and (2) do people become virtuous by being *taught* to be virtuous? Characteristically Protagoras uses social and political practices to cast light on moral questions. His answer to the first question – couched in the form of a myth – is that all members of a city must have a share of virtue, his argument being that without such a wide distribution of virtue citizens would not cooperate and the city would not survive. It follows that democracies are right, not naïve or irrational, to involve *all* citizens in decision-making, for it is a prerequisite of a city's survival that all citizens have the qualities that democracy expects to find in them.

Protagoras' answer to the second question is a resounding 'yes'. He cites as evidence what happens to people who are *not* virtuous: their fellow citizens do not regard their condition as unalterable, but actively correct them, thereby betraying a conviction that virtue can be instilled by correction. The correction often takes the form of punishment, but punishment is only rational if it is intended to deter – and so to make people different. (Protagoras' thoroughly social treatment of the morality of punishment can be contrasted with the treatment of this theme *outside* the social sphere in Platonic discussions of the afterlife.) One objection to Protagoras is that if virtue can be taught, we should expect there to be a correlation between good parents and good children – but there is no such correlation, as some admirable people have unremarkable or inferior children (and vice versa). But Protagoras ingeniously appropriates this evidence for his own argument. The lack of such a correlation reflects the ubiquity of lessons in virtue: learning virtue is a central part of *every* child's education, and the education continues into adulthood, for the city's laws show every member of the city how to behave (and, more obviously, how not to behave). Given that this is an education everyone receives, the children of good parents have no special advantage. Unimpressive though these children may seem to us, they are far better than they would be without the array of human and institutional teachers encountered each day.

The Great Speech is only part of Plato's portrait of Protagoras, and elsewhere in the *Protagoras* it is suggested that Protagoras offered to make his pupils powerful players in the political arena. But Plato himself suggests that Protagoras stood for more than the offer of power. In his Great Speech Protagoras seeks to show that people are not stuck with the characters handed out by forces beyond their control – and that everyone intuits as much already. As he says, people recognise that 'virtue comes not from nature or by luck; it is teachable and whoever attains it does so from deliberate effort' (323c). Protagoras' particular treatment of the nature/convention antithesis leads to the encouraging thought that it is in people's power to change themselves and to continue the formation of character begun by their educators. The sophist Prodicus is said to have represented Heracles facing a choice between Virtue and Vice, and submitting to the education of Virtue (Xenophon *Memorabilia* 2.1.34); notice the sophist's suggestion that the *Choice of Heracles* was Heracles' choice to make.

SOCRATES ON SELF-IMPROVEMENT, VIRTUE AND KNOWLEDGE

We are now able to appreciate a point of similarity between Socrates and sophists like Protagoras. Socrates, as represented in the dialogues of Plato and Xenophon, urges his contemporaries to improve themselves, evidently regarding self-improvement as being in their power. Sometimes this takes the form of encouragement: 'Socrates gave others confidence that if they attended to themselves nobility would be theirs' (Xenophon *Memorabilia* 1.2.2). The note of reproach – attend to yourself rather than to other things – is harder to miss in this self-description: 'I go around doing nothing but persuading both the young and the old among you not to attend to your bodies or wealth before, or as urgently as, ensuring that your soul is as good as possible' (Plato *Apology* 30a–b). Here too, however, it is assumed that improvement of one's soul – and so improvement of one's moral character – is possible.

Socrates claims for himself an important role in bringing about self-improvement in others. But at this point Socrates' admirers suggest contrasts between him and sophists. It is uncertain how many of these contrasts go back to the historical Socrates, but at the very least it is credible that Socrates attempted systematically to distinguish himself from sophists in his dealings with others. Above all, Socrates emphasised that self-improvement is improvement *by oneself* as well as *of oneself*. Socrates made a point of not offering too much: his job was not to teach or insert the desired expertise or character, but rather to find the line of questioning that would cause others to examine and then reform themselves. The exchange of short questions and answers, so ideally suited to making an interlocutor contradict himself (and thus to competitive display), thus acquires an ethical objective – as does the very process of making others contradict themselves. By getting interlocutors to contradict themselves, and thereby showing their ignorance or confusion (we shall see in a moment the connection between epistemic and moral qualities), Socrates removes the complacency that, left unchallenged, would prevent them from 'attending to themselves'.

What supports or explains Socrates' confidence that self-improvement is in people's power? Here too we find a contrast with sophists. When challenged, Protagoras looks for support to contemporary society and the widespread assumption that virtue can be instilled. As we have seen, this approach fits the sociological character of sophistic thought. Socrates goes elsewhere – to psychology, human nature and to what it *means* to be a good or virtuous human being. Within these large areas his admirers attributed to him various theories, and it is hard not to suspect that we are encountering later, fourth-century interpretations of Socrates' philosophy. All the same, the theories attributed to Socrates by sympathetic interpreters became a key part of Socrates' legacy to later philosophy. To begin with a less familiar example, Socrates' follower Phaedo, in his lost dialogue *Zopyrus*, uses an opposition between nature and training to explain how people can improve themselves. Phaedo argues that training can overcome the vices to which people are naturally susceptible, using Socrates himself to illustrate his point. In Phaedo's dialogue a physiognomist claimed that Socrates' appearance betrayed vices, and, when ridiculed by Socrates' companions, was rescued by none other than Socrates, who admitted being *naturally* prone to vices but said that he had avoided the vices through training. Phaedo's anecdote would be recalled in later philosophical literature on the possibility of changing one's character (Cicero *Tusculan Disputations* 4.80).

Plato's explorations of Socratic theory of course proved particularly influential, but extracting moral theories from the dialogues is not a simple matter. (See Chapter 3 below, by James Warren, which discusses the theories usually associated with Plato rather than Socrates, namely the Theory of Forms, the immortality of the soul and the division of the soul into three parts.) Sometimes, as for example in the *Apology, Gorgias* and *Crito*, Socrates reaches firm conclusions, usually because Plato wants to explain a decision Socrates made (not kowtowing to the jury in his trial and refusing to escape from prison). Elsewhere, however, such as in the *Euthyphro, Laches* and *Protagoras*, the dialogues exhibit not doctrinal conclusions so much as a kind of centripetalism. In these dialogues, Socrates takes the discussion towards some specific moral theories, but an objection or difficulty prevents him from reaching a verdict in their favour. Plato has translated into literature Socrates' insistence on improvement by oneself: readers of the dialogues must seek independently to resolve the problems presented in the dialogues.

One moral theory to which Socrates is attracted concerns the nature of the virtues or forms of human 'goodness'. Socrates takes there to be five virtues: wisdom, justice, piety, courage, and moderation or temperance (*sôphrosunê*, a term notoriously difficult to translate). But he aims to understand not the differences between them (what makes them number five?) but rather what they have in common (what makes them all virtues?). Socrates' conversations in Plato often move towards a conception of the virtues as forms of *knowledge or wisdom*, knowledge and wisdom here being treated as equivalent. An attraction of this conception of virtue, for sophists as well as for Socrates, is its implication for how virtue is acquired – not by luck or by nature, but (as Protagoras put it) from deliberate effort. If the virtues are all *knowledge*, then people can indeed be *taught* to be good – or rather, given Socrates' refusal to act as teacher of virtue, encouraged to learn to be good.

Courage is sometimes taken to be particularly resistant to this analysis – as Protagoras himself suggests, courage comes not from knowledge or intellectual training but 'from nature and good nurture of soul' (*Protagoras* 351a–b) – but Socrates suggests that courage, no less than the other virtues, is knowledge. Plato's major discussion of courage is his dialogue *Laches*, where Socrates and two generals attempt to define courage and almost arrive at a conception of courage as knowledge or wisdom. Once they agree that their discussion of courage should cover all cases of courageous behaviour, such as courage shown in illness (at first one general, Laches, considers only what Greek soldiers are standardly expected to do – stand their ground in battle), courage is first defined as 'endurance of soul'. Focussing on a quality of 'soul' is a step forward, inasmuch as it accommodates a wide variety of actions, but for Socrates they have not yet focussed on the right kind of mental quality: there must be something that makes the endurance admirable, and Socrates suggests that this is knowledge or wisdom. Laches is unable to specify the relevant kind of knowledge, but the other general, Nicias, suggests, following a remark of Socrates, that courage does not only require knowledge but *is* knowledge: knowledge of what should be dreaded and what should be confidently undertaken. Once people know what will be bad for them (and so should cause fear) and what will be good, or at least not evil (and so should not cause fear), they will have the resilience needed to make the right decisions; no further 'endurance' is necessary. Socrates himself then disrupts the movement towards a conception of the virtue as knowledge; he objects that a person with this knowledge would possess *all* the virtues, not the single virtue courage. (In a different context this may be precisely the conclusion at which Socrates wants to arrive.)

The conception of virtue as knowledge, and indeed Socrates' objection to it (how could someone with the relevant knowledge fail to be *completely* virtuous?), suggests that knowledge alone ensures the behaviour and characteristics expected of virtuous people. The obvious objection is that it is possible to know what one should do and yet act otherwise. According to Plato, Socrates' answer – his famous thesis that nobody does wrong willingly – was based on a robust monism about the object of human desires and the goal of human actions. Everyone desires *what is good*, and always acts in such a way as to obtain what is good, and so wrong-doing always depends on failure to recognise what is good. When this psychological claim is itself challenged and it is suggested that some people desire 'bad things' (it is better to retain the vagueness of the Greek), Socrates uses a dilemmatic argument to show otherwise (Plato *Meno* 77b–78a). *Either* these people believe that these bad things will benefit them, in which case they must think that the things are good, *or* they must recognise that the things will harm them: but they cannot help but see that harm will make them unhappy, and that alone will prevent desire – for nobody wants to be unhappy.

It remains to be shown that the pursuit of good things, informed by knowledge, conforms to our intuitions about virtuous behaviour. To meet this challenge Socrates needs to specify *which* things are good and so worthy of pursuit; one context where he does so is Plato's *Protagoras*, where, in a defence of his thesis that wrong-doing is involuntary, he surprisingly identifies the good as the 'pleasant' – but probably only in order to make his psychology persuasive to the non-intellectuals with whom he is arguing at that point. It is not clear that the pursuit of pleasure, even when informed by knowledge, need be *virtuous*, although the Epicureans would later try to establish precisely this point. We need now to consider Socrates' conception of goodness, and see how it compares with the sophists' discussions of goodness.

GOODNESS AND EVALUATION

Sophists and their followers are said to have emphasised the complexity of goodness, virtue and harm. Something beneficial in one context or relation turns out to be harmful in other contexts, and behaviour admired as virtuous in one person would be unbecoming in another. The sophists seem to have taken pride in recognising the full range of factors that should affect evaluation. Consider this outburst in Plato's *Protagoras*:

> Oil is utterly harmful to all plants and most opposed to the hair of all animals, except that of humans; for human hair it is useful, as it is for the rest of the body. And goodness is so complicated and varied that even in this area for the *external* parts of the body oil is good for people, but for *internal* parts this same thing is very harmful. (334b–c)

Protagoras is speaking. In the dialogue his remarks are admired by the other sophists and their pupils, and so Plato presumably intends to associate this kind of sentiment with sophistic thought more generally. At this point in the conversation Protagoras has become flustered, but he still achieves a telescoping effect in the relations he mentions: oil is harmful to plants, beneficial to humans, and even if we focus on one 'area', the effect of oil on humans, we continue to find both harm and benefit.

It is worth emphasising that Protagoras spells out the different *relata* – human hair, plants and so on – and does not try to arrive at the paradox that one and the same item is both harmful and beneficial in a non-relational sense. It is also worth emphasising that the relation is between oil and bodies, not oil and beliefs. Protagoras' point is not that people *believe* oil to be beneficial, and certainly not that plants believe it to be harmful, but simply that oil has different effects on different bodies and on different parts of the body. The benefit or harm, by some object on another object, is real, and it would be foolish to drink oil supposing otherwise. Contrast the following:

> In the sphere of politics, the noble and disgraceful, just and unjust, pious and impious, are really, for the city, such as each city *believes* when it sets them down in its laws, and in these matters nothing is wiser than anything else – individual than individual, or state than state. (Plato *Theaetetus* 172a)

This too is taken from a Platonic discussion of sophistry, in this case of Protagoras' *Truth*, but here Plato has indicated, with scruples not often found in ancient responses to predecessors, that this is not *echt* Protagoras. It is rather the most resilient version of Protagoras' dictum that 'man is the measure of all things', and the version held by those who do 'not entirely' follow Protagoras' doctrine (172b). It is combined with a realism about benefit: what is most beneficial to a state, in contradistinction to what is just or what is correct religious practice, is independent of what is believed in that state. In this different context, the *Theaetetus*, Plato suggests that Protagoras' own thesis was more comprehensive: what someone believes, on any subject, is true *for that person*. This is a different conception of Protagoras' philosophy from that explored in the *Protagoras*, and it is not certain that it accurately reflects the views of the historical Protagoras.

Emphasis on what made evaluation complicated was probably more characteristic of historical sophists. In another Platonic dialogue Meno, a young man who has fallen under Gorgias' spell, suggests that what constitutes virtue depends on age, sex and status: for a free man, virtue is preeminence and skill in the political sphere, used to benefit friends and harm enemies, whereas a slave should not aspire to such power, and for a free woman virtue is keeping a household to its budget and being obedient to her husband (*Meno* 71e). Socrates then argues that, on the contrary, women and men, old and young, become virtuous by attaining exactly the same characteristics. Good management of any kind, whether in politics or of a household, demands justice and moderation – two members of the standard list of Socratic virtues (*Meno* 72d–73c). Here we continue to rely on Plato's portrait of Socrates, but it may be significant that another follower of Socrates, Antisthenes, is said to have declared virtue to be the same in a man and in a woman (Diogenes Laertius 6.12). While sophists had avoided narrowness of vision by emphasising the difference made by age, sex and so on, Socrates achieved the same degree of comprehensiveness simply by framing his inquiry as an attempt to understand *human* goodness.

It might be thought that Socrates would have equally little sympathy for Protagoras' remarks on benefit and harm. Instead, as before, we find something more complex: Socrates appropriates this aspect of the sophists' thought, but uses it in the service of his own challenge or suggestion. In both Plato and Xenophon Socrates embraces the idea that 'beneficial' things turn out to be harmful as well – in other circumstances, in other relations, and so on. In Xenophon's *Memorabilia* (4.2.31–6) this occurs in a long attempt to undermine an interlocutor's self-belief. Socrates challenges his interlocutor, Euthydemus, to specify which things are good and which are bad, and then shows that the items suggested by Euthydemus as good, such as bodily health, can in some circumstances cause harm. Even wisdom and happiness can lead to harm – at least if happiness is understood as including physical attractiveness, strength, wealth and good reputation, all of which can give rise to harm. In Plato's dialogues Socrates' use of this argument is not so negative: he aims to show that there is an exception, some moral or intellectual quality that is consistently beneficial. Some of the same candidates as in Xenophon – health, strength, beauty and wealth – are considered and shown to be sometimes beneficial, sometimes harmful. But Plato's Socrates suggests that a single factor determines whether the possessor is benefited or harmed: are these items, such as wealth, used foolishly or with the relevant *knowledge*? Moving from external to internal so-called 'goods', he argues that admired qualities of the mind or soul, such as tough-mindedness or daring, also harm us, at least if not guided by knowledge or wisdom. (Plato makes it clear that he is not discussing the Socratic conception of courage as a kind of knowledge.) Knowledge alone is independently good and causes other possessions, such as daring, to *become* good (*Meno* 87e–89a; compare *Euthydemus* 279a–281e). Knowledge thus confers its essential goodness on the items used with knowledge.

A difficulty for Socrates is to explain how the knowledgeable person makes his or her choices, particularly when required to decide whether to pursue (rather than how to use) health or wealth. If these items possess no goodness independently of knowledge, as Socrates has argued, there seems no reason to choose one rather than the other – or even to choose health rather than illness. It is precisely this difficulty – what reason is there to pursue items that are not good? – that Stoics address in their own theory of value. Stoics presented themselves as Socrates' true heirs, and so it is not surprising to find them working through a difficulty in Socratic ethics. But Socrates' arguments for the unique status of knowledge or wisdom were a new application of a strand of sophistic thought. Through their interest in Socrates, as represented in Plato and Xenophon, Stoics were also reviving the arguments of sophists.

BIBLIOGRAPHY

An asterisk denotes secondary literature especially suitable for further reading.

Ahbel-Rappe, S. and Kamtekar, R. (eds.) 2006, *A Companion to Socrates*, Malden/Oxford: Blackwell
Barnes, J. 1982, *The Presocratic Philosophers*, London/New York: Routledge and Kegan Paul
Benson, H.H. (ed.) 1992, *Essays on the Philosophy of Socrates*, Oxford University Press
Bett, R. 2002, 'Is There a Sophistic Ethics?', *Ancient Philosophy* 22, 235–62*
Boys-Stones, G. and Rowe, C. 2013, *The Circle of Socrates: Readings in the First-Generation Socratics*, Indianapolis/Cambridge: Hackett
Brickhouse, T.C. and Smith, N.D. 2000, *The Philosophy of Socrates*, Boulder/Oxford: Westview Press
Broadie, S. 2003, 'The Sophists and Socrates', in D.N. Sedley (ed.), *The Cambridge Companion to Greek and Roman Philosophy*, Cambridge University Press, 73–97*
Curd, P. and McKirahan, R.D. 2011, *A Presocratics Reader*, 2nd edn, Indianapolis/Cambridge: Hackett

Decleva Caizzi, F. 1999, 'Protagoras and Antiphon: Sophistic Debates on Justice', in A.A. Long (ed.), *The Cambridge Companion to Early Greek Philosophy*, Cambridge University Press, 311–31

Kerferd, G.B. 1981a, *The Sophistic Movement*, Cambridge University Press

Kerferd, G.B. (ed.) 1981b, *The Sophists and their Legacy*, Wiesbaden: Steiner

Morrison, D.R. 2010, 'Xenophon's Socrates as Teacher', in V.J. Gray (ed.) *Xenophon*, Oxford University Press, 195–227

Morrison, D.R. (ed.) 2011, *The Cambridge Companion to Socrates*, Cambridge University Press*

Nails, D. 2002, *The People of Plato: A Prosopography of Plato and other Socratics*, Indianapolis/ Cambridge: Hackett

Nehamas, A. 1998 *The Art of Living: Socratic Reflections from Plato to Foucault*, Berkeley/Los Angeles/London: University of California Press

Notomi, N. 2010, 'Socrates versus Sophists: Plato's Invention?', in L. Rossetti and A. Stavru (eds.) *Socratica 2008: Studies in Ancient Socratic Literature*, Bari: Levante, 71–88

Pendrick, G.J. 2002, *Antiphon the Sophist: The Fragments*, Cambridge University Press

Taylor, C.C.W. 2000, *Socrates: A Very Short Introduction*, Oxford University Press

Vander Waerdt, P. (ed.) 1994, *The Socratic Movement*, Ithaca/London: Cornell University Press

Vlastos, G. 1991, *Socrates: Ironist and Moral Philosopher*, Cambridge University Press

Vlastos, G. 1994, *Socratic Studies*, Cambridge University Press

Woodruff, P. 1999, 'Rhetoric and Relativism: Protagoras and Gorgias', in A.A. Long (ed.), *The Cambridge Companion to Early Greek Philosophy*, Cambridge University Press, 290–310

3

Plato

JAMES WARREN

Plato's influence on the history of philosophy is enormous and is felt in the history of ethical philosophy no less than elsewhere.[1] However, any attempt to give a brief account of ethical philosophy in the works of Plato faces two significant and important difficulties. The first difficulty is that the various different dialogues explore questions of philosophical ethics in ways that can sometimes be in tension with one another. (Similar difficulties affect attempts to give a general account of any aspect of Plato's philosophical work.) The second difficulty is that there is no dialogue that deals solely in ethical matters. That is to say, although some dialogues more than others emphasize ethical matters, in the discussions depicted in the works the talk about values or virtues will also regularly and seamlessly take in questions about epistemology, metaphysics, politics, theology, and so on. That is just the way Plato does philosophy. In perhaps the most famous and most influential of his works – the *Republic* – the central question discussed by the participants in the dialogue is 'Why should I be just?' together with, as a necessary preliminary to that question, the definitional question 'What is justice?' But some of the most arresting parts of that work deal with questions about the nature of knowledge and belief and very basic questions of ontology since it turns out that a full answer to the central question involves dealing with such matters too.

Just as it is impossible to separate Plato's ethical thinking from his thinking about other areas of philosophy, so too Plato's exploration of metaphysics or epistemology is never free from ethical consequence. When he writes about knowledge and opinion, he is invariably also writing about the value of knowledge for a knower. When he is writing about the basic or fundamental

I would like to thank Thomas Land, Frisbee Sheffield, Voula Tsouna, and the editors of the volume for comments on earlier versions of this chapter.

[1] I shall use the broader term 'ethics' because Plato is concerned not only with 'morality' in the sense of determining which actions are correct or obligatory.

structure of reality he is also invariably writing about how reality is structured so as to be good and harmonious. What is more, coming to have knowledge of the nature of reality is supposed to have important and beneficial effects for the philosopher.

It is also difficult to draw a clear distinction between all the various ethical questions and ideas to be found in the works and what Plato himself thought about these matters. There are two principal reasons for this. The first is the difficult 'Socratic question'. Indeed, it is a familiar tactic in dealing with questions of differences or contradictions between claims made even by the same character, 'Socrates', in different Platonic dialogues to say that in one case we are dealing with the historical Socrates' view while in the other we are dealing with Plato's. I cannot settle this question here but will instead confine what I will say to works that are generally agreed not to reflect the views of the historical Socrates and in which ethical questions play a central role.[2] The second difficulty is that Plato's choice of an oblique form of writing expressly discourages us from thinking that what matters most of all is what the author himself thinks about some question or other. It is therefore in many ways a mistake to approach the corpus in search of 'Plato's ethical views'. The dialogues instead offer a series of ideas, arguments, provocations, challenges, and invitations to further reflection.

These difficulties make it almost impossible to give an informative and concise account of Plato's ethical thought as a whole.[3] But they also point towards a more positive route which can make a virtue of the way in which Platonic works engage the reader in a holistic philosophical enterprise. A shared feature of the Platonic works is the presentation of a picture of what it is like to think philosophically. They sometimes do this by presenting positive paradigms of philosophical thought. But they also do this by presenting incompetent or confused attempts and nefarious, counterfeit, or potentially damaging simulacra of philosophical thinking. Throughout, however, there is an insistence on the theme that the good and valuable human life is the philosophical life. In its strongest formulation this means that a good human life just is the life of a philosopher in the sense of someone who is dedicated to the acquisition and contemplation of philosophical truth, but this view may also accommodate the weaker idea that a good human life must be one that is informed by reflective philosophical thinking.

[2] See also Chapter 2 in this volume, by A.G. Long.
[3] Irwin 1995 is the most recent general account in English covering all the relevant dialogues.

VIRTUE AND THE GOOD LIFE

Plato inherited from Socrates a guiding framework for ethical thinking as well as a more general emphasis on the importance of critical inquiry and self-examination. Thinking in very broad terms, we can pick out two central ethical ideas. It is taken to be universally agreed that each person wants to live a good and happy life and therefore that the principal task of ethical inquiry is the identification of what makes a human life a good life and, if possible, the recommendation of how a given agent might come to live such a life.[4] The dialogues also take very seriously the common opinion that there are certain admirable and excellent states of character – virtues – the possession of which will lead an agent to act in laudable ways. A person in possession of the virtues will have a settled disposition to perform actions that display those virtues and will therefore act courageously, temperately, wisely, and so on. On this view, it is clear that ethical inquiry begins not with the assessment and recommendation of various kinds of acts or outcomes but with the identification and recommendation of traits of character that will lead inevitably to the right behavior – whatever that may be – in any given circumstance.

These two starting points are then related to one another by the contention that the possession of a virtuous character is what will guarantee that a person will live a good and happy life. Since everyone wishes to live a good life, everyone should wish to become virtuous. This last thought is perhaps the most difficult to defend since it appears that there are occasions when the virtuous agent will act in ways that are apparently detrimental to his well-being. A courageous person might undergo physical suffering and even die as a result of acting courageously. We can also imagine a person faced with an apparent choice between performing a just action and a beneficial action: perhaps he is faced with a choice between picking up some money lying in the street and pocketing it or handing it in to be reclaimed. In all these cases, we are supposed to come to see that in fact there is no genuine conflict between what is beneficial and what is virtuous: the virtuous action is what is beneficial to the agent because acting virtuously and possessing a virtuous character are both necessary and sufficient for living a good life.

A good life, then, is one in which the agent will possess and display various excellent traits of character – virtues – and so ethical inquiry must concentrate on the proper identification of those virtues and the recommendation of

---

[4] For a detailed exploration of the general structure of ancient ethical thinking see Annas 1993.

various recipes for their acquisition. At this point the dialogues often depart radically from common opinions about the virtues. Although it might be generally agreed, for example, that courage is a virtue of character that everyone should ideally strive to acquire and display, we should not rely on commonly accepted beliefs about the nature of courage and should not assume that commonly regarded authorities are indeed genuine experts whose opinions we should respect. (The *Laches* dramatizes this very point.) If, as a result of serious philosophical reflection, it should appear that courage is in fact something rather different from the commonly held ideals of martial prowess, then we should be guided by those reflections and be prepared to accept a revisionary picture of these valuable traits of character.

Since we are interested in certain excellent traits of character, ethical inquiry must be based on a proper understanding of character. In Plato's dialogues this crucially involves the proper understanding of the soul. A great deal of time and attention is spent on understanding the human soul: its nature, the way in which it is affected by its environment, by a person's upbringing, social interactions, and so on. Ethical inquiry therefore requires not only a deep psychological underpinning but also a close analysis of political, social, and aesthetic matters. This is perhaps an occasion when we can identify a difference between Socrates' insistence on a purely intellectual basis for psychological excellence and a new Platonic interest in non-intellectual elements in the soul. Socrates notoriously presents in some of the dialogues (e.g. *Protagoras*, *Meno*) the idea that 'no one does wrong willingly' in the sense that it is impossible to think some course of action better but nevertheless act on the basis of a desire for a worse action; human actions are guided exclusively by whatever it is that the person in question believes to be the better object of pursuit at the time and therefore there is no possibility of any genuine motivational conflict. (This is the claim sometimes known as the 'Socratic paradox' or the denial of 'weakness of will', *akrasia*. The thesis is supposed to hold no matter what are the particular agent's current criteria for determining what is better or worse. Of course, there is ample room for change and improvement in the criteria that are used.) One of the likely innovations of Plato's inquiries over those of Socrates is that in a number of other dialogues (e.g. *Republic*, *Timaeus*, *Phaedrus*), we are introduced to the idea that a human soul – at least when it is embodied so as to constitute a living human person – is a complex item. A living human can be faced with desires for physical pleasure and satisfaction, for fame and honor, and for truth and goodness. At different times different desires may be more powerful and guide the person's actions. And people may over time develop settled

characters in which one or other of these general motivations will be in control. Furthermore, people may be characterized by the various parts of their soul being in some kind of harmonious order or, alternatively, in some kind of constant tension and competition. The complexity of the soul is revealed most obviously in the various different and competing desires and motivations to which we are often subjected.

Perhaps the most sophisticated and elaborate examination of these psychological complexities is found in the *Republic*, where Socrates also draws on a political analogue to illustrate and investigate what is the best state for the soul. The complex psychology of the *Republic* is justified in part precisely on the basis of examples in which a person has a certain kind of desire for a better course of action but is led by another desire, for example because of an appetite for bodily pleasure, to do something he thinks is worse. (For example, someone might feel a desire for a particular kind of bodily gratification and, because of a commitment to propriety or the avoidance of shame, a simultaneous desire to abstain from that gratification.) Here, there is a genuine conflict between simultaneous and competing motivations and we are asked to assign each of these competitors to a different aspect or part of the soul. What emerges very clearly is that it is not enough merely for the parts of the soul or the parts of a city not to be in a state of conflict with one another. Certainly, the absence of conflict between its parts is an important characteristic of a well-ordered soul, but it does not offer a full explanation of why an excellent soul is in a good state. The three parts of the soul – the rational part, the spirited part, and the appetitive part – must be ordered in the right kind of hierarchical relationship with the rational part providing the governance and guidance for the whole soul. The appetites, for example, should be guided in desiring the pleasures that they do by the governance of what the rational part of the soul will recommend. So a person will be temperate, for example, not simply because he has developed the appetitive part of the soul in the correct manner but because the appetitive part of the soul is performing its proper function within a harmoniously ordered soul that is guided by reason. In fact, Socrates seems to assert that there cannot be any genuine order in the soul without such rational governance: someone who is dedicated entirely to the fulfilment of bodily appetites may experience no obvious internal psychological conflict but is not in truth a unified agent at all. He is instead a chaotic bundle of violent lawless desires (see e.g. *Republic* 574d–580a). The rational part of the soul, on this conception, is not a part of the soul tasked simply with instrumental reasoning or simply working out how to execute the desires of the other parts. (In fact, it seems that the

appetitive part of the soul is all by itself capable of some kinds of means–end reasoning in pursuit of its own goals.) The rational part of the soul pursues its own proper objects of desire – goodness and truth – and avoids what is bad (e.g. *Republic* 439c–d, 581b). At this point we have obviously begun to introduce some rather significant further premises which supplement this psychological analysis with additional metaphysical and meta-ethical claims.[5]

MORAL REALISM AND MORAL EXPERTISE

The Platonic dialogues base their inquiries into human happiness on a deep commitment to a form of moral realism combined with a teleological account of the fundamental nature of reality, the construction of the cosmos as a whole, and of humans in particular. The cosmos as a whole is good. Indeed, in the *Timaeus* the cosmos is said to be the product of a benevolent divine craftsman and in the *Republic* 'the Good' is said to be the first principle and cause of all reality. In making such assertions, the dialogues demonstrate a strong opposition to various other currents of philosophical thinking with which Plato was familiar. These include the various promises by sophistic teachers to impart virtue – for a fee – as a skill of persuasive rhetoric and various forms of moral, cultural, and epistemological relativism. Plato's works often stage a discussion between Socrates and supporters of these views and encourage the reader to diagnose and assess the various damaging consequences of the misguided ideas. Granted once again the difficulties of interpreting these carefully crafted discussions, there nevertheless emerges a reasonably clear favored point of view that we can without too many qualms identify as Platonic moral realism. It is regularly asserted, for example, that not only does the world contain various perceptible and transient instances of goodness and beauty but also that these instances of such moral properties are both inferior to and indeed caused to be good and beautiful to the extent that they are, by an imperceptible and intelligible, stable, eternal, and mind-independent objective, Goodness or Beauty. So, for example, a beautiful sunset, a beautiful young man, and a beautiful song are all made to be beautiful to the extent that each is beautiful by Beauty or 'Beauty itself': an everlasting, independent, objective, intelligible, and causally efficient item. 'Beauty itself' is the cause in the sense that the relationship between it and the

---

[5] For further recent discussion of Plato's moral psychology and the tripartite soul see Burnyeat 2006, Lorenz 2006, Ferrari 2007a, Moss 2008. For the analogy between the tripartite city and soul see Ferrari 2003.

sunset – sometimes put in terms of the sunset 'imitating' Beauty itself or 'participating in' Beauty itself – is what explains and is responsible for the sunset being as beautiful as it is. This is one aspect of what is often referred to as 'Plato's theory of Forms'.

For our purposes, there are two important aspects of this set of ideas. The first is that these Forms provide both the causal and ontological underpinning for the assertion of a moral realism: there are things that are good, beautiful, just, and so on regardless of whether anyone thinks that they are so and there is an objective standard to which things should be compared and ranked in these terms. An action or institution is just to the extent that it is because of its imitating or sharing in the Form of Justice. Although it will not be perfectly just in every way, there is nevertheless a genuine and objective measure of its justice that is independent of what people happen to believe about the matter. The second important aspect is that these evaluative Forms are offered as objects of knowledge and desire. The rational part of the soul desires to know them and, in its ideal state, will possess the knowledge of these Forms. The theory of Forms therefore holds out the promise of a kind of moral expertise. Looking again to the *Republic*, Socrates there asserts an extreme form of moral realism in which not only are there such objective moral properties but one of them – the Good – is elevated to the status of the single ontological principle responsible for everything that exists and, in turn, everything that merely comes to be and passes away. It is famously compared with the Sun: just as the Sun is the cause of making things grow and be visible, so the Good is the cause of making things exist and be knowable (508a–509b). Coming to know the Good is therefore the very pinnacle of human intellectual and moral achievement.[6] Other dialogues present similar views. In the *Symposium*, for example, Socrates gives a long exposition of the views of a wise woman – Diotima – about love. According to Diotima, in the context of the right kind of guidance, a person might progress from a desire for the beauty of a particular lover's body, through the recognition of a more general beauty in other bodies, also to see beauty in a soul and indeed in various institutions and practices. Finally, this same desire for beauty might lead someone to grasp and understand Beauty itself, a final culmination of this erotic ascent which is supposed to be intensely satisfying and also the cause of generating true virtue (211d–212b). Once again, the progression towards understanding the Form of Beauty is both an intellectual challenge

---

[6] See for further discussion of knowledge, Forms, and ruling in the *Republic*: Denyer 2007 and Sedley 2007.

and a gradual process of greater psychological satisfaction since the person's desires are gradually being trained on better and better objects. (Incidentally, the *Symposium* is just one of the dialogues in which Plato emphasizes the importance of proper and beneficial intimate interpersonal relationships of love and friendship in our lives for our chances of ethical improvement; the dialogues often represent examples of good and less successful such relationships in the exchanges between the characters.)[7]

The ethical consequences of such moral expertise can then be considered in two ways: the consequences for the knower himself and the consequences of the possibility of such knowledge for human societies more generally. First, just as Socrates seems to have asserted on the basis of a simple intellectualist model of the soul that knowledge of what is really good, really bad, and really neither is both necessary and sufficient for a person to live virtuously – sometimes he is tempted simply to assert that virtue is a kind of knowledge (e.g. *Euthydemus* 278e–282b, *Protagoras* 361a–c, *Meno* 87c–88d) – so too, even with the addition of the more complex psychology envisaged in other dialogues, it appears that possession of knowledge of the Forms will have a sufficiently powerful effect that it will guarantee the required harmony of the soul under the guidance and control of reason. In part, this assurance might be made more plausible by the thought that unless the non-reasoning parts of the soul are sufficiently under control in the first place, it is impossible to undertake the extremely demanding intellectual feats needed to come to know the Good. Certainly, Socrates emphasizes in the *Republic* not only how gruelling the preparation must be for coming properly to understand the Good – involving understanding various highly abstract and mathematical ideas – but also how this is not possible for people who are, for example, subject to violent and distracting appetitive desires.[8] Hence it is extremely important to make sure that even from birth we do our best to encourage the right kind of development of these non-rational motivations and avoid subjecting the soul to potentially disturbing forces. Nevertheless, once that knowledge is acquired and the person's reason is in full possession of this understanding, psychological harmony seems from that point on to be guaranteed and, in turn, so too will be the performance of actions in accordance with the excellent and virtuous traits of character that a harmonious soul will produce. It will also follow, therefore, that such a life will be a good human life.

---

[7] For a detailed account of the *Symposium* and its account of human happiness see Sheffield 2006.

[8] See e.g. Burnyeat 2000.

At this point, we should pause to notice that the good life is not something that can be achieved by all people. Most of us are sadly incapable of leading a genuinely good human life, largely because of our intellectual incapacity and poor early upbringing, and we must therefore make do with as close an approximation to the ideal as we can manage. Plato's ethical thinking, like his epistemology, is elitist in this sense. Not everyone – in fact, very few people – will attain full knowledge of the Forms and very few people will become moral experts and live a good human life.

There are several consequences of this picture of moral expertise for societies in general. In the first place, it seems to follow that the pursuit of such moral knowledge is of tremendous importance for everyone, not only those who might be so fortunate as to be able to acquire it themselves. Socrates is fond of using a comparison between expertise and the health of the body and expertise and the health of the soul. Just as someone without medical knowledge will listen to and obey the instructions of a medical expert in deciding how to foster his physical health, so too someone without moral expertise should listen to and obey the instructions of a moral expert in deciding how to foster his psychic health. The vast majority of humans will not be able themselves to acquire the knowledge of the Good and will therefore not be able to guarantee for themselves the kind of psychological excellence that a moral expert can. But they will be able to approach this state by relying on the knowledge that such moral experts have: they can bolster their own deficient reason by relying on the precepts set down by those experts. It is therefore in the interests of these people that they should be ruled by moral experts. This is one way in which the dialogues set out the deficiencies of a democratic regime in which majority opinion rather than knowledge is allowed to dictate what is treated as good and just. The desirability of being governed by knowledge of what is good trumps any purported value provided by everyone having some say in judgments about moral and political matters.[9]

What is more, the supreme importance of this moral expertise for everyone's chances of living as good a life as possible gives everyone good reason to do their utmost to foster the chances of those who might acquire this necessary knowledge. In the *Republic*, Socrates sets out how the ideal city is organized in order to foster as much as possible the right conditions for the acquisition and then the effective implementation of moral knowledge.

---

[9] See Keyt 2006 and, for a more general account of Plato's political philosophy, Schofield 2006.

These conditions extend beyond what might appear to be the narrow confines of educational policy into requirements for the right kind of architecture, artistic performances, familial relationships and the like. These often radical policies are all ultimately justified by the idea that everyone's good is best served by the promotion of the conditions for moral expertise.

There is one further important element to this vision. Once someone in such a city has acquired this knowledge he also recognizes an obligation to use that knowledge to legislate for and guide others for the best. Socrates thinks he is entitled to this claim not only because of the general understanding of the reasoning part of the soul as also motivationally efficient but also because, in the case of those who have acquired the moral expertise as a result of the assistance of their fellow citizens, it will be the just and good thing to do to repay this debt by undertaking to rule in the service of the city as a whole. And such 'philosopher kings' are all motivated to do what is just and good.[10]

SOUL AND BODY

Plato's inquiries into the psychological basis of human happiness involve not only an interest in the nature of the soul but also an interest in the nature of the relationship between the soul and the body. The dialogues share the view that a living human is composed of a body and a soul and that the soul is something immaterial that will survive after the dissolution of this body–soul pair. The soul therefore has various affinities with the immaterial Forms that are the proper objects of knowledge and is also closer to the divine than is the body. But the dialogues differ to some extent in their views about which of our human activities should be assigned to the body and which to the soul. Nevertheless, despite the differences of detail, there is a general commitment to the idea that embodiment is not the ideal state for the soul since, while in a body, it is hampered in performing its proper activities. This is perhaps given its strongest presentation in the *Phaedo*, where Socrates argues that the philosopher should strive as far as possible to separate the soul from the body by neglecting and denying value to merely bodily affections (e.g. *Phaedo* 79b–84b). In this way philosophy is 'a preparation for death' (67e). And the idea that the soul's natural state is to be disembodied is something to which

---

[10] The argument of this section of the *Republic* (519c–521a) remains extremely controversial. For some recent discussions see: Kraut 1999, Brown 2000, and Smith 2010.

Plato seems committed throughout his career. This has obvious important consequences for his ethical thinking and for the best way for humans to live their embodied lives. For one, the dialogues often explore the consequences of certain ways of embodied living for the fate of the soul once it is separated from the body at the person's death, often in the form of eschatological myths (see e.g. the myths at the end of the *Phaedo* (110b–115a), *Gorgias* (523a–527a), and *Republic* (614b–621d)). Souls that are affected as little as possible by their unfortunate embodiment will fare better once they have been freed from the body while souls that have been affected badly by being subjected to living a life committed to physical pleasures and indulgences will fare badly. Given the further claim that we should identify ourselves with our souls rather than either our bodies or the temporary combinations of bodies and souls (e.g. *Alcibiades I* 129b–130c), this concern for our own fate in the period after death should be an important guide for our behavior and values during life.

In other dialogues, however, the body is thought of in somewhat more positive terms. In Plato's *Timaeus*, for example, where we get an account of the nature and construction of the cosmos we find that – in line with the general framework of teleological cosmology – our physical bodies and sense-organs were designed by divine craftsmen in order best to allow our souls, when embodied, to come to recognize order, harmony and truth. Although the fact of being assaulted by information through perception and by bodily needs does threaten the soul's proper functioning, the gods who took care of the design of our bodies did their best to minimize the dangers. Timaeus recommends that we should look after our bodies (88a–89a) and also seems to grant an important role to perception, particularly the sense of sight, since it allows us to gaze at the harmonious revolutions of the heavens and thereby improve the revolutions of our own souls (90c–d).[11] Other dialogues emphasize the similar role that listening to the right kind of music can play in our psychic development by encouraging an affinity for harmony and order (e.g. *Laws* 669b–673d). Elsewhere, it seems that the sense of sight can provoke at least the initial stages of the intellectual journey towards knowledge of the Forms. In the *Symposium*, the apparent physical beauty of another body can provoke the desire that, properly harnessed, will lead to the ascent towards viewing Beauty itself. In the *Phaedo* and the *Republic* the recognition of the way perceptible items fall short of displaying perfect equality or appear to display a pair of contrary properties (e.g. the ring

---

[11] Two recent detailed accounts of the *Timaeus* are Johansen 2004 and Broadie 2012.

finger appears both large and small in comparison with the fingers either side of it) is a first step on the road that can eventually lead to knowledge of the Forms.

There is a similarly subtle account of the role of pleasure and pain in our ethical thinking and in the best kinds of life. While mere basic physical pleasures are never accorded a great value and will indeed often be a sign of a damaging interest in the body rather than in the soul, it is never denied that a good human life will be a pleasant life. In fact, it is asserted in the *Republic* that the best kind of life – the philosophical life – will be by some way the most pleasant life a person can lead. This is because of the presence in that kind of life of great intellectual pleasures – the pleasures of knowing the Forms – that come from satisfying the desires of the rational part of the soul. In the longest and most complicated analysis of the place of pleasures and pains in the good life – the *Philebus* – Socrates again admits that although they come very low on the final agreed list of goods, at least some pleasures are still a necessary part of a human life (62e–64a).[12]

BECOMING LIKE GOD

Finally, there is one last aspect of Plato's ethical thought that must be addressed. From the Hellenistic period onwards, anyone asking for a one-sentence summary of Plato's ethical ideal would in all likelihood have been told that according to Plato the goal of life (the *telos*) is 'becoming like god' or, expanded a little further, 'becoming as much like god as possible for a human' (see e.g. Alcinous' *Didaskalikos* 28). This slogan is found most prominently in the *Theaetetus* (176a–c) and the *Timaeus* (90a–d) but it occurs in the *Republic* (613a–b) and the *Symposium* (212b) too.

The idea that the best human life is one in which a person lives a life that is as divine as possible is in fact common ground between Plato, Aristotle, the Stoics, the Epicureans, and various others, although they differ from one another in both their accounts of the best life and their accounts of the nature of divinity. In Plato's case, the divine life amounts to a life spent in purely intellectual pursuits and is a further elaboration of the idea we met earlier that the good human life is the life of philosophy. More specifically, the philosophical life which is as divine as possible is a life spent in the contemplation of eternal truths rather than the shifting and contingent characteristics of our familiar perceptible world. Some dialogues – for example, the *Theaetetus* – choose to emphasize the way in which

---

[12] See Russell 2005.

this will draw a person away from mundane affairs and away from the concerns of politics and convention. Others – such as the *Republic*, as we have already seen – emphasize how the possession of such knowledge, given the right circumstances, will issue in a desire to make the familiar world as like as possible the perfect objects of this divine knowledge. (In this respect we might also imagine that the philosophical rulers of the ideal city are like the craftsman god of the *Timaeus* in so far as they are engaged in a project of making as close a likeness as possible to these perfect objects in the material with which they must work.) Through the knowledge of these things, as we have seen, such a person will not only be perfecting the very best part of himself – his reason – but will also himself become just and good, because he will know what is truly just and good.[13] In this way we see once again the close connection between possessing knowledge, particularly knowledge of moral truths, and being a just and good person. This close connection was in all likelihood something that Plato first saw being argued for by Socrates and it is a connection that he retained and elaborated throughout his career.

BIBLIOGRAPHY

An asterisk denotes secondary literature especially suitable for further reading.

Annas, J. 1993, *The Morality of Happiness*, Oxford University Press
Broadie, S. 2012, *Nature and Divinity in Plato's Timaeus*, Cambridge University Press
Brown, E. 2000, 'Justice and Compulsion for Plato's Philosopher-rulers', *Ancient Philosophy* 20, 1–17
Burnyeat, M.F. 2000, 'Plato on Why Mathematics is Good for the Soul', in T. Smiley (ed.), *Mathematics and Necessity*, Oxford: British Academy, 1–81
Burnyeat, M.F. 2006, 'The Truth of Tripartition', *Proceedings of the Aristotelian Society* 106, 1–22
Denyer, N. 2007, 'Sun and Line: The Role of the Good', in Ferrari 2007b: 284–309
Ferrari, G. 2003, *City and Soul in Plato's Republic*, Sankt Augustin: Academia Verlag
Ferrari, G. 2007a, 'The Three-part Soul', in Ferrari 2007b: 165–201
Ferrari, G. (ed.) 2007b, *The Cambridge Companion to Plato's Republic*, Cambridge University Press
Fine, G. (ed.) 1999, *Plato 2: Ethics, Politics, Religion, and the Soul*, Oxford University Press*
Irwin, T. 1995, *Plato's Ethics*, Oxford University Press*
Johansen, T. 2004, *Plato's Natural Philosophy*, Cambridge University Press
Keyt, D. 2006, 'Plato and the Ship of State', in Santas 2006: 189–213
Kraut, R. 1999, 'Return to the Cave: *Republic* 519–21', in Fine 1999: 235–54
Lorenz, H. 2006, 'The Analysis of the Soul in Plato's Republic', in Santas 2006: 125–45

---

[13] See Sedley 1999.

Moss, J. 2008, 'Appearances and Calculations: Plato's Division of the Soul', *Oxford Studies in Ancient Philosophy* 34, 35–68

Russell, D. 2005, *Plato on Pleasure and the Good Life*, Oxford University Press

Santas, G. (ed.) 2006, *The Blackwell Guide to Plato's Republic*, Oxford: Blackwell

Schofield, M. 2006, *Plato: Political Philosophy*, Oxford University Press★

Sedley, D. 1999, 'The Ideal of Godlikeness', in Fine 1999: 309–28

Sedley, D. 2007, 'Philosophy, the Forms, and the Art of Ruling', in Ferrari 2007b: 256–83

Sheffield, F. 2006, *Plato's Symposium: The Ethics of Desire*, Oxford University Press

Smith, N. 2010, 'Return to the Cave', in M. McPherran (ed.), *Plato's Republic: a Critical Guide*, Cambridge University Press, 83–102

4

Aristotle

MICHAEL PAKALUK

Aristotle's moral philosophy may usefully be viewed as the development and combination of two strands of thought and of ethical idealism, one drawn from Socrates and the other from Plato. The Socratic strand may be called the "protreptic," since it addresses the question, "How then shall I live?," and therefore is hortatory, and indeed it is found in its fullest form in a lost and then rediscovered dialogue of Aristotle, entitled *Protrepticus* (Johnson and Hutchinson 2005). The strand drawn from Plato may be called the "republican," because it looks at questions of individual well-being and flourishing mainly from the point of view of a lawmaker or citizen in a city-state, and its starting points are taken from Plato's dialogue, *Republic*. The protreptic strand disposes us to look at questions in moral philosophy from a first-person point of view, and the republican strand from a third-person point of view.

THE PROTREPTIC STRAND

The protreptic strand starts from an argument that we should direct ourselves to improving the soul, not the body: the task (*ergon*) of human life is to achieve something worthy of praise (*epaineton*); good and beautiful things ("noble," "honorable," "fine" – *kala*) are what are truly praiseworthy, and it is not the body but the soul which a human being truly is; but virtue (*aretê*) makes the soul good and beautiful, the way that health and fitness do for the body; therefore, the task of a human life is to make one's soul good and beautiful, by acquiring virtue (see *Protr.* 1.1–2.11).

The following abbreviations are used in this chapter: *DA – De Anima, EE – Eudemian Ethics, MM – Magna Moralia, NE – Nicomachean Ethics, Pol – Politics, VV – On Virtues and Vices.*

Note the presuppositions of even this simple argument: that human beings as a natural kind have some kind of role or place to play in nature; that considerations of how we should live depend upon considerations of what we are and how we are constituted; that considerations about the body can be used to draw conclusions by analogy about the soul; that beauty (involving form) and goodness (involving fruitfulness, benefit, and good functioning) are closely related; that the goodness of the soul, achieved through the virtues, is in various ways prior to the goodness of external things and the body; and that human life is reasonably understood as directed toward the achieving of something admirable and indeed even great.

In Aristotle's protreptic strand, this initial argument then gets developed mainly in two ways, first, to yield the conclusion that what one really needs to devote one's life to is the actualization and not the mere possession of virtue, and, second, to infer that a certain part or power of the soul deserves the same kind of prior attention, relative to the rest of the soul, that, it was originally claimed, the soul as a whole deserved over the body.

Consider first how the actualization of virtue naturally comes to be seen as most important. A certain incongruity results if a person attends to his body, its fitness and beauty, but fails to build up his soul: it is as if, Aristotle says, a master were to have rendered himself inferior to his slaves (*Protr.* 3.4). The disgracefulness of the disparity seems additional to the disgracefulness of simply the uncultivated soul itself. But this then suggests that the soul needs somehow to be at work, through the application of its virtue, in directing to its benefit those other things that have been identified as by nature ordered to it. Aristotle calls this application the "use" (*chrêsis*) and not mere "possession" (*ktêsis*) of virtue (using language that throughout his works he uses for the distinction between so-called first and second actuality) (see for example *NE* VII.3.1147a10–14).

It seems reasonable to pick out and give a name to the virtue of the soul insofar as someone makes good use of other goods by nature ordered to the soul. In the protreptic strand this is the first way in which Aristotle understands *phronêsis* ("practical wisdom"), which he will also refer to, at least initially, as "philosophy" (*philosophia*) (*Protr.* 9.1). With the identification of *phronêsis*, an ordering and hierarchy of goods appears within the soul also: *phronêsis* looks to be "better" than other virtues; other virtues are somehow "for" or "for the sake of" it. Aristotle supports this conclusion with various arguments which rely on a teleology supposed to be present in nature: for example, what comes later in a natural process of development may be presumed to be better, and *phronêsis* develops later than other virtues (*Protr.* 17.1–12).

Once an ordering among virtues is accepted at all, then the question can be raised of whether *phronêsis* really stands at the apex. To argue that it does not, first the possibility of some other, contender virtue needs to be established – which Aristotle does by holding that the part of the soul which *phronêsis* adorns and renders good, "the part which has or contains reason" (*to logon echôn*), has another operation besides the use and ordering of goods, and that a different virtue adorns and renders this part in that operation good. This other operation is "speculative" (*theôrêtikê*), that is, it involves doing nothing besides simply "seeing" and admiring the way the world is (*theôria*), and the virtue which adorns this activity as directed at the entirety of existence, and renders it good, is "wisdom" (*sophia*). But by various considerations one can establish that this virtue is at the apex and its activity is the best achievement of a human life, to wit: the activity of simply seeing is in general more valuable than useful goods, as shown by the fact that we happily pay money, giving up useful goods, to attend the theater and other spectacles, and, if so, then surely simply seeing the entirety of reality, which *sophia* enables us to do, is more valuable than all useful goods put together (*Protr.* 44.8); the activity of simply seeing is better than the activity of ordering and using, because its objects are better – they are even divine – while our ordering and use of goods pertains, of course, to things good *for us*, and thus the activity of *phronêsis* is restricted to the realm of the merely human (*to anthrôpinon*); we are busy in order to enjoy leisure, and so activities of leisure have the character of a goal (*telos*) and best good, but the activity of simply seeing is suited to leisure whereas the activity of *phronêsis* is not; and that activity which is most closely related to the gods would presumably be best, but the gods could hardly engage in any activity except simply seeing, and therefore human beings, to the extent that they engage in this activity as well, become like the gods and therefore would be beloved by the gods. Besides, the activity of simply seeing of itself leads to nothing else and is enjoyed just for its own sake, which is what one expects in a good at the top of a hierarchy of goods; and, in any case, *sophia* is in an important sense the *only* virtue of "the part of the soul which has reason" because it is the only virtue which is a virtue of just that part (*oikia*) – as the virtue of *phronêsis* can be seen to be bound up with other virtues of the soul.

The protreptic strand, in sum, aims to improve upon the Socratic exhortation to attend to virtue rather than corporeal goods by specifying one virtue in particular which deserves preeminent attention and by emphasizing that the ultimate good of a human life consists in the achievement of putting that virtue somehow into practice. This strand finds its fullest statement in the reconstructed *Protrepticus*, but Aristotle also brings it forward and gives it center stage at the conclusion of the *Nicomachean Ethics* (10.7–8), where nearly all the arguments of the *Protrepticus* are repeated in compressed form. This strand is addressed to the listener of the dialogue or of the lectures as if to an interlocutor. It makes no pretense of being a general claim about how human beings should live or even how society should be organized. It does not need to give an account of the virtues generally but simply to say enough to make it plausible that *sophia* would be the best among them. Its connection with any lines of thought in Aristotle that pertain to how we should act towards others in society takes place through the term that Aristotle typically uses to characterize that aspect of the world which makes it suitable simply to see, namely, *kalon*, which means literally "beautiful" or "admirable," but also by extension "honorable," "noble," "appropriate," or even "ingenious" and "excellent." The unifying idea is that what makes simply seeing worthy of choice is that its object is *kalon*, and what makes virtuous action worthy of choice in its own right is that such action is *kalon*, and the suggestion is either that thinking and doing are two different ways of possessing the *kalon*, or that action is inherently valuable on account of its somehow containing thinking which is inherently valuable (see Lear 2004).

THE REPUBLICAN STRAND

The rather different republican strand of thought takes its start from a main argument of Plato's *Republic* I, which is that authority in human affairs is based upon some kind of knowledge or expert skill (*technê*); expert skill of its nature aims at the good of the persons or things it acts upon, and certainly at some good other than the good of the person who practices that skill (except incidentally), or of the skill itself (which as a skill is perfect and needs nothing); political authority, too, is based upon expert skill; and therefore political authority, and the expert skill of which it should be an expression, of their very nature aim at the good of the ruled, not of the ruler. But now add some basic considerations which Aristotle presents in *Politics* 1.1 and in *Nicomachean Ethics* 1.1: political society (the *polis*, or *politikê koinônia*) is the form of human association to which all others are adapted and which marks the completion of other forms of sociability; the more complete the form of association, the more complete and ultimate the good at which it aims; and, thus, the good at which authority over the *polis* aims, strictly, is to make the citizens good human beings, by leading them through sound laws and customs to acquire the virtues (and to provide the conditions under which those virtues can find suitable realization).

But what makes a human being good? Aristotle attempts to be systematic, in cataloguing with precision what kinds of virtues there are, how they are to be defined, and exactly how many there are, and by explaining how they come into existence and can go out of existence. Of the four ethical works traditionally attributed to Aristotle, the *Nicomachean Ethics*, the *Eudemian Ethics*, the *Magna Moralia*, and *On Virtues and Vices*, the last is solely such a systematic catalogue of the virtues (and vices too), and the others are predominantly that. Aristotle regards this systematic cataloguing as the complete carrying-through of what his predecessors attempted. Socrates, he says, mistakenly regarded all the virtues as pertaining to "the part of the soul which has *logos*"; Plato improved upon Socrates through identifying additionally two virtues of character, which perfect the parts of the soul which do not of themselves "have *logos*": courage (*andreia*), related to the faculty of spiritedness (*thumos*), and moderation (*sôphrosunê*), related to the faculty of sense desire (or *epithumia*). Aristotle improves upon this scheme in turn by distinguishing, as we have seen, two main virtues of the part which has *logos*, corresponding to the two parts of this part (*phronêsis*, which is practical, and *sophia*, which is speculative). He adds a particular virtue of justice, which wants to realize equality in agreements and transactions. Finally, he adds virtues for each of the goods in the standard list of "external goods": money, honor, and companions. (Aristotle's general principle for enumerating virtues is to hold that there is a distinct virtue for each distinct part of the soul: Pakaluk 2011. Strictly there is no "money loving," "honor loving," or "companionship loving" part of the soul, presumably because the parts of the soul are properly those suggested by a sound human psychology, such as Aristotle thinks he presents in the *De Anima*, and the "external goods" do not correspond to biological needs but are artifacts of human social life. But the striving (*orexis*) for a good of this sort, as perduring, is akin to a part of the soul and can be thought of as having its own perfecting quality or virtue.)

Note that no one had attempted to define and enumerate virtues in this way before Aristotle. The final catalogue looks basically like this:

Parts of the soul	Virtues
The thinking part	
The part which has logos (*to logon echôn*)	
directed toward simply seeing (*theoretikon*)	wisdom, *sophia*
directed toward action (*praktikon*)	practical wisdom, *phronêsis*
The desiderative part	
The part which desires order and equality (*boulêsis*)	justice, *dikaiosunê*
The spirited part (*thumos*)	courage, *andreia*
The sense desiring part (*epithumia*)	moderation, *sôphrosunê*
Virtual parts	
Striving for money (*orexis chrêmatôn*)	
on a large scale	magnificence, *megaloprepeia*
on a small scale	liberality, *eleutheriotês*
Striving for honor (*orexis timês*)	
on a large scale	magnanimity, *megalopsuchia*
on a small scale	measured ambition, *philotimia*
Striving for companionship (*orexis philias*)	friendliness, *philia*
	truthfulness, *alêtheia*
	ready wit, *eutrapeleia*

The republican strand is of service to political authorities not simply as stating accurately what they should be aiming at in the citizens they govern but also as giving a portrait of what they themselves, precisely as rulers, should be like – since rulers, if not virtuous, will not seek the good of those they govern, Aristotle thinks. Non-virtuous rulers necessarily seek above all something good not as honorable (*kalon*), but rather as useful (*chrêsimon*) or pleasant (*hêdu*), which is therefore a good *for themselves*. Indeed, no one can be effective in political life without being good. Note that these concerns are similar to Plato's constant concern to channel the ambition of young aristocratic men and persuade them to become good before they acquire power; also, Plato's concern in the *Republic* to make the interests of rulers align with the interests of those ruled.

Aristotle uses his investigation of virtue as an occasion to introduce and cover anything closely related to the virtues, which is why, he says, he additionally covers friendship (*philia*), pleasure (*hêdonê*), and phenomena of weakness of will and self-control (*akrasia* and *enkrateia*). Friendship is the natural and most suitable context in which virtue is acquired, rendered stable, and actualized. Pleasure is of interest because pleasures associated with bodily functions (eating, drinking, sex, comfort) need to be demoted as goods, especially given that corrupt rulers, by seeking these pleasures, testify as it were that these are the greatest goods; yet pleasures which magnify, elicit, prolong, and focus activity need to be boosted and given prominence, as these are crucially important to the acquisition and realization of virtue. As for weakness of will and self-control, Aristotle finds these interesting because they look to be somehow intermediate between the two ostensible extremes of virtue and vice.

INTEGRATION OF THE PROTREPTIC AND REPUBLICAN STRANDS

The ethical works attributed to Aristotle, which together block out at least what could have been counted as in the Aristotelian tradition, contain the protreptic and republican strands to different extents. The *Protrepticus* cares not at all about virtue except to establish the superiority of the speculative kind. The probably spurious *VV* in contrast cares not at all about *sophia*. *MM*, of doubtful authenticity, mentions *sophia* briefly and says that *phronêsis* ministers to it, but it apologizes for introducing *sophia* into a discussion of republican virtue, and says it will deal with that virtue only because it would be improper to leave it out when all the other virtues were being covered. *NE* is famous for being mainly a catalogue of the virtues, with protreptic arguments breaking through and becoming decisive in the end.

Obviously one can try to explain the appearance of these distinct strands, and the differing emphases they receive, with some kind of developmental theory, or by a theory of different intended audiences, together perhaps with a dismissal of some of the mentioned works as spurious (Kenny 1978, Pakaluk 1998). Here it seems best to give a sketch of how Aristotle tended to conceive of these strands as integrated into his practical philosophy as a whole.

Aristotle holds that political society, the *polis*, is the naturally complete form of human association. But the *polis* is by nature composed of households. Within households free citizens have discretion in the ordering of their own lives, but subject to their first having met duties toward household life. Similarly, households and members of households have discretion in ordering their actions in public life, subject to their following the law of the *polis*, and given that duties toward the *polis* (such as military service) do not supersede. That is, citizens in their relationships and projects are subordinated to the households to which they belong, and those households to the *polis*, in a hierarchical relationship of authority like those sketched in *NE* 1.1 and 8.9. On this picture of how human social life arises by nature, practical philosophy has three subject areas: of the *polis*, or "politics" (*politika*); of the household, or "economics" (*oikonomika*);[1] and of an individual citizen and his character and practices, "ethics" (*êthika*). The protreptic strand speaks mainly to the question of what individuals should be like, and what they should ideally do, insofar as they have freedom over the use of their time, especially their time which is generally free of necessities ("leisure," *scholê*), and the republican to what individuals should be like usefully to occupy roles as members of households and of the *polis*.

To look for an Aristotelian "moral philosophy" other than in his complete philosophy of action, comprising all three subject areas mentioned, will inevitably lead to misunderstandings. For example, why does one find nothing like "moral law" in Aristotle's ethics? Because law is provided by the *polis*, and, at least in cases where rulers are reasonably aiming to rule for the good of the governed, legal obligation binds a citizen above all other duties and considerations. Again, why for Aristotle is it the case that one should not kill? Because any *polis* will for natural and obvious reasons set down laws against murder, and one is obliged to keep the laws of the *polis* before considering what one should do in one's own time or for one's own good.

For Aristotle, an individual does not begin ethical deliberation thinking about what is best for him and then somehow reasoning to why he should be just or why he should enter into political society or obey its laws; rather, an individual's ethical deliberation – a consideration of what kind of person one should be, and of the best use of the time at one's discretion – takes place in the context of political justice and law as already having force. These have force because an individual can reasonably come to regard himself, precisely as being the individual he is, as part of a larger whole whose good takes precedence over his own, if both cannot be attained. Here one must attend to the curious notion of a "common good" (*to koinêi sumpheron*). A clear example is found in the account of reproduction in *DA* II.4: animals want to imitate the divine and attain immortality, Aristotle says; but no animal composed of body and soul, and therefore inevitably mortal, can do this as an individual; however, the species as a whole can attain immortality, by reproduction of like by like for eternity; and so what an animal cannot achieve on its own it achieves through and with others of its own species. On this account, an animal's dying once it reaches maturity and reproduces is not contrary to that animal's good, because its good as a mortal being is

---

[1] Which considers the task which Aristotle thinks is distinctive of households, namely, wealth creation.

precisely to die and give way, as a part of the species, which continues to live. So too, Aristotle's account of courage presupposes that the good of an individual, by nature a part of the *polis*, in some circumstances is precisely to perish for the sake of the continuing existence of the *polis*. The individual who thus gives up his life can indeed see and affirm this: he is capable, then, of receiving the relevant law of the *polis* (say, "citizens are obliged to defend the *polis*, even unto death, if the *polis* is threatened") not as an alien restriction on an antecedent freedom, but rather as a reasonable prescription, trumping considerations of his own benefit (even his prospects for future speculative activity; see *NE* 3.9.1117b7–15), given his position as part of a greater whole.

Such is one way, then, by which the protreptic and republican strands are integrated for Aristotle. The other, as mentioned, involves the notion of the "noble," "admirable," or "beautiful," *kalon*, which Aristotle takes up following Plato in the *Gorgias* and *Symposium*. Aristotle gives no analysis of the *kalon*, but as it evidently means something like physical beauty, yet it is grasped by "the part which has *logos*," it must refer to the beauty of something precisely as grasped and understood. If it is a kind of beauty, then we can take it to have characteristics analogous to classical Greek ideals of beauty generally, and say that it involves some kind of symmetry, proportion, elegance, efficiency, fittingness of match, suggestion of fecundity, and radiance or clarity. That Aristotle might have characterized virtuous action, and the virtues themselves, as *kalon* is perhaps not difficult to see: virtues such as courage and moderation involve a subtle rational control and mastery not unlike what is admired in athletic accomplishments; courage in particular involves (as we have seen) the implicit affirmation, by the courageous soldier, that it is appropriate for a natural part of a social whole precisely to take its place as a part for the sake of the whole; justice displays appropriate proportion and a quasi-mathematical ideal of equality; magnanimity, as being a kind of "crown" of the virtues, draws attention to and expresses the beauty of virtue itself; a friendship is precisely a relationship in which considerations of condign reciprocity take precedence; and so on.

Considerations of the *kalon* serve of course to reinforce the picture of a human being as by nature a social animal. If it is by nature that a human being is fitted to live in political society, then it would be appropriate and *kalon* for an individual in effect to affirm this in his action, and wrongheaded, foolish, and misguided (*aischron*) for him in effect to deny this in his action. For a gifted philosopher to desert his friends on the battlefield on the ostensible grounds that he thereby can claim happiness for himself through a longer life becomes, at least, exceedingly incongruous. Such a person is open to the charge of choosing "mere living" over "living well." Aristotle additionally seems to hold, much along the lines of an argument in Plato's *Gorgias* (574c–584a), that no one is ever advantaged by doing something *aischron*, as an *aischron* action inherently deserves blame, and, if it cannot be corrected for – as an injustice can be corrected for – it is a standing occasion for shame and disgust felt towards oneself and reproach and repugnance felt by others. So if an *aischron* action can be corrected for, it should be, and therefore implies no advantage: the philosopher mentioned above, who deserted his friends in battle to save himself, if he were to seek again to attain the *kalon* without exception, would first of all be bound to turn himself in to the authorities and receive the due punishment for desertion.

But considerations of the *kalon* integrate the protreptic and republican strands in a more direct way. Aristotle regards true thought and good action as two varieties of attaining the *kalon*. His view depends upon particular understandings of both speculative thought and practical thought. For Aristotle, speculative thought is directed at things that cannot be otherwise; our purpose in thinking of them, therefore, cannot be to control or manipulate anything, but rather simply to admire, appreciate, and even wonder at them. Furthermore, because in the activity of thinking of something some kind of identity is forged between the thinker and thing thought of, to think of these wonderful things is to share ourselves in what makes them wonderful. As for practical thought, Aristotle seems to regard action and skillful making too as attractive because of the thought behind them, as both involve in broadest terms the imposition of form, which is an object of thought, upon matter. The author of *MM* goes so far as to say that if we could see directly what a virtuous person was purposing to do, there would be no need for him to do virtuous actions, for us to praise him. Apparently for Aristotle the sole advantage which actually doing a *kalon* action enjoys over the deliberate contemplating of it, itself *kalon* and praiseworthy, is that the action further realizes the existence of the person contemplating it (*NE* 9.7.1167b33–1168a9).

CONCLUDING OBSERVATIONS

It has been the concern of this introduction and overview to identify the most important presuppositions of Aristotelian ethical theory, which are taken for granted by him and implicit in the philosophical tradition which he inherits from Socrates and Plato. These presuppositions may be summarized as: nature is prior to convention and, as it is teleological, it sets down standards against which conventions, practices, and actions may be evaluated; by nature a human being is set with the task of speculative thought, that is, of simply seeing and admiring the world and its parts; in doing so a human being shares in the *kalon*, which is that which makes anything admirable; moreover, by his nature as a rational animal, and as a social animal, insofar as he must attend either on his own or together with others for the necessary conditions of human life, it is accordingly *kalon* for him to acquire the virtues and live with others in justice and friendship; there is a deep kinship between doing what is *kalon* and contemplating what is *kalon*; and the proper rule in life is without exception and above all to attain what is *kalon*. These presuppositions serve to group Aristotle with Socrates and Plato and set all three apart from much of the history of moral philosophy. It has likewise been a concern here to suggest explanations as to why what have seemed to be great difficulties for recent interpreters of Aristotle – such as the conflict between a "dominant end" and an "inclusive" conception of happiness (Hardie 1965, Ackrill 1974/1980); or the problem of why anyone should be moral if philosophizing is taken as a dominant end (Kraut 1991) – were at least not recognized by Aristotle as difficulties. Of course whether these problems ultimately are put to rest if these presuppositions are embraced cannot be decided here.

The standard tour through the highlights of Aristotle's moral theory has been avoided here, as there are many capable accounts which accomplish this (Bostock 2000, Broadie 1991, Pakaluk 2003, Urmson 1987). But the following points might profitably be touched upon specifically in relation to what has already been said.

"Happiness," eudaimonia. Aristotle takes it as commonplace that the term *eudaimonia* denotes the ultimate end of human life. He also regards it as commonplace that non-rational animals have no possibility of attaining *eudaimonia*, whereas God or the gods possess *eudaimonia* most fully; also, he thinks that human *eudaimonia*, insofar attained, is some kind of sharing in a life which properly and of itself is divine. What this implies is this. Not only is *eudaimonia*, for Aristotle, as is often said, a common standard for human beings and something objective (in the sense that someone could be wrong about whether he was happy or not); *eudaimonia* is also not something relative to type or kind but rather an absolute standard for the universe: *eudaimonia* is not merely the best possible achievement or realization for a living thing of some kind but rather a sharing in divine *eudaimonia* (Lawrence, 2005). It should also be noted, as we have in effect already noted, that Aristotle understands the *eudaimonia* at which a particular human being should aim as social: what he should aim at is his own *eudaimonia* as a part

of the *eudaimonia* of the *polis* as a whole. It follows directly and obviously from this that *eudaimonia* requires material conditions, just as the *polis* does. Indeed, an individual's possibility of sharing in some full way in speculative activity, according to Aristotle, depends upon the *polis*'s having developed sufficiently so as to create the possibility of leisure for some classes of citizen within the *polis*.

Virtue as a mean. Presumably Aristotle originally proposed his claim that each virtue of character lies in a mean between two vices at the extremes of deficiency and excess in order to reinforce the idea that some virtues are not entirely intellectual but involve the rational informing of parts of the soul that are by nature non-rational parts of the soul – since the rational part of the soul simply affirms or denies; and knowledge has only one contrary, ignorance; but correctness relative to an appropriate goal involving passions and actions of the body can go wrong by either excess or defect. Yet once this point is taken for granted and becomes settled, it evidently becomes easy in the Aristotelian tradition to think again of each virtue as opposed to only one vice, as is evident in the putatively late treatise, *VV*. Even in *NE* and *EE* there was typically only one vice that really needed to be taken into account for each virtue (e.g. cowardice as regards courage; self-indulgence as regards moderation), since, as *NE* takes pains to explain, frequently either because of the form of the action itself or because of tendencies in human nature there is only one extreme which it proves difficult to avoid. So virtue as a mean proves to be a doctrine of central importance mainly in a certain argumentative context.

"Right reason," *orthos logos*. Certainly Aristotle sometimes uses the multi-purpose word *"logos"* to mean a faculty, not an argument or an explanation (for example *NE* 3.12.1119b14–15), but the question of whether the phrase *orthos logos* means sometimes or mainly the virtue of practical reason (*phronêsis*) need not be settled here. Regardless of whether it is taken to be a faculty or rather simply a course of practical reasoning, what is significant about *orthos logos* is what is connoted by the term *"orthos,"* which means directedness or orientation toward a set goal. The goal toward which this *logos* is duly orientated, according to Aristotle, is the *kalon*: so *orthos logos* indicates a faculty or course of reasoning which properly directs towards the achievement of that goal. Hence Aristotle can re-describe the virtues of character as habits of the will which propose the goal of the *kalon* as regards different domains of action and feeling (which correspond to different parts and quasi-parts, as we have called them, of the soul). Thus, according to Aristotle, *phronêsis* cannot exist without the virtues of character, since then it would not take the *kalon* as its goal and would be reduced to mere cleverness, but the virtues of character similarly cannot exist without *phronêsis*, as they simply set the goal and imply a ductibility in moving toward that goal, but like merely natural virtues they could not reliably attain that goal on their own. Aristotle affirms the unity of the virtues only insofar as he affirms this mutual dependence. Note in this regard that if ethical action is fundamentally the application of form to matter, then it is obvious that successful ethical action must be marked by great sensitivity to facts and circumstances, as the expert shoemaker must be able to see how to adapt a pattern to the available leather, and even see when to throw out that pattern altogether and reach for another. To this extent it has always been a hallmark of Aristotelian ethical theory to stress the sensitivity of ethical judgment to particular facts and circumstances, the most important example of which is the sensitivity required to discern the intention of a lawgiver and apply a law to circumstances which were not and could not have been foreseen: Aristotle's name for this sensitivity, which he regards as refinement of the virtue of justice, is *epieikeia* (traditionally, "equity").

Friendship, *philia*. That one-fifth of *NE* and a comparable proportion of *EE* is devoted to friendship is sometimes taken to reflect the great importance placed on friendship in classical society. This is true, but not a sufficient explanation, since after all friendship in an ordinary sense occupies nothing like that position in Plato's ethical thought, for example. Aristotle has his own reasons. If ethics is, as has been explained, mainly practical philosophy of the individual considered as not antecedently bound by obligations to the *polis* or household, then friendship acquires great importance, as the type of sociability most characteristic of that domain and as the ordinary context in which virtue finds actualization. Again, Aristotle believes that human sociability by nature is meant to radiate out from self-love; its motives and habitual dispositions are impossible without genuine self-love and friendships of the right sort. The positive view developed in *NE* VIII and IX, and *EE* VII, is as it were the philosophical complement of the negative critique developed in *Pol* II, against Plato's communism. So a study of the "springs and sources" (*EE*) of the household and *polis* requires a suitable treatment of friendship in the discipline of ethics. Finally, friendship as a kind of fuller actualization of the relationship that a good person has with himself (*NE* 9.4, 9) in effect gives the best available picture of the human person as a moral agent and serves to explain why considerations of equality, transparency, reciprocity, and non-coercion are so central to our relationships with others.

Pleasure, *hêdonê*. Aristotle gives three accounts of pleasure: (i) it is a kind of perceptual activity which accompanies but is not the same as a bodily process by which some kind of bodily deficiency becomes remedied through replenishment; (ii) it is the unhindered activity of a nature constituted in its good and natural condition; and (iii) it is a kind of flower, or complementary realization, superadded to good activity. Interpreters argue over whether these accounts are consistent and whether the texts in which the different accounts are found in *NE* (7.10–14, and 8.1–5) belonged originally to the same work. The explanation given above of the protreptic and republican strands would suggest why there is a place for three accounts, as (i) argues in effect that what is valuable at all in the widely sought-after bodily pleasures is a kind of aesthetic activity, which therefore would suggest that better types of aesthetic activities are better than these pleasures; (ii) would be a natural way of describing pleasures inherent in the actions characteristic of the virtues of character – important to the republican strand – where the impeding of the activity is a possibility; and (iii) would capture the role of pleasure in the activity of simply seeing – important to the protreptic strand, as surely the grasping and taking thought of the *kalon* brings along with it its own kind of pleasure. Note that all three accounts have in common the thought that pleasure is somehow incidental and secondary to goodness, though in some cases inherently related to it, with the suggestion that it is misguided and ultimately self-defeating to seek pleasure directly and on its own.

BIBLIOGRAPHY

An asterisk denotes secondary literature especially suitable for further reading.

Ackrill, J.L. (1974/1980). "Aristotle on Eudaimonia," *Proceedings of the British Academy*, 60:339–59; reprinted in A.O. Rorty (ed.), *Essays on Aristotle's Ethics*. Berkeley: University of California Press, 15–34.

Bostock, David (2000). *Aristotle's Ethics*. Oxford University Press.

Broadie, Sarah (1991). *Ethics with Aristotle*. New York: Oxford University Press.*

Hardie, W.F.R. (1965). "The Final Good in Aristotle's Ethics," *Philosophy*, 40:277–95.

Johnson, Monte Ransome, and Hutchinson, D.S. (2005). "Authenticating Aristotle's *Protrepticus*," *Oxford Studies in Ancient Philosophy*, 29:193–294.

Kenny, Anthony (1978). *The Aristotelian Ethics*. Oxford University Press.

Kraut, Richard (1991). *Aristotle on the Human Good*. Princeton University Press.

Lawrence, Gavin (2005). "Snakes in Paradise: Problems in the Ideal Life in NE 10," Spindel Conference 2004, in *The Southern Journal of Philosophy*, 43(Supplement):126–65.

Lear, Gabriel Richardson (2004). *Happy Lives and the Highest Good: An Essay on Aristotle's Nicomachean Ethics*. Princeton University Press.

Pakaluk, Michael (1998). "The Egalitarianism of the *Eudemian Ethics*," *Classical Quarterly*, 48:411–32.

Pakaluk, Michael (2003). *Aristotle's* Nicomachean Ethics: *An Introduction*. Cambridge University Press.*

Pakaluk, Michael (2011) "The Unity of the *Nicomachean Ethics*," in Jon Miller (ed.), *Aristotle's Nicomachean Ethics: A Critical Guide*, Cambridge University Press.

Urmson, J.O. (1987). *Aristotle's Ethics*. Oxford: Basil Blackwell.

5

Epicureanism and Hedonism

VOULA TSOUNA

According to a famous allegory related by the sophist Prodicus, the Greek hero Hercules was confronted with the dilemma of choosing between the hard path of Virtue and the easy path of Pleasure, and opted for Virtue to the utter rejection of Pleasure. Most Greek philosophers, with the notable exception of Aristotle, followed Hercules' example, assuming (as Hercules had to assume) that the virtuous life and the pleasurable life represent two basic alternatives, exclusive and exhaustive, of which the former leads towards our moral perfection as rational beings whereas the latter caters to our lower, animal aspects. Epicurus, however, took the road of Pleasure positing it as the *telos*, the supreme good or ultimate goal of human life. Therefore his many critics, both ancient and modern, have consistently interpreted his ethics[1] as a theory advocating excessive physical indulgence.[2] Such interpretations rely on misunderstandings. For Epicurus and his followers developed their theory in deliberate contrast to the hedonism of the Cyrenaics, a Socratic school also accused of sybaritism because its third head, Aristippus the Younger (born c. 380/370 BCE), posited individual episodes of present pleasure, rather than pleasurable states enduring over time, as the only possible moral end. Consequently, Epicurus qualified his own concept of pleasure in such ways as to emphasize precisely the opposite: complete pleasure is a long-term stable condition and comprises one's present experiences as well as the pleasures experienced in the past and those anticipated in the future. Moreover, he suggested that this sort of pleasure goes together with a moderate if not ascetic lifestyle, and also he openly praised plain living.[3]

---

[1] For present purposes, 'ethics' and 'morality' are used interchangeably.

[2] Such criticisms are discussed by Sedley 1976; Hossenfelder 1986; and Erler and Schofield 1999: 643.

[3] It is debated whether Epicurus advocates a sort of asceticism (Erler and Schofield 1999), or considers luxurious pleasures as unproblematic as plain ones (Woolf 2009).

However, some Epicurean texts appear to support the idea that Epicurean ethics focuses on the gratification of the body. The declarations that the root of all good lies in the pleasures of the stomach (Athenaeus, *Deipn.* 546f)[4] and that the satisfaction of 'the cry of the flesh' so as not to be hungry or thirsty or cold makes one as happy as Zeus (*SV* 21) seem to point in that direction. The same holds for Epicurean references to the lowly pig as a positive symbol for humans,[5] and also for the founder's unambiguous hostility to entire domains of Greek *paideia*, culture, on the grounds that they are harmful to the attainment of happiness (D.L. X.5). The criticisms of sensualism and barbarism become even more pressing because the Epicureans were one of few Hellenistic schools that did not claim a Socratic heritage, but instead severed connections with the Socratic tradition and defined themselves in contraposition to the dominant Socratics of their era, the Stoics. Not only does Epicurean hedonism clash with the austere ethics of the Stoics, as well as with the ethics of the Cynics, the Peripatetics, and other groups, but, in addition, the Epicureans break away from the Socratic tradition in the domain of physics. Epicurus develops a modified version of Democritus' atomism and defends a thoroughly mechanistic, non-providential account of the universe and its contents, in sharp opposition to the providentialist creationism of the Stoics and their fellow Socratics of all periods. The surviving parts of Epicurus' major physical work *On Nature*, his *Letter to Herodotus* and *Letter to Pythocles* – both of which we are fortunate to have in their entirety – and the Latin poem *On the Nature of Things* by Lucretius (first century BCE) offer detailed materialist explanations of all sorts of phenomena in the physical world including, importantly, the constitution and functions of the human soul. Hence they convey a fair idea of the far-ranging implications of atomic physics for our understanding of the world and of ourselves, and of the extent to which atomism constitutes the basis of Epicurean hedonism. Throughout its long history, this latter also upholds an empiricist approach to matters of epistemology and scientific method, crucially pertinent to ethical analysis as well. Any attempt to assess Epicurean hedonism needs to take the above factors into account. And any answer offered at present is likely to be

---

[4] A goblet found in Boscoreale depicts Epicurus engaged in discussion with Zeno the Stoic and looking wistfully at a piece of cake lying on a table in front of him (Erler and Schofield 1999: 642–3).

[5] The pig is a positive symbol just in so far as it is tranquil and devoid of false or empty beliefs; however, this does not entail that a pig can attain perfect happiness nor that we ought to aspire to the mental and psychological limitations of that animal (see Warren 2002: 129–49).

reconsidered in future times in the light of fresh evidence found in hitherto inaccessible sources, notably the carbonized Epicurean papyri found in Herculaneum, which have become the object of intensive study. The account of Epicurean hedonism below relies on both earlier and later writings, some of which belong to the Herculaneum collection.

PLEASURE AND HAPPINESS

A good place to begin is the systematic exposition of Epicurean ethics by Torquatus, the Epicurean spokesman in Cicero's *On the Moral Ends* (*Fin.* I.29–30).[6] According to Torquatus, Epicurus said that pleasure is the only intrinsic value and pain the only intrinsic disvalue, while every other value is assessed by reference to those two; we may infer this from the natural behaviour of young and uncorrupted creatures, for as soon as they are born they all seek pleasure but avoid pain. Epicurus' own description of pleasure as 'the first and congenital good' alludes to the same reasoning: since all creatures in their natural state go after pleasure and avoid pain, these should be the goals of our choices or avoidances (*ad Men.* 129).[7] Thus, unlike later Epicureans who felt the need to argue for the goodness of pleasure and badness of pain (*Fin.* I.31), Epicurus held these truths to be self-evident: the natural behaviour of animals 'in the cradle' makes them plain to all observers. No formal proof is required in addition to the evidence of the senses – the foremost Epicurean criterion of truth. Nor is it possible that the concepts of pleasure and pain would be misapplied to congenital animal behaviour, for they are *prolêpseis* or preconceptions, empirically derived basic notions whose content and applications, like the content and use of sensory perceptions, is always reliable.[8] The Cradle Argument suggests that

---

[6] On the foundational structure of Epicurean ethics and the parallel structure in Epicurean physics, see Sedley 1998.

[7] Following Sedley 1998: 136–7, here the 'Cradle Argument' is interpreted as a form of reasoning in which the force of the normative inference ('we ought to pursue pleasure and avoid pain') derives, precisely, from the factual statement that all animals, when still uncorrupted, do seek pleasure but avoid pain. This is not a case of the naturalistic fallacy, for the fact that newborn animals behave this way already has a normative dimension: nature moves all uncorrupted animals in the right way, to seek what they ought (pleasure) and avoid what they ought (pain). A different interpretation of the Cradle Argument is proposed by Brunschwig 1986.

[8] See Torquatus' methodological agenda (*Fin.* I.29), which precedes the passage cited above, and also Woolf 2001: 13 n. 31. The proleptic use of the terms 'pleasure' and 'pain' should probably be distinguished from the appeal of some later Epicureans to the *prolêpsis* in order to justify the *goodness* of pleasure and the *badness* of pain (*Fin.* I.31).

Epicurus held a sort of psychological hedonism which, far from conflicting with ethical hedonism, actually entails it.[9] Assuming that 'ought' implies 'can', if it is psychologically impossible to pursue as the ultimate good anything other than pleasure, then there is nothing other than pleasure than one actually *ought* to pursue. Any other normative theory of choice and action would be bound to have no real object; it would be *empty* in just that sense. However, one might object that people *do* learn to be motivated by factors other than the pleasure or pain of an action or of its results; indeed, they act for non-hedonistic reasons much of the time.

To forestall that objection, Epicurus appears to have appealed to a central feature of his ethics, i.e. the hedonistic calculus. People do not shun pleasure because it is pleasure, but to gain greater future pleasure or avoid future pain; and they do not opt for pain because it is pain, but to avert greater future pain or to secure future pleasure (*ad Men.* 129; *Fin.* I.32). Thus, the attainment of the moral end depends on the relative calculation and appraisal of the affective value of our choices: the pleasures should counterweigh and exceed the pains in a regular manner and in the long run (*ad Men.* 129–30; *KD* VIII; *SV* 73).[10] The hedonistic calculus bears on the issue whether or not Epicurean hedonism encourages indulgence in bodily pleasures and a profligate life-style. On the one hand, failures in the calculus typically happen because of the overwhelming power of immediate pleasure (*Fin.* I.33), which makes this latter appear choiceworthy regardless of its future consequences. On the other hand, the successful performance of the calculus leads to a moderate and self-sufficient lifestyle, which enables us both to enjoy pleasure freely and to react appropriately to external constraints (*ad Men.* 130–2). However, late Epicureans debate the rôle of the calculus in moral choice: 'rustic' Epicureans

[9] Cooper 1999 forcefully argues that Epicurus was not a hedonist with respect to the psychology of human motivation and action (psychological hedonism), but rather a hedonist in his normative ethical theories of desire and pleasure (ethical hedonism). On the other hand, Woolf 2004 challenges Cooper's interpretation of the textual evidence and argues in a careful and detailed manner that, in fact, the relevant texts leave the psychological reading intact. On the view outlined here, these positions are compatible and, according to the Epicureans, psychological hedonism entails ethical hedonism (but not vice versa).

[10] Contrast the hedonism of mainstream Cyrenaics, which focuses on present experiences and may suggest that we should pursue present pleasures regardless of their long-term consequences. Regarding the tension between Cyrenaic presentism and the eudaimonistic framework of Greek ethics, see Annas 1993: 227–36, 338–9; Irwin 1991; and, for a response to both, Tsouna-McKirahan 2002.

believe that the right choices derive *directly* from the application of the cardinal principles of the system (*kuriôtata*), whereas 'sophisticated' members of the school contend that correct decisions are made on the basis of the calculus, which in turn is grounded on the cardinal principles (*De elect.* XI.7–20).

In balancing pleasures and pains, we must take into account the distinct ways in which two different categories of experiences, bodily and mental, contribute to the achievement of the supreme good. Bodily pleasures and pains are fundamental (PHerc. 1232, XVII.15, XVIII.10–17), either because their mental counterparts 'originate in the body and are based upon the body' (*Fin.* I.55; *Tusc.* III.38), or because mental pleasure and pain are ultimately about bodily feelings (*pathê*), or both. But despite whatever primacy bodily feelings have over mental ones, these latter exercise much greater influence with regard to the overall quality of one's life. For while bodily pleasures and pains are confined in the present, mental ones extend over all three temporal modes (D.L. X.137) and their force can be hugely increased by beliefs, especially when these are future-directed. The scope and intensity of mental affects and activities has a double edge. On the one hand, mental pleasures have the power to counterbalance bodily pain even if it is very severe. On the other hand, however, the mind can immensely magnify the effects of present pain or overcome whatever enjoyment we get in the present from physical pleasure. For this reason it is the affections and activities of the mind, not of the body, that constitute the focus of Epicurean moral therapy. More on this topic later.

Epicurus was probably the first to differentiate the concept of pleasure by introducing a controversial distinction between two kinds or aspects of pleasure: katastematic pleasure and kinetic pleasure (*Fin.* I.37–8; *Tusc.* III.41; D.L. X.136; Athenaeus, *Deipn.* 12, 546e–f).[11]

> Epicurus in his *On Choices* says this: 'freedom from disturbance (*ataraxia*) and freedom from physical pain (*aponia*) are katastematic pleasures; but joy (*chara*) and delight (*euphrosunê*) are viewed as kinetic activities' (D.L. X.136)

Dodging several interpretative problems, let us concentrate on the contrast between kinetic and katastematic pleasures, the ways in which they are

---

[11] Also, *ad Men.* 128 and *KD* XVIII probably allude to it. Several scholars have questioned or rejected the authenticity of the distinction: e.g. Gosling and Taylor 1982: 365–96; and Nikolsky 2001. Participants to the continuing controversy include Rist 1972; Giannantoni 1984; Striker 1993; Mitsis 1988: 45–52; Hossenfelder 1986; Purinton 1993; Konstan 2012; and, regarding Philodemus, Tsouna 2007: 15–17.

interrelated, Epicurus' reasons for introducing this distinction in his doctrine, and its philosophical implications for Epicurean hedonism.

On the interpretation advanced here, the main criterion by which Epicurus distinguishes between kinetic and katastematic pleasures is some sort of *kinêsis*, motion or change: the former pleasures essentially involve *kinêsis*, whereas the latter do not.[12] Moreover, the motions involved in kinetic pleasures may but need not be associated with processes of physical replenishment or mental desire-satisfaction, such as quenching one's thirst (*Fin.* II.9) or satisfying one's hunger (*SV* 33).[13] For kinetic pleasures are often presented also as variations of katastematic states when no process of restoration occurs (*KD* XVIII; *Fin.* II.10).[14] They belong to the body or the mind, just as katastematic pleasure is of the body (*aponia*, freedom from pain) or the mind (*ataraxia*, freedom from disturbance). And they have a limit: they cannot increase but can only vary beyond the point where all want has been removed (*KD* III, XVIII). Whether bodily or mental, kinetic pleasures are typically associated with the activity of the senses. Moreover, a quotation from Epicurus' lost *On the Moral Ends* (*Tusc.* III.41) suggests that kinetic pleasures are as integral (though not as valuable) elements of Epicurus' notion of pleasure as is katastematic pleasure. This holds for the kinetic pleasures experienced at present, but also for those that the mind anticipates or recollects: we feel active joy in the confident *expectation* of future pleasant activities, and the same holds regarding our *memory* of activities of similar sorts.

However, katastematic pleasure too can be the object of anticipation and probably of memory as well. Indeed, *On the Moral Ends* emphasizes the physical stability of the body and its ethical relevance to the tranquillity of one's mind. 'For the stable condition (*katastêma*) of the flesh and the reliable expectation concerning it (sc. the *katastêma*) contain the highest and most secure joy for those who are able to reach it by reasoning' (Plutarch, *Non posse...* 1089d). Even if there are agreeable motions supervening upon katastematic states, the above evidence indicates that katastematic pleasure cannot be identified itself with a motion; rather, it is the perfect natural condition of a well-functioning body or a well-thinking mind. On the present

---

[12] On a different interpretation of D.L. X.136 and of the other relevant evidence, what ultimately matters is not the katastematic state itself but the joy and delight that it gives us; and these are kinetic activities, just as Aristippus' *summum bonum* is kinetic: so Erler and Schofield 1999: 655–7.

[13] Contra Mitsis 1988: 45–6. See also Striker 1993: 15.

[14] See Long and Sedley 1987, vol. 1: 123–4.

account, then, katastematic pleasure has an important objective dimension. It is a physiological and psychological state, which satisfies certain physiological and psychological conditions and can be explained in objective terms. However, Epicurus indicates that katastematic pleasure also has a felt character in so far as it involves a *pathos*, feeling, by which we decide what to choose (*ad Men.* 129).[15] This element is important, especially because it could help defuse the criticism that katastematic pleasure is really no pleasure at all (*Fin.* II.20–32 and below).[16] To understand the provenance of that criticism a brief historical reference is in order. Philosophers associated with the Socratic tradition, notably Plato (*Phil.* 42c–44a), considered the absence of pain a *neutral* state, neither pleasurable nor painful. Significantly, this was the position of the Cyrenaic Aristippus the Younger, who compared pain and pleasure respectively with rough and smooth seas, and who claimed furthermore that there is a middle psychic state between pain and pleasure comparable to dead calm (Eusebius, *PE* XIV.18.31–2). By contrast, Epicurus and all his followers (e.g., Demetrius Laco, PHerc. 1012, I.1–8; Philodemus, *De Epic.*; PHerc. 1232, XVIII.10–17) call this state in which pain or disturbance are absent 'pleasure' – indeed, 'the highest pleasure'.[17]

This serves both a polemical and a philosophical purpose. In historical terms, the Epicureans deliberately differentiate themselves from their main hedonist rivals. Philosophically, they propose a sort of hedonism better attuned to the eudaimonistic framework of Greek ethics than the presentist hedonism of the Cyrenaics: *aponia* and *ataraxia* are conditions of stability and inner peace, whose formal requirements coincide with the formal requirements of *eudaimonia*, happiness, and whose positive description as 'the highest pleasure' enables them to be used as positive rules of ethical conduct.[18] While the negative formulas signalling the *absence* of pain or disturbance create the misleading impression that these states are affectively neutral, Epicurus' provocative act of identifying *aponia* and *ataraxia* with *pleasure* attracts attention to a substantive truth about them: being without pain or disturbance *feels* pleasurable to us; it feels wonderful.[19] As a bonus, positing katastematic pleasure as the supreme good would seem to exonerate the Epicureans from the charge of advocating luxurious extravagance and points to a frugal and sober lifestyle. For as we shall see, the Epicureans contend that

---

[15] So Woolf 2009: 172–5. [16] For this criticism cf. Hossenfelder 1986.

[17] Like the Cyrenaics, Epicurus too compares the absence of pain or disturbance to a storm that abates (cf. *ad Men.* 128).

[18] See Hossenfelder 1986; Mitsis 1988: 11–58; and Woolf 2009: 172–5.

[19] See Woolf 2009: 173–5.

it is easy to remove the pain of bodily want and, moreover, they claim to have the means of eradicating mental disturbance as well. In fact, it is significant that the capacity for physical katastematic pleasure (*aponia*) in a way is built in the flesh, which has its own goal and limit (*KD* XX) and cannot increase its pleasure once all pain has been removed (*KD* XVIII; Philodemus, *De elect.* IV.1–10, *De mort.* III.37). Nonetheless, it is ultimately not the body but the mind that dominates our pursuit of the supreme good. The flesh is limited to our awareness of the present and has no grasp of time, whereas the mind alone can comprehend the limits of pleasure and pain (*KD* IV), place them in temporal perspective (D.L. X.137), and perform the calculus so as to achieve perfect happiness.

Before proceeding, we should reflect on certain philosophical issues systematically raised by Cicero (*Fin.* II).[20] Regarding the Epicurean use of the Cradle Argument, one may retort, as the Stoics did, that the Epicureans misread the facts: newborn creatures are after self-preservation, not pleasure; and what gives animals the disposition of affectionate ownership towards themselves is nature itself, i.e. the foundation of the Stoic ethics of virtue.[21] Alternatively, one may question the extent to which we should rely on the behaviour of animals in order to draw normative inferences. For their nature can be corrupt without having been corrupted (*Fin.* II.33). Or it may be that their behaviour is simply not analogous to adult human behaviour. In response, the Epicureans could insist on the pleasurable character of early animal behaviour; argue that such behaviour is natural and not corrupt; and defend the grounds of the analogy between animals and humans in the early stages of their development. Further problems arise with regard to the Epicurean concept of pleasure. One cluster concerns the relation between katastematic and kinetic pleasures. While it is easy to understand how there may be variations of a poem or of a speech or even of pleasure (in the sense that different things produce different pleasures), it is less clear just how listening to music is a variation of absence of pain (*aponia*) (*Fin.* II.10). Other criticisms concern specifically katastematic pleasure. The idea that the absence of pain is pleasure is prima facie counterintuitive: *aponia* is not tied to any individual desire nor does it involve gratification in any obvious sense. Moreover, there appears to be residual tension between Epicurus' insistence that pleasure is inconceivable apart from the pleasures of eating, drinking,

---

[20] On Ciceronian dialogue, see Schofield 2008. On the composition of *Fin.* II, see Inwood 1990.

[21] See Chapter 6 in this volume, by Brad Inwood.

etc. and his claim that katastematic pleasure is the highest good (*Fin.* II.6–7). Besides, while Epicurus contends that pleasure is self-evident, many philosophers deny the self-evident goodness of the absence of pain, e.g. Plato, the Cyrenaics, and Cicero himself. The Epicureans could answer that the intuitive goodness of katastematic pleasure becomes self-evident once we have assimilated the truths disclosed by Epicurus. Also, they could evoke the dominant rôle of the mind to explain how katastematic pleasure is superior to kinetic gratification. Just how the mind can shape the good life becomes clearer in the light of the Epicurean theory of desire and passion, the account of the virtues, and the social and pedagogical views of the school.

DESIRES, EMOTIONS, VIRTUES, AND SOCIETY

One obvious way in which the mind determines one's hedonistic choices is by assessing the desires and beliefs motivating such choices. According to later Epicureans, who formalized Epicurus' original taxonomy of desires (D.L. X.127) in response to Academic criticism (*Fin.* II.9, 26), desires are divided into two genera, natural and non-natural or empty, of which the former are further subdivided into two subcategories, necessary and non-necessary (Philodemus, *De elect.* VI.7–21).[22] Accordingly, the evaluative beliefs involved in our desires are necessarily or contingently true or, in the case of empty desires, they are both false and harmful. And the corresponding pleasures should be chosen or avoided depending on whether they derive from the satisfaction of natural desires, which are the only ones we should seek to fulfill, or from empty ones, which should never receive satisfaction. Philodemus adds that the sources of our desires differ, as do the ways in which we experience them: they spring from our individual nature or from external factors, and they can have a strong or a weaker impact on us. Failure to understand such distinctions leads to moral error, i.e. mistaking alien desires for those congenial to our nature and pursuing ambition or luxury as we should not (*De elect.* V.4–21). Another, broader way in which the mind plays a crucial rôle in the attainment of tranquillity consists in acknowledging and understanding our deepest fears, and also in contributing to their therapy. In fact, the most attractive and valuable elements of Epicurean ethics are

---

[22] The desires for food and clothing are both natural and necessary. The desire for sex is only natural. The desires for luxury, power, or fame are empty: their objects have no real value.

found, precisely, in the analysis and cure of the passions, e.g. greed, anger, and the fear of death.

According to the so-called fourfold medicine (*tetrapharmakos*), which can be traced back to Epicurus, the four principal objectives of Epicurean therapy are that 'god gives no cause for fear, death no cause for alarm; it is easy to procure what is good, and also to endure what is bad' (Philodemus, *Ad* [. . .] IV.9–14). Beginning with the last two principles, the contention that pleasure is easily available gains plausibility in the light of Epicurus' theses that pleasure is limited in intensity and duration, the highest pleasure is the removal of pain, and this can be easily achieved by attending to our natural needs; no wealth, power, or other external factors are essential for that purpose (*KD* XV; *SV* 33, 59). Epicurus probably assumes that nature's provisions correspond to what we naturally need or want, while our further demands derive from empty opinion. However, it is more difficult to accept that pain is easy to endure (*KD* IV). For although Epicurus insists that pain is either severe but short or long but tolerable, we may agree with Cicero that pain can be both excruciating and long-lasting, and also that, for a hedonist, the memory of past pain and the prospect of experiencing it again in the future must be a fearful thing (*Fin.* II.94–5). Moreover, while the Epicureans contend that the pleasures of memory and anticipation ensure that we have katastematic pleasure even in physical adversity, critics may object that there are limits to our ability to control our affective memories (*Fin.* II.104–6) and hence to deal successfully with pain as and when it comes up. Anyway, the Epicureans assume that although it is natural to shun pain, the *intensity* of our fear of pain can only derive from empty beliefs; upon their removal, pain becomes psychologically manageable.

Empty opinions are also the reasons why people have difficulty following the first two axioms of the *tetrapharmakos*, concerning the gods and death. These principles have pride of place in Epicurus' *Letter to Menoeceus* (D.L. X.123–4, 124–9), and they are addressed at length by Lucretius in his poem. Also, Philodemus discusses the nature of the divine and of true piety towards the gods (*On the Gods, On Piety*), and treats systematically all sorts of fears concerning death (*On Death*). Following the founder, all known members of the school draw their arguments not only from psychology, but also from physics proper, i.e., Epicurus' theory of the atomic composition of everything in the universe, which precludes divine interference and the soul's survival after death.

It is debated whether Epicurus' gods are objectively existing entities, or, alternatively, thought-constructs created by the human mind.[23] Whatever their ontological status, however, the Epicurean gods play an all-important dual rôle in the ethics of the school: positive, because they represent a moral ideal that we should contemplate and emulate; negative, because the right conception of the gods removes all fears concerning the impact of the divinities on human lives. In brief, Epicurus and his followers present the gods as indestructible and blessed beings, who are not involved in or concerned with the workings of the world and the affairs of men. Although we cannot *see* them, we have the capacity to acquire clear knowledge of their essential attributes by means of thought. Specifically, indestructibility and blessedness are features of our *prolêpsis*, preconception, of the divine, which guarantees infallible access to the nature of divinity and leads to the acquisition of genuine moral knowledge. Epicurus contrasts the content of the *prolêpsis* with the false suppositions of the many, and urges us to closely attend to the *prolêpsis* of the gods in order to be truly pious: we should believe of the gods everything consistent with their imperishability and blessedness, but nothing incompatible with these (*ad Men.* 123; *KD* I; Cicero, *ND* I.43–9; Philodemus, *De piet.* V.131–44, VII.189–201 Obbink). Therefore, we should reject the popular belief that the gods meddle in any way with the workings of nature or the societies of man and, instead, we should think of the divinities as remote from our world and indifferent to it:[24] trouble, concern, anger, and fear are unworthy of them, but belong to weak and mutually dependent mortal beings (*ad Herod.* 76–7). Later Epicureans also defend these views and further highlight their ethical implications. Philodemus develops the contrast between our preconception of the divine and the distorted concepts of the many, and he speculates on the reasons why men came to ascribe to the gods features inconsistent with their true nature and fearsome for man (*De piet.* IX.234–3; XI.294 ff.). Also he explains Polyaenus' controversial assertion that divine nature is the cause (*aitia*) for us of goods and evils (*De piet.* XXXVIII.1096–7): the gods do not benefit or harm us by acting like moral agents, but by serving as perfect ethical paradigms for us to emulate and revere in worship (*De piet.* XXXVIII.1082–7, XL.1138–55, XLIV.1266–75). They are not 'the cause of death and life' (*De elect.* VII.17–20, X.12–15, IX.14–20,

---

[23] The former, 'realist' view is defended by Mansfeld 1993; Santoro 2000; Babut 2005; and Essler 2011. The latter, 'idealist' view is held by Long and Sedley 1987, vol. 1: ch. 23; Obbink 1989, 1996; Purinton 2001; and Sedley 2011.

[24] Again, this leaves open whether the gods live in the spaces between worlds (cf. *ad Pyth.* 89; *DRN* V.146–54; and Babut 2005: 86–9) or nowhere at all.

XII.8–9) and there is nothing to fear about them. On the contrary, whether or not they physically exist, the ethically important thing is to keep our conception of them pure, unimpaired, and free of accretions reflecting the wrong moral values.[25] If we succeed in this effort, then we shall enjoy perfect serenity and happiness and, so long as we are alive, we shall live a godlike life.

Partly related to the fear of the gods is the fear of death.[26] It is the 'greatest terror', a 'darkness of the soul' (DRN III.91; ad Men. 125), which nourishes also other vicious traits such as greed and injustice (DRN III.60–88), and which infects all sorts of anxieties, including fears concerning dying, the state of being dead, premature death, and even mortality itself.[27] Because the fear of death is so deep and fundamental, it poses the greatest threat to happiness. Removing it, then, is a decisive step towards the achievement of tranquillity and, moreover, viewing death in the right way is an essential aspect of the pleasurable life. The Epicureans advance two major arguments which are used, jointly or severally, in support of the second principle of the *tetrapharmakos*, that death is nothing to us: the so-called non-perception (*anaisthêsia*) and the non-identity arguments. According to the former argument, death is the dispersion of the compound constituted by one's soul atoms and one's body atoms; what is dispersed does not perceive, but, since the only intrinsic bad is pain, the only way in which we can be harmed is through perception; and since death entails complete loss of perception, it is nothing to us (ad Men. 124; KD II). Of course, one may deny that there are no unperceived harms, though one would have to specify just how one can be harmed without being aware of the harm.[28] According to the non-identity argument, a person is the combination of soul and body, and death is the destruction of that combination; when death is present, we are no more; but if something is to be bad for us, we must exist when the bad thing or event occurs; hence death is nothing to us (ad Men. 125). Again, critics of this argument must explain just how death can harm someone who no longer exists. Later Epicureans expand and refine these arguments. They further undermine the idea that death implies deprivation of any sort. And also, they address 'hard cases' of fears particularly difficult to remove (Philodemus, De mort. III.30–6, V.1–4, IX.1–12). Moreover, Lucretius and Philodemus introduce the so-called 'Symmetry Argument', which invokes a symmetry between the past and the future to conclude that,

[25] See Long and Sedley 1987, vol. 1: 146–7.
[26] One reason why people fear death is their belief in after-death punishment: see Tsouna 2007: 244–8.
[27] See Warren 2004: 1–6, Tsouna 2007: 256–311.
[28] See Nagel 1979, and the retort of Warren 2004: 24 ff.

just as the infinity of time preceding our birth has been nothing to us, so the time following our death shall also be nothing to us (*DRN* III.832–42, 972–5; *De mort.* XXII.24–8, XXIII.37–XXIV.5, XXVI.17–25). The Symmetry Argument can be interpreted as making either a factual claim, that our post-mortem existence will be nothing to us, or the following normative claim: as we look forward from a given point within our lifetime to a future time when we shall be dead, we should feel no distress about the fact that we shall not then be alive. Factually, Lucretius and Philodemus defend the principle that death is nothing to us on different grounds from any found in the surviving works of Epicurus: the postulated symmetry between prenatal and post-mortem time and the contention that our non-existence will be as complete after our death as it was before our birth, and as irrelevant in the one case as in the other. Normatively, it is interpreted as offering an explicit reason why we should not have regret about our mortality. The Symmetry Argument has had strong impact on contemporary philosophers. In outline, some of them reply by contending that the time of birth is a necessary condition for personal identity whereas the time of death is not;[29] others suggest that our attitudes towards past and future are inevitably asymmetrical.[30]

The Epicureans employ additional arguments as well, in order to treat cases in which it is especially difficult to accept death as we must. And they complement their arguments with a host of other techniques, all of them broadly cognitive and some of them especially intended to address not so much people's reason as their feelings, imaginings, etc. Such complex strategies are applied also to other emotions and character traits, e.g. flattery, arrogance, greed, and also anger and erotic love. The reason why the Epicureans combine argumentative techniques with rhetorical and literary speech is that they view the emotions and traits of character as complex states consisting of both cognitive and extra-cognitive features; and both these components need to be addressed, if the relevant passions and traits are to be corrected or removed. The Epicureans' approach to the emotions is intuitively plausible and philosophically defensible; and the strategies that they employ exhibit great variety and sophistication. In general, like other Hellenistic schools, the Epicureans endorse a medical model according to which the main purpose of philosophy is to purge the soul of psychic diseases and restore it to its healthy, natural state: pleasure or the complete absence of

[29] Kripke 1980: 110 ff. (the doctrine of the essentiality of origins). See Nagel 1979, 1986.
[30] Parfit 1984, especially 149–86.

pain. Their analyses of the passions and their modes of treatment are therapeutic in the sense that they pursue just that goal. As for the philosopher, whom the Epicureans liken to the doctor, he is expected to practise philosophical therapy as an ongoing activity integrated into the framework of ethical *praxis*. In addition to making therapy available to mankind by means of Epicurean writings (*ad Herod.* 35), the Epicurean teachers promote the hedonistic ideals of the founder by interacting with their peers and students within their schools. Philodemus' treatise *On Frank Speech* explains how the pedagogic and therapeutic method of *parrhêsia*, frank speech, is regularly used in such interactions in order to identify one's moral error and correct it by means of milder or harsher criticism. Teachers must take into account the patient's personality and character and never lose sight of the ultimate aim of the cure, namely the achievement of katastematic pleasure.

While the vices and the passions disturb or even destroy our chances for happiness, the virtues are essential to its pursuit. Epicurus conceives of them in a mild cognitivist way, i.e. as inner states importantly consisting of beliefs, on account of which they form some sort of unity (D.L. X.132). Moreover, he holds that the virtues and pleasure mutually entail each other[31] and that the pleasant life is inseparable from them. However, despite their unique and exclusive relation to pleasure, the virtues have a clearly instrumental status. Even the greatest virtue, wisdom, is desirable because of its capacity to control desire and rationally obtain pleasure; it is not desirable for its own sake (*Fin.* II.42). Temperance and courage also are valued as privileged means to pleasure, not in their own right (*Fin.* II.47–9). As for justice, it consists in a contract between fellow-citizens neither to harm others nor to be harmed (*KD* XXXI–XXXIII; *Fin.* II.50–3). Its precise character is determined by social factors (*KD* XXXVI) and its enforcement is choiceworthy so long as it proves beneficial. Even sages need to abide by that contract because they need protection from being harmed. All the same, justice has no independent value; it is valuable only instrumentally, insofar as it produces pleasure. In sum, the virtues are eliminated as candidates for the position of the supreme good, and pleasure remains the only victor in the field (*Fin.* II.54). So, it would seem that the Epicureans reject the choice of Hercules: they uphold hedonism and also retain traditional morality; they pursue pleasure and yet make room for virtue. Furthermore, it would appear that they shake off

---

[31] *De elect.* XIV.1–14 states only a one-way entailment, and also adds to the four canonical virtues several others.

successfully the charge of profligacy since, on their view, the virtues determine both the nature of the hedonistic calculus and its outcome. However, critics contend that, if virtue is practised because of one's fear of negative consequences, then it is a sham (*Fin.* II.69–71) and, generally, that Epicurean hedonism cannot account consistently for human motivation and action. Instead of maintaining that some ancestor had his son beheaded or exiled for the sake of egoistic advantage (*Fin.* II.34), it would have been preferable for Torquatus to argue that people of sound values would never perform such actions because they cannot be justified in hedonistic terms.

Similar considerations apply to the Epicurean doctrine of friendship. For Epicurus advances the claims that the sage will love his friend as much as himself (*Fin.* I.67–8) and will sometimes die for his friend (D.L. X.121), alongside the thesis that each agent's own pleasure is the moral goal. Hence Epicurus gives the impression of a more or less successful attempt to reconcile his self-interested and self-regarding ethics with the altruistic attitudes praised by conventional morality.[32] And also, he projects the image of an austere hedonism compatible with self-denial and self-sacrifice.[33] However, an opponent may retort that genuine friendship is fundamentally incompatible with the overarching pursuit of one's own pleasure and hence Epicurean friendship is not friendship at all (*Fin.* II.78–85). In response, some Epicureans maintained that, while friendship originates from self-regard, it eventually acquires independent value (*Fin.* I.67–8). However, whether their theory allows for genuine altruism can be debated.

In the public arena as in private life, Epicurean hedonism must face a final challenge that Cicero aptly identifies as 'the silence of history' (*Fin.* II.67): there are no recorded examples of distinguished persons who have justified their virtuous or altruistic actions by claiming that they were seeking their own pleasure. According to Cicero, the reason for this 'silence' is shame. But genuine moral beliefs must be sincere and public (*Fin.* II.77). We should not wear them 'like clothes, one set at home, another out of doors' (*ibid.*). In reply, the Epicureans can point to the fact that not only do they not conceal their hedonistic motivations, but they celebrate them in their worship of Epicurus: a man who professed and practised hedonistic values and thereby lived an exemplary moral life.

---

[32] See Mitsis 1988, ch. 3, and Annas 1993, ch. 11. Others maintain, however, that Epicurus values friendship only instrumentally: O'Keefe 2001a, 2001b, Brown 2002.

[33] See also *Fin.* I.67–70; *SV* 23 Brown 2002.

ABBREVIATIONS

ad Herod.	*ad Herodotum* (Epicurus)
ad Men.	*ad Menoeceum* (Epicurus)
ad Pyth.	*ad Pythoclem* (Epicurus)
D.L.	Diogenes Laertius
De elect.	*De electionibus et fugis* (Philodemus)
De Epic.	*De Epicuro* (Philodemus)
De mort.	*De morte* (Philodemus)
De piet.	*De pietate* (Philodemus)
Deipn.	*Deipnosophistae* (Athenaeus)
DRN	*De rerum natura* (Lucretius)
Fin.	*De finibus bonorum et malorum* (Cicero)
KD	*Kyriai Doxai* (Epicurus)
ND	*De natura deorum* (Cicero)
PE	*Praeparatio Evangelica* (*Eusebius*)
PHerc.	Papyrus Herculanensis
Phil.	*Philebus* (Plato)
SV	*Sententiae Vaticanae* (Epicurus)
Tusc.	*Tusculanae disputationes* (Cicero)

BIBLIOGRAPHY

An asterisk denotes secondary literature especially suitable for further reading.

Annas, J. (1993) *The Morality of Happiness*, Oxford University Press.
Babut, D. (2005) 'Sur les dieux d'Épicure', *Elenchos* 26: 79–110.
Brown, E. (2002) 'Epicurus on the Value of Friendship (Sententia Vaticana 23)', *Classical Philology* 97: 68–80.
Brunschwig, J. (1986) 'The Cradle Argument in Epicureanism and Stoicism', in Schofield and Striker 1986: 113–44.
Cooper, J. (1999) 'Pleasure and Desire in Epicurus', in J. Cooper, *Reason and Emotion*, Princeton University Press, 485–514.
Erler M. and Schofield, M. (1999) 'Epicurean Ethics', in K. Algra *et al.* (eds.), *The Cambridge History of Hellenistic Philosophy*, Cambridge University Press, 642–69.
Essler, H. (2011) *Glückselig und unsterblich: epikureische Theologie bei Cicero und Philodem (mit einer Edition von PHerc. 152/157, Kol. 8–10)*, Basel: Schwabe.
Giannantoni, G. (1984) 'Il piacere cinetico nell'etica epicurea', *Elenchos* 5: 25–44.
Gosling, J.C.B. and Taylor, C.C.W. (1982) *The Greeks on Pleasure*, Oxford University Press.
Hossenfelder, M. (1986) 'Epicurus – Hedonist *malgré lui*', in Schofield and Striker 1986: 245–63.

Inwood, B. (1990) 'Rhetorica Disputatio: The Strategy of *De Finibus* II', in M. Nussbaum (ed.), *The Poetics of Therapy, Apeiron* 23.4: 143–64.

Irwin, T. (1991) 'Aristippus against Happiness', *Monist* 74: 55–82.

Konstan, D. (2008) *A Life Worthy of the Gods*, Las Vegas/Zürich/Athens: Parmenides.*

Konstan, D. (2012) 'Epicurean Happiness: A Pig's Life?' *Journal of Ancient Philosophy* 4: 1–24.

Kripke, S. (1980) *Naming and Necessity*, Cambridge, MA: Harvard University Press.

Long, A.A. and Sedley, D.N. (1987) *The Hellenistic Philosophers*, 2 vols., Cambridge University Press.*

Mansfeld, J. (1993) 'Aspects of Epicurean Theology', *Mnemosyne* 46: 172–210.*

Mitsis, P. (1988) *Epicurus' Ethical Theory: The Pleasures of Invulnerability*, Ithaca, NY/London: Cornell University Press.

Nagel, T. (1979) *Mortal Questions*, Cambridge University Press.

Nagel, T. (1986) *The View from Nowhere*, Oxford University Press.

Nikolsky, B. (2001) 'Epicurus on Pleasure', *Phronesis* 46: 440–65.

Obbink, D. (1989) 'The Atheism of Epicurus', *Greek, Roman and Byzantine Studies* 30: 187–223.

Obbink, D. (1996) *Philodemus. On Piety I*, Oxford University Press.

O'Keefe, T. (2001a) 'Would a Community of Wise Epicureans Be Just?' *Ancient Philosophy* 21: 133–46.*

O'Keefe, T. (2001b) 'Is Epicurean Friendship Altruistic?' *Apeiron* 34: 269–305.

Parfit, D. (1984) *Reasons and Persons*, Oxford University Press.

Purinton, J. (1993) 'Epicurus on the *telos*', *Phronesis* 38: 281–320.

Purinton, J. (2001) 'Epicurus on the Nature of the Gods', *Oxford Studies in Ancient Philosophy* 21: 181–231.

Rist, J.M. (1972) *Epicurus. An Introduction*, Cambridge University Press.*

Santoro, M. (2000) 'Il pensiero teologico epicureo: Demetrio Lacone e Filodemo', *Chronache Ercolanesi* 30: 63–70.

Schofield, M. (2008) 'Ciceronian Dialogue', in S. Goldhill (ed.), *The End of Dialogue in Antiquity*, Cambridge University Press, 63–84.

Schofield, M. and Striker, G. (eds.) (1986) *The Norms of Nature*, Cambridge University Press.

Sedley, D. (1976) 'Epicurus and his Professional Rivals', in J. Bollack and A. Laks (eds.), *Études sur l'Épicurisme Antique*, Cahiers de Philologie 1, Lille: Centre de Recherche Philologique de l'Universite de Lille.

Sedley, D. (1998) 'The Inferential Foundation for Epicurean Ethics', in S. Everson (ed.), *Ethics*. Companions to Ancient Thought 4, Cambridge University Press, 129–50.*

Sedley, D. (2011) 'Epicurus' Theological Innatism', in J. Fish and K. Sanders (eds.), *Epicurus and the Epicurean Tradition*, Cambridge University Press, 9–52.

Striker, G. (1993) 'Epicurean Hedonism', in J. Brunschwig and M. Nussbaum (eds.), *Passions and Perceptions: Studies in Hellenistic Philosophy of Mind*, Cambridge University Press, 3–17.

Tsouna, V. (2002) 'Is There an Exception to Greek Eudaemonism?', in M. Canto and P. Pellegrin (eds.), *Le style de la pensée. Mélanges Jacques Brunschwig*, Paris: Les Belles Lettres, 464–89.

Tsouna, V. (2007) *The Ethics of Philodemus*, Oxford University Press.

Tsouna, V. (2009) 'Epicurean Therapeutic Strategies', in Warren 2009a: 249–65.*

Warren, J. (2002) *Epicurus and Democritean Ethics. An Archaeology of Ataraxia*, Cambridge University Press.

Warren, J. (2004) *Facing Death*, Oxford: Clarendon.*

Warren, J. (ed.) (2009a) *The Cambridge Companion to Epicureanism*, Cambridge University Press.

Warren, J. (2009b) 'Removing Fear', in Warren 2009a: 234–48.

Woolf, R. (trans.) (2001) *Cicero: On Moral Ends*, Cambridge University Press.

Woolf, R. (2004) 'What Kind of Hedonist Was Epicurus?' *Phronesis* 49: 303–22

Woolf, R. (2009) 'Pleasure and Desire', in Warren 2009a: 158–78.

6

Stoicism

BRAD INWOOD

Stoicism as a philosophical movement had a long and distinguished history, from its foundation in the late fourth century BCE until it yielded to Platonism in late antiquity. For over 500 years its well-coordinated theories in physics and cosmology, in ethics and in logic (including dialectic and rhetoric) exercised great influence on the development of other philosophical schools and on broader intellectual culture in the Greco-Roman world. In turn, Stoicism was consistently being shaped by debate with other schools. The Stoic school, especially in the area of ethics, was unambiguously in the Socratic tradition, like Peripatetic and Platonic philosophy. By contrast, though Epicurean ethics was influenced to some extent by the Socratic tradition, its basic approach was fundamentally different; for much of the Hellenistic period Epicureanism and Stoicism represented opposing but mutually influential approaches to the issue of how to live a good human life, which tended to be the central focus of ethical thinking in the ancient world.

An anecdote about the origins of Stoicism, preserved by Diogenes Laertius, sheds helpful light on its ethics. Zeno, the school's founder (died c. 262 BCE), came to Athens from Citium on the island of Cyprus. One day

> he went into Athens (he was thirty years old at the time) and sat down by a certain bookseller. The bookseller was reading the second book of Xenophon's *Memorabilia* [of Socrates]; he enjoyed it and asked where men like that spent their time. Fortuitously, Crates [the Cynic] came by and the bookseller pointed to him and said, 'Follow this man.' From then on Zeno studied with Crates, being in other respects fit for and intent on philosophy, but too modest for Cynic shamelessness . . .[1]

There can be little doubt that the excerpt which Zeno heard came from Chapter 1 of *Memorabilia* Book 2, a dialogue between Socrates and the

---

[1] Diogenes Laertius *Lives of the Philosophers* (hereafter D.L.) 7.2–3. Here and wherever possible translations are taken from Inwood and Gerson 2008.

hedonist Aristippus, in the course of which Socrates relates a parable first developed by Prodicus (a 'sophist' who was widely regarded to have been an influence on Socrates), about the Choice of Heracles (2.1.21–34). The upshot of this story was that Heracles, a human hero who ascended to join the gods because of his outstanding virtue and achievements, chose the hard life of virtue over the soft life of pleasure. Inspired by this, Zeno, the future head of the Stoic school, dedicated himself to the Cynic way of life under the tutelage of Crates (himself a student of Diogenes of Sinope, who had been taught by Socrates' follower Antisthenes, the founder of the Cynic movement).

Cynicism was a curiously anti-theoretical philosophical movement in the fourth century BCE. Opposed on principle to what they saw as the false values of ordinary society, Cynics pursued the best human life by following nature, stripping away superfluities and pretence. Like Socrates, the Cynics were willing to challenge and defy conventional values; they were if anything even more thorough-going in their anti-conventionalism. Eschewing wealth, marriage, householding, not to mention the risks and vanities of political life, they pursued virtue on its own, stripped down to what they regarded as the bare, natural essentials. Diogenes lived in a storage amphora and defied political convention, going so far as to be rude to Alexander the Great himself when the spirit so moved him. The Cynic lifestyle involved being satisfied with the plainest of food and the most direct satisfaction of physical desires. Sexual intercourse in a public place was nothing to be ashamed of, any more than the performance of other basic bodily functions. The nickname 'dog' (hence the label 'Cynic' from the Greek word *kuôn*) was inevitable, given such behaviour. This, of course, was the shamelessness which Zeno could not accept, even as he learned so much else from his master Crates.

The Cynics inherited the contrast between nature and convention, *phusis* and *nomos*, influential since the sophistic movement in the fifth century BCE. While not taking nature in quite the extreme way that Cynics did, Zeno made 'accordance with nature' the central tenet of his ethical theory. In one form or another, all Stoics from Zeno until the end of antiquity embraced the idea that one must live in full accord with nature if one is to live a successful human life. On this foundation (or, one might say, revolving around this fixed point) one can find all of the essential features of Stoic ethics. In this Stoic ethics was not unique. When faced with the choice between nature and contingent conventions as the determinant of ethical theory few philosophers have embraced mere convention. Pyrrhonist sceptics denied the existence of natural values and so recommended life in accordance with the customs and habits of one's society; and some of the sophists who had articulated the contrast of nature and convention held that there was nothing but convention to live by. It could be argued that some details of Aristotelian virtues should be thought of as depending on the conventions of the *polis*, but Aristotle himself regarded the *polis* as the natural way for human beings to live. If there is anything distinctive about the Stoic commitment to life according to nature it must lie in their conception of the nature in accordance with which people are supposed to live.

LIFE ACCORDING TO NATURE

Stoicism focussed on two senses of nature, the nature of the cosmos as a whole and the nature of humans. This, at least, is the mature form of the theory as expounded by Chrysippus, the third head of the school (c. 280–205 BCE): 'by nature, in consistency with which we must live, Chrysippus understands both the common and, specifically, the human nature. Cleanthes [the second head, c. 330–230 BCE] includes only the common nature, with which one must be consistent, and not the individual' (D.L. 7.89). It is not completely clear how Zeno, the founder, put the point, but it is safe to assume that his understanding of nature was not the stripped-down, antinomian version he learned from Crates. At the very least Zeno held that human nature was more robustly social than Cynics held, and in this respect Stoics aligned with mainstream values, as did Aristotle. Commitment to the intrinsic value of social bonds of various sorts was a defining feature of Stoicism, in contrast to Epicureanism, which regarded such relations, even friendship and family ties, as merely instrumental. Zeno advanced some form of 'cosmopolitanism' (treating all rational beings, gods and men, as parts of one 'civic' structure),[2] thus integrating human nature (with both its social and individual focusses) and cosmic nature (including the gods). Chrysippus seems to have reinstated this position in opposition to Cleanthes, whose focus on the nature of the whole cosmos gave his version of Stoicism a more theological aspect.[3] It is clear that there were differences of emphasis among Stoics about how best to conceive of the nature in harmony with which one should live, but the essential Stoic view is clear: living in accordance with one's rational nature as a human, one's social nature, and in conformity with

---

[2] Schofield 1991.

[3] Though theology was of critical importance to all Stoics, Cleanthes' *Hymn to Zeus* testifies to a particularly strong emphasis on the divine character of the cosmos whose nature humans are to harmonize with.

the cosmos (which was consistently understood as a teleologically organized, providential whole governed by a rational, divine plan) is the key to a good life. A life of that sort is the *telos*, or goal, for humans, and the best way to survey the range of views Stoics took on this issue is to consider their various definitions or characterizations of the *telos*.

THE AIM OF LIFE

In the *Eudemian* and *Nicomachean Ethics* Aristotle crystallized the notion of a highest good, a goal (*telos*) for the sake of which all rational action is ultimately done and is itself pursued for the sake of nothing else. Such an architectonic organizing principle provides a focus for thinking about values and right action, and the Stoics worked out their own version of this concept. There was considerable variety in the formulations of the *telos* during the school's history, but the underlying concept was quite stable. In one source (D.L. 7.87) we read that Zeno 'said that the goal was to live in agreement with nature, which is to live according to virtue; for nature leads us to virtue'. The built-in bias towards *aretê* (virtue, excellence) is a feature of Aristotelian and other mainstream teleological thinking about ethics in the ancient world; the Stoics were strongly committed to this approach, understanding virtue as a kind of 'completion' or perfection of human nature (see D.L. 7.90).[4] It is worth quoting one ancient survey of various Stoic formulations of the *telos* to illustrate this variety.

> Zeno defined the *telos* thus: 'living in agreement'. This means living according to a single and consonant rational principle [*logos*], since those who live in conflict are unhappy. Those who came after him made further distinctions and expressed it thus: 'living in agreement with nature', supposing that Zeno's formulation was an incomplete predication. For Cleanthes, who first inherited his school, added 'with nature' and defined the *telos* thus: 'the goal is living in agreement with nature'. Chrysippus wanted to make this clearer and expressed it in this way: 'to live according to experience of the things which happen by nature'. And Diogenes: 'to be reasonable in the

---

[4] The natural bias towards the development of virtue made it necessary for the Stoics to develop a robust theory of how human development goes wrong so systematically that virtually no one actually achieves virtue even though it is the goal of human life, just as excellence in its kind is the natural *telos* for anything in the natural world. See D.L. 7.89. Many ancient critics thought that the Stoic account of failure to develop virtue was unsuccessful.

selection and rejection of natural things'.[5] And Archedemus: 'to live completing all the appropriate acts' [*kathêkonta*][6]. And Antipater: 'to live invariably selecting natural things and rejecting unnatural things'. He often defined
it thus as well: 'invariably and unswervingly to do everything in one's power
for the attainment of the principal natural things'.[7]

Other characterizations of the *telos* are similar. Panaetius, we are told, said the
goal was 'to live in accordance with the inclinations given to us by nature';
Posidonius said it was 'to live in contemplation of the truth and orderliness of
the universe, helping to establish that order as much as one can, being in no
respect led astray by the irrational part of the soul'.[8] This more cosmological
formulation has unique features (the reference to an irrational component
within us which must be resisted, the focus on contemplation), but even this
way of expressing the *telos* coheres well enough with a fuller formulation
which seems to stem from Chrysippus: to live 'according to one's own nature
and that of the universe, doing nothing which is forbidden by the common
law [*nomos*], which is right reason, penetrating all things, being the same as
Zeus, who is the leader of the administration of things. And this itself is the
virtue of the happy man and a smooth flow of life, whenever all things are
done according to the harmony of the divinity [*daimôn*] in each of us with the
will of the administrator of the universe.'[9]

Stoic ethics, then, was in outline similar to Aristotelian eudaimonism: the
natural completion or perfection of human nature is the goal of life; distinctive views about human nature, then, determine what counts as human
excellence, or virtue. Practical reason (expressed in terms of selection and
rejection of 'natural things') is the realization of this virtue; and since human
nature is integrated with the nature of the cosmos, itself rational, providential
and divine, human excellence cannot, for the Stoics, be understood without
taking full account of how we fit into the cosmic scheme of things.

THE UNIQUENESS OF THE GOOD

The relationship of ethics to cosmology and theology is one of the features of
Stoic ethics that distinguishes it sharply from other movements in ancient ethics.
Another such feature is the Stoic emphasis on the uniqueness of the good. In

---

[5] 'Natural things' (*ta kata phusin*) are favourable or positive factors in the life of a given
kind of animal, things like health, prosperity, good social relations, etc. See below on
'preferred indifferents'.

[6] See below, n. 17.   [7] These three Stoics were prominent in the second century BCE.

[8] Clement *Stromates* 2.21.129.   [9] D.L. 7.88.

most ancient ethical systems there is a close connection between the conception of the good and happiness (*eudaimonia*), which is often described in terms of possessing or doing what is good. And on this the Stoics took a very strong position, claiming that the only properly good thing is virtue itself and what participates in virtue. Epicureans, of course, disagreed; for them as for Eudoxus[10] pleasure is the only truly good thing. Aristotelians held that there are three kinds of good (bodily, mental, external), whereas the Stoic position comes down to holding that only mental goods (goods of the soul) are genuine. Antipater, head of the school in the second century BCE, argued that even Plato held this view, writing a book entitled 'that according to Plato only the *kalon* is good'.[11]

But how did the Stoics defend their rather austere and restricted conception of the good? The answer lies, as is well known, in their interpretation of their Socratic heritage. It is of course important that Xenophon gives his readers a portrait of Socrates focussed relentlessly on moral virtue, and this no doubt encouraged the Stoics in their high-mindedness. More important, though, is an argument found more than once in Plato's dialogues[12] and also reflected in Xenophon:[13] the good is what is beneficial or useful, so anything that can harm as well as help cannot be genuinely good. This point was heartily embraced by the Stoics[14] and was the foundation of the doctrine that only virtue (which is unambiguously noble or fine, *kalon*) is good – anything else, even physical health and positive mental attributes such as good memory and quick wits, can in principle be harmful to the agent. So however much those positive features of life may accord with nature in one sense, they cannot be *good* and thereby make a decisive contribution to the happy life. Only virtue can be counted on to have that impact; hence it alone is good.[15] And conversely only vice is bad. Other defects and disappointing features of life (such as disease, pain and premature death) are not really bad. The way an agent reacts to or 'uses' such favourable or unfavourable circumstances is the only thing that is good or bad, and that use is exactly what depends on (that is, participates in) virtue.

But things like health, strength, a good memory and a supportive community are obviously positive features in a human life – they are 'according to nature' just as disease, premature death, mental weakness and social isolation are 'contrary to nature'. Although everything except virtue is indifferent to

---

[10] See Aristotle *Nicomachean Ethics* 10.2.
[11] In fact, the situation in Plato's dialogues is quite complex and could be interpreted along broadly Aristotelian or Stoic lines.
[12] *Gorgias* 467–8, *Euthydemus* 278–82, *Meno* 87–9. [13] *Memorabilia* 4.6.8. [14] D.L. 7.103.
[15] Along with things which are causally or conceptually dependent on it, i.e., what participates in virtue. This includes virtuous people and actions.

the happy life (in the sense that it does not guarantee it or even form an indispensable part of it) the positive features in life are naturally 'preferred' and the negative ones are naturally 'dispreferred'. These terms (*proêgmenon*, preferred; *apoproêgmenon*, dispreferred) are Stoic coinages and play a key role in Stoic value theory. Where Aristotelians recognized three kinds of goods (bodily, mental and external) the Stoics classified every positive value except virtue as a preferred indifferent and everything negative in life, except vice, as a dispreferred indifferent.[16]

Since the practice of virtue involves analysing, selecting and rejecting such natural values and disvalues, these 'indifferent' features of our lives clearly matter to the happy life; as Chrysippus put it, they are the principle under-lying 'appropriate action'[17] and the 'raw material' of virtue.[18] Hence it is deeply misleading to say that in Stoicism nothing matters except virtue and vice; Antipater coined the term 'selective value' for the feature of preferred indifferents which makes them worth pursuing in an intelligent way.[19] In fact, the proper 'use' of preferred and dispreferred things is indispensable to the virtuous and happy life. What Stoics emphasized, then, much more than other ancient moral theorists, is that simply coming to possess preferred things (and to avoid coming up against dispreferred things) cannot deter-mine whether one is successful in living a life in accordance with human nature, i.e., whether one is happy. For the value of our rational navigation through the contingencies of life is absolute and depends on how well, how rationally, it is done, even though such navigation would be meaningless if there were not a natural basis for preferring and avoiding the positive and negative 'indifferents' in life. It is reasonable, then, to describe the Stoics as dualists in their axiology, while recognizing that the one scale of value (virtue and vice) has an absolute priority over the quite distinct and incommensurable scale of value determined by things that are in accordance with or in conflict with our nature.

---

[16] They also recognized that some things are absolutely indifferent in that they aren't aligned with or against a natural human life. Such things (such as 'having an odd or even number of hairs on one's head') do not attract or repel us (stimulate an impulse towards or away from themselves); see D.L. 7.104–5.

[17] Appropriate action (*to kathêkon*) is action or behaviour which makes sense (that is, 'admits of a reasonable justification') for human beings (D.L. 7.107–9), though each natural kind has its own set of *kathêkonta* which accord with its specific nature. For rational animals, 'right actions' (*katorthômata*) are a special subset of appropriate actions.

[18] Plutarch *On Common Conceptions* 1069e, quoting Chrysippus.   [19] Stobaeus 2.83–5.

VIRTUE AND VICE

Following the example of Plato, Aristotle and their schools, the Stoics developed rich and complex descriptive taxonomies of the virtues and vices. Though some Stoics, such as Aristo of Chios, argued for a radically unitary conception of virtue, the mainstream view was that there are four cardinal or top-level virtues (wisdom, justice, self-control and courage) and a complex array of species and sub-species. The vices mirrored this classification. Since virtue is understood as a perfection and completion of human nature, the various virtues were generally held to be mutually entailing; if you had one you had them all, though each had its own distinct sphere of operation and characteristics. Similarly, as a perfection virtue did not, on the strict Stoic view of things, admit of degrees. There was no question of being more or less virtuous; either one had achieved perfection or not. This claim was not, obviously, in accord with common sense which, then as now, recognized degrees of goodness. Stoics certainly allowed for degrees of progress towards the goal of complete virtue, and that allowed them to account for the looser way of speaking (just as they could grant that preferred indifferents could be non-technically referred to as goods, provided one recognized this as a loose usage). But in the final analysis, virtue is a perfection (like straightness) which is either present or not. This had the effect of making virtue an effectively unachievable, aspirational goal. As a result, the Stoics claimed that virtuous people had been unbelievably rare in the history of the world – something which in no way detracted from the power of the ideal as a target for human improvement.

THE DEVELOPMENT OF GOOD CHARACTER

All ancient moral theories had something to say about how to make progress towards virtue and happiness. The extreme idealism of Stoic ethics was one factor that made this a greater challenge, but so too was their commitment to providential determinism. Everything in the world is causally determined and the active principle, the cause of it all, was a god who, like Plato's demiurge, aimed at producing the best possible outcome. So the fact that people born with natural inclinations to virtue *all* go astray needed an explanation. It was found readily enough in environmental and social influences (especially the corrupting influence of social conventions which the Cynics had rejected). These forces inevitably undermine our natural inclinations from very early childhood and the trajectory of moral education which follows is difficult and demanding. The rational capacities of children develop slowly as their concepts, including the concept of the good, are shaped by experience and instruction. Until their rationality is completed, at what may seem like an arbitrarily exact age of fourteen, children are not genuinely accountable for their choices; but once reason is in charge people become responsible for their own moral improvement.

Unlike Plato and Aristotle, Stoics tended not to believe that the passions and desires are distinct, potentially recalcitrant forces in the human soul; rather, once reason is in charge our desires and the behaviour based on them are determined by the opinions we hold, whether consciously or not. Self-knowledge is vital to moral progress, as one must learn to clarify one's values and to challenge the erroneous views inculcated by society. The later Stoic Epictetus puts particular emphasis on this path to moral improvement, but few if any of the Stoics would disagree with him. Moral progress was not a matter of taming and habituating a set of ineradicably irrational desires, but depended instead on the rational education of the unified soul of a mature agent; a deep and critical understanding of the virtues and the place of human beings in a cosmic community of reason was the goal. When and if this process was completed our life is perfected. There is no weakness of will in Aristotle's sense. Full rationality guarantees 'a smooth flow of life' and harmony both within oneself and with the larger rational world.

RELATIONS WITH OTHERS

Becoming virtuous is a personal achievement, but the nature which is perfected by this process is intrinsically social. Our first and deepest affiliation is to our own well-being (this is the *oikeiôsis*, or basic attachment to self-preservation and personal development), but that well-being cannot be realized without acknowledging and acting on our equally important commitment to the well-being of our fellow human beings. The most obvious 'proof' of this natural sociability lies in the universal commitment to family members; but the bonds which people feel to others in their community, nation, and indeed to all other humans as such are equally natural. Although eudaimonism, which rests on the cultivation of one's own character and personal fulfillment, can sometimes be interpreted as centred on oneself, the Stoic version of it makes personal perfection radically dependent on a deep commitment to other-regarding virtues. Stoics often think of the world as a cosmopolis, a universal community of gods and humans in which shared rationality is the foundation of a genuinely egalitarian communal life. Such an ideal community is the model we are to have in mind and to emulate in our more mundane lives as we pursue care for own moral well-being in the context of whatever social environment we find ourselves in.

ACTIONS AND PASSIONS

One of the distinguishing characteristics of Stoic ethics is their analysis of practical reason, actions, and passion. The adult rational soul is a unity, at least in the sense that the desires and passions we are subject to are reflections of, indeed are products of, our intellectual commitments and capacities. There are no 'brute' desires; if we have an unmanageable appetite for food or drink or an uncontrollable urge to lament the death of a loved one, that is not because something in us does not listen to reason. It is because (whether we realize it or not) we have overvalued those objects of concern. A critical reassessment of carnal pleasures or a more thoughtful approach to human mortality will not only change our beliefs but in addition it will thereby reshape our desires and emotions. This version of moral psychology makes practical reason sovereign over our affective lives as well as over our actions. This control is manifested most clearly in mental 'assent' – that is, the acceptance of the impressions on which an action or emotional reaction is based. In the rather schematic analysis that turns up most frequently in our sources, in adult humans actions and passions are proximately caused by such acts of assent, each of which reflects the agent's judgements about the value of things. If I have a raging thirst for fine wine and act on it, that is a result of my assent (on the relevant occasion) to the notion that fine wine is of paramount value in my life. If I have an overwhelming fear of death in battle, that is the result of my assent (perhaps unconscious, but in principle amenable to being brought to awareness) to the notion that death is an evil, more to be avoided than the shame of betraying my country by running away.

In a rather Socratic mode the Stoics assumed that once we understand our values and commitments and make conscious judgements about them we are in a position to revise those views and improve our lives accordingly. If we have a weak or uncertain attitude to such things the best plan is to withhold our assent, to reserve judgement and refrain from actions and feelings that are reckless and uncontrollable. Hence the Stoic advocacy of 'freedom from passions' (apatheia). Whereas Peripatetics urged that we should use our practical reason to moderate and regulate pleasure, pain and the passions generally, the life of the perfect wise person on Stoic principles involved complete freedom from all the passions (including pleasure and pain of the mental variety – there was no expectation that physical pleasure and pain could be eliminated; our job there was to recognize that such phenomena are indifferent rather than genuinely bad). In keeping with their classification of the virtues, Stoics provided a similar taxonomy of the passions: fear, appetite, mental pleasure, and mental pain (grief). The affective life of a virtuous person was not, however, barren. There is a rational counterpart of fear (cautious avoidance of what is actually bad), of appetite (the desire for genuinely good things) and of pleasure (joy at good things). The absence of a virtuous counterpart to grief is puzzling at first sight, but less surprising when one reflects that in the providential world as they saw it a truly wise person would find nothing to regret or grieve for since even the saddest outcomes are part of a benevolent divine plan.

RESPONSIBILITY AND DETERMINISM

In their physics, Stoics were committed to determinism (indeed to providential determinism). Since they were also committed to a form of physicalism which included the human soul, they were pressed by critics to justify holding people accountable for their actions. Critics claimed that if one's choices and decisions are part of a deterministic causal chain they won't be truly one's own. Since self-determination is presupposed by Stoic ethics, failure to respond to such criticisms would undermine their theory. A full discussion of Stoic compatibilism would be out of place here, but Chrysippus countered criticism from Academics in particular by emphasizing the role played by assent in the Stoic analysis of action and character. Responsible action is the result of assent to appropriate stimuli from the environment in the form of *phantasiai*, representations of states of affairs to which human response is appropriate. For example, a representation of a charging lion impinges on me, to which the appropriate practical response would be flight. Do I run? That depends on whether I give my assent to the notion that a danger is present for which flight is an appropriate response. I could in principle decline to assent, stand my ground and wrestle with the lion, or I could run away and survive. Clearly the approach of the lion is determined by causes beyond my control. But what determines my response? Certainly it will be causally determined, since my reactions and behaviours are as much a part of the web of causation as anything else that happens in the world of corporeal objects. My 'choice' of how to respond, then, is not a free and uncaused choice; there is no liberty of indeterminism. My response is caused by the state of my character and personality; if my soul is cautious in a certain way, then I assent to the idea of running away, and if it is reckless and bold I will not assent to running away but stand my ground and suffer the consequences. The determining causal factor is clearly the state of my character and the action is very much my own as a result – it is 'up to me'. The fact that I do not have absolute liberty to respond in any way at all does not make the action any less attributable to me; and the fact that I have not been the only cause of the development of my own character likewise does not make the action any less my own. The fact that the decisive cause is something internal to my own mind is enough, in Stoic eyes, to justify attributions of responsibility.

If the challenge is merely to show how agents can be causally responsible for their actions, including their character-shaping decisions, then this strategy ought to suffice and there is every reason to think that Stoics remained intellectually comfortable with this theory. The Aristotelian commentator Alexander of Aphrodisias (who advocated a radical liberty of indifference in his *De fato*) and later Platonists were not convinced and aimed to force Stoics either to reject full causal determinism for the material world or to admit that human agency involved an immaterial psychic starting point that was free of the nexus of causation.

PUZZLES AND PARADOXES

The compatibility of responsibility with determinism might seem paradoxical, but it was far from the most challenging Stoic doctrine. Throughout antiquity the Stoics were emphatic in their embrace of other ethical theses which their opponents and common sense recognized as deeply implausible – at least if one accepts the ordinary senses of the terms involved. No doubt they advocated paradox as an intellectual challenge and to underscore the distinctiveness of the conceptual foundations of their moral theory. Thus, since virtue is a perfect condition all states of vice are 'equal' and there are no degrees of virtue any more than there are degrees of straightness in geometry – a line is either straight or not and all deviations are equally deviations (even if they are not equal deviations). Similarly all right actions (*katorthômata*) and all moral mistakes (*hamartêmata*) are equal, at least in so far as they are all products of virtue and vice respectively. And the wise person is free of emotions – not in the sense that he or she has no feelings at all, but rather because the *pathê* are by definition vicious states of character. And only the wise are free, since everyone else is enslaved to passions and errors. And the wise man is a true king while all fools (everyone else) are slaves.

As a pedagogical tool these paradoxes no doubt did their intended job quite well, but they left the school chronically exposed to criticisms with which it is only natural to sympathize. And yet, as Seneca says, the underlying doctrines are not quite so crazy as they might sometimes appear. As he put the point in his *On Benefits* (2.35.2): 'some of the things we say seem rebarbative to our normal way of speaking, but then they come back around to it by an indirect path'. This is a point that one might make about Stoic ethics as a whole.

BIBLIOGRAPHY

An asterisk denotes secondary literature especially suitable for further reading.

Inwood, B. ed. 2003. *The Cambridge Companion to the Stoics* (Cambridge University Press).*
Inwood, B. and Donini, P.L. 1999. 'Stoic Ethics', in K. Algra *et al.* (eds.), *Cambridge History of Hellenistic Philosophy* (Cambridge University Press), ch. 21.
Inwood, B. and Gerson, L.P. 2008. *The Stoics Reader* (Indianapolis, IN: Hackett).
Long, A.A. 1974. *Hellenistic Philosophy* (London: Duckworth).
Long, A.A. 1996. *Stoic Studies* (Cambridge University Press).
Long, A.A. 2002. *Epictetus: A Stoic and Socratic Guide to Life* (Oxford University Press).*
Long, A.A. and Sedley, D.N. 1987. *The Hellenistic Philosophers* (Cambridge University Press).
Schofield, M. 1991. *The Stoic Idea of the City* (Cambridge University Press).
Schofield, M. and Striker, G. eds. 1986. *The Norms of Nature* (Cambridge University Press).

7

Ancient Skepticism

KATJA MARIA VOGT

Why assume that ancient skepticism made a contribution to the history of moral philosophy? Skepticism, it may appear, is first and foremost concerned with knowledge. Ancient skepticism, however, belongs to a Socratic strand in philosophy that refuses to draw a line between epistemology and ethics. Truth is taken to be so high a value that the good life must be a life of investigation. If there are norms of overriding importance, these are epistemic norms. But these norms are thought to bear immediately on whether one leads a good life. In other words, how to live is taken to be a question of how to think. In this chapter, I will focus on four topics: truth as an end; agency; disagreement; and the nature of value.

Before I begin, here is a minimal sketch of the protagonists. 'Ancient skepticism' refers to two philosophical movements. First, Academic skepticism, which emerges in Plato's Academy as a way of reading Plato and of adopting Socratic modes of investigation. Arcesilaus (316/315–241/240 BCE) and Carneades (214–129/128 BCE), both of them heads of the Academy, are its most prominent figures. Academic skepticism exerts influence on later thinkers mostly through Cicero (106–43 BCE), who writes two treatises called *Academica* and sees himself as doing philosophy in Academic spirit. Most of our knowledge about Academic skepticism derives from his writings, as well as from Pyrrhonian discussions about the differences between the two outlooks. Second, Pyrrhonian skepticism, which is rooted in long-standing metaphysical discussions about appearances. Pyrrho (365/360–275/270 BCE), the thinker in whose name later skeptics refer to themselves as 'Pyrrhonian', is almost a sage-like figure. He is less a founder of a school than an inspirer of successors, spread out over several centuries. Aenesidemus (first century BCE) and Agrippa (first to second century CE) devise famous modes of argument – the Ten Modes and the Five Modes – to be employed in skeptical investigation. The most comprehensive and sophisticated account of Pyrrhonian skepticism is formulated by Sextus Empiricus

Ancient Skepticism

(c. 160–210 CE). His *Outlines of Skepticism* (PH 1) offer a general account of skepticism. Sextus' further treatises consist of books on logic (standardly referred to as PH 2 and M 7–8), physics (PH 3.1–167 and M 9–10), ethics (PH 3.168–281 and M 11); and six books on other disciplines such as grammar and rhetoric (M 1–6). Pyrrhonian skepticism shares much with Academic skepticism. Both are inspired by sophistic and Socratic modes of argument: arguing 'for both sides' of an issue (*pros amphotera*); 'dialectically' exploring the premises of one's opponent without embracing them; and refuting proposals made by one's interlocutors.[1]

TRUTH AS AN END

The Greek word *skepsis* means investigation. This is what the skeptics, both Academic and Pyrrhonian, most centrally are: investigators. Sextus compares the skeptics to other philosophers, many of whom take themselves to have found the truth. The skeptics call them dogmatists (*dogmatikoi*), which literally means 'those who put forward theories'. Next, there is a camp that should not be confused with skepticism, namely those who declare things to be inapprehensible. For the skeptic, this counts as dogmatism. Something is said to be the case, whereas skeptics do not make claims about the way things are. Contrary to these other philosophers, the skeptics continue to investigate.[2]

Not only philosophers make assertions about 'how things are'. In ordinary life, cognizers accept any number of things as true that may turn out to be false. Hellenistic epistemologists, that is, those philosophers who are the skeptics' interlocutors, share with the skeptics the observation that it is difficult not to assent when appearances are compelling or when views are appealing. For the skeptics, this means that methods of argument must be developed that, on the one hand, prevent one from assent in everyday matters, and that on the other hand can be employed to test philosophical theories. In Academic skepticism, these methods resemble Socratic

---

[1] I refer to Sextus' writings as 'PH 1–3' and 'M 1–11'; and to Cicero's *Academica* in Brittain's edition (2006). 'DL' stands for Diogenes Laertius' *Lives of Eminent Philosophers*. Book 9 in DL provides a detailed account of Pyrrhonian skepticism; cf. Vogt 2015. Further evidence is collected in Long and Sedley 1987, abbreviated as LS. At times, I refer the reader to whole chapters in LS. 'LS 40', for example, references the chapter that collects fragments on the Stoic–Academic debate about criteria of truth; 'LS 40A' refers to the first entry in that chapter.
[2] PH 1.1.; cf. Cicero *Acad.* 2.7–8 for Academic skepticism.

techniques, as well as Epicurean methodology for examining impressions before judging something to be the case.[3] In Pyrrhonian skepticism, the Five Modes, Two Modes and Modes against Causal Explanations address the arguments that are employed to support theories (PH 1.164–86; DL 88–9). The Ten Modes target appearances, understood in a broad sense: something appears, either in a sensory or non-sensory way, to be so-and-so (PH 1.36–163; DL 79–88).

Both Academic and Pyrrhonian skeptics describe the state of mind that is generated by their investigations as suspension of judgment, *epochê*. This term presupposes Stoic philosophy of mind. According to Stoic premises, sense-perceptions and theoretical thoughts are impressions, *phantasiai*. Impressions move the mind toward or away from assent. There are three ways a cognizer can respond to an impression: assent, rejection, and suspension of judgment. Epistemic norms – norms of how to attain knowledge and avoid anything lesser than knowledge – are norms of assent. That is, a central component of Stoic philosophy addresses when and how one should (and should not) assent.[4]

Plato's Academy turns skeptical in a phase of intense epistemological debate. Arcesilaus overlaps in the Academy with Zeno, founder of Stoicism. The Stoics understand themselves as Socratics, rejecting the Forms as well as Plato's tripartite psychology. They embrace the views that the soul is reason and that virtue is knowledge. Knowledge of everything that pertains to life, namely physics, ethics, and logic, literally constitutes virtue (Aetius I, Preface 2, LS 26A). This systematic body of knowledge is hard to attain. In order to make progress toward knowledge, epistemic norms must be observed. One should assent in the ways in which a sage – a perfect cognizer – assents. This wise person does not hold any beliefs, *doxai*. When she accepts something as true, her assent constitutes a piece of knowledge. She assents only when she has a so-called cognitive impression, an impression that makes it clear that it presents things precisely as they are (DL 7.46, 54; Cicero *Acad.* 1.40–1, 2.77– 8; M 7.247–52). The cognitive impression is the Stoics' so-called criterion of truth.

But what makes an impression 'cognitive'? Indeed, is there such a thing as a cognitive impression? And more generally, is there *any* criterion of truth? A

---

[3] Cicero's discussion of Academic skepticism provides a general and detailed picture. Carneades develops a methodology for testing impressions that resembles Epicurean scientific methodology (cf. LS 18).

[4] Most of the relevant evidence is collected in LS, chs. 39, 40, 41 and 53.

criterion of truth, as Hellenistic epistemologists conceive of it, is crucial to the pursuit of knowledge. There are some impressions, the Stoics argue, that one can safely accept; though they may be few, one can build systematic knowledge by 'collecting' only those thoughts that are cognitive. The Epicureans argue that sense-perceptions are criteria of truth. Every sense-perception is true in the sense that it physically occurs: an image hits the eye, sound the ear, and so on; theories that are in conflict with sense-perception are to be rejected. But what if there is no criterion of truth, nothing that can safely be taken to be true just by itself? Another option may be to put forward proofs for one's theories and build knowledge from there. The criterion of truth on the one hand, and theories of proof on the other hand, are contentious topics for debates between skeptics and dogmatists.

When Sextus explains the motivation of skepticism, he describes the skeptics as philosophers: people who want to find out what is true and false (PH 1.12). They end up in on-going investigation, though not because they prefer suspension of judgment over discovery; they would like to find the truth. But as of yet, investigation continues because neither the dogmatists' criteria of truth nor their proofs appear compelling. Scholars dispute, however, whether this description is a good fit for philosophers who devise techniques that regularly lead to suspension of judgment. Truth and suspension of judgment may appear to be competing ends. Worse, some passages in Sextus suggest that Pyrrhonian skeptics pursue yet another end, namely a good life, understood as tranquility.[5]

To see how the ends of good life, truth, and suspension of judgment interrelate, turn briefly to Socrates. In Plato's *Apology*, Socrates says that an unexamined life is not worth living (38a5–6). Human beings have one eminently important task: to aim to lead a good life. But the question of how to live well is difficult. Those who presumably are experts – priests, sophists, and others whom Socrates talks to – cannot produce coherent answers. Investigation regularly leads into puzzles and perplexities. In response, one could turn away from investigation, as some of Socrates' interlocutors in early dialogues do. Notably, this is not Socrates' reaction. As difficult as it appears to be to lead a life guided by reason, this is what he argues needs to be attempted. That is, Socrates aims for a good life; for now, he must settle for a second-best life, namely one of on-going investigation instead of one that is based on knowledge of good and bad; he methodically

---

[5] Cf. Bett 2010a; Striker 2001; Vogt 2012: ch. 5, 'The Aims of Skeptical Investigation', pp. 119–39.

arrives at puzzlement which sustains this second-best state; and he is fundamentally motivated by the value of truth.

This is, roughly, the blueprint for the idea that a life of investigation is a pursuit of a good life. Both Arcesilaus and Sextus argue that skeptics live 'rightly'.[6] Suspension of judgment, though worse than discovery, is the best available state of mind as long as discovery has not been attained. Augustine, who is acquainted with Academic skepticism via Cicero, puts his finger on precisely this point. His *Contra academicos* takes this to be the crucial question by which to assess skepticism: whether it is possible to live happily without discovery of the truth, assuming that this discovery is what one's whole life is geared towards. Though a life of knowledge would be even better, the skeptics' reply, as I have sketched it, is 'yes'.

AGENCY

The dogmatists take themselves to have a damning objection against this sketch of the skeptics' life: agency is not possible without assent. Why does the skeptic walk through a door in order to leave a room, rather than run into the surrounding wall? As the dogmatists see it, one must assent to the impression 'there is the door' in order to successfully leave a room (Plutarch *Adv. col.* 1122A–F; LS 69A). Moreover, or so the argument continues, in order to decide what to do, say, whether or not to leave the room, an agent must assent to the thought that *this* is what she will do. That is, in order to survive and to lead an active life, agents must assent to impressions about how the world is and to impressions about what they should be doing. Beliefs about the world as well as evaluative and normative beliefs are indispensable for action, or so the dogmatists argue.[7]

The responses of Pyrrhonians and Academics to this so-called 'Apraxia Charge' differ.[8] Pyrrhonian skeptics follow appearances (PH 1.21–4). Adherence to appearances involves letting oneself be guided by affections, say, eating when hungry. It also involves learning skills by doing things the way they are done. Moreover, custom and law are considered appearances of a sort: the skeptic can go along with them. This last point has earned the

---

[6] Cf. M 7.158 and Cic. *Acad.* 2.37–9 for Academic skepticism; PH 1.16–17 for Pyrrhonian skepticism.

[7] The past three decades of scholarship on ancient skepticism take their starting-point from a paper by Michael Frede (1979), where he argues that the skeptics take themselves to have responses to the charge that without belief they cannot act.

[8] See Vogt 2010a.

skeptics much criticism. Hegel, among others, pointed out that Pyrrhonian skepticism is essentially conformist.[9] If one does not take a stand on how to act, and escapes inactivity simply by adhering to customary ways, one presumably leads a highly conventional life. The ancient version of this objection employs the following example, reminiscent of twentieth-century discussions about obedience in pernicious regimes: if a skeptic is asked by a tyrant to perform an unspeakable deed or else suffer the death penalty, it is assumed that the skeptic will obey.[10] Against this, skeptics argue that appearances can go either way (M 11.166). If the skeptic grew up in an environment of rebellious spirit, it may appear to her that resistance against a tyrannical regime is 'what one does'. This response, however, does not persuade many of the merits of a Pyrrhonian skeptic's life. The skeptics must admit that it is up to chance which way appearances guide her, not a matter of considering reasons for and against courses of action.

Arguably, Academic skepticism does better on this count. Arcesilaus and Carneades formulate criteria of action. The skeptics adhere to the 'reasonable' or to the 'convincing'. The reasonable, Arcesilaus' criterion, is roughly that which appears to an agent based on her best thinking about a given question (SE M 7.158; 7.150). One's best thinking is likely to fall short of getting things right. And yet the skeptic aims to deliberate as best as she can. Carneades' criterion, the convincing, is a sophisticated philosophical proposal, perhaps even intended as a criterion of truth, not merely of action (SE M 7.166–84). It is assumed that, in any number of contexts, we can just go with how things look; not much is at stake. But there are matters of importance in life. In these cases one ought to examine one's impressions. If you enter a dark room and some item looks like a rolled-up rope, do take a stick and poke at it, for perhaps it is a snake. The more something seems to matter, the more carefully one may deliberate.

Notably, this proposal does not acknowledge cases where, given how much is at stake and given how the arguments play out, we have fully understood what is right and wrong. Consider what the ancient skeptics would say in response to an argument often made against contemporary moral skepticism: you say you are doubting whether there is any moral knowledge; but don't you know any number of moral truths, for example,

---

[9] Cf., for example, Hegel 1977: para. 205.

[10] This is a much-debated example in ancient philosophy, perhaps in part inspired by Socrates, who is reported to have been commanded by the Thirty Tyrants to arrest an innocent man, which he refused to do. Cf. Aristotle, *Nicomachean Ethics* III.1, 1110a5–8.

that slavery is wrong? In response, today's moral skeptics may have to admit that they know this, as well as some similar moral truths. Thus they stand refuted. Academic skeptics, assuming they were around today, would react differently. They would argue that it took our culture quite long to agree that slavery is wrong. Rather than pride ourselves on this achievement we should suspect that it remains preliminary. They might point out that it may well be the case that any number of goods we buy today are produced under conditions that, if only we had a better understanding of what slavery is and why it is wrong, we would condemn and classify as slavery. So we should step back from seeing our current views as moral truths. Moreover, they would point out that they are not in the business of doubting what to others appears certain. They are investigating questions that, if others only paused to consider them, would appear also to them as worthy of further thought. Today's anti-skeptics may insist that even preliminary insights are insights. And yet as moralists they may also concede that the ancient commitment to investigation has some appeal: it pulls away from self-congratulatory notions of moral progress, and directs one's attention to what remains under-explored.

DISAGREEMENT

Early ancient ethicists consider disagreement a widespread phenomenon that philosophy has to respond to. Their starting-point is thus quite different from the starting-point of moral philosophers in the Christian era, who tend to assume that we largely agree in our moral notions, so that the task of philosophy is to clarify them. Arguably, this is one of the reasons why ethics of the sophistic–Socratic tradition is relevant to contemporary discussions. Today's ethicists also aim to address diversity, disagreement, and difference.

In the fifth century BCE, Herodotus as well as the sophists explore how one ought to respond to the fact that different people live according to different customs. Herodotus cites Pindar's saying 'custom is king'. He interprets the quote, suggesting that custom makes people believe that their own ways of doing things are natural while foreign ways are not only false, but unnatural and repellent. For example, Herodotus says, the Greeks burn their dead, while the Callatians eat them (*Histories* 3.38). Each consider their own funeral rites natural, and are disgusted by what others do. Once this observation is on the table, reliance on one's own commitment to one's customs and on one's abhorrence of other customs appears arbitrary. As philosophers today put it, those who disagree appear to be epistemic peers:

we ourselves are in no obvious way better suited to having found out how to live than other people.

Some of the sophists are associated with the contrast between nature and law, *phusis* and *nomos*, and with the resulting challenge regarding the naturalness of one's own customs. Moreover, the sophists are experts in a method of question-and-answer. The sophist asks his interlocutor 'is X A or B?', say, 'is virtue teachable or natural?' The interlocutor has to choose one answer and defend it. He loses if he ends up confused or contradicting himself upon further interrogation; he wins if the questioner is at a loss or contradicts himself. These themes and techniques are similar to Socrates', as he is presented in Plato's dialogues and as the skeptics see him. In the *Euthyphro*, Socrates points out that, when it comes to value, we have no established methods of resolving disagreement (7c–8a). Disagreement, moreover, occurs not just between different groups or peoples. It further occurs – and this takes center stage for Socrates – within the minds of individual cognizers, who regularly fail in sorting out their views about value.

One event in Carneades' life illustrates how Academic skeptics kept these preoccupations alive. Carneades was chosen, as one of three philosophers, to visit Rome in 155 BCE as ambassador from Athens. He disturbed the Romans with the following stunt. One day, he gave a speech advocating justice, to great acclaim. The next day, he gave a speech against justice, and was similarly persuasive. His aim in doing so, presumably, was to draw attention to the fact that the defenders of justice do not have the knowledge they claim to have, and that the nature of justice is as of yet ill understood (Lactantius, *Epitome* 55.8, LS 68M). In response, Carneades and his fellow-philosophers were expelled from Rome. With them, philosophy earned a bad reputation. However, when philosophy gained cultural relevance in Rome, Cicero, one of its main disseminators, picked up precisely where the Athenian embassy had left off. Arguably, philosophy was essentially associated with the very ideas that Carneades put on display: there are arguments for several sides of an issue, and one benefits from thinking through them with an open mind. Thus Cicero not only writes about Academic skepticism and claims to belong to this school. He also structures treatises of eminent influence in the Western tradition, among them *On Duties* and *On Ends*, as conversations between different philosophical parties, each of which is allowed to develop their point of view in detail.

Sextus defines skepticism as an ability to put appearances and thoughts into opposition. Suspension of judgment follows because, presumably, the arguments or appearances on both sides of any given question are of equal strength (PH 1.8). However, would it not seem that, more often than not, the opposing sides are unlikely to be of equal weight? The skeptic's reply is that skepticism is an argumentative ability. The Ten Modes of Aenesidemus provide tools for systematically putting into opposition appearances with appearances, appearances with thoughts, and thoughts with thoughts. This third option for generating suspension of judgment, which focuses on different theoretical proposals, is called 'the mode of disagreement (*diaphônia*)' in Agrippa's Five Modes.

How do these matters apply to ethics? The Tenth Mode generates suspension of judgment on customs, laws, religious beliefs, and doctrines about matters of value. Consider two of Sextus' examples, prayer and incest. Most people pray to the gods and are committed to this practice. However, Epicurus argues that the gods are elevated beings, too lofty to care for human prayer. If only you think through his arguments carefully, they seem as compelling as the practice of prayer (PH 1.155). Second, incest is condemned by Greek law. And yet the Stoics argue that there are cases where a wise person commits incest, and they cite actions of Olympian gods as evidence that this is not an outrageous proposal (PH 1.160 and 3.245). In both cases, one side of the opposition initially looks stronger: custom supports prayer and condemns incest. But arguments can be raised that give you pause, and that create a balance between two sides of the issue. Admittedly, skeptical oppositions at times read like collections of monstrosities and far-fetched illustrations.[11] In response, one may dismiss some of them as unsuccessful: there simply is no equal balance between the two sides. Or one may admit that there is something to the skeptic's enterprise: perhaps serious thought about value does take imagination and a willingness to entertain alien points of view.

THE NATURE OF VALUE

Ancient skepticism is not committed to any metaphysical view about value. Skeptical investigation implies neither what today we call anti-realism (that there are no attitude-independent normative facts), nor realism (that there are attitude-independent normative facts). Skeptical formulations, however, can seem to imply both of these positions. Indeed, Sextus' writings about ethics are particularly hard to assess. At times Sextus argues that, if agents disagree about the good, then there is nothing good by nature (e.g. PH 3.179). This is a metaphysical, and therefore non-skeptical claim. The best available reading

[11] Cf. Vogt 2008: 20–64.

of these passages says that here Sextus is integrating older Pyrrhonian material, inherited from Pyrrho and Aenesidemus, without adjusting it sufficiently to his own general outlook.[12] Sextus' considered formulations say what skeptical investigators should say, and what Academics say: disagreement leads to suspension of judgment and on-going investigations about value. But what about the other option, that skepticism implies a realist metaphysics? If investigation aims to find out the truth about value and the good life, this may presuppose that such a truth exists. Arguably, the skeptics aim to stay clear also of this implication. Investigation is open-ended both with respect to what is true and false *and* with respect to whether there are truths and falsehoods to be discovered.

Consider now the structure and upshot of Sextus' treatises on ethics, as compared to his treatises on logic and physics. In logic, there are two main questions, both of which affect any topic a philosopher may address: whether there is a criterion of truth, and whether there is a theory of proof. Sextus' discussions in physics cover major topics of ancient natural philosophy: whether there is motion, rest, void, causation, and so on. If suspension of judgment on all these questions were added up, the skeptic would quite generally suspend judgment on any and all aspects of the physical world. Sextus' treatises on ethics divide into two halves: on whether there is anything good, bad, and indifferent by nature; and on whether there is an art of life. If they are written with similar ambitions as those on logic and physics, these two questions should exhaustively cover the discipline. That is, a reconstruction of Sextus' project has to explain how these two questions exhaust the domain of ethics – or else the treatises on ethics are less systematic than those on logic and physics. Consider how this might work.

The basic question of ancient ethics is how to lead a good life. A Socratically inspired premise of Stoic philosophy – that is, of the skeptics' main interlocutors – is that knowledge of good and bad is both necessary and sufficient for leading a good life. That is, the person who knows what is good and bad and is thereby an 'expert' for living well, leads a good life. Accordingly, there are two ways in which a philosopher could demonstrate that there is ethical knowledge: either by laying out theories in such a way that no fault can be found with the arguments; or by pointing to a person who leads a good life. This person, if she existed, would have to be in possession of, as Sextus puts it, the 'art' (*technê*) of

---

[12] Cf. Richard Bett's reconstruction of both Sextus' writings on ethics and of Pyrrho's and Aenesidemus' metaphysical views: Bett 1997 and 2000.

life. Sextus' treatises on ethics target precisely these two options and are thus systematic in the same way as the treatises on logic and physics. Under the heading 'is there anything good, bad, and indifferent by nature?' Sextus examines theories of the good life, generating suspension of judgment at each step of his investigation. Under the heading 'is there an art of life?' he asks whether the 'product' of such an art, namely some agents who lead good lives, can be found. If not, then there is no art of life, or so the premises of his dogmatic interlocutors say. And if both questions lead to suspension of judgment, then the question of how to live well needs further investigation.

CONCLUSION

What, then, is the role of ancient skepticism in the history of moral philosophy? As I hope to have shown, the skeptics lead a life of on-going investigation, claiming that they are at ease even though the truth has not been found. In this, they are not unlike scientists today, who happily engage in research, and who would be quite disturbed by the suggestion that they should be miserable only because science has not yet found out the truth about the universe. Ethics, according to ancient skepticism, is like this: an on-going project of aiming to find out how to live, a project that is none the worse for not yet having been concluded.

BIBLIOGRAPHY

An asterisk denotes secondary literature especially suitable for further reading.

Annas, J. and J. Barnes (2000), *Sextus Empiricus. Outlines of Scepticism*, Cambridge University Press.
Barnes, J. (1997), *The Toils of Scepticism*, Cambridge University Press.
Bett, R. (1997), *Sextus Empiricus. Against the Ethicists*, Cambridge University Press.
Bett, R. (2000), *Pyrrho, his Antecedents, and his Legacy*, Oxford University Press.
Bett, R. (2002), 'Pyrrho', in E. Zalta (ed.), *Stanford Encyclopedia of Philosophy*: http://plato .stanford.edu/archives/fall2002/entries/pyrrho/, revised version 2006, http://plato.st anford.edu/archives/sum2006/entries/pyrrho/
Bett, R. (2010a), 'Scepticism and Ethics', in Bett 2010b: 181–94.*
Bett, R. (2010b) (ed.), *The Cambridge Companion to Ancient Scepticism*, Cambridge University Press.
Brittain, C. (2005), 'Arcesilaus', in E. Zalta (ed.), *Stanford Encyclopedia of Philosophy*: http://plato.stanford.edu/entries/arcesilaus/
Brittain, C. (2006), *Cicero: on Academic Scepticism* (Indianapolis: Hackett).
Broadie, S. and C. Rowe (2002), *Aristotle, Nicomachean Ethics. Translation, Introduction, and Commentary*, Oxford University Press.

Burnyeat, M. and Frede, M. (1997) (eds.), *The Original Sceptics*, Indianapolis, Ind. and Cambridge, Mass.: Hackett.*

Cooper, J. (2004), 'Arcesilaus: Socratic and Sceptic', in V. Karasmanis (ed.), *Year of Socrates 2001 – Proceedings*, Athens: European Cultural Center of Delphi. Reprinted in J. Cooper, *Knowledge, Nature, and the Good, Essays on Ancient Philosophy*, Princeton University Press, 81–103.

Frede, M. (1979), 'Des Skeptikers Meinungen', *Neue Hefte für Philosophie*, 15/16: 102–29. Reprinted as 'The Sceptic's Beliefs', in Burnyeat and Frede 1997, 1–24.

Frede, M. (1983), 'Stoics and Sceptics on Clear and Distinct Impressions', in M. Burnyeat (ed.), *The Skeptical Tradition*, Berkeley, Calif.: University of California Press, 65–94.

Hegel, G.W.F. (1977), *The Phenomenology of Spirit*, trans. A.V Miller, analysis and foreword J.N. Findlay, Oxford University Press.

King, P. (1995), *Augustine, Against the Academicians and* The Teacher, Indianapolis, Ind.: Hackett, 1995.

Long, A.A. (2006), *From Epicurus to Epictetus: Studies in Hellenistic and Roman Philosophy*, Oxford University Press.

Long, A.A. and D. Sedley (1987), *The Hellenistic Philosophers Vols. 1 and 2*, Cambridge University Press.

Striker, G. (1996), *Essays on Hellenistic Epistemology and Ethics*, Cambridge University Press.

Striker, G. (2001), 'Scepticism as a Kind of Philosophy', *Archiv für Geschichte der Philosophie* 83: 113–29.

Striker, G. (2010), 'Academics versus Pyrrhonists, Reconsidered', in Bett 2010b: 195–207.

Vogt, K.M. (2008), *Law, Reason, and the Cosmic City: Political Philosophy in the Early Stoa*, New York: Oxford University Press.

Vogt, K.M. (2010a), 'Scepticism and Action', in Bett 2010b: 165–80.

Vogt, K.M. (2010b), 'Ancient Skepticism', in E. Zalta (ed.), *The Stanford Encyclopedia of Philosophy* (Spring 2010 edn): http://plato.stanford.edu/entries/skepticism-ancient/.

Vogt, K.M. (2012), *Belief and Truth: A Skeptic Reading of Plato*, New York: Oxford University Press.

Vogt, K.M. (2015) (ed.), *Pyrrhonian Skepticism in Diogenes Laertius* (Greek–English), with Commentary and Essays, edited and with an Introduction by K.M. Vogt, SAPERE, Vol. **XXV**, Tübingen: Mohr Siebeck.

8

Neo-Platonism

ALEXANDRINE SCHNIEWIND

The Platonic philosophers of Late Antiquity, who were later called Neoplatonists, have been considered for a long time to be so otherworldly orientated that they could not be really interested in practical matters that involve moral philosophy and ethics. This opinion has recently changed and currently scholars concede the existence of ethics in Neoplatonism, but often reproach its elitist structure.[1] The great majority of the studies on the topic have been made on Plotinian ethics, whereas the later Neoplatonists, such as Porphyry, Iamblichus, Proclus, Simplicius and Damascius, have attracted less interest. It is true that Plotinus (204–270), the founder of the Neoplatonic school in Late Antiquity, set an example in focusing on the three principles (*hupostaseis*) that give the ontological structure to everything: the One (*to hen*), Intellect (*nous*) and Soul (*psuchê*).[2] He developed an ontology based on the derivation of a principle from another: Intellect proceeds from the One, Soul from Intellect. These three principles belong to the intelligible world, corresponding to a great extent to the Platonic world of Ideas. Ethics enter the picture only on the level of the sensible world. The sensible world results from the procession of the Soul, the last of the three principles. Individual souls proceed from the Soul-principle and enter sensible bodies in the sensible world. These souls have the specificity of maintaining a strong link to their origin in the intelligible world, as a part of them always remains anchored in the Soul-principle. Contrary to the intelligible world, the sensible world is characterized by its dispersion and multiplicity. Many things there happen randomly and individual souls who are attached to a body during their lifetime have to beware of not being too much attracted by the sensible world. For instance, an important risk for individual souls is to be distracted by constant multiple tasks (*polupragmosunê*) and to lose, thus, the

---

[1] See Dillon 1996; Smith 1999; Beierwaltes 2002; Schniewind 2003; Wilberding 2008; Pietsch 2013.

[2] For an introduction to Plotinus, see O'Meara 1993.

knowledge of their intelligible origin. This is to say that perceptions and emotions, as well as desires, may overcome a person and become stronger than her intellectual faculties. The soul is then overwhelmed by desires and is no longer able to form a counterpart, and may go so far as to forget that a part of it still remains in the intelligible realm.

Even though ethics has no place in the intelligible world, and even if metaphysics strongly determine all of Neoplatonic philosophy, it is still the case that ethics play a highly important role within the sensible world.[3] A person can only progress if she takes into account the fact that her ethical goal is to regain the intelligible world as quickly as possible, i.e., to separate her soul from her body as much as possible, as Socrates indicated in the *Phaedo*. Ethics, thus, has a strong moral component, as a person has the moral responsibility to improve herself as much as possible, in order to accomplish her highest faculties. This ontological and metaphysical world-view became the general setting for the whole Neoplatonic school that developed after Plotinus mainly in Athens and Alexandria and remained so until 529, when the Emperor Justinian closed the Neoplatonic schools because he considered them to be a threat to Christian thought.

Neoplatonic ethics has a particularity: it is mostly descriptive and preferably orientated towards the figure of the wise person, the accomplished sage (*spoudaios, sophos*). This is to say that Neoplatonic ethics do not consist of prescriptions, while being nonetheless normative.[4] Showing how the wise person lives, acts and thinks is a way to say how someone should live. It intends to be an exhortation for the ordinary person who aspires to lead a philosophical life. Neoplatonic ethics has two main topics: happiness (*eudaimonia*) and virtue (*aretê*), accompanied by connected topics such as the role of the good and the relation of *theoria* and *praxis*, contemplative or practical wisdom.

The privileged way of developing these topics occurs through the description of the sage. He is the perfectly virtuous person who is therefore happy. This of course had already been said by Aristotle and the Stoics. Aristotle in his *Ethics* had already developed the importance of virtue as the key to happiness and the Stoics also intimately linked a happy life to a virtuous life. Furthermore, the relation of contemplative wisdom to practical wisdom had also become a main issue in ethics from Aristotle on.

---

[3] See Bene 2013.
[4] For more details on this topic, see Schniewind 2003 and Gill 2005: 15.

The Stoics had already extensively enumerated all the supremely perfect qualities of the sage, mostly formulated as paradoxes as they stressed the inaccessibility of such a wise person.[5] The specificity of the Neoplatonic approach is to consider that an ordinary person can, and even should, strive to become as happy as a wise person. The detailed descriptions of the sage's behaviour towards himself and towards others seek to produce an effect on the ordinary person. These descriptions have a strong normative value.

The Neoplatonic philosophers use mainly two literary formats in order to describe the sage: treatises on happiness or on virtue, and biographies or Lives of famous philosophers (of the past such as Pythagoras, or of the present such as Plotinus and Proclus). In these Lives, they describe the fully happy person and show, often in great detail, how such a person realized the principles of life which one should strive to attain. This is to say that in Late Antiquity, the figure of the sage becomes the main vehicle of ethical demonstration. However, treatises on happiness and on virtue are being written, namely by Plotinus, but it is striking how little these treatises are theoretical.[6]

In the following, I will consider the two main notions of Neoplatonic ethics as represented by two philosophers over two different periods of Late Antiquity, and presented in two different texts: (1) the description by Plotinus of the sage, the fully happy person in his treatise *On Happiness*; (2) the description of the perfectly virtuous philosopher Proclus, drafted by his pupil Marinus in his *Life of Proclus*.

THE WISE AS A NORM

Over a long period of time Plotinus was not considered to have a consistent ethical theory. At best, he was attributed an elitist ethic, reserved, as it seems, for the sages.[7] Over the decades, a recurrent critique of Plotinus' ethics has been that it does not give sufficient practical indications to the ordinary person of how to become good. This opinion has been revised within the past decade.[8] For instance, it has been accepted that Plotinus developed thoughts on happiness since he wrote a whole treatise, *Ennead* I 4 [46],[9]

---

[5] See Hadot 2014. Hadot shows that Seneca first introduced the idea of a possible progression within ethics.
[6] See Schniewind 2015. [7] Dillon 1996. [8] See Schniewind 2003.
[9] The references indicate the place of the treatise within Plotinus' *Enneads*, as well as, between square brackets, the chronological position of the treatise. In the following, I will quote the passages of the *Enneads* according to the classical English edition established by Armstrong (1966–1988).

entitled *On Happiness* (*Peri eudaimonias*), dedicated to the topic. In this treatise, Plotinus gives a detailed description of the sage, who is presented as being perfectly happy. While this treatise offers Plotinus' longest sustained presentation of what it is to be happy, its theoretical part on happiness is much shorter. Plotinus describes the sage, presenting at length the deeds and thoughts of the *spoudaios*. We get thus an idea of what the *spoudaios* thinks about, i.e. what his epistemic state is. We also get to know how he behaves in normal life, how he interacts with other people, as well as how he interacts with himself (i.e. what he takes to be more worthy and what less).

Ennead I 4 [46] *On Happiness* gives the most detailed account of the *spoudaios* and gives us the opportunity to draw a rich picture of what the description of the sage might inspire. What is more, treatise I 4 shows that Plotinus develops his ethical theory by describing the ways of being and thinking of the *spoudaios*. We will have to imagine the impact this description has on the ordinary people, represented by the reader who might be taken as the typical kind of audience Plotinus addresses. But first, let us have a look at the range of aspects described by Plotinus as concerns the sage. Two main aspects can be distinguished: (1) the attitudes the sage has towards himself (thoughts, emotions, actions) and (2) the attitudes he has towards his fellow humans. These aspects are not described one by one, but are rather interwoven in the description of the sage.

The *spoudaios* is described as the fully happy person, who distinguishes himself from his other fellow humans precisely because of this happiness (the main distinction thus is made between a person who is actually happy and another who is actually not happy, even though potentially she would have access to happiness). The sage is described as being self-sufficient (*autarkês*) and not really needing the things which surround him. And here the wording is important: these outer things (*ta alla*, which are, at first, not specified by Plotinus) are described literally as being only surroundings (*perikeisthai*), a word often used by the Stoics while referring to the body that surrounds us (*to perikeimenon*).[10] And it turns out that this is indeed what Plotinus is referring to. The happy sage is in an attitude towards himself that designates his own body as being merely a kind of adjunct, like a coat one is wearing without being identified with it.

So far this is simply described as being a matter of fact. Only then is the question raised as to how it comes that the sage is in such a state of autonomy. The reason goes straight to the point: the *spoudaios* has a special

---

[10] For example Marcus Aurelius 8, 27; 10, 1.

relationship to the transcendent Good and this Good is the cause of the good within the *spoudaios*. The source of the sage's special attitude is to be sought in his having direct access to the transcendent Good. This shows that a metaphysical goal underlies the ethics. A strong anthropological aspect is also implied, as people differ from each other on the basis of who has access to the Good and who does not.

Let us briefly recall a central anthropological claim of Plotinus: the human soul is by nature "amphibious" (*amphibios*): it is partly intelligible and partly linked to the sensible world. Its intelligible part always remains in the intelligible realm.[11] The other part has come down to the sensible world and has entered a body. The difference between people is due to the different weighting one gives to these two parts, the intelligible or the sensible. The wise person gives full priority to her upper, intelligible part and is able to fully connect to that part; the ordinary person, on the contrary, is stuck more or less in her lower, sensible part which seeks strong connections with the body. Ordinary people are distinguishable on the basis of who is able to become aware of his upper part. Let us keep this in mind, as it will be of importance when we discuss on whom the description given of the wise person might have an effect.

For the present, let us go back to the *spoudaios* and his description. He possesses the good and this means, for Plotinus, that he has become his *own proper good* and therefore he is self-sufficient. Being so, he is not searching or seeking anything any more. This is an important specification, as it gives some insight into his epistemic state: traditionally, "search" (*zêtêsis*) is the word used to describe the philosophical activity. The search for principles is what constitutes a philosopher's most prominent drive. The sage is described not using that activity any more; one can deduce that he has already found the first principles and has access to them.

However, the wise person does not leave all the mundane things aside. He keeps searching for things in order to satisfy his bodily needs. Thus he keeps looking after his body, giving him the things he needs (food, drink, care). And for this purpose he is still in a seeking attitude, even though quite detached from it. However Plotinus stresses the fact that the wise person only does this because it is necessary and only as it is necessary to what belongs to him and not to what he himself is essentially.

Plotinus makes clear in what respect the *spoudaios* differs from other people: we get to know the source of his detached attitude (his direct access

---

[11] See *Enn.* IV 8 [6]; see also Schniewind 2005.

to his upper part), and we see the results of it in his attitude towards himself, namely towards his body. We see that he does not consider his body to *be* himself, but that he is willing to care for it within the limits of what is necessary.

What is more, *Ennead* I 4 provides us with supplementary information about how the sage is perceived by his fellow humans and also how he copes with his emotions. The sage is of course, as is every person, subject to the vicissitudes of fortune as well as to the death of members of his family or of close friends, but this will not affect his happiness. Neither will illness that affects his physical body diminish his happiness. It is noteworthy that in *Enn.* I 4, Plotinus does not bother to give the detailed doctrinal background of this capacity of the sage to stay unaffected by these unlucky events. This is a characteristic feature of Plotinus' ethics: he prefers to give detailed examples of the attitude of the sage and not so much of the doctrinal epistemic background. This is precisely the aim of the description of the sage. It says: "look at that sage and how he copes with unlucky events; see how he is able to remain happy." This in itself already has a strong pedagogical impact and does not need, at this stage, to be accompanied by more detailed information as to how he mentally deals with suffering, especially as we already know the most important thing from which we can deduce all the rest: the sage is able to behave like this only because of his linkage to the intelligible realm.

As concerns emotions, the sage is said to be sad when faced with the loss of a close person. But he knows that this sadness proceeds from his lower part and he will cope with these emotions, accepting them but not identifying himself with them. This is an interesting example, as Plotinus shows us that the sage is not exempt from emotions and that even an emotion like pain or sadness will affect him. But the difference is clearly shown: he will not be overwhelmed by these emotions and his true self will not be affected.

Does this mean that the *spoudaios* is a kind of cool and indifferent person in his inner self? Plotinus there too is quite specific and detailed in the description he gives: the *spoudaios* does have emotions, even in his inner self, but these are of a very special quality and are called "noble emotions" (*ta asteia*).[12] They consist in being purified of all kinds of intemperance (*akolaston*) and detached from bodily pleasures.[13] Furthermore, the sage will not be subject to excessive joy (*perichareias*). On the contrary, he will live in a joyful serenity (*to hileon*). He remains in a quiet peaceful state (*katastasis hêsuchos*) and is always content (*agapêtê*). These are the pleasures of the wise person: "If anyone looks

---

[12] *Enn.* IV 3 [26]. See Schniewind 2014.   [13] See *Enn.* I 4, 12.

for another kind of pleasure in life, it is not the life of virtue he is looking for."[14]

We see thus that *Ennead* I 4 draws a rich and consistent picture of the abilities of the sage. Obviously Plotinus is concerned by the fact that the description must have a pedagogical role and impact on those reading the treatise. For that purpose, the attitude of the sage toward his lower part is of high importance. At the beginning of his treatise he mentions the attitude of detachment the sage has towards his body; but he does not give much detail about how to achieve it. At the end of the treatise he comes back to this topic and this time stresses much more vehemently that the sage no longer considers himself as a composite of body and soul. And here comes a quite radical statement:

> There must be a sort of counterpoise on the other side, towards the best, to reduce the body and make it worse, so that it may be made clear that the real man is other than his outward parts.[15]

This statement is crucial for us as it makes clear that the sage is adopting here a pedagogical attitude in order to *show* to his fellow humans that his body is not what matters. Clearly, were he not bothered by the wish to show his fellow humans the path to happiness, he would certainly not bother to show anything to the outer world. But given the context, he seeks to make clear where the real values are and how to do so without words or teachings, but through his way of life and especially through his own attitude. In exaggerating his neglect and disdain of the body, he aims at showing that the real value that is important lies elsewhere. I take this to be a clear testimony of Plotinus' wish to provide ordinary people with a most useful and usable description of the sage. They would be able to look intently at the description and follow the attitudes described, keeping in mind the picture which has been drawn of the sage.

This picture is normative: this is how one has to be if one wants to be happy. But instead of proposing moral obligations or moral rules, Plotinus describes a perfectly wise and happy person and says: if you want to be happy too, just follow the example.

I take the detailed description of the sage of *Ennead* I 4 to be exemplary of the genre of the role and function of the description of a wise person in Neoplatonic ethics. To my mind, this description has the function of a strong recommendation that has its origin in some strong metaphysical claims. But

---

[14] *Enn.* I 4, 2, 11–12. [15] *Enn.* I 4, 14, 12–14.

it shows a constant concern for those individuals who are not yet wise people and for whom it will be of great help to hear (or read) such descriptions and to be taught by them. Is this not the most practical way to tell someone how to be good?

The question to be asked is: how does the description of the sage work as a model for the aspiration of ordinary people? If one meets a sage, what is going to motivate the wish to become a sage too? The relation of the sage to his body is important, as he is said to neglect it. How are we to take this kind of exaggeration in respect of the neglect of the body? As a way to indicate to the ordinary person that his aspirations should go elsewhere and should be directed towards knowledge of the intelligible world. Interestingly enough, this negative attitude toward one's body significantly changes in later Platonism, as soon as the scale of virtue becomes an essential part of ethics. Let us turn to this topic now.

THE PERFECTLY VIRTUOUS PHILOSOPHER: PROCLUS AND THE SCALE OF VIRTUE

The notion of virtue is strongly linked to ethics in ancient philosophy in general, but also to Neoplatonic ethics in particular. Plotinus already dedicated a whole treatise to that topic (*Ennead* I 2 [19] *On Virtues*) and Porphyry sought to give a more elaborated version of it (*Sentences*, ch. 32). Plotinus introduced the idea that there are two levels, the lower and the higher virtues which one can attribute to the four cardinal virtues. On their lower level, they are political virtues, helping us to live among fellow citizens in the sensible world and to have an appropriate attitude towards our desires and emotions.[16] On their higher level, they allow the soul to purify itself by separating from the body and to aspire thus to what was commonly called the "divinization" of the soul.[17] At this level the soul is able to apprehend the higher principles, Intellect and the One.[18] Plotinus stresses the fact that one necessarily needs to achieve the lower virtues in order to attain the higher ones, whereas it is not assured that one will attain the latter, having attained the former.[19] Porphyry elaborated in his book the *Sentences*, dedicated to chosen aspects of Plotinian philosophy, a more detailed version of Plotinus' theory of virtues, introducing four distinct levels of virtues: (1) political, (2) purificatory, (3) theoretical and (4) paradigmatic virtues. Both Plotinus and

---

[16] *Enn.* I 2, 2, 13–20. [17] See O'Meara 2003: 40–4. [18] *Enn.* I 2, 3, 22–31; 6, 23–7.
[19] *Enn.* I 2, 7, 10–12.

Porphyry highly influenced the later Neoplatonic philosophers, leading to a full scale of virtue one has to ascend in order to be perfectly virtuous. Iamblichus, who was a pupil of Porphyry, wrote a treatise *On Virtue*, which is lost. It seems that he elaborated the scale that was used in later Neoplatonism.[20]

Two centuries after Plotinus, Marinus of Neapolis (440–500) wrote a *Life of Proclus*. Intended as a funeral oration, it is a biography of Proclus (412–485), the famous Neoplatonic philosopher who had been his master and whose successor he became at the head of the Neoplatonic school of Athens.[21] Marinus wrote this biography in 486 for the first anniversary of Proclus' death. The aim of the *Life* is to show that Proclus had been fully virtuous and therefore completely happy. This means that Proclus accomplished in his own life the whole scale of virtue, ranging from the natural virtues all the way up to the paradigmatic virtues. Importantly, Marinus shows how the four cardinal virtues (wisdom, justice, temperance and courage) can be applied to Proclus at every level of the virtue scale. The scale contains the following steps: (1) natural virtues; (2) moral virtues; (3) political virtues; (4) purificatory virtues; (5) contemplative virtues; (6) theurgic virtues; (7) paradigmatic virtues.

The virtues appear in this progressive order that starts with virtues one has at birth (natural virtues) and which correspond to the good disposition of the bodily organs, as well as to the natural qualities of the soul. For example, Proclus is said to have been a beautiful child (advantages of the body) who learned everything very easily and quickly (good disposition of the soul).[22] Moral virtues[23] are acquired through education, from early age on. It was considered that some animals can acquire such virtues too, once they are well habituated; acquiring the right opinion is also trained at that level. This level needs special care by parents or teachers, as it does not engage the activity of reason in the child or animal. Its acquisition does not need an understanding of virtue by the child.

Political virtues[24] express themselves through virtuous actions. Contrary to the virtues of the previous level, they do require the activity of reason and are therefore considered to be the first properly human virtues.[25] Marinus

---

[20] See O'Meara 2003: 46.
[21] See the excellent edition and French translation of this text in Saffrey and Segonds 2001, and also Edwards 2000.
[22] *Life of Proclus*, § 3.8–6.23. [23] *Life of Proclus*, § 7–13. [24] *Life of Proclus*, § 14–17.
[25] O'Meara 2003: 48.

gives examples of Proclus' generosity and courage, as well as of his way of acting politically and being friendly towards his fellow citizens.

Purificatory virtues[26] express the intention of an individual to go beyond his bodily actions and to purify his soul from his body. Proclus is thus described as leading an abstinent life, accompanied by rituals of purification; furthermore he detached himself from bodily pains, as well as from his desires and negative emotions like anger.

Contemplative virtue[27] happens once the soul has been purified. Proclus was able to practise the virtues at a contemplative level, which means that he grasped them in their intelligible essence. This gave him the ability to develop philosophical issues to a high degree. For instance, Marinus says that it was the reason why Proclus was so prolific in his writings and always alert during the many teaching hours he had per day.

Theurgic virtues[28] show the ability of Proclus to produce miracles toward his fellow citizens. For example, he miraculously healed a woman. This shows that Proclus had a privileged relation to the gods (Athena, Asclepius, Pan).

Paradigmatic virtues correspond to the idea of virtue. Being able to grasp the paradigm of the virtues consists in knowing the principles.

What is striking throughout Marinus' description of the scale of virtue is the importance given not only to Proclus' intellectual faculties, but also to all his physical qualities. Contrary to what Plotinus claims about his sage's indifference towards his body and even the neglect that he might emphasize, Marinus wants to show how beautiful his master was and how perfect his bodily parts were. A contrast herein is also formed with Porphyry's description of Plotinus, as given in the *Life of Plotinus*, written 30 years after Plotinus' death. Porphyry stresses there that Plotinus was ashamed to have a body and that he declined any depiction of his bodily appearance.[29] Furthermore, he tells his readers that Plotinus died of a contagious bodily disease which had forced him to live as a recluse outside the city.[30] By contrast, the supremely happy person, according to Marinus, possesses a beautiful body throughout his lifetime. He even goes so far as to say that none of Proclus' bodily organs ever declined throughout his life. Not only are bodily beauty and perfect bodily functions attributed to Proclus, but so is bodily strength. There, too, the difference with Plotinus is striking: Plotinus indicates that it is not the strength of a body that determinates the inner strength of a person and that

---

[26] *Life of Proclus*, § 18–21. [27] *Life of Proclus*, § 22–5. [28] *Life of Proclus*, § 26–33.
[29] *Life of Plotinus*, § 1. [30] *Life of Plotinus*, § 2.

the wise person should not pay attention to it. Here we are told that, without his doing, Proclus had all these qualities naturally. That is to say that he naturally already had a huge advantage over others. We might see herein a hint that the aim is to say that Proclus was given by nature qualities and dispositions that his own action enhanced afterwards. This is indeed how the virtue scale is intended to be understood: excellent dispositions are a great advantage as they allow a person to better climb the virtue ladder.

To conclude, let us stress the central importance of happiness and virtue throughout Neoplatonism. A significant difference however is to be found in the attitude one adopts towards the body. Plotinus opts for the pedagogical attitude of the sage, who voluntarily neglects his body in order to show what counts most for a person. Marinus, on the contrary, stresses the perfect beauty and strength of Proclus. The risk of Marinus' description is to put Proclus on such a pedestal that nobody could attain its height. However, the scale of virtue is intended to be a step-by-step guide for the ordinary person. What counts is the effort to climb the rungs of the ladder and to integrate the virtues at their respective levels, irrespective of one's success in attaining the summit of the ladder.

BIBLIOGRAPHY

An asterisk denotes secondary literature especially suitable for further reading.

Armstrong, Arthur Hilary 1966–1988. *Plotinus: Enneads, including Greek (Henry & Schwyzer)*, 7 vols., Loeb Classical Library, Harvard University Press.

Beierwaltes, Werner 2002. "Das Eine als Norm des Lebens. Zum metaphysischen Grund neuplatonischer Lebensform," in T. Kobusch and M. Erler (eds.), *Metaphysik und Religion. Zur Signatur des spätantiken Denkens*, Munich, K.G. Saur, pp. 121–51.

Bene, László 2013. "Ethics and Metaphysics in Plotinus," in F. Karfík and E. Song (eds.), *Plato Revived*, Berlin/Boston, De Gruyter, pp. 141–61.

Dillon, John M. 1996. "An Ethic for the Late Antique Sage," in L. Gerson (ed.), *The Cambridge Companion to Plotinus*, Cambridge University Press, pp. 315–35.*

Edwards, Mark 2000. *Neoplatonic Saints. The Lives of Plotinus and Proclus by their Students*, Liverpool University Press.

Gill, Christopher 2005. "In What Sense are Ancient Ethical Norms Universal?," in C. Gill, *Virtue, Norms and Objectivity. Issues in Ancient and Modern Ethics*, Oxford University Press.

Hadot, Pierre 2014. *Sénèque. Direction spirituelle et pratique de la philosophie*, Paris, Vrin.

O'Meara, Dominic J. 1993. *Plotinus. An Introduction to the Enneads*, Oxford University Press.

O'Meara, Dominic J. 2003. *Platonopolis. Platonic Political Philosophy in Late Antiquity*, Oxford University Press.*

Pietsch, Christian (ed.) 2013. *Ethik des antiken Platonismus*, Stuttgart, Franz Steiner.

Saffrey, Henri Dominique and Segonds, Alain P. 2001. *Marinus, Proclus ou Sur le bonheur*, Paris, Belles Lettres.

Schniewind, Alexandrine 2003. *L'éthique du sage chez Plotin. Le paradigme du spoudaios*, Paris, Vrin.

Schniewind, Alexandrine 2005. "Les âmes amphibies et les causes de leur différence. A propos de Plotin, Enn. IV 8 [6], 4, 31–35," in R. Chiaradonna (ed.), *Studi sull' anima in Plotino*, Naples, Bibliopolis, pp. 181–200.

Schniewind, Alexandrine 2014. "Plotin et les émotions nobles: un accès privilégié par les vertus supérieures," in B. Collette-Ducic and S. Delcomminette (eds.), *Unité et origine des vertus dans la philosophie ancienne*, Bruxelles, Ousia, pp. 321–37.

Schniewind, Alexandrine 2015. "Plotinus' Way of Defining 'eudaimonia' in Ennead I 4 [46] 1–3," in O. Rabbas and E. Emilsson (eds.), *The Quest for the Good Life. Ancient Philosophers on Happiness*, Oxford University Press, pp. 212–21.

Smith, Andrew 1999. "The Significance of Practical Ethics for Plotinus," in J. Cleary (ed.), *Traditions of Platonism*, Aldershot, Ashgate, pp. 227–236

Wilberding, James 2008. "Automatic Action in Plotinus," *Oxford Studies in Ancient Philosophy* 34, pp. 443–77.

9

Early Christian Ethics

SARAH BYERS

G.E.M. Anscombe famously claimed that 'the Hebrew–Christian ethic' differs from consequentialist normative theories in its ability to ground the claim that killing the innocent is intrinsically wrong.[1] The legal character of this ethic, rooted in the divine decrees of the Torah, confers a particular moral sense of 'ought' by which this and other act-types can be 'wrong' regardless of their consequences, she maintained.[2]

There is, of course, a potentially devastating counter-example to Anscombe's characterization. Within the Torah, Abraham is apparently commanded by God to slaughter and set fire to his innocent son, Isaac.[3] For attempting to do so, he is praised in the Biblical passage and by later Jewish and Christian commentators.[4] The case cannot be dismissed immediately as uncharacteristic of the 'Hebrew–Christian ethic'; Abraham and

---

[1] Anscombe 1958: 10, 19. E.g., 'For it has been characteristic of that ethic [=Hebrew–Christian] to teach that there are certain things forbidden whatever *consequences* threaten, such as: choosing to kill the innocent for any purpose, however good . . . the prohibition of certain things simply in virtue of their description of such-and-such identifiable kinds of action, regardless of any further consequences, is certainly not the whole of the Hebrew–Christian ethic, but it is a noteworthy feature of it' (10).

[2] Anscombe 1958: 5–6, 10. E.g., ' . . . Christianity, with its *law* conception of ethics. For Christianity derived its ethical notions from the Torah' (5). Anscombe initially says that a law conception of ethics can in principle arise without belief in divine positive law (1958: 5, citing the Stoics), but later that it requires belief in God as a law-*giver*, comparing it to positive criminal law (1958: 6; strangely, she includes the Stoics again).

[3] Genesis 22:2. Regarding my qualifier 'apparently', see the second half of the section 'Conceptual Parameters' below.

[4] Genesis 22:16–17; Hebrews 11:17–19; James 2:21–3; sections 'Conceptual Parameters' (second half) and 'Early Christian Analyses' below.

Isaac are central figures in the Torah, which contains additional instances of God or Moses commanding the killing of civilians, including children.[5]

It would appear, then, that Anscombe is mistaken factually, about what the historical 'Hebrew–Christian ethic' taught, and in her conceptual claim that the role of law in this ethic is to ground stable content. Seemingly, killing the innocent was considered justified when it was done in order to propitiate God. And while it is true that defining 'right' action as 'lawful' action will ensure that the consequences of an act cannot alter its moral rightness, this will not by itself guarantee that certain act-types are always unlawful. Indeed, the content of decrees in the Torah appears inconstant. Although the Torah does, as Anscombe says, portray God as proscribing the killing of innocent human beings,[6] it also recounts God's contradictory command to kill Isaac and subsequent countermand not to kill Isaac after all.[7]

Christian authors from the third to the fifth centuries, some of whom were in contact with rabbinic glosses, addressed this Biblical story. A survey of their analyses will showcase the development of normative theory during this period, and allow us to assess more fully Anscombe's characterization of the 'Hebrew–Christian ethic'.

CONCEPTUAL PARAMETERS

The various early Christian commentaries invite comparisons with Plato's *Euthyphro* – where the conceptual question of the gods' relation to morality was famously raised – and with rabbinic interpretations of the episode. Although the Christian authors rarely cite the *Euthyphro* by name,[8] we frequently find them employing concepts discussed there. These parallels, rather than questions of direct textual transmission, are the objects of my focus. Similarly for the rabbinic background: I will concentrate on relevant shared content, only alluding to *Quellenforschung* in passing.

---

[5] Deuteronomy 7:1–2, 20:16–18; Numbers 31:7–18. Cf. Dawkins 2006: 31.

[6] Exodus 23:7 ('Do not kill the innocent'; cf. Exodus 20:13; Deuteronomy 5:17); 'innocent' indicates non-murderers or non-attackers (e.g. Genesis 9:5–6; Exodus 22:2; Jeremiah 2:34).

[7] Genesis 22:12.

[8] Eusebius, *Preparation for the Gospel* 13.4 (quoting *Euthyphro* 6a–c). The lack of frequent references is not surprising given the relaxed approach to citation in antiquity; it may also indicate reluctance to quote the text directly, given its polytheistic context.

It should have occurred to any classically educated early Christian writer who knew the *Euthyphro* to evaluate the Abraham–Isaac episode in light of the notions of piety, justice, and normativity discussed by Plato. Both texts deal with the killing of an innocent or possible innocent, and both contrapose piety toward God or the gods with the attempted killing of a family member.[9]

There are two senses of 'piety' in the *Euthyphro*, which we might call particular and general piety. Both are employed in analyses of the Abraham–Isaac episode during late antiquity.

We find particular piety, that is, the proper ritual worship of the gods, discussed at the end of the dialogue. Euthyphro and Socrates agree that these pious acts are just, though not every just act is pious (11e–14e). Similarly, it is a commonplace amongst authors in late antiquity – Christian and pagan – that the particular virtue of piety is a species of the virtue of justice.[10] 'Justice' is often defined in this later period as giving what is due: hence piety is giving due worship to God or to the gods. There is a similar understanding, without an explicit analysis into genus and species, in rabbinic commentaries redacted in late antiquity,[11] as we shall see later in this section.

General piety is the main focus of the *Euthyphro*, and will receive most of our attention. Socrates and Euthyphro agree that the morally good is what the gods love (7d–e; cf. 5d). And being pious is defined as doing what the gods love (6e–7a). It follows that being pious is doing what is morally good. 'Piety' in this sense is not a special virtue amongst others, or a species of some one virtue. Rather, whoever is a thoroughly good person is pious and *vice versa*.

This general sense of 'piety' is in play when Socrates raises the problem of metaphysical ground. Are actions good independently of the gods' loving them, in recognition of which the gods love them, or are they good because they happen to be beloved of the gods (10a)?

---

[9] Euthyphro charges his father with intentional homicide, a capital offense, for killing-by-neglect a servant who killed a slave while drunk. The father's guilt is disputed as is (Plato seems to imply) the servant's, given his drunkenness (*Euthyphro* 4b–e, 9a; MacDowell 1963: 45–6, 59–60, 110–21; Phillips 2007: 89–90, 99; Phillips 2013: 89–90; Plato, *Laws* 865a–874d). Isaac appears to be innocent of any crime when his father attempts to kill him.

[10] Cicero, *On the Nature of the Gods* 1.116, 2.153; Cicero, *On Goals* 5.23.65; Apuleius, *On Plato and his Philosophy* 2.7; Basil of Caesarea, *Rule Q.* 170; Ambrose, *On Duties* 1.27.127. Cf. Jones 2006; Mikalson 2010: 196.

[11] *Genesis Rabbah* (GRab.), believed to have been redacted c. 400–450 CE.

Since Socrates and Euthyphro agree that the gods' loves are belief-based (*hêgountai*, 7e), and also that the gods are not mistaken,[12] the philosophical question raised here is: why are the gods' beliefs not mistaken? Either (1) because the gods perceive accurately what is good in itself, owing to their mental acuity, or (2) because the mere opinion of the gods is determinative of what is good. Socrates' question therefore bears comparison with the debate about whether 'knowledge' – including ethical knowledge[13] – 'is simply perception', in *Theaetetus* 151e–183c. 'Knowledge is simply perception', we are told, asserts that opinion (*doxa*) is knowledge: each individual's experience and belief is the criterion or 'measure' of truth (152a, 152c, 161d–e, 178b). Socrates' option (2) in *Euthyphro* 10a would say this of the gods' perceptions, whereas (1) would deny it. Socrates is of course presented as favoring (1). As a shorthand way of referring to (1) and (2), it will be useful to employ Kretzmann's nomenclature: Theological Objectivism (TO)[14] and Theological Subjectivism (TS), respectively.[15]

In the *Euthyphro*, the violation of the principle of non-contradiction entailed by TS when multiple divine perceivers simultaneously hold contradictory opinions about the same thing[16] is avoided by stipulating that the gods are in perfect agreement (9d). This effectively reduces the number of divine perceivers to one. But it remains an implication of TS that there is no such thing as an intrinsically evil act.[17] For it also follows from the perception theory (and TS) that when the opinion of a single perceiver (here, the set of gods) changes, an act-type must shift from being good to not-good or the reverse.[18] This is the outstanding issue in the *Euthyphro*, given that the gods' opinions are not said to be immutable.

This brings us back to the Torah's successively contradictory divine commands. Although the commands might seem to suggest a voluntaristic God without comparison to Socrates' and Euthyphro's intellectualist gods, in the Hebrew Bible divine commands about child sacrifice are said to be based on God's thoughts,[19] and in the Socratic dialogues, the gods are presented as commanding.[20] More importantly, philosophically TS requires divine

---

[12] Cf. Evans 2012: 28.   [13] *Theaetetus* 157d, 167c, 172b.

[14] For the variant 'internalist TO', see the Conclusions.

[15] Kretzmann 1983: 35, though his TS is not intellectualist.

[16] *Euthyphro* 7b–8b; *Theaetetus* 152b, 171b.   [17] Cf. *Theaetetus* 157d.

[18] *Euthyphro* 6a–c on the changeable Homeric gods; *Theaetetus* 152d–e, 172b.

[19] Jeremiah 19:5, *dienoêthên* (the extant Greek text is believed to be older than the Masoretic text).

[20] *Apology* 28e, 29d.

commands, and TO allows for them. Because perception and opinion are by definition perspectival and personal,[21] in TS the only way for non-gods to know what the moral status of an action is, is for the gods to tell them. And since the gods' opinions are merely asserted to be right, not justified by any publicly accessible intelligible features of the world, this 'telling' cannot be an *explanation of how or why* an act is good or bad,[22] but must be simply a statement of what is to be done, a command. In a TO universe, anyone with sufficient mental acuity could in principle know acts' moral statuses and the reasons why they are good or bad; but commands could nevertheless be useful as instruction for those who *happen* to be ignorant, or to remind and encourage those who already know. Of these two roles for law, the TO model seems implied by the general disapproval of murder in Genesis 9:5–6 insofar as this text offers an explanation of why murder is wrong, namely that humans are in the image of God.

Turning to rabbinic interpretations of the divine command to kill Isaac, we find that they do not advocate TS. First of all, they conceive of the would-be action of killing Isaac as the pious offering of 'first-fruits'[23] – Isaac being the first produce of the marriage of Abraham and Sarah – and thus as an instance of the general moral duty to pay back what is owed.[24] We can now see the similarity to Christian and pagan accounts that define piety as a kind of justice, giving to God what is due. The rabbis do not think the killing of Isaac is justified on consequentialist grounds, to return to Anscombe's concern. Nor is its justice or injustice dependent on changing divine opinions and commands. Instead, it is just in itself because Isaac is God's. When in Genesis 22:12 God ultimately excuses Abraham from repaying this debt, it is mercy. We may not understand why God calls in his debts in some cases and not others, but there is no real conflict with morality – so this reasoning goes.

Of course, this rationale fails to address the divergence between the Torah's murder prohibitions, and the initial divine command that Abraham kill Isaac. Justice is at issue here, for the Biblical passages which stipulate that innocents may not be killed but non-innocents may be[25] imply that killing the innocent is wrong because it is unfair.

[21] *Theaetetus* 160c.   [22] *Theaetetus* 161d–e.
[23] *GRab.* 22.5 (re Genesis 4:3–4); Genesis 22:2; Exodus 22:29–30; Deuteronomy 18:4; Leviticus 20:1–8.
[24] E.g. Psalm 37:21. The rationale for first-fruits is that God, the maker of the earth, is the rightful 'owner' of all produce; first-fruits signify gratitude and recognition of this dominion.
[25] See note 6.

More interestingly, some of the rabbinic commentary – which is not homogenous – alleges that God never commanded Abraham to kill Isaac. This exegetical tradition argues that Abraham misunderstood the verb *alah* in the command he received, taking it to mean '*offer [send up in smoke] him* there as an offering' when he should have understood God to say '*make him [Isaac] ascend* there for an offering.' In other words, Abraham was actually being told to take Isaac up the mountain so that the two could sacrifice there some other thing.[26] Since the former reading accords with the conventions of Hebrew syntax and semantics (the sense of the verb is indicated by the presence of the cognate 'as an offering' (*olah*)),[27] these rabbis are choosing to disregard grammatical convention to arrive at a theologically acceptable interpretation.

We might expect that their motivation here was to make the story consonant with the Torah's moral law, much as Kant later claimed that if an Abraham were apparently commanded to kill an Isaac, the command would have to be illusory, given its conflict with the moral law.[28] But in fact they do not invoke the prohibitions on murder in support of their exegesis. Instead, they decry the 'unnaturalness' of a father killing his own son, note that a command to kill Isaac would contradict the divine promise of a lineage through Isaac, and observe that in Genesis Abraham assures the bystanders that Isaac will return with him from the sacrifice.[29]

EARLY CHRISTIAN ANALYSES

Turning now to the early Christians, we find a repeated identification of the Abraham–Isaac case as an instance of 'killing a relative' (*parricidium*), which is also the feature emphasized as salient in the *Euthyphro* murder case. Some of these Christian authors engage the notion of particular piety, examining whether the sacrifice of Isaac would be worship owed to God. Most centrally, however, these writers care about general piety and 'justice' in the sense of general righteousness, asking whether Abraham acted morally correctly in carrying out God's command to kill Isaac.[30] On the normative question – whether God's conflicting commands signify that actions become pious from

---

[26] *GRab.* 56.2, *GRab.* 56.8. Cf. Kalimi 2010: 5.
[27] Thanks to David Vanderhooft for consultation on the Hebrew.
[28] *The Conflict of the Faculties*, trans. Gregor 1979: 115.
[29] Respectively: *GRab.* 56.5; *GRab.* 56.8 and *GRab.* 56.10 (cf. Genesis 17:15–19); *GRab.* 56.2 (re Genesis 22:5).
[30] Origen is an exception; he reads the story figuratively but not morally (*Homilies on Genesis* 8.6–7; cf. *GRab.* 56.3 and 56.9). Cf. Cavadini 2002.

not-pious, and just from not-just – the texts fall into three groups: employment of what we have called TS, ambiguity or vacillation between TS and TO, and endorsement of TO. These approaches are not necessarily mutually exclusive for a given author; some writers change their minds.

Ambrose apparently subscribes to a TS position in the year 393. Arguing that a command from God makes honorable what would ordinarily be a dishonorable act (*obprobrium, turpitudo*), he asks rhetorically, 'Could he[31] believe that to be dishonorable (*turpe*) which God enjoined? ... Abraham ... received a very great reward, because he believed that at God's command, even the killing of a relative might be piously (*pie*) carried out' (*Letters* 6.27.14).[32]

In the category of ambiguous accounts, we have a number of texts. Cyprian of Carthage (martyred 258) says that Abraham is among the morally righteous (*iusti*) because he was prepared to kill a relative in order to please God (*On Mortality* 12).[33] Yet later in the same text, he avers that 'God does not ask for our blood, but for our faith. For neither Abraham, nor Isaac, nor Jacob were slain' (18).[34] Does Cyprian think that God consistently does not want this kind of act because it is intrinsically wrong (TO) and that Abraham was ignorant of this, but nevertheless morally praiseworthy because he had a good intention? Or does Cyprian mean that although God happens not to want human blood, he could have wanted it, in which case it would have been just to kill Isaac (TS), and that Abraham was praiseworthy because he recognized that TS is true? Similarly, Ambrosiaster (active c. 375–400) asserts that God did not desire Isaac's blood, but also that Abraham's justice (*iustitia*) was increased by his attempt to kill Isaac and by his belief that God wanted Abraham to kill a relative despite God's previous threat to punish homicide (*homicidium*).[35] Again, Chrysostom's *Homily on Genesis* (c. 385–398) states that God did not intend (*oude thelôn*, 47.11–12) for Isaac to be killed, citing the conclusion of the story, while it praises Abraham's belief (*hê gnômê*) that God did want it, and intention (*hê prohairesis*) to cut his child's throat (47.17; cf. 47.5–6, 47.9). In sum, these analyses praise Abraham for being committed to what we have called TS, while stating that God did not want the killing of Isaac, leaving it unclear whether God did not want it because killing the innocent is intrinsically wrong.

[31] Isaiah (Ambrose compares his commanded indecent exposure to Abraham's commanded killing).
[32] Trans. Walford 1881 (therein numbered Letter 58), amended.
[33] Cf. *The Good of Patience* 10.   [34] Trans. Wallis 1868.
[35] *Questions on the Old and New Testament* (*Quest.*) 43.2; 117.6 (alluding to Genesis 4:15).

Worse than ambiguous is Ambrose's self-contradictory gloss in his eulogy for his brother (dated 379). Here he claims that Abraham 'knew' (*sciebat*) – not just believed – both that 'his son would be *more acceptable to God when sacrificed than when whole (sanum)*' and that '*God is appeased not by blood* but by dutiful obedience ... and so Abraham was not stained with his son's blood' (*On the Passing of Brother Satyrus* 2.97–8, my emphasis).[36]

None of these authors cites the Torah's prohibition on killing the innocent as relevant to Isaac. In the case of Cyprian, this seems to be because he generally reserves the descriptor 'innocent' for Christ and the martyrs, on the grounds that they are the paradigmatic and 'truly' innocent ones. But while Ambrose and Ambrosiaster sometimes repeat this prophetic interpretation of Exodus 23:7, they do employ the wider sense of 'innocent' as 'non-aggressor' elsewhere in their writings. They just do not apply it to Isaac. Apparently they believe that if God commanded the slaying of Isaac, it could not be wrong to do it, and any investigation of *how* it could be right would be merely academic.

More sophisticated is Augustine, though he too is ambiguous from 397 to at least 413.[37] Here we see him attempting to remain faithful to earlier exegesis while using a form of what we have called TO. Like Ambrose, Augustine asserts in Sermon 8 that killing a relative, which would have been cruelty if undertaken without a command, became (*facta est*) piety when God commanded it (8.14). However, Augustine strikes out on his own when he gestures toward a *rationale* for how the command was just. He cites the Israelites' taking booty from the Egyptians at the command of Moses during the exodus,[38] mentioning that 'perhaps' (*forte*) this was not stealing but the recouping of a wage owed to the Israelites for their slave labor (8.16). The parallel with Isaac is not spelled out, but presumably it is that Isaac was not actually innocent, just as the Egyptians did not rightfully own what the Israelites took.

Additional detail is available in the *Against Faustus*. Here Augustine classifies the killing of Isaac as a deed 'placed in a middle position' (*medio quodam loco*) between good and bad by the 'eternal law' (22.73). That is, the act-type *killing* is in itself indifferent morally, and becomes right or wrong owing to one's intention, or the circumstances (22.71–8).[39] (Note how this anticipates

---

[36] Trans. Romestin 1896.
[37] Sermon 8, c. 400–411; *Against Faustus*, c. 397–405; *Confessions*, c. 397–401; *City of God* (*City*, begun 413), 1.21, 1.26.
[38] Exodus 12:35. [39] Cf. *Confessions* 3.7.13–3.8.16.

Aquinas' division of acts into object, end, and circumstances, and his stipulation that a defect in any of these renders an action wrong.)[40] If, Augustine
says, Abraham had undertaken to kill Isaac of his own initiative rather than in
obedience to a divine command, the motive would have been cruelty and
hence the act would have been wrong (22.73).[41] This motive could have
rendered the act morally wrong even if the act-type was correct in itself (res
recta) (22.74). Regarding the circumstances, Augustine implies that Isaac was
not innocent, comparing Abraham's killing of him to killing the enemy in a
justified war. God has superior knowledge of who is guilty, and the best
moment for their punishment (22.71–5). Apparently, then, Augustine thinks
that Isaac had done something deserving of death, which is unknown to us.
Similarly, the Egyptians deserved to have things taken from them as the
recouping of a wage (22.71), though the Israelites did not realize this until
Moses commanded them to do it.

Clearly Augustine is attempting a version of what we are calling TO; yet
there is, simultaneously, an insistence on the necessity of the command for
the act's liceity, which savors of TS. In keeping with TO, he argues that God's
global view of the situation allows him to see how justice is to be applied in
each case. It follows that if humans had such epistemic prowess, they could
decide correctly in each situation, rendering commands from God unnecessary. But Augustine also insists that humans are incapable of knowing the
relevant circumstances (22.72, solus Deus novit), which strains credibility. That
the Israelites' labor deserved recompense from the Egyptians is easily inferred
from a basic notion of fairness; and if Isaac had done something that merited
capital punishment, surely his father could have known about it.[42]
Apparently Augustine asserts universal invincible ignorance merely to
make the command somehow necessary, out of loyalty to earlier exegetes'
friendliness toward TS.

It is worth remarking how these early Christians' conflict of loyalty to TS
and TO differs from the dichotomous model proposed by Kierkegaard. If we
take Kierkegaard at his word, he thinks that the divine command to kill Isaac
imposes an absolute religious duty to obey God, which has precedence over
and thus can 'suspend' morality, 'reducing' universal moral norms 'to the
relative' while they remain ethical duties.[43] So the command does not render

---

[40] Summa theologiae IaIIae Q. 18. [41] Cf. City 1.21, 1.26.
[42] Possibly Augustine assumes Isaac's sharing in the corporate human guilt of the
original sin; but he fails to say so.
[43] Fear and Trembling, trans. Hannay 1985: 60, 98.

what would otherwise be unethical ethical, nor is the command justified by its conformity to objective criteria of justice. Rather, in such a case an *unethical* act is *pious*. That scenario cannot arise for our authors, for whom obeying divine commands always coincides with moral righteousness (via either TS or TO), and particular piety falls within the class of morally just actions.

We finally come to an analysis of the Isaac story that approximates Anscombe's 'Hebrew–Christian ethic' in Augustine's *Questions on the Heptateuch* 7.49 (dated 419–420). Bringing to the fore the apparently consequentialist rationale for sacrificing Isaac, Augustine asks whether the story of Abraham and its near-parallel, the tale of Jephthah,[44] signify that human sacrifice is acceptable for the sake of an eternal reward from God. He emphatically answers that on the contrary, God 'hates this kind of sacrifice' (*odisse talia sacrificia*), citing the general prohibitions on child-sacrifice elsewhere in the Torah,[45] and the climactic divine command *not* to kill Isaac. Although Augustine does not quote the more general Biblical prohibitions on killing innocent humans, he implies that these are the grounding principles when he says that this story about *child* sacrifice shows that God does not want *human* sacrifice (*hominis immolatio*). Why, then, did God order Abraham to offer up his son? It served to create a teaching moment. By dramatically preventing the sacrifice of a human being, God shows (*ostendit*), prior to the Mosaic Law's prohibition, that it is wrong. The lesson was needed because Abraham, the first Jew, was surrounded by religions that normally sacrificed children.[46] The episode also taught particular piety by instituting the 'buying back' ritual for human first-fruits (codified later),[47] with the ram being the substitute sacrifice.[48]

Augustine's exegesis here must be indebted to Ambrose's *On Virginity* 2.5–9 (written 377–384),[49] but he improves upon it. According to *On Virginity*, the Isaac episode was a divine pedagogy (*exemplum*) given because people were ignorant of the status of human sacrifice. It taught (*docuit*) that God does not approve of killing one's child (*parricidium*), and that firstborn children should be dedicated to God, though not as holocausts. Ambrose

---

[44] Jephthah sacrificed his daughter in fulfillment of a vow (Judges 11:30–9).

[45] Quoting Deuteronomy 12:29–31, alluding to 'many others.'

[46] Deuteronomy 12:29–31, cited by Augustine, on the Canaanites west of the Jordan (=Abraham's home in Genesis 22:2–12); cf. Deuteronomy 18:10; Jeremiah 7:18, 4:31, 7:31–2; Xella et al. 2013; Smith et al. 2013. On child sacrifice to the Ammonite god Molech (east of the Jordan), see 1 Kings 11:7, 2 Kings 23:10, Leviticus 18:21.

[47] Exodus 13:13, 13:15.   [48] Genesis 22:13.   [49] Adkin 2003: 32 n. 15, 387.

here implies that God never intended for Isaac to be killed, a gloss which he probably owes to the rabbis.[50] However, Ambrose backtracks, calling into doubt whether he thinks God opposes child sacrifice because it is objectively unjust. He claims that God's cancellation of the killing of Isaac was divine 'mercy' (rather than a defense of Isaac's life), which the father and son earned by believing that God is merciful. In contrast, he surmises, God allowed Jephthah to kill his daughter as punishment for failing to believe that God would mercifully intervene. Augustine says, more consistently, that it was Jephthah's *vow to kill his daughter* that God punished, of which God disapproved because he hates human sacrifice as such.

It might be objected against Augustine's *Questions on the Heptateuch* interpretation that it has merely replaced a murderous God with a lying God. For according to Augustine, God told Abraham to kill his son while not actually intending that he do so. This seems particularly problematic, given that Augustine wrote two treatises insisting that lying is always wrong. But note that Augustine's definition of a 'lie' is 'telling a falsehood with the intent to deceive.'[51] According to this criterion, God was not lying, since a command is not a proposition, and hence cannot be false.[52] Apparently Augustine thinks that God's filicidal command should be understood as a case of antiphrasis.[53]

CONCLUSIONS

We have investigated about 200 years of rabbinic and early Christian analyses of the Abraham–Isaac episode, and find that only if we make Augustine's late (c. 420) writing the standard of what is 'characteristic' of 'Hebrew Christian ethics' can we say that Anscombe's description of that ethic is true in this case. It is hasty generalization to speak of a unitary ('the') Hebrew–Christian ethic that is always characterized by its opposition to killing the innocent. Moreover, to defend Anscombe's assertion that the Torah teaches that killing the innocent is always forbidden regardless of its consequences, one would need to use the kind

---

[50] He does not reason from the ambiguity of the verb, however (the LXX *anapherein* is ambiguous), but from the conclusion of the story. On Ambrose and rabbinic glosses, see e.g. Rueling 2006.

[51] In *On Lying* (c. 395), Augustine says the combination of these two conditions is sufficient for a lie, but leaves it open whether both are necessary conditions (4.4); however, in *Against Lying* (c. 420, contemporaneous with *Questions on the Heptateuch*), Augustine says both are necessary (10.23–4, 12.26), *pace* Griffiths 2004: 25–31.

[52] Diogenes Laertius, *Life of Zeno* 7.65, 7.68; Byers 2013: 8–22, 29 on Augustine's reception.

[53] See *Against Lying* 12.26.

of hermeneutical method employed by Augustine. His approach makes the Bible's *general* prohibitions on killing non-aggressors *determinative* of the meaning of the *particular* demand to kill Isaac. This procedure requires an idiosyncratic reading of the Hebrew of Genesis 22:2, or interpreting it as antiphrasis.

Furthermore, we can accept Anscombe's conceptual claim that this (Augustinian) defense of the innocent Isaac is grounded in a 'law conception of ethics' only if we equivocate on 'law.' By the 'legal character' of the 'Hebrew–Christian ethic' Anscombe understands divinely given prohibitions.[54] In contrast, Augustine's ultimate criterion of ethics is 'eternal law', which is not divine legislation but God's set of simple ideas of justice, prudence, moderation, and fortitude. These ideas subsist in God irrespective of whether they are positively given to humans. Augustine's model, which could be called 'internalist TO', is derived from Neoplatonic and Stoic conceptions of eternal 'law' (*ho nomos, lex*);[55] herein God's ethical ideas are called 'law' because they are immutable and because living in accord with them yields a consistent and well-ordered pattern of life. God's simple ideas when articulated in words are ethical axioms and definitions (for instance, 'justice is giving what is deserved');[56] these are to be applied variously in differing circumstances.[57] The proposition 'Killing the innocent is unjust' is always true because 'innocent' specifies the relevant circumstance.[58] Augustine does think that a comprehensive divine positive law (*lex generalis*) 'Do not kill the innocent' was issued at a particular time and recorded in the Torah.[59] But he holds that the function of this and more particular decrees such as 'Do not kill children as sacrifices' was to inform people who happened to be ignorant about what objective justice entails, rather than to be the ultimate criterion of rightness and wrongness.[60]

BIBLIOGRAPHY

An asterisk denotes secondary literature especially suitable for further reading.

Adkin, Neil 2003. *A Commentary on the Libellus de Virginitate Servanda (Letter 22)*. Cambridge: Francis Cairns.
Anscombe, G.E.M. 1958. 'Modern Moral Philosophy', *Philosophy* 33.124: 1–19.

---

[54] See note 2.
[55] Plotinus, *Enneads* 5.9.5 ll. 28–9, cf. 5.9.10 ll. 2–4; Chrysippus in Marcian (Long and Sedley 1987: 67R); Arius Didymus in Eusebius, *Preparation for the Gospel* 15.15; Cicero, *Republic* 3.33.
[56] *On Free Choice* 2.10.29; cf. *City* 19.4.   [57] *Confessions* 3.7.13–8.16.
[58] Cf. *Commentaries on the Psalms* 61.22.   [59] *Against Gaudentius* 1.11.12ff.
[60] Cf. Byers 2013: 167–9.

Appelbaum, Alan 2012. 'Rabbi's Successors: The Later Jewish Patriarchs of the Third Century', *Journal of Jewish Studies* 63.1: 1–21.

Byers, Sarah 2013. *Perception, Sensibility, and Moral Motivation in Augustine*. Cambridge University Press.*

Cavadini, John 2002. 'Exegetical Transformation: The Sacrifice of Isaac in Philo, Origen, and Ambrose', in P. Blowers *et al.* (eds.), *In Dominico Eloquio*, Cambridge: William B. Eerdmans Publishing Company: 35–49.

Coogan, Michael (ed.) 2010. *The New Oxford Annotated Bible*. Oxford University Press.

Dawkins, Richard 2006. *The God Delusion*. Boston: Houghton Mifflin.

Evans, Matthew 2012. 'Lessons from *Euthyphro* 10A–11B', *Oxford Studies in Ancient Philosophy* 42: 1–38.

Gregor, Mary (trans.) 1979. *Immanuel Kant: The Conflict of the Faculties*. New York: Abaris Books.

Griffiths, Paul 2004. *Lying: An Augustinian Theology of Duplicity*. Grand Rapids: Brazos Press.

Hannay, Alastair (trans.) 1985. *Kierkegaard:* Fear and Trembling. London: Penguin Books.

Jones, Rusty 2006. 'Piety as a Virtue in the *Euthyphro*: A Response to Rabbås', *Ancient Philosophy* 26.2: 385–90.

Kalimi, Isaac 2010. '"Go, I Beg You, Take Your Beloved Son and Slay Him!" The Binding of Isaac in Rabbinic Literature and Thought', *Review of Rabbinic Judaism* 13.1: 1–29.

Kretzmann, Normann 1983. 'Abraham, Isaac, and Euthyphro: God and the Basis of Morality', in D. Stump *et al.* (eds.), *'Hamartia': The Concept of Error in the Western Tradition*, New York: Edwin Mellen Press: 27–50.

Long, Anthony and Sedley, David 1987. *The Hellenistic Philosophers*. Vols. 1–2. Cambridge University Press.

MacDowell, Douglas 1963. *Athenian Homicide Law in the Age of the Orators*. Manchester University Press.

Mikalson, Jon 2010. *Greek Popular Religion in Greek Philosophy*. Oxford University Press.

Phillips, David 2007. '*Trauma ek Pronoias* in Athenian Law', *The Journal of Hellenic Studies* 127: 74–105.

Phillips, David 2013. *Law and Society in the Ancient World*. Ann Arbor: University of Michigan Press.

Romestin, H. de (trans.) 1896. *Some of the Principal Works of Saint Ambrose*. Oxford and London: Parker and Company.

Rueling, Hanneke. 2006. *After Eden: Church Fathers and Rabbis on Genesis 3: 16–21*. Leiden: Brill.

Smith, Patricia *et al.* 2013. 'Age Estimations Attest to Infant Sacrifice at the Carthage Tophet', *Antiquity* 87: 1191–8.

Thompson, John 2001. *Writing the Wrongs: Women of the Old Testament among Biblical Commentators*. Oxford University Press.

Walford, Henry (trans.) 1881. *The Letters of Saint Ambrose, Bishop of Milan*. Oxford: James Parker and Co.

Wallis, Robert (trans.) 1868. *The Writings of Cyprian, Bishop of Carthage*. Edinburgh: T. & T. Clark; London: Hamilton & Co.; Dublin: John Robertson.

Xella, Paolo *et al.* 2013. 'Phoenician Bones of Contention', *Antiquity* 87: 1199–1207.

10

Boethius, Abelard and Anselm

JOHN MARENBON

The subjects of this chapter, Boethius (476–524/525), Anselm (1033–1109) and Abelard (1079–1142) span six centuries, as long as the whole period between Ockham in Chapter 14 and Wittgenstein in Chapter 50. These pages can, therefore, offer no more than three isolated flash photographs of figures in a landscape which, because it lies in darkness, should not be considered unpopulated. These pictures, moreover, will not be portrait but detail mode, focusing in each case on a single, philosophically interesting discussion. Their purpose, it might seem, is to show that, contrary to the impression given by most histories, moral philosophy was flourishing in the period from Boethius to Abelard.[1] But that, as the closing remark will explain, would be the wrong conclusion![2]

BOETHIUS: THE MORAL COMPLEXITY
OF THE 'CONSOLATION OF PHILOSOPHY'

Complexity seems to be precisely what is lacking from the moral discussions in the *Consolation of Philosophy*. Boethius used his own position – a once rich

---

[1] I use the term 'moral philosophy' – in line with the title of this whole volume – to refer in general to philosophical thinking about values in connection with the actions of rational (and super-rational) beings. Were the distinction to be made, as by Williams 2010, between ethics in general and morality as a 'peculiar institution', then 'moral' would need to be replaced throughout by 'ethical', but this substitution would yield some odd results (e.g. 'ethical psychology') and so it has been avoided.

[2] The following abbreviations are used for primary texts: *Coll.* – Abelard *Collationes* (Abelard 2001); *CP* – Boethius *Consolation of Philosophy* (Boethius 2005); *OFD, OH, OT* – Anselm *On the Fall of the Devil, On the Harmony of Prescience, Predestination and the Grace of God with Free Will, On Truth* (Anselm 1946–1961). The latter is the standard edition, edited by F.S. Schmitt. The philosophical works are in vols. 1 and 2. They are translated well in Anselm 2007 and, sometimes unreliably, in Anselm 1998. References are to the (book and) chapter, and to the volume, page (and if necessary lines) in Schmitt's edition.

125

and powerful man, now unjustly imprisoned as a traitor awaiting execution –
to provide a dramatic setting for a prose and verse dialogue in which a
personification of Philosophy reasons with him.[3] Boethius depicts himself,
the Prisoner, complaining that the good suffer and the wicked prosper, and
doubting that providence has any concern for humans. Philosophy gradually
convinces the Prisoner that, despite appearances, the good are rewarded and
the wicked punished in a justly ordered universe. She uses great rhetorical
power and literary sophistication, and draws on a range of Platonic themes,
to present her case, but it is a simple one, and its chief support is a monolithic
conception of the Highest Good, which is identified with God and argued to
be that alone which can bring happiness. It is hardly surprising that most
historians of philosophy have left the first four books of the *Consolation*,
which are devoted to this discussion, to the literary specialists and turned
their attentions to the treatment of prescience and contingency in Book Five.[4]

According to one reading, however, the *Consolation* does indeed put
forward a complex theory. The complex interpretation differs from the
standard one by distinguishing between two different, and incompatible,
arguments used by Philosophy in order to console the Prisoner. The first
argument proposes a variegated conception of true good. It has two stages.
The first stage begins by considering what are called the 'goods of fortune':
goods or apparent goods which a person gains and loses through external
causes. Philosophy quickly establishes (*CP* II.4.23–9)[5] that such goods are not
sufficient for a happy life because they are unstable, and the fear of losing
them precludes true happiness. She has already made a distinction among
goods of fortune between those, on the hand, which are, in the Prisoner's
words, 'ornaments', such as wealth, high office, power and fame, and on the
other hand certain goods 'dearer than life' – his father-in-law, wife and sons
(*CP* II.4.4–10). She then goes on to argue that the ornamental goods of fortune
are unstable and, in any case, of little value: not only are they limited and

[3] For background information on Boethius, see Marenbon 2003b and 2009, and Kaylor
and Philipps 2012. There are many translations available: Boethius 2001 is particularly good.

[4] There is, in consequence, little literature about Boethius as a moral thinker. In
Marenbon 2003a and 2003b: 99–124, I give a detailed account on the same general
lines as I present here. An excellent presentation of a different view is given by
Magee 2009. Peter King (2013) suggests that Boethius concentrates centrally on the
'Problem of Desert'.

[5] The references in brackets are to the Books, (prose) sections, and sub-divisions of the
Consolation.

often bring difficulties with them, but they do not truly belong to those who have them and they can be possessed by wicked people as well as by good ones (CP II.5–7). The second stage of the argument considers much the same list of ornamental goods of fortune, but it introduces a new idea about them (CP III.1–8). They are, Philosophy says, the false goods for which people strive as a result of error. What everyone desires to gain is true happiness, the state in which he or she possesses every true good. But instead of pursuing the true goods of sufficiency, respect, power, fame and joy, people pursue one of the false goods in the place of each of them: they wrongly believe that riches will give them sufficiency, status respect, rule of kingdoms power, glory fame and sensual pleasures joy. Philosophy's new idea helps to explain why the ornamental goods of fortune turned out, on examination, to be of such little value. They do not satisfy those who desire them, because they are what they only think they desire, not what they really want. By contrast, the true goods will satisfy people's desires, and they are also highly stable and proof against fortune. But Philosophy has not so far tried to show that the true good for humans is entirely invulnerable to external events. She leaves it open that moderate amounts of the ornamental good of fortune help towards happiness, and she has said nothing to question the true value of the nonornamental, but vulnerable, goods – those whom we love.

Philosophy goes on, however, to develop an entirely different line of reasoning, which proposes not a variegated, but a monolithic, conception of the true good. Rather than human error mistaking false goods for a variety of true ones, its fault is now diagnosed as being to separate what is simple and undivided (CP III.9.4). The words which she had used for the true goods are, Philosophy now insists, all names for one and the same substance (CP III.9.15). She goes on to identify this single substance with God (III.10) and to say that what people really desire when they pursue false goods are not, as she previously held, the various corresponding true goods, but the one true good alone (CP III.10.36–42). On the monolithic view, the true good is completely stable and true human happiness, which consists in gaining it, entirely invulnerable. Unlike the variegated conception, which allows for some description of what the truly happy human life would be, the monolithic view does not explain what it is for a person to gain the true good, which is God, and so happiness. But it is clear that, unlike the variegated conception, the monolithic view entirely excludes goods of fortune as requisites for human happiness.

According to most interpreters, however, Philosophy does not pursue two different lines of reasoning, but a single one: she leads the Prisoner *through* the variegated conception *to* the monolithic one. In support of this reading, they can point out, first, that Philosophy describes her arguments in medical terms as progressively stronger remedies (*CP* II.1.7; II.5.1; III.1.2); second, that Philosophy goes on to treat the happiness of the good and punishment of the wicked in a way which presupposes the monolithic view; and third, that the monolithic conception is what the Platonist outlook, which Philosophy clearly champions, requires.

All three points can, however, be answered. First, the scheme of increasingly stronger remedies is used *within* the presentation of the variegated conception, and not when the monolithic conception is introduced. Second, it is certainly true that Philosophy, using but distorting the argument of the *Gorgias*, shows (*CP* IV.1–4) that, on the basis of the monolithic conception of the good, the wicked gain nothing of any value through the goods of fortune, and the good lose nothing of any value, whatever losses and suffering they must endure. But the Prisoner challenges her position. There is, he believes (*CP* IV.5.2), 'something of good and evil in the popular conception of fortune'. With his own personal change of circumstances in mind, he contends that no wise man would choose to be a shamed, destitute exile, rather than flourishing in honour and riches in his own city, and that the community as a whole gained from having such people in authority, and imprisonment and execution being reserved for the wicked. Philosophy responds (*CP* IV.6) not by reiterating the monolithic conception of the good, but by explaining how divine providence so orders things that, even on a variegated view of the good, they are for the best in the long run.

As to the third point, the personification of Philosophy is indeed a Platonist and her preferred view of the good seems to be the monolithic one. But the *Consolation* is a dialogue, and although the outlook of Boethius the Prisoner at the beginning is clearly not the author's, it should not be taken for granted that the authorial view is identical with Philosophy's. Its prose and verse form puts the work into the genre of Menippean Satire, where there is an expectation that the statements of an authoritative figure will be questioned or ridiculed.[6] Moreover, Philosophy personifies a tradition of pagan thought, whereas Boethius is a Christian writing for a Christian audience. Although Boethius the author has great respect for Philosophy, he may be suggesting that she is not able to reach a definitive answer to the problems raised by the Prisoner (a judgement which is supported, arguably, by the discussion of

---

[6] On the importance of its Menippean form for understanding the *Consolation*, see Relihan 2006 and the criticisms of his view in Shanzer 2009.

divine prescience and human freedom at the end of the work.)[7] The ethical doctrine of the *Consolation* on this reading is, therefore, complex on two levels. First, a complex, variegated conception of the good and human happiness is not dismissed by the progress of the argument, but remains as a possible view within the dialogue. Second, there is a higher-order complexity for the readers, who are required to think about the inconclusiveness of the ethical arguments within the dialogue and perhaps to draw from them their own conclusion about the limitations of purely philosophical discussion.

ANSELM: AN UNKANTIAN REJECTION OF EUDAIMONISM

Whatever the complexity of his overall position, Boethius's moral psychology is a straightforward eudaimonism, widely shared in the ancient world. People act to gain what they believe will bring them happiness, but they are often mistaken in what they seek, pursuing false goods instead of true ones (or the one true good). Those who are not mistaken act in a way which is both good and will bring them genuine happiness. Anselm has a more complex view of both moral motivation and moral desert. He develops it in a set of three master–pupil dialogues (*On Truth, On the Freedom of the Will, On the Fall of the Devil*), which provide superb examples of how to analyse concepts philosophically, and in his final treatise (*On the Harmony of Prescience, Predestination and the Grace of God with Free Will*), where he refines and clarifies his thinking.[8]

At the centre of Anselm's view is a contrast between two sorts of good and evil. The first sort he calls 'the agreeable' (*commodum*) and 'the disagreeable' (*incommodum*). All sensitive and rational beings find some things agreeable and some things disagreeable. Agreeable things are what make the being in question happy (*beatus*). The agreeable things appropriate for one sort of animal are not always appropriate for another sort: sensual pleasures, for instance, are appropriate agreeable things for irrational animals, but not for humans (*OH* 3.13; 2: 286). Examples of the agreeable which are appropriate for humans are life and health (*OH* 3.11; 2: 281). The second sort of good and evil are justice (*iustitia*) and injustice. Only rational creatures (human and angels) can be just or unjust, and the evil which is

---

[7] See Marenbon 2003b: 144–5.
[8] On Anselm as a moral philosopher, see Brower 2004 and Visser and Williams 2009: 171–221.

injustice, unlike the disagreeable, is not made by God and is not anything: it is a mere failure to be just (*OH* I.7; 2: 258–9).

The wills of rational creatures are related to these two sorts of good in a very particular way. A will, Anselm thinks, moves automatically to will what the agent perceives as good. So long, however, as a rational agent is able only to will in this automatic way, it is not capable of being just or unjust. Anselm brings out this point in a thought-experiment he makes in *On the Fall of the Devil*. He imagines God creating an angel in stages. First, it has the mere capacity to will, but no object has been set for its will, and at this stage it wills nothing. Then God sets up happiness as the aim for its will. Anselm argues that when such an angel wills to be similar to God (Lucifer's sin), it is being neither unjust nor just, because, since its will is set only to will happiness, it cannot but will this supreme happiness (*OFD* 13; 1: 257 ll. 4–10). He then imagines that God gives the angel a will directed only, not to happiness, but to rightness (or – synonymously – what is fitting).[9] Is the angel just when it wills what is right? No, argues Anselm, the angel will still be neither unjust nor just, because, since its will is directed only to what is fitting, it cannot will otherwise. Anselm goes on to explain that, in order to give the angel the chance to be just, God gave it two wills, one set to happiness, and the other to the right (*OFD* 14; 1: 258 ll. 18–30).[10] Later, in *On Harmony*, Anselm puts the same idea more elegantly, by supposing that there is a single will (in the sense that the will is an instrument) in each angel and human, which has two 'affections' or ends to which it moves – what is agreeable and what is right (*OH* 3.11; 2: 281).

As will be clear, the division that Anselm makes here between the two wills, or affections of the will, does *not* correspond on both sides to his central distinction between two types of good. On the one side of the contrast there is, indeed, the agreeable, but it is set against not what is just, but what is right.[11] The relationship between justice and rightness (*rectitudo*) is, for

---

[9] In *OH* (3.11; 2: 281 ll. 7–16), he uses 'rightness'; in *OFD* 14 he talks of a will for 'what is fitting' (which the rubric of Chapter 14 describes as a will for 'rightness') (1: 258 ll. 6–22).

[10] Cf. *OH* 3.11; 2: 281 l. 3–282 l. 2.

[11] Almost all recent commentators, however, describe the two wills as being for agreeableness and for what they describe either as 'justice', or (as if the two terms meant the same) as 'rightness' or 'justice' (for example, Rogers 2008: 69; Visser and Williams 2009: 179; King 2011: 369; King 2012: 273 – all of these, none the less, in other respects very valuable studies.) Ekenberg 2005: 97–106 sees that Anselm distinguishes rightness from justice, but then concludes that the will other than that for agreeableness is *not* for rightness but for justice.

Anselm, a subtle one. Justice is a special sort of rightness. He treats rightness as a very broad concept. Things or people are right when they do what they ought to do: the meaning of a phrase is right, when it signifies what is the case; when fire does what it ought, by heating, it can be said to make rightness, as can humans when they act well (OT 2–5; 1: 177–83). Justice, explains Anselm, is the sort of rightness which is worthy of praise. A stone which falls, or a horse which feeds on the grass, is doing what it ought to do and so is right, but they do not merit praise, because they do not know they are doing what is right. Only rational agents can know that they are acting rightly, and so they alone can be just. But if a rational being acts rightly but does not will to do so, it will not be worthy of praise. Justice, therefore, is rightness of the will. But, Anselm points out, if someone wills what is right by accident (as when I will to close the door, thereby happening to bar access to a murderer who, unknown to me, is lurking in the next room), this is not an instance of justice. Nor is it one when someone does the right thing for the wrong reason, as when someone feeds the hungry in order to show off their wealth. A will, therefore, deserves praise, and so is not merely right but just, when it follows rightness *for its own sake* (OT 12; 1: 191–4).

What marks out willing rightness for its own sake? Anselm's underlying idea seems to be that it is not some accompanying or preceding thought, but rather the lack of any other reason for the choice. At times he even seems to go as far as denying that a will directed towards what is right is just when the end happens also to be agreeable (or to avoid what is disagreeable), and he certainly always concentrates on the cases where the agent wills a right end which is not, or is not believed to be, agreeable. This perspective emerges particularly clearly when Anselm discusses the degree of knowledge which Lucifer had about the consequences of rebelling against God. Whilst, as a rational creature, he knew that, if he rebelled, it would be just for him to be punished, he did not know, Anselm insists, that God would punish him. Had he known that by rebelling he would be made wretched, he could not freely will to rebel, and therefore 'he would not have been just in refraining from willing what he ought not to do, because he could not have willed it' (OFD 23; 1: 270 ll. 22–3).[12]

Since the distinction between the agreeable and the just seems to correspond to that which some more modern philosophers would draw between non-moral and moral goodness, it is tempting to see in Anselm an anticipator of Kant's rejection of eudaimonism.[13] It is only when an agent does not

---

[12] King 2012: 273–81 analyses Anselm's presentation of Lucifer's decision to sin.
[13] See e.g. Recktenwald 1998: 26; Goebel 2001, esp. 404–8; Wilks 2012: 588–92.

131

pursue happiness that he is capable of moral goodness. Yet, although Anselm is not a eudaimonist, he is far from being a proto-Kantian. First, Anselm recognizes in humans a natural, God-given tendency to will what is right. Merely following this tendency does not in itself make people behave in a morally good, as opposed to a naturally good way, but they need just to take one further step, and follow it where it conflicts with the natural tendency to will what leads to happiness. Second, the pursuit of justice is justified in terms very far from Kant's autonomous reason. God, says, Anselm, gave humans 'happiness as an end because it was agreeable for them, and justice as an end so that they would honour him.' (OH 3.13; 2: 286).[14] The problem which drives the argument in the three dialogues is not that of human moral values, but the need to explain how it is that creatures have nothing except what God has given them, and yet God is not responsible for sin and did not make injustice. It is only in the light of this emphasis and direction that we can make sense of Anselm's apparent undercutting of his whole theory, when he says that, if (counterfactually) the angels who remained true to God were unable to sin just because of their knowledge of Lucifer's punishment, it would be 'to their glory' (OFD 25; 1: 272 ll. 22–5).[15] Here Anselm is willing to allow that even the most perfect creatures might in principle be motivated by purely eudaimonic considerations.

ABELARD AND THE METAPHYSICS OF MORALS

Peter Abelard, too, has been seen as proto-Kantian in his ethics, because of a feature different from that just discussed in Anselm, though it is one found in Anselm too, but less emphatically. Abelard, like Kant, makes underlying intentions alone the subject for moral judgements. For Kant they are good in so far as they accord with the moral law, whilst for Abelard they are good in so far as they follow God's law. Abelard develops a quite elaborate theory. With cases of reluctant action in mind, Abelard explains how an agent can intend an act ('consent to it') without willing it. And he shows how, whilst it is agents' subjective attitude to God – whether or not their action shows contempt for God – which determines whether or not they sin, the awareness all have of natural law stops this subjectivism from excusing moral laxity.[16]

---

[14] OH 3.13; 2: 286.
[15] It is made clear at OFD 25; 1: 273 ll. 25–30 that this is just a counterfactual example. In fact, the angels who persevered can no longer sin because they have been raised to a level where they have no will to do so.
[16] See Marenbon 1996: 251–81.

Abelard's moral theory is, indeed, the widest-ranging and most fully elaborated of any medieval thinker's before the reception of Aristotle's *Ethics* in the thirteenth century, and, when its various different facets (including a theory of virtues, practical ethics and meta-ethics) are taken into account, the resemblance with Kant starts to seem even more dubious than in the case of Anselm.[17]

One of his most remarkable ethical discussions is the final section of a dialogue called *Collationes* ('Comparisons'), where Abelard explores the meanings of the word 'good' and brings out some deep connections between his ideas about morality and his views on ontology and providence.[18] He recognizes that 'good' is often used attributively, so that its meaning is affected by the thing which it qualifies: a good horse is one that is strong and swift, a good person is one who is morally good (*ex moribus*), a good craftsman exercises his craft skilfully and a good thief is proficient in stealing (*Coll.* 201). Many philosophers today would stop here, but Abelard thinks 'good' also has a non-attributive, unqualified meaning. Most medieval thinkers agreed with him, but usually they held a distinctive view about the extension of 'good' when understood in this unqualified way: they believed that all things are good, simply by virtue of existing. Boethius had written a short treatise explaining this idea, and from the thirteenth century onwards good was considered to be among the transcendentals, properties had by all existing things.[19] Supposed things which are obviously not good, such as evil itself, or sin, or blindness, were considered not to be things at all, but merely privations.[20]

---

[17] For an attempt to bring together the various parts of Abelard's ethical thought, see Marenbon 1996: 213–331, and on Abelard and Kant (with further references), see Marenbon 2013: 115–16.

[18] The *Collationes*, probably written c. 1130, consists of two dialogues, one between the Philosopher (who bases his arguments on reason, without reference to a revealed law) and a Jew, the other between the Philosopher and a Christian. The ideas discussed here are put forward by the Christian; although the Christian is not simply Abelard, these views do seem to be straightforwardly his own and will be treated so here. For further background information, see the Introduction to Abelard 2001. References (preceded by '*Coll.*') are to the paragraphs of this edition, which has a parallel translation.

[19] *Opuscula sacra* III: Boethius 2005: 186–94; Boethius 1973: 39–51 for (parallel-text) translation; and cf. MacDonald 1988 and (for thirteenth-century development) 1992.

[20] There were some exceptions, though, such as pain according to Anselm: OH 1.7; 2: 258. Examples of the disagreeable for Anselm are pain and blindness. Whilst blindness is not a thing but merely a privation of something, pain is a real thing.

Abelard did not follow this way of thinking. The most remarkable feature of his definition of 'good' in the unqualified sense is that it leaves room for there to be a variety of real, evil things. A good thing, says Abelard, 'is (a) what is fitted for some use and (b) the worth (*dignitas*) or agreeableness (*commodum*) of nothing else is, as a matter of necessity, obstructed by it' (*Coll.* 203). Part (a) of this definition turns out to carry little weight, since Abelard goes on to explain that anything, good or bad, can serve a useful purpose (*Coll.* 207–8). Part (b) is designed so that just one class of things fails to meet it and so, according to Abelard, these things are evil (*Coll.* 203). There are some accidents which have contraries: life, for instance, is contrary to death, happiness to sadness, health to sickness and knowledge to ignorance. One of a pair cannot remain in the same substance as its contrary: sadness necessarily destroys happiness, health sickness, death life and ignorance knowledge. Happiness, health, life and knowledge each bring some worth or agreeableness which is, then, necessarily lost when their contraries replace them. Therefore accidents such as these *do* necessarily obstruct the worth or agreeableness of something and so are evil, not good.

Surprising though the standard medieval view that every existing thing is good may seem to readers today, there was a strong reason for holding it. The perfectly good creator God of Christian belief seems to leave no room for evil things, since few Christians would be willing to admit either that some things are not created by God, or that God created any evil things. How then could Abelard, who also believed in a perfectly good creator God, justify his unusual view that a variety of things are indeed evil? It follows from his definition that no *substance* can be evil, since it is only accidents which, by being contrary to one another, are such as necessarily to impede the worth or agreeableness of something (*Coll.* 224). But it is unlikely that Abelard would have accepted that accidents were not created by God. He does, however, have a way of explaining how a perfectly good God created evil things.[21] As

---

[21] Earlier in *Coll.* (143–6), the Philosopher had adumbrated some of the distinctions which would be developed by the Christian in the passage discussed here. The Philosopher says that, according to Christians, 'there is nothing in God's creation which is not good' (*Coll.* 144). But then, having anticipated the idea that all substances are good, the Philosopher points out that 'in its very creation the good substance of human nature is made to participate in many evils', and he mentions some of the same things as will be said by the Christian later on to be evil: mortality, sickness and stupidity (this becomes, later, ignorance). The Christian does not take issue with these points, and so the passage provides some evidence that Abelard did indeed countenance the idea that God created evil non-substance things.

well as the sorts of items in the Aristotelian universe – substances and essential and accidental attributes – Abelard's account of reality includes the *dicta* of propositions, although he denies that they are things of any sort. These *dicta* ('what are said') are, as the word itself indicates, what propositions say. For example, the proposition 'John is drinking tea' says *that John is drinking tea*. Philosophers now would call a *dictum* (at least as envisaged in the *Collationes*) a fact or state of affairs.[22] 'Good', explains Abelard, can be used not just of things, but of *dicta*. In this use 'good' means that the state of affairs is necessary in order to fulfil God's best plan (*Coll.* 225). The example of a *dictum* Abelard gives is telling. It is the *dictum* 'that there is evil'. We can affirm, he believes, that it is good that there is evil, although evil is in no way good (*Coll.* 202). Abelard could, then, argue that God's beneficence is seen at the level of the states of affairs (*dicta*) which he brings about or allows to be brought about. The way he disposes things is always best, but this disposition involves the existence of evil things (and so even their creation by God).

CLOSING REMARK

With four or five times as much space, these three snapshots could be expanded into larger pictures, showing how Boethius, Anselm and Abelard (especially) each answered a variety of the questions which are now considered part of ethics. Yet none of these depictions would be a portrait, even a partial one. Each would bring together blocks of material from different areas of the writer's thought, connecting it to make a whole (what is called 'the Ethics of Anselm', for instance) which never existed in his thought, whilst disregarding the links between the blocks and other, non-ethical and often, at least from today's perspective, unphilosophical questions. For the same reason, trying to depict the landscape of early medieval ethics would not succeed, even as an exercise in mapping. No such terrain is to be found. The enterprise of looking in the early medieval texts for answers to questions of interest in moral philosophy today remains valuable, but only so long as investigators who wish to go beyond an introduction like this one are willing to follow the grain of the material and regard their point of departure as no more than that.

---

[22] On *dicta* in Abelard, see King 2004: 105–8, the essays in Maierù and Valente 2004: 1–80 by Rosier-Catach, Guilfoy and Marenbon, and Marenbon forthcoming.

BIBLIOGRAPHY

An asterisk denotes secondary literature especially suitable for further reading.

Abelard, Peter (2001) *Collationes*, ed. John Marenbon and Giovanni Orlandi, Oxford University Press.

Anselm (1946–1961) *Opera omnia*, ed. F.S. Schmitt, Edinburgh: Nelson.

Anselm (1998) *The Major Works*, ed. Brian Davies and Gillian R. Evans, Oxford University Press.

Anselm (2007) *Basic Works*, ed. and trans. Thomas Williams, Indianapolis and Cambridge: Hackett.

Boethius (1973) *The Theological Tractates. The Consolation of Philosophy*, trans. H.F. Stewart, E.K. Rand and D.J. Tester, Cambridge and London: Harvard University Press.

Boethius (2001) *Consolation of Philosophy*, trans. Joel C. Relihan, Indianapolis: Hackett.

Boethius (2005) *De consolatione Philosophiae. Opuscula sacra*, ed. Claudio Moreschini, Munich and Leipzig: Saur, revised edn.

Ekenberg, Thomas (2005) 'Falling Freely: Anselm of Canterbury on the Will', PhD thesis, University of Uppsala.

Goebel, Bernd (2001) *Rectitudo. Wahrheit und Freiheit bei Anselm von Canterbury. Eine philosophische Untersuchung seines Denkansatzes*, Münster: Aschendorff.

Kaylor, Noel H. and Philip E. Phillips (2012) *A Companion to Boethius in the Middle Ages*, Leiden and Boston: Brill.

King, Peter (2004) 'Metaphysics', in *The Cambridge Companion to Abelard*, ed. Jeffrey E. Brower and Kevin Guilfoy, Cambridge University Press, 65–125.

King, Peter (2011) 'Scotus's Rejection of Anselm: The Two-Wills Theory', in *Johannes Duns Scotus 1308–2008: Investigations into his Philosophy*, ed. Ludger Honnefelder et al., Münster: Aschendorff, 359–78.

King, Peter (2012) 'Angelic Sin in Augustine and Anselm', in *A Companion to Angels and Medieval Philosophy*, ed. Tobias Hoffmann, Leiden: Brill, 261–81.

King, Peter (2013) 'Boethius on the Problem of Desert', in *Oxford Studies in Medieval Philosophy*, ed. R. Pasnau, vol. 1. Oxford University Press, 1–22.

MacDonald, Scott (1988) 'Boethius's Claim that all Substances are Good', *Archiv für Geschichte der Philosophie* 70: 245–79.

MacDonald, Scott (1992) 'Goodness as a Transcendental: The Early Thirteenth-Century Recovery of an Aristotelian Idea', *Topoi* 11: 173–86.

Magee, John (2009) 'The Good and Morality: *Consolatio* 2–4', in Marenbon 2009: 181–206.

Maierù, A. and L. Valente (eds.) (2004), *Medieval Theories on Assertive and Non-Assertive Language*, Florence: Olschki.

Marenbon, John (1996) *The Philosophy of Peter Abelard*, Cambridge University Press.

Marenbon, John (2003a) 'Rationality and Happiness: Interpreting Boethius's *Consolation of Philosophy*', in *Rationality and Happiness: From the Ancients to the Early Medieval*, ed. Jiyuan Yu and Jorge J.E. Gracia, University of Rochester Press, 175–97.

Marenbon, John (2003b) *Boethius*, New York: Oxford University Press.

Marenbon, John (ed.) (2009) *The Cambridge Companion to Boethius*, Cambridge University Press.

Marenbon, John (2013) *Abelard in Four Dimensions. A Twelfth-Century Philosopher in his Context and ours*, University of Notre Dame Press.

Marenbon, John (forthcoming) 'Suigenerism', in *Facts and States of Affairs*, ed. Laurent Cesalli and John Marenbon, Turnhout: Brepols.

Recktenwald, Engelbert (1998) *Die Ethische Struktur des Denkens von Anselm von Canterbury*, Heidelberg: Winter.

Relihan, Joel C. (2006) *The Prisoner's Philosophy: Life and Death in Boethius's Consolation*, with a contribution on the medieval Boethius by William Heise, University of Notre Dame Press.

Rogers, Katherin (2008) *Anselm on Freedom*, Oxford University Press.

Shanzer, Danuta (2009) 'Interpreting the *Consolation*', in Marenbon 2009: 228–54.

Visser, S. and T. Williams (2009) *Anselm*, Oxford University Press.*

Wilks, Ian (2012) 'Moral Intention', in *The Oxford Handbook of Medieval Philosophy*, ed. John Marenbon, New York: Oxford University Press, 588–604.

Williams, Bernard ([1985] 2010) *Ethics and the Limits of Philosophy*, London and New York: Routledge (new edn).

Medieval Jewish Ethics

TAMAR RUDAVSKY

In this chapter I explore the status of Jewish ethics in medieval Jewish philosophy.[1] The very notion of Jewish ethics can only be understood against the backdrop of the Mosaic commandments. The 613 commandments articulated in the Pentateuch covered a myriad of situations: they include rituals, sacred attitudes toward the Deity, and inter-personal relationships. These latter actions are commonly considered to comprise the moral domain. While I focus primarily upon the status of law and ethical theory in the works of Moses Maimonides (c. 1138–1204 CE), brief discussions of ethical works composed by Maimonides' predecessors Saadiah Gaon (882–942 CE), Bahya ibn Pakuda (eleventh century), and Solomon ibn Gabirol (c. 1021–c. 1058) enable us to situate Maimonides' discussions within the context of contemporary views regarding the rationality or universality of the commandments.

The very exercise of trying to provide the underlying rational reasons for particular commandments, a technical rabbinic process known as *ta'amei ha-mitzvot*, dates back to Talmudic times, and continued throughout the medieval period. It is based on the suggestions of earlier rabbis that some commandments (in fact the very ones reflected in the Noahide Laws, more on which below) are said to be "inherently" or "intuitively" obvious,

I would like to acknowledge the help of OSU graduate student Miriam Rudavsky-Brody in researching and helping to edit this paper.

[1] The following abbreviations will be used in this chapter: *BBO* refers to book, chapter and page number of Saadia Gaon (1948), *The Book of Beliefs and Opinions*; *CT* (*Laws Concerning Character Traits*) refers to Maimonides 1975b; *DH* refers to book, chapter and page number of Bahya ibn Pakuda (2004), *The Book of Direction to the Duties of the Heart*; *EC* refers to chapter and page number in Maimonides (1975a), *Eight Chapters*; *NE* refers to book, chapter and page number in Aristotle (1995), *Nicomachean Ethics*; *GP* refers to part, chapter and page number of Maimonides (1963), *Guide of the Perplexed*; and CM Avot refers to chapter and part number of Maimonides (1972), "Commentary on the Mishnah, Avot."

ascertainable through reason, and not totally dependent upon divine command. While Maimonides is associated most famously with this attempt to both rationalize and universalize the Law, we shall see that his predecessors engaged in this enterprise as well.

NATURAL LAW AND RATIONALITY OF THE COMMANDMENTS IN SAADIAH GAON

The sense of a grounding for some of the commandments independent of divine command is articulated by the tenth-century Jewish philosopher Saadiah Gaon, one of the leaders of the intellectual circle of Jews in Babylonia and a strong opponent of Karaism. Rabbinic law relies on circuitous arguments that often diverge from a straightforward (*peshat*) reading of Scripture. The eighth-century Babylonian sage Anan ben David rejected the rabbinic tradition and advocated a return to the text of the Bible itself. Many Babylonian Jews, surrounded by Muslims who referred to the Qur'an as the central authoritative Scripture of Islam, were compelled by Anan ben David's arguments to reject the rabbinic tradition and to seek truth in the text of the Bible itself, not in external interpretations. This anti-rabbinic movement came to be called Karaism.[2] In an ongoing effort to invalidate polemical Karaite claims, Saadiah and other rabbis of his time were devoted to validating the legitimacy of rabbinical Judaism. In *The Book of Belief and Opinions* [*Kitab al-Amanat wa-al-I'tiqadat (Sefer ha-Emunot ve-ha De'ot)*], a work much influenced by Islamic Kalam epistemology and cosmology, Saadiah distinguished between the rational commandments (*al-shara'i' al-'aqliyyah; mitzvoth sikhliyyot*), which in theory are discoverable by means of reason, and the traditional laws (*al-shara'i' al-sam'iyyah; mitzvoth shimm'iyot*), which comprise rituals and ceremonial laws (such as the dietary laws) that are not rooted in reason. Saadiah is the first Jewish philosopher to frame his discussion of ethical precepts in the context of rational apprehension.

Saadiah's discussion is framed in the context of a basic theory of knowledge. In the introduction to the work, Saadiah distinguishes four sources of reliable knowledge (*'ilm*): sensation (*'ilm al-shahid; yedi'at hanir'eh*), reason or *nous* (*'ilm al-'aql; mada' ha-sekhel*), logical inference (*'ilm ma dafa'at al-darura 'ilayhi; yedi'at mah sheha-hekhreh mevi elav*), and reliable tradition (*al-khabr al-sadiq; ha-hagadah ha-ne'emenet* or *ha-masoret ha-amitit*). Sense perception and reason both function as epistemic foundations. Knowledge of the senses is

---

[2] See Greenstein 1984.

based on empirical contingents and is posited as the basis for logical inference and reliable tradition, both of which are rooted in this indubitable epistemic foundation. Reason represents the faculty of immediate, intuitive knowledge by means of which we apprehend self-evident axioms of reason. Reason, Saadiah tells us, emanates ultimately from God, resulting in an innatist theory according to which ideas are "implanted" in the mind – the word "implanted" connotes a source for knowledge that lies outside the realm of human consciousness. Saadiah claims, for example, that we are able to "recognize" a violation of the law of non-contradiction, even though it is not based on the senses (*BBO*.II.13).

In contradistinction to reason, reliable tradition is not universal, but is common to "the community of monotheists." If, however, reason, with the help of this outside source, enables humans to determine both the self-evident axioms and necessary principles of thought, what becomes of tradition? Saadiah relegates to tradition two roles: first, tradition enables us to determine the particulars necessary for observing the more general rational precepts; and second, tradition also speeds up the rather tedious process of discovering these rational principles. Thus while reason allows us a limited amount of epistemic authority, tradition with the aid of revelation enables us to achieve salvation.

Based on these epistemological distinctions, the foundations for moral obligation are delineated primarily in Book III, while details on how to achieve the good life are to be found in Book X. The classification of ethical precepts into rational and revelatory is straightforward: rational commandments are those whose "approval" has been implanted in our minds (*BBO.* III.2.140). In other words, humans have an intuitive grasp of the content of these commandments inasmuch as they determine right action. Saadiah further argues that the rational commandments are inherently related to the dictates of reason, and that they represent logical inferences from these dictates (*BBO*.II.5.106; III.1.139). Revelatory commandments, which constitute the second general division of law, are not inherently dependent upon the above-mentioned rational dictates, but rather are imposed by God without regard to their inherent rationality. Thus the approbation of these laws implies no more than simple submissiveness to God. As we shall see, however, Saadiah discerns a social utility for nearly all these laws. Thus, Saadiah will want to argue that although these laws are not grounded in reason, nevertheless they too may be justified by rational argument. Saadiah offers many examples (sanctifying certain times rather than others; the dietary laws, etc.) to explicate the overall social utility of the traditional laws. Saadiah's system thus incorporates a theory of rational obligation into the rubric of revelatory commandments. We can therefore acknowledge Saadiah's sustained efforts to articulate the underlying idea that ethical theorizing is fundamentally objective, based on human nature, and accessible to human reasoning.

SOLOMON IBN GABIROL

Solomon ibn Gabirol (c. 1021–c. 1058) was a prominent but reclusive member of Andalusian Jewish intellectual society. Representing the flourishing of Jewish intellectual life in Andalusia just after the enlightened reign of the Umayyad caliphate, Ibn Gabirol was one of the first Jewish philosophers in Spain to benefit from the intellectual ferment of this Golden Age. What little is known of him biographically is mostly gleaned from statements in his poetry which scholars have interpreted as reflective of his real life circumstances.[3] Both a poet and a philosopher, Ibn Gabirol composed poetic and non-poetic texts which incorporate themes of medieval Neoplatonism. He is known primarily for his metaphysical writings: his major philosophical work *Meqqor Hayyim* is a purely metaphysical treatise which presents a rigorously defined Neoplatonic cosmology. Ibn Gabirol's major contribution to ethical literature is his work *Tiqqun Middot ha-Nefesh (On the Improvement of the Moral Qualities)*. Written in 1045 in Saragossa, this work is available in the original Arabic (*Aslah al-Akhlaq*), as well as in a Hebrew translation by Judah ibn Tibbon dated 1167, which has been reprinted in many versions.

Tiqqun Middot ha-Nefesh is primarily a treatise on practical morality, in which, like Saadiah, Ibn Gabirol develops a system of ethics dependent upon the rule of reason. Although his ideas are supported by biblical references, he also includes quotations from Greek philosophers and Arab poets. Notably, he does not reference the Talmud. Many of the standard elements of his work can be readily found within classical Jewish Neoplatonism. However, as Schlanger has pointed out,[4] Ibn Gabirol does introduce an original element into his work, namely the connection between the moral and physiological makeup of the human. Ibn Gabirol describes the qualities and defects of the soul, with particular emphasis upon the doctrine of the Aristotelian mean. The qualities of the soul, according to Ibn Gabirol, are made manifest through the five senses of sight, hearing, smell, taste, and touch. Each

---

[3] Scheindlin 1986: 12.   [4] Schlanger 1968.

sense additionally governs four main moral qualities: sight corresponds to pride and humility, modesty and impudence; hearing to love and hate, mercy and cruelty; smell to anger and favoritism, jealousy and diligence; taste to joy and grief, confidence and remorse; and touch to generosity and parsimony, bravery and timidity.[5] Harvey notes that Ibn Gabirol's correlative pairs do not have an explicit precedent in philosophic literature, but rather seem to be drawn from Hebrew idioms. "He must have presumed," writes Harvey, "that ancient Hebrew idioms reliably reflect human physiology and psychology and therefore may be used to construct a theory of moral qualities."[6]

Ibn Gabirol describes humans as representing the pinnacle of creation; inasmuch as the final purpose of human existence is perfection, they must overcome their passions and detach themselves from this base existence in order to attain felicity of the soul. The soul distinguishes man from other living beings and, by developing his own soul, an individual can increase his spiritual perfection. The body as well as the soul must participate in the person's aspirations toward felicity: "In the actions of the senses as well as in the moral actions, one must reside in the mean and not fall into excess or defect."[7] In effect, Ibn Gabirol has delineated a complete parallel between the microcosm as represented by the human being, and the macrocosm, which is the universe.

BAHYA IBN PAKUDA (fl. 1050–1090)

Bahya ibn Pakuda, Ibn Gabirol's younger contemporary, is best known for his system of Jewish ethics, which appeared in 1040 in Arabic and was later translated into Hebrew by Judah ibn Tibbon. This work, entitled *Sefer Hovot ha-Levvavot* (*The Book of Direction to the Duties of the Heart*), is one of the first attempts to present ethical laws and duties espoused by Judaism in a coherent philosophical system. Bahya describes his motivation for compiling his ethical system in the introduction of the work. It was his impression that many Jews either paid little attention to the duties of Jewish law, or paid exclusive attention to duties performed by the body. He was underwhelmed by the supposed evidence that people were obeying and cultivating duties of the heart, from which the work gets its title. Bahya's ethics is the first medieval Jewish work whose ideas evolved from Jewish thought. Unlike

---

[5] Harvey 2012: 88; Wise 1902.　[6] Harvey 2012: 88.　[7] Schlanger 1968: 18.

Ibn Gabirol, who refrained from quoting the Talmud and other rabbinic sources, Bahya referenced both biblical and rabbinical literatures.[8]

In *Duties of the Heart* Bahya distinguishes between two types of duties: duties of the heart and external duties. The former are purely rational and intellectual, and the latter are practical. The two types of duties are linked, as external duties (such as moving one's limbs or helping one's neighbor) are impossible without internal duties (consent of the mind in the former instance, and love or respect of one's neighbor in the second). The ideal state, which Bahya terms "whole-heartedness," is reached when man achieves complete accord of the mind and body. When "whole-heartedness" is impossible, then an unrealized intention is preferable to a correct deed completed without intention. In other words, inner spirituality is of greater importance than external behavior. *Duties of the Heart* is divided into ten chapters, representing the ten roots, or "gates" of the duties of the heart. These roots lead to a *wholehearted* belief in God.[9]

In *Duties of the Heart* III.10 Bahya presents a list of twenty moral qualities, borrowed from those of Ibn Gabirol; unlike those pairs found in Ibn Gabirol, however, Bahya's list is grouped into contrary pairs: 1) joy and sorrow; 2) fear and hope; 3) bravery and timidity; 4) modesty and impudence; 5) favor and anger; 6) mercy and cruelty; 7) pride and humility; 8) love and hate; 9) generosity and parsimony; 10) idleness and diligence (*DH*:III.10.218–20).[10] He claims to have recorded the qualities as he thought of them, and in no particular order.

MOSES MAIMONIDES (C. 1138–1204)

Maimonides is unarguably one of the greatest figures in the medieval Jewish period. Born in Córdoba, Spain, Maimonides' family fled to al-Fustād, where he became a physician and served as Saladin's vizier. In his major philosophical work *Guide of the Perplexed* (*Moreh Nevukhim*), Maimonides applies Aristotelian principles of mathematics and logic to religious doctrines in order that his intended audience, comprised of devout religious individuals who also admire science and law, might potentially assuage their "perplexities." His discussion of ethical behavior occurs in a number of works, including *Eight Chapters*, *Laws Concerning Character Traits*, and *The Guide of the Perplexed*.[11] In his introduction

---

[8]   Dan 2007.   [9]   Harvey 2012: 89; Mansoor 2004.   [10]   See Harvey 2012: 89.

[11]   The *Eight Chapters* is part of Maimonides' *Commentary on the Mishnah* (an introduction to the *Chapters of the Fathers* (*Pirqei Avot*)) in which Maimonides brought

to *Eight Chapters*, Maimonides is explicit in his borrowings from both the sages and from "the discourse of both the ancient and modern philosophers" (*EC*: I.60). Not wanting to dissuade his readers from taking these "alien" ideas seriously, he takes care not to identify the authors of his sources. We know, however, that Aristotle, al-Fārābī, and to some extent Plato lurk in the background of Maimonides' discussions in both *Eight Chapters* and the *Guide*.[12] Although Maimonides does not quote al-Fārābī explicitly, there are nevertheless many passages in the *Guide* that intimate the importance of the philosopher in the domain of public affairs. For these reasons, any discussion of Maimonides' theory of morality must incorporate social and political philosophy, as well as ethical thought.

Moral Character

While Maimonides is interested in both actions and character traits, his ethical works focus primarily on the latter. In *Eight Chapters* he reserves the terms "virtuous" and "vicious" for character traits rather than for actions. Maimonides emphasizes the propaedeutic nature of moral virtues: "the improvement of moral habits is the same as the cure of the soul and its powers" (*EC*:I.61). Note that the terms "virtue" and "vice" pertain not to human actions, but to characteristics in the human soul. While there is a connection between "inner" and "outer," and our outward behavior provides the best access we have to these inner characteristics, nevertheless the "outer" actions are not themselves virtuous or vicious. This point is made both in *Eight Chapters* and in *Character Traits*.

Maimonides agrees with Aristotle that ethics is *not* an exact science. Although we should expect the sort of accuracy common to any study, ethics does not contain the sort of accuracy found in the demonstrative sciences. For Aristotle, our manner of investigation consists in beginning with the common views on virtue (*endoxa*) and then seeking out the "wise person's view." The wise and virtuous are the best judges of those areas in which they have knowledge and experience (*NE*:I.3,1095a).

Like Aristotle and al-Fārābī, Maimonides distinguishes in *Eight Chapters* between two types of virtue: rational and moral. Rational virtues include wisdom and intelligence, which in turn comprise theoretical intellect,

together a number of ethical ideas. *Laws Concerning Character Traits* is a short work, part of the *Mishneh Torah*, devoted to ethical matters.

[12] Berman 1991 emphasizes the importance of Aristotle's *Nicomachean Ethics* for Maimonides. Cf. also Pines 1963; Davidson 1987.

acquired intellect, and what he calls "brilliance and excellent comprehension" or intuition (*EC*:II.65). Moral virtues are found in the appetitive part of the soul, not the rational part, and include a number of characteristics: moderation, liberality, justice, gentleness, humility, contentment, and courage. This separation between intellectual and moral virtues raises a concern however about the epistemological status of ethical knowledge.[13] In the *Guide* Maimonides emphasizes that imagination must *not* be confused with intellect (*GP*:I.2). He is very clear that only intellectual knowledge can lead to rational virtue, while imagination represents a lesser faculty of the soul and leads to social perfection.

The implications of this distinction between intellect and imagination are important when we turn to the justification of ethical claims in general. Maimonides argues that good and evil, as opposed to true and false, are not intellectual concepts, but rather are notions that arise as a result of the act of the imagination. More specifically, terms such as "good" (*tov*) and "bad" (*ra'*) signify what Maimonides calls generally accepted opinions, things "generally accepted as known," and are not rooted in reality itself (*GP*:I.2; II.33; III.10). The relativism of ethical terms can be contrasted with the propositions of mathematics and physics, which we can know through the science of demonstration. Unaided reason (based on demonstration) can come to know objective concepts rooted in reality, but not subjective concepts such as "good" and "bad."[14]

Because moral values reflect particular situations, the highest moral knowledge must ultimately derive from intellectual knowledge. *Character Traits* 1:3 and 1:4 are saturated with normative language – the *good* and *right* way that *ought* to be followed. Maimonides offers both rational and halakhic considerations to exhort his reader to adhere to a normative way of life. Reflecting Aristotle, Maimonides argues that acting in a "good" and "right" way enables us to be a completed person; he then follows up with halakhic considerations, telling us that "We are commanded to walk in these middle ways" (*CT*:I.5.30). Maimonides is very clear as to the end of human existence (viz. intellectual perfection). He argues that whatever directs us toward that ultimate goal – presumably developing one's intellectual character will best achieve this aim – ought to be actualized.

Reflecting the Platonic dictum in the *Euthyphro* that the gods command pious acts because they are pious, Maimonides is suggesting that there exists

---

[13] For discussion of this difficulty, see Twersky 1980: 453–9; Kellner 1990; Weiss 1991; Fox 1990; Pines 1990; Schatz 2005.

[14] See Harvey 2012.

a rational, autonomous nature of what is right: these actions have been commanded *because* they are intrinsically good and right. Theoretically (although such a person does not exist in actual fact) an individual ruled entirely by intellect, and not at all by his affections, would not entertain the notions of good and evil; such terms would be either meaningless or redundant.[15]

We have noted the importance of character development in determining the value of moral action. Maimonides, following Aristotle and al-Fārābī, emphasizes the repetition of habitual actions for proper character formation. The very title of *Character Traits* (*Hilkhot Deot*) reinforces the importance of character. The first four chapters set forth the morality of the wise individual who follows the middle way. Chapter 5 concerns the discipline of such a person and is concerned with actions rather than character traits, focusing on social interactions. Maimonides follows al-Fārābī and claims that inculcation of virtues requires habitual repetition of "right actions": according to Maimonides, "a man shall habituate himself in these character traits until they are firmly established in him. Time after time, he shall perform actions in accordance with the character traits that are in the mean. He shall repeat them continually until performing them is easy for him and they are not burdensome and these character traits are firmly established in his soul" (*CT:* I.7.30). Virtues are not innate; the most we can say is that individuals may have a natural proclivity toward particular virtues.

Doctrine of the Mean

We come now to the heart of Maimonides' discussion of moral virtue, which incorporates Aristotle's doctrine of the mean. Aristotle's well-known doctrine of the mean is presented in *Nicomachean Ethics* Book II, and represents an intermediate between excess and defect. Aristotle explains the intermediate as "that which is equidistant from each of the extremes, which is one and same for all men," while at the same time emphasizing that the intermediate is relative to the agent (*NE:*II.6, 1106a.30). In other words, we must distinguish between the arithmetical mean, which represents a strict arithmetical proportion between two extremes, and the mean relative to us, which takes into account personal properties and situation. Thus, for example, the amount of

---

[15] Harvey (1981) draws the interesting parallel between Maimonides' discussion and that of Spinoza in the *Ethics*. According to Harvey, neither is fully a moral relativist, although both relegate the terms good and evil to the realm of the imaginative faculty.

training required by a marathon runner will be more than that required by a 10-km runner, and the amount of food required by the former will be more than that required by the latter. Moral virtue, then, must aim at the mean: to feel fear, confidence, appetite, anger, pity and the like "at the right times, with reference to the right objects, towards the right people, with the right motive, and in the right way, is what is both intermediate and best, and this is characteristic of virtue" (NE:II.6, 1106b.20–2).

Maimonides reiterates Aristotle's theory, as mediated by al-Fārābī, and presents the middle way, or life in accordance with the mean, as a way of achieving both personal serenity and communal well-being. Chapter 4 of *Eight Chapters* concerns the doctrine of the mean: "good actions are those balanced in the mean between two extremes, both of which are bad: one of them is an excess and the other a deficiency" (EC:IV.67). Virtues are defined as "states of the soul and settled dispositions in the mean between two bad states [of the soul], one of which is excessive and the other deficient" (ibid.). Maimonides then gives a number of examples: moderation is the mean between lust and insensibility; liberality is the mean between miserliness and extravagance; humility is the mean between haughtiness and abasement; generosity is the mean between prodigality and stinginess. Maimonides says that these virtues can be firmly established in the soul by repeating the actions pertaining to a particular moral habit over a long period of time, resulting in our "becoming accustomed to them" (EC:IV.68).

Both Maimonides and Aristotle recognize counter-instances to this general doctrine. Aristotle lists adultery, murder and theft as exceptions to the mean, claiming that these actions are never appropriate and so cannot be analyzed in terms of finding an intermediate action. Maimonides' list of exceptions, including the virtues associated with anger and humility, and the doctrine of asceticism in general, are more problematic, however. We turn now to Maimonides' attempt to reconcile the doctrine of the mean with the Law.

Saintliness, Asceticism and the Mean: Is the Hasid' a Sinner?

So far we have emphasized the moderating tendencies in Maimonides' theory of virtue. Agents should aim toward the intermediate between extremes in order to cultivate a virtuous character; the commandments themselves have as one of their aims the cultivation of virtuous actions resulting from this middle way. Acts exceeding a slight deviation may be prescribed occasionally to heal a diseased psychological characteristic, but Maimonides insists that they may not be performed continuously: extreme behavior, Maimonides asserts, runs contrary to God's will and results in "vices" in the soul.

But what about the fact that Torah law mandates many actions that do not reflect the mean? How do we account, for example, for the dietary laws, many of which clearly do not reflect a doctrine of the mean? More generally, what correlation can we draw between acquisition of moral virtue and acquiescence to the commandments? Further, what do we do with Maimonides' characterization of the *Hasid* or saint, whose radical behavior reflects an apparent repudiation of the mean? Recognizing these difficulties, Maimonides adopts a less moderate position in the cases of humility and anger, claiming that the truly pious individual or *Hasid* recognizes the harm brought about by pride, and inclines to utter meekness "so as to leave not even a trace of pride in their soul" (CM Avot 4.4). In this regard he appears to deviate markedly from Aristotle, who, in *Nicomachean Ethics*, presented both proper pride and appropriate anger as virtues to be achieved (*NE*:IV. 3, 1123b14).

Whereas Aristotle values proper pride and anger, Maimonides' discussion is more conflicted and reflects the tension between Aristotelian moderation and the extreme humility found in rabbinic texts. On the one hand, Maimonides advocates the mean in all actions, including anger and pride. In *Character Traits* I.4–5 and II.1–3 he follows Aristotle in suggesting that "the right way is the mean in every single one of a man's character traits"; in the case of anger, a person should aim for the mean and "only become angry about a large matter that deserves anger so that something like it not be done again" (*CT*:I.4.29). Yet other passages in the same work eschew the mean in these two cases. With respect to pride, Maimonides introduces a new motif, and claims that "whoever moves away from a haughty heart to the opposite extreme so that he is exceedingly lowly in spirit is called a pious man; this is the measure of piety. If he moves only to the mean and is humble, he is called a wise man; this is the measure of wisdom" (*CT*:I.5.30). This point is expressed even more explicitly in II.3, when Maimonides suggests that in the case of haughtiness and anger, not just the pious saint (*Hasid*), but *everybody* ought to aim to the extreme: "the good way is not that a man be merely humble, but that he have a lowly spirit, that his spirit be very submissive" (*CT*:II.3.31). Similarly, anger is now seen to be "an extremely bad character trait," and one must train oneself not to become angry, even over something that Aristotle would have argued that it is proper to be angry about. Maimonides goes so far as to suggest that occasionally one might want to simulate anger in order to impress others, but "his mind shall be tranquil within himself, like a man who feigns anger but is not angry" (CT:II.3.32). Individuals should train themselves not to feel anything, even in situations that provoke what Aristotle would have considered proper anger.[16]

The Rationality of the Commandments

Our final topic has to do with the overall rationality of the Law, returning us to the issue with which we started. While Maimonides' analysis of the commandments reflects Saadiah's distinction between rational and ritualistic commandments, Maimonides is more radical in his claim that *all* the commandments are rational: both the laws (*mishpatim*) and the statutes (*huqqim*) have beneficial ends, the only difference being that the former are recognizable to all, whereas the latter possess ends that are only manifest to the wise. The laws correspond to Saadiah's rational commandments, while the statutes correspond (in general) to Saadiah's listing of ceremonial laws and rituals. For Maimonides, however, both laws and statutes have a basis in reason.

Aspects of a natural law sentiment can be found throughout Maimonides' work. Maimonides is clear that "governance of the Law is absolute and universal" (GP:III.34.534). In *Guide* III.25 Maimonides offers several proofs based on philosophical reasoning for the rationality of law. He argues that to attribute to God non-purposive and non-rational actions, namely laws that are the arbitrary result of God's will, would be blasphemous, for frivolous actions are the most demeaning. Furthermore, he argues that in order to command the respect of the nations of the world, Jewish law must be rational. In an interesting aside, Maimonides claims that were the Law not rational, the peoples of the world would not look up to the Jews, and they would lose their standing among the moral peoples.

Turning specifically to the utility of commandments, Maimonides distinguishes between the generalities and the particulars of a commandment. While the generalities of the commandments were given for utilitarian reasons, the particular details may not have the same utilitarian value. While the overall purpose of the particulars is to purify the people (GP: III.26.508), Maimonides castigates those who try to find causes for every particular detail in the laws. Such individuals are stricken with "madness" and "are as far from truth as those who imagine that the generalities of a commandment are not designed with a view to some real utility" (GP: III.26.509). In fact, Maimonides goes to great lengths to warn his reader that

[16] See Rudavsky 2010 for further discussion of Maimonides' attempts to resolve the tension between Aristotle and the rabbinic sources.

for some particulars no cause can be found. Why, for example, did the Law prescribe the sacrifice of a ram rather than a lamb? No reason can be given, but one or other particular had to be chosen.

Maimonides argues further that the commandments serve to support social and political beliefs. In an extended passage, Maimonides offers a historical deconstruction of the Law (GP:III.29.514–22; III.32.525–31; III.37. 540–50; III.45.575–46.592). In order to explain the importance of sacrifices, he traces the laws back to Moses' attempts to combat Sabianism. The Sabians were a polytheistic tribe steeped in magic and myth. In the context of refuting the idolatry of the Sabians who "explicitly asserted that the stars are the deity and that the sun is the greatest deity" (GP:II.29.514), Maimonides tells us that the first intention of the Law as a whole is to put an end to idolatry: "it is explicitly stated in the text of the Torah that everything that was regarded by them as worship of their gods and as a way of coming near to them, is hateful and odious to God" (GP:III.29.517). According to Maimonides' deconstructive analysis, Moses knew that weaning the Israelites away from idolatry and sacrificial rituals would be an arduous task, and so in order to do so gradually, the commandments regarding sacrifice were relaxed to require sacrifices only to God, the idea being that eventually they would be abandoned altogether.

Maimonides thus distinguishes two intentions in the mind of God: the first intention is that humans reject idolatry, while God's second intention is the satisfaction of the commandments. Because human nature is inherently fallible, and humans cannot always act in their own best interest, God must occasionally resort to secondary intentions in order to achieve primary goals. Sabianism represents one form of idolatry, but Maimonides knew that because of their corporeal nature, human beings are always tempted by some form of idolatry or other. Even if there had been no Sabianism to combat, presumably God's second intention would have remained inviolable, and so the commandments would have served God's purposes. Let us grant Maimonides the claim that God needed to resort to second intentions in order to achieve God's aims. But ought these rationally graspable and intelligible reasons for the commandments be divulged to the public? Maimonides clearly states that "all laws have causes and were given with a view to some utility" (GP:III.26.507). This utility is applicable to both welfare of the soul (achieved by acquisition of true beliefs) and welfare of the body (achieved by practical and moral virtues). Might not the very process of uncovering the reasons for the commandments lead to a sort of philosophical anti-nomianism among the masses, if they were to understand both the causes and goals of particular commandments? Could not this understanding lead to the seductive conclusion that these prescribed actions are dispensable? If the goal of human existence (namely intellectual perfection) can be achieved in a way that does not require performance of the commandments, does that not render the commandments otiose? Maimonides' successors were quite aware of the untoward implications of the *Guide*; subsequent centuries struggled with these very issues.

CONCLUSION: NATURE AND HUMAN PERFECTION

I have presented a view, developed in medieval Jewish philosophy, according to which humans have an intuitive sense of what is right and wrong; this intuitive sense is reflected in the commandments and supported by generally accepted opinions. Further, by a careful reasoning process, we can often uncover the inherent rationality of the laws, rooted in our nature as human beings. This understanding incorporates both moral and intellectual perfection, and it is reflective of our nature *qua* both corporeal and spiritual beings. Thus, on the reading I have presented, medieval Jewish philosophers, drawing upon ingredients found already in rabbinic sources, were moving toward a natural law theory according to which moral truths are universally binding, reflective of our human nature, and accessible to human reasoning.

BIBLIOGRAPHY

An asterisk denotes secondary literature especially suitable for further reading.

Aristotle (1995), "Nicomachean Ethics," in Barnes, Jonathan (ed.), *The Complete Works of Aristotle* (Princeton University Press).
Bahya ibn Pakuda (2004), *The Book of Direction to the Duties of the Heart*, trans. Mansoor, Menahem (Oxford: The Littman Library of Jewish Civilization).
Berman, Lawrence (1991), "The Ethical Views of Maimonides within the Context of Islamicate Civilization," in Kramer, Joel (ed.), *Perspectives on Maimonides: Philosophical and Historical Studies* (Oxford University Press for the Littman Library), 13–32.
Dan, Joseph (2007), "Ethical Literature," in Skolnik, Michael and Berenbaum, Fred (eds.), *Encyclopaedia Judaica* (Detroit: Macmillan Reference USA), 525–31.
Davidson, Herbert A. (1987), "The Middle Way in Maimonides' Ethics," *Proceedings of the American Academy for Jewish Research*, 54, 31–72.
Fox, Marvin (1990), "The Nature of Man and the Foundations of Ethics: A Reading of *Guide* 1.1–2," *Interpreting Maimonides: Studies in Methodology, Metaphysics, and Moral Philosophy* (University of Chicago Press), 152–98.
Greenstein, Edward L. (1984), "Medieval Bible Commentaries," in Holtz, Barry W. (ed.), *Back to the Sources* (New York: Summit Books).

Harvey, Warren Zev (1981), "A Portrait of Spinoza as a Maimonidean," *Journal of the History of Philosophy*, 19, 151–72.

Harvey, Warren Zev (2012), "Ethical Theories among Medieval Jewish Philosophers," in Crane, Elliot N. and Dorff, Jonathan K. (eds.), *The Oxford Handbook of Jewish Ethics and Morality* (Oxford University Press), 84–98.*

Kellner, Menachem (1990), *Maimonides on Human Perfection* (Atlanta: Scholars Press).

King, Peter (2013), "Boethius on the Problem of Desert," in Pasnau, R. (ed.), *Oxford Studies in Medieval Philosophy*, vol. 1 (Oxford University Press), 1–22.

Maimonides, Moses (1963), *The Guide of the Perplexed [Arabic: Dalalat al-hairin; Hebrew: Moreh Nevukhim]*, trans. Pines, Shlomo (2 vols; University of Chicago Press).

Maimonides, Moses (1972), "Commentary on the Mishnah, Avot," in Twersky, Isadore (ed.), *A Maimonides Reader* (New York: Behrman House), 387–400.

Maimonides, Moses (1975a), "Eight Chapters [Introduction to Commentary on Mishnah Avot]," *Ethical Writings of Maimonides* (New York: Dover), 60–104.

Maimonides, Moses (1975b), "Laws Concerning Character Traits," *Ethical Writings of Maimonides* (New York: Dover), 27–58.

Mansoor, Menahem (2004), "Translator's Introduction," *Bahya ibn Pakuda, The Book of Direction to the Duties of the Heart* (Oxford: The Littman Library of Jewish Civilization), 1–65.

Pines, Shlomo (1963), "Translator's Introduction: The Philosophical Sources of *The Guide of the Perplexed*," in Maimonides 1963: lvii–cxxxiv.

Pines, Shlomo (1990), "Truth and Falsehood versus Good and Evil," in Twersky, Isadore (ed.), *Studies in Maimonides* (Cambridge, MA: Harvard University Press), 95–157.

Rudavsky, Tamar (2010), *Maimonides* (Malden, MA: Wiley-Blackwell).*

Saadia Gaon, ben Joseph al-Fayyumi (1948), *The Book of Beliefs and Opinions*, trans. Rosenblatt, Samuel (New Haven: Yale University Press).

Schatz, David (2005), "Maimonides' Moral Theory," in Seeskin, Kenneth (ed.), *The Cambridge Companion to Maimonides* (Cambridge University Press), 167–93.

Scheindlin, Raymond (1986), *Wine, Women and Death: Medieval Hebrew Poems on the Good Life* (Oxford University Press).

Schlanger, Jacques (1968), *La philosophie de Salomon Ibn Gabirol* (Leiden: E.J. Brill).

Twersky, Isadore (1980), *Introduction to the Code of Maimonides (Mishneh Torah)*, (New Haven: Yale University Press).

Weiss, Raymond L. (1991), *Maimonides' Ethics: The Encounter of Philosophic and Religious Morality* (University of Chicago Press).

Wise, Stephen (1902), "Introduction," *The Improvement of the Moral Qualities: An Ethical Treatise of the Eleventh Century by Solomon ibn Gabirol* (New York: Columbia University Press), 1–28.

12

Moral Philosophy in the Medieval Islamicate World

ANNA AKASOY

What is moral philosophy in the medieval Islamicate world?[1] The term 'philosophy' already constitutes an important limitation. Rather than meaning systematic thought in a general sense, the Arabic term *falsafa* referred to a rational tradition of thought inspired and informed by the legacy of Greek philosophy and science. While the designation 'secular' for this intellectual approach betrays a modern understanding of religion, medieval authors in the Islamicate world frequently distinguished Islamic from foreign branches of knowledge.[2] Such classifications of knowledge also contain useful information as to how contemporary scholars defined moral philosophy and adapted Greek traditions of practical philosophy.

In al-Fārābī's (d. 950/951) *Enumeration of the Sciences* (*Iḥṣā' al-'ulūm*), morals loom large. Since his definition is going to serve as a starting point here, it is worth quoting it in some length. Al-Fārābī distinguishes five kinds of sciences: language sciences, logic, mathematics, natural science and 'political science' or 'the science of the city' (*al-'ilm al-madanī*).[3] The definition of this last category begins as follows:

> Science of the city investigates the various kinds of voluntary actions and ways of life; the acquired talents (*malakāt*), morals (*akhlāq*), natural inclinations (*sajāyā*), and inborn character traits (*shiyam*) that lead to these actions and ways of life; the ends for the sake of which they are performed; how they

---

[1] I am using Hodgson's term 'Islamicate' in order to refer to literature produced in an area under Islamic rule. While Islamic rule and 'culture' are significant for this literature, the Islamic religion in a narrow sense does not provide an exclusive framework. Hodgson 1974: 57–60.

[2] See the examples in Rosenthal 1994: 62–73. The authors discussed in this chapter fall within the broader purview of *falsafa*. Studies which consider a wider field include Donaldson 1953; Hourani 1971 and 1975; Fakhry 1991, but see Gutas 1997.

[3] Gutas 2004. Gutas's argument hinges on the identification of al-Fārābī's concern as noetics rather than politics.

must exist in human beings; how to order them in human beings in the manner in which they must exist in them; and the way to preserve them for them. It distinguishes among the ends for the sake of which the actions are performed and the ways of life are practiced. It explains that some of them are true happiness, while others are presumed to be happiness although they are not. That which is true happiness cannot possibly be of this life, but of another life after this, which is the life to come; while that which is presumed to be happiness consists of such things as wealth, honor, and the pleasures, when these are made the only ends in this life. Distinguishing the actions and ways of life, it explains that the ones through which true happiness is attained are the goods, the noble things, and the virtues, while the rest are the evils, the base things, and the imperfections; and that they [must] exist in human beings in such a way that the virtuous actions and ways of life are distributed in the cities and nations according to a certain order and are practiced in common.[4]

At the outset of his definition, al-Fārābī focusses on issues which are crucial to moral philosophy in the medieval Islamicate world. He distinguishes presumed happiness with its this-worldly desires and vicious actions from true happiness which requires virtuous behaviour, fostered by a virtuous environment, and which can only be fully attained in the afterlife. Al-Fārābī continues with deliberations regarding the significance of virtuous rule for the moral life. Classical elements are easily discernible. The emphasis on happiness brings Aristotle's *Ethics* to mind and al-Fārābī, like Aristotle, distinguishes different kinds of happiness, the contemplative life being the highest form. The text had been translated into Arabic in ninth-century Baghdad and left traces in philosophical writing in the Islamicate world.[5] It circulated under the title *Akhlāq*, which designated ethics as a philosophical discipline. Literally, as above, it also means 'morals', which already suggests that the line between ethics and morals is difficult to draw.[6]

Al-Fārābī's own undertakings in practical philosophy were broader than Aristotle's *Ethics* and reflect the definition of the 'science of the city'. As is

---

[4] Modified translation by Fauzi Najjar in Lerner and Mahdi 1963: 24–30, 24. For the Arabic text al-Fārābī 1996: 79–80.

[5] Zonta 2003; Akasoy and Fidora 2005 and Ullmann 2011–2012. Al-Fārābī wrote a lost commentary on the text. See also his *Directing Attention to the Way to Happiness* in McGinnis and Reisman 2007: 104–20.

[6] For further comments on the terminology and the relationship between morals and habits see also Rundgren 1976: 86–8. For the relationship between ethics and moral philosophy in the context of the medieval Islamicate world see also Ramón Guerrero 2011: 317–18.

obvious above, moral philosophy cannot be separated from communal life and the political order of the city in which people pursue true happiness. Material conditions are critical: '. . . man cannot attain the perfection, for the sake of which his inborn nature has been given to him, unless many (societies of) people who co-operate come together who each supply everybody else with some particular need of his'.[7] Not every city allows this. The 'excellent city' requires people who form perfect associations as well as perfect rulers. Given his detailed discussion, it is no surprise that al-Fārābī reigns supreme in scholarship concerned with early Arabic political thought.[8]

While other authors too have written about issues of the 'science of the city', their texts are not primarily classified as philosophical writing. Dimitri Gutas has distinguished three kinds of ethical literature in the Islamic world: 1) wisdom literature and gnomology, 2) popular philosophical, and 3) mirrors for princes.[9] The following writers exemplify some of the salient features of these categories.

AL-KINDĪ (C. 800–870)

Before al-Fārābī, philosophers in the Islamicate world wrestled with issues of true happiness and the virtuous life. Al-Kindī flourished at the time of the early translation movement when Greek texts on philosophy and science were translated into Arabic, sometimes via Syriac. His works reflect this continuous influx of philosophical premises and methods of argumentation.

Al-Kindī's ethical treatises have to be read with some caution since most texts of this prolific writer, including most of his practical philosophy, are lost. The preserved eclectic ethical works reveal a holistic interpretation of philosophy which combines knowledge and action. The title of al-Kindī's most important ethical treatise provides a good idea of its contents and ambition: *On the Means of Dispelling Sorrows.*[10] Written in an engaging literary style, the text gained some popularity. The philosopher's intention may have been to challenge commonly held views and draw uninitiated readers into the study of philosophy.[11] Readers of the treatise must already have had some familiarity though with philosophical views such as the rational soul as the essence of human beings.[12] This and other principles are taken for granted in the text.

---

[7] Al-Fārābī 1985: 229.   [8] Daiber 1996.
[9] Gutas 1990. For other divisions see also Gutas's review (1997).
[10] Translation in McGinnis and Reisman 2007: 23–35.   [11] Druart 1993a.
[12] Adamson 2007a: 155.

Al-Kindī begins his deliberations with a popular view: the absence of external goods leads to sorrow. In fact, al-Kindī argues in his text, it is the obsession with these goods which causes sorrow. The remedy for this disease is an intellectual asceticism. Instead of fixating on the value of material objects which, by their very nature, will not last, we should love what is stable: our intellect. Al-Kindī criticizes those who fail to eradicate their own misfortune with sharp words: 'This is the sign of the unjust, uncouth, miserable, and stupid man, because the unjust man is one who drags out misfortune.'[13]

The literary imagery in On the Means of Dispelling Sorrows sometimes points to philosophical trends. The parable of life as a journey on a ship already appears in the Stoic Epictetus's Enchiridion, although al-Kindī describes in greater detail how different people spend their time whenever the ship lands and the passengers disembark. While some deal only with the necessary obligations, others get distracted, lose the best seats and are weighed down by goods which they can ultimately not keep.[14]

The hero who looms large, however, is Socrates.[15] Another of al-Kindī's preserved writings is a collection of The Sayings of Socrates. This compilation is hardly informed by Plato's dialogues and betrays misunderstandings which circulated more widely in the medieval Islamicate world. Socrates was oftentimes conflated with Diogenes, whose asceticism contributes a prominent feature in the former's Cynic representation by al-Kindī. In The Sayings of Socrates, he advocates a stern principle of avoiding external goods since they are considered bad.

If On the Means of Dispelling Sorrows is meant as an invitation to philosophy, al-Kindī's other works contain more details about this enterprise. In the version of his On the Definitions and Descriptions of Things used by Isaac Israeli (c. 855–955), one of the definitions given for philosophy is an imitation of God's actions.[16] Al-Kindī's Socrates too has features associated with God such as wisdom and justice.[17]

YAḤYĀ IBN ʿADĪ (893–974)

A later member of the Baghdad philosophical scene had a similar message for his readers. Yaḥyā ibn ʿAdī belonged, like his teacher al-Fārābī, to an influential group of Aristotelians. Unlike the other authors discussed here, Yaḥyā

---

[13] McGinnis and Reisman 2007: 27.   [14] Ibid., 31–3.   [15] Adamson 2007b.
[16] Druart 1993a: 337.   [17] Adamson 2007a: 147–9.

belonged to the Syrian Orthodox church. Christians like Yaḥyā, who was also a translator, played an important role in the transmission of Greek learning into Arabic. The commonalities with Muslim scholars engaged in the same intellectual project are an argument against the label 'Islamic philosophy', as has often been pointed out. Yaḥyā's religious identity is rarely visible in the book discussed here, *The Reformation of Morals (Tahdhīb al-akhlāq)*.[18]

The author begins with a positive anthropology: 'The worthiest thing a man chooses for himself is his own fulfillment and perfection' (RM 5). This, however, is a difficult task. While we have, as Galen believed, good and bad states of our souls, the bad states tend to dominate. Laws and rulers are necessary to keep us from giving in. Like other authors, Yaḥyā uses the Platonic tripartition of the soul into appetitive, irascible and rational. Humans alone have a rational soul which allows us to distinguish good from bad deeds and control our lower faculties. Natural disposition, upbringing and environment determine our chances for human perfection and moral leadership.

Like other authors, above all Miskawayh, Yaḥyā presents his own list of twenty vices and virtues each, but gives them a peculiar twist by discussing them for different social classes. 'The forebearance of a lower-class person toward someone of a higher class is not to be reckoned a virtue' (RM 33). Greed is 'abhorrent for everyone except for kings. An abundance of money, of stores, and of goods gives support to a reign' (RM 47). 'Lying is to be considered repugnant in kings and leaders most' (RM 55). Some characteristics can be virtue or vice. Renunciation is commendable for scholars, monks and other religious authorities, but not for kings (RM 63). While Yaḥyā warns his readers not to confound wealth and virtue, he does not abhor money, as long as it is spent in the right way (RM 69). As with al-Kindī, the rational sciences are critical for reformation (RM 83), as are patience and love. The ultimate aim of human perfection and a state close to angels (RM 93), however, is only attainable for the select few.

Yaḥyā wrote for those who could recognize themselves in his description of the perfect human being (RM 9). Beyond its philosophical message, the text's purpose may have been to make a plea for support for scholars and a fair treatment of non-Muslims.[19]

ABŪ BAKR AL-RĀZĪ (864–925/932)

In his works *Spiritual Medicine* and *Philosopher's Way of Life*, Abū Bakr al-Rāzī presented a rather unusual moral philosophy.[20] Rāzī, the Latin physician

---

[18] Ibn ʿAdī 2002, hereafter RM.   [19] Griffith 2003.
[20] Druart 1993b. For a translation see McGinnis and Reisman 2007: 36–44.

Rhazes, belonged to a small group of medieval freethinkers. Rather than making Himself known through revelation, he believed, God had given humans reason as spiritual guidance. Unlike other approaches to moral philosophy which focus on virtues, Rāzī's ethics is based on six normative principles which breathe the spirit of Plato's *Timaeus* and reflect the author's familiarity with Galen:[21]

> We have a state after death that is either praiseworthy or blameworthy, depending on the way we lived during the time our souls were with our bodies. The noblest thing for which we were created and to which we are directed is not the pursuit of bodily pleasures but rather the acquisition of knowledge and the application of justice, both of which lead to our liberation from this world in the world in which there is neither pain nor death. Both nature and whim le[a]d us to prefer the pleasure of the present, while the intellect often calls on us to give up present pleasure in favor of things that *it* prefers. The Lord of us all, from whom we anticipate reward and fear punishment, watches over us, is merciful with us, does not seek to harm us, loathes our injustice and ignorance, and loves our justice and knowledge. For this Lord will punish in fair measure those of us who cause harm and those who deserve to suffer pain. We are not required to suffer pain in place of a pleasure that is preferable to that pain in quantity and quality. The Creator (mighty and high is He) has placed in our trust things particular to our needs, such as the cultivation of land, the craft of weaving cloth, and other such things that allow for the maintenance of the world and our livelihood. Let us accept these principles as valid so that we may build upon them.[22]

Al-Rāzī shares much with the other authors discussed in this chapter. He picks up Plato's tripartite soul and assigns to the rational soul the responsibility of controlling the two lower souls in order to live a virtuous life and secure a pleasant afterlife for ourselves. This brings Ibn ʿAdī to mind as well as al-Kindī. In a like manner, al-Rāzī pointed out that human pleasures always involved pain since we become used to them and demand more.[23] He also embraces the principle of *imitatio Dei*, in particular by acquiring knowledge and being just. Unlike the other authors, however, the freethinker al-Rāzī believed in reincarnation and included other animals in his moral philosophy. Sentient creatures should only be harmed if necessary. At the same time, the

---

[21] Druart (1993b) discusses parallels in Plato and Galen in some detail. See also Bar-Asher 1989 and, for Galen, Klein-Franke 1979.

[22] McGinnis and Reisman 2007: 38–9.

[23] Druart 1993b: 177. Miskawayh is indebted to Plato for a similar statement. See Adamson 2007c: 44.

philosopher advocated a strict utilitarianism in which his principles could be applied in an almost mathematical manner. A horse can be sacrificed to help a human escape from his enemy, 'especially if that person is learned and virtuous or is rich in some other way that will be of benefit to all people'.[24] Such solutions extend to conflicts among humans. If two men are stranded in the desert with little water, the more useful man should drink and survive. Carnivorous and poisonous animals should be destroyed since this would reduce the harm done to others and the harm these animals inflict on their own souls.

While much separates al-Rāzī and al-Kindī, both used Socrates conflated with Diogenes as a model. The *Philosopher's Way of Life* begins with an apology, in which al-Rāzī defends himself for his professional activity. Although this is not in accordance with the radical asceticism of the younger Socrates, he argues, it does reflect the Greek philosopher's later attitude.[25] Given the significance of human responsibility in al-Rāzī's philosophy and the God-given potential for improving our situation, it is not surprising that he defended an active lifestyle for a philosopher.

MISKAWAYH (d. 1030)

One of the best-known authors from the Islamicate world to write on happiness and friendship, Miskawayh has been identified as a 'humanist' and stands at the beginning of Islamicate Persian literature on ethics.[26] He wrote several treatises on moral philosophy, among which his own *Refinement of Character* (*Tahdhīb al-akhlāq*) is the best known.[27] The book begins with the statement that in order to achieve a character which allows good deeds, one has to study the soul first. Miskawayh's theory of the soul betrays Platonic and Neoplatonic influence.[28] Like many other philosophers in the medieval Islamicate world, Miskawayh considered Aristotle the greatest authority, but could not accept the implication of his theory of the soul as the 'form of the living body'. Instead, he maintained that the soul was

---

[24] For this and the following McGinnis and Reisman 2007: 40.   [25] Ibid., 36–7.

[26] Naṣīr al-Dīn al-Ṭūsī (1201–1274) used the treatise in his own *Akhlāq-i Nāṣrī*. See al-Ṭūsī 1964. See also Madelung 1985 and Kraemer 1993: 222–33.

[27] See Miskawayh 1968 (hereafter RC). The title is the same as that of Ibn ʿAdī's treatise; I am using the title of Zurayk's translation for the purpose of disambiguation. For other texts see Arkoun 1982; Marcotte 2012; Miskawayh 1964; Fakhry 1975a.

[28] About the underlying theory of the soul see Adamson 2007c. See also Fakhry 1975b.

immaterial and survived death. This notion is critical to all ethical literature discussed here. A list of virtues equally testifies to the influence of Plato's theory of the soul. Miskawayh uses his tripartition of the soul and locates them, like al-Rāzī and their common model, the *Timaeus*, in the brain, the heart and the liver respectively (RC 15). Furthermore, Miskawayh reproduces Plato's cardinal virtues which are associated with the soul: wisdom, courage and temperance as well as justice as the result of these. Each cardinal virtue comes with a list of sub-virtues (RC 17–22). Like Aristotle, he defines virtues as means between extremes, which are vices (RC 22–5).

In *The Refinement of Character*, scholars have paid most attention to the chapter on friendship and love, where Miskawayh's indebtedness to Aristotle is remarkable.[29] Like Aristotle, Miskawayh distinguishes different kinds of friendship depending on how easily they form and disintegrate. He highlights the friendship of virtuous people, which is lasting (RC 125). The law fosters such friendships by institutionalizing regular meetings in mosques and rituals (RC 127–8). Miskawayh is adamant that virtuous life requires society: 'the nature of human happiness ... cannot be achieved without bodily actions, civic conditions, good assistants, and sincere friends' (RC 150). Ascetics who withdraw to caves are unable to achieve moral virtues. As with al-Kindī and al-Rāzī, philosophy is critical for human perfection.[30]

The virtuous life of the mind in inspiring company, however, is only the first form of happiness. Ultimate happiness can only be found in approaching the divine. Miskawayh quotes Aristotle to this effect: 'Man's aspirations should not be human, though he be a man ... He should rather aim with all his capacities to live a divine life. For though man is small in body, he is great by his wisdom and noble by his intellect' (RC 152).

KUTADGU BILIG (WRITTEN 1069/1070)

Mirrors for princes constitute an important category of ethical literature in the medieval Islamicate world. Attributions to Aristotle, invariably inaccurate, associate some of these texts more closely with philosophy even though they are devoid of a systematic approach to the subject.[31] Treatises which offer wisdom for princes echo views expressed in texts more unambiguously characterized as philosophical. The example chosen here is one of the earliest

---

[29] Goodman 1996.   [30] Gutas 1983: 232.
[31] An important category is pseudo-Aristotle's letters to Alexander the Great. Doufikar-Aerts 2010: 93–133.

pieces of literature written in Turkish. In 1069/1070, Yūsuf of Balasagun presented his *Kutadgu Bilig* ('The Wisdom that Conduces to Royal Glory or Fortune') to the Karakhanid ruler of Kashgar. The text takes the form of a story, much of it in the form of dialogue or letters, of four allegorical characters. At the beginning stands the king, Rising Sun, who represents justice. He seeks a vizier and finds a suitable companion in Full Moon, who represents fortune. This becomes obvious when he dies: fortune is unreliable. Before he died, Full Moon had recommended his son, Highly Praised, to the king. The son becomes Rising Sun's advisor and reveals himself to represent the principle of wisdom or intellect. When the king seeks further advisors, Highly Praised recommends Wide Awake, an ascetic more virtuous than himself, who has withdrawn to a mountain. Despite great efforts, Wide Awake refuses to join the court, which would bring only distractions. He does, however, agree to visit Rising Sun briefly. King and vizier become persuaded of the ascetic's point of view, but maintain their functions. The story ends with Wide Awake's death after he has already had a dream vision to this effect.

In the course of the story, Highly Praised offers practical advice for rulers and behaviour at court when Wide Awake contemplates accepting the invitation. Elsewhere, the characters expound on ethical principles. Not unlike Ibn ʿAdī's prescriptions, these principles are primarily presented for the benefit of the ruler and those higher up in society whose actions affect a great number of people, but they can serve commoners as well.

Yūsuf alienates modern readers with his misogyny and radical social and intellectual elitism. 'Two sorts of noble men there are, one the prince, the other the sage, head of humankind. All beside them are cattle.'[32] While Yūsuf explains how the just and wise behaviour of a ruler benefits himself as well as his subjects, his anthropology also has a universal streak. Like Miskawayh, Yūsuf states, 'Man's chief glory is wisdom and intellect' (WRG 44). This disposition allows humans, or at least men, to cure the illness of their soul, to become noble and successful. Although Yūsuf pays particular attention to speech, 'interpreter to intellect and wisdom', he stresses repeatedly the importance of good actions (WRG 44 and 46ff). Time and again, he reminds his reader that life inevitably comes to an end and urges us to pay heed to his

---

[32] Yūsuf Khāṣṣ Ḥājib 1983 (hereafter WRG): 48. The misogyny is present throughout the text, but most obvious in the section about women at court. In general, Highly Praised comments, it would be better not to have daughters at all or if they at least died soon after birth.

advice. The consequences of good and evil deeds are not exclusively other-worldly. One's fate after death mirrors success or failure during one's life-time. Virtuous behaviour is conditioned by the challenges of social ascent and requires effort, but it pays off. By allowing others to become wealthy, for example, the ruler gains a reputation for generosity. (Compare this to Ibn ʿAdī, who justifies royal greed on similar grounds.) Commoners too have the opportunity to rise. Humility and loyalty are crucial transactional and instrumental virtues, and Rising Sun sounds like al-Rāzī when he states that 'a useless man should die when he is born' (WRG 146). While wisdom can be acquired, intelligence is God-given.[33] Quite conveniently, a virtuous disposition is also visible in a person's physical beauty. Full Moon 'was a young man, of quiet demeanor, intelligent, and wise of heart. His face was of dazzling beauty, his speech was soft, charm poured from his tongue' (WRG 55). The prince is expected to be upright, God-fearing, devout, calm, modest, honest, wakeful, just, brave, bold, steadfast, generous, humble and compassionate, but also handsome and trim (WRG 103–8).

With the introduction of Wide Awake, the *Kutadgu Bilig* takes a curious turn for a mirror for princes. The realm to which the practical advice of the first part pertains is relegated to a secondary position and only of interest because it benefits the masses. Even though Highly Praised is superseded by Wide Awake, who represents man's last end, the arguments for this view on morality are entirely rational. The message of the *Kutadgu Bilig* resembles that of Miskawayh: even though our ultimate happiness lies beyond this world, we have to do our duty by our fellow humans, especially if we have the mental, moral and material resources to do so. 'Strive to be good, O king, for the people are good in the measure that their ruler is. The people are like sheep and their ruler, their shepherd. The shepherd must have compassion for his flock' (WRG 85).

IBN ṬUFAYL (1105–1185)

About a century later, Ibn Ṭufayl made similar points at the opposite end of the Islamic world. Several Andalusi philosophers authored important works about ethics. Ibn Ḥazm (994–1064) wrote a book on virtues, vices, knowledge, love, friendship and other moral topics.[34] Ibn Bājja (1095–1138)

---

[33] Yūsuf Khāṣṣ Ḥājib 1983: 68 and 94–5, 98–9. Similarly Miskawayh, Adamson 2007c: 44.
[34] Abu Laylah 1990.

developed a rather negative view of contemporary human society in his *Rule of the Solitary* and *Farewell Message*. Rather than focusing, like al-Fārābī, on how a virtuous city allows its citizens a virtuous and happy life, he realized that the cities of his time were all corrupt and that a happy life was possible in isolation only.[35] Ibn Rushd (1126–1198) composed a commentary on the *Nicomachean Ethics* which is preserved in Latin and Hebrew translations.[36]

Ibn Ṭufayl's only preserved philosophical work sticks out because of its literary form and mystical twist. He begins by addressing a friend who had asked him about esoteric knowledge. While he is unable to describe the knowledge acquired during a mystical journey, Ibn Ṭufayl is able to offer a second-best account of the truth, which uses philosophical language. He then tells the story of the text's eponym, Ḥayy ibn Yaqẓān ('Alive, Son of Awake'), who grows up on an island uninhabited by other humans. While he learns practical skills during his early childhood by imitating other animals, his rational mind awakens when his deer mother dies and he cannot solve the problem of her demise. As he becomes older, Ḥayy ibn Yaqẓān abstracts and theorizes, drawing all the right conclusions about the nature of his self, the world, the heavenly bodies and God. Once he has realized that thinking about God provides pleasure and happiness, he imitates the heavenly bodies. He avoids killing animals and provides water for plants. This post-humanist care is reminiscent of al-Rāzī and representative of Ḥayy's entire attitude to other creatures. Taneli Kukkonen has read this disposition of Ḥayy as a reflection of Ibn Ṭufayl's Neoplatonic cosmology and larger causalities at work in the universe.[37] Ḥayy's impulse of kindness towards other creatures can also be read as a display of empathy, a subject of interest to primatologists.[38] Such a recognition of the suffering of another sentient being is obvious in the first encounter with Absāl, a man from another island, who seeks refuge on Ḥayy's island from his narrow-minded literalist compatriots. Full of curiosity, Ḥayy chases and tackles the other man, but realizes from his behaviour that Absāl is afraid. 'He could make out the signs of fright and did his best to put the other at ease with a variety of animal cries he knew. Ḥayy also patted his head, rubbed his sides and spoke soothingly to him, trying to show how delighted he was with him. Eventually Absāl's trepidation died down and he realized that Ḥayy did not mean him any harm.'[39]

---

[35] Translation by Lawrence Berman in Lerner and Mahdi 1963: 122–33. See also Harvey 1992.
[36] See Zonta 2003: 195–6. [37] Kukkonen 2008. [38] De Waal 2009.
[39] Ibn Ṭufayl 2009: 159.

After some effort to establish communication, Absāl realizes that Ḥayy has developed a pure approach to the divine. They return to Absāl's island, but fail to convince the local scholars of their path. Frustrated, they seek happiness in isolation on Ḥayy's island. Ibn Ṭufayl's conclusion resembles that of Ibn Bājja: virtuous and happy life requires withdrawal from the corrupting influence of society. Unlike Ibn Bājja, however, and somewhat like Yūsuf of Balasagun, Ibn Ṭufayl envisages this supreme level of knowledge as holding up to rational argument as well as to superior spiritual principles, which have a clearly mystical character for the latter.

CONCLUSIONS

The authors introduced here represent prominent trends of moral philosophy in the medieval Islamicate world: the combination of Platonic and Neoplatonic theories of the soul with Aristotelian views on humans as 'political animals', philosophy as the key to happiness and as preparation for the afterlife or the *imitatio Dei* as ultimate human purpose, lists of virtues and vices and their positive and detrimental effects. They reflect some differences too, such as divergent views on social obligations or on piety.

Among the many areas for future research, some concern the larger context of philosophical discourses on morality. How do they relate to other contemporary views on ethics and morality? For all authors, we can assume that more explicitly Islamic or Christian views marked the predominant discourse on morality and ethics. (The same is true for Jewish authors such as Maimonides, who partook in the same tradition.) Al-Rāzī is one of the few authors who did not subscribe to such a framework and the terminology he used for his moral philosophy suggests that he tried to challenge normative systems based on revelation.[40] The position of philosophical ethics within Islamicate literature has been the subject of several publications.[41] Issues of morality, however, were not monopolized by scholars. As Michael Meeker has pointed out, for example, the epic stories of the Turks known as the *Book of Dede Korkut* clearly reflect ethical principles of tribal life.[42] While Meeker sees personal values at stake in individual heroic actions, which are often aggressive, these also need to be compatible with social values, emotional bonds and cohesion within society. Dede Korkut's stories deal with the resulting conflicts, ending with trust in God and reintegration of the tribe.

[40] Druart 1993b: 170 and 181.   [41] See note 2 above.
[42] Meeker 1992. For Persian literature see de Fouchécour 1986.

While such traditions do not theorize about morals, they are important parts of the larger tapestry of ethical thought in the medieval Islamicate world.

BIBLIOGRAPHY

The Arabic prefix 'Al-' is ignored for the purposes of alphabetization.

An asterisk denotes secondary literature especially suitable for further reading.

Abu Laylah, Muhammad 1990. *In Pursuit of Virtue. The Moral Theology and Psychology of Ibn Hazm al-Andalusi [384–456 AH/994–1064 AD] with a Translation of his Book Al-Akhlaq wa'l-Siyar*. London: TaHa.

Adamson, Peter 2007a. *Al-Kindī*. Oxford University Press.

Adamson, Peter 2007b. 'Stoic, Cynic, Platonic: al-Kindī's Version of Socrates', in Trapp, M.B. (ed.), *Socrates, from Antiquity to the Enlightenment*. Aldershot: Ashgate, pp. 161–78.

Adamson, Peter 2007c. 'Miskawayh's Psychology', in Adamson, Peter (ed.), *Classical Arabic Philosophy. Sources and Reception*. London: The Warburg Institute, pp. 39–54.

Akasoy, Anna and Fidora, Alexander (eds.) 2005. *The Arabic Version of the Nicomachean Ethics*, With an Introduction and Annotated English Translation by Douglas M. Dunlop. Leiden: Brill.

Arkoun, Mohammed 1982. *Contribution à l'étude de l'humanisme arabe au IVe/Xe siècle: Miskawayh, philosophe et historien (320/325–421) = (932/936–1030)*. Paris: Vrin.

Bar-Asher, Meir M. 1989. 'Quelques aspects de l'éthique d'Abu Bakr al-Razi et ses origines dans l'oeuvre de Galien', *Studia Islamica* 69: 5–38 and 70: 130–47.

Daiber, Hans 1996. 'Political Philosophy', in Nasr, Seyyed H. and Leaman, Oliver (eds.), *History of Islamic Philosophy*, vol. 2, London: Routledge, pp. 841–85.

D'Ancona, Cristina 1998. 'Al-Kindī on the Subject-matter of the First Philosophy. Direct and Indirect Sources of *Falsafa al-ūlā*, Chapter One', in Aertsen, Jan A. and Speer, Andreas (eds.), *Was ist Philosophie im Mittelalter?* Berlin and New York: Walter de Gruyter, pp. 841–55.

de Fouchécour, Charles-Henri 1986. *Moralia. Les notions morales dans la littérature persane du 3e/9e au 7e/13e siècle*. Paris: Éditions recherche sur les civilisations.

De Waal, Frans 2009. *Primates and Philosophers. How Morality Evolved*. Princeton University Press.

Donaldson, Dwight M. 1953. *Studies in Muslim Ethics*. London: S.P.C.K.

Doufikar-Aerts, Faustina 2010. *Alexander Magnus Arabicus. A Survey of the Alexander Tradition through Seven Centuries: from Pseudo-Callisthenes to Ṣūrī*. Paris: Peeters.

Druart, Thérèse-Anne 1993a. 'Al-Kindi's Ethics', *Review of Metaphysics* 47: 329–57.

Druart, Thérèse-Anne 1993b. 'Al-Razi (Rhazes) and Normative Ethics', in Boileau, David and Dick, John A. (eds.), *Tradition and Renewal. Philosophical Essays Commemorating the Centennial of Louvain's Institute of Philosophy*, vol. 2, Leuven University Press, pp. 167–81.*

Fakhry, Majid 1975a. 'Justice in Islamic Philosophical Ethics: Miskawayh's Mediating Contribution', *Journal of Religious Ethics* 3: 143–54.

Fakhry, Majid 1975b. 'The Platonism of Miskawayh and its Implications for his Ethics', *Studia Islamica* 42: 39–57.

Fakhry, Majid 1991. *Ethical Theories in Islam*. Leiden: Brill.*

Al-Fārābī 1985. *Al-Farabi on the Perfect State. Abū Naṣr al-Fārābī's Mabādi ᵓ ārā ᵓ ahl al-madīna al-fāḍila*. A Revised Text with Introduction, Translation, and Commentary by Richard Walzer. Oxford: Clarendon Press.

Al-Fārābī 1996. *Iḥsā ᵓ al-ᶜulūm*. Ed. ᶜAlī Bū Malḥam. Beirut: Dār wa-Maktabat al-Hilāl.

Goodman, Lenn 1996. 'Friendship in Aristotle, Miskawayh and al-Ghazali', in Leaman, Oliver (ed.), *Friendship East and West: Philosophical Perspectives*. Richmond: Curzon, pp. 164–91.

Griffith, Sidney 2003. 'The "Philosophical Life" in Tenth-Century Baghdad: The Contribution of Yaḥyā ibn ᶜAdī's *Kitāb Tahdhīb al-Akhlāq*', in Thomas, David (ed.), *Christians at the Heart of Islamic Rule. Church Life and Scholarship in ᶜAbbasid Iraq*, Leiden: Brill, pp. 129–49.

Gutas, Dimitri 1983. 'Paul the Persian on the Classification of the Parts of Aristotle's Philosophy: A Milestone between Alexandria and Baġdād', *Der Islam* 60: 231–67.

Gutas, Dimitri 1990. 'Ethische Schriften im Islam', in Heinrichs, Wolfhart (ed.), *Orientalisches Mittelalter*, Wiesbaden: AULA, pp. 346–65.*

Gutas, Dimitri 1997. Review of Fakhry 1991, *Journal of the American Oriental Society* 117: 171–5.

Gutas, Dimitri 2004. 'The Meaning of *Madanī* in al-Fārābī's "Political" Philosophy', *Mélanges de l'Université Saint Joseph* 67: 259–83.

Harvey, Stephen 1992. 'The Place of the Philosopher in the City according to Ibn Bājja', in Butterworth, C.E. (ed.), *The Political Aspects of Islamic Philosophy. Essays in Honor of M.S. Mahdi*. Cambridge: Harvard University Press, pp. 199–233.

Hodgson, Marshall G.S. 1974. *The Venture of Islam. Conscience and History in a World Civilization*, vol. 1, *The Classical Age of Islam*. Chicago University Press.

Hourani, George F. 1971. *Islamic Rationalism. The Ethics of ᶜAbd al-Jabbār*. Oxford: Clarendon Press.

Hourani, George F. 1975. 'Ethics in Medieval Islam: A Conspectus', in Hourani, George F. (ed.), *Essays on Islamic Philosophy and Science*. Albany: State University of New York Press, pp. 128–35.

Ibn ᶜAdī, Yaḥyā 2002. *The Reformation of Morals*, A Parallel Arabic–English Edition, Translated and Introduced by Sidney H. Griffith. Provo: Brigham Young University Press.

Ibn Ṭufayl 2009, *Ibn Tufayl's Hayy ibn Yaqzan. A Philosophical Tale*, Translated with an Introduction and Notes by Lenn Evan Goodman. University of Chicago Press.

Klein-Franke, Felix 1979. 'The Arabic Version of Galen's Περὶ ἐθῶν', *Jerusalem Studies in Arabic and Islam* 1: 125–40.

Kraemer, Joel L. 1993. *Humanism in the Renaissance of Islam. The Cultural Revival during the Buyid Age*, 2nd edn. Leiden: Brill.

Kukkonen, Taneli 2008. 'No Man is an Island. Nature and Neo-platonic Ethics in Hayy ibn Yaqẓān', *Journal of the History of Philosophy* 46: 187–204.*

Lerner, Ralph and Mahdi, Muhsin 1963. *Medieval Political Philosophy. A Sourcebook*. Toronto: The Free Press of Glencoe.

Madelung, Wilferd 1985. 'Naṣīr ad-Dīn Ṭūsī's Ethics between Philosophy, Shiᶜism and Sufism', in Hovannisian, Richard G. (ed.), *Ethics in Islam*. Malibu: Undena, pp. 85–101.

Marcotte, Roxanne D. 2012. 'Ibn Miskawayh's *Tartīb al-Saᶜādāt* (The Order of Happiness)', in Langermann, Y. Tzvi (ed.), *Monotheism and Ethics. Historical and Contemporary Intersections among Judaism, Christianity, and Islam*. Leiden: Brill, pp. 141–61.

McGinnis, Jon and Reisman, David C. 2007. *Classical Arabic Philosophy. An Anthology of Sources*, Translated with Introduction, Notes, and Glossary. Indianapolis: Hackett.

Meeker, Michael E. 1992. 'The Dede Korkut Ethic', *International Journal of Middle East Studies* 24: 395–417.

Miskawayh 1964. *An Unpublished Treatise of Miskawaih on Justice or Risāla fī Māhīyat al-ʿAdl li-Miskawaih*, ed. and trans. M.S. Khan. Leiden: Brill.

Miskawayh 1968. *The Refinement of Character. A Translation from the Arabic of Aḥmad ibn-Muḥammad Miskawayh's Tahdhīb al-akhlāq*, trans. Constantine K. Zurayk. American University of Beirut.*

Ramón Guerrero, Rafael 2011. 'Ethics, Arabic', in Lagerlund, Henrik (ed.), *Encyclopedia of Medieval Philosophy: Philosophy from 500 to 1500*. Dordrecht: Springer, pp. 317–23.

Rosenthal, Franz 1994. *The Classical Heritage in Islam*. London: Routledge. (Originally published 1975.)

Rundgren, Frithiof 1976. 'Das Muxtaṣar min Kitāb al'Axlāq des Galenos. Einige Bemerkungen', *Orientalia Suecana* 23–4: 84–105.

Al-Ṭūsī, Naṣīr al-Dīn 1964. *The Nasirean Ethics*, trans. G.M. Wickens. London: Allen & Unwin.

Ullmann, Manfred 2011–2012. *Die Nikomachische Ethik des Aristoteles in arabischer Übersetzung*, 2 vols. Wiesbaden: Harrassowitz Verlag.

Yūsuf Khāṣṣ Ḥājib 1983. *Wisdom of Royal Glory. A Turko-Islamic Mirror for Princes*, Translated, with an Introduction and Notes by Robert Dankoff. University of Chicago Press.

Zonta, Mauro 2003. 'Les éthiques. Tradition syriaque et arabe', in Goulet, Richard (ed.), *Dictionnaire des philosophes antiques*, Supplément. Paris: Éditions du Centre National de la Recherche scientifique, pp. 191–8.*

13

"Christian Aristotelianism"?
Albert the Great and Thomas Aquinas

TOBIAS HOFFMANN AND JÖRN MÜLLER

The development of moral philosophy in Scholasticism was tremendously shaped by the reception of Aristotle's *EN*.[1] Its complete translation into Latin by Robert Grosseteste around 1246/1247 sparked significant interest in moral philosophy among medieval theologians, and marked a new beginning of ethics as a philosophical discipline from the second half of the thirteenth century onwards (see Wieland 1982). But this forceful re-entry of Aristotle was bound to produce tensions because it clashed in several areas with traditional moral theology in the vein of Augustine. The most noteworthy differences concerned the attainability of happiness in this life, the character of the virtues (either natural or supernatural), and the normative foundation of moral precepts (theocentric or anthropocentric).

Albert the Great (1200–1280) and his student Thomas Aquinas (1225–1274) tried to come to terms with Aristotelian philosophy in general and with the *Nicomachean Ethics* in particular, on which they both wrote commentaries. Therefore, they are usually credited with being the founding fathers of "Christian Aristotelianism." But this label tends to blur the nuanced differences in their individual appropriation of Aristotle's ethics and to obscure the complexity of their own conceptions of morality. In what follows, we will pay particular attention to the question of how they conceived of the relationship between philosophical ethics and moral theology with regard to the three challenges mentioned above. This also involves a closer look at the way in which they elaborate on Aristotle's account by drawing on other philosophical (above all Stoic and Neoplatonic) sources. At the end, we will provide a meta-ethical evaluation of their positions.

---

[1] Abbreviations used in this chapter: *EN* = Aristotle, *Nicomachean Ethics*; *Eth.* = Albert the Great, *Ethica*; *SE* = Albert the Great, *Super Ethica* (1968–1972); *ST* = Aquinas, *Summa theologiae*.

ALBERT THE GREAT: ETHICS AS A PRACTICAL SCIENCE AND THE HAPPINESS OF THE PHILOSOPHERS

Albert the Great commented on the *Nicomachean Ethics* twice: in 1250–1252 (*Super Ethica*, 1968–1972) and in 1262 (*Ethica*, 1891 and 2002). This in itself attests to the significance the *EN* had for Albert. In both commentaries he intends not simply to elucidate the meaning of Aristotle's text but also to develop a truly philosophical ethics, one which would offer a view of morality wholly independent of any religious or theological commitments. This endeavor stands in marked contrast to the pre-1250 commentaries on earlier partial translations of the *Nicomachean Ethics*, which produced a grossly harmonizing theological reading of Aristotelian key concepts like happiness (see Celano 1986 and Celano 2016, ch. 4).

The first step in Albert's moral project is to secure a domain in which philosophical ethics is wholly competent on its own. Therefore, he distinguishes neatly between theological and philosophical virtues with regard to their efficient and final cause: while theological virtues are infused directly by God (*virtutes infusae*) and are exercised for His sake, philosophical virtues owe their existence to human actions as their immediate cause (e.g. teaching or habituation) and are exercised by the agent in order to achieve personal happiness. Albert separates these two areas of discourse consistently by using the phrases "speaking theologically" (*loquendo theologice*) and "speaking philosophically" or "ethically" (*loquendo philosophice/ethice*). This difference of perspective even accounts for opposite judgments: whereas in the area of natural morality lying does not necessarily harm acquired virtue, it is always harmful from the theological standpoint (*SE* 4.14, pp. 288–9). Albert certainly does not intend to set up philosophical ethics as a competitor to moral theology, but he maintains that their statements are ultimately incommensurable (see Tracey 1999: 33–65). Thus theological views can never be the epistemological touchstone or even the criterion of truth for philosophical ethics, which enjoys at least a partial autonomy in the domain of natural morality. This includes everything which is in man's own power without supernatural grace and which can be understood on the basis of natural reason, without divine illumination or revelation.

In a second step, Albert underpins this autonomous status of philosophical ethics with innovative scientific considerations concerning the subject, method, character, and aim of this discipline.[2] The principal problem he

---

[2] Cf. *SE*, prol., pp. 1–4; *Eth.* 1.1.1–7, critically edited in Müller 2001: 308–58. For a detailed analysis of these texts see ibid., 256–307.

addresses is whether there can be a science of ethics, since it has to deal with contingent and ever-changing human actions which seem to be devoid of the universality and necessity required for scientific demonstrations. Albert solves this problem by distinguishing between moral phenomena in their real existence (*mos secundum id quod est*) and their underlying essential and conceptual structure (*mos secundum rationem et intentionem*). A particular token of bravery, say that of Achilles, cannot be the subject of science in the strict sense, but it can be regarded as an essential type, namely the virtue of fortitude. Fortitude itself is a universal species of moral dispositions to which specific differences and properties (like holding the mean with regard to fear and confidence) necessarily belong. Furthermore, the generic notion of virtue itself can be subdivided into the species of moral, intellectual, heroic, etc. virtues. Albert frequently compares the ethicist to the natural philosopher because both have to identify unchanging forms which are universal in a world of ever-changing enmattered particulars (*SE* 8.7, p. 619). The conceptual scheme which emerges from this analysis allows for scientific demonstrations as the basis of a moral doctrine satisfying the high scientific standards of Aristotle's *Posterior Analytics*. As a science of the principles of ethics, which Albert calls an *ethica docens*, it produces genuine syllogistic proofs based on necessary premises and is therefore completely precise. Albert is thus even more ambitious than Aristotle himself, who thought ethics was a science that can only be done "in outline" (*tupôi*), ultimately lacking the precision of the theoretical disciplines (*EN* 1.3.1094b19–27).

But being a practical science (*scientia practica*), ethics does not consist solely of this demonstrative part but also contains an *ethica utens*, i.e. an applied and action-guiding ethics. This part of ethics proceeds on a persuasive basis (*modus persuasorius*) and comes closer to rhetoric in that it uses incomplete syllogisms and examples. Consequently, *ethica utens* will not produce exceptionless moral principles but rather rules of thumb, which are closer to particular actions than the universal principles of *ethica docens* while lacking the latter's scientific exactness, since they only hold in most cases (*ut in pluribus*).

This obvious gap between *ethica docens* and *utens* calls for a disposition in the soul which partakes in both and possesses the ability to apply their rules correctly to the particular situations. This role is fulfilled by the virtue of prudence (*prudentia*). Its most important task is to determine the mean of the ethical virtues and to "inform" them with it in concrete situations. Thus prudence ensures that the ethical universals are adequately put into practice. This requires experience in moral matters as well as a firm grasp of the universal norms of human behavior. These are accessible to prudence as a kind of innate knowledge of the principles of natural law (*ius naturale*) which are to be applied by it (see Payer 1979). Albert closely links natural law to the classical notion of conscience in that they guide us in similar ways: both produce particular judgments based on universal principles, following the scheme of Aristotle's practical syllogism, e.g.:

Fornication is to be avoided.
Sleeping with this woman would be an act of fornication.
Sleeping with this woman is to be avoided.

The competence of prudence not only pertains to both premises but also to the conclusion, which is a practical judgment (*sententia*) and an action-guiding rational order (*imperium*) given by prudence to the other powers of the soul. Because prudence is concerned with universals as well as with particulars, it is itself twofold, *docens* and *utens*, and constitutes a perfect "operative knowledge" (*scientia operativa*). In the final analysis, prudence is in a kind of middle state between the moral and the intellectual virtues (*Eth.* 6.4.1, Albert the Great 1891: 456b). Accordingly, Albert sums up the practical character of ethics: "It is not possible to act well without moral virtue, but moral virtue cannot be had without prudence, which in turn is instructed by moral teaching. Thus it is not possible to act well without moral doctrine (*doctrina moralis*)" (*SE* 10.17, p. 778). This underscores the importance of *ethica docens* for the full development of the moral life.

The main subject of ethics as a practical science is happiness and how it is to be achieved. Following Aristotle's approach, Albert distinguishes two forms of happiness:

(1) Civil happiness (*felicitas civilis*) is constituted by the act of prudence in its role of ordering the complete moral life. Albert views the civil life as an ordered whole in which the external goods are solely instrumental and the moral virtues only dispose towards prudence and its activity as the pinnacle of the moral life (*SE* 6.17, p. 499).

(2) Contemplative happiness (*felicitas contemplativa*) is a higher form of human perfection since it pertains to our intellect, the highest part in us. In this activity the human being is able to have an immediate knowledge of separate (i.e. immaterial) substances, that is, God and angels, which constitute the realm of the highest intelligible beings. Especially in his second commentary, Albert ascribes this beatific contemplation to the highest stage the human intellect can reach in this lifetime, namely the "acquired intellect" (*intellectus adeptus*), which has a direct knowledge of separate substances without any

need of abstraction from sense-impressions or imaginations (*Eth.* 10.2.3–4, Albert the Great 1891: 628a–632a). This doctrine of the acquired intellect, which is foreign to the *EN* and for which Albert draws heavily on Arabic sources like al-Fārābī, Avicenna, and Averroes, links psychology, epistemology, and ethics in a quite sophisticated manner (see Müller 2006). It proved to be very influential for a wide-ranging variety of later Latin thinkers, from the so-called Averroists or radical Aristotelians in the Parisian Arts faculty, like Siger of Brabant, to the German Dominican school of the fourteenth century, such as Dietrich of Freiberg (see de Libera 1990: 215–66).

The focal point of Albert's doctrine of speculative happiness that sparked this tremendous reception was the idea that this kind of contemplation constituted a substantial realization of this-worldly happiness. While many of his predecessors and contemporaries in ethics adhered to Augustine's belief that "all men are necessarily miserable as long as they are mortal" (*De civitate Dei* 9.15) and thus relegated happiness entirely to the afterlife, Albert transformed Aristotle's notion of the theoretical life with the help of the *intellectus adeptus* into a kind of beatific vision of the higher intelligible entities. He argued that it lacked nothing in itself and was therefore complete (or even perfect) in its worldly order, thus freeing this happiness from all theological constraints. The gist is that the acquired intellect and the happiness stemming from it are not to be understood as gifts of supernatural grace but as the crowning achievement that supervenes on a life spent in the study of philosophy. In this way, Albert not only establishes ethics as a practical science but also forcefully reinvigorates the ancient idea of doing philosophy as a way of life (see Bianchi 1987).

Albert's innovative understanding of human happiness is ultimately based upon a mind–body dualism in which "man, insofar as he is man, is only intellect" (*Eth.* 9.2.1, Albert the Great 1891: 571b). This prompts Albert to counsel that everything else ought only to be done for the sake of the (acquired) intellect, and nothing for our body or for the rest of the soul that is still connected with the material world. This does not sit too well with Aristotle's hylomorphic anthropology, according to which the rational soul is not an independent substance but the form of the living human body. It lends his philosophical ethics a very intellectualist touch, which can be spotted in different areas.

First, the civil life and its happiness is in the end completely subordinate to contemplative happiness. Possessing sufficient external resources, having the moral virtues, and being guided in their activity by prudence are thus necessary requirements for achieving the acquired intellect, but they are not an essential part of the fulfillment of human nature in its highest (i.e. intellectual) part. This exclusivism of Albert's intellectual happiness as the single aim of human life is accompanied by the loss of the organic unity between ethics and politics so dear to Aristotle.

Second, Albert tends to limit the contribution of the non-rational parts of the soul to the moral life. In his theory of natural law, he deliberately turns away from any biological impulses stressed in the preceding tradition and views natural law (*ius naturale*) basically as a law of reason (*ius rationis*) which has to impose a rational order on the sensual powers of the soul.

Third, in his theory of virtue, Albert ends up replacing Aristotle's moral virtues with Plotinus's "virtues of the purged mind" (*virtutes purgati animi*), which do not moderate the passions but rather extirpate them in Stoic fashion (see Müller 2001: 192–8). Especially in his *Ethica*, Albert thus portrays the happy man as a kind of ascetic who focuses completely on his intellectual development and despises sensuality.

These intellectualist tendencies offer ample evidence for the hypothesis that Albert's philosophical ethics is, despite its heavy reliance on the *Nicomachean Ethics* in its mode of procedure and its key concepts, rather a Platonizing approach in Aristotelian disguise. It is an important part of a larger cosmological project on which Albert was focused from his early *De bono* onwards (see Cunningham 2008, esp. 93–111), namely the development of a comprehensive Neo-Platonic metaphysics of goodness as a framework for the notion of the specific human good (*Eth.* 1.2.1–7, Albert the Great 2002). In this conception, man's cognition of the highest intelligible realm in contemplative happiness is at the same time a return to its first source from which the human intellect initially came (see Anzulewicz and Rigo 2002). The acquired intellect thus constitutes, as Albert repeatedly claims, the "root of immortality" (*radix immortalitatis*, *Eth.* 1.6.6, Albert the Great 1891: 92b), and Aristotelian moral philosophy ends up being drafted into the service of a Platonizing view of the universe as an overarching intellectual order. Nevertheless, Albert is to be credited as the first Scholastic thinker who developed a truly free-standing view of natural morality deliberately conceived as independent from theology.

THOMAS AQUINAS: TWOFOLD HAPPINESS, NATURAL LAW, AND PRUDENCE

Aquinas's appropriation of the *Nicomachean Ethics* is not limited to his own commentary on it (*Sententia libri Ethicorum*; written around 1271/1272) but extends to large portions of his theological writings (see Hoffmann, Müller, and Perkams 2013). Although Aquinas's understanding of Aristotle was certainly influenced by his teacher's views as they were laid down in Albert's *Super Ethica* (which was edited by Aquinas himself), there are some notable differences between the ways in which they make use of Aristotelian concepts.

A major discrepancy between them concerns the notion of the final end: while Albert the Great emphasizes the attainability of happiness for human beings already before death, Aquinas explicitly labels Aristotle's ideal of the philosophical life in this world as an "incomplete" or "imperfect happiness" which is only a foreshadowing or a beginning of the true and perfect happiness (*beatitudo perfecta*) enjoyed by the blessed in the afterlife (*Summa contra Gentiles* 3.48; *ST* 1–2.5.3). The highest aim of human nature is the beatific vision of God in and through his essence, but this activity can only be realized after death and with the aid of supernatural grace.[3] This different understanding of the scope of worldly beatitude is ultimately due to substantial epistemological and anthropological differences between him and his teacher, in which Aquinas sticks closer to an Aristotelian hylomorphic vision of man as a composite of soul and body than does the rather dualist-minded Albert (see Steel 2001).

Aquinas thinks that his understanding of perfect happiness in the afterlife as the fulfillment of the human quest for happiness is ultimately compatible with Aristotelian ethics and results implicitly from Aristotle's own claim in his *Metaphysics* (1.1.980a21) that "all men by nature desire to know." This thirst for knowledge can only be completely quenched by the perfect vision of the highest intelligible object and the ultimate truth, i.e. God's essence, and this ideal must be attainable because "nature does nothing in vain" and hence does not instill in man a pointless desire. But Aquinas very consciously avoids "baptizing" Aristotle by directly ascribing to him this Christian understanding of the happy afterlife (*Scriptum super libros Sententiarum* 4.49.1.1.4). On the contrary, Aquinas's own conception of happiness is explicitly intended as an elaboration of Aristotle's purely natural or philosophic ethics by means of theological speculation. Since according to Aquinas grace does not destroy but rather perfects nature, theological ethics does not completely subvert moral philosophy but rather completes it. By seeing God, man finally participates fully in the divine good. Human happiness thus becomes part of an overarching metaphysical framework in which all creatures ultimately

---

[3] For this highly complex and controversial topic see Bradley 1997, esp. ch. 9, and Feingold 2010.

strive for God as the highest end by realizing the particular goals inscribed in their nature (see *Summa contra Gentiles* 3.2–3 and 3.16–24; *ST* 1-2.2.8).

As Aquinas's doctrine of happiness already shows, his ethics emphasizes strongly that there is a fundamental order within which human beings seek their good. What the human good consists in is set by human nature, independently of a person's individual makeup, preferences, history, and particular practical considerations. At the same time, Aquinas makes room for subjective criteria for good and evil in a way that was original in his time.

How am I to act? Aquinas starts answering this question by pointing to the most general guidelines of human action, which in his view are offered by natural law. All the so-called precepts of the natural law are based upon the statement that "the good is to be done and to be pursued, and evil to be avoided." This "first principle in practical reason" is self-evident to those who have an adequate grasp of its terms. The notions of "good" and "end" coincide: the good is an end which one pursues or should pursue. Most fundamentally, we desire happiness, but in order to know how we should act we need more particular principles. The human good is constituted by various more specific goods. What these are is not discoverable by means of a purely conceptual analysis, say, of the notion of happiness and the definition of the human being. Nonetheless, we need to know something about human nature in order to know what the more specific human goods consist in: we have to know what human beings are ordered towards by nature. For Aquinas, this is revealed in man's "natural inclinations" (*inclinationes naturales*). Some of his examples are the inclinations to conserve one's being, to sexual union, and education of the offspring, to know the truth about God, to live in society, and to act according to reason. The human goods revealed in these inclinations, then, are life itself, the propagation of life, knowledge of truth, communal life, and a life governed by reason, which is a virtuous life. Since one must do good and avoid evil, everything that promotes these goods is to be done and what harms them is to be avoided (*ST* 1-2.94.2–3). Accordingly one arrives at positive precepts, such as to take care of one's offspring, as well as negative precepts, such as to avoid ignorance. Aquinas calls these the precepts of the natural law.

Aquinas's theory of natural law thus has two foundations. One is human nature with its natural inclinations that point to the things that by nature are our ends, the human goods. The other is reason, which understands the self-evident principle that good is to be done and evil to be avoided, and which discovers the human goods, that is, the genuine ends to which the natural inclinations point. In Aquinas, then, the fundamental ethical principles are rooted in a law of nature, and not merely in a law of reason as they are for Albert.[4] For Aquinas, natural law itself has an even more fundamental foundation in the "eternal law." The eternal law regulates the entire universe, which is subject to divine providence. Natural law is "the participation of rational creatures in the eternal law." It is thanks to the eternal law that all things receive inclinations "to their proper acts and ends" (*ST* 1-2.91.1–2). This explains the foundational role of the natural inclinations for natural law, for they express the divine intention regarding which ends humans are to seek and attain.

The bridge from the general principles of morality, which are the precepts of the natural law, to concrete action here and now, is made in one way by conscience and in another by prudence. Aquinas holds that each human being has a fundamental moral awareness, called "*sunderesis*," of the general principles of the natural law (*De veritate* 16.1, *ST* 1-2.94.1 ad 2). A judgment of conscience consists in the application of a general principle to the concrete case, which Aquinas, just like Albert, describes by means of a practical syllogism. While the awareness of the general principles is infallible, its application can be erroneous. But even when one's conscience is mistaken, e.g., when one falsely thinks that one is obliged to commit this act of fornication, conscience "binds," that is, one must not act against it. For if one did, one would act contrary to what one thinks is good. Yet an erring conscience is not necessarily excused, for it may be one's own fault that it is insufficiently or falsely informed. But contrary to his own contemporaries, Aquinas allows for the possibility that, without fault, one may blamelessly do something that is objectively bad. Despite a general insistence on an objective order of what is good or evil, Aquinas thus also acknowledges subjective factors in moral evaluation (*ST* 1-2.19.5–6).

The complementarity of objective and subjective dimensions in ethics is even more pronounced in Aquinas's account of prudence. When he discusses the general moral principles which constitute the precepts of the natural law and which are dispositionally present in *sunderesis*, he emphasizes that these principles are known to us by nature and without error. But Aquinas distinguishes between two kinds of moral principles: general and particular. In practical matters, the principles are the ends that are or should be pursued.

---

[4] For overviews of Aquinas's theory of natural law, see Lisska 1996, Finnis 1998: 79–102, and Jensen 2015. Aquinas does not found his ethics in a metaphysics of the good, as does Albert, but it does have a metaphysical foundation in human nature with its natural inclinations. Mistaken conceptions of natural inclinations as felt urges or drives are corrected in Cunningham 2012.

While the universal practical principles, which concern the most general ends (e.g., to do the good; to shun ignorance), are known by nature and are incorruptible, the particular practical principles, which concern the end the individual pursues here and now, can be corrupted by passion (*ST* 1-2.58.5). Thus for the weak willed, the universal principle that good is to be pursued remains intact throughout, but the particular principle that now one should be temperate is corrupted because of sensual desire (*ST* 1-2.77.2). Prudence, which is the virtue of right reason in concrete actions, requires that both the universal principles and the particular principles be intact. Thus prudence is a very personal virtue: no one can substitute for the individual in the correct assessment of what is to be done here and now. The particular principle of action, that is, the proximate end pursued here and now, is kept intact by the moral virtues that order the individual's affections and that make it connatural to the individual to judge correctly about the proximate end (*ST* 1-2.58.5; *De veritate* 5.1; see also Hoffmann 2013).

Aquinas also expresses the relationship between the naturally given remote end and the affective conditions for a correct assessment of the proximate end in more general terms, in commenting on Aristotle's notion of practical truth. Aristotle makes practical truth – that is, truth concerned with action – depend on right desire (*EN* 6.2.1139a21–31). But it would seem that right desire itself needs to be measured by some standard of truth, and so Aristotle's conception of the relation between right desire and right judgment may appear to be circular. Aquinas escapes this dilemma by distinguishing between right desire for the ultimate end and right desire for that which promotes this end. The ultimate end of human action is determined by nature, as we have already seen in his account of happiness and of natural law. The truth of practical reason, then, is measured by the right desire toward the remote end which is given by nature. But the desire of the things that promote this end is measured by practical reason. So practical truth is measured by a right desire which in turn is measured by the end given by nature. For Aquinas, then, the ultimate criterion for morality is given with the nature of the human being and hence is universally the same, rather than assessed relative to the ideals of a particular culture.

Like Aristotle's ethics, Aquinas's ethics, too, is fundamentally eudaimonistic. His theory of happiness underlies the whole of his ethical writing. But whereas Aristotle does not have any explicit doctrine of natural law, Aquinas harmoniously integrates this doctrine into his ethics. His theory of natural law serves to further specify what the human good consists in and makes explicit the relation of ethics to human nature. But the greatest contribution of Aquinas's ethics consists not in a further elaboration of the foundation of ethics, but rather in his unrivaled account of moral virtues. Aquinas anchors his doctrine of virtue in both his theory of natural law and in his account of happiness. Since humans have a natural inclination to live according to reason, that is, to live virtuously, natural law orders one to practice all the virtues (*ST* 1-2.94.3). In accordance with his distinction of a twofold happiness, one consisting in activities within human capacities, the other exceeding human nature, Aquinas distinguishes between naturally acquired virtues that order humans toward each other and divinely infused virtues that order them towards God (*ST* 1-2.62.1).

ALBERT AND AQUINAS IN META-ETHICAL
AND HISTORICAL PERSPECTIVE

Viewed from the meta-ethical angle of contemporary philosophy, Albert's and Aquinas's moral theories share some significant features.

First, both thinkers are *moral cognitivists* in that they both rely on a notion of practical truth which can be grasped and put into practice by prudence.

Second, they conceive this moral truth as *objective* and *universalist*, i.e. valid for all human beings and societies. Normative claims are ultimately anchored in a metaphysical order of the whole universe; this proves sufficiently stable to safeguard thick ethical universals but still allows for a certain flexibility when it comes to particular rules and virtues under specific historical circumstances. These universals are the basis for the construction of a genuine moral science which clearly surpasses the rather weak methodological requirements that Aristotle himself postulated for ethics.

Third, both theories are *naturalist* in the sense that they are built on strong claims concerning the nature of man as well as the nature of the whole universe as created by God. But they differ in what they take to be the morally relevant essence of man. Albert favors a Platonizing version of man as an intellect which has to "acquire" itself by separating itself gradually from all corporeality. Aquinas, in contrast, favors a hylomorphic picture of man as a composite of soul and body and gives more weight to the non-intellectual elements of the human make-up, like emotions. This anthropological discrepancy profoundly affects their disagreement on several issues, ranging from their understanding of moral virtues to their conceptions of ethical principles. For example, Albert's purely rationalist version of natural law tends towards a direct derivation of moral norms from metaphysics, while

Aquinas inserts the natural inclinations as foundational for a genuine law of nature.

The most striking difference between their theories is their view of the relationship between philosophical ethics and theology. Albert very consciously establishes a separatist reading of natural and religious morality which explicitly safeguards the autonomy of philosophical ethics. Aquinas, by contrast, presents a unifying or complementary interpretation in which the philosophical analysis is ultimately subordinated to moral theology and cannot be truly separated from it and its purposes (see Bradley 1997). He uses Aristotle's ethics as a suitable starting-point for a broader theological inquiry into the nature of perfect happiness which is not limited by the bounds of natural reason. Thus his overall view of happiness proves to be decidedly eschatological. Consequently, in the concrete elaboration of his ethics centered on the cardinal virtues, he ends up paying little attention to the differences between naturally acquired and supernatural virtues, while Albert keeps them clearly separate.

Since neither of them tries to baptize Aristotle's ethics, the still widespread notion of Christian Aristotelianism is misleading as a common label for Albert's and Aquinas's moral theories. Both offer sophisticated emendations and elaborations of Aristotelian ideas with respect to the notions of virtue and happiness as well as regarding the construction of a genuine moral science based on universal practical principles. While Aquinas transcends Aristotle's concept of nature on the eschatological level, Albert operates from the start within a Platonizing frame of thought. These remarkable differences between student and teacher – as well as between them and Aristotle – bear witness to the complexities involved in discussing ethical Aristotelianism in the Middle Ages.

BIBLIOGRAPHY

An asterisk denotes secondary literature especially suitable for further reading.

Albert the Great 1891. *In X Ethicorum*, ed. Auguste Borgnet (Paris: Vivès).
Albert the Great 1968–1972. *Commentum et quaestiones super Ethica*, ed. Wilhelm Kübel (Münster: Aschendorff).
Albert the Great 2002. *Ethica*, Book 1, Treatise 2, in J. Müller (ed.), "Der Begriff des Guten im zweiten Ethikkommentar des Albertus Magnus," *Recherches de Théologie et Philosophie Médiévales*, 69 (2), 318–70.
Anzulewicz, H. and Rigo, C. 2002. "*Reductio ad esse divinum*: Zur Vollendung des Menschen nach Albertus Magnus," in J.A. Aertsen and M. Pickavé (eds.), *Ende und Vollendung: Eschatologische Perspektiven im Mittelalter* (Berlin: de Gruyter), 388–416.

Bianchi, L. 1987. "La felicità intellettuale come professione nella Parigi del Duecento," *Rivista di Filosofia*, 78, 181–99.

Bradley, D.J.M. 1997. *Aquinas on the Twofold Human Good: Reason and Happiness in Aquinas's Moral Science* (Washington, D.C.: The Catholic University of America Press).*

Celano, A.J. 1986. "The Understanding of the Concept of *felicitas* in the Pre-1250 Commentaries on the *Ethica Nicomachea*," *Medioevo*, 12, 29–53.

Celano, A.J. 2016. *Aristotle's Ethics and Medieval Philosophy: Moral Goodness and Practical Wisdom*. Cambridge University Press.

Cunningham, Sean B. 2012. "Aquinas on the Natural Inclination of Man to Offer Sacrifice to God," *Proceedings of the American Catholic Philosophical Association*, 86, 185–200.

Cunningham, Stanley B. 2008. *Reclaiming Moral Agency: The Moral Philosophy of Albert the Great* (Washington D.C.: The Catholic University of America Press).*

De Libera, A. 1990. *Albert le Grand et la philosophie* (Paris: Vrin).

Feingold, L. 2010. *The Natural Desire to See God according to St. Thomas Aquinas and His Interpreters*, 2nd edn (Ave Maria, Fla.: Sapientia Press).

Finnis, J. 1998. *Aquinas: Moral, Political, and Legal Theory* (Oxford University Press).

Hoffmann, T. 2013. "Prudence and Practical Principles," in Hoffmann, Müller, and Perkams 2013: 165–83.

Hoffmann, T., Müller, J., and Perkams, M. (eds.) 2013. *Aquinas and the Nicomachean Ethics* (Cambridge University Press).*

Jensen, S.J. 2015. *Knowing the Natural Law: From Precepts and Inclinations to Deriving Oughts* (Washington, D.C.: The Catholic University of America Press).*

Lisska, A.J. 1996. *Aquinas's Theory of Natural Law: An Analytic Reconstruction* (Oxford University Press).

Müller, J. 2001. *Natürliche Moral und philosophische Ethik bei Albertus Magnus* (Münster: Aschendorff).*

Müller, J. 2006. "Der Einfluss der arabischen Intellektspekulation auf die Ethik des Albertus Magnus," in A. Speer and L. Wegener (eds.), *Wissen über Grenzen* (Berlin: de Gruyter), 545–68.

Payer, P.J., 1979. "Prudence and the Principles of Natural Law: A Medieval Development," *Speculum*, 54, 55–70.

Steel, C. 2001. *Der Adler und die Nachteule: Thomas und Albert über die Möglichkeit der Metaphysik* (Münster: Aschendorff).

Tracey, M., 1999. "The Character of Aristotle's Nicomachean Teaching in Albert the Great's *Super Ethica Commentum et Quaestiones* (1250–1252)," PhD dissertation, University of Notre Dame.

Wieland, G. 1982. "The Reception and Interpretation of Aristotle's Ethics," in N. Kretzmann, A. Kenny, J. Pinborg, and E. Stump (eds.), *The Cambridge History of Later Medieval Philosophy* (Cambridge University Press), 657–72.

14

Duns Scotus and William of Ockham

TOBIAS HOFFMANN

Duns Scotus and William of Ockham, who are arguably the most prominent theologians of the fourteenth century, develop their moral theories within the intellectual tradition of Scholasticism, which is greatly indebted to Augustine and, from the thirteenth century onward, to Aristotle. While deeply embedded in this context, the moral theories of Scotus and Ockham are highly innovative and point in important ways to modernity. Although Ockham often takes issue with particular doctrines of Scotus, he shares with him important presuppositions and often sets up the questions in the same way. In particular, Scotus and Ockham are both concerned to go beyond the naturalistic tendencies of more Aristotelian moral theories such as that of Thomas Aquinas. This is especially manifest in their theories of the will, of virtue, and of normativity. Their virtue theory depends on how they conceive of the human will, while their normative theory depends on how they conceive of the divine will.[1] So I start by presenting their conception of the will and of its freedom.

THE WILL AND FREE WILL

The dominant conception of the will in the thirteenth century was that of a rational appetite, an Aristotelian concept transmitted to the Latin medievals by

I wish to thank Cyrille Michon and Thomas Osborne for helpful suggestions while writing this chapter.
[1] For good introductions to Scotus's and Ockham's ethics and action theory, see Möhle 2003, Williams 2003b, and Kent 2003 (on Scotus), as well as King 1999, Adams 1999, McGrade 1999 (on Ockham), Williams 2013, and Osborne 2014 (on Scotus and Ockham). Williams 2017 and Wolter 1997 provide translations (and Wolter also introductory expositions) of key texts by Scotus on moral psychology and ethics; Wood 1997 translates Ockham's most extensive treatment of the virtues and provides a historical and doctrinal introduction. Abbreviations of bibliographical references are listed at the end of the chapter.

way of the twelfth-century translation of John Damascene's *De fide orthodoxa* (Burgundionis versio 36.8–15). For Aquinas, the definition of the will as rational appetite implies that the will can only desire or choose what is known under the guise of the good (*Summa theologiae* [= *ST*] 1-2.8.1), and this in turn implies in his view that whatever one desires, one desires for the sake of happiness, which is the ultimate end of rational creatures (*ST* 1-2.1.6–7). While the will desires happiness necessarily, it does not desire or choose this or that particular good necessarily – unless it is manifest that happiness cannot be reached without it (*ST* 1.82.1–2; *ST* 1-2.10.2). Other thirteenth-century theologians writing before and after Aquinas are in fundamental agreement with him on these points. Scotus and Ockham, however, break with this teleological and eudaimonistic conception of the will. For Scotus, if the will were merely a rational appetite, it could not help pursuing happiness-maximization and hence it would not be free. Instead, the will has not just a natural inclination toward one's own happiness (*affectio commodi*), but moreover an inclination (or capacity) to affirm freely what is ethical in its own right (*affectio iustitiae*), even when it goes against one's happiness (*Ordinatio* [= *Ord.*] 2.6.2nn49–51, Vat. 8: 48–51). Although for Scotus it is not necessary that one desire happiness, one cannot desire to be miserable or not to be happy.[2] For Ockham, likewise, the will is not bound to desire happiness; not, however, because it has two complementary inclinations, but rather because it has no inclinations, strictly speaking (*In Sent.* 1.1.6, O: *OT* 1: 507; *In Sent.* 3.6, O: *OT* 6: 175–6). Ockham still holds that the will always acts for the sake of some end, but it freely sets its own end (*In Sent.* 1 prol. 10, O: *OT* 1: 291). In his view one can even desire not to be happy (*In Sent.* 1.1.6, O: *OT* 1: 503–7; *In Sent.* 4.16, O: *OT* 7: 350–3).

For Aquinas, the will is free precisely because it is a rational appetite, that is, because its desire or choice follows upon rational rather than merely sensory knowledge of goods. Thus the intellect can evaluate a particular good from different perspectives as either choiceworthy or not, and accordingly the will is free to choose it or not. The will in turn can move the intellect to exercise its act, that is, to think or stop thinking about something (e.g., *ST* 1-2.10.2, *De malo* 6). Scotus and Ockham reject the idea that the will's freedom derives from the intellect's knowledge or is consequent upon the interaction of intellect and will. For them, the intellect cannot be the cause of the will's freedom, because the intellect itself is not free; it does not control whether it understands something

---

[2] Scotus, *Lectura* 1.1.2.2n118, Vat. 16: 100; *Ord.* 1.1.2.2nn151–2, Vat. 2: 103–4 (here Scotus is somewhat hesitant); *Ord.* 4.49.1.6n354–5, Vat. 14: 378–9; *Quodlibet* 16nn22–4 in Scotus 2007: 170–1.

or not, or whether it assents to a proposition or dissents from it. To the extent that there is freedom in the intellect, it is derived from the will.[3] The will, in contrast, has immediate control of whether it elicits an act or its opposite, and it can choose either alternative under the exact same circumstances.[4] The will can even act contrary to the practical judgment about what is to be done here and now.[5] The will is unique in its ability to act differently under the same circumstances. All other causes or powers fall under the label of "nature": in a given set of circumstances, they act in one determinate way. Thus will and nature, or free and natural causes, are fundamentally distinct.[6] The upshot is that an individual has immediate control only of the act of the will; all other control, such as the control of the intellect or of bodily members, must be traced to the control exercised by the will.[7]

THE VIRTUES AND THEIR CONNECTION

At the heart of Aristotle's ethics are the moral virtues as stable dispositions (*hexeis*, in Latin *habitus*) that render us worthy individuals and that make us act well in every aspect of our lives. The point of life is to obtain the virtues, for our happiness consists in virtuous activity. The moral virtues go hand in hand with prudence, the intellectual virtue that concerns what is conducive to the good life as a whole. For Aristotle, prudence is a single intellectual virtue that directs all the moral virtues. Prudence in turn presupposes all the moral virtues because

---

[3] Scotus, *In Metaph.* 9.15nn36–41, Scotus 1997–2006 (hereafter S: *OP*), 4: 684–6; *Ord.* 4.49.1.4n240, Vat. 14: 351; Ockham, *Quaestiones variae* (hereafter QV), 7.3, in O: *OT* 8: 370; *In Perihermenias* 2.7§5, O: *OP* 2: 481; *In Sent.* 4.16, O: *OT* 7: 358–9.

[4] Scotus, *In Metaph.* 9.15nn21–2, S: *OP* 4: 680–1; *Lectura* 2.25n74, Vat. 19: 255; Ockham, *Quodlibet* 1.16, O: *OT* 9: 89.

[5] Scotus, *Ord.* prol. 5n237, Vat. 1: 161; *Ord.* 3.36n64 and n72, Vat. 10: 245–6 and 249; *In Metaph.* 9.15n55, S: *OP* 4: 692; Ockham, *In Phys.* 2.8§1, O: *OP* 4: 319–20; *In Sent.* 1 prol. 10, O: *OT* 1: 286–7; *In Sent.* 3.11, O: *OT* 6:355, *In Sent.* 3.12, O: *OT* 6: 421; *Quodlibet* 1.16, O: *OT* 9: 88; QV 7.3, O: *OT* 8: 363–71.

[6] Scotus, *In Metaph.* 9.15nn22–3, S: *OP* 4: 680–1; *Lectura* 2.25n93, Vat. 19: 261; Ockham, *In Perihermenias* 2.7§5, O: *OP* 2: 481; *In Sent.* 1.1.6, O: *OT* 1: 501; *In Sent.* 1.10.2, O: *OT* 3: 335–8. While Scotus and Ockham agree that the will differs from natural causes in that it has leeway (the ability to choose differently in the same circumstances), for Scotus, unlike for Ockham, the core difference lies in the will's sourcehood rather than leeway. Even when the will acts in the mode of necessity, that is, without alternative possibilities, its act is not determined or caused by prior causes, but rather self-determined. See Scotus, *Quodlibet* 16nn63–4 in Scotus 2007: 192–4. For further differences between their theories, see Adams 1986: 10–11.

[7] Scotus, *Ord.* prol. 5n234, Vat. 1: 159; Ockham, *In Sent.* 1 prol. 10, O: *OT* 1: 292.

they guarantee the pursuit of good ends, while vices corrupt the right perception of which ends are truly worth pursuing. Because of this interdependence, all the moral virtues are connected in such a way that one cannot have any one of them without having them all (*Nicomachean Ethics* 1.7, 2.5–6, 6.5, 6.12–13, 10.6–8). While none of the medieval theologians appropriated Aristotle's ethics without making important adaptations, Aquinas and many other thirteenth-century theologians shared Aristotle's view about the centrality of the moral virtues for the moral life and about their connection with each other and with prudence. Scotus and Ockham, too, tend to present their theories as being in continuity with Aristotle's ethics, but they work a more radical transformation of virtue theory. They acknowledge the importance of the moral virtues, but they shift the emphasis away from virtuous dispositions toward good acts of the will. The role of the virtues is no longer to provide happiness, but to perfect the will in willing what right reason and God command. Furthermore, Scotus and Ockham hold that the virtues can be had independently of each other.

To understand the importance of the moral virtues, we must ask what they actually do. For Aristotle, they make individuals good and make them perform their work well (*Nicomachean Ethics* 2.6.1106a22–4). Do they really? For Scotus, a virtuous disposition (*habitus*) does not contribute anything to the moral goodness of an act – at least not directly – for the act's moral goodness does not depend on whether it is caused by a disposition, but rather on whether it conforms to right reason. Thus the moral virtues' causality regarding an act's moral goodness must be traced to prudence as its proper cause (*Ord.* 1.17.1nn62–7, nn92–8, Vat. 5: 163–9, 184–9). Furthermore, dispositions, taken by themselves, are natural causes, not free causes. Accordingly, the way they exercise their causality is not in the agent's control, and were our dispositions the total causes of our acts, our actions would not be free. Then an act of love, for example, would not be meritorious (*Ord.* 1.17.1n24, n26, Vat. 5: 148, 149). For Scotus, dispositions act either as partial causes or as inclinations, and in either case they act in conjunction with, but subordinate to, the will. Virtuous dispositions allow the individual to act with ease, delight, promptness, and without impediment, and they make the act itself more intense (*Ord.* 1.17.1nn32–54, Vat. 5: 152–60).

Ockham agrees with Scotus that a disposition is not the cause of moral goodness; in fact, properly speaking, only acts are virtuous, while dispositions can be called virtuous only by "extrinsic denomination," namely insofar as they incline to a virtuous act (*In Sent.* 3.11, O: OT 6: 359). But he disagrees with Scotus that an act's moral goodness is caused by the act's conformity with right reason. God could produce in my will an act that is conformed to right reason, but it would not be virtuous, because it would not be in the control of my will.

A virtuous act must certainly conform to right reason, but its goodness must be intrinsic to the act and not caused by something extrinsic, as if the act were in itself morally indifferent and then obtained its goodness from its relation to right reason. He argues that moral goodness comes about in only one of two ways: either it originates from within an act, that is, from a "necessarily and intrinsically virtuous act," or it is derived from an act which is already intrinsically virtuous. A "contingently virtuous act," that is, an act which is not intrinsically virtuous, can only be rendered virtuous by something that is intrinsically virtuous. Going to church, for example, is contingently virtuous, for external acts are morally neutral and can be done with a good or bad intention, but "willing to do something because it is divinely commanded," "willing to pray for the sake of God's honor and because it is commanded by God in accordance with right reason" or "loving God above all and for his sake" are necessarily virtuous acts that cannot be done badly, unless God commands differently. Only acts of the will can constitute these necessarily and intrinsically virtuous acts, for two reasons. First, because only acts of the will are fully in the will's control, whereas exterior acts can cease to be so (as when someone who jumps off a cliff changes her mind, but can no longer avoid falling). Secondly, because praiseworthiness belongs at its root only to acts of the will; other acts are only derivatively praiseworthy or blameworthy, insofar as their praiseworthiness or blameworthiness depends on whether they are done from a good or bad intention.[8]

The moral virtues are generated by acts of the will: for Scotus, by choices in accord with right reason (*Ord.* 3.33nn43–4, Vat. 10: 161–2); for Ockham, by intrinsically virtuous acts (*QV* 7.1, 7.2, O: *OT* 8: 328, 340). They are dispositions that are "located" in the will and that incline it to make right choices. This is how Scotus and Ockham understand Aristotle's definition of virtue as *hexis prohairetikê, habitus electivus* – a disposition to make choices.[9] The dispositions in the sensory appetite are not virtues properly speaking. For Scotus, this is because these sensory dispositions are not *habitus electivi* (*Ord.* 3.33n45, Vat. 10:163); for Ockham, because the acts of the sensory appetite cannot be intrinsically virtuous (*In Sent.* 3.11, O: *OT* 6: 359–62, 366, 369). Why does the will need any virtues? One reason Scotus gives is that the will is free not to follow reason; thus a virtue in the will determines it to choose rightly (*Ord.* 3.33nn22–4, Vat. 10: 152–3). By contrast, Ockham rejects this explanation, since the will remains

---

8 Ockham, *In Sent.* 3.11, O: *OT* 6: 387–90; *QV* 7.1, 7.2, 7.4, O: *OT* 8: 327–30, 338, 379–81, *Quodlibet* 3.14, O: *OT* 9: 253–7.
9 Aristotle, *Nicomachean Ethics* 2.6.1106b36; Scotus, *Ord.* 3.33n7, Vat. 10: 143; Ockham, *In Sent.* 3.11, O: *OT* 6: 351.

free to choose well or badly even with a disposition. A virtuous disposition in the will merely increases the perfection of the act and the inclination and facility to choose it, as is manifest in the continent person who previously did not resist his bad desires but now resists them, because he has now a disposition in the will which makes him more inclined not to follow them (*In Sent.* 3.11, O: *OT* 6: 363–5).

If the moral virtues are dispositions of the will, and if the will is fundamentally free with or without such dispositions – free even to act contrary to the practical dictate of the intellect – then the moral virtues cannot be connected as tightly among each other and with prudence as Aristotle would have it. According to Scotus and Ockham, the acts of the moral virtues are not connected, for one can act temperately and thus obtain temperance without having courage – after all, one may simply lack the occasions to act courageously.[10] So the moral virtues are not directly connected. Nor are they indirectly connected by way of prudence. Scotus and Ockham admit that all the moral virtues require prudence, for no choice is right if it does not conform to right reason. But contrary to Aristotle, they hold that each moral virtue has its own prudence. Furthermore, prudence does not guarantee the possession of the moral virtues, for the intellect may well pronounce the correct practical dictate without the will following it.[11] In their view the moral virtues are not prerequisites for prudence as though they were necessary for avoiding the corruption of practical knowledge. Scotus argues that the will is unable to corrupt the judgment of the intellect (*Ord.* 3.36n65, Vat. 10: 246–7), and Ockham holds that the judgment of prudence is naturally caused, that is, not in our power (*QV* 7.4, O: *OT* 8: 380, 400). Scotus and Ockham, then, do not conceive of prudence as practical wisdom concerning life as a whole, but more like Aristotle's craft knowledge (*technê, ars*), that is, as partial competences which can be acquired separately and which have no affective preconditions.

NATURAL LAW AND DIVINE PRECEPTS

Having left behind a eudaimonistic conception of the will and of ethics in general, Scotus and Ockham face a new problem. In Aquinas's account of natural law, moral norms indicate ways toward human flourishing, and hence they can be in a sense read off human nature. But Scotus and Ockham sever the

---

[10] Scotus, *Ord.* 3.36n26, nn32–3, Vat. 10: 229–30, 233–4; Ockham, *QV* 7.3, O: *OT* 8: 345–6, 350.

[11] Scotus, *Ord.* 3.36n42, nn64–72, nn88–9, n92, n96, Vat. 10: 239, 245–9, 256–9; Ockham, *In Sent.* 3.12, O: *OT* 6: 421–2; *QV* 7.2, 7.3 O: *OT* 8: 331, 362–3, 371; see also note 5 above.

tie between moral norms and flourishing. What, then, is the basis for moral norms? As Scotus puts it, is an action good (or bad) in its own right and therefore divinely commanded (or prohibited), or conversely is an act good (or bad) precisely because it falls under a divine precept (*Ord.* 3.37n9, Vat. 10: 275)? For Scotus and Ockham, this is a problem not only of normative theory but also of metaphysics, for it concerns the dependence of the created order upon God's creative power. Both hold that God can will anything non-contradictory, and both hold that whatever he wills with regard to creatures he wills contingently, that is, in such a way that he could also will its opposite – and do so justly.[12] While they agree upon this premise, Ockham is willing to concede more leeway to God's legislative will than Scotus.

Because God is free in his relation to the created world and its order, Scotus argues that God cannot be obliged to will certain precepts, for example, that one's neighbor must not be killed or hated and that theft must not be committed (*Ord.* 3.37n14, Vat. 10: 277–8). While Scotus's normative theory is premised on his theory of God's freedom, he sets up the problem of divinely commanded norms from a different angle: he asks whether all the precepts of the Decalogue belong to the natural law. His answer steers a middle course between two extremes. The first extreme is the view that all precepts of the Decalogue belong to the natural law, because they are all either self-evident or can be deduced from self-evident propositions. If so, then what is commanded is so commanded because it is good, not vice versa. Hence God could not dispense from any precepts, because they would concern what is unlawful as such, and hence they would not be subject to any legislative will. According to the other extreme view, not all commandments belong to the natural law, since God did indeed give dispensations from some commandments of the Decalogue. Biblical examples show that he dispensed certain human beings from the prohibitions of homicide, theft, and prostitution: he ordered Abraham to sacrifice his son, the Israelites to despoil the Egyptians, and the prophet Hosea to have children of whoredom (*Ord.* 3.37nn9–10, nn2–4, Vat. 10: 274–5, 271–2).

Scotus argues that all the commandments of the Decalogue belong to the natural law, but he distinguishes between the natural law in the narrow and the broad sense. In the narrow sense, only self-evident practical propositions

---

[12] Scotus, *Lectura* 1.39nn53–4, Vat. 17: 496–7; *Ord.* 1.8.2n255, nn263–92, Vat. 4: 297, 302–21; *Ord.* 1.44nn3–8, Vat. 6: 363–6; *Ord.* 4.46.1n25, nn29–32, Vat. 14: 204–6; Ockham, *In Sent.* 2.3–4, O: *OT* 5: 55; *In Sent.* 2.15, O: *OT* 5: 342–3, 353; *Quodlibet* 6.2, O: *OT* 9: 589–91.

TOBIAS HOFFMANN

and the conclusions that can be demonstrated from them belong to the natural law. These are contained in the first table of the Decalogue (the first three commandments, which concern our obligations to God), and from these God cannot dispense us. Scotus's examples are the principles that "if God exists, he alone is to be loved as God," "no one else than God is to be worshiped as God." Without these principles the ultimate end, which consists in loving God, cannot be attained. But God can dispense from the precepts that belong to the natural law in the broad sense, which are contained in the second table (the last seven commandments, which concern our obligations to other creatures). To the natural law in this extended sense belong also those precepts that are neither self-evident nor demonstrable propositions, but that are harmonious with these propositions (*Ord.* 3.37nn16–29, Vat. 10: 279–84). Although the natural law in the broad sense is contingent upon the divine will, Scotus holds that it is de facto so harmonious with the natural law in the strict sense that it does not change over time and that it is in principle knowable to all (*Ord.* 4.17n19, n21, Vat. 13: 162–3). Yet since many actually ignore it, it is fitting that God revealed it (*Ord.* 3.37n41, Vat. 10: 289–90, *Ord.* 4.26nn39–40, Vat. 13: 346). If God dispensed from a precept of the Decalogue for a period of time, he would make this known. For example, God dispenses from monogamy in situations in which procreation is particularly urgent for preserving the human race, such as after the Fall of Adam and Eve and after the Flood, or in general after war, destruction, or the plague. But polygamy can only be allowed if right reason dictates it on account of such necessity, and if it is sanctioned by a special divine precept. Scotus thinks this could happen by some revelation that God would make to the Church (*Ord.* 4.26n44, n74, Vat. 13: 347, 355; *Ord.* 4.33.1nn15–24, Vat. 13: 426–9). The way Scotus discusses this example suggests that he does not think of God as an arbitrary legislator. Yet whether Scotus thinks that God's legislation of the second table is fundamentally restricted by God's justice and by human nature is debated.[13]

Since moral norms depend on God's legislation, what counts as a mortal sin, that is, as an impediment to eternal life, depends for Scotus on the divine will and is known not by moral philosophy but rather by Holy Scripture (*Ord.* 2.34–7nn57–8, Vat. 8: 390). Ockham agrees that an act is a sin precisely because one is obliged by a divine precept to avoid it. But he goes further than Scotus in drawing the implications. God himself is not subject to any

---

[13] Wolter 1997 takes Scotus to advocate such restrictions, while Williams 1998 argues against this view.

obligations: "He is debtor to no one."[14] Thus God could issue commands contrary not only to the second table of the Decalogue, but also to the first. As it happens, hatred, theft, and adultery are evil, and by divine precepts we are bound to avoid them. But God is free to command them, and then they would be done meritoriously. Yet they would have to be called by different names, for the words hatred, theft, and adultery connote that a divine precept obliges us to avoid them.[15] Ockham famously held that God could even command us to hate him and not to love him. Could we obey such commands? Ockham maintains earlier in his career that we could obey his command to hate him (*In Sent.* 4.16, O: *OT* 7: 352), and later he argues that we could not obey his command not to love him, for if we did, we would be loving God by the very fact that we were obeying him (*Quodlibet* 3.14, O: *OT* 9: 256–7).

Clearly then, for Ockham, moral norms have their source in the divine legislative will. Yet Ockham also grants that right reason is an indispensable criterion for moral actions. Whether for Ockham right reason is an additional and in some sense independent source for moral norms is debated.[16] What is clear, however, is that for Ockham it is self-evident that we should follow divine commands, and that God wants us to follow right reason.[17] What we do not find in Ockham is a doctrine of natural law that would ground moral norms on natural reason in unison with the teleology expressed in our natural inclinations (as Aquinas believes, *ST* 1-2.91.2 and 94.2), or on natural reason alone (as Scotus claims), independently of a revealed divine law. Ockham speaks of the natural law only in his later political writings, and there he identifies it with the divine law contained in Holy Scripture, which means that the natural law is nothing but the de facto divinely instituted moral order.[18]

CONCLUSION

The ethics of Scotus and Ockham has many typically modern traits, as can be seen in a rough comparison with Kant. Human freedom is not bound by

[14] Ockham, *In Sent.* 2.3–4, O: *OT* 5: 59; *In Sent.* 2.15, O: *OT* 5: 343; *QV* 7.4, O: *OT* 8: 389–90.
[15] Ockham, *In Sent.* 2.15, O: *OT* 5: 352. See also *In Sent.* 1.47, O: *OT* 4: 680–5, where, without committing himself to any particular view, Ockham discusses the possibility of God commanding evil.
[16] According to Adams 1986: 24 and 1999: 266, it is, whereas for Osborne 2005 it is not.
[17] Ockham, *QV* 7.3, O: *OT* 8: 366; *QV* 8, O: *OT* 8: 436; see Adams 1986: 26.
[18] Ockham, *Dialogus* 3.2.3.6, www.britac.ac.uk/pubs/dialogus/w32d3btx.html.

natural necessity, not even in its desire for happiness. So nature and freedom constitute two fundamentally distinct domains, and ethics is situated on the side of freedom rather than of nature. Like Kant, Scotus and Ockham abandon eudaimonism in favor of deontology. Although Kant cuts off any tie between moral obligations and the divine will, he agrees with Scotus and Ockham that human nature is ultimately not a source of moral norms. The moral virtues are still part of Scotus's and Ockham's ethics, as they are of Kant's, but they lose their centrality. Prudence is no longer a *sui generis* intellectual virtue which presupposes the right ordering of our affections, but rather it is merely a practical skill, cleverness, or carefulness, which entails that prudence is no guarantee for moral agency.

ABBREVIATIONS

O: *OP*	Ockham 1974–1988. *Opera philosophica*
O: *OT*	Ockham 1967–1984. *Opera theologica*
QV	*Quaestiones variae*, in O: *OT* 8
ST	Aquinas, *Summa theologiae*
S: *OP*	Scotus 1997–2006. *Opera philosophica*
Vat.	Scotus 1950–. *Opera omnia* (Vatican Edition)

BIBLIOGRAPHY

An asterisk denotes secondary literature especially suitable for further reading.

Adams, Marilyn McCord 1986. "The Structure of Ockham's Moral Theory," *Franciscan Studies* 29: 1–35.*

Adams, Marilyn McCord 1999. "Ockham on Will, Nature, and Morality," in Spade 1999: 245–72.

Aquinas, Thomas 1882–. *Opera omnia*, ed. the Dominican Fathers (Rome: Typographia Polyglotta).

Damascene, John 1955. *De fide orthodoxa*, ed. Eligius M. Buytaert (St. Bonaventure, N.Y.: The Franciscan Institute).

Kent, Bonnie 2003. "Rethinking Moral Dispositions: Scotus on the Virtues," in Williams 2003a: 352–76.*

King, Peter 1999. "Ockham's Ethical Theory," in Spade 1999: 227–44.*

McGrade, A.S. 1999. "Natural Law and Moral Omnipotence," in Spade 1999: 273–301.*

Möhle, Hannes 2003. "Scotus's Theory of Natural Law," in Williams 2003a: 312–31.*

Ockham, William of 1967–1984. *Opera theologica*, ed. Gedeon Gál *et al.* 10 vols. (St. Bonaventure, N.Y.: The Franciscan Institute).

Ockham, William of 1974–1988. *Opera philosophica*, ed. Philotheus Boehmer *et al.* 7 vols. (St. Bonaventure, N.Y.: The Franciscan Institute).

Ockham, William of 2011–. *Dialogus*, ed. John Kilcullen, John Scott *et al. Auctores Britannici medii aevi* (Oxford University Press). Preliminary editions are published on www.britac.ac.uk/pubs/dialogus/wtc.html

Osborne Jr., Thomas M. 2005. "Ockham as a Divine-Command Theorist." *Religious Studies* 41: 1–22.

Osborne Jr., Thomas M. 2014. *Human Action in Thomas Aquinas, John Duns Scotus, and William of Ockham* (Washington, D.C.: The Catholic University of America Press).*

Scotus, John Duns 1950–. *Opera omnia*, ed. Carolus Balić *et al.* (Vatican City: Typis Polyglottis Vaticanis).

Scotus, John Duns 1997–2006. *Opera philosophica*, ed. Girard J. Etzkorn *et al.* 5 vols. (St. Bonaventure, N.Y.: The Franciscan Institute).

Scotus, John Duns 2007. "Beati Ioannis Duns Scoti Quodlibetum quaestio 16," ed. Timothy B. Noone and H. Francie Roberts, in Christopher Schabel (ed.), *Theological Quodlibeta in the Middle Ages: The Fourteenth Century* (Leiden: Brill), 160–98.

Spade, Paul Vincent (ed.) 1999. *The Cambridge Companion to Ockham* (Cambridge University Press).

Williams, Thomas 1998. "The Unmitigated Scotus." *Archiv für Geschichte der Philosophie* 80: 162–81.

Williams, Thomas (ed.) 2003a. *The Cambridge Companion to Duns Scotus* (Cambridge University Press).

Williams, Thomas 2003b. "From Metaethics to Action Theory," in Williams 2003a: 332–51.*

Williams, Thomas 2013. "The Franciscans," in Roger Crisp (ed.), *The Oxford Handbook of the History of Ethics* (Oxford University Press).

Williams, Thomas 2017. *John Duns Scotus: Selected Writings on Ethics* (Oxford University Press).

Wolter, Allan B. 1997. *Duns Scotus on Will and Morality*, ed. William Frank (Washington, D.C.: The Catholic University of America Press).

Wood, Rega 1997. *Ockham on the Virtues* (West Lafayette, Ind.: Purdue University Press).

15

Humanism

SABRINA EBBERSMEYER

The term 'humanism' is highly ambiguous, and therefore requires some specification. In its most general meaning it refers to an attitude of thought, in which the human being is central and marks the essential point of reference.[1] In a more specific historical sense, commonly used with the epithet 'Renaissance', it refers to a movement of intellectual renewal which started in Italy in the second half of the fourteenth century and spread all over Europe during the fifteenth and sixteenth centuries.[2] During this period the term 'humanism' was not in use; it was introduced into scholarship only in the nineteenth century.[3] There are, however, some reasons for using it now. The humanists refer frequently in their writings, especially when addressing friends and colleagues, to their humanity (*humanitas*) as a shared ideal for their life and work, and they exhort each other to follow and practise the *studia humanitatis*. In addition, the term 'humanist' in its Latin and Italian form came into use during the fifteenth century to designate students and teachers of these studies,[4] which included moral philosophy alongside grammar, rhetoric, poetics and history.[5]

The humanists represented a new type of intellectual. They were seldom professors of philosophy at universities; more often we find them as scribes,

---

[1] See, for instance, the definition given by F.C.S. Schiller: 'Humanism is really in itself the simplest of philosophic standpoints; it is merely the perception that the philosophic problem concerns human beings striving to comprehend a world of human experience by the resources of human minds' (Schiller 1907: 12).

[2] The literature on Renaissance humanism is endless. Eugenio Garin and Paul Oskar Kristeller were probably the most influential scholars on humanism of the twentieth century: see especially Garin 1965 and Kristeller 1961. For the political dimension of humanism and the notion of 'civic humanism', see Baron 1955 and 1988, Bec 1975 and Hankins 2000. The volume edited by Mazzocco 2006 presents various contemporary approaches towards Renaissance humanism.

[3] See Niethammer 1808 and Voigt 1859.   [4] Campana 1946 and Giustiniani 1985.

[5] Sforza 1884: 380, cited by Kristeller 1951: 109.

diplomats or teachers at princely courts or the Curia, or in schoolrooms or the newly founded academies. And for the first time in history, a considerable number of women participated in the learned world. Moral questions were one of the humanists' major concerns. Using various text forms such as letters, dialogues, invectives, poems and treatises, they wrote on a great variety of topics, such as virtue, the highest good, fate and free will, nobility, love and friendship, education, marriage, civic duties and many other subjects. However, the humanists are not known for developing entirely new, original or complex theories on morals or moral agency. Despising the academic philosophy of their own age with its scientific approach to moral questions, they propagated an alternative attitude towards moral philosophy. In fact, they introduced and established a new style of thought, which led to a fundamental transformation of moral philosophy with consequences well into the seventeenth century. This style of thought is characterized by a certain type of argumentation with an emphasis on persuasion, intelligibility and diversion.

Humanism is also characterized by a pragmatic, sometimes almost utilitarian approach to moral questions. This pragmatic and realistic view shaped the understanding of human agency in a particular way and led to fundamental reconsiderations in moral matters, such as the reassessment of human nature in the face of the divine, of the active life as against the contemplative life, and in general of usefulness as opposed to divine truth.[6]

THE EMERGENCE OF HUMANIST MORAL THOUGHT: CRITICISM OF SCHOLASTIC PHILOSOPHY

It is widely agreed that the humanist movement had its origin with Petrarch. Petrarch was one of the first figures to criticize Scholastic philosophy in a sharp and often polemical way, and propagated openly a different approach to philosophy which drew on the authors of Roman antiquity. In addition, he disseminated this new conception through his extensive letter-writing. His immediate followers regarded him as the founder of a new intellectual era.[7] Petrarch's ethical ideas were strongly shaped by his critique of Scholastic

---

[6] In this chapter I rely on the material presented in my book *Homo agens*: see Ebbersmeyer 2010.

[7] See especially the letters written by Coluccio Salutati in Salutati 1891–1911, vol. 1: 176–87; 334–42 and vol. 4.1: 126–45, and Leonardo Bruni, *Le vite di Dante e di Petrarca* [1436], in Bruni 1928: 50–69.

philosophy. This critique has various aspects, but they all spring from the same source, namely from the conviction that philosophy implies an existential commitment and should provide advice for guiding one's life. With regard to this purpose, Petrarch held that Scholastic philosophy failed in almost all respects.

Firstly, Petrarch criticized the professional approach towards moral philosophy as such. Professional philosophers were actually a recent invention at Western universities, arising during the thirteenth century as philosophers started to remain at the arts faculties and thus became independent of the higher faculties of theology, law and medicine.[8] As professional philosophers, the *cathedrarii philosophi* did not necessarily have much interest in conducting their lives in accordance with the doctrines they taught.[9] Rather, they exhibited a theoretical and scientific approach towards morals, as during this period moral philosophy, like many other disciplines, was being reshaped according to Aristotelian standards of scientific reasoning and was gaining the status of a science: *scientia moralis*.[10] In contrast to this understanding of moral philosophy, Petrarch held that practising moral philosophy does not imply being a professional philosopher – it entails performing in one's own life what one is teaching to others. He extolled 'those true [philosophers], who are always few in number, and I don't know if there are now any at all, who exhibit what they profess publicly, the love and pursuit of wisdom'.[11]

In addition, Petrarch criticized the marginal place which moral philosophy occupied in the academic context, especially when compared with natural philosophy, which was extensively studied and had a much more prominent place in the curriculum. In Petrarch's view, a preoccupation with natural philosophy distracts from the essential questions of human life:

> Of what use is it, I pray, to know the natures of the animals, birds, fish and snakes, if we do not know the nature of men, what we are born for, where we come from and where we are going, and if we spurn these questions?[12]

Many humanists followed Petrarch in this respect and regarded moral philosophy as much more important than natural philosophy.[13] This also led to a

---

[8] Bianchi 1987 and Libera 1991.

[9] Petrarca 1975, 1: 500. Petrarch is referring to Seneca who already criticized the *cathedrarii philosophi* of his own days. See Seneca *De brevitate vitae* 10.1.

[10] For this development see Wieland 1981 and 1990.   [11] Petrarca 1975, 1: 500.

[12] Ibid., 1: 104.

[13] See, for instance, Bruni *Isagogicon moralis disciplinae*, in Bruni 1928: 21 and Palmiere *Della vita civile*, in Palmieri 1982: 29 and 59.

re-evaluation of the philosophers of the past. No longer Aristotle, but now Socrates was regarded as the model for the true moral philosopher, as he was the one who directed the search of the philosopher away from the stars and nature to the exploration of the heart. He became the 'first artist of moral philosophy' and the 'best master of life'.[14]

Finally, Petrarch criticized the method and style that accompanied the scientific approach towards moral philosophy. Devoted to dialectical analysis, the scholastics failed to perform the main task of moral philosophy, which is to move and engage the hearer:

> Thus the true moral philosophers and valuable teachers of virtues are those whose first and last purpose is to make their students and readers good. They not only teach the definitions of virtue and vice, haranguing us about virtue's splendor and vice's drabness. They also instil in our breasts both love and zeal for what is good, and hatred and abhorrence of evil.[15]

Academic philosophy is unfit to meet this task, but Petrarch found support elsewhere: 'Anyone looking for such exhortations will find them in Latin authors, especially in Cicero and Seneca.'[16]

Although Petrarch has a broad-brush view on scholastic philosophy, there is a kernel of truth in it. His critique is a reaction to a development within academic philosophy, namely the increasing tendency to apply logical analysis to every given philosophical problem, which led to a highly abstract and complicated way of dealing with it. This critical attitude towards scholastic philosophy, especially in the field of moral philosophy, became a main characteristic of humanist thought. Juan Luis Vives, for example, followed the same line of thought in his work *On the Causes of the Corruption of the Arts*:

> The scholastics have turned the discipline of morals [*disciplina morum*], which aims at action, into mere verbal jousting. They discuss ethics not in order to become better or to make others better, nor in order to determine the truth about the virtues and about life, but rather in order to quibble.[17]

This critique can be found in many other humanists, such as Bruni, Valla, Erasmus and Montaigne, and can even be traced to early modern authors such as Hobbes and Descartes.[18] So given that the overall aim of moral philosophy is understood by the humanists not as a theoretical but as a

[14] Petrarca 1945: 33. [15] Petrarch 2003: 316–18. [16] Ibid., 314–15.
[17] Vives 1997: 102–3. For Vives' opponents concerning moral philosophy see Di Liscia 2007.
[18] Hobbes, *Leviathan* IV. 46, in Hobbes 2012 3: 1052–1102; Descartes, *Discours de la méthode* VI, in Descartes 1996 6: 61–2.

practical one, i.e. acquiring virtue, giving advice, providing orientation in
practical matters, what are the appropriate means for doing this?

The humanists cultivated text forms and methods of argumentation which
set them apart from the academic approach common to the schools, where
commentaries written on the moral works of Aristotle and addressed to
trained students of philosophy constituted the major part of moral writings.
Rather the humanists wrote texts for a wider audience, avoiding technical
expressions and preferring classical Latin. Many texts were written in dialogue form, which allowed for the setting out of the pros and cons of the topic
under discussion. The dialogue form also had some impact on the validity
and truth of the opinions presented, and led to a certain openness regarding
dissenting positions.[19] Often the opponents did not reach mutual consent,
which left the ending of the dialogue open and allowed the reader to draw
conclusions. For instance, Poggio's dialogue on *True nobility* ends with the
comment 'everyone is free to think what he wants'.[20]

Letter-writing, another text form cultivated by the humanists, allowed
advice to be given to individual cases in singular circumstances, and enabled
the author to adjust general maxims to the specific and individual needs of the
addressee. Petrarch was well aware of this fact. When reflecting on his own
letter-writing he stated:

> The varieties of human beings are infinite, there is no greater likeness of
> minds than of faces; and as the same food does not always please not only
> different, but also the same stomach, so likewise the soul should not always
> be nourished in the same style.[21]

Later Montaigne wrote essays, fragmentary works, which show repeatedly
that trying to generalize human behaviour and establish certain general rules
is a vain undertaking. His scepticism concerning general assumptions about
human nature led him to write about himself, to observe and analyse his own
life: 'Thus, gentle Reader my selfe am the ground-worke of my booke.'[22]

These text forms went along with different methods of argumentation.
Mocking the sterile syllogistic argumentation and intricate analyses of terms
commonly used in the schools, the humanists preferred rhetorical strategies

[19] For more detail see Hempfer 2002. [20] Poggio Bracciolini 2002: 38.
[21] Petrarch *Familiares* I, 1 (29) in Petrarca 1933–1942 1: 9.
[22] *Preface to the reader*, Montaigne 1603 sig. [A6v].

intended to divert, engage and persuade the reader.[23] Rhetoric was understood not as mere verbal jousting in order to show one's own verbal skills – rather it was conceived as the appropriate method to follow when dealing with contingent facts, as is the case with human agency, the subject of moral philosophy.[24] The science of rhetoric, as Salutati put it, 'is a battle and a dispute about what has been done or what should be done'.[25]

The use of exempla, one of the central means of rhetorical argumentation, became crucial and characteristic for humanist moral thought. Whereas in a scientific context examples serve mainly as illustrations of an otherwise proven truth, they reveal a more relevant power in the realm of moral counselling.[26] Examples do not provide explanations, as they do not refer to the causes of human action, but they show what others have done under similar circumstances. Thus, they provide advice for future action; they inspire and offer orientation, as Petrarch states:

> As a face in the mirror, so the morals of men are easily corrected with an exemplar; moreover, as we walk more safely along a path which has been marked out by the footsteps of others, so in life we adhere more easily to the examples of others than if we were to undertake a new way without any guide.[27]

Historical works in particular provide many examples. Salutati praised history because it contains a treasure-trove of human experience conserved in books, which can be of great value for different people in diverse situations:

> For the knowledge of the past deeds exhorts the princes, instructs the people and informs the individuals about what one has to do at home and what outside the home, what as an individual, what with the family, what with citizens and friends, and what one has to do in private and in public.[28]

According to Salutati, historical works are an even better form of instruction than traditional moral advice in the form of theological or philosophical doctrines, as the latter tend to overwhelm the mind, leading ultimately to disgust.[29] In contrast, historical examples do not weary the mind, but refresh it.[30]

---

[23] Some scholastic authors were likewise unhappy with the method of moral philosophy and claimed that rhetoric should be applied to it; see Roger Bacon *Moralis philosophia* in Bacon 1953: 250–1 and Buridan's preface to his commentary on Aristotle's *Ethics*, Buridan (1968 [1513]), iira–iiva.

[24] For more detail see Kessler 2013.   [25] Salutati 1891–1911, 2: 295.

[26] On the meaning of the example see Aristotle, *Topic* VII, 1; 157a; *Rhetoric*, I. 2; 1356b1–10; *Analytica priora*, II. 24.

[27] Petrarca 1945: 133.   [28] Salutati 1891–1911, 2: 291–2.   [29] Ibid., 292.   [30] Ibid., 295.

Along with this devotion to history and historical examples as a means of
moral orientation, the humanists showed an increasing openness to using
empirical observation. They placed emphasis on describing man as he really
is, rather than prescribing how he should be.[31] As Poggio put it, 'the life of
mortals according to the scales of philosophy cannot be demanded from us'.[32]
The willingness to observe human behaviour unbiasedly, and to challenge
traditional moral assumptions in the light of this, had various consequences.
Lorenzo Valla, for instance, undertook in his dialogue *On Pleasure* a reconsideration of the cardinal virtues of moderation, courage and justice; with sharp
observational skills he unmasked apparently virtuous acts and revealed their
true selfish character.[33] This critical attitude was much cultivated by
Montaigne, who became a sceptic concerning the legitimacy of forming any
general moral judgment as such, for in his view it requires diligent investigation
of all the aspects relevant for a certain behaviour and cannot be determined
beforehand: 'lo here the reason why when we judge of a particular action, we
must first consider many circumstances, and thoroughly observe the man, that
hath produced the same before we name and censure it'.[34] Montaigne avoided
drawing conclusions and looking for essentials in moral thought and
behaviour, but was eager to describe a great many singular cases with detailed
accuracy and to point out phenomena that were previously overlooked; in this
way he demolished the traditional foundations of morality. According to
Montaigne, general moral norms and laws in a given society cannot claim to
be true in themselves; rather their validity is due to convention and habit:

> The lawes of conscience, which we say to proceed from nature, rise and
> proceed of custome; every man, holding in special regard, and inward venera-
> tion the opinions approved, and customes received about him, cannot without
> remorse leave them, nor without applause applie himself unto them.[35]

REASSESSMENTS OF THIS LIFE

This new attitude towards morality challenged many traditional assumptions about human nature, and led to a reconsideration of the place and
tasks of man in the world. Despite many disagreements, the humanists
shared the belief that human activity should be valued by its usefulness with

---

[31] See Palmieri *Della vita civile*, in Palmieri 1982: 7 and 63 or Machiavelli, *The Prince*, ch.
15, in Machiavelli 1989, vol. 1: 57.
[32] Poggio Braccolini 1994: 80. [33] Valla 2004: 96–190.
[34] *Essays* II.11, in Montaigne 1603. [35] *Essays* I.22, in Montaigne 1603.

regard to this life. The effects of this commitment can be observed in various realms.

Firstly, human nature as such was reconsidered. It was no longer regarded as deficient, and even its sensual and affective components were seen as sound and adequate.[36] In reply to the tradition of *miseria hominis* literature, the humanists accentuated the specific human dignity which was located in man's ability to act and to design his own destiny. Thus Giannozzo Manetti referred in his treatise *On the Dignity and Excellence of Man* (1452) to the ability to think (*intelligere*) and act (*agere*) as man's characteristic features, and Giovanni Pico della Mirandola pointed in his famous speech *On the Dignity of Man* to man's capacity for self-determination.[37]

Another striking example is the demolition of the ideal of contemplation and its related life form, the *vita contemplativa*. In a long and influential tradition going back to the days of Plato and Aristotle, contemplation was esteemed as the noblest occupation of man and as his ultimate end in life.[38] In consequence, practical concerns were seen as subordinate. This ideal lived on in the Christian tradition and was revered in the arts faculties of Western universities.[39] Many humanists, however, did not follow this path. Salutati, for example, concluded that the 'active life' has to be preferred to 'speculation'.[40] Caring more about man's human nature, with all its needs and pleasures, than about his ties of filiation with the divine, the humanists laid the greatest emphasis on what was useful for this life. In a famous letter Leonardo Bruni states that 'not the contemplative, but the active life, is the proper life of man. For one does not contemplate insofar as one is human, but as something divine and separate.'[41]

In accordance with this appreciation of the active life, the traditional order of virtues and vice shifted. Prudence, for instance, became more prominent and gained more relevance when compared with wisdom. Defined by Aristotle as 'right reason applied to practice' (*recta ratio agibilium*), prudence was for Salutati the virtue that fulfils (*perficit*) wisdom.[42] Palmieri defined prudence as 'the true ability to examine rationally and understand all things that are good or bad for the people',[43] and subordinated the intellectual virtues of intellect, science, art and wisdom to prudence, as their task is merely to assist the prudent to choose what is right.

[36] See Ebbersmeyer 2013.   [37] Pico della Mirandola 1948: 225.
[38] See, for instance, Plato *Phaido* III, 5; 82c–84b, Aristotle *Nicomachean Ethics* X, 6–8; 1176a30.
[39] See Bianchi 1987.   [40] Salutati 1990: 183.   [41] Bruni 1928: 135–6.
[42] Salutati 1990: 178–9.   [43] Palmieri 1982: 32.

This development becomes even more striking in a dialogue written by Poggio Bracciolini, *On Avarice*. While avarice was traditionally regarded by philosophers as a vice and by theologians as a sin,[44] Poggio tentatively presents the opposite view, namely that avarice can be understood as a virtue. His arguments are based on empirical observations and an unprejudiced interpretation of the activities of man, and from them he infers that avaricious behaviour contributes to the blossoming of culture and the well-being of society. The pursuit of personal wealth is no longer considered to be an unnatural inclination that destroys the common good, but as a beneficial natural inclination:

> ... nature has instilled an instinct for survival in all living creatures; for this reason, we seek food and whatever else is necessary for the care and nurture of the body. And unless we are quite foolish, we buy these things with money. So is it surprising if I am covetous, if I seek bronze, gold, or silver, without which one cannot have the necessities of life? If this be avaricious, then (as it was asserted before) avarice is not against nature but instilled in us and imprinted on us by nature itself, just like the other desires with which we are born.[45]

In accordance with this appreciation of the active life and devotion to worldly affairs, usefulness was regarded as the basic motive for human actions. All of man's activity is by nature aligned to its expected benefits, as Poggio declared:

> ... whoever undertakes anything without hope of it [profit]? The more evident the profit, the more willingly we enter into the enterprise. All follow gain, all desire it. Whether you consider the military profession, or business, or agriculture, or the arts, both liberal and mercenary, the desire for money is innate in everyone. Everything we treat, work at, or undertake is directed at getting as much profit as possible. For its sake we undertake hazards and run risks.[46]

A notable example of this new evaluation of avarice, wealth and economic success is Leon Battista Alberti's work *Della famiglia* (1434–1441). The whole management of family life – looking for a spouse, dealing with friends, caring for one's children – is subjected to a strictly economic perspective. On Alberti's view we should assist sick people not because this is what charity prescribes, but rather because it will be cheaper and more economical in the

---

[44] Aristotle *Nicomachean Ethics* IV, 1–3; 1119b21–1122a18; Cicero *De officiis* I, 7, 24; 1 *Tim* 6,10; Augustine *De Genesi ad litteram* 11, 15.
[45] Poggio Bracciolini 1994: 76–7; English translation from Poggio Bracciolini 1989.
[46] Poggio Bracciolini 1994: 261–2; English translation from Poggio Bracciolini 1989.

long run.[47] In what is virtually an early capitalistic analysis, even time can be 'lost' and becomes a resource that has to be used and applied for one's own profit and wealth.[48] In this context the Stoic doctrine of self-preservation gained significance. It served as a first principle which humanists referred to when arguing for engagement with worldly affairs, especially when legitimizing interest in wealth and material goods.[49] This is also true for Alberti, who took up the Stoic doctrine in the first two parts of his work on household matters, when legitimizing a strictly economic perspective on family life.[50]

GENDERED VIRTUES

When moral philosophers wrote about the human being, its virtues, duties and actions, they were referring implicitly or explicitly only to men, not to women. In a long tradition going back to antiquity, women were not regarded as equal to men in moral matters. With reference to the physiological difference between the sexes, it was argued that women had weaker judgment and consequently needed to be supervised by men. This is particularly true for the Aristotelian tradition, which became dominant in Western philosophical thought from the thirteenth century onwards.[51] Although the Christian doctrine implied in general the moral equality of the sexes, differences in moral matters were still to be found in the Christian tradition, supported by biblical precepts for women to remain silent, not to teach, and to be subordinate to men.[52] In addition, for centuries women were excluded from any formal education, as they were not allowed to attend universities. The humanist movement, however, opened its gates to women too, albeit in a restricted sense.

The education of women became a concern of many humanists. Treatises were written promoting and defending the education of girls and women and providing curricula for them. Gradually women, too, began to contribute to the discussion on female education and to put forward their right to it. In a letter on the *Defence of a Liberal Education for Women*, Laura Cereta claimed that 'the licence for learning is given equally to everyone by nature'.[53] A

---

[47] Alberti 1960: 237.   [48] Ibid., 176.
[49] Poggio Bracciolini 1994: 76–7; Palmieri 1982: 60–3.
[50] Alberti 1960: 31–2; see also 133.
[51] See Aristotle *On the Generation of Animals* 737a25ff; 775a13ff; *Politics* 1259a39–b4; *Nicomachean Ethics*, 1160b24ff. See also Plato *Timaeus* 91e.
[52] See 1 Cor. 14, 34–6; 1 Tim. 2, 11–15; Eph. 5, 22–4.
[53] Laura Cereta, *Epistolae* (letter 65), Cereta 1640: 191.

hundred years later, Marie de Gournay, editor of Montaigne's *Essays*, wrote an essay on *The Equality of Men and Women* (1622), in which she stressed the importance of education for the equality of the sexes.

However, even those who supported the idea of female education saw no need for equality between the sexes. The curricula for women differed from those for men and were adjusted to their different social roles. For instance, knowledge of rhetoric was not regarded as desirable for women as they were not supposed to speak in public.[54] Their presence in the public sphere as letter-writers was tolerated, but only during a certain period of their life, namely as young girls; to remain in the public sphere thereafter carried the risk of being publicly accused as unchaste.[55]

The virtues were also regarded differently in the case of men and women. Male authors tend to stress the importance for women of the virtues of chastity, silence, obedience, and concern for domestic affairs. Chastity in particular, which was hardly ever taken up in treatises on virtuous behaviour in men, became one the main concerns of defenders of women's education.[56] Women faced a long tradition of misogynistic literature in which their moral inferiority was proclaimed,[57] and although some male humanists supported the request of women for education and participation in public life, and praised their worth,[58] this older tradition was still strong and influential.

One of the first women to raise her voice against this prejudice was Christine de Pizan (1365–1430). Her *Book of the City of Ladies* (1405) can be understood as a moral defence of women against unjust accusations and assaults. Christine took up the traditional prejudices against women, explained their origin, and refuted them. She did so by using the literary tradition of collections of exempla and transforming this genre for her own purposes. She presented exempla of virtuous women from antiquity up to her own time, thus proving that women are capable of virtuous behaviour. This genealogy of virtuous women constitutes an intellectual refuge for women: 'Now a New Kingdom of Femininity is begun.'[59] The moral defence of women was taken up by many later female humanists, such as Isotta Nogarola (1418–1466), who asked rhetorically in a letter – after citing numerous exempla of virtuous women – 'whether women are superior to men in verbosity or rather in eloquence and virtue?'[60] Although it still took centuries

---

[54] See Bruni's curriculum addressed to Battista da Montefeltro, in Bruni 2002: 92–125.
[55] King 1980.   [56] See Vives 2000.   [57] See Clack 1999 and Holland 2006.
[58] Capra 2001 [1525], Agrippa 1529 and Domenichi 1549.
[59] *The Book of the City of Ladies*, II.12. Christine de Pizan 1982: 117.
[60] Nogarola 2004: 100.

for women to be granted equal rights and to participate on equal terms in the discussion of moral questions, what the female humanists had begun was pursued during the seventeenth century and found its expression especially in the French salon, where several women, such as Madeleine de Scudéry and Madeleine de Souvré, contributed to the moral discussions of their time.[61]

THE LEGACY OF HUMANISM

What place do the humanists hold in the history of moral philosophy? Their historical significance lies on the one hand in breaking with the previous academic traditions of dealing with moral philosophy, and on the other hand in laying the foundations for the empirically-based analyses of moral action which became characteristic of the early modern period. The humanists rejected the sterile and abstract way of treating moral problems common within the schools, and with its radical subjectivism and relativism, and its emphasis on rhetoric and on what is useful, their thought resembles in many ways the ethical thought of the Sophists and Rhetoricians of ancient Greek and Roman culture. They took up the pragmatic approach of Cicero and Seneca, their leading authorities, and used it to combat scholastic philosophy.

The impact of humanism on later thought can be clearly seen. Firstly, the humanists looked at human nature and human agency from a new perspective that was determined not by idealistic concepts but rather by the observation of the empirical world. Many of them, perhaps especially Petrarch and Montaigne, consider individual cases and reject general rules and norms. The French moralists of the seventeenth century, such as La Rochefoucauld and Pascal, took up this approach. The humanists' tendency not to prescribe but rather to describe human behaviour without prejudices became a *topos* in the seventeenth century.[62] This is also true of their use of the principle of self-preservation as an explanation of moral behaviour, which became prominent in the moral writings of Hobbes and Spinoza.[63] Moreover, insofar as the humanists emphasized the useful as the most fundamental value for humans and championed it against 'nobler' transcendental values, while also focusing on the actual conditions of humans in this life, they form a part of that strand of the philosophical past that led eventually to the formation of the theory of

---

[61] See Conley 2002.

[62] See Mandeville 1924 [1732] 1: 39; Spinoza *Tractatus politicus* I, § 1 in Spinoza 1925 3: 273.

[63] Hobbes *De cive* I.1 in Hobbes 1983: 89–90; *Leviathan* chap. XIV, in Hobbes 2012 2: 198; Spinoza *Ethics*, IVp18d in Spinoza 1925 2: 221–2.

utilitarianism. Finally and more generally, we can recognize that they have contributed to a fundamental readjustment which is distinctive of the modern period, namely the devaluation of the theoretical paradigm in favour of the practical, which is traceable in Kant's famous dictum of the primacy of pure practical reason regarding the theoretical and was then echoed in Fichte's *System of Ethics*.[64]

BIBLIOGRAPHY

An asterisk denotes secondary literature especially suitable for further reading.

Agrippa, Henricus Cornelius 1529. *Declamatio de nobilitate et praecellentia foeminei sexus.* Antwerp.
Alberti, Leon Battista 1960, *Della famiglia,* in: *Opere Volgari II,* ed. Cecil Grayson. Bari: Laterza.
Bacon, Roger 1953. *Moralis philosophia,* ed. Eugenio Massa. Zurich: Thesaurus Mundi.
Baron, Hans 1955. *The Crisis of the Early Italian Renaissance. Civic Humanism and Republican Liberty in an Age of Classicism and Tyranny,* 2 vols. Princeton University Press.
Baron, Hans 1988. *In Search of Florentine Civic Humanism. Essays on the Transition from Medieval to Modern Thought,* 2 vols. Princeton University Press.
Bec, Christian 1975. *L'umanesimo civile. Alberti, Salutati, Bruni, Bracciolini e altri trattatisti del '400.* Turin: Paravia.
Bianchi, Luca 1987. 'La felicità intellettuale come professione nella Parigi del Duecento', *Rivista di filosofia* 78: 181–99.
Bruni, Leonardo 1741. *Epistolarum libri VIII,* ed. Laurentius Mehus, 2 vols. Florence: Paperinius.
Bruni, Leonardo 1928. *Humanistisch-philosophische Schriften mit einer Chronologie seiner Werke und Briefe,* ed. Hans Baron. Leipzig: Teubner.
Bruni, Leonardo 1987. *The Humanism of Leonardo Bruni: Selected Texts,* ed. Gordon Griffiths, James Hankins and David Thompson. Binghamton: Center for Medieval and Early Renaissance Studies, State University of New York at Binghamton.
Bruni, Leonardo 2002. *The Study of Literature (De studiis et litteris),* in *Humanist Educational Treatises,* ed. and trans. C.W. Kallendorf. Cambridge, Mass.: Harvard University Press, 92–125.
Buridan, John 1968 [1513]. *Quaestiones super decem libros ethicorum Aristotelis ad Nicomachum.* Paris: Ponset le Preux. Facsimile repr., Frankfurt a.M.: Minerva.
Campana, Augusto 1946. 'The Origin of the Word "Humanist"', *Journal of the Warburg and Courtauld Institutes* 9: 60–73.
Capra, Galeazzo Flavio 2001 [1525]. *Della eccellenza et dignità della donna.* Rome: Bulzoni.
Cereta, Laura 1640. *Epistolae.* Padua: Sardi.
Christine de Pizan 1982. *The Book of the City of Ladies,* trans. Earl Jeffrey Richards. London: Pan Books.

[64] Kant 1908 [1788]: 119–21; Fichte 1798.

Clack, Beverley 1999. *Misogyny in the Western Philosophical Tradition: A Reader.* Basingstoke: Macmillan.

Conley, John J. 2002. *The Suspicion of Virtue: Women Philosophers in Neoclassical France.* Ithaca, N.Y.: Cornell University Press.

Descartes, René 1996. *Œuvres.* 11 vols., ed. C. Adam and P. Tannery. Paris: Vrin.

Di Liscia, Daniel A. 2007. 'Kalkulierte Ethik: Vives und die "Zerstörer" der Moralphilosophie (Le Maistre, Cranston und Almain)', in S. Ebbersmeyer and E. Kessler (eds.), *Ethik – Wissenschaft oder Lebenskunst? Modelle der Normenbegründung von der Antike bis zur Frühen Neuzeit / Ethics – Science or Art of Living? Models of Moral Philosophy from Antiquity to the Early Modern Era.* Berlin: LIT Verlag, 75–105.

Domenichi, Lodovico 1549. *La nobiltà delle donne di M. Lodovico Domenichi.* Venice: Gabriel Giolito.

Ebbersmeyer, Sabrina 2010. *Homo agens. Studien zur Genese und Struktur frühhumanistischer Moralphilosophie.* Berlin: de Gruyter.*

Ebbersmeyer, Sabrina 2013. 'Passions for this Life', in *Rethinking Virtue, Reforming Society: New Directions in Renaissance Ethics, 1400–1600*, ed. S. Ebbersmeyer and D. Lines. Turnhout: Brepols, 193–213.

Ebbersmeyer, Sabrina, Kessler, Eckhard and Schmeisser, Martin (eds.) 2007. *Ethik des Nützlichen. Texte zur Moralphilosophie im italienischen Humanismus* (Latin/German). Munich: Fink.*

Erasmus von Rotterdam, Desiderius 1979. *Moriae encomium id est stultitiae laus*, ed. Clarence H. Miller [=*Opera omnia Desiderii Erasmi Roterdami* 4, 3]. Amsterdam, Oxford: North-Holland Publishing Company.

Fichte, Johann Gottlieb 1798. *Das System der Sittenlehre nach den Principien der Wissenschaftslehre.* Jena: Gabler.

Garin, Eugenio 1965. *Italian Humanism. Philosophy and Civic Life in the Renaissance.* Oxford: Basil Blackwell.

Giustiniani, Vito R. 1985. 'Homo, Humanus, and the Meaning of "Humanism"', *Journal of the History of Ideas* 46: 167–95.

Hankins, James (ed.) 2000. *Renaissance Civic Humanism. Reappraisals and Reflections.* Cambridge University Press.

Hankins, James 2003. *Humanism and Platonism in the Italian Renaissance. Humanism.* Rome: Edizione di Storia e Letteratura.*

Hempfer, Klaus (ed.) 2002. *Möglichkeiten des Dialogs. Struktur und Funktion einer literarischen Gattung zwischen Mittelalter und Renaissance in Italien.* Stuttgart: Steiner.

Hobbes, Thomas 1983. *De cive*, ed. Howard Warrender. Oxford: Clarendon Press.

Hobbes, Thomas 2012. *Leviathan.* 3 vols., ed. Noel Malcolm. Oxford University Press.

Holland, Jack 2006. *Misogyny: The World's Oldest Prejudice.* Philadelphia, Pa.: Running Press.

Kant, Immanuel 1908 [1788]. *Kritik der praktischen Vernunft*, in Gesammelte Schriften, vol. 5, ed. Paul Natorp. Berlin: Georg Reimer.

Kessler, Eckhard 2013. 'The Method of Moral Philosophy in Renaissance Humanism', in D.A. Lines and S. Ebbersmeyer (eds.), *Rethinking Virtue, Reforming Society: New Directions in Renaissance Ethics, c.1350–c.1650.* Turnhout: Brepols, 107–29.

King, Margaret L. 1980. 'Book-lined Cells: Women and Humanism in the Early Italian Renaissance', in *Beyond their Sex: Learned Women of the European Past*, ed. P.H. Labalme. New York University Press, 66–90.

King, Margaret L. 1991. *Women of the Renaissance*. University of Chicago Press.*

Kristeller, Paul Oskar 1951 [1945]. 'Humanism and Scholasticism in the Italian Renaissance', in *Renaissance Thought: The Classic, Scholastic, and Humanistic Strains*. New York: Harper & Row, 92–119.

Kristeller, Paul Oskar 1961 [1955]. 'The Humanist Movement', in *Renaissance Thought: The Classic, Scholastic and Humanist Strains*. New York: Harper & Row, 3–23.

La Rochefoucauld, François de 1964. *Œuvres complètes*, ed. L. Martin-Chauffier, rev. Jean Marchand. Paris: Gallimard.

Libera, A. de 1991. *Penser au Moyen Âge*. Paris: Éditions du Seuil.

Machiavelli, Niccolò 1989. *The Chief Works and Others*. 3 vols., trans. Allan Gilbert. Durham, N.C.: Duke University Press.

Mandeville, Bernard 1924 [1732]. *The Fable of the Bees or Private Vices, Publick Benefits*, ed. F.B. Kaye. 2 vols. Oxford: Clarendon Press [repr. Indianapolis, Ind.: Liberty Classics, 1988].

Mazzocco, Angelo (ed.) 2006. *Interpretations of Renaissance Humanism*. Brill: Leiden.

Montaigne, Michel de 1603. *The Essayes, or Morall, Politike and Millitarie Discourses of Lo[rd] Michaell de Montaigne*. Trans. John Florio. London.

Niethammer, Friedrich 1808. *Der Streit des Philanthropinismus und des Humanismus in der Theorie des Erziehungs-Unterrichts unsrer Zeit*, Jena: Frommann.

Nogarola, Isotta 2004. *Complete Writings*, ed. and trans. Margaret L. King and Diana Robin. The University of Chicago Press.

Palmieri, Matteo 1982. *Vita civile*, ed. Gino Belloni. Florence: Sansoni.

Petrarca, Francesco 1933–1942. *Le Familiari*, ed. Vittorio Rossi and Umberto Bosco, 4 vols. Florence: Sansoni.

Petrarca, Francesco 1945. *Rerum memorandarum libri*, ed. Giuseppe Billanovich. Florence: Sansoni.

Petrarca, Francesco 1975. *Opere latine*. 2 vols., ed. Antonietta Bufano. Turin: Unione Tipografico–Editrice Torinese.

Petrarch, Francesco 2003. 'On his Own Ignorance and That of Many Others', in *Invectives*, ed. and trans. David Marsh. Cambridge, Mass.: Harvard University Press.

Pico della Mirandola, Giovanni 1948. 'On the Dignity of Man', trans. Elizabeth Livermore Forbes, in *The Renaissance Philosophy of Man*, ed. E. Cassirer, P.O. Kristeller and J.H. Randall. University of Chicago Press, 223–54.

Poggio Bracciolini, Gian Francesco 1989. *On Avarice*, in *The Earthly Republic*, ed. Benjamin Kohl and Ronald G. Witt. Philadelphia, Pa.: University of Pennsylvania Press, 241–92.

Poggio Bracciolini, Gian Francesco 1994. *De avaritia* (Latin/Italian), trans. Giuseppe Germano. Livorno: Belforte.

Poggio Bracciolini, Gian Francesco 2002. *De vera nobilitate*, ed. Davide Canfora. Rome: Edizioni di Storia e Letteratura.

Salutati, Coluccio 1891–1911. *Epistolario di Coluccio Salutati*, ed. Francesco Novati, 4 vols. Rome: Forzani e C. Tipografi del Senato.

Salutati, Coluccio 1990. *Vom Vorrang der Jurisprudenz oder der Medizin / De nobilitate legum et medicinae*, trans. Peter Michael Schenkel. Munich: Fink.

Schiller, Ferdinand Canning Scott 1907. *Studies in Humanism*. London: Macmillan and Co.

Sforza, G. 1884. 'La patria, la famiglia ed i parenti di papa Niccolò V', *Atti della Reale Accademia Lucchese di Scienze, Lettere ed Arti*, 23: 1–400.

Spinoza, Baruch de 1925. *Opera* ed. Carl Gebhardt. Heidelberg: Carl Winters Verlagsbuchhandlung.

Valla, Lorenzo 1977. *De voluptate*, trans. A. Kent Hieatt and Maristella Lorch. New York: Abaris Books.

Valla, Lorenzo 2004. *Von der Lust oder Vom wahren Guten*, ed. and trans. Peter Michael Schenkel. Munich: Fink.

Vives, Juan Luis 1997. *On the Causes of the Corruption of the Arts: Book VI: On the Corruption of Moral Philosophy (De causis corruptarum artium, liber sextus, qui est de philosophia morali)*, trans. J. Monfasani, in *Cambridge Translations of Renaissance Philosophical Texts, I: Moral Philosophy*, ed. J. Kraye. Cambridge University Press, 91–107.

Vives, Juan Luis 2000. *The Education of a Christian Woman, a Sixteenth-century Manual (De institutione feminae Christianae)*, ed. and trans. Charles Fantazzi. University of Chicago Press.

Voigt, Georg 1859. *Die Wiederbelebung des classischen Alterthums oder das erste Jahrhundert des Humanismus*. Berlin: Georg Reimer.

Wieland, Georg 1981. *Ethica – scientia practica. Die Anfänge der philosophischen Ethik im 13. Jahrhundert*. Münster: Aschendorff.

Wieland, Georg 1990. 'The Reception and Interpretation of Aristotle's *Ethics*', in Norman Kretzmann, Anthony Kenny and Jan Pinborg (eds.), *The Cambridge History of Later Medieval Philosophy*. Cambridge University Press, 657–72.

16

The Protestant Reformation

JESSE COUENHOVEN

The Protestant Reformation was a diverse spiritual, intellectual, and political revolution. It spanned multiple countries – particularly the areas we now call Germany, Switzerland, and Great Britain – though its influence was felt throughout Europe. Even France, under Henry IV, flirted with disestablishing Catholicism. Partly because of its gradual political progress, the Reformation worked its influence out over decades of European history, with seminal figures appearing in different places at a variety of times. Thus, it might be more accurate to talk of reformations than of a single reformation movement. This suggestion is substantiated by the lasting divisions between the main churches born of the Reformation, the Lutheran, Reformed, and Anglican denominations.

It should not be forgotten that alongside these reformations another revolution of thought and practice was taking place – the "Radical Reformation," which birthed such movements as the Mennonites and Brethren, among others. These diverse, often populist reformers sought to make radical changes to the ethos of their day, experimenting with the abolition of hierarchies of authority, permitting women to preach, living in communities that shared goods in common, and practicing pacifism.

Because of the Reformation's complexity, it is not possible to speak with any accuracy of "the moral philosophy of the Protestant Reformation" as if there were one such thing. Consider, for example, the attitude of leading reformers towards ancient philosophy. Although Martin Luther was bitterly opposed to Aristotle's influence on the moral theology of his day, his favored follower Phillip Melanchthon was openly deeply influenced by Aristotle, and their sometime ally and opponent Huldrych Zwingli drew on Stoic as well as Greek philosophy in his defense of divine predestination.[1] The Reformation

---

[1] For helpful introductions to these figures and other important Reformation thinkers, see Bagchi and Steinmetz 2004.

held under its umbrella multiple philosophies, albeit with family resem-
blances enough that the major aims and teachings of its leading figures can
be recognized as sharing a reforming impulse that sought to correct abuses of
Catholic practice and teaching, return to the Biblical texts, and re-emphasize
the priority of divine grace for the Christian life. Rather than attempt to cover
any significant number of the leading figures of the Reformation, this essay
focuses on the thought of the two most influential members of its first and
second generation, Martin Luther and John Calvin.

LUTHER AND CALVIN'S ATTACK ON SCHOLASTICISM

It is widely thought that these reformers said little of interest to philosophers.
This overlooks the fact that most of the theological thought of their time, not
to mention the medieval era before them, was also philosophical. Given that
reality, they could hardly help engaging a variety of philosophical ideas as
they responded to the Scholastic theologies influential in Europe. It is true
that they were committed to distinguishing philosophy from theology, saw
themselves as doing the latter, and mistrusted much of what they considered
the speculative errors of Aristotelian and especially Ockhamist philosophers.
Their distinction between philosophy and theology pertained not to subject
matter, however, but sources. They were focused not only on writing about
God or "religion" but on writing about (and only about) matters on which
God had shed light in the revelations given to the Church. Thus, they often
wrote on philosophical topics, including questions about freedom and
epistemology.

Luther, who was born in Germany in 1483 and died in his hometown of
Eisleben in 1546, is famously the theologian who challenged Catholic teaching
about indulgences with the argument that salvation is a divine gift that
cannot be earned. Calvin, who was born in France in 1509 and died in
Geneva, Switzerland in 1564, made clear his tremendous debts to Luther,
but his training as a humanist and his different cultural context clearly
differentiated the two thinkers. Luther and Calvin had important disagreements (for instance, over the nature of the Eucharist), and even where they
did not disagree they often differed in the emphasis they placed on certain
themes or the extent to which they developed those themes. That and their
marked differences in writing style have sometimes obscured how harmonious their thought often was. This is particularly true of their moral
philosophies, a topic where Calvin developed a number of claims Luther
had made before him.

An important point of agreement between Luther and Calvin, though one that went without saying, was their conviction that ethics is a derivative discipline. They had a number of reasons for taking this view. As Calvin wrote at the beginning of his *Institutes*, "man never achieves a clear knowledge of himself unless he has first looked upon God's face."[2] Calvin believed that we cannot understand the nature of the claims upon us without first having a deep knowledge of ourselves – and that we can understand ourselves only if we understand our relationship to God. Anthropology informs ethics, therefore, and theology informs anthropology. A second reason for thinking of ethics as derivative related to their well-known mistrust of human reason. What moral norms a person can know in the light of reason alone, if any, is a contested topic in Luther and Calvin scholarship. Both agreed, however, that the true nature and goal of moral law can be known only in the light of revelation. This was not only an epistemic claim but also a reference to the origin of norms, which are promulgated by divine command.

The discussion below follows the order of thought just mentioned, discussing Luther and Calvin's conception of human nature and agency as a background to explicating their moral philosophies. It should be noted that Luther, unlike Calvin, was not a systematic thinker, and his approach often lacked nuance. He saw himself as a pioneering "rough woodsman" whose task was to hew through thorns and briars in order to clear a new path; he referred those who preferred a more subtle theology to Melanchthon. Calvin sought, to some extent, to tidy up after Luther, though he too resisted "speculation," the temptation to develop his claims in ways that went beyond what Scripture clearly mandated.

Luther was clear about his negative philosophical agenda: undermining Aristotle's influence. Luther wrote that "He who wishes to philosophize by using Aristotle without danger to his soul must first become thoroughly foolish in Christ."[3] Accordingly, he had the courses on Aristotle at Wittenberg replaced by courses on Augustine. This does not mean he was ignorant about Scholastic philosophy, or Aristotle.[4] Unlike Calvin, who lacked theological training early in his career, Luther was well acquainted with the theological schools of his day. Luther even lectured on Aristotle for a time, and one of his first works, now lost, was a commentary on Aristotle's *Physics*.

The reformers were skeptical of Ockhamist philosophy because they were convinced that it understood morality and spirituality in a fundamentally

---

[2] Calvin 1960, I.1.2.   [3] Luther 1957b: 41.   [4] See, for instance, Luther 1957a.

backwards manner.[5] Aristotle took for granted that the point of the moral life is to strive to do the best one can with one's natural powers. The Ockhamists' Christian addendum to this pagan concept of the good life was that God would reward those who did their best and be gracious to them.[6] By contrast, Luther believed that reading Augustine and *Romans* had converted him from pagan ethics, which requires human beings to earn their own value, to the true Christian philosophy that God gives us the value that we have without our having first earned it. Challenging Aristotelian claims that righteousness is achieved by doing good and that a proper education teaches what we should strive for, Luther defended what he considered the true Christian view. Only those who are already righteous can genuinely do good; we cannot incrementally work our way up into virtue because our intent must be right in order to do good. A proper Christian moral education, therefore, teaches what someone else has done for me.[7] Luther's ethos is apparent in his comment that good works "should be done as fruits of righteousness, not in order to bring righteousness into being. Having been made righteous, we must do them; but it is not ... that when we are unrighteous we become righteous by doing them."[8]

A corollary of this view is that human worth is a gift, not a task. The reformers believed that the error of thinking that we can and must earn our worth had led the Catholic church into a number of errors. One was a kind of Pelagianism, the belief that human beings can come to deserve God's love without relying on God's help. Another was its teaching about indulgences, which suggested that it is possible to buy divine favor.

It is widely believed that Luther and Calvin's views were based on their low estimate of human capacities after the fall into sin. On this reading, their point was that we cannot make ourselves righteous because we are too weak. There is some truth in this claim. Luther and Calvin were not optimistic about the agential powers of sinners, and they considered the Scholastic philosophical theology with which they were familiar generally mistaken about the nature of human psychology, responsibility, and free will. However, the point Luther made in the quote above was mainly conceptual. Although the effects of the fall played a significant role in Protestant thought, Luther and Calvin's approach to ethics, merit, and agency was not contingent on the fall.

---

[5] We will see, however, that Calvin was more appreciative of Aristotle, whose ideas he appropriated eclectically.

[6] Cf. Kolb 2005: 19.   [7] Luther 1963: 91. See Meilaender 1988 for helpful commentary.

[8] Luther 1963: 169.

The core of their moral philosophy was based on their conception of God's plan in creation. Even before the fall the Christian life was not about striving to be worthy of God's love – it was a matter of living out of the love God had already given, celebrating the worth Adam and Eve already had. For Adam and Eve, too, then, the point of human existence was not to make themselves good but to return God's love with their own. This fundamental claim had a number of significant ramifications that Luther developed insightfully, if not always as carefully as Calvin.

LUTHER AND CALVIN ON HUMAN AGENCY

When Luther wrote that the sinner is unable to earn God's favor through his works, he had in mind both the basic theological claim just mentioned – that human beings are only ungrateful if they seek to earn the favor God freely bestows – and an additional claim about human psychology. *The Bondage of the Will* in particular clarified this second assertion, which is that "a person does what is in him."[9] Luther's re-interpretation of this Scholastic saying was that human beings choose only what they are motivated to choose. Moreover, human motives express aspects of personality that are too deeply imbedded within human hearts and minds to be objects of choice. We make our choices because of who we are; we are not, Luther thought, able to choose who we are. Luther developed this claim with two striking metaphors. The most famous was his image of the human will as a beast of burden, subject to one of two riders, either God or Satan. To be subject to God is "royal freedom" but to be subject to Satan is mere bondage.[10] Similarly, Luther often referred to human beings as trees, bearing whatever fruit is the natural result of the sort of roots a person has. These metaphors were his own, but in using them Luther was following Augustine's anti-Pelagian writings (as he and Calvin often pointed out).

Luther's moral psychology was less complex than Augustine's had been – perhaps because Luther sought to avoid speculating about matters not directly implied by revelation, or perhaps because he did not see such work as part of the task given to him. Nevertheless, the outlines of his view were distinctly Augustinian, beginning with his picture of personal volition as flowing from a person's basic orientation. This was good news for those who put their trust in God's love, but bad news for sinners as such, who can do nothing to save themselves. Indeed, Luther argued, moral and religious

[9] Cf. Luther 1957b: 50–1.   [10] Luther 1972: 65.

law had been promulgated precisely to teach sinners to despair of their own abilities and to seek help from outside themselves.

Original sin, Luther insisted, left human beings "without the capacity to do anything but sin" and thus without significant choices.[11] The sinners' fundamental problem, from which all other sins stem, is lack of belief in God, in whose love the sinner is not content to rest. The choices of original sinners flow from this basic and flawed source, the unwillingness to let God be God, and the attempt to be creators of value in God's place. At times Luther made it sound as though his belief in divine foreknowledge and divine immutability had led him to believe in a complete divine determinism, but his theology as a whole nuanced this claim in two ways. First, like most theologians he considered it impossible for God to be the author of sin. Evil wills, he concluded, are not caused by God though they are permitted by God for God's own, often inscrutable reasons (which Luther found it counterproductive to inquire into). This suggested that although the overall outcomes of happenings in God's creation are planned by God, God does not directly and personally micromanage each and every aspect of creation. Second, Luther granted that "you might perhaps rightly attribute some measure of choice to man, but to attribute free choice in relation to divine things is too much."[12] His claim was that human beings have choice with regard to "what is beneath them," meaning spiritually insignificant matters such as decisions about one's apparel. Free choice is lacking, however, with regard to "what is above them," matters that pertain to salvation.[13]

Luther was no libertarian about human free will. It was precisely libertarian ideas that Luther had in mind (under a different name, of course, since that term did not exist in his day) when he made his more extravagant statements about there being no such thing as free choice. His point was that the sort of choice sought by leading thinkers of his time, including his onetime ally Erasmus, is nonexistent. Erasmus thought of free choice as the ability to choose or turn away from the things that lead to salvation. Luther argued that fallen human beings have no power worthy of the name free choice.

Luther's sweeping unwillingness to speak of postlapsarian human free will has led many to view him as a fatalist who did not take human agency seriously, or some kind of radical divine command theorist who held that God was just no matter what God decreed or how those decrees related to their objects. Luther was indeed a divine command theorist who held that

---

[11] Ibid., 272. [12] Ibid., 103. [13] Ibid., 70.

because obligations are created by God's commands, God has no obligations to the creation. However, Luther did not simply hold that God made moral claims or assessments by fiat. Though Luther often found God's ways hidden, on this topic he discerned a logic in the divine judgments that followed the order God set up in creating and redeeming humanity, and which referred back to the goodness of God's own nature. The order of the divine commands was not something that Luther considered even unfallen human minds capable of deeply understanding, but he affirmed that it follows a high logic that we can sometimes follow.

A key to properly assessing Luther's view of human agency is recognizing the fact that he followed Augustine in reserving the term "freedom" for those who are good – only God and human beings and angels who live within God's grace are free. Correspondingly, his understanding of human agency was that of a "compatibilist" (or "soft determinist"). That modern term for thinkers who consider responsibility compatible with necessity is, of course, anachronistic. Luther's view fits neatly into the category, however, and it is better to call Luther something he would not have called himself than to mistake him for a fatalist.

Readers who prescind from Luther's polemical tone find his claims more subtle than he sometimes let on. I have mentioned that Luther granted the possibility that we often make free choices about "lower" matters. In the light of his convictions that what God foreknows will necessarily happen, and that God foreknows everything about the created order, it would not seem to make sense for Luther to have had libertarian free choices in mind, unless he was being inconsistent. But he did indicate that we should expect a basic "civil" righteousness not only from Christians but from pagans and other theists as well. Laws are meant to keep wickedness within bounds, and by and large Luther took for granted that anyone is able to follow such laws. This seems to suggest that sinners have the power to follow certain aspects of the law. Even if they necessarily do what God foresees them doing, that only proves that they act without alternatives, not that they act for any particular reason, or that they act because God made them do so. Thus, Luther granted that human agents have some power for good with regard to "lower" things.

The ability not to violate state law is not especially laudatory, however, because the law is enforced by coercion and keeping the law is therefore at least partially motivated by self-interest. No matter how good one's life may appear, Luther thought that those who have not been specially graced by God lack the ability to make choices of ultimate significance. Human powers extend to many things, but not far enough to make a difference to our final end. We lack significant choices because as beings who live out of ourselves, we cannot remake ourselves. Thus, although the motivational powers we have been given may allow us to choose how, by worldly standards, to be a success or whether to be one, they do not give us the ability to live up to God's standards, which require of us a trust and humility that is at once the simplest and hardest possible thing. Such persons are not free.

Luther might have made his point more clearly had he developed a more complex philosophy of action, but he made no attempt to offer an account of the meaning of "free will" or "free choice" that challenged the dominant paradigm of his day. Rather than recasting free choice as the ability to do what you will (as we will see Calvin did), Luther simply argued that there is no such thing as free choice. He found other views sophistical in their sophistication.

As a compatibilist, Luther's answer to the question of what makes post-lapsarian sinners responsible before God for the unbelief that they cannot help having was not (merely) that God says so. Divine judgment on sinners is a clue that points to the sort of agency human beings have. Although Luther did not argue the point explicitly, he took for granted that only human beings and angels can be blamed as sinners because only they have the volitional and rational powers that allow persons to be either the image or the anti-image of God. He highlighted the fact that Judas and other Biblical sinners were not under compulsion when they sinned. God does not force them to sin, he insisted, nor does God take away their agency; they acted willingly. So while sinners cannot do what they ought, that is because they do not want to. And not wanting to be good was, for Luther, irreducibly blameworthy.

Luther employed a corresponding distinction between two kinds of necessity: the necessity of "immutability" and the necessity of compulsion. The former pertains to the inability of the will to change its basic orientation: "when a man is without the Spirit of God he does not do evil against his will, as if he were taken by the scruff of the neck and forced to it . . . but he does it of his own accord and with a ready will."[14] The necessity of compulsion, by contrast, takes place when one is forced into something against one's will. Postlapsarian human beings are under the necessity of immutability, which seems similar to the inability to abandon one's commitments some recent authors have named "volitional necessity."[15] Because sinners cannot believe that their worth and standing come from outside themselves, and as a result continually seek to justify their own existence, they cannot turn from sin. But

---

[14] Ibid., 64.   [15] See, for instance, Watson 2002.

they are not typically under compulsion. If they are, they are excused from blame.

Because the sinner cannot help being a sinner, Luther viewed the "ought" promulgated in the moral and the spiritual law not as a guide for right action but as a goad that teaches human beings where to place their hope. When it becomes clear that humanity is unable to rise to the demands of the law, the lesson that we ought to learn is not to try harder, which only exacerbates our problems, but that we should call for help. For Luther, therefore, "ought" did not imply "can," if "can" refers to the unaided power of individual human wills. However, what is commanded can be done with God's help.

This brings us to Luther's conception of Christian agency. One aspect of salvation is God's gracious re-making of the sinful will. Luther described the sinner as "incurvatus in se," turned in on oneself. The need to validate oneself focuses one's gaze upon oneself. Those who are genuinely good, by contrast, look outwards without fretting about themselves. Grace frees them to attend to others. This grace cannot be resisted, but since the will itself undergoes repair, those who are sanctified do not resist, and are not compelled. It was important for Luther that Christians say "I am yours" to the Spirit, even though they cannot say "I am not yours." God recreates Christians not to overwhelm their agency but so that they might cooperate with him.[16] God does not work within us without us, Luther wrote.

In a sense, the Christian is "slave and captive" to the Spirit, but in Luther's view human beings are always worshipping some god. The question is not whether we make some principle central to our lives but which one. Bowing to our creator and redeemer, who gives us our worth and asks us to rest in it, is the only way to have the royal freedom that makes it possible to be so free from existential need that we can follow Christ in being lords of all and yet at the same time the servants of all. This particular sort of elevated servitude counts as freedom because freedom is a concept he, like Augustine, understood primarily in normative terms. Those who are free require certain capacities in order to be free, but a power for alternatives was not among Luther's requirements. After all, the devil is not free, even though he has a mind and will of the highest order. If so, freedom must be characterized not only by the ability to act of one's own accord but by the life in love that is divine. Only human beings who are "little Christs" are free.

* * *

[16] Luther 1972: 243.

Calvin attempted to follow Luther's lead on these topics. His efforts to deal with some of the questions raised by Luther's views sometimes led him to make alterations, but he did so to preserve what he took to be Luther's main point. Calvin, therefore, sought to nuance and develop Luther's compatibilism.[17]

In support of the claim that actions and good or bad character can be both voluntary and necessary, Calvin particularly cited Augustine and Bernard of Clairvaux. Both had noted that although God is good of necessity, we nonetheless praise God. This is appropriate, they claimed, because God's goodness is voluntary.[18] Calvin followed Luther in arguing that the converse point is true of the devil and other sinners; they are culpable because they sin voluntary, even if they also sin necessarily.

Luther's suggestion that everything happens by necessity had been met with consternation, and Calvin made use of the traditional Aristotelian distinction between absolute and contingent necessity to clarify that most of what happens in the created order could have happened otherwise, had God willed it.[19] Yet because God's will cannot be thwarted, Calvin insisted that Luther was basically right: what God wills, or knows, must happen. He was careful to add that the Christian view differs from the mechanical chain of necessity associated with Stoicism.[20] What God makes necessary is made so by an active and ongoing presence, not simply a causal process set in motion long ago. At the same time, Calvin was more insistent than Luther that it is unhelpful to say that God merely permits some evils, as Luther had indicated. God is finally responsible for everything, and Calvin argued that God in one way or another is behind all events in history.

However, God cannot be blamed, and for two reasons. First, Calvin agreed that God could not be in the wrong, since right is established by divine commands. God cannot violate a duty because God has none. Second, Calvin argued that God is always good because God's intentions are never bad.[21] The implication of this claim is that no actions are intrinsically bad, at least for God; everything depends on intent. And it is possible for God to intend for good what human beings intend for evil – the death of Christ on the cross is the obvious example, but Calvin found similar events throughout Scripture.

In response to widespread concern that Luther's picture of human agency was too passive, Calvin offered a somewhat richer account of the human activity that responds to prevenient grace. While maintaining the priority of

---

[17] On Calvin's compatibilism, see, for instance, Helm 2010.   [18] Calvin 1996: 4.333.
[19] Calvin 1997: 177–8.   [20] Calvin 1996: 2.257.   [21] Calvin 1997: 179–82.

God's love, Calvin went beyond Luther's somewhat vague claims about God working with us by appropriating Aristotle. He wrote that the *habitus* of the will is reoriented by God's grace.[22] This specified how receiving sanctifying grace changes a person. The will has a new "form" after its encounter with God, one that reorients it toward the good.

Calvin also interpreted Luther's claim that human beings have choice over "external and public" affairs. Sinners have free choice in a compatibilist sense only. Insofar as "free" means "not coerced" sinners have free choice – they are not forced to act as they do but sin by their own evil intent.[23] Without God's grace, however, they lack the power to save themselves, much like the coward who cannot bring himself to challenge an adversary. This bondage is voluntary, composed of the sinner's own foolish and misdirected will. Because it is self-determined, Calvin granted that there is a sense in which the bondage of sin is free. Yet it is also strange to call those who are slaves to sin free, and indeed it is confusing to the many people who immediately think that free choice implies a power for self-control that sinners lack. Moreover, Calvin agreed that sinners cannot, of themselves, fulfill God's commands even though they ought to do so.[24] Thus, he too preferred not to speak of free choice in sinners. Like Luther, Calvin understood freedom not to primarily mean having options, or even self-determination, but to have the positive meaning of sharing in God's life.

LUTHER AND CALVIN'S ANTI-EUDAIMONISM

These ideas made Luther and Calvin's thought anti-moralistic, and in some ways anti-eudaimonistic. This is not to say that they were not virtue theorists; they were concerned with states of character more than right action. However, they did not see personal happiness as the end of the good life, at least in this life, and they did not believe that personal flourishing was the main goal of those who must die. Those who are united to Christ should follow his example and forget themselves. They found conventional morality more a danger to the soul than a help, since it is misleading to believe that we can make ourselves good by following rules when what is needful is new delights and sorrows. Calvin particularly resisted offering praise to human moral achievements, since without God's help we only do less than we ought.

---

[22] Calvin 1996: 6.378.   [23] Ibid., 2.279.   [24] Ibid., 4.331–2.

The reformers did defend a positive, if secondary, role for moral laws in fallen societies that need to create minimal peace and order. However, because they considered it impossible even for graced sinners to exhibit anything more than deeply flawed virtue they saw moral codes as a pragmatic necessity that made space for the work of the Gospel. The first use of the moral law, they agreed, was to convince us of the hopelessness of trying to make ourselves better.

Calvin added that there is a tertiary, positive use for the law, for those who have been baptized into Christ's life. In practice, Luther could only agree. Luther implicitly defended a positive role for ethical principles when he counseled spouses about how to interact, women about their role in leadership, or princes and peasants about their obligations to one another. Nonetheless, Calvin was clearer about this so-called "third use" of the law, and it was more central to his theology and the practices of his people in Geneva. Calvin's corrections to Luther's views led him to emphasize the activity of the Christian agent somewhat more, with the result that Calvin tended to develop themes of human perfectibility more than Luther, whose characteristic emphasis lay on God's forgiveness of us.

Yet both Luther and Calvin believed in the imperfectibility of humanity, until the life to come. This plus their conviction that God bestows worth on humanity as a gift rather than as a merited reward led them to challenge standard conceptions of ethics. They discerned a gap between what humanity is able to be and what is properly asked of us, and they resisted attempts to mitigate that gap by expecting humanity to do more, whether those attempts expressed themselves in Ockhamist theories of free agency or short-cuts such as indulgences.[25] They also resisted attempts to lower the moral demands placed upon humanity, or to mitigate the blame due for human bondage to evil. The solution to our failure to be what we ought, they believed, has been given to us. Accepting that offer was a lifelong task in which ethics and spirituality coincided.

BIBLIOGRAPHY

An asterisk denotes secondary literature especially suitable for further reading.

Bagchi, David, and David C. Steinmetz, ed. 2004. *The Cambridge Companion to Reformation Theology.* Cambridge University Press.*

[25] I owe the idea of the "moral gap" to Hare (1996).

Calvin, John. 1960. *Institutes of the Christian Religion*. Translated by Ford Lewis Battles. Edited by John T. McNeill. Philadelphia, PA: The Westminster Press.

Calvin, John. 1996. *The Bondage and Liberation of the Will: A Defence of the Orthodox Doctrine of Human Choice against Pighius*. Translated by Graham I. Davies. Edited by A.N.S. Lane. Grand Rapids, MI: Baker Books.

Calvin, John. 1997. *Concerning the Eternal Predestination of God*. Translated by J.K.S. Reid. Louisville, KY: Westminster John Knox Press.

Hare, John E. 1996. *The Moral Gap: Kantian Ethics, Human Limits, and God's Assistance*. New York: Oxford University Press.

Helm, Paul. 2010. "Calvin the Compatibilist." In *Calvin at the Centre*. New York: Oxford University Press, 227–72.

Kolb, Robert. 2005. *Bound Choice, Election, and Wittenberg Theological Method: From Martin Luther to the Formula of Concord*. Grand Rapids, MI: William B. Eerdmans Publishing Company.

Luther, Martin. 1957a. "Disputation against Scholastic Theology." Translated by Harold J. Grimm. In *Luther's Works*, vol. 31: *Career of the Reformer I*, edited by Helmut T. Lehmann and Harold J. Grimm. Philadelphia, PA: Fortress Press, 3–16.

Luther, Martin. 1957b. "Heidelberg Disputation." Translated by Harold J. Grimm. In *Luther's Works*, vol. 31: *Career of the Reformer I*, edited by Helmut T. Lehmann and Harold J. Grimm. Philadelphia, PA: Fortress Press, 35–70.

Luther, Martin. 1963. *Lectures on Galatians 1535: Chapters 1–4*. Translated by Jaroslav Pelikan. In *Luther's Works*, vol. 26, edited by Jaroslav Pelikan. Saint Louis, MI: Concordia Publishing House.

Luther, Martin. 1972. *The Bondage of the Will*. Translated by Philip S. Watson and Benjamin Drewery. In *Luther's Works*, vol. 33: *Career of the Reformer III*, edited by Helmut T. Lehmann. Philadelphia, PA: Fortress Press.

Meilaender, Gilbert. 1988. "The Examined Life is Not Worth Living: Learning from Luther." In *The Theory and Practice of Virtue*. South Bend, IN: University of Notre Dame Press, 100–26.

Watson, Gary. 2002. "Volitional Necessities." In *Contours of Agency*, edited by Sarah Buss and Lee Overton. Cambridge, MA: The MIT Press, 129–59.

17

Descartes's Provisional Morality

LISA SHAPIRO

In Part Three of his *Discourse on the Method for Rightly Conducting Reason*, first published in French, in 1637, Descartes introduces what he characterizes as "a *morale par provision* consisting of three or four maxims" (CSM 1:122; AT 6:23).[1] There are a number of issues, both interpretive and philosophical, concerned with this *morale par provision*. In many ways, these issues derive from understanding this peculiar expression itself. In what way do these maxims constitute a *morale*, that is, a moral code or an ethics? How can they guide us in our practical lives, in helping us determine what we ought to do? And what does it mean for this moral code to be *par provision*? Because the answer to this last question can inform the answer to the other two, I begin there. However, it will be helpful to have an initial overview of the maxims themselves.

The first maxim on its face adopts a blend of conservatism and moderation: "to obey the laws and customs of my country, holding constantly to the religion in which by God's grace I had been instructed since my childhood, and governing myself in all other matters according to the most moderate and least extreme opinions" (ibid.). The second maxim – "to be as firm and decisive in my actions as I could, and to follow even the most doubtful opinions, once I had adopted them, with no less constancy than if they had been quite certain" (CSM 1:123; AT 6:24) – prescribes resoluteness in one's decisions. The third maxim concerns self-mastery: "to try always to master myself rather than fortune, and change my desires rather than the order of the world" (CSM 1:123; AT 6:25). The fourth maxim consists of choosing as his

---

[1] References to Descartes's writings are cited internally as follows: CSM vol.: page = Descartes (1984–91), vols. 1–2; CSMK page = Descartes (1984–91), vol. 3; AT vol.: page = Descartes (1996). Translations of Descartes's correspondence with Princess Elisabeth are my own, cited as ED (Princess Elisabeth and Descartes 2007). Translations of *Passions of the Soul* are drawn from Descartes 1989, and cited internally as Voss page.

life's occupation "to continue with the very one I was engaged in, and to devote my whole life to cultivating my reason and advancing as far as I could in the knowledge of the truth, following the method I had prescribed for myself" (CSM 1:124; AT 6:27), but Descartes does not recommend that everyone pursue the life of a philosopher. Indeed, he suggests that it is not likely to be suited to everyone.

PAR PROVISION

"*Morale par provision*" has been widely translated as "provisional morality," thereby implying that the set of maxims Descartes offers in the *Discourse* is temporary, a stop-gap measure put in place to allow one to make practical decisions while in the grip of skeptical worries. Until recently, this reading of the *Discourse* maxims dominated considerations of Descartes's ethics. (See Gilson 1976; Rutherford 2008.) There are both philosophical and textual reasons for going down this route.

First, as is well known, Descartes's philosophical project is grounded in a skeptical method, and a radical skepticism in particular. The Cartesian goal is to arrive at a set of beliefs, all of which are true, and that goal is achieved not by considering each belief on its own, as it becomes salient, but rather by doubting all our beliefs at the outset, and taking them to be false. Such radical doubt, however, presents real practical challenges: if one truly rejects *all* of one's beliefs, it is not clear how one could ever take action, including the basic actions through which we preserve ourselves and manage to get by in the world. If we genuinely take it that the apple that appears to be before us is not there, within arm's reach, on what basis would we move to grab the apple and take a bite? If we are genuinely taking even the most evident truths to be dubious, how are we going to engage with our neighbors to procure goods and services? In order to ensure that we remain around and intact long enough to achieve our epistemic goals, it seems that we will have to take some actions. What, however, ought the basis for those actions to be? It is tempting to read the *morale par provision* in the *Discourse* as addressing this question. The maxims, on this reading, are meant to provide agents with a set of principles to guide actions that can ensure that the conditions for achieving the overriding epistemic goal are met. Such a reading recognizes that the *morale* has pragmatic value, but it also presumes that while under the cloud of skepticism we have no rational basis for thinking that this pragmatic value tracks real value or the good.

This reading gains traction from the way in which Descartes introduces the maxims, drawing an analogy between the shelter one secures while rebuilding one's house and the maxims to guide his actions while he suspended his judgement in his search for truth (CSM 1:122; AT 6:22). The implication seems to be that the maxims are temporary guides just as is the place in which one lives during a major renovation. The metaphor of the tree of philosophy Descartes offers in the Preface to the French edition of the *Principles of Philosophy* keeps this reading on course. According to the model put forward in the metaphor, morals is a branch of the tree, growing out of the trunk of physics (or natural philosophy), which is in turn rooted in metaphysics. However, Descartes specifies morals as "the highest and most perfect moral system," one which "presupposes a complete knowledge of the other sciences and is the ultimate level of wisdom" (CSM 1:186; AT 9B:14). Given that the *morale par provision* is presented from the skeptical position, it certainly cannot presuppose "complete knowledge of the other sciences." It thus cannot be, so it seems, "morals" properly speaking, but something put in place until we arrive at the true morality. It makes sense, then, to think of the *morale* as provisional.

Michelle LeDoeuff (1989) has suggested a different reading of *"par provision,"* distinguishing that expression from *"provisionnelle."* LeDoeuff maintains that *"par provision"* invokes a juridical context and ought to be read as meaning "'what a judgement awards in advance to a party' . . . The provision is not liable to be put in question by the final judgement" (LeDoeuff 1989: 62). This re-interpretation, along with attention to Descartes's articulation of his moral philosophy in his correspondence with Princess Elisabeth of Bohemia and in the *Passions of the Soul*, has opened up other ways of understanding Descartes's *morale par provision*.

One way to go, consistent with LeDoeuff's reinterpretation, is to maintain that while the *morale* is not Descartes's final moral philosophy, there remains a continuity between the *morale* and Descartes's perfect moral system. On this view, the *morale* is understood as not merely of pragmatic value but rather as a fledgling moral theory in and of itself. It is a first approximation of a moral theory, one that will require revision and modification. (See Marshall (1998) as an exemplary version of this line.) This line of interpretation has the advantage of being able to accommodate the context of skepticism in which the maxims are introduced, whilst at the same time recognizing the maxims as a genuinely moral code.

Nonetheless, this reading would seem to predict that Descartes's ethical views ought to develop from the *Discourse morale* through his other works. Instead, there is a remarkable constancy from the *morale* articulated in the *Discourse*, to the remarks in correspondence with Princess Elisabeth of

Bohemia and Queen Christina, to the *Passions of the Soul*. Consider the second maxim: "to be as firm and decisive in my actions as I could, and to follow even the most doubtful opinions, once I had adopted them, with no less constancy than if they had been quite certain" (CSM 1:123; AT 6:24). In his correspondence with Princess Elisabeth in 1645, in commenting on what he thinks Seneca ought to have said in his *De vita beata*, Descartes sets out explicitly just in what he takes virtue to consist: "a firm and constant resolution to carry out whatever reason recommends" (to Elisabeth, 4 August 1645, ED 98; AT 4:265). The similarity between this definition of virtue and the second maxim is evident, and Descartes himself appeals to the *Discourse* in setting out this account to Elisabeth. Moreover, as the correspondence continues, he reiterates this point numerous times. In his letter to her of 18 August 1645 he writes: "In order to have a contentment that is solid, it is necessary to follow virtue – that is to say, to have a firm and constant will to execute all that we judge to be the best, and to employ all the force of our understanding to judge well" (ED 104–5; AT 4:277). And the same point is made in another letter to Elisabeth of 1 September 1645: "Thus, we know of no exercise of virtue (that is to say, what our reason convinces us we ought to do) from which we do not receive satisfaction and pleasure" (ED 107–8; AT 4:284). Descartes also makes the same claim about the nature of virtue to Queen Christina in his letter of 20 November 1647:

> I do not see that it is possible to dispose it [the will] better than by a firm and constant resolution to carry out to the letter all the things which one judges to be the best, and to employ all the power of one's mind in finding out what these are. This by itself constitutes all the virtues; this alone, finally, produces the greatest and most solid contentment in life. So I concluded that it is this which constitutes the supreme good. (CSMK 325; AT 5:83)

Moreover, this same account of virtue is carried forward into the *Passions of the Soul*, where, in article 148, he writes:

> For anyone who has lived in such a way that his conscience cannot reproach him for ever having failed to do anything he judged to be the best (which is what I call following virtue here) derives a satisfaction with such power to make him happy that the most vigorous assaults of the passions never have enough power to disturb the tranquility of his soul. (Voss 101; AT 11:442)

Descartes's clear commitment to this second maxim, and his leaving its formulation essentially unchanged, argues against the view that the *morale* maxims are merely provisional, or a stopgap measure. It also undermines the reading that understands the *morale* to be an approximation. It is worth noting that Descartes also reaffirms the first and third maxims of the *morale* in correspondence with Elisabeth, as well as in the *Passions of the Soul*, further arguing against the standard readings. (See CSMK, 257f, AT 4:265ff; CSMK, 263f, AT 4:284ff; CSMK, 267, AT 4:294ff; as well as *Passions* articles 144–6, Voss 97–100, AT 11:436ff.) The *morale* of the *Discourse* thus seems to be quite close to Descartes's ultimate view.

The consistency of the position raises another question. If, in fact, Descartes is committed to the moral maxims he first articulates in the *Discourse*, on what basis does he hold these maxims? Namaan-Zauderer (2010) argues that while Descartes took at least some of the maxims to be well grounded from a practical point of view, he nonetheless wanted them to be fully supported by metaphysical and scientific investigations. The provisional character of the maxims consists in their awaiting this full grounding. Recent work by Cimakasky and Polansky has argued that the maxims of the *morale* parallel the rules constituting the method for rightly conducting reason as outlined in Part Two of the *Discourse* (Cimakasky and Polansky 2012). They take seriously Descartes's own suggestion that the maxims follow from the method (see in particular CSM 111; AT 6:1 and CSM 142; AT 6:61). Though the first maxim of the *morale* would seem to contravene Descartes's first rule of the method – "to include nothing more in my judgements than what presented itself to my mind so clearly and so distinctly that I had no occasion to doubt it" (CSM 1:120; AT 6:18) – they argue that aspects of the first maxim require the same critical attitude articulated in the first rule. The first moral maxim requires one to follow the "most moderate and least extreme opinions," and this would seem to entail an evaluation of which opinions are the most sensible, an evaluation involving the attitude of doubt which hones in on clear and distinct perceptions. Similarly, they argue that the distinction of relevant alternatives presupposed in the resolute decision to pursue an action, called for in the second maxim of the *morale*, is analogous to the injunction of the second rule to resolve a problem into its component parts. The third maxim of the *morale*, which exhorts us to master ourselves rather than fortune, and identifies nothing as "entirely in our power but our thoughts" (CSM 1:123; AT 6:25), clearly resonates with the third rule of the method, "to direct my thoughts in an orderly manner" (CSM 1:120; AT 6:18). And finally, the fourth maxim seems to be a direct result of applying the fourth rule – "to make enumerations so complete, and reviews so comprehensive, that I could be sure of leaving nothing out" (CSM 1:120; AT 6:19) – to the practical sphere: Descartes's conclusion to pursue the philosophical life is not only a direct result of a survey of a full slate of other possibilities, it is also pursued precisely because doing so involves a commitment to the method. On this reading, the *morale* is grounded in the same way as the method for rightly conducting reason. It is fitting then that the *morale* is first articulated in the *Discourse*, whose aim is to defend Descartes's methodological commitments, in part by arguing just how fertile it is.

However, if the *morale* is to be understood as the method for rightly conducting reason applied to the practical sphere, it is not clear how to understand Descartes's allusions to a perfect moral system. If the maxims are indeed grounded by the rules of the method, in what sense are they perfectible? If they are properly grounded, what more needs to be articulated about the *morale*? If they are not fully grounded, what more support needs to be provided?

Approaching the maxims of the *morale* by looking at the historical context in which Descartes was writing can perhaps help in addressing these questions. The seventeenth century saw a revival of Stoic philosophy owing largely to the recovery of Stoic texts and the work of Justus Lipsius in laying out Stoic philosophy from its physics to its ethics. There has been a growing effort at tracing the impact of this Stoic revival on early modern ethical theories. (See Levi 1964, Rutherford 2004.) That Hugo Grotius (*The Laws of War and Peace*) was influenced by Stoic texts is well documented and, equally, it is widely recognized that works of the French moralists Pierre Charron and Guillaume Du Vair, among others, served to popularize Stoic ethics in France. (Charron was also influenced by the revival of skepticism.) Equally, Descartes's moral writings are increasingly seen as having a distinctly Stoic aspect. The Stoic sage was characterized by his success at self-mastery, that is, aligning his desires with the order of nature, and this is precisely what the third maxim of the *morale* demands. Equally, just as the second maxim calls for resoluteness in action, so too must the Stoic sage be guided solely by his proper understanding and not turned by external influences. The affinity between Descartes's maxims and Stoic ethics certainly suggests a line of influence. (For a more detailed accounting of the Stoic influence implicit in these maxims see Namaan-Zauderer 2010.) Equally, Descartes's selection of Seneca to read with Princess Elisabeth is evidence of an interest in Stoic thought, and his commentary shows him to be drawing on and appropriating Seneca's Stoic ethics to his own ends. (Rutherford 2004 works through some of the details.) Looking more closely at Stoic ethics might well help us to better understand Descartes's *morale par provision* and its relation to his notion of a perfect moral system. (The discussion that follows draws on Shapiro (2010).)

Of particular interest is the aim of some strands of Stoicism to articulate a complete set of *kathêkonta*. The term is often translated as "duties" or "obligations" but also as "proper functions" and "befitting actions." The *kathêkonta* were meant to lay out an array of rules governing every action of daily life, and to which a sage would adhere in the situations in which he found himself. Within this set of rules, some were understood to be general, or "unconditional obligations." It is important to highlight just how general these unconditional obligations were. They included, for example, prescriptions to tend to one's health and to one's sense organs. In so far as these rules are to guide us unconditionally, they set out constraints on all our other decisions, and so frame the way we are to live our lives. In this sense, they were rules a sage would adhere to in his actions in *all* circumstances. The Stoics also set out highly particular rules, or "circumstantial obligations." These rules explain how the virtuous person, or sage, would act in very specific circumstances. They might, for instance, demand that we give away all our possessions, if we find ourselves to be one of very few "haves" among many "have-nots."

Given the seventeenth-century context of the revival of Stoicism, it makes sense to read the maxims of the *morale par provision* as a set of unconditional duties. The maxims are presented as general rules, applicable in all circumstances. Being firm and decisive in one's actions, aiming to master oneself rather than fortune, and cultivating one's reason are clearly not principles of conduct tailored to a particular set of circumstances. And while it might seem that following local customs and abiding by the least extreme opinions is circumstance-specific, the maxim is presented as a rule to apply no matter the customs and opinions in which one is immersed. All four maxims serve as principles that guide one's approach to one's life; they serve to frame the context in which one will make particular decisions. In this way they are themselves not dependent on the conditions in which those particular decisions will be made. They are similar both in kind and in function to Stoic unconditional duties.

On this interpretation of the *morale*, we get a better sense of what Descartes might intend in invoking a "perfect moral system." Insofar as Descartes's ethics is influenced by Stoic ethics, we should expect Descartes's perfect moral system to include not only a set of unconditional duties which frame our general approach to life but also a complete set of rules governing the particular decisions we make in the course of life, that is, a complete set of circumstantial duties. Thus, the Cartesian perfect moral system would include not only the maxims of the *morale par provision* but also rules for action we would arrive at were we to have a comprehensive understanding of the world – that is, a complete physics. Moreover, this reading is consistent with the account of the grounding of the *morale* maxims in Descartes's method offered by Cimakasky and Polansky (2012).

On this understanding of the *morale par provision* and the Cartesian perfect moral system, the standard approaches miss the mark. The maxims of the *morale* are not to be understood as pragmatic stop-gap measures put in place until we arrive at the true and perfect moral system. Nor are they to be understood as approximations for the rules for action arrived at with perfect knowledge. With perfect knowledge, we will arrive at new rules for action, but these rules are not meant to supersede the maxims of the *morale*. Rather the *morale* provides us with the unconditional duties that frame our approach to the conduct of life. Once we have complete knowledge we will be able to supplement those general rules with a set of particular rules meant to govern our actions in all the circumstances of life. This set of circumstantial duties does not preclude but rather presupposes the validity of the unconditional duties.

WHAT IS A *MORALE*?

One way of thinking of a moral code is as a guide to action, as those rules that highlight one alternative over an array of others as we are faced with a decision about what to do. If this is what a moral code is supposed to be, the *morale* of the *Discourse* is somewhat unsatisfying. As we have already noted, the *morale* hardly specifies how we ought to make decisions. While it might seem that this might help the standard reading of the *morale* as a stop-gap measure, since it is not supposed to be a full-blown moral code after all, in fact it further undermines it. The *morale* is meant to be a stop-gap measure precisely to help us make decisions under conditions of metaphysical instability, but it is not much help in doing that at all. And of course this lack of guidance for determining particular courses of action is even more of a problem for a reading which takes the *morale* to be continuous with Descartes's moral philosophy

How then is Descartes thinking of a moral code if it is not to help directly in decision-making? If we understand the maxims as providing a framework for a general approach to life, we can see Descartes's provisional morality as providing the core of a virtue ethics. For the purposes of this discussion, a virtue ethics is defined first and foremost by its setting an end for all human actions, an end that is tied to a conception of human nature. This setting of an end, in turn, provides the measure through which we evaluate decisions we are faced with, and pursuing virtue thus cultivates in us a disposition to do the right things for the right reasons. For Descartes, as he expressly articulates to Elisabeth in his letters of 4 August 1645 and 18 August 1645, virtue is being resolved to do what reason recommends, that is, "to have a firm and constant will to execute all that we judge to be the best, and to employ all the force of our understanding to judge well" (ED 105; AT 4:277). The second maxim of the *morale par provision* articulates just this view, but the way in which it is articulated brings out the peculiarity of Descartes's conception of virtue. Descartes recognizes that our best judgements can be wrong, and so, for him, we can do what appeared to be the right thing, even for the right reasons, and yet still have things not transpire as we had hoped. This conception of virtue is at odds with Aristotelian and Stoic accounts that insist that in order to be virtuous we need to have actually succeeded in acting well.

If we can err and still remain virtuous, how then does Descartes's account provide a framework for making decisions? The first and third maxims provide the answers to this question. The first maxim seems to encourage a kind of conservatism in asking us to follow the customs of those around us, even while looking for the most sensible of our community as guides to action. But it is also an acknowledgement of our limited nature in acting. Not only do we not act in a vacuum, but rather in a particular context, we also act with only limited experience, and do better if we can incorporate the experience of others into our decision-making. Nonetheless, others are just as limited as we are, so mere imitation will be inadequate to making good decisions. We still need to judge the best we can for ourselves. The third maxim gives us insight into what it is to judge the best we can: we need to distinguish what depends on us from what does not, and act only in accordance with what does depend on us. Again this maxim has two sides. On the one hand, it advises us to act only where we have influence, and to remain unperturbed when the world does not conform to our desires. While there is something to this advice, it also seems facile. Usually, the contexts in which we are faced with a practical decision are those in which the boundary between what depends on us and what does not is blurry. On the other hand, for Descartes, the only thing that does depend on us is our free will. Understanding that we have a free will, for him, involves understanding what it is to use that will well, and the good use of the will is nothing other than the method of thinking, the same method that grounds the maxims themselves. We judge well, for Descartes, in conducting our reason rightly, even if our reasonings are unavoidably incomplete.

Understanding Descartes's *morale par provision* in this way also helps to explain the somewhat peculiar fourth maxim – the choice of philosophy as a vocation. While Descartes frames this as his personal choice, there is some disingenuousness in his doing so. For what philosophy is for him, and arguably for anyone, is quite simply the willful pursuit of rationality, a pursuit through which we realize our freedom, and thereby arrive at the method that grounds the moral maxims and reveals the nature of virtue. (See Beyssade 2001 and Cottingham 1998 for further discussion.) Even if we were to pursue some other vocation, in learning the lessons the *Discourse* aims to teach we would all also be philosophers.

RELATION OF DESCARTES'S MORAL PHILOSOPHY
TO HIS EPISTEMOLOGY AND METAPHYSICS

Interpretations of Descartes's provisional morality are intimately connected to how the relation between his theoretical and practical philosophy are conceived. The standard reading assumes that the *morale par provision* is orthogonal to Descartes's metaphysics and epistemology. In so far as it is to serve as a stop-gap measure, it cannot depend on the metaphysics that is in the process of being sorted out. The alternative readings that have been developed in recent years situate the provisional morality within the context of his other works, and demonstrate that Descartes consistently maintains his views regarding practical philosophy over time. This consistency then leaves open the question of the relation between Descartes's theoretical and practical philosophy.

As already mentioned, in the Preface to the French edition of the *Principles of Philosophy* Descartes invokes the metaphor of a tree to depict the relationship between different elements of philosophy. Metaphysics serves as the roots that ground the trunk of physics, or natural philosophy. With that stability, the branches of mechanics, medicine and morals are able to grow, and thrive. The metaphor certainly implies that Descartes takes these different philosophical domains to be interrelated. The question is how. Though it denies that the *morale par provision* is the perfect moral system, the standard reading takes the true morality to be deduced from physics, which is itself deduced from metaphysics. It can be tempting to preserve the idea that Descartes takes morality to be deducible from natural philosophy. However, to do so involves ignoring a central feature of the tree metaphor. A tree is a living thing, and as such regenerates itself. So while it is certainly true that the roots of a tree support its trunk, which supports its branches, the branches also bear fruit, which nourish and reseed the soil. Attending to this feature suggests that the relationship between metaphysics and morals is more complicated than an inferential relationship.

Rodis-Lewis (1987) argues that *générosité* ("generosity," which is the term Descartes prefers to the older "magnanimity") – the knowledge that we have a free will and the resolve to use it well, and the key to all the virtues according to Descartes – is also at the core of his metaphysics and is central to the method for avoiding error that the meditator arrives at in the Fourth Meditation. If this is correct, then there is an intimate interconnection between Descartes's metaphysics and epistemology and his ethics. Theoretical philosophy and practical philosophy are not two separate domains of philosophy for him, but rather intertwined through their shared commitment to using our free will well by adhering to a method for arriving at good reasons for belief and action. It is noteworthy that this method involves properly ordering a set of *our* thoughts, that is, thoughts had by *human* beings. Descartes recognizes that human thinkers are also feeling things, and reasoning well, whether it be in the theoretical or the practical context, involves well-regulated passions. (See Shapiro 2005 and 1999.)

BIBLIOGRAPHY

An asterisk denotes secondary literature especially suitable for further reading.

Beyssade, J.-M. 2001. "Sur les 'trois ou quatre maximes' de la morale par provision," in *Descartes au fil de l'ordre*. Paris: Presses Universitaires de France, 237–57.

Charron, P. 1986 [1601/1604]. *De la sagesse*. Paris: Librairie Arthème Fayard. (Original work published in 1601, revised in 1604.)

Cimakasky, J. and R. Polansky. 2012. "Descartes's Provisional Morality," *Pacific Philosophical Quarterly*, 93, 253–72.

Cottingham, J. 1998. *Philosophy and the Good Life: Reason and the Passions in Greek, Cartesian and Psychoanalytic Ethics*. Cambridge University Press.

Descartes, R. 1984–1991. *Philosophical Writings of René Descartes*. 3 vols. Ed. J. Cottingham, R. Stoothoff and D. Murdoch with A. Kenny for vol. 3. Cambridge University Press.

Descartes, R. 1989. *Passions of the Soul*. Ed. and trans. S Voss. Indianapolis, IN: Hackett Publishing.

Descartes, R. 1996. *Œuvres*. 11 vols. Ed. C. Adam and P. Tannery. Paris: Vrin.

Du Vair, Guillaume. 1945 [1600]. *De la sainte philosophie: philosophie morale des stoïques*. Paris: Vrin.

Gilson, E. 1976. *Discours de la méthode, texte et commentaire*. Paris: Vrin.

Grotius, H. 1962 [1625]. *De jure belli ac pacis [On the Law of War and Peace]*. Trans. Francis Kelsey and Arthur Boak. Indianapolis, IN: Bobbs-Merrill.

LeDoeuff, M. 1989. "Red Ink in the Margins," in *The Philosophical Imaginary*. Trans. C. Gordon. Stanford University Press.

Levi, Anthony. 1964. *French Moralists: The Theory of the Passions 1585–1649*. Oxford: Clarendon Press.

Marshall, John. 1998. *Descartes's Moral Theory*. Ithaca, NY: Cornell University Press.

Marshall, John. 2003. "Descartes's *Morale par Provision*," in B. Williston and A. Gombay (eds.), *Passion and Virtue in Descartes*. Amherst, NY: Humanity Books.

Morgan, Vance. 1993. *Foundations of Cartesian Ethics*. Atlantic Highlands, NJ: Humanities Press.

Namaan-Zauderer, Noa. 2010. *Descartes's Deontological Turn: Reason, Will and Virtue in the Later Writings*. Cambridge University Press.

Princess Elisabeth of Bohemia and René Descartes. 2007. *The Correspondence of Princess Elisabeth of Bohemia and René Descartes*. Ed. and trans. L. Shapiro. University of Chicago Press.

Rodis-Lewis, Geneviève. 1998 [1957]. *La morale de Descartes*. [Descartes's Moral Philosophy.] Paris: Presses Universitaires de France.

Rodis-Lewis, Geneviève. 1987. "Le denier fruit de la métaphysique cartésienne: la générosité," *Etudes Philosophiques*, 1, 43–54.

Rutherford, Donald. 2004. "Descartes vis-à-vis Seneca," in S. Strange and J. Zupko (eds.), *Stoicism: Traditions and Transformations*. Cambridge University Press, 177–97.

Rutherford, Donald. 2008. "Descartes' Ethics," in E. Zalta (ed.), *Stanford Encyclopedia of Philosophy*: http://plato.stanford.edu/entries/descartes-ethics/ (substantive revision 1 December 2008).

Shapiro, Lisa. 1999. "Cartesian Generosity," in T. Aho and M. Yrjönsuuri (eds.), *Norms and Modes of Thinking in Descartes*. Acta Philosophica Fennica, 64, 249–75.

Shapiro, Lisa. 2005. "What are the Passions Doing in the *Meditations*?," in J. Jenkins, J. Whiting and C. Williams (eds.), *Persons and Passions: Essays in Honor of Annette Baier*. Notre Dame, IN: University of Notre Dame Press, 14–33.

Shapiro, Lisa. 2010. "Descartes's Ethics," in J. Broughton and J. Carriero (eds.), *A Companion to Descartes*. Oxford: Blackwell.*

18

Hobbes

S.A. LLOYD

The English philosopher Thomas Hobbes (1588–1679) is best known for his absolutist political philosophy according to which subjects are to obey the commands of an unlimited, undivided sovereign authority in all matters except those that would jeopardize immediate self-preservation or eternal salvation. That political philosophy is grounded in a moral philosophy that radically revises Hobbes's inherited natural law tradition.[1] Basic moral requirements to regulate the interactions of people in communities, expressed in a set of natural laws discoverable through an exercise of unaided natural reason, unfold a core normative ideal of reciprocity. Applications of the core requirement of reciprocity yield a duty to submit to government, and settle both the authority of government and its limits. Although Hobbes's moral philosophy is developed in the service of political theory, and only so far as it is needed for that purpose, it nonetheless stakes out a position original to its time and, on at least some of its interpretations, not unattractive today.

"The laws of nature," Hobbes writes, "are immutable and eternal ... [a]nd the science of them, is the true and only moral philosophy ... and therefore the true doctrine of the laws of nature, is the true moral philosophy" (*Leviathan* XV.38–40).[2] Scholarly disagreement over how to understand

---

[1] By the term "a moral philosophy" I mean a system that orders ideas of rightness, goodness, and virtue into a more or less coherent scheme and offers an account of the justification of that scheme, including an account of its relation to human motivation. Aristotle, Kant, and Bentham each offer a moral philosophy in the sense I use the term. Rawls terms the comparative study of such systems "moral theory," which he sees as a part of the discipline, "moral philosophy," that seeks to understand the general and abstract properties of such systems.

[2] Hobbes wrote several versions of his political philosophy, including *The Elements of Law, Natural and Politic* (also under the titles *Human Nature* and *De corpore politico*) published in 1650 (herein cited by part, chapter, and paragraph), *De cive* (1642),

Hobbes's moral philosophy concentrates in disagreement about the status of the laws of nature and the way in which Hobbes derives those laws as theorems of reason. Are these merely prudential recommendations to the agent concerning how best to preserve his own life? Are they exception-less rule-egoistic moral principles? Or are they commands from God, the moral status of which depends on their having been so commanded? Or are they rules for the preservation of human communities derived from the necessary desire of any rational agent to secure an environment in which her agency may be effectively exercised?[3] According to the interpretation I describe

published in English as *Philosophical Rudiments Concerning Government and Society* in 1651 (cited by chapter and paragraph), and the English *Leviathan* (similarly cited by chapter and paragraph) published in 1651, and its Latin revision in 1668.

[3] Interpretations of Hobbes's intended derivation of the laws of nature may be roughly divided into three types: duty based, desire based, and definitional. Duty-based derivations of Hobbes's laws of nature include divine-command interpretations (Hood 1964; Martinich 1992; Taylor 1965; Warrender 1957) that understand the normativity of Hobbes's laws of nature to be a function of their having been commanded for our observance by God. Some of these interpretations argue that Hobbes's moral theory is independent of his psychological theory and is a strict deontology. The rationally required end interpretation (Gert 2001) derives the laws of nature from a duty of self-preservation imposed on us by reason itself, which specifies required ends, as well as finding means to our idiosyncratic ends. Desire-based derivations of Hobbes's laws of nature present those laws as necessary means for obtaining peace, which is in turn desired instrumentally as a necessary means to the individual's self-preservation (Curley 1994; Gauthier 1969; Hampton 1986). A rule-egoist variant of desire-based derivations developed by Kavka 1986 holds that Hobbes sought to justify the laws of nature by showing that the best strategy for securing self-preservation is always to conform to, or at least to accept and try to conform to, the laws of nature, even in those particular cases in which violating the laws can be seen to be in one's interest. Definitional derivations of the laws of nature seek to use only definitions and premises analytic to the theory, in accordance with Hobbes's stated "geometrical" method according to which all genuine knowledge is a matter of correct inference from correct definitions of words. Some definitional derivations attempt to derive the laws of nature from Hobbes's definition of a law of nature (Deigh 1996; McNeilly 1968), while another takes Hobbes to have derived them from his definition of man as a rational agent (Lloyd 2009). Another disputed question among interpreters of Hobbes's moral philosophy concerns the source of moral motivation. If the laws of nature are merely precepts of personal prudence, that source might be a self-interested desire for personal preservation or profit; if they are divine commands, it might be a desire to do God's will or a fear of divine punishment. If the laws of nature are reasonable constraints on interpersonal behavior, the motivation to observe them might stem from the desire to justify oneself to others as a rational agent.

below, Hobbes offers a constitutivist account of the authority of natural law, grounding its authority in human practical agency, and a constructivist account of the content of natural law. What distinguishes Hobbes's theory from other natural law theories is how it grounds natural law, how it specifies its content, and the relation between natural and positive law it settles, "self-effacing" natural law directing us to defer to positive law even in interpretation of its own requirements.

HOW THE NEED FOR MORAL NORMS ARISES

The need for moral norms, and in turn for political governance, arises from the fact of humans' pervasive disagreement in private judgment. Individuals disagree in their judgments of what is to be done, what is theirs or others', good or bad, right or wrong, what is equitable, just, or sinful, as well as in what honors they are due, how best to govern themselves, the requirements of true religion, and most every other question. Hobbes's account of this disagreement in private judgments is multi-faceted. Our differing private judgments reflect differences in upbringing, experiences, bodily constitution, tastes and interests, education and values. Even when our plans are not in conflict, a failure to coordinate our activities effectively may lead us to interfere with one another. Hobbes observes that unlike ants and bees and other "naturally sociable" creatures, humans do not enjoy hardwired harmony in their interactions with others of their kind, and so they need both moral norms for guidance, and a public authority to settle disputes over the interpretation and application of those norms. Because of pervasive disagreement, a condition of universal individual self-government by private judgment such as is the notorious "state of nature" will involve perpetual, irresoluble conflict with concomitant human frustration and even misery.

Hobbes emphasizes throughout his political writings that individuals tend to call things good or evil according to whether they like or dislike them. We use these terms to express our attitudes, even though we take ourselves to be talking about independent properties of actions, objects and states of affairs. But naturally, as our likes and dislikes differ from those of others, so do our judgments of good and evil. For this reason, Hobbes thinks that sound moral arguments cannot profitably begin from claims about what is good, because the term 'good' has no settled universal signification. Further, although it is a fact that people use the terms to track their likes and dislikes, such use is improper, on Hobbes's view. Hobbes condemns the schools of the Grecians as unprofitable, in part for the reason that

Their moral philosophy is but a description of their own passions. For the rule of manners, without civil government, is the law of nature; and in it, the law civil; that determineth what is honest, and dishonest, what is just, and unjust; and generally what is good and evil. Whereas they make the rules of good and bad by their own liking and disliking: by which means, in so great diversity of taste, there is nothing generally agreed on; but everyone doth, as far as he dares, whatsoever seemeth good in his own eyes, to the subversion of commonwealth. (*Leviathan* XLVI.11)

To take one's own affections as the standard for good and evil is only human, but it is an error, and not just an error, but a social catastrophe. For a condition in which every individual governs himself according to his own private judgment, which Hobbes terms the condition of mere nature, promises so much irresoluble conflict and insecurity that no one can have a reasonable expectation of being able to accomplish any of his plans, no matter what they are. Because people's uncoordinated actions create sufficient interference that none can be sure of gaining and maintaining access to the material resources and unimpeded movement needed to pursue his ends, flourishing human lives require the abridgment of a condition of action on universal private judgment. Humans are, by definition in Hobbes's view, rational agents, and *qua* rational and agents, they must desire to make their agency effective. This is a necessary desire – perhaps the only real candidate for a necessary desire, in contrast to desires for such things as wealth and temporal bodily self-preservation that may mean less to many people than the pursuit of honor, eternal salvation, or the welfare of their family or nation. The dismal state of nature is precisely the condition in which private appetite is the measure of good and evil, and is dismal for that very reason.

Hobbes characterizes the insistence on taking one's own likes and dislikes as the standard of good and evil as a form of excessive pride, or *hubris*. He names his treatise on how to create a stable state Leviathan after that "king over all the children of pride" invoked in the Biblical Book of Job. The sorts of private judgments that Hobbes thinks most disrupt social order (as they did during the English civil war) are judgments about what God wants, what is just, righteous, sinful, etc.; and a person willing to take up arms to impose his own such judgments, in defiance of the civil sovereign, must feel very certain that he knows better than anyone whose judgments differ from his own. Hobbes takes this prideful self-assurance in the superiority of one's own opinions to be condemned by God himself, as related not only in the Book of Job, but in the Genesis account of God's anger with Adam and Eve for taking on themselves to judge good and evil by eating from the tree of knowledge, and subsequently judging their nakedness, in which God saw fit to create them, as shameful.

Unmediated affect, then, cannot provide a moral standard. But harmonious human life requires one, which reason discovers in the laws of nature dictating the rules of "peaceable, sociable, and comfortable living" (*Leviathan* XV.40). Reciprocity is the common core of these various laws. Stated as a positive principle, they command that we do to others whatever we require that they should do to us, and that we love others as ourselves. Hobbes writes, "Thou shalt love thy neighbor as thyself . . . is the natural law, having its beginning with rational nature itself" (*Philosophical Rudiments* XVII.8), and characterizes the required sort of love behaviorally rather than as an experience of affectionate feeling: "To love our neighbor as ourselves, is nothing else but to grant him all we desire to have granted to ourselves" (*Philosophical Rudiments* IV.12). It is "so to be understood as that a man . . . should esteem his neighbor worthy of all rights and privileges that himself enjoyeth . . . [He] should be humble, meek, and content with equality" (*Elements of Law* I.V.6). Stated negatively, Hobbes variously formulated the reciprocity requirement of natural law as prohibiting doing what one would not have done to oneself; doing what one thinks unreasonable to be done by another to oneself; doing what one would not approve in another; reserving to oneself any right one is not content should be reserved to all the rest; and allowing to oneself that which one denies to another.

   Reciprocity, then, requires that each of us applies our own set of standards consistently to everyone, without exempting ourselves from the demands or judgments we apply to others. Hobbes derives reciprocity as a theorem of reason from the axiom that man is by nature a rational agent: To be rational is to offer justifying considerations for one's actions. But to offer something as a justifying consideration for one's own action commits one to accepting that same consideration as justifying the like actions of others, *ceteris paribus*. We do not count an act as contrary to reason unless we are prepared to fault the agent for performing it. So when one does what one is prepared to fault others for doing, one acts contrary to reason. Thus, humans' rational nature commits us to reciprocity.

   Reciprocity suggests a test for discerning whether one's actions comport with the law of nature, namely, that the agent should imagine herself on the receiving end of the action she proposes to perform and consider whether from that vantage point she would fault the action as unreasonable:

[T]here is an easy rule to know upon a sudden, whether the action I be to do, be against the law of nature or not ... [namely] *[t]hat a man might imagine himself in the place of the party with whom he hath to do, and reciprocally him in his.* (*Elements of Law* I.IV.9)

Here instantly those perturbations which persuaded him to the fact, being now cast into the other scale, dissuade him as much. And this rule is not only easy, but it is anciently celebrated in these words, *quod tibi fieri non vis, alteri ne feceris: do not do that to others, you would not have done to yourself.*
(*De cive* 3.26)

FROM STATE OF NATURE TO POLITICAL SOCIETY

Hobbes seeks to show that this traditional moral principle entails a duty to submit to a system of government. If, as Hobbes argues, a condition of universal private judgment threatens danger and frustration for everyone, rational agents must will the abridgment of that condition. Most desirable, from the point of view of the agent, would be to retain her own right of private judgment while requiring others to give up theirs. But reciprocity rules out any such asymmetrical solution. Instead, abridging a universal right to act according to private judgment will involve taking some questions out of the purview of private judgment for everyone, and submitting them to arbitration by a public judgment. A sovereign/government/political authority is most basically the repository of public judgment, empowered to make that judgment effective in regulating conduct. Thus reason, making appeal to reciprocity, requires submission to government.

Were one to inhabit a state of nature and to think it blameworthy of others not to join oneself in submitting to government upon equal terms, reciprocity would require one to join with willing others in transferring to a public authority that portion of private judgment one thinks it must have in order to secure peace and defense, and be content with the same degree of residual liberty of private judgment one is willing to allow to others. This requirement is just Hobbes's second Law of Nature, *"that a man be willing, when others are so too, as far-forth, as for peace, and defense of himself he shall think it necessary, to lay down this right to all things; and be contented with so much liberty against other men, as he would allow other men against himself"* (*Leviathan* XIV.5).

For those already living under a government that is effective in protecting them, Hobbes can urge the duty of political obedience on the simple ground provided by reciprocity itself. If we cannot be willing that others should exempt themselves from obeying the authority who without obedience cannot secure the protection we enjoy, then, under reciprocity, neither may we legitimately exempt ourselves from obedience. In general, to enjoy the benefits of our fellow subjects' obedience without ourselves obeying is contrary to the requirement of reciprocity, which licenses only symmetrical behaviors, and never such asymmetrical arrangements as when some free-ride on the cooperation of others. The condition of mere nature, in which all are granted the right to be judge and jury over all matters, is one conceptual possibility under reciprocity; that all submit equally to a public judgment that supersedes the private judgment of each is another possibility under reciprocity. What is not possible under that theorem is the asymmetrical outcome that only some people retain rights that they deny to others.

When applied to ordinary sorts of social interactions, the abstract reciprocity requirement yields specific ought-principles (presented in *Leviathan* Chapters XIV, XV, and Review and Conclusion) which may be summarized as *requiring*:

1. the effort to make peace with willing others
2. the reciprocal surrender of a part of our natural right
3. that we keep our valid covenants
4. gratitude to benefactors
5. that we accommodate the needs and interests of others
6. pardoning offenders who repent and promise not to repeat their offense
9. that we acknowledge others as our equals by nature
11. equity from judges in their judging
12. common use of indivisible resources
13. taking turns, or assignment by lot of things that cannot be used in common
14. first seizure or primogeniture to determine distributions of goods assigned by natural lottery
15. that those who mediate peace be allowed safe conduct
16. the submission of disputes to an arbitrator
19. the use of witnesses in determining factual disagreements,
20. that everyone in times of war do their utmost to protect the authority by which they are protected in times of peace

and as *prohibiting*:

7. punishing for revenge
8. expressing hatred or contempt toward others
10. denying to others rights we claim for ourselves
17. being judge of one's own case
18. using arbitrators who are not impartial.

These laws of nature concern only the behavior of "men in multitudes," that is, of people living together in groups, whose actions may either harm or benefit their neighbors. Hobbes indicates that there may be other rules of reason prohibiting certain self-regarding vices such as gluttony or drunkenness, but does not include them in his discussions of the laws of nature, which, he explains, "are called the laws of nature, for that they are the dictates of natural reason, and also moral laws, because they concern the manners and conversations of men, one towards another" (*De corpore politico* V.1). Those he does include facilitate peaceful, sociable, and comfortable living within communities.

The laws of nature articulate a set of natural duties, the claim of which on us does not depend on our having agreed or promised to follow them. Ingratitude to benefactors or partiality in judging or iniquity is blameworthy regardless of whether or not one has agreed to be grateful or impartial or fair. Hobbes notes that even during war, gratuitous cruelty is forbidden by the law of nature; it would certainly be no moral defense to explain that one had never undertaken any obligation to refrain from such cruelty. However, although the laws of nature articulate a set of "eternal and immutable" duties, from observance of which only children, madmen, and those who lack reason are generally excused, Hobbes allows that when no one else is performing them, and our doing so would cause our ruin, we are excused from unilateral performance. That the laws of nature do not bind *in foro externo* in that extreme case reflects our judgment that it would be unreasonable to fault us for refusing to sacrifice ourselves for the benefit of others none of whom are themselves willing to observe the requirements of morality. As Hobbes explains,

> These laws of nature . . . in case they should be observed by some, and not by others, would make the observers but a prey to them that should neglect them, leaving the good both without defence against the wicked, and also with a charge to assist them . . . Reason therefore, and the law of nature over and above all these particular laws, doth dictate this law in general, *That those particular laws be so far observed, as they subject us not to any incommodity, that in our own judgments may arise, by the neglect thereof in those towards whom we observe them.* (*Elements of Law* I.IV.10)

Hobbes's theory imposes weak reciprocity and perspectival universality requirements on justified action that pick out a *moral minimum* intermediate between egoism and full generality, and yields both reasonable and rational constraints. It describes a consistency requirement on the individual's attitude toward an action under a description: one acts contrary to reason when one does what one would fault others for doing, no matter how well such action might serve one's ends. We may, of course, fault others for actions we deem imprudent or irrational for themselves, and so act contrary to reason if we imitate those actions. But in the realm of actions that may have deleterious effects on others, over which the laws of nature operate, when we fault others for iniquitous, unjust, or uncharitable actions, we act unreasonably to engage in those actions ourselves. Hobbes's notion of contrariety to reason thus broadly encompasses both the irrational and the unreasonable.

It is an implication of Hobbes's perspectival theory that individual differences in judgment result in marginal differences in moral duties. What Hobbes terms "cases in the law of nature" (*Elements of Law*, Dedicatory Epistle) are determined by applying the reciprocity test to an action under a description. The person who faults others for slovenliness acts wrongly to be slovenly herself, while the uncritical slob does not. Those who condemn interfaith marriage or usury or gambling place themselves under moral requirements not to engage in those practices that do not bind their less judgmental fellows. Because the sorts of behaviors governed by the laws of nature so centrally impact the social environment in which all must attempt to operate, all can be expected to fault violators of those norms, and so all are bound to observe them. Disagreements may arise over the correct description of action-types, as for instance when the religious missionary views her proselytization as teaching true religion, while her target population regards it as corrupting true religion. In this sort of case, the law of nature requires us to adopt the least abstract *uncontested* description when adjudicating the dispute. Hobbes himself condemns the efforts of missionaries to alter religion in another country on the ground that the missionary "does that which he would not approve in another, namely, that coming from hence, he should endeavor to alter the religion there" (*Leviathan* XXVII.4).

MORAL DUTIES OF SOVEREIGNS AND SUBJECTS

Hobbes appeals to the laws of nature not only to establish the requirement of submission to government, but also to determine the duties of both government and citizens. The most important class of what Hobbes terms cases in the law of nature applies that law to the sovereign's behavior, yielding the norms of Hobbes's art of government. Sovereigns are bound by all of the laws of nature, because, these being divine, no person or commonwealth can alter nor abrogate them (*Leviathan* XXIX.9). For instance, all are bound by equity "to which, as being a precept of the law of nature, a sovereign is as much subject, as any of the meanest of his people" (*Leviathan* XXX.15). It is true that the sovereign has final authority to interpret what equity requires of subjects and of himself, but that does not mean that equity just is whatever the sovereign thinks it is; "there is no judge subordinate, nor sovereign, but may err in a judgment of equity" (*Leviathan* XXVI.24). Sovereigns may be mistaken, but their interpretations and applications of the laws of nature are nonetheless to be treated as authoritative. Only God may hold them accountable for their errors. Strikingly, the law of nature itself dictates submission to a public political authority *to interpret and enforce its own content*. Hobbes's law of nature is in this way *self-effacing*, directing people to subject themselves to political authority and to treat its positive laws as authoritative even as they specify or interpret natural law.

The sovereign's moral duties are office-specific. Hobbes writes that "[t]he office of the sovereign ... consisteth in ... the procuration of the safety of the people; to which he is obliged by the law of nature, and to render an account thereof to God, the author of that law, and to none but him. But by safety here is not meant a bare preservation, but also all other contentments of life, which every man by lawful industry, without danger, or hurt to the commonwealth, shall acquire to himself" (*Leviathan* XXX.1). Hobbes asserts in *De cive* that "the benefits of subjects, respecting this life only, may be distributed into four kinds. 1. That they be defended against foreign enemies. 2. That peace be preserved at home. 3. That they be enriched, as much as may consist with public security. 4. That they enjoy a harmless liberty" (XIII.6).

Harmless liberties include such things as "the liberty to buy, and sell, and otherwise contract with one another; to choose their own abode, their own diet, their own trade of life, and institute their children as they themselves think fit; and the like" (*Leviathan* XXI.6). Hobbes considers that valid covenants or contracts can make actions that were before morally indifferent now either morally required or impermissible; and because the third law of nature prohibits violating valid covenants, some people may be faulted for actions that others may perform blamelessly. For instance, the man who voluntarily enlists in the military undertakes an obligation not to plead fear as an excuse for running from battle (and is morally fault-worthy if he does so). However, some contracts or personal arrangements do negatively impact the public good and so should be regulated. Hobbes offers the examples of contracts forming private leagues or unions that may divide subjects' loyalties, or incestuous marriages that may decrease the intelligence of future generations.

As distinct from "harmless liberty," the law of nature carves out a special group of exemptions from obedience that Hobbes terms the "true liberties of subjects." As discussed in Chapter XXI of *Leviathan*, these are the rights which cannot be transferred by valid covenant. Subjects are morally blameless when acting in defense of these rights; although sovereigns may legitimately command actions that threaten the interests these rights protect, subjects may legitimately disobey those commands. Commands to kill, wound, or maim oneself, to abstain from things necessary to preserve one's life, to incriminate oneself or one's loved ones, or not to resist punishment may permissibly be disobeyed. It may seem that these sorts of liberties are far from harmless, but Hobbes suggests that acknowledging them really does not threaten public safety, for two reasons. First, it is not necessary to public safety that subjects obey commands to, for instance, execute themselves, because there are others to carry out the sovereign's execution orders. Second, the improbability that individuals will reliably obey such commands would render any presumed obligation to do so of no practical importance. Even if subjects could divest themselves of the true liberties, there is no need for them to do so because the sovereign's ability to promote the public good does not depend on that.

Hobbes insists that it is also a part of the sovereign's duty under the law of nature of procuring the common good that it regulate doctrine and religion so that subjects do not develop false beliefs that pit moral or religious beliefs, or the claims of private conscience, against their duty of civil obedience. Taking educational measures against the "poison of seditious doctrines" is especially important because sovereign power ultimately depends on people's opinions of the sovereign's rights, especially on the opinions of those people who are supposed to coerce compliance with the sovereign's commands. The needed education could be accomplished, Hobbes suggests, by teaching his book *Leviathan* in the universities, and having its essentials disseminated to the common people from the pulpit.

Finally, "Forasmuch," Hobbes writes, "as eternal is better than temporal good, it is evident, that they who are in sovereign authority, are by the law of nature obliged to further the establishing of all . . . they believe the true way thereunto. For unless they do so, it cannot be said truly, that they have done the uttermost of their endeavor [for the good of the people]" (*Elements of Law* II.IX.2). It does not necessarily follow from this that morality requires sovereigns to dictate the profession and practice of religion to their subjects, for a conscientious belief in the value of free faith would condemn such imposition. Still, sovereigns are required to take whatever measures they think needed to help their subjects toward a happy afterlife while nevertheless acknowledging that the reciprocity requirement of natural law forbids faulting subjects for insisting on private religious conscience, "for who is there, that knowing there is so great danger in an error, whom the natural care of himself, compelleth not to hazard his soul upon his own judgment, rather than that of any other man that is unconcerned in his damnation?" (*Leviathan* XLVI.37).

BIBLIOGRAPHY

An asterisk denotes secondary literature especially suitable for further reading.

Curley, E. (1994) "Introduction to Hobbes's Leviathan," in E. Curley (ed.), *Leviathan*, Indianapolis: Hackett Publishing Company, Inc.

Deigh, John (1996) "Reason and Ethics in Hobbes's Leviathan," *Journal of the History of Philosophy* 34: 33–60.*

Gauthier, D. (1969) *The Logic of 'Leviathan': The Moral and Political Theory of Thomas Hobbes*, Oxford: Clarendon Press.

Gert, Bernard (2001) "Hobbes on Reason," *Pacific Philosophical Quarterly* 82: 243–57.

Hampton, Jean (1986) *Hobbes and the Social Contract Tradition*, Cambridge University Press.

Hood, F.C. (1964) *The Divine Politics of Thomas Hobbes*, Oxford: Clarendon Press.

Kavka, Gregory S. (1986) *Hobbesian Moral and Political Theory*, Princeton University Press.

Lloyd, S.A. (2009) *Morality in the Philosophy of Thomas Hobbes: Cases in the Law of Nature*, Cambridge University Press.*

Martinich, A.P. (1992) *The Two Gods of Leviathan: Thomas Hobbes on Religion and Politics*, Cambridge University Press.

Martinich, A.P. (2005) *Hobbes*, New York: Routledge.

McNeilly, F.S. (1968) *The Anatomy of Leviathan*, London: Macmillan.

Taylor, A.E. (1965) "The Ethical Doctrine of Hobbes," in K.C. Brown (ed.), *Hobbes Studies*, Oxford: Blackwell.*

Warrender, H. (1957) *The Political Philosophy of Hobbes: His Theory of Obligation*, Oxford: Clarendon Press.

19

The Cambridge Platonists

SARAH HUTTON

But virtue has no master; by honoring or dishonoring it, each will have a greater or lesser share of it. The responsibility is the chooser's; god is not to be blamed.

(Plato *Republic* 10.617e)[1]

The moral philosophy of the Cambridge Platonists is a distinctive strand of English ethical thought, in a century where the history of moral philosophy is dominated by Descartes, Hobbes and Locke, and natural law theory.[2] Committed to the idea that goodness is intrinsic to all things, and that the good can be grasped rationally, the Cambridge Platonists discuss such themes as the nature and knowledge of the good, moral accountability and moral autonomy, in the service of an ethics which is both rational and practical.

The main figures associated with this group were Benjamin Whichcote (1609–1683), Peter Sterry (1613–1672), John Smith (1618–1652), Nathaniel Culverwell (1619–1651), Henry More (1614–1687) and Ralph Cudworth (1617–1688). Neither John Smith nor Benjamin Whichcote wrote systematically on ethics. Smith's *Select Discourses* is based on a collection of posthumously edited sermons, while Whichcote's moral thought is contained in his sermons and the 'select notions' excerpted from them. Neither Sterry nor Cudworth ever published on ethics in their lifetime. Sterry's *A Discourse of the Freedom of the Will* (1675) is incomplete. Cudworth's main published writings on ethics are his *Treatise of Eternal and Immutable Morality* and his *Treatise of Freewill*, both of which were first published posthumously (in 1731 and 1838 respectively), and some of his ethical writings remain unpublished to this

---

[1] Plato 2013.

[2] In this paper I treat the terms 'ethics' and 'moral philosophy' as equivalent. This accords with the Cambridge Platonists' own use of these terms, illustrated in the title of More's handbook of ethics: *Enchiridion ethicum, præcipua moralis philosophiæ rudimenta complectens* (1668), reprinted in an English translation in 1690 with the title *An Account of Virtue*.

day.[3] However, there is partial statement of his ethical views in his sermons, especially his great sermon to the House of Commons in 1647 and his *True Intellectual System of the Universe* (1678; hereafter *TIS*). More's treatise on ethics, his *Enchiridion ethicum* (1668), was reprinted in an English translation in 1690 with the title *An Account of Virtue*. In this essay I shall focus on the three whose moral philosophy was most fully developed: Nathaniel Culverwell, Henry More and Ralph Cudworth. Between them they represent both the common features and individual variation that characterise the group.

Although the Cambridge Platonists shared much in their outlook and ideas, they did not uniformly subscribe to the same tenets. Common to all of them is a broad consensus on theological matters which colours their philosophy. There is considerable overlap between their moral theory and their religious principles, in both the theoretical and the practical aspects of their ethics. Key elements of their theological formation are their opposition to Calvinist voluntarism and their receptivity to the Platonising Patristic philosopher, Origen. A major point of convergence between their theology and their ethics is their critique of voluntarism and determinism. As Christian philosophers, they regarded moral philosophy as integral to a Christian outlook. This, however, was neither narrow nor dogmatic. To a degree unusual for their time, they placed emphasis on the moral content of religion, to the point of almost equating religion and morality: as Whichcote put it, 'morals . . . are nineteen parts in twenty of all religion'.[4] Their religious open-mindedness extended to those who did not share their faith: to quote Whichcote again, 'The Good nature of a Heathen is more Godlike than the furious Zeal of a Christian.'[5] As Christian thinkers, they were concerned about the disjunction which they perceived to have developed between theological doctrine and the fundamentals of Christianity, in particular the gospel message of love. Their moral objection to voluntarism was that it saps the foundations of morality by rendering moral principles arbitrary, thereby undermining individual moral accountability. Worse, the logic of extreme voluntarism, according to which the will of God is totally unconstrained, made God potentially the author of evil. Instead of insisting on the primacy and omnipotence of divine will, as voluntarists did, the Cambridge Platonists emphasised divine goodness and sought to revitalise Christian conduct, by

---

[3] Both Cudworth 1838 and 1996 reproduce British Library MS Additional, 4978. The other, unpublished treatises on Liberty and Necessity are MSs Additional, 4979–82.

[4] Whichcote, *Moral and Religious Aphorisms*, in Patrides 1969: 332.

[5] Whichcote, *Aphorisms*, in Taliaferro and Tepley 2004: 135.

de-emphasising predestination, playing up the value of reason as a guide in matters of faith and emphasising free will. Their belief in human capacity for self-direction is a central feature of their anthropology and a key element in their ethics. The Origenist strand in their theology feeds into their sense of the compatibility of Platonism and Christian belief.

The descriptor 'Platonist' by which these Cambridge philosophers have come to be known is misleading. Although there is no question of their drawing on Plato and Plotinus, Platonism was only one of several strands of philosophy with which they engaged. Along with Platonism, Stoicism and Cartesianism are of key importance in shaping their moral philosophy, as were, in a negative sense, Hobbes and Epicureanism. The Cambridge Platonists were philosophers trained in the traditions of Renaissance humanism, who responded to the challenges and possibilities afforded by both ancient and contemporary philosophy. Generally speaking, they repudiated the traditions of the schools and engaged with a broader spectrum of philosophy, ancient and modern. Like the philosophers of the Scottish Enlightenment, most of them lived and worked in an academic environment. In consequence their thought reflects, to varying degrees, their acquaintance with the scholastic Aristotelian framework which maintained its hold in the universities. They were thus familiar with the debates generated by modern scholastics, such as Francisco Suarez. Although their ethical position was not originally formulated in opposition to Hobbes, several themes were developed in their response to what they saw as the atheism, determinism, egoism and ethical relativism of Hobbes's philosophy. They regarded Hobbism as an extreme summation of a wider spectrum of issues emerging in the wake of Cartesianism and the revival of Epicureanism. Chief among these were the mechanical philosophy with its deterministic model of causation and denial of final causes, which threatened to negate morality by reducing human beings to automata and undermining ideas of purposive action. The foundational principles of morality were further undermined by the revival of the Epicurean notion that pleasure is the end we seek, and that self-love, or self-interest, is the fundamental motivator of human behaviour. In facing these challenges, they accepted the new notion that morality be considered a science, 'no less demonstrable than Mathematics'[6]. They also assimilated Descartes's theory of the passions, and adapted Epicurean ethical views which linked happiness with pleasure.

If there is variation in point of style and content as to how the Cambridge Platonists discussed ethics, the fundamental element on which they could all

---

[6] More 1668: 6

agree was on the Platonist foundations of their ethics. They held to the real existence of the immutable principles of goodness, knowledge of which is accessible to the mind by virtue of its 'participation' in God. Since God is essentially good, goodness is intrinsic to all created things. As Cudworth put it, 'The *Goodness*, or *Justice*, or *Righteousness* is intrinsicall to the thing itself.'[7] Moral principles are discernible by reason and available to all. However, the Cambridge Platonists recognised that mere knowledge of the good is insufficient to ensure moral behaviour, and they also had to account for moral fallibility. Although they aspired to a rationally demonstrable ethics, they recognised that, to act morally, we must be able and inclined to seek the good and act in conformity with it. Knowledge of the good must not just be easy to obtain, but we must be free to direct our own actions towards the good. The foundations of moral behaviour are two essential attributes of human nature, reason and free will. And an important part of their ethical theory is their development of the notion of free will, and with it the attention they give to moral psychology. At its simplest, this relies on a conception of reason as affective reason, or reason coloured by feeling. However, Cudworth and More elaborated more complex psychologies, in which they drew on Stoicism and Plotinus to formulate the conception of will as self-determination, or having power over oneself, which they term variously the *autexousion, eph' hêmin* ('self-power') or *hêgemonikon*.

NATHANIEL CULVERWELL

While Nathaniel Culverwell differs from his Emmanuel College colleagues by his recourse to natural law as the basis of ethics, he nevertheless shares extensive common ground with them. Like them he was an anti-voluntarist and he agreed on the rational basis of morality. His *Elegant and Learned Discourse of the Light of Nature* (1652) was published posthumously. There is no indication that he was aware of the challenge to natural law theory posed by Hobbes's use of it. Although Culverwell was the only one of their number to discuss morality in terms of natural law, he was not the only one to discuss natural law. The other Cambridge Platonists certainly agreed with natural law theorists that the law of nature is right reason, and that this is intrinsic to the soul. But they disagreed on the relation of reason and goodness to the will

[7] *TIS*: 897. The Cambridge Platonists were not uncritical of aspects of Platonism, in particular the theory of anamnesis and the pre-existence of souls. Culverwell's critique of Plato on these points has contributed to misunderstanding of his relationship to Cambridge Platonism, and has led some to deny that he was a member of the group.

or command of the legislator. For them, since goodness is intrinsic to nature it is antecedent to all law. Right and wrong cannot be legislated. Cudworth, for example, denies that moral good and evil are 'Theticall or Positive things' which exist 'by Law or Command', but they are intrinsic to the nature of things, and they exist '*phusei*', 'by Nature'. Henry More concurred. 'What is unjust in its own nature', he writes, 'Cannot by any external Consideration be made just'.[8] The good has force of itself, requiring no law to oblige us to seek it. Whichcote likewise considered that 'Moral Laws are Laws of themselves, without Sanction of Will; and the Necessity of them arises from the Things themselves.'[9] Nevertheless, there are some places where they discuss goodness and law. Henry More, for example, makes a distinction between 'Right Natural' and 'Right Legal', but concedes that what is right in nature is 'not . . . always clear and intelligible without reference to some law'.[10] Cudworth discusses the relationship of law, will and the good at some length in his critique of Hobbes in *A Treatise Concerning Eternal and Immutable Morality*, where he allows that positive law of human command obliges, by virtue of the fact that the 'liberty of commanding' accruing to a lawful ruler rests on natural justice. However, should that ruler exceed 'the bounds that nature sets him . . . his commands will not oblige'.[11]

Culverwell's *Discourse of the Light of Nature* is a lengthy discussion of the nature of reason as the distinguishing feature of human nature, and that by which human beings are capable of morality. He agrees with his Cambridge Platonist colleagues that goodness is intrinsic to the nature of things, and that we are free to choose the good. Rational beings have a 'competent liberty and enlargment' such that each may 'willingly consent to its own happiness'.[12] The difference between Culverwell and the other Cambridge Platonists is largely a matter of the point where he sits on the scale between the voluntarist and intellectualist views of the relationship of divine will and divine goodness, and the role of human reason in the divine order. According to the Preface, Culverwell stated that his aim in his *Discourse* was 'to vindicate the use of Reason in matters of Religion, from the passions and prejudices of some weaker ones in these times'. Culverwell conceives God to be 'a most knowing and most intellectual being'[13] and he held that reason was an important means of communication between God and man. He also held that our reason is aided by experience of the external world which manifests

---

[8] More 1690: 116.
[9] Whichcote, *Moral and Religious Aphorisms*, printed in Patrides 1969: 329.
[10] More 1690: 112. [11] Cudworth 1996: 21. [12] Culverwell 1652: 59. [13] Ibid., 114.

divine God's wisdom in the fixed order of divine providence. Culverwell argues that all human minds are furnished with 'cleare and undelible Principles' of reason and morality,[14] but he denies that such principles are 'connate' or present from the moment of the creation of the soul, a view which he associates with the Platonic doctrine of pre-existence of souls, of which he is highly critical. The 'light of nature' of the book's title is human reason, which he also calls 'the candle of the lord'; and the 'intellectual lamp' placed by God in the human soul is a disposition of mind which enables mankind to understand the law of nature, or '*nomos graphos*', written in our hearts. The law of nature is therefore accessible even to those who have not had the benefit of revelation – Culverwell shared Whichcote's view that many pagan philosophers had led better lives than many Christians, although they were not among the elect of God. While Culverwell held the view that goodness is intrinsic to all things, and that moral principles do not depend on the will of God, he took the view that there is no obligation without law, and that moral obligation is imposed by law.[15] Thus, although Culverwell held that reason and free will are preconditions for knowledge of the moral law and the obligation to obey it, his position is closer to both Richard Cumberland and Suarez in holding that moral obligation requires the force of legislation. In this respect he tries to hold the balance between rationalism and voluntarism.[16]

HENRY MORE

Henry More's ethics is coloured by his Origenism. Unlike both Cudworth and Culverwell, who rejected it, he believed in the doctrine of pre-existence of the soul before its life in the body. This was a theory particularly associated with Origen. More's reasons for holding it are relevant to his ethics in two respects. First of all, the doctrine of the pre-existence of souls vindicates divine goodness because it accounts for suffering and punishment of the apparently innocent by explaining it as punishment for the sins of souls in their pre-existent state. Secondly, pre-existence maximises God's goodness because, by creating all souls at the beginning of the world, God

[14] Ibid., 55.   [15] Ibid., 34, 68–9.
[16] See Haakonssen 1996. Prominent among the authorities which Culverwell cites are Francisco Suarez's *De deo legislatore*, John Selden, and Grotius's natural law classic, *De jure belli ac pacis*. But he also draws extensively on ancient philosophy and was conversant with the philosophy of Descartes, Herbert of Cherbury and Francis Bacon, as well as Agostino Steuco's *De perenni philosophia* (1540).

maximises the number of good things created, and thereby the conditions for exercise of virtue. Maximum goodness only ever exists in possibility, since souls from the beginning were created free to choose to pursue good or evil.[17]

Such metaphysical issues aside, it is a fundamental principle of More's anthropology that human beings have free will. And he conceives free will as a principle of self-control, or self-determination, which, like Cudworth, he terms the *autexousion*. One of the earliest invocations of this principle is in More's refutation of Hobbes in *Of the Immortality of the Soul* (1659). Against Hobbes's view that the will is essentially a passive response to external impulse, More argues that 'the *Soul* being endued with *Understanding* as well as *Will* . . . is not *necessarily* determined to will by external impresses'. The proof of this is that mind has control over its activities, being able to 'excite' the images it retains of external objects, 'change and transpose them at her own will'. Mental activity is thus an exercise of will and choice, 'an arbitrarious act'. This '*Liberty* and freedom in ourselves' is most apparent in situations of moral conflict, especially when 'we refuse the good, and chuse the evil, when we might have done other wise'. This is an argument based on experience of the mind's self-awareness, and thus presupposes consciousness, since the mind is aware of its ability to choose or to refuse to act and aware subsequently that we might have acted differently: 'we are conscious to our selves of that Faculty which the Greeks call *autexousion*, or a *power in our selves*'.[18]

Henry More's fullest treatment of moral philosophy is his manual of ethics, *Enchiridion ethicum* (1668). This work blends identifiably Stoic, Platonic, Cartesian and even Aristotelian elements in a new synthesis which anticipates later developments, particularly Shaftesbury's conception of the moral sense. More's purpose in writing it was, he states, the emendation of human life (*Humanae nimirum vitae emendatio*). More defines ethics in classical terms as the art of living well and happily (*ars bene beateque vivere*), and argues that happiness arises from the exercise of virtue. For More, virtue is an extreme (he explicitly rejects Aristotle's account of virtue as a mean between extremes), and the image of God in man. His treatise considers the knowledge of happiness and how we acquire it, addressing the problem that reason alone is not sufficient to motivate people to act virtuously.

More accords right reason an essential role in how we recognise the good: right reason is 'a sort of Copy or Transcript of that Reason or Law eternal

---

[17] *Of the Immortality of the Soul*, chs. 12–14, in More 1662.   [18] Ibid. in More 1662: 70–3.

which is registred in the Mind Divine', and the height of virtue is 'constantly to pursue that which to Right Reason seems best'. More also sought to prove the principles of morality by means of rational demonstration. When discussing knowledge of the good in Chapter 4, he provides a set of twenty-five propositions or 'noêmata of morality' as the basis of a rational demonstration of how we can arrive at knowledge of the good. These noêmata provide a summary of all the principles of ethics – for example, 'The Good is that which is grateful, pleasant, and congruous to any Being which hath Life and Perception.'

Although he claims that we can know the good by the exercise of right reason, and that 'Moral Good is Intellectual and Divine',[19] More insists that virtue cannot be taught by mere theory or precepts ('definitions or divisions'). Virtue is 'an intellectual power of the Soul', and living virtuously entails active pursuit of the good. The moral agent must, therefore, be capable of self-direction. He makes direct reference to his critique of Hobbes in the *Immortality of the Soul* to restate his conception of free will as *autexousion* or 'having a Power to Act with in ourselves'.[20]

For all his emphasis on rationality of ethics and moral action, there is a hedonistic element in More's moral philosophy. For More defines happiness as pleasure arising from the sense of virtue. This is apprehended not by reason, but by a faculty of mind which he calls the 'boniform faculty' and describes as 'the most elevated and most divine Faculty of the Soul'. The 'boniform faculty' is the seat of happiness and it performs its function by a kind of sensation: we recognize virtue by tasting it – More writes of the 'relish' of the good. More's idea that goodness can in some way be apprehended sensually as well as by reason is connected with another distinctive feature of his ethical theory, and that is the role which he accords to the passions. In seventeenth-century terms this is a modern feature of his moral philosophy, reflective of his debt to Descartes. More conceives of the passions as physical effects which affect the soul either adversely or beneficially. The passions have the capacity to destabilise the soul by disabling reason: a passion is a 'corporeal Impression, which hath force enough to blind the Mind'.[21] But rightly controlled and guided by virtue or 'an inward power of the soul', the passions serve to purge or aerate the spirits and to inspire affection in the soul towards its object. They are thus 'a most certain and solid Treasure of the Soul', and 'our Souls are not able, without such Passions, to wed the Object, and, as it were, to intermix it with our Sense and Life'.[22] Most

[19] More, 1690: 28. [20] Ibid., 175, 176. [21] Ibid., 33. [22] Ibid., 39.

of More's treatise, in fact, is taken up with an account of individual passions. His list of passions is taken from Descartes, though classified differently in four groups headed by admiration, love-and-hatred, cupidity, joy-and-grief.

RALPH CUDWORTH

Ralph Cudworth is traditionally regarded as an ethical rationalist, and is classified accordingly in histories of ethics.[23] This is correct in so far as it is rests on Cudworth's most important published work on moral philosophy, his *A Treatise Concerning Eternal and Immutable Morality*, which argues for the real and immutable existence of moral principles, on an *a priori* basis. However, *A Treatise* is only a partial statement of Cudworth's ethics, which is developed further in a set of three writings 'On Liberty and Necessity', two of which remain unpublished. The third of these, 'Of Freewill', was not published until the nineteenth century.[24] The central topic discussed in these writings is Cudworth's conception of free will, or, more exactly, self-determination, supported by a moral psychology.

Prior to the publication of *A Treatise of Freewill*, Cudworth's ethical views would have been known to his contemporaries through his published sermons, and through scattered discussion in his major work, *The True Intellectual System of the Universe* (1678). This book was originally planned as the first part of a larger treatise which would cover the themes discussed in the unpublished ethical writings. In fact *The True Intellectual System* establishes the governing principles of his other ethical writings. In this work Cudworth grounds the eternal unchanging character of goodness and justice in God himself, and argues that mind and conceptual realities are first in the order of nature. For Cudworth, as for Descartes, God is 'a Being Absolutely Perfect', but also as for Plato, God is 'The very Idea or Essence of Good' (Cudworth quotes Plato's very words in *Republic* 6).[25] It follows that God creates all things 'according to his Own Nature (his Essential Goodness and Wisdom) and therefore according to the Best Pattern, and in the Best manner Possible, for the Good of the Whole'. Thus God is both architect and archetype of the best possible world, goodness is intrinsic to the nature of things (creation), and essential goodness is eternal and unchanging. From the existence and nature of God, Cudworth derives not just the principles of morality, but the basis of moral conduct. For he argues that moral action is accountable. Thus in order to be accountable for their actions, moral agents

[23] Selby-Bigge 1897.   [24] See note 3 above.   [25] *TIS*: 204.

must be free to act, and freedom of action requires that they must have the power to act. These fundamental ethical principles are constitutive of the 'intellectual system' of Cudworth's *True Intellectual System*. As he states in the Preface, the basic constituents of the 'true' system are,

> First, ... that there is an Omnipotent Understanding Being, Presiding over all. Secondly, That this God, being Essentially Good and Just, there is ... Something in its own Nature, Immutably and Eternally Just, and Unjust; and not by Arbitrary Will, Law, and Command onely. And Lastly, That there is Something *eph' hêmin*, or That we are so far forth Principles or Masters of our own Actions, as to be Accountable to Justice for them.[26]

Goodness is thus absolute in nature, and moral accountability is built into the fabric of creation. The exercise of goodness is, furthermore, active and not passive: moral action is not brought about by external compulsion, for that would remove accountability. Freedom to act is essential to ethical conduct. The exercise of goodness requires active internal self-determination. Free will, therefore, entails not just the possibility of acting otherwise than we do, but the power to pursue the course of action which we choose to follow. Cudworth's moral rationalism is supported by a moral psychology which he only begins to outline in *A Treatise*, but which is elaborated in his analysis of the nature of mind and moral action in the writings on 'Liberty and Necessity'. The main feature of this is his re-conception of the will as a power of self-determination, which he calls the *hêgemonikon* or *autexousion*. This ruling principle of the soul integrates its various functions into one unified control centre, bringing together what had traditionally been regarded as separate faculties. By combining the higher functions of the soul (will and reason) with the lower, animal, appetites of the soul, the *hêgemonikon* bridges the divide between will and intellect familiar from scholastic philosophy and that between soul and body that characterises Cartesianism. This is the seat of moral responsibility, because it gives one

> a power over oneself, either of intending or remitting and consequently of determining ourselves better or worse; which is the foundation of commendation or blame, praise or dispraise, and the object of retributive justice, remunerative or judicative, rewarding or punishing.[27]

---

[26] Cudworth, *TIS*, sig. A3v. The classic study of Cudworth's philosophy is Passmore 1951.
[27] Cudworth 1996: 185.

As a power by virtue of which we may direct ourselves towards the good or away from it, the *hêgemonikon* is both a 'self-improving power and a self-depressing power'.

INFLUENCE

In the seventeenth century, Culverwell and More were the most widely read of the Cambridge Platonists – Culverwell's *Elegant and Learned Discourse of the Light of Nature* (1652) was reprinted four times, twice in Oxford.[28] More's *Enchiridion ethicum* (1668) was used as a textbook in England and Scotland. More's moral axioms were later appended by James Tyrell to his popular abridgement of Richard Cumberland's *De legibus naturae*, published as *A Brief Disquisition of the Laws of Nature* in 1690. In the longer term, however, the moral philosophy of Cudworth was the most influential and enduring of that of all the Cambridge Platonists. However, Cudworth's legacy is complicated by the fact that, as already explained, most of his work on ethics remained unpublished in his lifetime. As a result there have been different perceptions of his ethical thought in different periods. His reputation today as moral rationalist derives from *A Treatise concerning Eternal and Immutable Morality*, which appeared during the rationalist-sentimentalist debates of the Scottish Enlightenment, in which Cudworth was aligned with Samuel Clarke against Francis Hutcheson and Shaftesbury. The philosopher most indebted to Cudworth's *Treatise* was Richard Price, in his *A Review of the Principal Questions in Morals* (1757). Since the recovery of Cudworth's manuscripts (then unknown) it has been suggested that Cudworth may also have influenced moral sentimentalism through Shaftesbury.[29] Another intriguing possibility, as yet untested, is that *A Treatise* was known to Kant in Mosheim's Latin translation, published in Jena in 1733.[30]

BIBLIOGRAPHY

An asterisk denotes secondary literature especially suitable for further reading.

Cudworth, Ralph 1678. *The True Intellectual System of the Universe*. London.

[28] Culverwell's *Discourse of the Light of Nature* was reprinted in London, 1654, 1661, and Oxford, 1659, 1669.
[29] Passmore 1951; Gill 2004.
[30] Johan Lorenz Mosheim delayed publication of his Latin translation of *TIS* in order to publish a translation of *A Treatise* with it. See the Introduction to Cudworth, 1996.

Cudworth, Ralph 1838. *A Treatise of Freewill*, ed. J. Allen. London.

Cudworth, Ralph 1996. *A Treatise concerning Eternal and Immutable Morality; with, A Treatise of Freewill*, ed. S. Hutton. Cambridge University Press.

Culverwell, Nathaniel 1652. *An Elegant and Learned Discourse of the Light of Nature*. London.

Cumberland, Richard 2005. *A Treatise of the Laws of Nature*, trans. John Maxwell, ed. Jon Parkin. Indianapolis, IN: Liberty Fund.

Darwall, Stephen 1995. *The British Moralists and the Internal 'Ought', 1640–1740*. Cambridge University Press.*

Gill, Michael B. 2004. 'Rationalism, Sentimentalism, and Ralph Cudworth', *Hume Studies*, 30: 149–81.*

Gill, Michael B. 2010. 'From Cambridge Platonism to Scottish Sentimentalism', *The Journal of Scottish Philosophy*, 8: 13–31.*

Haakonssen, Knud 1996. *Natural Law and Moral Philosophy from Grotius to the Scottish Enlightenment*. Cambridge University Press.

Hutton, Sarah 2012. 'From Cudworth to Hume: Cambridge Platonism and the Scottish Enlightenment', *Canadian Journal of Philosophy*, 42, Iss. Sup. 1, 8–26.*

More, Henry, 1662. *A Collection of Several Philosophical Writings*. London.

More, Henry, 1668. *A Divine Dialogues*. London.

More, Henry 1690. *An Account of Virtue*. London [English translation of *Enchiridion ethicum, præcipua moralis philosophiæ rudimenta complectens*, 1668].

Passmore, J.A. 1951. *Ralph Cudworth. An Interpretation*. Cambridge University Press.

Patrides, C.A. (ed.) 1969. *The Cambridge Platonists*. Cambridge University Press.

Plato 2013. *Republic*, ed. and trans. Chris Emlyn-Jones and William Preddy. Cambridge, MA: Harvard University Press.

Selby-Bigge, L.A. (ed.) 1897. *British Moralists, Being Selections from Writers Principally of the Eighteenth Century*. Oxford: Clarendon Press.

Sterry, Peter 1675. *A Discourse of the Freedom of the Will*. London.

Taliaferro, Charles and Alison Tepley (eds.) 2004. *Cambridge Platonist Spirituality*. New York: Paulist Press.

Tyrell, James 1690. *A Brief Disquisition of the Laws of Nature*. London.

20

Bayle

JEAN-LUC SOLÈRE

Pierre Bayle did not write a systematic treatise on moral philosophy, but moral and ethical concerns are addressed throughout the entirety of his body of work.

PLEASURE

A good place to start is Bayle's intervention in the polemical disagreement between Antoine Arnauld and Nicolas Malebranche. Arnauld had taken Malebranche to task for writing: "pleasure is a good, and in effect makes happy whoever enjoys it, while he enjoys it and as far as he enjoys it" (*Search after Truth*, 4: 10) – i.e. any pleasure, even sensory pleasures. Bayle wrote in support of Malebranche that this statement is a self-evident truth.[1] Its obviousness, though, had not been granted by philosophers in previous centuries – quite the opposite; and Arnauld was upholding the classical Socratic–Stoic paradox by contending that libertines who live a life dedicated to pleasure are *not* happy, contrary to what they may believe, but are in fact miserable. Malebranche's and Bayle's claim must be understood in the context of a reaction against neo-Stoicism and of the rehabilitation of Epicureanism undertaken by Pierre Gassendi, who had shown that hedonism does not lead to an immoral life. Moreover, the preeminence which Epicureanism gives to the search for pleasure is consistent with the widespread Augustinian view of a fallen human nature exclusively governed by concupiscence in the absence of grace.[2] True, neither Malebranche nor Bayle endorses Epicurean ethics; still less do they recommend indulging in sensory pleasures. Their admission that a

---

[1] *Nouvelles de la République des Lettres*, August 1685, in Bayle 1964–1990 = *Œuvres diverses* (*OD*), 1: 348a.

[2] Epicurus's ideas are much more adapted to our present condition than are those of the Stoics, Bayle notes (*Nouvelles . . .*, January 1686, *OD* 1: 475b).

present pleasure makes us happy is immediately followed by a warning: it is not always advantageous to enjoy pleasure and it is sometimes advantageous to endure pain, given that God will punish illegitimate pleasures and reward pious sufferings by eternal pleasure. This is no incitement to loose morals. Nevertheless, this warning itself has a distinctive Epicurean ring, as it amounts to a calculation of pleasure. The classical eudaimonism of Plato, Aristotle, and the Stoics acknowledged that the pursuit of happiness is the essential driving force of the soul, but also held that happiness results not from any pleasure whatsoever, but rather only from what is our *true* good. With Malebranche's and Bayle's hedonism, the main opposition is no longer between apparent and real happiness, but between small and large pleasures, or momentary and durable pleasures. Grace itself is a holy pleasure.

As for sensory pleasure specifically, the view of classical eudaimonism, which Arnaud defended against Bayle, is inseparable from the idea that each class of things has its own natural ultimate end, which is also a norm for the things in that class. Our true good and duty is to reach our ultimate end, namely, the accomplishment of the potentialities of our human nature, characterized by reason and free will. Sensory pleasures are only the means for safeguarding our bodies or the species. Taking them as final goals is therefore a fundamental moral disorder.

Bayle, however, rejects this hierarchical system of ends.[3] The category of pleasure is homogeneous: corporeal pleasure has the same nature as holy pleasure, because a pleasure is always a modification of the soul, whatever its cause. Bayle bases his rationale on Malebranche's view that body and soul do not interact at all. The belief that certain pleasures belong to the body, and, as such, are by nature inferior to pleasures of the mind, reflects a failure strictly to distinguish the two substances. In fact, there is nothing psychological in the body; it is pure extension and mechanism. All sensations, as mental events, are modifications of the soul. Therefore, there is no "physical" pleasure *per se*; all pleasure is "spiritual." Moreover, as the body does not act on the soul, it does not produce in the latter any feeling. It is God who directly modifies the soul and makes it experience certain feelings on the occasion of certain modifications of the body. Therefore, no pleasure is more "spiritual" than another by virtue of its efficient cause, since God is in every case the sole efficient cause. Pleasure can be said to be more or less spiritual only in regard to its occasional cause. That is why, in theory, there is no pleasure that could not make us eternally happy. God is free to choose what will be the

---

[3] *Réponse de l'auteur des Nouvelles . . .*, OD 1: 454a–455b.

occasional cause of what. Therefore, if God linked the pleasure we at present experience on the occasion of eating chocolate to seeing his essence in the afterlife, beatitude would be just that pleasure stretched to eternity. In Epicurean terms, God would transform a kinetic pleasure into a katastematic one. Sensual pleasures are sinful because they are forbidden by God, and not forbidden by God because they are sinful. That is why one can warn libertines that sensual pleasures will have dire consequences, but not that they do not make them happy.

However, what if we are talking to atheists, who do not fear retribution in the afterlife? Does that entail that they have no morals, except indulging in whatever makes them happy here and now?

THE VIRTUOUS ATHEIST

One of Bayle's most famous and provocative theses was that an atheist can be virtuous.[4] Before Bayle, being an atheist was tantamount to having no reason to refrain from acting on any of one's impulses. As a result, an atheist was seen as bound to be immoral, indeed to be a monster.

Bayle objects that the fear of hell or the hope of salvation do not deter most of the people who are nominally Christian from committing numerous sins. This proves that beliefs and theories have little or no influence on our conduct.[5] We choose a course of action not because of abstract notions, but as a result of the particular judgment we formulate in given circumstances and in view of a certain object we desire or fear. Generally, this judgment conforms not to theoretical views about *dos* and *don'ts* but to what will bring us more pleasure, in accordance with the passion that is dominant in us at that moment or with our temperament and habits. Reason, actually, is rarely the cause of our actions. In language that is evocative of Hume, Bayle explains that mere mental representations are powerless to counteract passions. For instance, the idea of God's wrath is quite different from a genuine feeling of fear and therefore cannot thwart a violent desire.[6]

Since human beings rarely act in keeping with their own principles, and since, in particular, religious beliefs are generally not a barrier to sin, it is unlikely that the lack of such beliefs would provoke the unleashing of

---

[4] This thesis is not part of a direct plea in favor of atheism: Bayle presents it in defense of his claim that, of the two evils, idolatry is worse than atheism.

[5] *Pensées diverses sur la comète* [=PD] §§134–6 (*OD* 3: 87–8).

[6] *Continuation des Pensées diverses* [=CPD] §139 (*OD* 3: 388a).

passions allegedly contained by them. Inclination to evil comes not from negating the existence of God, but from human nature, which is deeply corrupt: as crooked a timber as ever Kant would find it to be.[7] A believer is not more poised than an atheist to live a virtuous life. If the decisive factor is, for instance, temperament, it may well be that an atheist is endowed with a calm disposition and is therefore less of a sinner than a believer who has a disposition towards bodily pleasures, anger, and so on.

However, one might reply that although it is true that most nominal Christians are not real followers of Christ, Christian societies (or other religious societies) nevertheless subsist because of certain values and promises that foster social bonds. By contrast – it was firmly believed before Bayle – an atheist society is impossible: it would immediately collapse, as there would be no incentive to temper the raw egoism that would pit its members against each other.

But Bayle cleverly uses an idea that was also commonplace in his days, namely, St Augustine's claim that the so-called "virtues of the pagans" were actually "superb sins," due not to their love of God but to pride. Why would atheists not be able to act in the same way as the ancient Romans? They could accomplish heroic deeds and display abnegation, for the sake of glory or out of love for their country. Admittedly, not everyone would act that way. Strict laws would have to be enforced. But is that not the case in Christian societies?[8]

In addition, an important factor is at work in all social interaction: we care about the opinion of others; we want to be liked by them. Why are women generally less prone to lapses in sexual ethics? Not because they have less of a sex drive, Bayle suggests, but, except for those who are really godly, because they are subjected to the laws of honor that men impose on them.[9] If they could satisfy their desires without damaging their reputation, they would be as unfaithful as men, but fear of infamy is a potent reason for them to remain chaste. Similarly, if it was as honorable for men to live chastely as it is to face an enemy without fleeing, men would be far less prone to philandering. This motivation has nothing to do with religious feelings, so why would it not have the same effect on atheists? Admittedly, the search for pleasure would be the ultimate cause of their acts, but this is also true of believers, and gaining the esteem of others is a pleasure as well, which leads to civilized interactions. As the "deep psychology" promoted by Pierre Nicole and

---

[7] *CPD* §23 (*OD* 3: 220a).   [8] *PD* §146 (*OD* 3: 94).   [9] *PD* §162 (*OD* 3: 104).

François de La Rochefoucauld has shown, self-interest pursues its goals by disguising itself as politeness, altruistic behavior, modesty, and so on.

Thus, fear of civil punishment, fear of others' scorn, and thirst for their praise would be sufficient "repressing principles" among atheists. They would yield the same results as in religious societies, where they take effect independently of beliefs (or sometimes against them). An atheist society would not be worse than a society of believers. In fact, Bayle notes, the society that would not be viable is one composed of true Christians, as strict evangelical ethics would prevent it from defending itself against external aggression. But, he sarcastically adds, one does not have to worry about the fate of the so-called Christian states. The rules of "Nature" prevail in these states; the lure of profit and relentless aggressiveness make them thrive.[10] In a fashion that anticipates Mandeville's *Fable of the Bees*, Bayle even points out that some vices are beneficial to public prosperity – for instance, the taste for luxury puts money into circulation and gives work to artisans.

Bayle pushes his provocation still further. He contends that, beyond self-interested motives, an atheist might also have insight into moral rectitude (the *honestum* of the Stoics), that is to say, into what should be done just because it is right, not because it is useful or pleasant.[11] This idea was often vehemently denied, on the grounds that by definition an atheist cannot recognize that the foundation of all moral values is God, and consequently cannot know these values. But Bayle maintains that gifted atheist philosophers would be able to discover moral distinctions (between good and evil, just and unjust, etc.) because these distinctions belong to the nature of things. For theistic metaphysics, God creates existences, but not essences (Bayle rejects Descartes's thesis of the "creation of eternal truths"). They are what they are independently of God's choice. So thorough materialists, who claim that a Nature devoid of thought produces all things, could nevertheless discover the difference between lie and truthfulness, ingratitude and gratitude, etc., just as they would discover the difference between a square and a circle, namely by comparing their properties. Moreover, they could realize that moral values impose duties upon us. This would be on a par with abiding by the laws of logic. Just as rules of reasoning are necessarily what they are, there are rules for the will, the most general being that humans must want what conforms to reason, because such is our nature as rational beings. As it is a defect not to comply with logic when we think, it is a defect to want a thing without observing this rule of the will. If atheists are able to discover

---

[10] *CPD* §124–5 (*OD* 3: 360b–362b).   [11] *CPD* §151–2 (*OD* 3: 405–10).

the necessity of the laws of logic, why should they be unable to discover the necessity of the laws of ethics? Why should they be unable to realize that keeping one's promises or being grateful to a benefactor are requirements of reason, that is to say, objective duties?

If moral obligation does not result from sanctions or rewards attached to the law but is just a fact of reason, it is tempting to translate this into the Kantian language of autonomy. Thus, it appears that the language that Bayle was speaking to the libertines, in the dispute with Arnauld, was not that of morality, but rather was the heteronomous rhetoric of religious persuasion. It may be that atheists, unconcerned with promises of happiness or threats of punishment, have a purer view of moral rectitude.[12]

However, the fact that they know about moral laws does not entail that atheists live in an ethical way. Since, according to Bayle, humans rarely act in keeping with their principles, atheists may be able to know everything about virtue, but for the most part they will not practice it, yielding instead to some dominant passion or particular pleasure like other human beings. When their conduct conforms externally to moral standards, it is probably because of a motivation such as ensuring reciprocation from others or concern for their reputation, as we saw earlier. Or it will be a matter of chance: if an atheist has a non-sensual temperament and finds pleasure in virtue, then he will be virtuous; if not, not.[13] That would be a case of what we call today "moral luck." That kind of luck is rather rare. Bayle conjures up the exemplary lives of Epicurus, Vanini, Spinoza, or some remote Chinese Confucian or Buddhist as concrete examples of virtuous atheists, but the list is bound to be short. Moreover, while atheists may have a clear view of moral standards and strive to abide by them because it is right to do so, their intention is not "pure" in a Kantian sense. Bayle specifies that their righteousness is not an exception to the rule of self-love – in fact, it is a refined love of oneself. These atheists can act according to what is right and wrong without an extrinsic incentive, but they would do it for the sake of the internal satisfaction of having chosen rectitude over vice and of having proven to themselves their strength of character. "Nothing is sweeter than being pleased with oneself."[14] A subtle but exquisite pleasure is the final cause of their conduct. Thus, even if we leave aside the pleasure of being esteemed by others, the conduct of virtuous atheists would conform to the laws of morality, but they would not be totally disinterested.

---

[12] *CPD* §91 (*OD* 3: 317b). [13] *CPD* §150 (*OD* 3: 404b–405a).
[14] *CPD* §153 (*OD* 3: 413a.) Cf. §152, note *r* (410b).

Only acting for the love of God is purely moral ("the most beautiful morality," as Bayle calls it),[15] but this requires the influence of God's grace. In fact, when Bayle writes that there are only two motivations of our will – either grace, or self-love[16] – he seems to take up the traditional, Augustinian opposition between, on the one hand, the true Christians, regenerated by grace, who belong to the city of God, ruled by charity; and, on the other hand, all the other humans, who obey the law of the terrestrial city, self-love. However, there are relative degrees of wrongness within the terrestrial city. As its inhabitants are not illuminated by grace, the reason why some are not as evil as others does not lie in their views on religion. It is related to their private passions (some love praise, others prefer sensual pleasures to their neighbors' esteem) or to their natural disposition to a dispassionate life. What made Bayle's theory scandalous in his day is that he affirms that a good-natured atheist acting in accordance with mere reason would be more ethical than common believers who abstain from sinning because of their fear of punishment.

MORALITY AND GOD

As we have just seen, Bayle is a rationalist in ethics, even if he is more of a skeptic in many theoretical matters. Although our reason has lost the power to control passions, because of original sin, "natural light" does not fail us as far as the eternal laws of morality are concerned.

What reason shows us, however, does not square with what Revelation tells us about God's actions. A conflict ensues, as reason is supposed to be given by God to guide us and make us see these moral truths which are not contingent on God's will but are, so to speak, true for God himself. Is God not bound by them as well? Indeed, God seems to be outright immoral – this is the other quite scandalous aspect of Bayle's theses. Among the several episodes of the Bible in which God appears to be cruel, let us mention only the major one: the Fall of Adam and Eve. This narrative has been used by theologians to account for the presence of evil in the Creation. If God is all-benevolent, almighty, and omniscient, how is it that there are evils such as plagues, earthquakes, serial killers, wars, and so on? The usual response is that evil comes from the disobedience of Adam and Eve, who were endowed by God with free will. They alone are responsible for original sin, and from that first act of evil derive all the evils that humanity commits (moral evil) or

---

[15] *CPD* §153 (*OD* 3: 412b, note o).   [16] *CPD* §153 (*OD* 3: 411a).

has to endure (physical evil). Bayle mercilessly refutes that explanation. Free will is supposed to be the ultimate gift that God gave to mankind, but the problem is that God, among his infinite perfections, has foreknowledge of all events, including the volitions of human beings, and therefore must have known in advance that Adam and Eve would put their free will to bad use. But common sense says that if you are certain that the potential recipient of a gift would use it for harming himself or others, you should withhold that gift, or you will be held morally responsible for the consequences. Your love for that person would also be questioned. Using several quaint comparisons, Bayle dismisses all the reasons for which God could have allowed to happen what he knew was going to happen. To make redemption possible and display his forgiveness? Anyone knows that it is a greater act of goodness to prevent a man from falling into a hole than to let him fall so he can be rescued an hour later. To manifest his glory? God would be like a surgeon who lets his children break their legs so that he can show his skill at repairing them. To not infringe upon Adam's and Eve's freedom? God would be like a mother who allows her young daughters to go to a party where she knows that they will be mixed up in drug trafficking, and is "satisfied with exhorting them to be virtuous and with threatening to disown them"[17] (I slightly modernize Bayle's example). In short, what we know of God's action flies in the face of our moral convictions. Our reason clearly shows us, as an axiom of morality, that someone who can prevent an evil but refrains from doing so is responsible for that evil.

As a result, given the conjunction of the divine attributes of foreknowledge and almightiness, it is a mere sophism to contend that God made it possible for Adam and Eve to sin but is not responsible for their actual sin. His conduct appears to be lacking any goodness, as the consequence of the Fall is the infinite suffering of generations of humans on Earth and the eternal damnation of the great majority of them. Even if a greater good resulted from that evil, the cost was too high, and God, who was free to create or not to create, should have refrained from creating. The existence of evil has been chosen by him; he is the author of sin as much as human beings are. Therefore, God seems to be immoral.

Does Bayle endorse that conclusion? I will not enter into the debate about his supposed atheism. I will only note that Luther and Calvin had already said that by the standards of human reason God is cruel and unjust. Their answer is that faith makes the believer uphold, against all appearances, that God is good

[17] Bayle 1995, article "Pauliciens," remarks E and F.

and just. Turning this position into a philosophical one, Bayle, a Calvinist by
education, explains[18] that the picture of God's goodness that we draw from
Revelation does contain some of the characteristics that are included in our
rational, "common notion" of goodness (for instance forgiveness), but does
not contain other characteristics that are also comprised by this common
notion (for instance, preventing evil as much as one can). Moreover, we do
not see how acts that are incompatible with our notion of goodness (for
instance, ordering the killing of innocents) could be compatible with God's
goodness. But we only have "imperfect and confused" ideas of God and of his
attributes, given the disproportion between infinite and finite. Since we do not
comprehend all of God's goodness (which is identical to God's essence) nor its
connection with other attributes (for instance justice), we cannot be certain
that the characteristics of goodness that we do not see are in effect absent, and
that certain actions of God are definitely incompatible with his goodness. We
can only postulate that all of this meshes in a way which is worthy of the all-
perfect being but which we cannot understand. By a sort of rational faith, on
the basis of the premise that God is an absolutely perfect being, we can believe
in the truth of the conclusion that everything that God does is good, without,
however, being able to align what God does with morality. So Bayle is strongly
committed to rationalism in ethics, but it may be that the principles that our
reason grasps are only part of the total truth. Yet we are required to stand by
those truths that God has made accessible to our reason and not to give our
imagination free rein to supplement or change them. Reminding us of the laws
we are bound by is the role of conscience.

CONSCIENCE AND TOLERANCE

The set of moral truths consubstantial to God is known as the "eternal law"
and from it derives the set of obligations for creatures known as the "natural
law." Our practical reason is called "synderesis" when it grasps the practical
principles, that is, the primary axioms of ethics contained in the natural law. It
is called "conscience" when it carries out practical reasoning, that is, draws
conclusions which apply the principles to the concrete situation we face and
pronounces a command: this action ought to be done.[19] Since such conclusions come directly from the eternal law in God, ultimately, then, when our
conscience dictates something, it is God who orders it, and disobeying one's

[18] *Entretiens de Maxime et de Thémiste* I, chs. 1, 2, 7 (*OD* 4: 7b, 11b, 21a).
[19] *Systema totius philosophiae* (*OD* 4: 259–62).

conscience amounts to holding God in contempt. This is why it is the supreme principle of morality that we must always obey our conscience. This standard holds even if our practical judgment is not correct, that is to say, even if we make a mistake in our deductions. What an erroneous conscience dictates is still a moral duty, because to disregard knowingly what *appears* commanded by the moral law amounts to holding God in contempt just as if it was in fact commanded.[20]

Consequently, acting against one's conscience is always worse than the opposite, even if what we do is in fact wrong because our conscience is erroneous. Suppose that someone comes to your door to collect money for charity, and you *mistakenly* believe that he is a swindler.[21] Your conscience tells you not to give him money because the sum would be put to better use by helping persons in real need. Suppose that you obey your conscience, but that in addition you erroneously believe that it also is your duty to beat up the alleged swindler to teach him a lesson. Your action is objectively bad, because in fact one should not be violent towards anybody. By contrast, imagine that, against your conscience, you give money because you dare not refuse out of patholo- gical shyness. It turns out that your action is going to benefit the destitute. However, the second action is morally worse than the first because no moral goodness can be found in it at all: neither in the mind's judgment ("this person is a swindler," which is false), nor in the volition (which goes against conscience), nor in the action as a physical event (handing over a banknote, which a machine can do). That it is beneficial for the destitute does not confer on it any ethical value, because the effect was unintended. Only a wrong action done in violation of conscience can be worse (for instance, beating up the alleged swindler while knowing that this is bad). By contrast, in the first case, although the action of beating is objectively bad, there is nevertheless one element of goodness, namely, the fact that the action is in accordance with conscience. (Note, however, that this does not make it a virtuous deed: only an objectively good action in agreement with conscience qualifies as ethical.)

The conscience principle finds a remarkable application to the domain of religious toleration (which was a novelty at the end of the seventeenth century.) Since it is immoral not to follow one's conscience, forcing people not to do what their conscience tells them to do – that is to say, to be immoral – is also

---

[20] *Commentaire philosophique sur ces paroles de Jésus-Christ, Contrains-les d'entrer …* [=CP] II.9 (*OD* 2: 432b).
[21] Cf. *CP* II.8 (*OD* 2: 423a–b).

immoral.[22] Therefore, believers of each persuasion should be left alone. Bayle does not ground tolerance on relativism: it may well be that one faith is true and all the others wrong. But an erroneous conscience obligates as much as a correct conscience. So alleged heretics may be misguided, but not to obey their conscience would make things still worse. Moreover, an error is blameworthy when it was avoidable and we have let negligence or passions lead us astray. Ignorance of moral truths is never unavoidable, because they are accessible to anybody who pays attention to natural light, Bayle says in a Malebranchist fashion.[23] These truths are composed of clear and distinct notions. But religious dogmas cannot claim for themselves the same kind of obviousness: what pertains to God is largely inaccessible to reason. Therefore, errors in that domain are unavoidable and heretics who sincerely strive after truth but fail to find it can be excused.[24] What matters, for God, is orthopraxy (correct action), not orthodoxy (correct belief).[25] As in the atheists' case, theoretical errors do not necessarily imply immorality. Vice is not the cause of heresy, and a heretic can be a good person.

BIBLIOGRAPHY

An asterisk denotes secondary literature especially suitable for further reading.

Bayle, Pierre 1964–1990 (reprint). *Œuvres Diverses*. Hildesheim, Georg Olms.
Bayle, Pierre 1995 (reprint). *Dictionnaire Historique et Critique*, 5th edn. Geneva, Slatkin.
Labrousse, Elisabeth 1963. *Pierre Bayle*. The Hague, M. Nijhoff.*
Solère, Jean-Luc 1995. "Tout plaisir rend-il heureux? Une querelle entre Arnauld, Malebranche et Bayle," *Chroniques de Port-Royal*, 44: 351–79.*
Solère, Jean-Luc 2010. "Scepticisme, métaphysique et morale: le cas Bayle," in Bost, H. and McKenna, A. (eds.), *Les "Eclaircissements" de Bayle*. Paris, Honoré Champion, 499–524.*
Solère, Jean-Luc 2016. "The Coherence of Bayle's Theory of Toleration," *Journal of the History of Philosophy*, 54/1: 21–46.*

---

[22] *CP* I.6 (*OD* 2: 384b). Given what Bayle says in *PD*, as we have seen in 'The Virtuous Atheist' above, conscientious believers are certainly a tiny minority. But, precisely because of the fragility of humans' morals, it is important not to induce them into temptation.
[23] *CP* I.1 (*OD* 2: 368b).   [24] *CP* II.10 (*OD* 2: 439a–440b, 442a–b).
[25] *CP* II.10 (*OD* 2: 436a–438b).

21

Leibniz

GREGORY BROWN

Leibniz's moral philosophy is in large part driven by the need to reconcile his psychological assumption, that all deliberate action is done for the sake of the agent's own perceived good, with the demand of justice, that we ought to seek the good of others for its own sake. After briefly recounting Leibniz's deduction of rights and obligations in his early *Nova methodus discendae docendaeque jurisprudentiae* (1667; hereafter, *NM*), I consider in turn his account of what moves us to act, of what moves us to act justly, and what obligates us to act justly. Finally, I consider how his doctrine of disinterested love enables him to reconcile his psychological assumption with the demand of justice.

THE DEDUCTION OF RIGHTS, OBLIGATIONS AND THE 'THREE GRADES OF THE RIGHT OF NATURE' IN NM

In §14 of Part II of his earliest systematic work on moral philosophy[1] and natural law, the *Nova methodus discendae docendaeque jurisprudentiae*, Leibniz proposed to 'elicit a sound method [for learning and teaching jurisprudence] from the definitions of things themselves' and proceeded, in this and the following six sections, to deduce a series of rights and obligations for all rational beings. He began by defining jurisprudence as 'the science of actions insofar as they are said to be just or unjust' and added that '*justice* [. . .] and *injustice* are whatever is useful or harmful to the public' (A.VI.1: 300). In §14[a] he argued that 'the *morality* . . ., i.e. the Justice, or Injustice of actions, arises from a quality of a person acting in turn so as to produce an action born from preceding actions, which is called *moral Quality*'. Leibniz then qualified this by

---

[1] I use the term 'moral philosophy' here because in the *NM* Leibniz defines justice as 'whatever is useful . . . to the public' and '*morality*' (*moralitas*) as 'Justice' (*Justitia*) (A. VI.1: 300, 301). See the end of the chapter for abbreviations used in bibliographical references. All translations are my own, although I have also included reference to a standard English translation where one is available.

adding, 'but as the real Quality in turn for bringing about an action is twofold, the power of acting [*potentia agendi*] and the necessity of acting [*necessitas agendi*], so moral power is called *Right* [*Jus*] and moral necessity is called *Obligation* [*Obligatio*]' (A.VI.1: 301). He went on to deduce the rights of freedom (*libertas*), faculty (*facultas*), and authority (*potestas*) and the corresponding obligations not to hinder the freedom, faculty, or authority of others. Leibniz's initial deduction ends in §19, where, in referring to the previous six sections, he concludes that 'in this way, therefore, we have deduced the highest source of all Right' (A.VI.1: 304).

In §§73–5 of NM, Leibniz continued his deduction with the 'three grades of the Right of Nature', which, ranked in increasing order of perfection, are: '*strict Right* (*Jus strictum*), *equity* (*aequitas*), *piety* (*pietas*)' (A.VI.1: 343). For Leibniz these three grades of right or justice correspond to the three precepts of law (*juris precepta*) given at the beginning of Justinian's *Institutes*: 'not to injure another' (*alterum non laedere*), 'to give to each his own' (*suum cuique tribuere*), and 'to live honourably' (*honeste vivere*) (*Institutes* I.i.3). In §73, Leibniz states that

> strict or *pure right* derives from the definition of terms, and it is, if you judge correctly, nothing other than the Right of War and peace . . . From which it is evident that the unique precept of the pure Right of Nature is *to harm no one*, let him not be given the Right of war. (A.VI.1: 343)

Hence strict right relates to what Leibniz says in §17 of his earlier deduction, where he argued that '*injury* in the completely natural state gives the harmed party . . . the Right of war against the offending violator of society' (A.VI.1: 303).

In §74 Leibniz states that '*equity* or equality, that is, the ratio or proportion of two or more, consists in harmony or congruence' and that 'it requires that against him who harms me, not that I should set about an internecine war, but towards the attainment of restitution', as well as the principle 'that what you do not wish for yourself is not be done to another . . . Hence that precept: *To give to each his own*' (A.VI.1: 344).

In §75 Leibniz asserts that '*piety* is . . . the third grade of *the Right of Nature*, and it gives perfection and effect to the others' (A.VI.1: 344). How piety does this is shortly revealed:

> Whenever strict Right and equity are without Physical bond, God, becoming an accessory, brings it about that whatever is useful to the public, that is, to the human race and the world, is made useful even for individuals. And thus every honourable thing is useful and every base thing is harmful. Because God has established rewards for the just and punishments for the unjust

based upon his wisdom: and what the reason of omnipotence resolves to
achieve prevails. (A.VI.1: 344)

Thus piety perfects strict right and equity by providing a motive to act justly
when 'physical bond' fails. But what that bond is, and the conditions under
which it might fail, are explored in later works.

WHAT MOVES US TO ACT?

In the *Discours de Métaphysique*, Leibniz explains that the actual world is
founded on two decrees of God, 'upon the first free decree of God, which
inclines him always to do what is the most perfect, and upon the decree that
God has made (on the basis of the first) with respect to human nature, which is
that man will always do (although freely) what appears the best' (A.VI.4: 1548/
AG.46). Thus 'the object of the will is the apparent good, and nothing is desired
by us except under the aspect of an apparent good', which, he observed, is 'a
most ancient and common dogma' (A.VI.4: 1380). Consequently, a deliberate
act of will presupposes a judgement that something is good, a doctrine that was
explicitly stated in the very early NM: 'every action of the soul is a thought, for
even to will is nothing other than to reflect upon the goodness of a thing'.[2] And
it becomes clear from many other passages that the good that Leibniz thought
moves us to act is *our own perceived good*. Thus in the fourth set of notes for
Elementa juris naturalis (hereafter, *EJN*), Leibniz wrote:

> prudence cannot be separated from our own good, and whatever they may
> say against it is both empty and alien to the practice itself of those speaking.
> There is no one who deliberately does anything except on account of his own
> good, for we even seek the good of those whom we love on account of our
> own pleasure, which we receive from their happiness.
> (A.VI.1: 461/L.134; cf. A.II.3: 369/W.565; Preface Mantissa/L.424)

Leibniz was a motivational hedonist, declaring in *Theodicy* §289 that 'in truth
we will only that which pleases us' (G.6: 289/H.303) and in the *Nouveaux essais*
that 'in substances which are capable of pleasure and pain every action is an
advance towards pleasure and every passion an advance toward pain' (A.VI.6:
210/RB.210). But Leibniz defined the good in various ways. Sometimes he
defined it as 'what contributes to pleasure' (A.VI.4: 1358, cf. A.VI.4: 303, 1412,

---

[2] A.VI.1: 284/L.88. In a later revisionary note to this passage (c. 1697–1700), Leibniz
wrote that 'to will is nothing other than a striving from thought, i.e., to strive for
something on account of its goodness perceived by thought' (A.VI.1: 284 Z.4–6 D/
L.91; cf. A.VI.4: 1412).

1419, 2760, 2773, 2810), or 'what contributes more to [a creature's] joy than to its sorrow' (A.VI.4: 2761). And so in a list of definitions from c. 1701–1705, he wrote that 'the *good of each thing* is what contributes to its happiness' (Gr.667). But he also defined 'the good' as 'what contributes to perfection' (A.VI.4: 405), the 'true good' as 'that which serves in the perfection of intelligent substances' (M.48/R.50), and the 'general good' as 'the advance toward perfection of men' (K.10: 11/R.105). These different senses of 'good' are related through Leibniz's definition of pleasure as 'the perception of perfection' (A.VI.4: 2803/W.568; cf. A.VI.6: 194/RB.194; A.VI.4: 2810). Thus what 'serves in the perfection of intelligent substances' will also contribute to their pleasure. The good is what contributes to pleasure, but not all pleasures are good, since some pleasures, bodily pleasures in particular, can often lead to pain. It is the business of right reason to determine what contributes to the happiness of a person, where happiness is 'lasting joy' (A.VI.6: 90/RB.90; cf. A.VI.6: 189–90/ RB.189–90). But Leibniz often suggests that it is our perfection – the perfection of our intellect and will in particular – that constitutes our happiness, since the perfection of the mind is the stable and enduring source of our highest pleasures: 'happiness consists in the perfection of mind'.[3] Moreover, we shall see that for Leibniz the good of others, that is, their happiness or perfection, is something that can be desired in itself because it is an immediate source of our own pleasure. Thus unlike theorists with whom we are perhaps more familiar, Leibniz did not hold that something that is desired in itself is desired independently of concern for one's own good; and this, as we shall see, holds the key to the reconciliation of his egoistic psychological assumptions with his belief that we can, and morally ought to, desire the good of others for its own sake.

WHAT MOVES US TO ACT JUSTLY?

Given that on Leibniz's view we are, as a matter of natural law, bound to choose that which appears best[4] – and best *for us* in particular – it is clear that

---

[3] A.VI.4: 1992/L.279. For a more detailed account of the relationship between pleasure, happiness, and perfection in Leibniz, see Brown 2011, especially 286–303.
[4] But the act is contingent in Leibniz's sense because it is only hypothetically necessary, i.e., necessary on the assumption of God's second free decree:

> the event has noting in it to make it necessary and which does not permit one to conceive that a completely different thing could happen instead. And as for the connection of the causes with the effects, it only inclined the free agent without necessitating it, as I have just explained: thus it

we are moved to act justly just insofar as doing so appears to us to be in our own best interest.

In his *Monita quaedam ad Samuelis Puffendorfii principia*, Leibniz wrote:

> Grotius has noted well that there would be a certain natural obligation [*naturalem obligationem*] even if it were granted – which cannot be granted – that God is non-existent – or even if the divine existence is set aside for the moment, since certainly care for one's own preservation and benefit requires many things from men towards others, which even Hobbes has observed in part: and alliances of thieves confirm this bond of obligation [*obligationis vinculum*] by example, while enemies to others, they are forced to cultivate a certain sense of duty toward each other, although, as I have already noted, a law of nature that proceeds from this alone would be very imperfect.
>
> (Du.IV.3: 279–80/R.71; cf. Du.IV.3: 281/R.73)

Similarly, in the *Méditation sur la notion commune de la justice*, following his definition of justice as the charity of the wise, Leibniz added:

> Wisdom, which is the knowledge of our own good, brings us to justice, that is to say, to a reasonable advancement of the good of others. We have already adduced one reason for this, which is the fear that we may be harmed if we should do other wise. But there is also the hope that others will do the same for us.
>
> (M.58–9/R 57; cf. M.55/R.54)

It is not surprising, then, that in the *Méditation* Leibniz deduced the three grades of the right of nature solely by appeal to concern for a person's own good (see M.55–9/R54–7). But the reason Leibniz suggests that a natural law based on 'care for one's own preservation and benefit' alone would be imperfect is not because such a law would not be genuinely binding, but rather because, as he noted in the *Nouveaux essais*, 'there are some cases in which there would be no way of demonstrating that the most honourable thing is also the most useful. It is thus only the consideration of God and immortality that makes the obligations [*obligations*] of virtue and justice absolutely binding [*indispensables*]' (A.VI.4: 201/RB.201).

There are two kinds of cases that Leibniz had in mind here: (1) those in which men could violate the demands of strict right and equity to their own advantage without being caught (see, for example, A.II.1: 47; M.60/R.58; Du.4: 277/R.67–8), and (2) those in which honour requires a man to give up every-thing, even including his own life, for the sake of the public good (A.VI.1: 431;

---

does not bring about even a hypothetical necessity, if something outside of it is not added to it, namely this maxim itself, that the strongest inclination always prevails.   (G.6: 131–2/H.152)

Du.IV.3: 276–7/R.67–8; G.3: 388/R.173). In the first kind of case, the threat of future punishment in an afterlife would make 'the obligations of virtue and justice absolutely binding'; in the second kind of case, the future reward in an afterlife would make it possible to make the most extreme sacrifices for the public good without being guilty of 'magnificent folly [*splendida stultitia*]' (Du. IV.3: 277/R.67).

The physical or natural bond of strict right and equity, what moves us to act justly, is concern for our own welfare and happiness; and thus in his *Titulus 1. de justitia et jure*, Leibniz specified 'three . . . principles by which we are moved to act justly':

> *The first* is personal utility, namely, that we harm no one, that we neither harm anyone nor in turn arouse others against us; and then that we help everyone, as much as we can, because the common good flows back to us; *a second* is a sense of humanity and honour . . . In fact, since that sense of humanity is innate in all men, from this source arises the pang of conscience, as for example a man who acts badly does not satisfy himself and feels within himself a certain anguish and sting, and this punishment is natural. *The third* principle is religion. Now since the sense of humanity and the goad of conscience may be blunted in many, and individual utility may alone prevail, which cannot keep men sufficiently protected from men as long as there is hope of impunity, for that reason the highest perfection of natural law is to be sought in the veneration of God, of a most intelligent and powerful substance, whom no one can elude or escape. Whence it is that the useful and the honourable are the same, that there is no sin without punishment, that no honourable action is unprofitable.　　(A.VI.4: 2778–9)

The fact that Leibniz says in the *Nouveaux essais* that it is 'only the consideration of God and immortality that makes the obligations of virtue and justice absolutely binding' suggests that concern for our own welfare and happiness is not only what *motivates* us to act justly, but it is also what *obligates* us to act justly.[5] Stephen Darwall has noted that because 'he reserved "obligation" for the state a person enters by laying down a right', 'Hobbes would not have said that an agent is obligated to do something simply by virtue of the fact that action is necessary to achieve an inescapable end'. However, he also notes that Hobbes 'was prepared to say that the laws of nature *oblige* on these grounds' and that

> by the turn of the century . . . many British moralists would come to find this way of thinking and speaking both sensible and familiar. They frequently

---

[5] Cf. A.VI.6: 96/RB.96: 'I admit that there is scarcely any precept to which one would be indispensably obliged if there were not a God who leaves no crime without punishment nor any good action without reward.'

posed the question Why be moral? by asking whether there is an obligation to be virtuous. And they often sought the answer to this question in whether or not the virtuous life conduces most to an agent's interest, taking for granted that this is an end all rational human beings seek.[6]

Despite the fact that Leibniz regarded natural law as an a priori science, and that he undertook in *NM* to deduce 'from the definitions of things themselves' a number of rights and obligations for all rational beings, he was nonetheless very much of the same mind with those British moralists mentioned by Darwall on the question of the obligation to be virtuous.

WHAT OBLIGATES US TO ACT JUSTLY?

In the very first paragraph of the first set of notes for *EJN*, Leibniz commented on something that the great Dutch natural lawyer, Hugo Grotius, had said in the Prolegomena to his *De jure belli ac pacis*:

> *H. Grot. proleg.* introduces Carneades as asserting that justice is either nothing or the height of folly, because having regard for the interests of another harms oneself. Grotius denies that it is folly to have regard for the interests of another to one's own loss. *But I do not doubt* that this is folly, to such a great extent that if this is not folly, then nothing is. For what, I beseech you, is folly if not negligence of one's own advantage (for he who does not know it neglects it, as well as he who knows it but does not attend to it in acting). Cicero rightly denies that advantage must be excluded from honour.
>
> (A.VI.1: 431)

And in his roughly contemporaneous letter of 23 January 1670 to Herman Conring, Leibniz repeats this judgement, but with a nod in the direction of Hobbes as well as Carneades:

> I suppose with Carneades (and Hobbes agrees) that justice without one's own advantage (whether present or future) is the height of folly, for the arrogant boastings of the Stoics and the Sadducees about virtue practised for its own sake are far removed from human nature. Consequently every just thing must be personally beneficial. (A.II.1: 47)

At the very beginning of his studies for *EJN*, Leibniz was deeply concerned with the question of how it could ever be reasonable for a person to act justly if it is assumed that justice is not personally beneficial. And already at the very beginning it is clear that he had come to accept, along with Hobbes and

---

[6] Darwall 1995: 80.

Carneades, the view that no reasonable person would deliberately act contrary to his own interest or advantage. But given Leibniz's account of deliberate, voluntary action – that no one can, as a matter of natural law, act deliberately except on account of his own good – and given that for him 'ought' implies 'can', Leibniz was committed to the view that no one *can*, in a fairly strong sense of that term, be obligated except by concern for his own good. A judgement about what appears to a person to be in his own best interest is integral to the decision about what he ought morally to do, since such a judgement is integral to any decision to act at all. Thus motivation is intrinsic to obligation itself: what cannot move us cannot obligate us, and we have seen that the three principles that Leibniz believed move us to act justly all involve a concern for our own good, even if only to avoid the pang of conscience.[7] And thus in the fourth set of notes for *EJN*, Leibniz wrote:

> it is not possible that anyone be obligated to his own harm, nor that anyone be obligated except to his own good. For since justice is something that a prudent man can be persuaded to accept, and it is not at all possible to be persuaded except for reasons derived from the utility of the listener, it is necessary that every duty be useful. Thus we have two propositions derived

---

[7] In two recent papers, Christopher Johns has attempted to establish, contrary to the vast majority of commentators, that Leibniz's moral theory is actually a deontological theory, having more in common with Kantian moral theory than with any form of consequentialism, that Leibniz was committed to the view that rational beings as such are capable of acting 'independently of natural desires and causes' (Johns 2009: 559; cf. Johns 2006/2007: 139), and that obligation for Leibniz is established independently of motivation. Furthermore, he suggests that for Leibniz 'it is ... the mark of moral strength (virtue) to be motivated by the force of right' rather than by 'rational self-interest' (Johns 2009: 574). But such views are wildly at odds with Leibniz's actual doctrines, as I hope this chapter has shown to some extent. The suggestion that Leibniz thought that virtuous action is 'motivated by force of right' is particularly odd in light of the passage, discussed above, in which Leibniz specifies 'three ... principles by which we are moved to act justly', all of which have to do with motives of self-interest and none of which has anything remotely to do with a 'force of right', free from all concern for one's own good. Johns' interpretation, for the most part, results from his uncritically reading into Leibniz's early *NM* a number of doctrines taken from the works of Samuel Pufendorf, while ignoring the fact that, despite what he sometimes suggests, Pufendorf himself seems to have thought that there could be no obligation without fear of punishment from God or man (see, for example, *Elementorum jurisprudentiae universalis libri duo* Bk. I, Def. 12, §16; see also Darwall 2012, especially 230–7, and Schneewind 1998: 134–8). Johns also seriously misconstrues Leibniz's mature theory of action. I do not have space to pursue these points further here, but I hope to have dealt with them in detail in Brown 2016.

from the common view of those who use these words: first, everything necessary is just, and second, every duty (injustice) is useful (harmful).

(A.VI.1: 462/L.134)

In the sixth set of notes for *EJN*, Leibniz wrote:

Injustice is what, being done by a good man, is absurd or implies a contradiction. Therefore Grotius calls Right and Obligation moral qualities; it should thus be understood that they are attributes of the good man.

(A.VI.1: 480–1)

But if right and obligation are attributes of the good man, it would appear that only the good man can actually be obligated to be virtuous. Things Leibniz says elsewhere reinforce this impression. For example, he states that 'obligation ... is a moral necessity certainly imposed on him who wishes to preserve the name of a good man' (A.VI.4: 2850). But a more accurate view is to be found in the following passage:

And since *right* is a power, and *obligation* a necessity assigned or imposed on him who practises justice, it will also be applicable to him who desires to be unharmed. Whoever is wise already understands, and he who is not wise will learn by his misfortune, that the wise man cannot do those acts that violate piety and justice or modesty, and that are contrary to good morals, and, in short, things that ought not to be done; and, on the contrary, that to strive for virtue and praise, and especially to cultivate piety, is the most useful thing for everyone. (M.2)

There is an obligation for both the just and the quasi-just alike, and for both the obligation arises out of a concern for their own good. But the truly just man finds his good in the just act itself, whereas the quasi-just man acts justly only in the hope of an external reward or of evading punishment:

In the view of the wise, religion and honour, or love of virtue, are the same. For they understand that to live happily is to strive for perfection, to follow nature the guide, to be disposed in the best way towards the universe, and to be convinced that the providence of the supreme author of all things governs in the best way. Now it is necessary that he who is thus disposed loves God above all things. Likewise, he cannot fail to be secure and happy, for he knows that by loving God everything is changed to good and that in turn good men are the friends of God. Thus they may not be moved by reward or punishment, yet they delight in happiness as if in a necessary bonus of virtue, or rather, the virtue of the wise is itself the reward for itself since it produces pleasure of the mind. If anyone does not in fact attain true wisdom, religion superadds some degree of honour to him. (A.VI.4: 2779–80)

Since the quasi-just man acts in accord with the demands of justice only for the sake of an external reward or to avoid punishment, he is not truly just. But since he does act justly, even if from the wrong motivation, religion – fear of God – 'superadds some degree of honour to him'. But again,

> he who does not act virtuously from hope or fear of a superior, but acts virtuously by an inclination of the soul, is so far from not acting justly that that very one acts justly in the best way, by a kind of human imitation of divine justice. Now he who does good from love for God or neighbor finds pleasure in the act itself (for that is the nature of love) and does not need any other incentive, or the command of a superior: and of such a man it is said that the law is not established for the just. To so great an extent is it opposed to reason that the law or constraint alone make just, although it must be granted that those whose soul does not reach that degree of perfection are obligated [*obligari*] only by hope and fear and that it is especially in the expectation of divine vengeance, which it is not permitted to escape by death, that they can discover the absolute and universally valid necessity of observing law and equity.[8]

Unlike those who act to avoid punishment or seek reward, the truly just man acts from a certain kind of love, which is the source of his own pleasure.

DISINTERESTED LOVE

In the fourth set of notes for *EJN*, and referring to his earlier claim that 'there is no one who deliberately does anything except on account of his own good', Leibniz wondered: 'But how are these views reconciled with what was said above, where we said that nothing can be desired by us except on account of our good [*boni nostri causa*], when we now deny that another's good is to be desired for the sake of our own [*propter nostrum*]?'[9] His answer was that 'it is doubtless brought about by a certain principle observed by few, from which a great light can be thrown on true jurisprudence as well as theology. Without doubt this matter hinges on the nature of love' (A.VI.1: 463–4/L.136). In his *Initium institutionum juris perpetui*, Leibniz observed:

[8] Du.IV.3: 280–1/R.72; cf. M.60–3/R.57–9. Note that Leibniz is contrasting the *motives* of the just and unjust man. He says that the unjust man is *obligated* by his *motives* of hope and fear, which clearly suggests that the just man is obligated by his motive of taking pleasure in acting justly. For the connection between motive and obligation, see also M.60, 64/R.58, 60, Du.IV.3: 279–80/R.71.

[9] For a detailed discussion of Leibniz's technical use of the terms '*boni nostri causa*' and '*propter nostrum [bonum]*', see Brown 2011, especially 279ff.

Prudence is the science of right, i.e., the science of freedom and duties, or the science of right in some proposed case or fact. I call it a science, even if practical, because all its propositions can be demonstrated from the definition of the good man alone and do not depend on induction and examples, even if they are made remarkably clear by the harmony of various laws, and by the written and unwritten agreement of the prudent, and by the common voice of the people, and even confirmed in the works of men incapable of demonstrations.   (M.1–2)

The reason the science of right can be deduced from the definition of the good man alone is because, in the fifth and sixth set of notes for *EJN*, Leibniz defines the good man as 'whoever loves all men' (A.VI.1: 466, 481), and, after stating that 'we love those whose happiness pleases us', he observes that 'from this definition many very beautiful Theorems of importance in Theology and morality [*re morali*] can be demonstrated' (A.VI.1: 482).

Perhaps the most important theorem that Leibniz thought could be derived from his definition of love is that we can, and ought to, seek the good of others for its own sake. In his fourth set of notes for *EJN*, Leibniz wrote:

There is a twofold way of desiring the good of others; one is for the sake of our good [*propter nostrum*], the other is as if it were our good [*quasi nostrum*]. The former is that of the calculating man, the latter is that of the lover. The former is the affection of a master toward his servant, the latter of a father toward his son; the former of one in need toward an instrument, the latter of a lover toward his beloved. One is desired for the sake of something other than the good of others, another for the sake of the good of others itself. But, you ask, how is it possible that another's good be the same as our own, and yet sought for its own sake? For another's good can be our own good in another way, as a means, but not an end. In truth, and on the contrary, I reply: it can be our good as an end and desired in itself when it is pleasant. Now all pleasant things are desired in themselves, and whatever is desired in itself is pleasant; other things are desired for the sake of what is pleasant, according as they produce it, preserve it, or eliminate opposing things.

(A.VI.1: 464/L.136)

And later in the same work he concluded: '*Justice* therefore will be the habit of loving others (or seeking the good of another and delighting in another's good in itself) as long as it can be done prudently (or as long as it is not the cause of greater pain)' (A.VI.1: 465). And among the theorems that Leibniz deduced in his fifth set of notes for *EJN* from his definitions of the good man and love, nearly two pages of them are theorems relating the notions of justice and love, beginning with 'every just thing is understood by some case of loving all men' and ending with 'whatever is not necessary for loving somebody (anybody) is not a duty' (A.VI.1: 472, 473).

The love that moves us to seek the good of others for its own sake is what Leibniz came to call 'disinterested love': '*to love* truly and disinterestedly is nothing other than to be led to find pleasure in the perfections or in the happiness of the object' (A.II.3: 441/W.566). On Leibniz's view, our pleasure actually results from the perception of our own *increasing perfection*,[10] which itself results from the perfection of other things being somehow transferred into us when we perceive or understand it. For example:

> *Pleasure is the feeling of some perfection*, and this perfection which causes pleasure can be found not only in ourselves, but also elsewhere. For when we ourselves are aware of it, this knowledge itself excites some perfection in us because the representation of perfection is also a perfection. This is why it is good to familiarize oneself with objects which have much perfection. And it is necessary to avoid hatred and envy which impede us from taking pleasure in it. (Gr.582; cf. G.7: 86/L.425)

It is in the nature of *disinterested* love to cause us to take pleasure in the very act of benefitting those whom we love. Because the truly virtuous man takes pleasure in the perfections of God that he perceives in those whom he loves, he is moved to preserve and augment their perfection. But he increases the perfection of his own will by exercising his moral virtue, and the perception of his increasing moral perfection is pleasing to him. The increasing perfection of those whom he benefits also produces pleasure by being transferred into him, and he is moved to love them more and is thus disposed to benefit them further. By the same token, those who are benefitted perceive their own increasing perfection and thus are pleased; and if they love their benefactor, as they should, they will be infected with, or inspired by, his perfection and hence be disposed to benefit him in turn, as well as others whom they love, to the degree that they perceive the perfections of God within them. A community of disinterested lovers is Leibniz's moral ideal because such a community is driven continuously toward greater perfection by a feedback mechanism based on the infectious nature of perfection itself and of the love that results from it: the perfection of each is reinforced and augmented by the perfection of others, and so the perfection of all is constitutive of the perfection of each.[11]

---

[10] See, for example, A.VI.4: 2760, 2849, 2871.

[11] Thus Leibniz observed that 'there is no doubt that he who often keeps company with excellent people and things also becomes more excellent as a result' (G.7: 86/ L.425).

'Wisdom in my sense', Leibniz wrote, 'is nothing other than the Science of Happiness ... Wisdom, which is knowledge of our own good, brings us to justice, i.e., to a reasonable advancement of the good of others' (M.54, 58/R.54, 57; cf. A.II.3: 441/W.567). And in his fourth set of notes for *EJN*, Leibniz introduced his discussion of the science of right in this way:

> Now it will suffice to sow the seeds of that science which shows why individuals must yield to the good of all men if they should want happiness, increased by reflection, to flow back upon themselves. To have shown this is to have handed down the Elements of Law and Equity, which we now undertake to accomplish with blessings from heaven.
>
> (A.VI.1: 460/L.133)

The wise man knows that the happiness of others is constitutive of his own. Since the wise and truly just man finds his own good in the good of others, his natural desires align with his duty to seek the good of others for its own sake: 'The moral is what right reason, or prudence, or care for one's own good makes equivalent to the natural' (Gr.721); and so for Leibniz, as we have seen, 'he who does good from love for God or neighbor finds pleasure in the act itself (for that is the nature of love) and does not need any other incentive' (Du.IV.3: 280–1/R.72). Thus in a letter of 14 May 1698 to the scholar and poet Claude Nicaise, Leibniz wrote:

> I explained my definition [of love] in the preface to my *Codex diplomaticus juris gentium* ... because I needed it in order to give the definition of *justice*, which in my opinion is nothing other than charity regulated by wisdom; now since charity is universal benevolence, and *benevolence* is a habit of loving, it was necessary to define what love is. And since *to Love* is to have a feeling that finds pleasure in what accords with the happiness of the object loved, and since *Wisdom* (which makes the rule of justice) is nothing other than the science of happiness, I showed by this Analysis that happiness is the foundation of justice, and that those who would give the true Elements of jurisprudence, which I do not yet find properly written, ought to begin by establishing the science of happiness, which does not yet appear well established, although the books on moral philosophy are full of discourses on the blessedness of the sovereign good. (A.II.3: 441/W.567)

In the end, it is disinterested love, and the happiness it generates, that are for Leibniz the true foundation of natural law and morality.

ABBREVIATIONS

A   German Academy of Sciences (ed.) *G.W. Leibniz: Sämtliche Schriften und Briefe.* Berlin: Akademie Verlag, 1923–. References are to series, volume, and page number.

AG   Ariew, R., and Garber, D. (eds. and trans.) *G.W. Leibniz: Philosophical Essays.* Indianapolis, Ind.: Hackett, 1989.

Du   Dutens, L.L. (ed.) *G.G. Leibnitii Opera Omnia,* 6 vols. Geneva, 1768. References are to volume, part (if applicable), and page number.

G   Gerhardt, C.I. (ed.) *Die Philosophischen Schriften von Leibniz,* 7 vols. Berlin: Weidmann, 1875–1890; reprinted Hildesheim: Georg Olms, 1971. References are to volume and page number.

Gr   Grua, G. (ed.) *G.W. Leibniz: Textes inédits d'après des manuscrits de la Bibliothèque provincial d'Hanovre.* Paris: Presses Universitaires de France, 1948.

H   Huggard, E.M. (trans.) *G.W. Leibniz: Theodicy: Essays on the Goodness of God, the Freedom of Man, and the Origin of Evil.* LaSalle, Ill.: Open Court, 1985.

K   Klopp, O. (ed.) *Die Werke von Leibniz,* erste Reihe, eleven vols. Hannover: Klindwort, 1864–1884. Vols. 7–11 reprinted Hildesheim: Georg Olms, 1970–1973. References are to volume and page number.

L   Loemker, L.E. (ed. and trans.) *G.W. Leibniz: Philosophical Papers and Letters,* 2nd edn. Dordrecht: Reidel, 1969.

M   Mollat, G. (ed.) *Mittheilungen aus Leibnizens ungedruckten Schriften.* Leipzig: H. Haessel, 1893.

Mantissa Leibniz, G.W. *Mantissa codicis juris genium diplomatici.* Hannover, 1700.

R   Riley, P. (ed. and trans.) *The Political Writings of Leibniz.* Cambridge University Press, 1972.

RB   Remnant, P., and Bennett, J. (eds. and trans.) *G.W. Leibniz: New Essays on Human Understanding.* Cambridge University Press, 1981.

W   Wiener, P.P. (ed. and trans.) *Leibniz: Selections.* New York: Scribner's and Sons, 1951.

BIBLIOGRAPHY

An asterisk denotes secondary literature especially suitable for further reading.

Brown, Gregory 1995. 'Leibniz's Moral Philosophy', in Jolley 1995: 411–41.*

Brown, Gregory 2016. 'Leibniz on the Ground of Moral Normativity and Obligation', *The Leibniz Review* 26: 11–62.*

Brown, Gregory 2011. 'Disinterested Love: Understanding Leibniz's Reconciliation of Self- and Other-Regarding Motives', *British Journal for the History of Philosophy* 19: 265–303.*

Darwall, Stephen 1995. *The British Moralists and the Internal 'Ought'*. Cambridge University Press.

Darwall, Stephen 2012. 'Pufendorf on Morality, Sociability, and Moral Powers', *Journal of the History of Philosophy* 50: 213–38.

Hostler, John 1975. *Leibniz's Moral Philosophy*. London: Duckworth.*

Johns, Christopher 2006/2007. 'Deontic Foundations in Leibniz's Practical Philosophy', *Studia Leibnitiana* 38/39: 131–55.

Johns, Christopher 2009. 'The Grounds of Right and Obligation in Leibniz and Hobbes', *The Review of Metaphysics* 62: 551–74.

Jolley, Nicholas 1995. *The Cambridge Companion to Leibniz*. Cambridge University Press.

Schneewind, J.B. 1998. *The Invention of Autonomy*. Cambridge University Press.

22

Spinoza

STEVEN NADLER

In his philosophical masterpiece, the *Ethics* (*Ethica*), Benedictus (Baruch/Bento) de Spinoza (1632–1677) famously identifies God with Nature, argues for a strict causal determinism throughout all of Nature, and insists that the human mind and the human body are 'one and the same thing', albeit considered under different 'attributes' of Nature (Thought and Extension). But to concentrate only on the metaphysical and epistemological theses of the work is to miss Spinoza's primary project: to provide an account of human freedom and well-being grounded in the proper use of reason and the exercise of virtue.[1]

EGOISM

In Part Three of the *Ethics*, after having explained the metaphysical and episte-mological foundations of human nature, Spinoza turns his attention to what he calls, alternately, 'the power of acting [*potentia agendi*]' or 'force of existing [*vis existendi*]'. Every individual thing in nature is a partial and determinate expression of one and the same infinite power of God or Nature. Every individual mind is a finite expression of God or Nature's infinite power through thinking; likewise, every particular body is a finite expression of God or Nature's infinite power in matter and motion. This finite quantum of power that constitutes each individual thing is what Spinoza calls *conatus*, which can be variously translated as striving, tendency or endeavor.

In any particular thing, this finite determination of power manifests itself as a striving to persevere as that individual. 'Each thing', he says, 'as far as it can by its own power, strives to persevere in its being' (IIIp6).[2] There is in all

[1] Studies specifically of Spinoza as moral philosopher include Curley 1973, Garber 2004, Garrett 1996, LeBuffe 2010, Kisner 2011, the essays in Kisner and Youpa 2014, Matheron 1971, and Miller 2005.

[2] References to the *Ethics* are by the standard notation of Part (roman numeral), definition (def), proposition (p), demonstration (dem), scholium (s), and

things – bodies and minds – a kind of existential inertia by which they resist any attempts to destroy them or change them for the worse, and even actively seek what will aid their preservation. The metaphysical notion of *conatus* lies at the heart of Spinoza's moral psychology.

Spinoza defines the affects or emotions generally as changes in *conatus*, as transitions from a greater to a lesser power of striving or vice versa. The passive affects, or passions, are those transitions in an individual's power that are caused by external things; joy (*laetitia*), for example, is a transition to a greater power of acting, while sadness (*tristitia*) is a transition to a lesser power of acting, both brought about by some object. Such changes in *conatus* or power form the fundamental motivational basis for the things that agents do. Their pursuits and avoidances of things, their choices of action and judgments about what is good and bad are all moved by joy and sadness, love and hate, and pleasure and pain, by the modifications in the striving to persevere in existence. We desire and pursue the things we do because we love them, and we love them because we are conscious of the way in which they bring about an increase in our capacities. 'We strive to further the occurrence of whatever we imagine will lead to joy, and to avert or destroy what we imagine is contrary to it, or will lead to sadness' (IIIp28). Put another way, we always and necessarily desire and strive after those things that we believe promote our well-being. In Spinoza's view, then, human beings are thoroughly egoistic (or hedonistic) agents.[3]

GOOD

Spinoza begins Part Four of the *Ethics* with a preface in which he considers some basic ethical language: good and evil, perfect and imperfect. He insists that such terms do not refer to absolute and intrinsic features of things, properties that they have independently of anything else (especially human agents). It follows from Spinoza's naturalism that nothing is, taken by itself and without relation to something else, good or evil or perfect or imperfect, least of all when these words are understood in the normative sense. Whatever *is* just *is*, period.

What 'good' and 'evil' (and 'perfect' and 'imperfect') in the normative sense do refer to, if not intrinsic, non-relational features of the world, is an evaluative measure of the degree to which a thing corresponds to some stipulated standard

---

corollary (c). I use the following abbreviations for Spinoza's works: G = Spinoza 1925; C = Spinoza 1984.

[3] Whether Spinoza's view of conscious motivation is best considered as a kind of egoism or hedonism is discussed by LeBuffe 2010: 128–36.

or model. The most obvious case in which this is so is the evaluation of an artifact. A building, for example, is deemed more or less perfect depending upon the extent to which it matches the architect's original conception, which serves as a standard to which the finished product is compared. This evaluative practice gets extended to natural objects when human beings form universal ideas of kinds of things in nature. For example, from experience we conceive some ideal model of what a horse is, or a tree. We then call some particular horse or tree 'perfect' or 'imperfect' depending upon how well it matches with that randomly created and arbitrarily adopted model.

The same analysis applies to the terms 'good' and 'evil'. These evaluative labels are, likewise, always to be understood in the context of a thing's relationship to a standard or model. Something is 'good' if it is an effective means to an end. More particularly, since every individual is naturally and necessarily striving to maximize its power, something is 'good' if it promotes what appears to that individual to be its well-being and helps move it closer to a stipulated ideal condition; and something is 'evil' or 'bad' if it is detrimental to what is perceived to be an individual's power and well-being. The result is that 'good' and 'evil', like 'perfect' and 'imperfect', are totally relative terms (relative, that is, to the conception of some individual's interest), and in many cases what is good for one person may not be good for another person (IV, Preface, G 2:208/C 1: 545).

Now the standards or models themselves that are ordinarily used for determining how perfect an individual is or whether some thing is 'good' for an individual seem to be highly subjective. One person's conception of what constitutes an ideal tree or an ideal human being will differ from another person's conception, given the differences in their experiences and thus in the particulars from which they abstract their general notion, as well as in the features they focus on in creating that notion. For this reason it is appropriate to refer to what is 'believed to be' in someone's interest, and it will be the case that something will be 'good' if, given what one believes about an ideal life and an individual's interests, one believes it to be good (as a means to that ideal). But there is no guarantee that one's beliefs about these things are true, nor even that they will be shared by others. Indeed, the framing of standards and models is strongly dependent on an individual's very particular desires, and thus so will be judgments about what is good and perfect.

If this was all Spinoza had to say about 'good' and 'evil', then he would be saddled with a subjectivist analysis of those important moral terms. However, he notes that while 'good' and 'evil' do not refer to real intrinsic features of the world, nevertheless 'we must retain these words', but without giving up their relativist meaning. This is because Spinoza thinks they can, while remaining context-relative, also bear a more objectivist burden. Spinoza believes that there is, in fact, a specific ideal that can serve as an objective standard according to which things can be judged as truly 'good' for a human being. There is a particular kind of person and life that represents, objectively, a perfection of human nature.

> Because we desire to form an idea of man, as a model of human nature which we may look to, it will be useful to us to retain these same words with the meaning I have indicated. In what follows, therefore, I shall understand by good what we know certainly is a means by which we may approach nearer and nearer to the model of human nature that we set before ourselves. By evil, what we certainly know prevents us from becoming like that model. Next, we shall say that men are more perfect or imperfect, insofar as they approach more or less near to this model. (IV, Preface, G 2: 208/C 1: 545)

This does not mean that 'good' and 'evil' are not relative terms. It is still the case that nothing, taken in and of itself and without comparison with or utility for some standard or model, is good or evil. However, the subjectivism suggested by the claim that 'good' and 'evil' are relativized to only haphazardly formed conceptions or standards is now replaced by a more objective, metaphysically grounded model. 'Good' now means 'useful for making a human being closer to what is truly a more perfected specimen of humanity'.[4] What that more perfected specimen of humanity consists in is an individual of maximal power of persevering as a human being, or maximal human activity. Something is 'good' if it truly contributes to an increase in an individual's *conatus*.

Spinoza thus defines 'good' in Part Four as 'what we certainly know to be useful to us' (IVdef1), and 'evil' as 'what we certainly know prevents us from being masters of some good' (IVdef2). It is also what he has in mind when, as of IVp14, he begins speaking of 'the true knowledge of good and evil', as opposed to merely 'a knowledge of good and evil' (see, for example, IVp8). The latter refers to one's affective perception of something as bringing about some increase in some partial aspect of his capacities. Some things are judged 'good' because they are a source of joy and pleasure. This judgment is often grounded only in the passions, however, and thus based on inadequate knowledge of the thing and of oneself. But the 'true knowledge of good and evil' is one's rational perception – derived from adequate ideas and not just random experience, based on understanding and not (in a short-sighted way) simply on the positive way something happens to affect one's body and one's mind – of what benefits a person in a

---

[4] Thus, Miller (2005) rightly distinguishes between circumstantially and non-circumstantially relative value in Spinoza.

more complete and essential manner, truly bringing him as a whole individual to a more powerful condition. The difference is summed up by Spinoza in the demonstration of IVp35: 'What we judge to be good or evil when we follow the dictate of reason must be good or evil.'

VIRTUE

An agent's power or striving may be directed either by random sense experience and the imagination (or 'inadequate ideas') or by knowledge ('adequate ideas'). When a person's *conatus* or desire is guided by the senses and the imagination, he pursues those things that he believes, on a deficient basis, to be good for him; when *conatus* is guided by knowledge, on the other hand, he will regularly and reliably do those things that really *do* increase his power of acting.

Spinoza initially defines virtue, in IVdef8, simply as power. But in IVp18s – in a statement that strongly recalls the ancient Stoic doctrine of virtue as 'acting in accordance with nature' – he says that 'virtue . . . is nothing but acting from the laws of one's own nature'. Now the nature of any thing is just its *conatus*, or striving to persevere in existence. Thus, the laws of any thing's nature prescribe that the thing strive to preserve its being. Therefore, as Spinoza concludes, 'the foundation of virtue is this very striving to preserve one's own being'. More precisely, the virtuous person is the person who properly follows the laws of his own nature and acts so as to preserve his own being. Virtue, in other words, is not simply the exercise of power but the *successful* striving for preservation (IVp20dem). The person lacking virtue or power, by contrast, 'allows himself to be guided by things outside him, and to be determined by them to do what the common constitution of external things demands, not what his own nature, considered in itself, demands' (IVp37s1).

It is when Spinoza turns to specifying what 'following the laws of one's own nature' and 'striving to seek one's own advantage' really mean and how a person can put these notions to work in his life that his moral rationalism comes into play. Spinoza identifies 'living according to one's own nature' with 'living according to the guidance of reason'. This is because a human being lives according to his own nature when the things he does have their adequate cause in that nature alone and not in the ways external things affect him; that is, he lives according to his own nature when he is active, not passive. And a human being is active – he *acts* rather than *suffers* – when what he does follows from his own adequate ideas, from his rational knowledge of things, and not from inadequate ideas or the passions.

Reason's guidance comes embodied in what Spinoza calls (in IVp18) the 'dictates of reason [*dictamina rationis*]'. These rational dictates are grounded in the individual's *conatus* and represent a kind of enlightened propositional expression of that natural striving. They demand

> that everyone love himself, seek his own advantage, what is really useful to him, want what will really lead man to a greater perfection, and absolutely, that everyone should strive to preserve his own being as far as he can.
>
> (IVp18s)

More important, reason also provides guidance on how to achieve these common human ends. It does so universally and objectively, without regard to a person's particularities.

Among the first things that reason demands is that 'we ought to want virtue for its own sake, and that there is not anything preferable to it, or more useful to us'. Reason also prescribes that we should strive to possess the 'many things outside us which are useful to us' (IVp18s). Spinoza's virtue, in other words, does not lead to an ascetic withdrawal from the world, but rather a more knowledgeable and successful navigation within the world and a more efficient use of things in it. The virtuous person is able to determine what is *truly* conducive to his well-being and what is not. The virtuous person accurately discerns what is in his own best interest and actively desires and pursues that which will best serve his own power of persevering. He knows, in other words, what is truly good and strives for it.

It turns out, moreover, that what is truly good for a rational being is knowledge. In particular, the person who is led by reason pursues what Spinoza calls 'adequate ideas', a deep understanding of Nature itself, and especially of one's own place in Nature. What such rational knowledge reveals is the necessity of all things, of the fact that any bodily or mental event is 'determined by an infinite connection of causes to exist and produce effects'. This understanding, in turn, leads to a moderating of the passions and the turmoil they bring to our lives. Spinoza claims that 'insofar as the mind understands all things as necessary, it has a greater power over the affects, or is less acted upon by them' (Vp6). This is because when a person sees the necessity of something, he is less moved or troubled by it. His desire or anxiety, his hope or fear, are diminished by the perception that the attainment or loss of that thing is not subject to his will but necessitated by an infinite number of causal factors.

Spinoza has shown that all of the human emotions, in so far as they are passions, are constantly directed outward, towards things and their tendencies to affect us one way or another. And aroused by our passions and desires, we seek or flee those things that we believe cause joy or sadness. Such is the troubled life of bondage (*servitus*). He says that it is a kind of disease to suffer too much love for a thing that is mutable and never fully under our power, even when we do, for a time, have it within our possession.

> Sickness of the mind and misfortunes take their origin especially from too much love toward a thing which is liable to many variations and which we can never fully possess. For no one is disturbed or anxious concerning anything unless he loves it, nor do wrongs, suspicions and enmities arise except from love for a thing which no one can really fully possess.   (Vp20s)

When a person sees the necessity of all things, however, and especially the fact that the objects that he values are, in their comings and goings, not under his control, that person is less likely to be overwhelmed with emotions at their arrival and passing away. We see that all bodies and their states and relationships – including the condition of our own body – follow necessarily from the essence of matter and the universal laws of physics; and we see that all ideas, including all the properties of minds, follow necessarily from the essence of thought and its universal laws. When we come to this level of understanding, we realize that we cannot control what nature brings our way or takes from us, and consequently we are no longer anxious over what may come to pass and are no longer obsessed with or despondent over the loss of our possessions.

> The more this knowledge that things are necessary is concerned with singular things, which we imagine more distinctly and vividly, the greater is this power of the Mind over the affects, as experience itself also testifies. For we see that Sadness over some good which has perished is lessened as soon as the man who has lost it realizes that this good could not, in any way, have been kept.   (Vp6s)

A person who sees the necessity of things regards them with equanimity, and is not inordinately and irrationally affected in different ways by past, present or future events. He will bear the slings and arrows of outrageous fortune with self-control and a calm mind (G 2: 136/C 1: 490). The resulting life is more tranquil, and not given to sudden disturbances of the passions. The virtuous person, the individual who follows 'the order of nature', will experience 'true peace of mind' (Vp42s); by contrast, the ignorant person is 'troubled in many ways by external causes'. What the virtuous person achieves is happiness, blessedness, even 'salvation'.

DOING UNTO OTHERS

Of course, ethics, ordinarily understood, is not just about one's own self-preservation, self-development, and well-being. It must also have something to say about how one is to treat other human beings, even if it turns out that this is itself to be motivated by the pursuit of self-interest. Spinoza's egoism – like any egoism – can certainly allow for activity that is directed at the welfare of other people, with no *conscious* thought of how such activity redounds to one's own benefit. Spinoza does not deny that there is or can be altruistic behavior; what he must reject is only that such behavior is altruistically motivated.

One way in which a moral philosophy based on egoism might ground treating other human beings in ways that pass ethical muster is captured by the Golden Rule: 'Do unto others as you would have others do unto you.' An egoistically motivated agent can be moved to act benevolently toward others because that makes it more likely that they will act benevolently toward him in return.

However, the virtuous person of the *Ethics* is not going to rely on merely creating good will from others by means of his own considerate actions. This person, guided by reason, is out not simply to modify the actions of those with whom he must interact in society. Rather, he wants to transform those individuals themselves, to modify their character. Spinoza's virtuous person wants to make other people into virtuous individuals as well, to *improve* those among whom he must live. He wants, in fact, to make them more like himself.

Another possible Spinozistic route to traditionally virtuous behavior toward others might arise from the imagination and the inadequate ideas that arise as a result of random experience. Love understood as a passive affect is defined by Spinoza as 'joy with the accompanying idea of an external cause' (IIIp13s). That is, one loves the external thing that brings about an increase in one's power. Spinoza then demonstrates that a person will strive to benefit individuals who cause him joy, whom he loves (IIIp39), as well as those whom he believes to love him. But such considerate and benevolent treatment of others is grounded in the passions, an unstable and unpredictable foundation for ethical behavior in so far as it depends upon the way a person is affected by other people or things outside himself. Similar considerations apply to a person who acts benevolently toward others out of pity. To the extent that a person's *conatus* and desire are directed by the passions of love and hate or pity, he is in a state of bondage, not virtue; his actions are dictated by what happens to affect him with pleasure and pain, not by what he *knows* to be a true good (IVp37s1).

Passionate affect is not what moves the truly virtuous and rational person to treat others in a benevolent and ethical manner. He does not care for the welfare of others out of passionate love, hope for reciprocation, fear of being treated miserably, sympathy, pity, or threats. He does it because reason tells him to (IVp50s).

Spinoza begins his discussion of benevolence in Part Four with the claim of IVp31: 'insofar as a thing agrees with our nature, it is necessarily good'. A thing that agrees with my nature is good for me because such a thing will necessarily aid the preservation of that nature. A thing that shares my nature must, like anything, strive to preserve its own nature; and because its own nature is like my nature, it is therefore necessarily striving to preserve *my* nature. He adds that 'the more a thing agrees with our nature, the more useful or better it is for us'. Spinoza's point is essentially that things that agree in nature are good for each other and necessarily contribute to each other's flourishing.

Spinoza thus concludes that nothing is better for preserving one's own being than uniting oneself with something that shares one's nature – that is, another human being who is very much like oneself. Therefore, the person who is acting rationally – acting out of virtue and according to the dictates of reason – will behave in such a way that he promotes the virtue and rationality of other human beings in order that their natures will be more like his own. That is, he will treat others in such a way that their own *conatus* or power of acting is increased (which is what virtue is) and that their life is thereby improved. And he will do so because he, egoistically motivated as he is, recognizes through reason alone that it is to his own benefit to do so.

But how exactly is one's own welfare promoted by helping other people improve themselves and move toward lives of virtue and reason (and thereby become more like oneself)?

One answer seems to be a rather straightforward quantitative one: basically, two heads are better than one, especially if they are in agreement about such important matters as what is good and what is bad.

> For if, for example, two individuals of entirely the same nature unite with one another, they compose an individual twice as powerful as each one. To man, then, there is nothing more useful than man. Man, I say, can wish for nothing more helpful to the preservation of his being than that all should so agree in all things that the minds and bodies of all would compose, as it were, one mind and one body; that all should strive together, as far as they can, to preserve their being; and that all, together, should seek for themselves the common advantage of all. (IVp18s)

Spinoza seems to be arguing here that two human beings represent a strengthening (by doubling) of one and the same power. Two things of the same nature, thus two things striving on behalf of the same goal (i.e., the preservation of that nature), will increase the power working on behalf of that goal and thus the likelihood of its successful achievement.

Of course, human beings are also useful to each other – especially in society – insofar as they are *not* like each other and complement each other's skill sets. But Spinoza's deeper point here is that human beings are good for and useful to each other only to the extent that they agree with one another in nature and thus share a common project and a common vision of things. It is our differences and particularities, not our commonalities, that divide us and set us against each other. And nothing contributes more to our mutual differences than the passions. Our biggest differences and disagreements are in the ways in which we perceive and feel about things (IVp33). Human discord is based on our passionate desires for things, along with a basic fact about the things that, through our inadequate ideas, we value: namely, not everyone can equally share in their possession. Passionate desires tend to be directed at finite, mutable goods that, very often, only one or a few people can obtain. Thus, they (and, consequently, their subjects) frequently come into conflict (IVp34d).

On the other hand, virtuous human beings who live according to reason 'agree in nature' (IVp35). This should be understood both in a negative sense and in a positive sense. In the negative sense, they agree in nature because those factors that, above and beyond what is common in human beings, lead to differences – i.e., the passions – are diminished. More important, in a positive sense, individuals who live according to reason value the same things and pursue the same goods. Unlike the case of passionate rivals, however, the good that virtuous rational people value and pursue is not a finite commodity but something that is eternal, imperishable, and capable of being shared equally by all: knowledge.

> IVp36: The greatest good of those who seek virtue is common to all, and can be enjoyed by all equally.
>   Dem: To act from virtue is to act according to the guidance of reason (by IVp24), and whatever we strive for from reason is understanding (by IVp26). Hence (by IVp28), the greatest good of those who seek virtue is to know God, i.e. (by IIp47 and IIp47s), a good that is common to all men, and can be possessed equally by all men insofar as they are of the same nature, q.e.d.

To the extent that a person is guided by reason, he does only what is truly good for his nature, that is, for human nature. But this nature is exactly what he has in common with all other human beings. Thus, what the rational person strives for is what is good not only for himself but for all human beings. The rational other person strives properly for the improvement of his own nature; but his nature is *my* nature, too; so the rational other strives ultimately for my improvement, or so Spinoza argues. 'Insofar as men live according to the guidance of reason, they must do only those things that are good for human nature, and hence, for each man, i.e. (by IVp31c), those things that agree with the nature of each man' (IVp35d).

A rational person pursues true goods that are good for everyone and acts in such a way that he aids the human striving for perseverance. This is why Spinoza concludes that 'there is no singular thing in nature that is more useful to man than a man who lives according to the guidance of reason' (IVp35c1), and that 'men will be most useful to one another when each one most seeks his own advantage [according to the guidance of reason]' (IVp35c2). The virtuous person will know that he is better off surrounded by other virtuous, i.e. rational, individuals, all of whom are striving for the same thing: the maximization of the true human good – knowledge and understanding – and thus the perfection of their common nature. He will therefore undertake, through his actions, to help others reach this condition of rational virtue. That is, he will act toward other human beings with benevolence, nobility, justice, and charity. And he will do so even toward – perhaps especially toward – those who are most under the sway of harmful passions. 'He who lives according to the guidance of reason strives, as far as he can, to repay the other's Hate, Anger, and Disdain toward him, with Love, or Nobility' (IVp46).

This appears to be the upshot of Spinoza's main argument for an egoistic grounding of the rational virtue of benevolence toward others and for working to improve their lives. But the utility to me of another virtuous person goes beyond the general (and, it should be said, rather vague) metaphysical fact that the things he pursues are what are good for human nature, hence good for everyone, hence good for me. There are in Spinoza's account additional connections between the virtue and flourishing of others and my own well-being such that I should, for my own sake, promote their flourishing.

First, a person guided by reason will be useful to me in my own rational striving for perseverance because he will be free of such divisive and even harmful passions as jealousy, envy, and hate – just those affects that would make him oppose me in my endeavors. Indeed, because a person guided by reason is striving for the same non-finite goods as myself (knowledge and well-being), he is likely to be of *positive* assistance to me in this project, especially since he will clearly see that the more rational *I* become, the more free I will be of the divisive passions and thus the more useful I will be to *him*. So there is, in fact, a sense in which I aim to aid him in leading a better life for the sake of the aid he will actively provide me in return – not, however, because of reciprocated good will, but because of mutual enlightened self-interest. That is, it is in my best interest to make him into the kind of person who will see that helping me increase my power of acting is in his own best interest.

Second, Spinoza also seems to believe that surrounding myself with rational and virtuous individuals will do much to positively reinforce my own desire to live according to reason and thus my own pursuit of perfection, and this the rational person recognizes to be a good thing. Spinoza says, in his analysis of the affects, that 'if we imagine that someone loves, desires, or hates something we ourselves love, desire or hate, we shall thereby love, desire or hate it with greater constancy' (IIIp31). Seeing someone else who loves virtue and desires knowledge will make me love and desire virtue and knowledge all the more. Thus, it is useful to me and in my interest to have others love virtue and desire knowledge.[5]

> The good which man wants for himself and loves, he will love more constantly if he sees that others love it (by IIIp31). So (by IIIp31c), he will strive to have the others love the same thing. And because this good is common to all (by IVp36), and all can enjoy it, he will therefore (by the same reason) strive that all may enjoy it.   (IVp37d2)

Finally, seeing an improvement in a being similar to oneself – that is, seeing another human being experience the true joy (or increase in the power of acting) that comes through virtue – causes one to feel a sympathetic joy and undergo a similar increase in one's power. 'If we imagine a thing like us, toward which we have had no affect, be affected with some affect, we are thereby affected with a like affect' (IIIp27). Thus, again, it is to my own good that there are other virtuous people.

The upshot of all this is that a person guided by reason, who sees what is truly in his own best interest, will strive to bring other people to the same level of rational perfection as himself. That is, the benevolence toward others exhibited by the rational person does not consist merely in considerate and tolerant behavior in his interactions with them. Virtuous or rational benevolence is not merely a passive attitude of forbearance toward the foibles of

---

[5] For an analysis of this argument, see Della Rocca 2004.

one's fellow human beings. Nor is it simply a kind of classically liberal and value-neutral generosity whereby one provides to others the things they need to pursue what they believe (rightly or wrongly) to be good and thereby accomplish their goals and projects, whatever they may be. Rather, the virtuous and rational person will be actively engaged and take steps to insure that other people are also guided by reason and pursue the true good, knowledge. For this is what will maximize their utility to him as he strives for his own perfection. 'The good which everyone who seeks virtue wants for himself, he also desires for other men' (IVp37). In other words, a rational and virtuous person will act so that other people also become rational and virtuous. He will behave toward them in such ways as will help *them* achieve the life of reason. But because it is also in *their* best interest to be rational and virtuous, all this is just to say that the person guided by reason will strive to further the interests of others, to act in ways that truly benefit them, albeit from selfish and not altruistic motives.

'The desire to do good generated in us by our living according to the guidance of reason, I call morality [*pietas*]' (IVp36s1). The person who is virtuous in Spinoza's idiosyncratic sense will also exhibit those traits of character and modes of behavior that are traditionally regarded as 'virtues' – ethical and social virtues – all of which follow naturally from his rational pursuit of self-interest. 'A man who is guided by reason' will have 'strength of character'. He 'hates no one, is angry with no one, envies no one, is indignant with no one, scorns no one, and is not at all proud'; he will avoid 'whatever he thinks is troublesome and evil, and moreover, whatever seems immoral, dreadful, unjust, and dishonorable' (IVp73s).

Spinoza's view, in short, is that rational egoism leads in fact not to the rampant disregard of the well-being of others but to the highest ethical behavior. As he insists, 'I have done this to win, if possible, the attention of those who believe that this principle – that everyone is bound to seek his own advantage – is the foundation, not of virtue and morality, but of immorality' (IVp18s).[6] Spinoza's virtuous person is not just engaged in kind, considerate behavior toward others; he is not simply responding to them with love or treating them in fine ways out of pity, sympathy, or hope for reciprocal consideration. As Spinoza puts it at the end of Part Two of the *Ethics*, his 'doctrine contributes to social life insofar as it teaches . . . [that each person] should be helpful to his neighbor, not from unmanly

---

[6] Bennett (1984), for one, is not impressed with these propositions of the *Ethics*: 'Spinoza fails at every step in his journey towards his collaborative morality' (306).

compassion, partiality, or superstition, but from the guidance of reason, as the time and occasion demand' (IIp39s). Through his actions, the virtuous person, like Socrates, wants to improve them, to make them more virtuous, and thus more happy.

BIBLIOGRAPHY

An asterisk denotes secondary literature especially suitable for further reading.

Bennett, Jonathan 1984, *A Study of Spinoza's Ethics* (Indianapolis: Hackett Publishing).

Curley, Edwin 1973, 'Spinoza's Moral Philosophy', in *Spinoza: A Collection of Critical Essays*, ed. Marjorie Grene (Notre Dame: University of Notre Dame Press), 354–76.

Curley, Edwin 1988, *Behind the Geometric Method* (Princeton University Press).

Della Rocca, Michael 2004, 'Egoism and the Imitation of the Affects in Spinoza', in *Spinoza on Reason and the Free Man*, ed. Yirmiyahu Yovel and Gideon Segal (New York: Little Room Press), 123–48.

Garber, Daniel 2004, 'Dr. Fischelson's Dilemma: Spinoza on Freedom and Sociability', in *Spinoza on Reason and the Free Man*, ed. Yirmiyahu Yovel and Gideon Segal (New York: Little Room Press), 183–208.

Garrett, Don 1996, 'Spinoza's Ethical Theory', in *The Cambridge Companion to Spinoza*, ed. Don Garrett (Cambridge University Press), 267–314.

Kisner, Matthew J. 2011, *Spinoza on Human Freedom: Reason, Autonomy and the Good Life* (Cambridge University Press).

Kisner, Matthew J. and Andrew Youpa, eds. 2014, *Essays on Spinoza's Ethical Theory* (Oxford University Press).*

LeBuffe, Michael 2010, *From Bondage to Freedom: Spinoza on Human Excellence* (Oxford and New York: Oxford University Press).*

Matheron, Alexandre 1971, *Individu et communauté chez Spinoza* (Paris: Editions de Minuit).

Miller, Jon 2005, 'Spinoza's Axiology', *Oxford Studies in Early Modern Philosophy* 2: 149–72.

Nadler, Steven 2014, 'The Lives of Others: Spinoza on Benevolence as a Rational Virtue', in *Essays on Spinoza's Ethical Theory*, ed. Matthew Kisner and Andrew Youpa (Oxford University Press), 41–56.

Spinoza, Baruch 1925, *Spinoza Opera*, ed. Carl Gebhardt, 5 vols. (Heidelberg: Carl Winters Universitaetsbuchandlung).

Spinoza, Baruch 1984, *The Collected Works of Spinoza*, trans. Edwin Curley, vol. 1, (Princeton University Press).

23

Pascal

DESMOND M. CLARKE

Nature is corrupt.[1]

During his relatively brief life (1623 –1662), Pascal published only a few short reports of experiments designed to prove atmospheric pressure and, more famously, the letters that he published anonymously and that came to be known as the *Provincial Letters* (1656–1657). The posthumous publication of other draft writings provided a vivid picture of someone who had struggled emotionally and intellectually with his conception of an avenging God, with Augustinian themes about the corruption of human nature by the sin of Adam, with the theology of predestination and eternal damnation, and with an overpowering awareness of the fragility and finitude of human existence in the infinite space and time of the universe. In particular, the notes that Pascal collected for an *apologia* on behalf of Christianity, which appeared in 1670 under the title *Pensées*, record outline arguments and critical comments about a wide range of topics. However, they are often unclear about his own opinions, and the history of their collection and editing fail to confirm even the order in which they were composed. In a sense, we know what Pascal was thinking about during the 1650s, without always knowing which thoughts he affirmed or denied, and one often has to look elsewhere to decide if he endorsed or merely entertained the views that were summarized in the aphoristic prose of the *Pensées*.

These hermeneutic reservations apply especially when reviewing Pascal's moral theory, since he never published a philosophical ethics. However, some themes appeared so consistently in his posthumous writings that they may be

---

[1] I cite Pascal (2000), by volume and page number; for the *Pensées*, I also include the Fragment number of this edition. The epigraph was a *liasse* title, without accompanying text (2: 615). The same sentiment occurs in Frag. 4 (2: 544), Frag. 395 (2: 675), and Frag. 436 (2: 709). Most editions provide a concordance for the alternative numbering systems adopted by the Brunschvicg, Lafuma, and Sellier editions.

accepted as reflecting his considered opinion. Among the topics to which he often returned, especially during the final decade of his life, was a theological interpretation of moral decision-making that he borrowed from Augustine.

THE MORAL LAW AND CORRUPT NATURE

In the *Provincial Letters*, Pascal assumed and frequently claimed that there are some human actions that are unquestionably immoral. Thus he wrote to the Jesuits in the Fourteenth Letter:

> The permissions to kill that you grant in so many contexts show that on this point you have so forgotten the law of God, and so extinguished the light of nature, that you need to be restored to the basic principles of religion and common sense. For what could be more natural than this opinion: An individual has no right over the life of another? 'We are so well informed about this within ourselves', says Saint Chrysostom, 'that when God established the commandment not to kill, he did not add that this is because homicide is evil; because ... the law assumes that we have already learned this truth from nature'.[2]

In the same letter he claims that capital punishment is justified by 'the principles of public peace and safety, which were accepted at all times and in all places, and on which all the legislators of the world, sacred or profane, have based their laws. Even pagans have never introduced an exception to this rule ...'[3] He writes, in similar terms, in Letter Fifteen about the 'law of God, nature and the Church'[4] and quotes with approval the decision of a judge in Paris, Monsieur de Montrouge, who rejected the defence offered by a domestic employee who had been charged with theft and who pleaded, as an excuse, the advice of his confessor that it is sometimes permissible to steal from one's employer to compensate for inadequate wages. The judge described that defence as 'an unlawful, pernicious doctrine, contrary to all laws, natural, divine and human'.[5] Pascal made a similar implicit appeal to a law of nature in a pamphlet published on behalf of the secular priests of Paris

[2] Pascal (1967) 207 (2000, I: 735). All subsequent citations of the *Provincial Letters* are to Kralsheimer's translation (1967), which is identified simply as *Letters*, and the corresponding page in Pascal's original works (2000). Where the translation is amended, I add 'trans. amend.' The passage quoted in this citation is from St. Chrysostom, Homily XII, Migne (1862), vol. 49: 131, in which Chrysostom writes about God implanting 'natural law' in human beings at their creation, so that it is known through their 'conscience'.

[3] *Letters*, 209 (I: 737).   [4] Ibid., 232 (I: 757).   [5] Ibid., 100 (I: 646).

in 1658, the *Factum for the Curés of Paris*: 'There is no place among pagans or savages where it is not forbidden to say that calumny is not a crime and where one is not allowed to kill one's neighbour merely in defence of one's honour.'[6] These allusions to a law of nature assume an understanding of what that law requires, and of how people could come to know its provisions.[7]

One of Pascal's most insistent criticisms of Jesuit casuistry focused on their suggestion that it is possible to 'direct the intention' of a human action and thereby modify its moral character. He attributes to his Jesuit interlocutor a 'method of directing the intention, which consists in proposing something that is allowed as the objective of one's action'.[8] The Jesuit distinguished between the perspective of a judge who considers only the externals of an action and that of casuists who 'look primarily at the intention'.[9] If 'the intention ... determines the quality of an action' and if Jesuit confessors could not prevent some forbidden action from occurring, they could at least purify its intention and thereby correct the evil of the action by the purity of its assigned objective.[10] For example: one may not kill another if motivated by revenge, which is never lawful, but it may be permissible to kill another to protect one's honour; one may not engage in a duel with the intention of doing so (which is immoral) but may turn up at the location where a duel is scheduled to defend one's honour, since that involves merely walking about in a field and then defending oneself if challenged; one may even use a mental reservation to make a promise without intending to keep it or accept interest on a loan without breaching the prohibition on usury. The moral quality of external actions, and even the very meaning of one's words, could thus be radically altered by a purely mental act on the part of the agent.

The *Provincial Letters* stop short of specifying Pascal's alternative to this theory of moral actions based on intentions, except to say that 'the whole of Christian morality [is] overturned by such strange aberrations' and

No directing of the intention can justify slander and even if the conversion of the whole world were at stake, it would not be permissible to damage the reputation of innocent people, because one should not commit the least evil to realize the greatest good.[11]

---

[6] *Écrits des curés de Paris: Factum* (1: 842).
[7] Despite his appeals to nature, Pascal includes 'natural law' among the unfamiliar words that his opponents exploit to make scholastic distinctions; *Letters*, 186 (1: 717).
[8] 1: 649.   [9] 1: 656.   [10] 1: 679, 649.   [11] 1: 703–4. The final phrase alludes to Rom. 3.8.

Pascal's unequivocal condemnation of this morality of intentions suggests that he thought of human actions as having an objective moral character independently of their consequences and of any mental activity, on the part of the agent, that might accompany their performance. He needed to explain, therefore, how those objective moral truths can be known; among the potential methods of discovery, consulting moral casuists was least likely to succeed.

The Jesuit 'doctrine of probable opinions' (or probabilism) was as unacceptable to Pascal as the moral principles that relied on it. This principle for guiding consciences or moral deliberations did not result from a mathematical theory for calculating probabilities, although on at least one occasion Pascal described it as the doctrine of probability.[12] According to this doctrine, 'an opinion is called probable when it is founded on reasons of some importance' and 'anything approved by well-known authors is probable and safe in conscience'.[13] Consequently, inconsistent opinions could be accepted as probable, and one could even follow the least probable among many alternative probable opinions, on condition that some acknowledged author proposed it.[14] Pascal rejected this kind of relativism, and pointed out that judges do not accept probable opinions as an excuse for illegal actions, thereby implying that the moral law should be understood by analogy with civil laws as forbidding certain kinds of human action. Some actions are illegal or immoral, and the opinions of commentators cannot change their status any more than the mental substitution of permissible objectives could change the immorality of impermissible actions.

Having rejected probabilism, Pascal reverted to what he identified as the only three reliable sources of belief: religious faith, reason, and sensation. His confidence in the veracity of sensations supported his famous argument that five propositions that were condemned by Pope Innocent X as heretical did not occur in the writings of their alleged author, Cornelius Jansen.[15] While he did not dispute the Pope's authority to decide what Catholics should believe, Pascal rejected the claim that matters of fact could be decided by appeal to any authority, including that of the Pope.

---

[12] 'La doctrine de la probabilité' (1: 732).   [13] Letters, 82 (1: 631); 204 (1: 732).
[14] Thirteenth Letter: 'The probability of an opinion does not prevent the probability of the contrary opinion ... it is permissible to follow the less probable and less certain opinion, while ignoring the more probable and more certain opinion': Letters, 204–5 (1: 733).
[15] Papal condemnation, Cum occasione, 31 May 1658.

How then do we learn the truth about facts? It will be from our eyes, Father, which are their legitimate judges, as reason is the judge of natural and intelligible things, and the faith the judge of things that are supernatural and revealed.[16]

In light of this clarification of what he calls the 'principles of our knowledge', Pascal argued that the only way to decide if the condemned propositions were in Jansen's book was by examining the book; 'matters of fact are proved only by the senses'.[17] He contentiously illustrates this general rule about how to decide factual claims by referring to the condemnation of Galileo:

It was in vain too that you obtained from Rome the decree against Galileo that condemned his view about the earth's motion. That will not prove that the earth remains at rest; and if one had consistent observations that showed that it is the earth which revolves, all the men in the world would not prevent it from rotating nor prevent themselves from turning with it.[18]

Although Pascal could not have invoked sensation to discover the moral principles of the natural law, there was a matter of fact (or many such alleged facts) involved in his claim about the universality of some prohibitions, such as the prohibition of homicide. The empirical evidence of modern anthropology, however, does not confirm the 'facts' to which he appealed in this context. One has to conclude that, rather than appeal to the senses, Pascal projected onto disparate cultures a claim about universal moral customs that suited the rhetorical objectives of his dispute with the casuists of his day. Nonetheless, even if empirical evidence had supported his factual claims, it would still not have established the obligatory character of allegedly universal norms. To convert universal customs into moral principles, Pascal had to appeal either to reason or faith.

Pascal's account of the corruption of nature excluded the first of these options.[19] He summarized his consistently negative assessment of the scope of our intellectual powers in the *Pensées*, where he wrote: 'There are

[16] *Letters*, 294 (1: 810), trans. amend.
[17] 1: 813. Compare the Fourth Letter where, in relation to the experience of being tempted to sin, Pascal asked: 'Must we appeal to Scripture to prove something that is so obvious? This is not a matter of faith, or of reasoning. It is a matter of fact. We see it, we know it, we sense it' (1: 619).
[18] 1: 813.
[19] Baird (1975) argues that, according to Pascal's theory of three orders and the impossibility of crossing from one order to another by incremental steps, the order of nature and what we know about nature by reason could never support a morality that depends essentially on grace.

undoubtedly natural laws but this fine reason, having been corrupted, has corrupted everything.'[20] He illustrated this defection from natural law in the customs that allow someone to kill another simply because their respective monarchs are at war with each other. 'Could there be anything more silly than that someone would be entitled to kill me because he lives beyond the sea and his prince is quarrelling with mine, although I have no quarrel with him?'[21] However, while the corruption of nature might be accessible to some extent by reason, it is ultimately based on religious faith.

> From my point of view, I admit that once the Christian religion reveals this principle, that human nature is corrupted and has fallen away from God, it opens our eyes to see the nature of this truth everywhere. For nature is such that it exemplifies everywhere a God who has been lost, both within man and outside man, and a corrupt nature.[22]

Thus religious faith reveals the corruption of nature and the limited capacity of natural intelligence to identify the moral law. In contrast with the account of natural law that was given by Aquinas, which suggested that the primary principles of natural law could be discovered by reason, Pascal was so convinced of human corruption that he seems to have understood natural law as a mere shadow of a moral order that originated with God, that had been accessible to human beings in their pre-lapsarian condition, but can no longer be known reliably except through revelation.

The *Pensées* frequently reiterate the theme of human wretchedness and corruption, and attribute this condition to the sin of Adam. It is clear that this was a matter of faith for Pascal, and he almost revelled in its incomprehensibility:

> However, it is a surprising thing that the mystery that is furthest from our knowledge – which is that of the transmission of [original] sin – is something without which we cannot have any knowledge of ourselves. For there can be no doubt that nothing shocks our reason more than saying that the sin of the first man made guilty those who, far removed from this source, seem incapable of having participated in it. This contamination seems to us to be not only impossible but it also seems to be unjust; for what is more contrary to the laws of our miserable justice than to damn eternally infants who are incapable of willing for a sin in which they seem to have so small a part that it was committed six thousand years before they were born?[23]

Pascal does not attempt to explain original sin or make it rationally intelligible. He even compares it with the incomprehensibility of God's existence:

---

[20] Frag. 56 (2: 560).   [21] Ibid.   [22] Frag. 436 (2: 709).   [23] Frag. 122 (2: 581–2).

'Incomprehensible that God should exist and incomprehensible that he should not ... incomprehensible that original sin should exist and that it should not.'[24]

There is nothing novel in Pascal's interpretation of Christian soteriology, except perhaps his assessment of the extent and depth of the consequences of original sin and his attribution of liability for so much human misery to a unique mythical event in the Garden of Eden. He also seemed to assume that the degree and scope of the natural wretchedness he described provided independent confirmation of his theological interpretation of its source. 'That nature is corrupt, [shown] by nature itself. That there is a Redeemer, [shown] by Scripture';[25] the reality of nature's corruption is almost self-evident, and the doctrine of original sin makes sense of a reality that would otherwise be both evident and incomprehensible.

Following Adam's sin, therefore, human reason is inadequate to the challenge of discerning the moral law, which is finally revealed only as the law of Christ. Pascal wrote in 1658 about 'true morality, which ought to have nothing other than divine authority as its principle', and he contrasted this situation with one in which – if Jesuit casuists succeeded – 'the law of God would be destroyed and natural reason alone would be our guide in all our actions'.[26] In the same context, he rejected the suggestion that 'natural reason alone' could guide our conscience because, as opponents alleged, the same natural reason determined monarchs to decide who may be lawfully killed.[27] For Pascal, even monarchs could not decide the justice or otherwise of capital punishment simply by recourse to reason. God made that decision, and then delegated the relevant authority to monarchs.

Thus, even if Adam had never sinned and human nature were still in the unblemished state in which God created it, so that the intellectual and emotional weaknesses and self-interest that deceive us were entirely absent, Pascal seems to locate the unique source of the categorical moral principles to which he appeals in the jurisdiction of God as creator of human beings. On this account, one need not think of God as initially creating human nature and then issuing arbitrary moral commands that could have been otherwise. One should think of God as creating human beings and determining what was good (and evil) for them by the choice of nature with which He had endowed them. Whether Pascal understood these divine decisions as one creation or as two, the alleged near universal recognition of some moral principles was a reflection of the fact that God's commands have not been

---

[24] Frag. 665 (2: 816).   [25] Frag. 4 (2: 544).   [26] 2: 834, 839.   [27] 2: 840.

completely obscured by human corruption.[28] Given this level of obscurity, if we wish to know what is morally required of us we have no alternative but to consult the commandments as revealed in Scripture and to observe scrupulously their unequivocal provisions.[29]

THE MORAL AGENT: NATURE AND GRACE

One of the objectives of Pascal's unrelenting engagement in religious controversy on behalf of Port-Royal was to clarify the voluntariness of immoral actions and the extent to which blame or praise should be attributed to agents who failed to satisfy the high ideals to which he was committed. He seems to have adopted a traditional analysis of voluntariness, inherited originally from Aristotle, while defending unwaveringly an interpretation of nature and grace that he attributed to Augustine.

The Jesuit interlocutor in the Fourth Letter had claimed that an agent acts immorally only if they know that their action is immoral and if they decide to act against the inspiration to act morally that accompanies such knowledge. When expressed in the language of sin, this meant that 'an action cannot be imputed as sinful unless God gives us, before we commit it, knowledge of the evil involved in it and an inspiration that motivates us to avoid it'.[30] To support this principle, he appealed to Aristotle's distinction between voluntary and involuntary actions, and argued that 'an action cannot be blameworthy if it is involuntary'.[31] In the ensuing dispute about the definition of 'voluntary', Pascal appealed to the *Nicomachean Ethics*, III, i, where Aristotle clarifies the kind of ignorance that renders an action involuntary:

> An action is not properly called involuntary ... if the agent is ignorant of what is beneficial, because it is not ignorance in rational choice that causes the involuntariness (that rather causes wickedness), nor ignorance of the

---

[28] In the expression adopted by Aquinas, natural law represents a limited participation by human reason in the divine law: *Summa theologiae*, IaIIae, q. 91, a. 4.

[29] When Aquinas discussed this transition from natural law to the law of the gospel, he presented it as if there were various intermediate stages between human nature before the Fall and the full revelation of God's law in the New Testament. For Aquinas, the law of the Old Testament was revealed as an interim measure to compensate for 'the deficiencies of reason' at a time when 'natural law began to be obscured by reasons of the proliferation of sin': *Summa theologiae*, IaIIae, q. 98, a. 6. In Fourteenth Letter, Pascal also claims that the prohibition on killing others that is explicit in the New Testament confirmed the prohibition of the old law.

[30] *Letters*, 62 (1: 614–15), trans. amend.   [31] Ibid., 70 (1: 622).

universal (since people are blamed for that), but ignorance of particulars –
the circumstances of the action and what it is concerned with. For it is on
these that pity and pardon depend, since someone who is ignorant of any of
them is acting involuntarily.[32]

Pascal concludes that ignorance of the moral law does not excuse one of
responsibility for one's actions, whereas ignorance of particular facts about
the circumstances in which the action is performed may imply involuntari-
ness. For example, someone may hold a mistaken belief that a given liquid is
wine when it is poison, or may mistake as an enemy someone who happens
to be their own father. That kind of mistaken belief about particular matters
of fact could render one's action involuntary.

To confirm that interpretation, Pascal suggests that it would be safer to
follow the exposition of his favourite theologian, Augustine, rather than that
of Aristotle, and he quotes with approval from Book I of Augustine's
Retractions:

> Those who sin through ignorance perform their action only because they
> want to do so, although they sin without wishing to sin. Thus even this sin of
> ignorance can be committed only by the will of the person committing it,
> although the will is directed towards the action and not towards sin.
> Nevertheless, this does not prevent the action being a sin, because for that
> it is enough to have done what one is obliged not to do.[33]

On this account, an action is immoral if the agent fails voluntarily to observe a
divine command. This voluntary failure could be attributed to the corruption
of human nature, and that in turn was indicative of the necessity of a special
support from God to overcome the moral inertia that results from original sin.

This issue about the necessity of grace was the focus of extremely acrimo-
nious disputes between theologians in various Christian churches in the
seventeenth century. It arose from a number of doctrinal decisions that had
been made over many centuries concerning the freedom with which Adam
sinned, the freedom with which God saves human beings from the results of
Adam's sin (so that 'grace' is never deserved or owed in justice to those who

---

[32] Aristotle (2000), 1110b28–1111a2. For a commentary on this text, see Meyer (2011),
171–6.

[33] *Letters*, 73 (1: 624), trans. amend.; the original text was: '*Nam et qui nesciens peccavit,
non incongruenter nolens pessasse dici potest, . . . Quia voluit ergo fecit, etiamsi non quia
voluit peccavit, nesciens peccatum esse quod fecit. Ita nec tale peccatum sine voluntate esse
potuit, sed voluntate facti non voluntate peccati, quod tamen factum peccatum fuit; hoc
enim factum est quod fieri non debuit*' (Augustine (1984), 47).

inherited liability for Adam's sin), and the freedom with which those to whom this grace is given can accept or reject assistance that is necessary to overcome the effects of original sin. Apart from the apparently competing freedoms of the interlinked agents, Pascal had to address another dimension of this conceptual thicket: the efficacy or adequacy of the grace provided by God – so that He did not appear impotent in relation to the damage caused by Adam – and the foreknowledge traditionally attributed to God, which made it seem (from the perspective of human agents) as if He decided who would be saved or damned before any human agents act.

The axiom that 'ought implies can' highlights some of the philosophical questions implicit in this controversy. When applied to divine commands, this principle means that those to whom the commands are directed are capable of obeying them. The sixth session of the Council of Trent addressed this question in 1547, in which it taught that 'God does not command what is impossible' and condemned those who believed that 'God's commands are incapable of being observed even by someone who is justified and established in grace'.[34] In his commentary on this decree, however, Pascal argued that 'there is no necessary connection between possibility and power' and that 'all the things that may happen to someone are not always within the power of that subject'.[35] He used an example that reflected his own experience of the ill-health he experienced for most of his life: while it is possible for someone to live to the age of sixty, it is not within their power to make that happen. Likewise, the word 'possible' may be understood in such a way that it is not inconsistent to say that it is possible for human beings to obey divine commands, but they may not be able to do so, because the grace required to turn what is possible into action is not provided to everyone. That suggests a query about Pascal's understanding of moral agents who are not 'saved' in the relevant theological sense.

There is little doubt that Pascal assumed that compliance with God's commands is possible only for those to whom He freely grants the disputed grace required for salvation. In the seventeenth letter, Pascal denied that he had ever been a *solitaire* at Port-Royal and that his only allegiance was to the Catholic Church:

> . . . I have no allegiance on earth except exclusively to the Catholic, apostolic, Roman church, in which I wish to live and die, in communion with the pope,

[34] Tanner (1990), 2: 675, 680. For Pascal's commentary on this, see *Écrits sur la grâce*, 2: 211–87.
[35] *Écrits sur la grâce*, 2: 240.

its sovereign head, and outside of which I am very convinced there is no salvation.[36]

This traditional expression of the necessity of church membership for salvation results from Pascal's theology of original sin. He argued, in his *Writings on Grace*, that 'God could not justly impose precepts on Adam and innocent human beings without giving them the necessary grace to fulfil them'.[37] Accordingly, God gave Adam all that was necessary to observe the moral law so that, by his 'free will', he could comply fully with divine commands. Once Adam sinned, however, the whole of humanity was corrupted. Consequently, there are now three kinds of people: 'those who never acquire the faith, those who acquire it but fail to persevere and then die in mortal sin, and finally those who acquire the faith and persevere in it with charity until their deaths'.[38] Although he had conceded the incomprehensibility and apparent injustice of God holding everyone responsible for Adam's sin, Pascal effectively rejected the principle that 'ought implies can' because many of the so-called 'damned' are morally required to observe God's commands although they are unable to do so; God has freely decided not to give them the means necessary to comply. 'In the state of corruption, God could justly damn the whole mass of mankind; and those who continue to be born today without being rescued from that state by baptism are damned.'[39]

For a minority of human beings, therefore – those who are baptized and then persevere in a virtuous life until their death – the question remains about how they succeed in obeying categorical divine commands, with which they are incapable of complying without a special assistance from God. The Jansenist position that Pascal defended was opposed to two other accounts of grace that were taught by Dominicans and Jesuits in the names, respectively, of two Spanish theologians, Luis de Molina (1535–1600) and Domingo Báñez (1528–1604).[40] Pascal was not a professional theologian. He was not educated in scholasticism, and his familiarity with many of the details of these disputes seems to have been acquired indirectly through discussions with Arnauld and other leading members of the Jansenist movement. Despite

---

[36] *Letters*, 260–1 (1: 781), trans. amend. The *solitaires* lived a life of humility and asceticism at Port-Royal. Their movement was often linked to Jansenism.

[37] *Écrits sur la grâce*, 2: 287. [38] Ibid., 2: 262. [39] Ibid., 2: 261.

[40] The possibility of divine middle knowledge, on which Molina relied to protect human freedom despite God's foreknowledge of future possible events, is discussed in Adams (1997) and Freddoso (1988). There were also competing theological views within Calvinism, which I have not mentioned in the text above.

these intellectual shortcomings, however, he tried to explain how God's absolute freedom and foreknowledge were compatible with the kind of voluntariness that he presupposed in any human action that is subject to moral evaluation. The question was, as he expressed it in *Writings on Grace*, 'whether the salvation of some human beings and the damnation of others results from the fact that God wills it or from the fact that human beings will it'.[41]

Pascal had described Adam, prior to the Fall, as having 'a free will equally disposed towards good and evil' and as having sufficient grace to choose the good: God 'gave Adam a sufficient grace, that is, one such that none other was necessary in order to comply with the precepts [of the moral law] and to live a just life'.[42] After the Fall, however, the free will of all human beings was weakened by concupiscence, and their understanding of good and evil was dulled:

> Free will has remained disposed to good and evil, but with this difference: whereas, in the case of Adam, there was no inclination towards evil and knowing what was good was sufficient for him to enable him to follow it, now evil has such a strong attraction and sweetness as a result of concupiscence that the free will infallibly moves towards it of its own accord as if it were its good, and chooses evil voluntarily, very freely and joyfully as the object in which it finds its bliss.[43]

This contrast implies a freedom of indifference in Adam prior to the Fall, when he was 'equally' disposed to good and evil and, after the Fall, an infallible disposition in all human beings towards evil, although Pascal describes the will even then as acting 'voluntarily'. To counteract this attraction to evil, God's 'medicinal grace' provides a compensating attraction towards what is good, although it is given only to those who are baptized.

> ... grace ... which is nothing other than a sweetness and delectation in the law of God ... which not only equals but exceeds the concupiscence of the flesh and fills the will with a greater pleasure in what is good than concupiscence offers the will in what is evil; thus free will itself ... chooses infallibly God's law for the simple reason that it finds therein more satisfaction and experiences its bliss and happiness there.[44]

This account of free choice coincides with Fragment 90 of the *Pensées*, which adopts Aristotle's distinction between voluntary and involuntary actions in

---

[41] *Écrits sur la grâce*, 2: 259.   [42] Ibid., 2: 287–8.   [43] Ibid., 2: 289.

[44] Ibid., 2: 289–90. The word 'infallibly' is used twice on p. 290 to describe the certainty with which God's grace is efficacious.

terms of factors that are internal or external to the agent. 'Concupiscence and force are the sources of all our actions. Concupiscence causes voluntary actions, force causes involuntary ones.'[45] According to this definition, the will chooses freely as long as the factors that affect a choice are internal to the agent. Thus, when Adam's will was attracted to evil, it was free; likewise, when the will of those who are saved by God's grace is attracted to what is good, they too are free.

> ... those to whom God is pleased to grant this grace, bring themselves of their own accord by their free will infallibly to prefer God to creatures. For that reason one may say indifferently either that free will brings itself there of its own accord by means of this grace ... or that this grace brings free will there ...[46]

Those who persevere in accepting God's infallibly efficacious assistance, according to Pascal, overcome their concupiscence 'by their own choice and the movement of their free will, which is carried there of its own accord voluntarily and freely'.[47]

If one were to set aside Pascal's theological interpretation of moral decision-making – which includes a mythical account of the corruption of human nature in the Garden of Eden and its partial restoration by the free intervention of an angry and indignant God[48] – his moral theory adopts a pessimistic picture of human psychology, in which the attractiveness of what is morally impermissible tends to overpower the attraction of the good. He concedes almost no room for doubt about what is morally required, and assumes that even pagans are informed of the most fundamental principles of morality (which originate in divine commands) through the reduced light of natural reason. The moral life, therefore, is a constant struggle for the acquisition and consolidation of those virtues that dispose us to act morally or, in theological language, a struggle between the concupiscence of the flesh and efficacious divine grace. This internal struggle is what makes the resulting actions voluntary, because they result from the deliberation of the agent rather than from some external determining factor.

In retrospect, one might regret that the rhetorical skill, absolute conviction, and unrelenting vigour with which Pascal defended Jansenism masked the need for a philosophical defence of an ethics that relied ultimately on the certainty of his religious beliefs. Despite the famous phrase in the *Pensées* to

---

[45] Frag. 90 (2: 570). [46] *Écrits sur la grâce*, 2: 291. [47] Ibid.
[48] Pascal describes 'the mass of humankind' as being 'the just object of God's anger and indignation' (2: 261).

the effect that a human being is a 'thinking reed', Pascal's moral theory reflects his fundamental evaluation of the unreliability of reason when compared with faith and the inability of human beings without grace to discover or implement the moral law.[49]

BIBLIOGRAPHY

Adams, R.M. 1997. 'Middle Knowledge and the Problem of Evil', *American Philosophical Quarterly*, 14, 109–17.

Aristotle 2000. *The Nicomachean Ethics*, trans. Roger Crisp. Cambridge University Press.

Augustine, Saint 1968. *The Retractions*, trans. Mary I. Bogen. Fathers of the Church, vol. 60. Washington, DC: Catholic University of America Press.

Augustine, Saint 1984. *Retractionum Libri II*, ed. A. Mutzenbecher. Corpus Christianorum, Series Latina, vol. 57. Turnhout: Brepols.

Baird, A.W.S. 1975. *Studies in Pascal's Ethics*. The Hague: Nijhoff.

Freddoso, F. 1988. *On Divine Foreknowledge*. Ithaca, NY: Cornell University Press.

Meyer, Susan Sauvé 2011. *Aristotle on Moral Responsibility*.Oxford University Press.

Migne, J.-P., ed. 1862. *Patrologia Graeca*, vol. 49. Paris.

Pascal, Blaise 1967. *The Provincial Letters*, trans. A.J. Krailsheimer. London: Penguin.

Pascal, Blaise 2000. *Œuvres complètes*, ed. Michel Le Guern. 2 vols. Paris: Gallimard.

Tanner, Norman P. 1990. *Decrees of the Ecumenical Councils*, 2 vols. London: Sheed & Ward.

---

[49] Frag. 104 (2: 574).

24

Locke and Butler

STEPHEN DARWALL

On the face of it, the ethical philosophies of John Locke and Bishop Joseph Butler could hardly be more starkly opposed. Butler saw himself as defending the "ancient" doctrine that virtue accords with our nature both in the sense of arising naturally from resources moral agents have within them and of realizing their natural end or good.[1] Locke, by contrast, saw morality as externally imposed through God's superior authoritative command on creatures who, left to their own devices, would find themselves, if not in a Hobbesian war of all against all, in a mutually disadvantageous situation even so.

This is a familiar theme of Locke's political philosophy. Though Locke believes the state of nature is a state of natural right and not of war, the mutual disadvantages of lacking a common umpire of civil authority are sufficiently clear to give everyone reason to bind themselves by mutual contract and create the state.

This is no less a theme of Locke's moral philosophy than of his political philosophy. Like legal rights, natural rights and obligations are also established by an exercise of authority, except that here the relevant authority is nothing any human being has, but a superior authority that only God can exercise through command. God's commands have a similar function and role in Locke's moral philosophy to that of the social contract in his political philosophy – they save human beings from a situation that would be worse for all. Since human motivation is ultimately self-regarding, God can enable human beings to escape conflict and turmoil only by commanding them to act in mutually beneficial ways and backing his commands with eternal sanctions. Like earthly legislators, God makes use of self-regarding, sanction-avoiding

---

[1] In this sense, Butler might be thought to carry on an "Aristotelian naturalist" tradition of the sort described in Irwin 2008. For Irwin's discussion of Butler, see vol. 2: 539–57.

human motivation to get people to act for mutual advantage in ways they would not naturally.

All of this seems very far away indeed from Butler. Butler is perhaps most famous for having "refuted" *psychological egoism*, the view that all human behavior results from self-regarding motives. As Butler saw it, human beings can act rightly for mutual advantage out of benevolence or, more importantly, out of moral conscience, and not just from fear of divine retribution. Butler believes, moreover, that morality is not something that could, even in principle, be imposed on a moral agent from without, not even by God's command.

Any genuinely moral law must ultimately be grounded somehow in the moral agent herself. Butler takes as the defining text of two of his most famous sermons "Upon Human Nature" St Paul's saying that the "Gentiles" to whom God's law has not been explicitly communicated are nonetheless "a law unto themselves." A central claim of Butler's ethics is that morality is only possible because a moral agent has within himself a "superior" "authoritative" principle, conscience, that makes him "a law to himself" (Pr.29).[2] Without this moral agency and morality itself would be impossible.

Locke's focus is entirely on moral *conduct*. For him, indeed, *"Mora[l] Good and Evil . . . is only the Conformity or Disagreement of our Voluntary Actions to some Law"* (*Essay*, 351).[3] In this way, virtue or moral goodness is effectively reduced to right action, to *what* we do regardless of why we do it. Butler, by contrast, is more fundamentally interested in moral agency as it is expressed in the moral agent's practical reasoning. Whether conduct is virtuous depends not on what the agent does, but on her reasons for so acting.

Butler holds, moreover, that genuine virtue is realized only through the agent's guiding herself by the faculty that makes her a moral agent, her own conscience. By Locke's lights, no such source of human motivation exists. What matters is simply our conduct's conforming to the law, God's authoritative command, and that is made possible by fear of God's retribution.

Despite these fundamental differences, however, there are also significant commonalities between Locke and Butler. Most importantly, both can be seen as modern moral philosophers in ways that depart from ancient Greek ethics and even from the classical natural law tradition of Aquinas. There are various aspects of this, but the most important is that both Locke and Butler

---

[2] See Butler 1983. References to Preface (pr.) or Sermon number and paragraph will be placed parenthetically in the text.
[3] See Locke 1975. References will be placed parenthetically in the text.

develop and defend a conception of *morality* that purports to provide a normative standard – the morally *right* – that differs from that of the good. Both Locke and Butler pursued "modern moral philosophy" in the sense that Anscombe complained about in her famous eponymous essay.[4]

What does this putative difference between ancient and modern ethics amount to? Anscombe argues that the "modern" concepts of "*moral* obligation and *moral* duty," hence "of what is *morally* right and wrong, and of the *moral* sense of 'ought,'" cannot be found in ancient thought.[5] Unlike ancient Greek conceptions of the good, these modern notions are modeled on the idea of law, essentially including "juridical" notions of obligation, culpability, and guilt (30–1). The point is not that the modern view makes no distinction between the moral and the legal. Rather it identifies a peculiar kind of law that differs conceptually from local, national, or even from international law. In Locke's version, morality consists in divinely created law.

Ancient ethical thought employs juridical notions also, of course, but mostly in political thought and not in any fundamental normative standard of individual conduct. When, for example, Socrates answers Glaucon and Adeimantus's question "why be just?" in Plato's *Republic*, he does so by arguing that justice realizes an intrinsic human *good*, harmony of soul. Sidgwick makes the same point:

> [I]n Platonism and Stoicism, and in Greek moral philosophy generally, but one regulative and governing faculty is recognised under the name of Reason – however the regulation of Reason may be understood; in the modern ethical view, when it has worked itself clear, there are found to be two, – Universal Reason and Egoistic Reason, or Conscience and Self-love.[6]

Like Anscombe, Sidgwick also stresses that "conscience" in modern ethical thought is essentially conceived with "quasi-jural notions" of obligation, "duty," and right.[7] We can put Sidgwick's claim by saying that whereas the ancients recognized only one fundamental normative or ethical standard, the good, modern ethical thought recognizes two: the good and the right.

The classical natural law tradition deriving from Aquinas also employs the notion of moral right, of course, but not as a fundamental normative standard and not as essentially *obligating* in a distinctively juridical sense. For Aquinas, natural law is simply "eternal law" – a teleological perfectionist standard inherent in any being – graspable by human beings who are able to follow or

---

[4] See Anscombe 1998.
[5] Anscombe, 1998: 26. Further references will be placed parenthetically in the text.
[6] Sidgwick 1964: 198.   [7] Sidgwick 1967: 106.

flout it by virtue of their rational nature. What natural law requires is thus no different from what realizes the agent's good. They are ultimately the same standard.

Locke and Butler disagree with classical natural law on this fundamental point. The title of Chapter 8 of Locke's *Essay on the Law of Nature* is: "Is Every Man's Own Interest the Basis of the Law of Nature? No." And conscience and self-love function as two independent "principles" in Butler's moral psychology.

More, the modern idea of right or obligation depends upon a distinction between moral advice or "counsel" and what morality requires or "commands," a distinction Suarez initially posed as an objection to the Thomistic theory of natural law. Genuinely obligating law does not merely counsel or advise prudent acts; it purports to require action and to make those subject to it answerable for conformance. Suarez objected that Aquinas's theory of natural law couldn't account for this essentially deontic or juridical aspect. The idea that morality's distinctive power to obligate cannot be accounted for by any such prudential counsel is one that is central to modern moral philosophy from Grotius on.[8]

Second, Locke and Butler also develop, though in very different ways, another core idea of early modern ethical thought: *autonomy*. We have already glimpsed this in Butler's claim that morality and moral agency involve a person's being "a law to himself." Moral virtue, for Butler, involves the excellent exercise of the faculty that makes a person a moral agent in the first place, determining her conduct by her own conscientious judgment. But autonomy turns out to be important to Locke's moral philosophy also, although in a very different way.

Locke denies the very possibility of autonomy as Butler conceives it, both because the moral law is imposed externally by God and because Butlerian conscience is no possible form of human motivation. At the same time, however, Locke holds that morality does indeed depend on autonomy of a kind. Unless human beings were capable of determining themselves within their own practical reasoning to comply with the moral law, then God could hardly hold them responsible for compliance. To accommodate this, Locke argues that God endows human beings with a kind of autonomy or "liberty" consisting in the power to step back from and "suspend" current desires, reflectively consider their objects, make considered judgments of long-term

---

[8] For defense of this, see Darwall 2012.

good or pleasure, and thereby determine themselves to do what is morally right (*Essay*, 263).

Thus both Locke and Butler distinguish the morally right from the good and develop the idea that complying with right involves autonomy. For Butler, moral agents act morally by determining themselves conscientiously by their own moral judgments. For Locke, this is impossible, but it is possible nonetheless, indeed, it *must* be possible, for human agents to determine themselves autonomously to do what is morally right. Although the ideas of moral right and good are fundamentally distinct for Locke no less than for Butler, Locke holds that morality nonetheless depends upon human agents having reasons of their own good (owing to God's sanctions) *and* that they can determine themselves by these reasons to do what is morally right.

JOHN LOCKE

Let us turn now to laying out the main outlines of Locke's and Butler's ethics, beginning with Locke. Locke's ethical philosophy is squarely within the modern natural law tradition that begins roughly with Grotius's *The Rights of War and Peace* (1625).[9] People today are much more familiar with Locke's political philosophy, especially his *Second Treatise of Government*, which sets out a doctrine of natural rights and a justification of the state as necessary to protect them and so arising by mutual consent through the social contract. Locke's political ideas exercised great influence in the seventeenth and eighteenth centuries – the phrases "unalienable rights" of "life, liberty, and the pursuit of happiness" of the American Declaration of Independence have clear Lockean overtones. For Locke, the state exists to protect "property," which includes "life, liberty, and estate."[10] And Locke's political ideas retain much of their power today.

Locke's moral philosophy is less well known, but it provides the necessary underpinnings for his better-known political ideas. It is no accident, then, that his ethics are fundamentally juridical, a theory of natural law. An interesting way to begin to appreciate this is through Locke's famous discussion of personal identity in the *Essay Concerning Human Understanding*. It is impossible to understand what personal identity, as opposed, say, to bodily identity, consists in, Locke thinks, unless we understand what it is to be a person. "Person," Locke says, is a juridical or "forensick term appropriating actions and their merit" (*Essay*, 346). In order to be "accountable," someone must be

---

[9] Grotius 2005. [10] Locke 1988: 323.

able to "own and imput[e] to itself past actions," and thereby be "capable of a law" (*Essay*, 346). The very idea of a person, in other words, is of a being that is subject to law. To be subject to law is to be accountable for compliance through owning and imputing actions to oneself.

Locke gives an initial formulation of his natural law theory in his *Essays on the Law of Nature*.[11] There he argues that human beings are bound by a law of nature that derives from God's superior authoritative will:

> All the requisites of a law are found in natural law. For, in the first place, it is the decree of a superior will, wherein the formal cause of a law appears to consist; . . . Secondly, it lays down what is and what is not to be done, which is the proper function of a law. Thirdly, it binds men, for it contains in itself all that is requisite to create an obligation. (111–13)

Experience shows us that human existence derives from God's creative power and, therefore, "that there exists another more powerful and wiser agent who at his will can bring us into the world, maintain us, and take us away" (153). "On the evidence of the senses," therefore, "reason lays down that there must be some superior power to which we are rightly subject, namely God" (153–5).

It is important to appreciate that Locke is not reducing God's superior authority to his superior power. Rather God's power and authority together give him the *right* to rule, and thereby to obligate, and not just compel, us to act. "All obligation," Locke writes, "lays a bond on the mind itself, so that not fear of punishment, but a rational apprehension of what is right, puts us under an obligation" (183).

Locke does not hold, like some theological voluntarists, that morality derives from God's arbitrary will. Like Aquinas and Suarez, he holds that there must be "a harmony between this law and human nature, in so far as it is rational" (104). God's benevolent wisdom leads him to command us to act in ways that are mutually beneficial. However, unlike Aquinas and Suarez, Locke does not believe that the law simply directs us to act for our good, since, unlike them, Locke does not believe that individuals' goods naturally harmonize; these sometimes conflict. Collective compliance with God's commands could not lead to mutual benefit, consequently, if these simply directed us to pursue our own goods individually. To the contrary, Locke writes, "a great number of virtues, and the best of them, consist only in this:

---

[11] Locke 1954. Composed in the 1660s, unpublished in Locke's lifetime. Further references will be placed parenthetically in the text.

that we do good to others at our own loss" (207). "Every man's own interest" cannot be "the basis of the law of nature" (205).

It is not far wrong to think of God's commands as intended to solve a very large collective action problem or "prisoners' dilemma." Natural law's function is to direct people to mutually beneficial conduct when collective guidance by self-interest would be mutually disadvantageous. But although the legitimacy of God's commands, and their power to obligate and "law a bond upon the mind itself," is independent of self-interest, Locke believes, quite unlike Butler, that human beings are incapable of guiding themselves by their judgment of what is morally right unless they have self-interested motives for doing so. This is clearest in the *Essay*, where Locke makes explicit divine sanctions' role in motivating rightful conduct: "the Power to enforce [the law] by Rewards and Punishments of infinite weight and duration, in another Life . . . is the true touchstone of *moral Rectitude*" (352). Even in the *Essays*, though, Locke says that "law is to no purpose without punishment" (173).

For Locke, the thought that an action is morally right or obligatory is motivationally inert. Human agents can only be moved by thoughts of their own pleasure or good.

> The pleasure that a man takes in any action or expects as a consequence of it is indeed a Good in it self able & proper to move the will. But the Moral Rectitude of it considered barely in it self is not good or evill nor in any way moves the will but as pleasure & pain either accompanies the action it self or is looked on to be a consequent of it. W^ch is evident from the punishments & rewards god has annexed to moral rectitude or pravity as proper motives of ye will wch would be needless if moral rectitude were it self good & moral pravity evil.[12]

In order to make natural law to some "purpose," therefore, God must give human beings the motivation to follow it through eternal sanctions.

Locke's disconnecting moral obligation from motivation may seem unsatisfying – it certainly must have to Butler – but his ideas fit together in a fairly neat, distinctively modern, way. Morality is the solution to the problem that arises when individuals' goods do not or, at least, cannot be known to, harmonize naturally. Morality's directives are normatively distinct from the good, but if individuals collectively comply with them, they will realize mutual benefit. Humans cannot, however, be moved to act morally directly.

---

[12] This is from Locke's Commonplace Book, in the Lovelace Collection held in the Bodleian Library, Oxford University, MS C28, fol. 114.

But just as God provides the source of morality's distinctive authority, so also does he give human beings motives to act morally through eternal sanctions.

By the time Locke wrote the second edition of the *Essay*, however, this package must have seemed a little too neat. If human beings are "accountable" for complying with natural law, it will not be enough that long-term self-interest coincides with divinely sanctioned right conduct, if human beings are unable to determine their conduct by knowing this. As Locke put it in an example of syllogistic reasoning that he added to the *Essay* even later, God's sanction can amount to "Just Punishment" only if wrongdoers "could have done otherwise," if their circumstances made "Freedom" and "self-determination" possible (*Essay*, 673).

For Locke, this cannot mean that moral agents have the ability to determine themselves to act morally through *conscience*, as Butler will later hold. Only thoughts of good are motivating; deontic thoughts are not. The problem, as Locke poses it in the *Essay*'s second edition, is that agents are moved not, as he had earlier believed, by their greatest good as they perceive it, but rather by their strongest current desire, by their greatest "present uneasiness" (*Essay*, 254). Even if we know that acting rightly is best for us in the longest run, we will act wrongly if we are motivated by a stronger current desire, for example, for some nearer-term good. In order to determine ourselves to act rightly we need a way that we *ourselves* can bring the strengths of our current desires into line with what we know about our long-term good.

And this is precisely what Locke goes on to argue we have: a form of deliberative reasoning that is "the source of all liberty" (*Essay*, 263). Although the most "pressing" uneasiness moves us "for the most part," it does "not always" (*Essay*, 263):

> For the mind having in most cases, as is evident in experience, a power to suspend the execution and satisfaction of any of its desires, and so all, one after another, is at liberty to consider the objects of them, examine them on all sides, and weigh them with others. In this lies the liberty man has; and from the not using of it right comes all that variety of mistakes, errors, and faults which we run into in the conduct of our lives, and our endeavours after happiness. (*Essay*, 263)

This ability to step back self-reflectively from desires, affect their strengths by deliberative thought, and thereby determine ourselves in a "reasons responsive" way is one thing contemporary philosophers mean by autonomy. We could fairly characterize Locke, therefore, as developing an account of autonomous agency as a necessary complement to his concept of moral persons as accountable agents "capable of a law."

BISHOP BUTLER

Unlike Locke's ethics, but perhaps more like Locke's political philosophy, Butler's ethics have had a profound and continuing influence. Butler's impact on Hume, Hutcheson, and Adam Smith was substantial. And the *Sermons* were reprinted more during the nineteenth century than any other British ethical work.[13] Sidgwick's *Methods of Ethics* is full of references to Butler. Sidgwick's famous "dualism of practical reason" recapitulates the modern contrast between "Universal" and "Egoistic Reason," which Sidgwick also puts in Butler's terms of "Conscience" and "Self-Love."[14]

Analytical moral philosophy of more recent times is also greatly indebted to Butler. Butler was a master of subtle, important distinctions. "Everything is what it is, and not another thing," he wrote in the *Sermons'* preface (*Sermons*, Pr.40). G.E. Moore made Butler's saying the epigraph for his path-breaking work of twentieth-century analytical ethics, *Principia Ethica*.[15] Butler's distinction between *"mere power* and *authority"* (*Sermons*, II.8) antici-pates Sidgwick's contrast between non-normative and normative, "ethical judgments" as well as Moore's juxtaposition of naturalistic properties and the irreducible property of goodness.[16] Finally, W.D. Ross's famous "deontolo-gical" objections to Moore's "ideal utilitarianism" – that considerations other than the goodness of consequences "make right acts right" – bear a clear relation to Butler's objections to Hutcheson's claim that "virtue is resolvable into benevolence" in the former's *Dissertation Concerning Virtue*. There Butler argues, anticipating Ross, that we "condemn falsehood, unprovoked vio-lence, [and] injustice" and "approve of benevolence to some preferably to others, abstracted from all consideration, which conduct is likeliest to pro-duce an overbalance of happiness or misery."[17]

Butler is perhaps noted most, however, for his sophisticated and systema-tic moral psychology, for his penetrating analysis of different motivational sources within the human psychic "economy" or "constitution," and for his powerful, suggestive ideas of how these fit together within moral agents, indeed, of how agents fit them together themselves in determining their own

---

[13] See Schneewind 1977: 7.   [14] Sidgwick 1967: 373–407. Sidgwick 1964: 198.
[15] And Saul Kripke invokes it; also Kripke 1981: 94.
[16] Sidgwick 1967: 23–38 and Moore 1993: 53–88.   [17] *Dissertation*, para. 8, in Butler 1983.

moral conduct. Perhaps Butler's most significant idea, however, is that this capacity for self-determining, self-constituting moral agency is necessary for the very possibility of morality.

It can be difficult to keep in mind how little of Butler's life was actually devoted to ethical philosophy. When Hume listed Butler as one of "some late philosophers in England, who have begun to put the science of man on a new footing," he was judging Butler on the strength of a few sermons preached at the Roll Chapel in London and published as part of a collection in 1726.[18] Although others in the collection have continuing interest, for example, those on resentment and self-deceit, Butler's central ethical ideas are mainly laid out in only five sermons, three on human nature and the superior authority of conscience, and two on the "love of our neighbor," along with a short essay or "dissertation" on virtue. Butler's only other philosophical work was his massive *Analogy Concerning Religion, Natural and Revealed* (1736), which argued that revealed religion is fully consistent with then current experimental natural philosophy. Mostly, Butler was an Anglican clergyman, then bishop, who devoted himself to church affairs.

According to Butler, the human psychic economy consists of various particular "passions and affections" which, though some be "private" and tend to our individual good and others "public," tending toward the good of others, are nonetheless distinct, respectively, from self-love and benevolence. Butler is careful to distinguish desires, emotions, and attitudes by their different "intentional objects," as we might now call them, by what they are specifically "of" or "for." For example, "desire of esteem from others, contempt and esteem of them, love of society as distinct from affection to the good of it, indignation against successful vice," these are all "public affections or passions" in the sense that they frequently lead us to benefit others. But these all have different objects from benevolence. None aims directly at others' benefit (*Sermons*, II.7). Similarly "private" passions, like hunger, can lead us to benefit ourselves. But unlike self-love, hunger's *object* is not one's own good *per se*.

Benevolence and self-love also differ from other public and private passions and affections by virtue of being, as Butler analyzes it, second-order rather than first-order motivational states. A central tenet of Butler's case against psychological egoism is that "the very idea of interest or happiness consists in this, that an appetite or affection enjoys its object" (*Sermons*, Pr.37). The reason not all actions can be motivated by a desire for one's own good is that the object of the latter is just the satisfaction of some of one's *other*

---

[18] See Hume 2000: 5.

desires. So, happiness is so much as possible for a being only if that being has some other, first-order desires. It simply cannot be that our only desire is for our own happiness. And only a self-reflective being can even conceive of welfare or happiness and desire it, whether of others (benevolence) or one's own (self-love).

Butler makes a related point about the psychological hedonist idea that all action is done for the sake of pleasure. All "particular appetites and passions" are for particular objects "distinct from the pleasure arising from them," and "there could not be this pleasure" unless we are such as to like or find enjoyable the object itself.[19] "There could be no enjoyment or delight from one thing more than another, from eating food more than from swallowing a stone," if we did not like eating delicious food more than swallowing stones (*Sermons*, IV.6). In principle, moreover, others' good is no less a possible object of human desire than is anything else. Butler argues that the empirical evidence massively supports the proposition that human beings are capable of desiring and being moved directly by the weal and woe of others.

Benevolence and self-love are alike in standing above particular public and private desires, respectively, not yet in any order of justification, but in the sense that an agent must be able to be able to view first-order desires with reflective distance even to have these second-order sources of motivation. But while benevolence and self-love are both reflective in this way, both are also distinct from what Butler calls "the principle of reflection":

> There is a principle of reflection in men, by which they distinguish between, approve and disapprove their own actions. We are plainly constituted such sort of creatures as to reflect upon our own nature. The mind can take a view of what passes within itself, its propensions, aversions, passions, affections, as respecting such objects, and in such degrees; and of the several actions consequent thereupon. In this survey it approves of one, disapproves of another, and towards a third is affected in neither of these ways, but is quite indifferent. This principle in man, by which he approves or disapproves his heart, temper, and actions, is conscience. (*Sermons*, I.8)

Conscience has a distinctive "superintendent" role in the human psychic economy or constitution. Because we have conscience, "our constitution is put in our own power. We are charged with it; and therefore are accountable for any disorder or violation of it" (*Sermons*, Pr.14). "It is by this faculty, natural to man, that he is a moral agent, that he is a law to himself" (*Sermons*, II.8).

---

[19] Such an intentional object might be an experience, of course.

Butler holds that self-love and conscience are both "superior" principles in the sense that when they conflict with particular passions and affections, an agent should act on them. As we might put it these days, considerations of moral right and the agent's own good provide weightier normative reasons for acting than do any deriving from or associated with particular passions. At one point, indeed, Butler says that "reasonable self-love and conscience" share the honor of being "the chief or superior principles in the nature of man," in a passage that led Sidgwick to see a Butlerian pedigree for his "dualism of practical reason" (*Sermons*, III.9).

Nevertheless, Butler clearly maintains that "judgment, direction, and superintendency" are essential to the very idea of conscience in a way they are not to self-love. "You cannot form a notion of this faculty" without bringing these in. They are "constituent part[s] of the idea, that is, of the faculty itself, and to preside and govern, from the very economy and constitution of man, belongs to it" (*Sermons*, II.14).

Self-love is self-reflective and "superior" to particular desires and affections, but is nonetheless like them in being a desire, Butler says, "a [person's] general desire of his own happiness" (*Sermons*, IV.5). Conscience, by contrast, is a faculty of normative judgment; it is the faculty through which we are able to judge, among other things, the superiority of self-love to particular passions. Self-love cannot make that judgment itself. Only "*the* principle of reflection" can.

Butler allows that it can seem a sensible question whether we should always follow conscience, and he devotes *Sermon* II to answering it. Partly he argues that conscience's *function* is clearly superintendent, so God's manifest purpose must be that we should follow it. But such an argument risks ending up either with Locke's idea that we should follow conscience because God wills it or with the ancient eudaimonist notion that normativity is grounded ultimately in the good, or with some combination.

A more interesting interpretation is what we might call a "transcendental" one, according to which having a conscience and giving it authority is a presupposition of the very possibility of moral agency. "It is by this faculty," Butler writes,

> natural to man, that he is a moral agent, that he is a law to himself: by this faculty, I say, not to be considered merely as a principle in his heart, which is to have some influence as well as others; but considered as a faculty in kind and in nature supreme over all others, and which bears its own authority of being so. (*Sermons*, II.8)

To be so much as capable of moral agency, a being must be able to step back from its various sources of motivation, to make normative judgments which she should act on and to act on those judgments. When she finds herself judging that she should do something, she can of course question her judgment in the sense of asking herself whether her judgment is really correct. But if she is convinced it is, then there is no further sensible question of whether she should act on it or not. In Butlerian terms, she must presuppose the "supreme authority" of her principle of reflection or conscience sensibly to deliberate at all.

Butler's *Sermons* have proven a treasure trove of other ideas that have had great influence in the history of ethics. Butler is the source of Sidgwick's "paradox of egoistic hedonism," that we often best advance our aims and good by not directly aiming at them.[20] As Butler puts it, "disengagement is absolutely necessary to enjoyment; and a person may have so steady and fixed an eye upon his own interest, whatever he places it in, as may hinder him from attending to many gratifications within his reach, which others have their minds free and open to" (*Sermons*, IV.9). Somewhat similarly, Butler argues that God's desire for the greatest possible human happiness is best accomplished if we are endowed with a conscience that is deontological rather than an act utilitarian one that approves of acts based only on their consequences.

> Were the Author of nature to propose nothing to himself as an end but the production of happiness, were his moral character merely that of benevolence; yet ours is not so. Upon that supposition, indeed, the only reason of his giving us the ... disapprobation of falsehood, unprovoked violence, and injustice, must be, that he foresaw this constitution of our nature would produce more happiness, than forming us with a temper of mere general benevolence.[21]

In the end, however, Butler's most powerful ideas concern the mutual dependence of the ideas of morality and moral agency, and how the constitution of the former depends upon the self-constitution of the latter, through an agent's excellent exercise of the faculty that makes her a moral agent.

BIBLIOGRAPHY

An asterisk denotes secondary literature especially suitable for further reading.

Anscombe, G.E.M. 1998. "Modern Moral Philosophy," in *Virtue Ethics*, ed. Roger Crisp and Michael Slote. Oxford University Press, pp. 26–44.

---

[20] Sidgwick 1967: 136.   [21] *Dissertation*, para. 8, in Butler 1983.

Butler, Joseph 1983. *Five Sermons, Preached at the Rolls Chapel and a Dissertation upon the Nature of Virtue*, ed. Stephen L. Darwall. Indianapolis, IN: Hackett Publishing Inc.

Darwall, Stephen 2012. "Grotius at the Creation of Modern Moral Philosophy," in *Archiv für Geschichte der Philosophie* 94: 296–325.

Grotius, Hugo 2005. *The Rights of War and Peace*, 3 vols., ed. Richard Tuck. Indianapolis, IN: Liberty Fund.

Hume David 2000. *A Treatise of Human Nature*, ed. David Fate Norton and Mary J. Norton. Oxford University Press.

Irwin, Terence 2008. *The Development of Ethics*. Oxford University Press.*

Kripke, Saul 1981. *Naming and Necessity*. Malden, MA: Blackwell Publishing.

Locke, John 1954. *Essays of the Law of Nature*, ed. with an intro. by W. von Leyden. Oxford University Press.

Locke, John 1975. *An Essay Concerning Human Understanding*, ed. by Peter H. Nidditch. Oxford University Press.

Locke, John 1988. *Second Treatise of Government, in Two Treatises of Government*, ed. Peter Laslett. Cambridge University Press.

Moore, G.E. 1993. *Principia Ethica*, ed. with an intro. by Thomas Baldwin. Cambridge University Press.

Schneewind, Jerome B. 1977. *Sidgwick's Ethics and Victorian Moral Philosophy*. Oxford University Press.

Sidgwick, Henry 1964. *Outlines of the History of Ethics for English Readers*, with an additional chapter by Alban G. Widgery. Boston, MA: Beacon Press.

Sidgwick, Henry 1967. *The Methods of Ethics*, 7th edn. London: Macmillan.

25

Shaftesbury, Hutcheson and the Moral Sense

JAMES A. HARRIS

In 1897 L.A. Selby-Bigge published *British Moralists: Being Selections from Writers Principally of the Eighteenth Century*. The book had two volumes, one containing 'the three principal texts of the sentimental school – Shaftesbury, Hutcheson and Butler, followed by Adam Smith and Bentham', the other containing 'S. Clarke, Balguy and Price, with extracts from Cudworth and Wollaston, and additional extracts from Balguy in the Appendix, as representatives of the intellectual school' (Selby-Bigge 1897, vol. 1: vi).[1] These two schools, Selby-Bigge explained in his Introduction, 'are primarily distinguished by their adoption of reason and feeling respectively as the faculty which perceives moral distinctions, a faculty declared in each case to be peculiar and not identifiable with ordinary reason or ordinary feeling' (xxviii). Yet, Selby-Bigge is clear, this was not in eighteenth-century Britain a self-standing philosophical question. It was not merely an early round, so to speak, of the fight between realists and anti-realists, or cognitivists and non-cognitivists. For sentimentalists and intellectualists were in agreement about what they took to be a more important question, the question posed by Hobbes, and then posed again by Mandeville, concerning the reality of the distinction between virtue and vice. Hobbes and Mandeville argued that moral distinctions are wholly artificial, that they are legislated into existence by the state (Hobbes) or invented by scheming 'politicians' (Mandeville), that morality is altogether a matter of arbitrary convention, and that our reasons to be moral are no different from our reasons to be polite or fashionable. Sentimentalists and intellectualists both believed that Hobbes and Mandeville were deeply, and dangerously, wrong. They disagreed only about the best means of showing Hobbes and Mandeville to be wrong, which is to say, about the best means of showing, in Selby-Bigge's words, 'that virtue is real

---

[1] Hume was omitted because Selby-Bigge had recently produced editions of the *Treatise* (1888) and the *Enquiries* (1893).

and is worth pursuing in itself; that virtue and the motive to it are irreducible to a merely animal experience of pleasure and pain' (xxviii). The principal topic of this chapter is the role played by the idea of a 'moral sense' in the cases made for the reality and intrinsic worth of virtue by Shaftesbury and by Hutcheson.

THE ORIGINS OF MORAL SENSE THEORY

In the second half of the seventeenth century it seemed to many that the best answer to Hobbes was to show that, far from being merely a matter of human artifice and convention, moral principles are principles of reason, as necessarily true as principles of logic and mathematics. The most influential version of this line of thought was Pufendorf's picture of the rules of morality as laid down by a divine law-giver, yet also deducible from the fundamental principle of human sociability. Of course, it was possible to argue that Pufendorfian morality was in a sense just as conventional as Hobbesian morality, in that it too had its ultimate origins in a pure act of will, albeit on God's part, rather than on the sovereign's. However, Pufendorf denied that the bindingness of God's commands lies simply in God's omnipotence. God made us sociable when he was under no obligation to do so, and this fact should inspire a gratitude manifesting itself in obedience. Locke followed Pufendorf's lead: morality, though not innate, is a science capable of demonstration, independently of any consideration of positive law. Ordinary moral agents may not be able to see the full extent of the rational system of morality, but they have the resources to reason their way, albeit fallibly, to certain moral conclusions, to sure knowledge of the laws they must obey. Our point of departure in our autonomous moral reasoning, Locke claimed, is our ideas of pleasure and pain. The conclusions we reach are conclusions about what will give us most pleasure and most pain – and what biblical revelation tells us about heaven and hell makes it clear that it is always in our interests to do as God commands. There was, again, scope here for worry about the ultimate arbitrariness of the moral laws that reason identifies as issuing from God's will. Locke was confident that God could be proved to be good as well as omnipotent, but he left it unclear how such a proof was supposed to proceed. As a result it seemed to the Cambridge clergyman Thomas Burnet that Locke 'resolve[d] all into the will and power of the law-maker'. '[H]as the will of a law-maker no rule to go by?', Burnet asked in a set of 'remarks' on Locke's *Essay* published anonymously in 1697. 'And is not that

which is a rule to His will a rule not also to ours, and indeed the original rule?'
(Burnet 1989: 25).

Burnet, a disciple of the Cambridge Platonists, held that there is 'a more
immutable distinction' between good and evil, virtue and vice, than Lockean
reason is able to provide. 'This I am sure of', he declared:

> that the distinction, suppose of gratitude and ingratitude, fidelity and infide-
> lity, justice and injustice and such others, is as sudden without any ratiocina-
> tion, and as sensible and piercing, as the difference I feel from the scent of a
> rose and assafoetida. 'Tis not like a theorem which we come to know by the
> help of precedent demonstrations and postulatums, but it rises as quick as
> any of our passions, or as laughter at the sight of a ridiculous accident or
> object.   (25)

In further sets of remarks on Locke, published in 1697 and in 1699, Burnet
pressed his case for the non-rational, or pre-rational, status of our awareness
of the distinction between right and wrong. This 'natural conscience' or
'inward sense' works, he claimed, independently of conceptions of 'natural
good and evil – pleasure or pain, conveniences or inconveniencies'. It does
not violate Locke's strictures against innate ideas and principles, no more
than does our pre-reflective awareness of the difference between tastes,
odours and sounds. And just as the natural 'gratefulness' or 'unwelcomeness'
of tastes, odours and sounds generate natural inclinations and aversions, so
also the moral sense should be recognised to be 'a spring and motive of our
actions' (25). There is no need to try to explain the actions prompted by the
moral sense in terms of hedonistic self-love. Nor is there a need to bring in
awareness of the requirements of law, natural or divine, as essential to the
definition of virtue. Burnet's view, in effect, was that Locke had conceded far
too much to Hobbes. Another kind of answer was possible.

SHAFTESBURY

This was the opinion also of another disciple of the Cambridge Platonists,
Anthony Ashley Cooper, third earl of Shaftesbury.[2] Shaftesbury believed that
Locke had made morality 'depend only on law and will'. According to
Locke's philosophy, therefore, 'neither right nor wrong, virtue nor vice are
any thing in themselves; nor is there any trace or idea of them naturally

[2] As Ernst Cassirer put it, Shaftesbury 'was able to penetrate [the Cambridge
Platonists'] scholastic exterior, and get at the moral and religious core of their
doctrine in its pure form' (Cassirer 1953: 161).

imprinted on human minds' (Shaftesbury 1716: 40–1). To Shaftesbury, as to Burnet, it appeared obvious that, on the contrary, human beings are indeed fitted with a natural sense of right and wrong. In 'An Inquiry concerning Virtue, or Merit', published as part of *Characteristicks of Men, Manners, Opinions, Times* in 1711,[3] Shaftesbury describes this sense as in the first instance an agent's inwardly-directed, 'reflected', awareness of the motives of her actions. It makes such affections as pity, kindness and gratitude 'the subject of a new liking', and it makes the contraries of those affections the subject of 'dislike' (Shaftesbury 2001, vol. 2: 16). This 'liking', Shaftesbury says, is a matter of awareness of merit, and of awareness of deserving praise. Thus the 'dislike' that one feels toward oneself when one voluntarily does harm to another 'cannot fail to create an apprehension and fear of like harm', an apprehension and fear that is a matter of knowing that one deserves to be punished. The natural sense of right and wrong, then, 'must consist in a real antipathy or aversion to injustice or wrong, and in a real affection or love towards equity and right, for its own sake, and on account of its own natural beauty and worth' (24–5). Shaftesbury rejected the egoism of Hobbes and Locke, and held that it is obvious that human nature comprises, in addition to love of self, affections that interest us in the good of others, indeed in the good of human kind as a whole. He calls these 'natural' affections. Moral goodness in an agent lies in the right balance between natural affections and 'self-affection'. But there is more to virtue than the state of one's affections. Virtue, as Shaftesbury puts it, is something other than 'mere goodness' (16). A being only counts as virtuous in so far as she is consciously and reflectively aware of her motives, and approves of what is good in them and disapproves of what is bad. Virtue, as distinct from goodness, consists in 'a certain just disposition, or proportionable affection of a rational creature towards the moral objects of right and wrong' (23).

Shaftesbury's principal concern in the 'Inquiry' is with the relation between virtue and religion. His question is whether virtue necessarily involves religious belief, or, 'whether it be a true saying, That it is impossible for an atheist to be virtuous, or share any real degree of honesty and merit' (4). Shaftesbury rejected outright the idea that there might be anything virtuous about living one's life in fear of punishment and hope of reward, even if the punishments and rewards were taken to be dispensed by God himself. No matter how perfectly such a person lived in accord with moral law, her goodness would be nothing but servility, no different in kind from

---

[3] An unauthorised edition of the 'Inquiry' had been published by John Toland in 1699.

'innocence and sobriety in a monkey under the discipline of the whip' (32). Locke's grounding of morality in divine punishment and reward was thus just as pernicious as Hobbes's grounding of morality in the will of the sovereign. The natural sense of right and wrong, according to Shaftesbury, functions independently of religious belief. It works just as well in an atheist as in the believer. Indeed, and following Bayle, Shaftesbury regarded 'corrupt religion, or superstition' as much more likely than atheism to damage the sense of right and wrong (27). In Book Two of the 'Inquiry' Shaftesbury completes his case against the need for a religious foundation for virtue with an argument intended to show that there is no reason to think, as many of his contemporaries did, that life in this world is for the virtuous person bound to be a life of self-dislike and self-denial. It is not the case that our affections or passions set us at odds with our sense of right and wrong. It is not the case that interest and duty are incompatible. To think so is to misunderstand the nature of happiness, which, according to Shaftesbury, is found in its purest and most satisfying form in the satisfaction of the natural, or 'publick', or 'social', affections. In the longest section of the whole 'Inquiry' Shaftesbury strives to make it apparent 'how much natural affection is predominant; how it is inwardly join'd to us, and implanted in our natures; how interwoven with our other passions; and how essential to that regular motion and course of our affections, on which our happiness and self-enjoyment so immediately depend' (80).[4]

It is important that this argument of Shaftesbury's be understood in the context of his larger case against Locke's way of joining morality with religion. The argument is a reply to the person who claims that there is no real happiness for the virtuous person except in the life to come. It is not meant as an answer to the moral sceptic who wants reasons why he should be virtuous rather than vicious. Shaftesbury took a great deal from the Stoics, including the thesis that virtue is a love of goodness considered in itself, not a love of goodness merely for the sake of the happiness that it brings. Virtue does bring happiness, in the here and now, but making this clear was not for Shaftesbury a way of arguing the reader into virtue. No such argument is needed provided that the sense of right and wrong is working properly. The sense of right and wrong is, as we have seen, characterized by Shaftesbury in terms of a love of goodness 'for its own sake, and on account of its own natural beauty and worth'. Virtue is very often described by Shaftesbury as a

---

[4] Shaftesbury does allow, however, that (natural) religion plays a significant role as an indirect support to virtue: see Shaftesbury 2001, vol. 2: 33–44.

kind of beauty, the beauty in question being that of the 'measure, arrangement, and disposition' of the several parts of human nature (16). The mind, Shaftesbury says, 'feels the soft and harsh, the agreeable and disagreeable, in the affections; and finds a foul and fair, a harmonious and a dissonant, as really and truly here, as in any musical numbers, or in the outward forms or representations of sensible things' (17). Shaftesbury's language is slippery here, but his view seems to be that moral beauty is an intrinsic property, an objectively existing feature of human beings. Shaftesbury certainly speaks elsewhere as if he regards the beauty of the universe as a whole as lying in the arrangement, proportion and harmony of its parts.[5] The moral sense as Shaftesbury understands it would seem to be the means whereby human beings perceive themselves as elements of that larger whole. Spelling out precisely the epistemology and metaphysics implicit in talk of a 'natural sense of right and wrong' is, however, not Shaftesbury's project in the 'Inquiry'. It is implied throughout that anyone not in the grip of false philosophy, or of false theology, will know exactly what he means.

HUTCHESON

In the 'Search into the Nature of Society' added to the 1723 edition of *The Fable of the Bees* Mandeville expressed scepticism about the existence in all human beings of a single and uniform sense of the nature of virtue and its difference from vice. Mandeville's complaint was, simply, that experience gives us no reason to believe that any such sense exists. Moral codes vary just as much as do codes of manners and customs – and just as much as do conceptions of beauty. 'Plurality of wives is odious among Christians . . .', Mandeville notes: 'But polygamy is not shocking to the Mahometan. What men have learned from their infancy enslaves them, and the force of custom warps nature, and at the same time imitates her in such a manner, that it is often difficult to know which of the two we are influenced by' (Mandeville 1988, vol. 1: 330). Hunting after what is beautiful and good in itself, the Stoic *pulchrum et honestum*, is 'not much better than a wild-goose-chase that is but little to be depended upon' (331). When it was published in 1725, Francis Hutcheson's first book, *An Inquiry into the Original of Our Ideas of Beauty and Virtue*, advertised itself on its title-page as intended to explain Shaftesbury's principles and to defend them against Mandeville. In later editions, though, there is

---

[5] See 'The Moralists' in Shaftesbury 2001, vol. 2; esp. Theocles' speech in Part II, Section IV (159–66).

no mention of an explanation and defence of Shaftesbury on the title-page, perhaps because Hutcheson had come to see that his answer to Mandeville's scepticism about a natural sense of right and wrong was significantly different from Shaftesbury's answer to Locke and Hobbes. Hutcheson's case for the naturalness of a sense of virtue involves an outright rejection of the idea that there is an important connection between virtue and rationality. His principal target is the view that moral judgments are – as Locke claims they are – judgments about what is in our long-term self-interest. But he is hostile also to there being a place for reflection of any kind in the definition of virtue. In the *Inquiry* it is argued that 'Instinct may be the spring of virtue.' 'I know not for what reason', Hutcheson says, 'some will not allow that to be virtue, which flows from instincts, or passions' (Hutcheson 2008: 133). He might well have had Shaftesbury's distinction between virtue and 'mere goodness' in mind as he wrote this. In the *Illustrations upon the Moral Sense*, published in 1728, he explicitly criticized Shaftesbury on just this score. 'Some alledge', he says, 'that merit supposes, beside kind affection, that the agent has a moral sense, reflects upon his own virtue, delights in it, and chuses to adhere to it for the pleasure which attends it'. A footnote directs the reader to 'Part One' – presumably Book One is meant – of Shaftesbury's 'Inquiry'. 'We need not debate the use of this word *merit*', Hutcheson continues: "tis plain, we approve a generous action, tho the agent had not made this reflection' (Hutcheson 2002: 186).[6]

Whereas Shaftesbury draws his account of the natural sense of right and wrong from the agent's introspective awareness of the motives on which she is disposed to act, Hutcheson concentrates upon a spectator's third-person judgment of the actions of others. What we approve in an agent, he claims, is benevolence, the doing of good to others. What we blame is malevolence, the doing of harm to others. Half of the 'Inquiry Concerning the Original of our Ideas of Virtue or Moral Good' (the second part of Hutcheson 2008) is taken up by Hutcheson's case for the naturalness of benevolence and against the claim, lately repeated by Mandeville, that all human actions are selfish. The other half of the 'Inquiry' is Hutcheson's argument for the existence of a moral sense, a sense by means of which we are given an immediate pleasure in the perception of benevolent actions, without any thought of how those actions might be to our own advantage. As for Thomas Burnet in his remarks on Locke, it is the immediacy of moral judgment that is crucial for Hutcheson. He pours scorn on the idea that praise and blame might need

---

[6] Hutcheson does allow, however, that such reflection 'is a great security to character'.

to wait upon judgments, sometimes necessarily very complex, about what is
and is not in our long-term interests.

> [M]ust a man have the reflection of Cumberland, or Puffendorf, to admire
> generosity, faith, humanity, gratitude? Or reason so nicely to apprehend the
> evil in cruelty, treachery, ingratitude? Do not the former excite our admira-
> tion, and love, and study of imitation, wherever we see them, almost at first
> view, without any such reflection; and the latter, our hatred, contempt and
> abhorrence? Unhappy would it be for mankind, if a sense of virtue was of as
> narrow an extent, as a capacity for such metaphysicks.
>
> (Hutcheson 2008: 94)

Hutcheson reminds the reader that it is a familiar fact of experience that we
make moral judgments about actions that have no possible bearing on our
own situation: we praise or condemn persons that we read about in history,
or who live in faraway regions of the world. It may be true that there is a way
of arguing from the fact that these actions contribute to the good of humankind as a whole to the conclusion that we do in fact benefit from them in
some small way. But that only goes to show that there is an explanation to be
given of why the moral sense operates as it does. It does not make it plausible
that an unconscious calculation as to one's own gain or loss must precede
such judgments.

Hutcheson was as concerned as Shaftesbury to emphasize that the sense of
morality has no direct connection with religious belief. '[M]any have high
notions of honour, faith, generosity, justice', he observes in the *Inquiry*, 'who
have scarce any opinions about the deity, or any thoughts of future rewards;
and abhor any thing, which is treacherous, cruel, or unjust, without any
regard to future punishments' (96).[7] This got him into trouble with those, like
John Clarke of Hull, who held that ordinary people needed belief in future
rewards and punishments if they were to remain committed to virtue even
once exposed to Hobbesian and Mandevillean scepticism (Clarke 1726: 41–
111). Others attacked Hutcheson on account of the way he disconnected the
moral sense from the faculty of reason. It was such criticism on the part of
Gilbert Burnet (chaplain to George I, and second son of the eponymous
historian and bishop of Salisbury) that caused Hutcheson to write *Illustrations
upon the Moral Sense* (Hutcheson 2002). In letters published in *The London
Journal* in 1725, Burnet argued that Hutcheson had elided the distinction
between moral good and evil considered in themselves, and the effect upon

---

[7] As with Shaftesbury, however, Hutcheson gives an important supporting role to
religious belief: see Harris 2008.

us of the perception of moral good and evil. Good and evil cannot be defined as what give us certain kinds of pleasure and pain, because that would entail that, if our moral sense worked differently, good and evil would be different as well. Hutcheson had failed, in other words, to find a way of answering Mandeville, a way of showing the reality of the distinction between moral good and evil. That could only be done if there were allowed to be something immutable in virtue of which Hutcheson's moral pleasures and pains can be said to be right or wrong, or appropriate and inappropriate, and, according to Burnet, such an immutable rule can only be provided by reason and its perception of the difference between truth and falsity. The pleasures and pains of the moral sense are, he urged, 'only the consequence of finding that we judge right, and according to reason': for '[t]hings do not seem to us to be true or right, because they are beautiful, or please us; but seem beautiful, or please us, because they seem to us to be true or right' (G. Burnet 1735: 12). Yes, the sense of beauty or pleasure often rushes ahead of the perception of truth or right, but it is also true that often, on reflection, we find our sense of beauty or pleasure to be mistaken, just as we sometimes find, on reflection, our other senses to be mistaken.

This line of argument did not discomfort Hutcheson. His response was to claim that it was Burnet who had failed to show the real difference between virtue and vice. When the question of why we judge as we do in moral matters is pushed as far as it can be pushed, we are bound to end up saying, if we are to say anything at all, simply that it pleases us that one course of action is chosen and not its contrary. Thus, as Hutcheson puts it in the *Illustrations*, 'Justifying reasons presuppose a moral sense' (Hutcheson 2002: 145). We approve of actions that tend to the public good. Why? Because, we might say, that is what God wants of us. Why is it good to do what God wants of us? Because, we might say, God is our benefactor. Why is it good to concur with the will of a benefactor? 'Here', Hutcheson claims, 'we must recur to a sense' (ibid.). We might alternatively say that we approve of actions that tend to the public good because it is best that all be happy. But what does 'best' mean here? Either we say in reply 'best' means 'morally best', and so get caught up in a circle; or we say that what is best about the state where all are happy is that it is the most happy state. If we take the latter option, Hutcheson says, we then face the question 'most happy for whom? for the individual, or for the system as a whole?' To say that it is assurance of the happiness of each and every individual that makes a state most happy is to explain moral approval in terms of what furthers private happiness, not in terms of intrinsic rightness. To say that it is the happiness of the system as a whole that makes a state most happy is to be faced with the further question of why the happiness of the system as a whole should be taken as a moral good, and, here again, Hutcheson claims, 'we must recur to a sense or kind affection' (145–6).

In the *Illustrations* Hutcheson engages not only with Burnet, but also with other rationalists, or 'intellectualists', including John Balguy, Samuel Clarke and William Wollaston. At no point does he concede that describing the moral faculty as a sense entails giving up on a real distinction between virtue and vice. He was as committed as Shaftesbury to the project of recovering the Stoic notion of the good in itself in the face of the claim that the difference between moral good and evil is a matter of artifice and convention. Once Hutcheson moved in 1729 from Dublin to take up the chair of moral philosophy at Glasgow, he was fighting also on another front, against the extreme voluntarism of traditionally-minded Scottish Calvinist theologians. Like Shaftesbury, Hutcheson understands the goodness of the world God has created to be a matter of the way parts fit together to make a larger organized whole. However, the overall system is characterized by Hutcheson not, as with Shaftesbury, in terms of its intrinsic beauty, but rather in terms of the way it maximizes happiness. The manifest goodness of the universe, and the goodness of the God who created the universe and sustains it in existence, is a major theme of Hutcheson's final work, the posthumously published *System of Moral Philosophy*.[8] In the *System* the moral sense is shown to be an essential means to the realization of God's providential purpose. 'Without a distinct consideration of this moral faculty', Hutcheson argues, 'a species endued with such a variety of senses, and of desires frequently interfering, must appear a complex confused fabrick, without any order or regular consistent design. By means of it, all is capable of harmony, and all its powers may conspire on one direction, and be consistent with each other' (Hutcheson 1755, vol. 1: 74). The reliability and authority of the moral sense is evidenced by the fact that it points the way to order and harmony and happiness, both in the soul and in social and political relations between human beings.

SENTIMENTALISM AFTER HUTCHESON

Large claims have been made for Hutcheson's influence on subsequent moral philosophy in Britain. He has been said to be 'the father of the Scottish Enlightenment'.[9] His biographer claims that he was a 'leader of the Enlightenment' in Britain more generally.[10] Certainly his case against

[8] See Moore 2000.   [9] See Campbell 1982.   [10] See Scott 1900, ch. 13.

rationalism persuaded Hume, who, in the section of the *Treatise* entitled 'Moral distinctions not deriv'd from reason', did little more than summarize arguments that Hutcheson had already made. In *The Theory of Moral Sentiments* Smith did not think it necessary to rehearse the reasons for adopting the sentimentalist approach to morals. Yet neither Hume nor Smith recognized the existence of a Hutchesonian moral sense. Both looked instead to sympathy as the source of moral judgment, arguing that to do so was to have a more direct way of vindicating the moral faculty than Hutcheson was able to provide. A sympathy theory, in other words, did not need the support of the scheme of divine providence. The faculty of sympathy could show itself to be worthy of approval in the way that the moral sense could not. 'Those who resolve the sense of morals into original instincts of human nature, may defend the cause of virtue with sufficient authority', Hume remarked in the 'Conclusion' of Book Three of the *Treatise*; 'but want the advantage, which those possess, who account for that sense by an extensive sympathy with mankind. According to their system, not only virtue must be approv'd of, but also the sense of virtue: And not only that sense, but also the principles, from which it is deriv'd' (Hume 1978: 470). Smith made the same point in explicit criticism of Hutcheson. It is a major failing, according to Smith, that the supposed moral sense is, as Hutcheson concedes it is, unable to approve of itself. On the sympathy theory, this fact can be accommodated and explained (see Smith 1982: 321–7).

What Hume says follows from Hutcheson's critique of rationalism, that '[m]orality . . . is more properly felt than judg'd of' (Hume 1978: 470) should not, therefore, be taken as a straightforward endorsement of Hutcheson's postulation of a moral sense. Hume was sceptical also about the extent to which human nature could by itself, without need for supplementation by reflection and invention, explain every instance of the distinction between virtue and vice. He argued that less of morality was natural, in the sense of being original and prior to education and socialization, than Hutcheson had been prepared to acknowledge. Hutcheson was squarely in Hume's sights when he declared that 'nothing can be more unphilosophical than those systems, which assert, that virtue is the same with what is natural, and vice with what is unnatural' (475) – and so was Shaftesbury. Sentimentalists in England also questioned the explanatory need for a special moral sense. Thus John Gay, in the 'Preliminary Dissertation Concerning the Fundamental Principle of Virtue or Morality' prefixed to Edmund Law's 1731 translation of William King's *De origine mali*, rejected Hutcheson's theory as an instance of 'rather cutting the knot than untying it'. The origin of our ideas of morality could be explained without the need of (what Gay regarded as) a mysterious sixth sense. The ultimate ground of moral approval is rational self-love, but the reason why particular actions are approved of is often obscured by habitual reflexes of approval and disapproval that are the work of the association of ideas (Gay 1731: esp. pp. xiii–xv, xxx–xxxiii). Gay was a key influence on David Hartley, and Hartley in turn was a key influence on Bentham.[11] A full history of what Selby-Bigge characterized as 'sentimentalist' moral thought in Britain would show that the idea of a special moral sense was in fact of limited significance and influence. Selby-Bigge's other 'principal text of the sentimentalist school', Joseph Butler, had more impact on later developments than did either Shaftesbury or Hutcheson. But that is another story, told in another chapter of this volume.

BIBLIOGRAPHY

An asterisk denotes secondary literature especially suitable for further reading.

Burnet, Gilbert 1735. *Letters Between the Late Mr. Gilbert Burnet and Mr. Hutchinson [sic] Concerning the True Foundation of Moral Goodness.* London.

Burnet, Thomas 1989. *Remarks on John Locke.* Ed. George Watson. Doncaster: Brynmill Press.

Campbell, T.D. 1982. 'Francis Hutcheson: "Father" of the Scottish Enlightenment', in R.H. Campbell and Andrew S. Skinner (eds.), *The Origins and Nature of the Scottish Enlightenment.* Edinburgh: John Donald, pp. 167–85.

Cassirer, Ernst 1953. *The Platonic Renaissance in England.* Trans. James P. Pettegrove. Edinburgh: Nelson.

Clarke, John [1726]. *The Foundation of Morality in Theory and Practice Considered.* York.

Darwall, Stephen 1995. *The British Moralists and the Internal 'Ought': 1640–1740.* Cambridge University Press.*

Gay, John 1731. 'Preliminary Dissertation Concerning the Fundamental Principle of Virtue or Morality', in William King, *An Essay on the Origin of Evil*, trans. Edmund Law. London, pp. xi–xxxiii.

Gill, Michael B. 2006. *The British Moralists on Human Nature and the Birth of Secular Ethics.* Cambridge University Press.*

Halévy, Elie 1934. *The Growth of Philosophic Radicalism.* Trans. Mary Morris. London: Faber.

Harris, James A. 2008. 'Religion in Hutcheson's Moral Philosophy', *Journal of the History of Philosophy* 46: 205–22.

Hume, David 1978. *A Treatise of Human Nature*, ed. L.A. Selby-Bigge, rev. P.H. Nidditch. Oxford: Clarendon Press.

[11] See Halévy 1934: 6–9.

Hutcheson, Francis 1755. *A System of Moral Philosophy*. Glasgow and London. 2 vols.

Hutcheson, Francis 2002. *An Essay on the Nature and Conduct of the Passions and Affections, with Illustrations on the Moral Sense*, ed. Aaron Garrett. Indianapolis, IN: Liberty Fund.

Hutcheson, Francis 2008. *An Inquiry into the Original of Our Ideas of Beauty and Virtue*, ed. W. Leidhold. Revised edn. Indianapolis, IN: Liberty Fund.

Mandeville, Bernard 1988. *The Fable of the Bees: or, Private Vices, Publick Benefits*, ed. F.B. Kaye. Indianapolis, IN: Liberty Fund. 2 vols.

Moore, James 2000. 'Hutcheson's Theodicy: The Argument and the Contexts of A System of Moral Philosophy', in Paul Wood (ed.), *The Scottish Enlightenment: Essays in Reinterpretation*. University of Rochester Press, pp. 239–66.

Scott, William Robert 1900. *Francis Hutcheson: His Life, Teaching and Position in the History of Philosophy*. Cambridge University Press.

Selby-Bigge, L.A. (ed.) 1897. *British Moralists: Being Selections from Writers Principally of the Eighteenth Century*. Oxford: Clarendon Press. 2 vols.

[Shaftesbury, Anthony Ashley Cooper, third earl of] 1716. *Several Letters Written by a Noble Lord to a Young Man at the University*. London.

Shaftesbury, Anthony Ashley Cooper, third earl of 2001. *Characteristicks of Men, Manners, Opinions, Times*, ed. Douglas Den Uyl. Indianapolis, IN: Liberty Fund. 3 vols.

Smith, Adam 1982. *The Theory of Moral Sentiments*, ed. D.D. Raphael and A.L. Macfie. Indianapolis, IN: Liberty Fund.

Yaffe, Gideon 2002. 'Earl of Shaftesbury', in Steven Nadler (ed.), *A Companion to Early Modern Philosophy*. Malden, MA: Wiley-Blackwell, pp. 425–36.*

26

Hume

PAUL GUYER

HUME'S SCIENCE OF MAN AND THE AIMS OF MORAL PHILOSOPHY

Hume's moral philosophy, like his theoretical philosophy, was originally conceived as part of a comprehensive "science of MAN," a thorough acquaintance "with the extent and force of human understanding, . . . the nature of the ideas we employ, and of the operations we perform in our reasonings," which can itself be solidly founded only "on experience and observation." In Hume's view, even *Mathematics, Natural Philosophy, and Natural Religion*" must be grounded on the science of man, and all the more obviously so must "the other sciences, whose connexion with human nature is more close and intimate," including "*Logic, Morals, Criticism,* and *Politics.*" Thus, "The sole end of logic is to explain the principles and operations of our reasoning faculty, and the nature of our ideas: Morals and criticism regard our tastes and sentiments: And politics considers men as united in society, and dependent on each other."[1] The over-arching argument of Hume's "science of man" is then that principles that have traditionally been assumed to be founded in reason, such as the principle that every event has a cause, but also the principles of morals and politics, are not founded on reason at all, but on "sentiments," feelings produced from experience through the mechanisms of custom and imagination.

---

[1] Hume, *A Treatise of Human Nature* (2007b). The text of Hume's *Treatise* is contained in vol. 1 of this edition, while vol. 2 contains only editorial material, so the volume number 1 will be omitted from citations to it. The present quotations come from the Introduction, paragraphs 4, 5, and 7, p. 4. Quotations from the body of the work, to be abbreviated as "*T*," will be given by Book, Part, section, and paragraph number, followed by page number.

Norman Kemp Smith went so far as to argue that Hume's development of his sentimentalist account of moral principles was the motivation for his development of his whole "science of MAN" and thus of his application of his sentimentalist method to theoretical principles too.[2] But there is a crucial difference between Hume's application of his method to "logic" in the first Book of the *Treatise* and to "morals" in the second and third Books of the *Treatise* as well as in his subsequent popularization of those books in his 1751 *Enquiry Concerning the Principles of Morals*.[3] This is that, while Hume's application of his method to theoretical principles such as the principles of causality is supposed to leave our practices untouched (*T*, 1.4.7.9, p. 175), the realization that the most fundamental principles of morality are founded on no authority other than our own natural sentiments of approbation of actions and characters that are agreeable and useful to self and others and disapprobation of their opposites is clearly intended to undermine the grip of, on the one hand, a Hobbesian ethics of self-interest but also, on the other, of "the whole train of monkish virtues" – "Celibacy, fasting, penance, mortification, self-denial, humility, silence, solitude" – which cannot be founded on the natural sentiments of human beings but only on "the delusive glosses of superstition and false religion" (Hume, *EPM*, 9.1.3, p. 73).[4] The natural sentiments of mankind can only approve of qualities that are agreeable and useful to their owners and to the others affected by those owners or, most often, to both (Hume, *EPM*, 9.1.6, p. 75). This implication of Hume's science of man was not hidden from his contemporaries, so it is no wonder that Hume's application for the Edinburgh chair in moral philosophy after the publication of the *Treatise* and his later application for a similar chair at Glasgow were rebuffed by the Presbyterian ministers and town councils who controlled the universities.[5]

---

[2] See Smith 1941.

[3] Hume, *An Enquiry Concerning the Principles of Morals* (1998). Citations from this work will be located by the abbreviation *"EPM"* followed by section or appendix number, section part number when there is one, paragraph number, and page number. *An Enquiry Concerning Human Understanding* (2000; *"EHU"*) will be cited in the same way.

[4] Hume foregrounds the classification of the virtues into those that are agreeable or useful to self or others in the *Enquiry* (Sections 2 and 5 through 8), but this formulation is already present in the *Treatise* as well (3.3.1.27–30, pp. 376–7).

[5] For these episodes, see Ernest Campbell Mossner 1954: 153–62 and 240–56. That Hume's "catalogue of virtues" is revisionary, "a young rebel's attempt to topple a puritan establishment," has been particularly stressed by Baier 1991, especially ch. 9 (the quotation is from p. 203).

"MORAL DISTINCTIONS NOT DERIV'D FROM REASON" BUT FROM "A MORAL SENSE"

Hume put forward his moral theory in Book III of *A Treatise of Human Nature* (1739–40). Here he first presented what we would call his meta-ethics, and then the normative ethics grounded upon that theory. The key to Hume's meta-ethics is his conception of reason combined with the empiricism he inherited from John Locke. The central idea of such empiricism is what is called Hume's "copy principle," the assumption that the contents of the mind are only original "impressions" of external or internal states and "ideas" which are copies of such impressions; such ideas can be considered in isolation from the original contexts of the corresponding impressions and combined in ways not originally experienced, but cannot be created *ab novo* except perhaps in fringe cases like the "missing shade of blue," where Hume allows that the mind might be able to create an idea that fills in a gap in an otherwise consistent series of previously experienced impressions.[6] Hume's view of reason is that it is confined to the recognition of identities and differences among ideas, or to the recognition of *"philosophical* relations" among ideas such as their resemblance, identity, spatial contiguity and temporal succession, quantity, and contrariety (*T*, 1.1.5.1–9, pp. 14–15), but that knowledge of any further relations of ideas, their "natural" relations, depends on experience rather than mere reason. The most obvious natural relation is causation (*T*, 1.3.2.4, p. 53); existence might seem to be another natural relation, although since Hume equates judgments of the existence of (external) objects corresponding to our ideas with judgments that our ideas have been caused by such objects, he does not need to treat existence separately (see especially Hume, *EHU*, 4.1.4, p. 25). In the 1748 *Enquiry Concerning Human Understanding*, Hume replaces his distinction between philosophical and natural relations with one between "relations of ideas" and "matters of fact" (*EHU*, 4.1.1, p. 24), but the essence of the view remains the same: in the terms that Kant would subsequently use, reason can deliver only analytic judgments, while synthetic judgments – any judgment that an idea corresponds to an extant object, or that one state of an object has caused or will cause another – can come only from experience. On the basis of these assumptions, Hume then constructs his diagnosis of the non-rational character of our causal inferences. First, since our impressions of external objects

---

[6] For the "copy principle" generally, see *T*, 1.1.1.1–5, pp. 7–8; for the missing shade of blue, see *T*, 1.1.1.10, pp. 9–10.

include those of their succession and contiguity but contain no impression of necessity from which we could copy an idea of necessity, reason cannot ground any causal inferences of the form "Condition C must be followed by condition E" on any idea of necessity included in the complex idea of the relevant object (T, 1.3.2.12, p. 55). So it could resort only to "custom" or experience; but since experience consists only of a finite number of *past* impressions, it could not license any inference as to what must follow what in the *future* except on the basis of the assumption that the future must resemble the past. However, *that* assumption cannot be warranted by reason alone – its contradiction is not self-contradictory or a denial of any other "philosophical" relation – nor by experience, since that would be circular: without that premise, experience can only prove that *in the past* the future has resembled the past (T, 1.3.6.4–11, pp. 62–4; *EHU*, 4.2.16–21, pp. 30–2). So, Hume concludes, the basis for our causal inferences, which are the entire foundation of our knowledge of the external world and of human behavior as well, is nothing more than the tendency of the mind to form *vivid* ideas on the basis of past experience (T, 1.3.7.5, p. 67; *EHU*, 5.1.8, p. 39; 5.2.11–13, pp. 40–1). Of course, Hume's story about causal inference is itself a story about how the mind is *caused* to form beliefs, and depends upon the assumption that the *mind* will work in the future much as it has in the past; for this reason, Hume calls his account a "sceptical solution" to his "sceptical doubts" about causation. But none of this is meant to imply that our practice of causal belief is *irrational* in the everyday sense of being *unreasonable*; on the contrary, Hume holds that it would be unreasonable of us to try to *change* this practice: "I must yield to the current of nature, in submitting to my senses and understanding" (T, 1.4.7.10, p. 175).

Hume's argument that moral principles are derived not from reason but from a moral sense is similarly supposed to be an argument that such principles cannot be derived from any mere analysis of ideas and their philosophical relations but only from the operations of feeling, in this case our natural feelings of approbation and disapprobation to actions seen as signs of various human characters. Or, as Hume says in the 1751 *Enquiry Concerning the Principles of Morals*, the foundation of morals can be nothing other than a "sentiment," namely "a feeling for the happiness of mankind, and a resentment of their misery" (*EPM*, Appendix 1.4, p. 84). Hume means his position to contrast to those moral rationalists "who affirm that virtue is nothing but a conformity to reason; that there are eternal fitnesses and unfitnesses of things, which are the same to every rational being that considers them; that the immutable measures of right and wrong impose ... obligation," and that such fitnesses and unfitnesses, hence such obligations, are "discern'd merely by ideas" (*T*, 3.1.1.4, p. 294). Hume attacks specific versions of this view due to such rationalists as Samuel Clarke and William Wollaston, but beyond them stands the larger figure of the dean of the late seventeenth-century Cambridge Platonists, Ralph Cudworth, whose *Treatise Concerning Eternal and Immutable Morality* was posthumously published in 1731, thus just at the start of the decade in which Hume wrote the *Treatise*.[7] Hume's argument is that the principles of "morals" must "have an influence on the actions and affections," or "produce or prevent actions," but that "reason alone," confined as it is to the recognition of philosophical relations, "is utterly impotent in this particular," or "can never have any such influence" on our actions and affections; thus the principles of morals must instead be grounded on naturally occurring "passions," sentiments that are self-evidently capable of moving us to actions. Hume allows that reason has a subsidiary role in determining us to action in conjunction with appropriate sentiments, for it is reason that must inform us whether the "proper object" of our passion actually exists, that is, whether the situation that calls for an action by arousing a passion is the situation we think it is, and whether the "connexion of causes and effects" obtains that would "afford us a means of exerting any passion," or allow us to act effectively as passion directs (*T*, 3.1.1.12, p. 295). But even in this extended sense of reason, which now includes the ability to make existential judgments and causal inferences that had previously been attributed to experience, reason alone still does not *inspire* action.[8] That, Hume contends, can be done only by passion or sentiment.

Hume does not attempt to argue for the premise that morality must have an influence on action; that must seem too obvious to him to need an argument. He does attempt to buttress his claim that reason alone cannot move us to action. In Book II of the *Treatise*, he argues that it is "the prospect of pain or pleasure from any object" that moves us to action by disposing us "to avoid or embrace what will give us this uneasiness or satisfaction," and then that reason, even construed broadly to include our capacity to discover

---

[7] Cudworth 1996.

[8] Hume is often represented as holding that action is motivated entirely by desire, with reason involved only in determining the means to the ends set by desire. Rachel Cohon has argued that on Hume's account action is actually motivated by belief about desire and the means to fulfilling it; see Cohon 2008, chs. 2–3. But then without the occurrence of desire, the relevant belief will not be formed; belief alone does not generate desire.

causal connections, can discover what objects might promise us pleasure or pain, but is not what *makes* them pleasurable or painful; that can be only our natural constitution to respond to certain things with pleasure and others with pain. It is in this context that Hume makes his famous statement that "Reason is, and ought only to be the slave of the passions, and can never pretend to any other office than to serve and obey them" (*T*, 2.3.3.3–4, p. 266), meaning by this bit of hyperbole that reasoning broadly construed can tell us *how* to obtain pleasure and avoid pain but not *that* we should – only the experience of our own sentiments can do that. (The "ought only" must mean simply that it is a waste of effort to try to get a faculty to do something that it cannot do.)

In Book III of the *Treatise*, Hume adds arguments that the kinds of relations that are recognized by reason are not capable of moving us to action. These arguments, which are in fact taken over from Francis Hutcheson's 1728 *Illustrations upon the Moral Sense*, along indeed with the more general position that "*Instincts*" determine "us to desire *Ends*, without supposing any previous *Reasoning*," and that the "use of our *Reason*" is merely to "find out the Means of obtaining our *Ends*,"[9] are directed against the views of Clarke and Wollaston. Wollaston, who held that what is wrong with an immoral act is that it is a lie or conveys a falsehood, is easily dispensed with: to be sure, reason is the faculty for discerning truth, and may even be allowed its own interest in discerning and disseminating truth; but if all that were wrong with an immoral act is that it conveys a falsehood, then I could avoid conveying any falsehood while indulging "myself in … liberties with my neighbour's wife," for example the falsehood that she is my wife, simply by taking "the precaution of shutting the windows" (*T*, 3.1.1.16, note, p. 297). Yet of course, Hume reasonably supposes, we would *feel aversion* to this action even if, or all the more so if, truthfully informed about it. More generally, "this whimsical system … leaves us under the same difficulty to give a reason why truth is virtuous and falsehood vicious, as to account for the merit or turpitude of any other action" (ibid.): even if we could reduce all vice to untruthfulness, we would still need to posit a foundational approbation of truthfulness and

---

[9] Hutcheson 2002, Section I, p. 148. Hutcheson's argument against Wollaston is found in Section III of this work, "Mr. Woolaston's Significancy of Truth, as the Idea of Virtue considered," and his argument against Clarke and other "fitness" theorists in Section II, "Concerning that Character of Virtue and Vice, The Fitness or Unfitness of Actions." Could it be that Hume's unacknowledged debt to Hutcheson was at least part of the cause of the latter's coolness to Hume's attempts to secure a professorship of morals?

disapprobation of untruthfulness that comes from sentiment rather than reason.

Hume's argument against Clarke's view that morality is grounded in certain eternal relations of fitness and unfitness which are just the sort of thing that reason alone can discern is not quite so witty but is still quite pointed. He argues that if, for example, what were wrong with parricide were just that it is the relation of an offspring killing its own progenitor, then we should find a sapling "which at last overtops and destroys the parent tree" just as "horrid and unnatural" as a case of human parricide – but obviously we do not. Yet the relations of parenthood and killing, which are all that reason is concerned with, are precisely the same in both cases, so the moral "characters" of the two actions must not be "discover'd merely by reason" (*T*, 3.1.1.24, p. 300): rather, we *feel* differently about human parricide from how we feel about arboreal parricide. To the objection that the relations are not the same, that the action of the human parricide is intentional and voluntary while that of the sapling is not, Hume initially makes the feeble reply that "the same relations" may "have different causes; but still the relations are the same" (ibid.); but his deeper response is that relations among objects alone, even that of action to voluntary intention, do not constitute virtue and vice, and that you can never find what is wrong in an action or character "till you turn your reflection into your own breast, and find a sentiment of disapprobation, which arises in you, toward this action" or character, and likewise in the case of one that is right (*T*, 3.1.1.26, p. 301). Hume initially describes his result by saying that "morality consists not in any relations, that are the objects of science," nor "in any *matter of fact*, which can be discover'd by the understanding," but he quickly revises this to say that "Here is a matter of fact; but 'tis the object of feeling, not of reason" (ibid.). Morality is grounded in facts, but in facts about what feelings of approbation and disapprobation we have, not in any other kind of facts. This is the meaning of Hume's famous statement that "In every system of morality, which I have hitherto met with," there has been an imperceptible and unexplained slide from "*is*, and *is not*" to "*ought*, or *ought not*" (*T*, 3.1.2.27, p. 302): Hume's position is not that "ought" can never be derived from "is," but that it must be derived from the *right kind* of "is," namely a claim about human feelings of approbation and disapprobation and not any claim about abstract relations that does not mention human feelings.

Having argued that our moral principles are not grounded in reason, Hume nevertheless offers an explanation of why the opposite has been so widely assumed. His explanation is that reason operates with "calmness and tranquillity"; that the sentiments on which our moral principles do rest, "benevolence ..., the love of life, and kindness to children; or the general appetite to good," indeed even "resentment" at unwarranted injuries, also operate with calmness and tranquility, or are calm rather than violent passions; so we tend to mistake these sentiments for "determinations of reason" that "proceed from the very same faculty . . . which judges of truth and falsehood" (*T*, 2.3.3.8, p. 268). But they do not. However, as we turn from Hume's meta-ethics to his normative ethics, we will see that his interest in calmness and tranquility goes deeper than just explaining this error about reason; in fact, calmness and tranquility rank very high on Hume's list of virtues, thus what Hume takes to be the normal human sentiment in favor of calmness and tranquility is itself one of the sentiments grounding our moral principles.

It may certainly be debated whether Hume's meta-ethics rests on too narrow a conception of reason, as merely the ability to discern truth and falsehood and other abstract relations. Kant, for example, conceives of reason as our ability to *universalize*, and argues in his *Groundwork for the Metaphysics of Morals* that the fundamental principle of morality is nothing more than the requirement to universalize our proposed maxims for action, to act only on maxims that we would be willing to have everyone act upon. But even Kant seems compelled to posit an *interest* in reason, or in being reasonable, to explain why we feel obliged by this fundamental principle, and it is at least not obvious that this interest is anything more than a natural aversion of healthy and mature human beings to making an exception of themselves or allowing themselves liberties they are not prepared to concede to others. It is not obvious that Hume's sentimentalist position is immediately undermined by a more Kantian conception of reason and its powers.

HUME'S NORMATIVE ETHICS: THE NATURAL VIRTUES

Now let us turn from Hume's meta-ethics to his normative ethics, or catalogue of virtues, for it is here that the revisionist and rebellious character of Hume's moral philosophy becomes obvious.

Hume divides the virtues into "natural" and "artificial" ones. The former are qualities of mind or character that are "naturally fitted to be useful to others, or to the person himself, or which [are] agreeable to others, or to the person himself" (*T*, 3.3.1.30, p. 377). The latter, which can be summed up as the virtue of justice, are patterns of action and sentiments associated with them that make sense and earn our approval only given certain social practices and institutions. The distinction between natural and artificial is misleading, however, because it is entirely natural for human beings to develop the institutions and sentiments of justice: although institutions and laws of property as well as approbation of behavior that supports such institutions and disapprobation of behavior that damages them do not exist in a state of raw nature, they naturally develop in any human society, indeed they inevitably develop within and from an institution that is essential to any human existence at all, the family.[10] Moreover, although in both the *Treatise* and the *Enquiry Concerning the Principles of Morals* Hume expounds the artificial virtue of justice before expounding the natural virtues, justice can be understood as a virtue that is useful to both self and others, and that because of that becomes agreeable to both self and others. So Hume's approach to the virtues can be best understood if we reverse his order of exposition and begin with the natural virtues. And it is by means of his account of the natural virtues that Hume rejects the "monkish virtues" of contemporary Christianity.

Hume's quadripartite division of the natural virtues into those agreeable or useful to oneself or others can also be misleading, for the same virtues can often fit under several of Hume's pigeon-holes. We can see the problem if we begin with Hume's lists of the natural virtues. In the *Enquiry*, he begins with qualities useful to oneself; these include discretion, industry, frugality, strength of mind, and a good memory (*EPM*, 6.1.8–19, pp. 49–52); these can clearly make one useful to others as well. The qualities "immediately agreeable to ourselves" include cheerfulness, "spirit and dignity of character, or a proper sense of what is due to oneself," courage, and above all "that undisturbed philosophical TRANQUILLITY, superior to pain, sorrow, anxiety, and each assault of adverse fortune" (*EPM*, 7.1–16, pp. 59–63), which allows one to be content no matter what fortune brings one's way. The last is of course a Stoic virtue – Hume explicitly invokes Epictetus in his exposition of it – and represents a definite alternative to a Christian conception that the misfortunes of this life can be made good by bliss in the next; for Hume the necessary condition of happiness is calm in the face of the misfortunes of this life alone.[11] Qualities "immediately agreeable to others" include "good manners or politeness," "wit and ingenuity," "modesty and self-diffidence" that at

---

[10] On the difficulty of Hume's distinction between natural and artificial virtues, see among others Whelan 1985, ch. 4.

[11] For a similar emphasis on the importance of moderation to Hume, Jones 1982: 149–60.

the same time do not exclude "a noble pride and spirit," and "decency and cleanliness" (*EPM*, 8.1–12, pp. 67–70), while qualities useful to others may be summed up under the (Hutchesonian) term "benevolence," which includes "beneficence and humanity, friendship and gratitude, natural affection and public spirit, or whatever proceeds from a tender sympathy with others, and a generous concern for our kind and species" (*EPM*, 2.1.5, p. 9). Of course being agreeable and/or useful to others can also be agreeable and/or useful to oneself.

But this overlap of natural virtues is not an objection to Hume. On the contrary, his picture of what makes life agreeable and what virtues make it possible to live an agreeable life is thus both individual and social: tranquility will make contentment possible even in isolation, but throughout life much of our joy comes from sharing our happiness with others and sharing their happiness ourselves.

HUME'S NORMATIVE VIRTUES: THE ARTIFICIAL VIRTUE OF JUSTICE

The key point here is that justice is a virtue that is useful to both ourselves and others, and thus it fits into Hume's division of the natural virtues once we realize that the boundary between utility to ourselves and others is not strict. It is also part of Hume's account that once we come to recognize the utility of justice, we tend to develop feelings of approbation toward compliance with its demands, and thus the boundary between what is merely useful and what is immediately agreeable also tends to become blurred. Before we further consider Hume's account of justice, however, there is another point that needs to be made. In his account of the natural virtues, Hume argues that we respond to any particular action "only as a sign of some quality or character," because particular actions "not proceeding from any constant principle, have no influence on love or hatred, pride or humility; and consequently are never consider'd in morality" (*T*, 3.3.1.4, p. 367). That is, we ordinarily do not and should not judge ourselves or others on the basis of isolated actions, for they might be accidents that do not reveal a person's real character. But Hume's position cannot be that our interest in actions is always merely epistemic, that we are interested in actions merely as signs of character, thus that our substantive interest is an interest in character for its own sake rather than in actions and their consequences. Rather, we approve of the character-trait of benevolence because it tends to yield actions that ameliorate the condition of others, and even more obviously we approve of a strong sense of justice because it tends to yield useful actions, even if in particular cases, such as the repayment of a debt to a rich man when there is a poor man who could use the money more, the action is not useful considered in isolation but only considered as promoting a pattern of action that is generally useful. For example, "When I relieve persons in distress, my natural humanity is my motive," and my beneficent action is helpful and approved of in the absence of any special practices or institutions, but when I repay a debt to a rich man who does not need the money, although my action is not immediately useful to him, we nevertheless approve of it because the practice of making and repaying loans is generally useful. The action and the approval of it would indeed be unnatural in the absence of the general practice, and it is to that extent "artificial," but, as previously suggested, it is entirely natural for human beings to evolve such practices and feelings of approbation toward actions that maintain them.

Hume's account of justice is thus an account of the utility of this virtue in society, its natural evolution, and the natural evolution of appropriate sentiments of approbation and disapprobation along with the former. Hume illustrates his account with the simple example of two people rowing a boat: it does not take much for each to realize that the boat will go faster if they coordinate their efforts than if they do not, so without any "promises to each other" or any other antecedent pact, "Two men, who pull the oars of a boat," form "an agreement or convention" to coordinate their efforts (T, 3.2.2.10, p. 315), each expecting that the other will do his part out of his own recognition of the benefits of so doing to himself but also, through the natural mechanism of sympathy, to the other – there is no reason why the artificial virtue of justice would have to be constructed on the basis of self-interest alone. People will naturally come to similar recognitions about the exchange of labor and of goods: If "Your corn is ripe to-day" and "mine will be so tomorrow," we can both realize that "'Tis profitable for us both, that I shou'd labour with you to-day, and that you shou'd aid me tomorrow" (T, 3.2.5.8, p. 334); and if we have each some claim to private property, then "it will be for my interest to leave another in the possession of his goods, *provided* he will act in the same manner to me" (T, 3.2.2.10, p. 315). Labor contracts and private property do not exist in a state of raw nature, but it is not hard for human beings to see the benefits of establishing such institutions and acting in ways to maintain them, even in particular cases, such as the repayment of a debt to a rich man, where there is nothing else to be said in favor of the relevant performance.

The origin of the institutions of justice and of conformity to the practices that support them does not seem like much of a puzzle for Hume; for him, the bigger puzzle is how we come to invest conformity to or violation of these practices with the same sorts of feelings of approbation and disapprobation that we have toward natural virtues and vices. He answers this puzzle with a little story about the family, the most natural of human institutions. Sheer "natural appetite betwixt the sexes" attracts a man and a woman to each other, but when children follow from sex, as they often do, "a new tye takes place" between the man and the woman "in their concern for their common offspring," and they naturally take on certain obligations toward those children and toward each other with regard to those children, and naturally invest the fulfillment of those obligations with feelings of approbation and their violation with disapprobation. The children, in turn, are naturally equipped with feelings of affection toward their parents and toward each other, but at the same time compete with each other for limited resources, and naturally, with the natural help of their parents, introduce some rules for avoiding conflict. "In a little time, custom and habit operating on the tender minds of the children, makes them sensible of the advantages, which they may reap from society, as well as fashions them by degrees for it, by rubbing off those rough corners and untoward affections, which prevent their coalition" (T, 3.2.2.4, p. 312). But since the children naturally have some affection toward each other, they naturally also feel approbation toward the welfare of their siblings, not just toward their own, and so observance of rules of justice that are naturally worked out within the family is also invested with the moral sentiments. Then, Hume argues, people come to see the benefits of extending their practices of justice toward the larger society beyond the family, and the moral sentiments naturally follow.

It is certainly less than clear that the little drama Hume describes has to re-enact itself in every family in every generation; perhaps ontogeny does recapitulate phylogeny, and some of the learning about the benefits of cooperation took place in the early history of mankind or pre-human hominids or primates and has been encoded into the genes of later generations. It is also unclear that Hume needs an elaborate story to explain how the natural sentiments of approbation and disapprobation become attached to the artificial virtue of justice; as earlier suggested, the natural occurrence of sympathy alongside self-interest might suffice to explain why we care about how others fare under the practices and institutions of justice as well as how we fare ourselves. What remains clear, however, is that Hume's account of the artificial virtue of justice is itself naturalistic, and should be seen as a part of rather than as an alternative to his account of the natural virtues.

BIBLIOGRAPHY

An asterisk denotes secondary literature especially suitable for further reading.

Árdall, Páll S. 1967. *Passion and Value in Hume's Treatise*. Edinburgh University Press.

Baier, Annette C. 1991. *A Progress of Sentiments: Reflections on Hume's Treatise*. Cambridge, Mass.: Harvard University Press.

Baier, Annette C. 2010. *The Cautious Jealous Virtue: Hume on Justice*. Cambridge, Mass.: Harvard University Press.

Baillie, James 2000. *Routledge Philosophy Guidebook to Hume on Morality*. London: Routledge.*

Botros, Sophie 2006. *Hume, Reason and Morality: A Legacy of Contradiction*. London: Routledge.

Bricke, John 1996. *Mind and Morality: An Examination of Hume's Moral Psychology*. Oxford University Press.

Cohon, Rachel 2008. *Hume's Morality: Feeling and Fabrication*. Oxford University Press.

Costelloe, Timothy M. 2007. *Aesthetics and Morals in the Philosophy of David Hume*. London: Routledge.

Cudworth, Ralph 1996. *A Treatise Concerning Eternal and Immutable Morality, with A Treatise of Freewill*, edited by Sarah Hutton. Cambridge University Press.

Hardin, Russell 2007. *David Hume: Moral and Political Theorist*. Oxford University Press.

Harris, James A. 2015. *Hume: An Intellectual Biography*. Cambridge University Press.

Hume, David 1932. *The Letters of David Hume*, edited by J.Y.T. Grief. 2 vols. Oxford: Clarendon Press.

Hume, David 1954. *New Letters of David Hume*, edited by Raymond Klibansky and Ernest Campbell Mossner. Oxford University Press.

Hume, David 1976. *The Natural History of Religion* and *Dialogues concerning Natural Religion*, edited by A. Wayne Colver and John Valdimir Price. Oxford: Clarendon Press.

Hume, David 1983. *The History of England*, with a foreword by William B. Todd. 6 vols. Indianapolis, Ind.: Liberty Fund.

Hume, David 1987. *Essays Moral, Political, and Literary*, edited by Eugene F. Miller. Revised edn. Indianapolis, Ind.: Liberty Fund.

Hume, David 1998. *An Enquiry concerning the Principles of Morals*, edited by Tom L. Beauchamp. Oxford: Clarendon Press.

Hume, David 2000. *An Enquiry concerning Human Understanding*, edited by Tom L. Beauchamp. Oxford: Clarendon Press.

Hume, David 2007a. *A Dissertation on the Passions* and *The Natural History of Religions*, edited by Tom L. Beauchamp. Oxford: Clarendon Press.

Hume, David 2007b. *A Treatise of Human Nature*, edited by David Fate Norton and Mary J. Norton. 2 vols. Oxford: Clarendon Press.

Hutcheson, Francis 2002. *An Essay on the Nature and Conduct of the Passions and Affections, with Illustrations on the Moral Sense*, ed. Aaron Garrett. Indianapolis, Ind.: Liberty Fund.

Jones, Peter 1982. *Hume's Sentiments: Their Ciceronian and French Context*. Edinburgh University Press.

Mackie, John L. 1980. *Hume's Moral Theory*. London: Routledge & Kegan Paul.

Mercer, Philip 1972. *Sympathy and Ethics: A Study of the Relationship between Sympathy and Morality with special reference to Hume's Treatise*. Oxford: Clarendon Press.

Miller, David 1981. *Philosophy and Ideology in Hume's Political Thought*. Oxford: Clarendon Press.

Mossner, Ernest Campbell 1954. *The Life of David Hume*. Austin, Tex: University of Texas Press.

Norton, David Fate 1982. *David Hume: Common-Sense Moralist, Sceptical Metaphysician*. Princeton University Press.

Passmore, John A. 1952. *Hume's Intentions*. Cambridge University Press.

Radcliffe, Elizabeth S. (ed.) 2008. *A Companion to Hume*. Oxford: Blackwell.

Russell, Paul 1995. *Freedom and Moral Sentiment: Hume's Way of Naturalizing Responsibility*. New York: Oxford University Press.

Russell, Paul (ed.) 2016. *The Oxford Handbook of Hume*. Oxford University Press.

Smith, Norman Kemp 1941. *The Philosophy of David Hume: A Critical Study of its Origins and Central Doctrines*. London: Macmillan.

Stroud, Barry 1977. *Hume*. London: Routledge & Kegan Paul.

Whelan, Frederick G. 1985. *Order and Artifice in Hume's Political Philosophy*. Princeton University Press.

27

Smith and Bentham

CRAIG SMITH

Adam Smith and Jeremy Bentham are somewhat unusual figures in the history of moral philosophy: unusual in the sense that the primary source of their reputation lies outside pure philosophy in the fields of political economy and jurisprudence. Yet both thinkers generally do have some place in university courses based around the history of moral philosophy. Bentham is a regular fixture on moral philosophy syllabi as the proponent of a particularly stark form of classical utilitarianism and is often used as a foil for the apparently more sophisticated account given by John Stuart Mill. Smith's fame largely rests on his *Wealth of Nations* with his *Theory of Moral Sentiments* having, until recently, been largely ignored by moral philosophers.

In what follows I aim to achieve three things: First, to provide an indication of the main tenor of the thought of Smith and Bentham; second, to illustrate their importance in the development of the relationship between moral philosophy and public policy; and third, to indicate the sharp divergence in their thought through the related issue of the justification of punishment. The two thinkers were familiar with each other's work. Bentham was an admirer of Smith's economic writings but in his *Defence of Usury* (1787) disagreed with Smith on that issue. In the *Wealth of Nations* Smith argued that it would be reasonable for the government to regulate the rate of interest applied by private banks because excessive interest would encourage 'prodigals and projectors'[1] who would create financial instability by encouraging risky investments. In response to this Bentham defended the idea of freely floating interest rates on what he saw to be Smithian grounds. Given Smith was willing to trust the market to set prices and individuals to act in their best interest, then there is sufficient reason to expect the market also to do this more efficiently than a government regulator in the field of interest rates. This point is a handy illustration of the more significant fact that Smith was

---

[1] Smith 1976a: 357.

not the unthinking advocate of laissez-faire economics of popular caricature, while Bentham, for all his focus on reform of the state, remained committed to a high degree of individual freedom.

The pair also operated in a shared philosophical tradition. Both Smith and Bentham were influenced by the work of Bernard Mandeville and the response to it of Smith's teacher Francis Hutcheson. Smith and Bentham develop different aspects of Hutcheson's thought. Smith, while rejecting the idea of a distinctive moral sense, takes on the sentimentalism and interest in sociability and sympathy that characterise Hutcheson's thought. Bentham instead develops the notion of the 'greatest happiness for the greatest numbers'[2] and the interest in quantification that Hutcheson began to develop in the search for an ethical principle to direct political activity. Both thinkers are also heavily influenced by David Hume. Smith clearly saw himself as working in his friend's tradition of the 'science of man' and draws on his methodology and his account of causation. However, when it came to moral philosophy, they differed on a number of important issues – particularly the role of utility in the development of moral and political judgment. It is precisely on this point that Bentham claimed that on reading Hume the 'scales had fallen from my eyes'[3] as he saw the potential of utility as an explanatory and justificatory principle.

THE THEORY OF MORAL SENTIMENTS

Smith's contribution to moral philosophy lies chiefly in his *Theory of Moral Sentiments*.[4] First published in 1759 and revised several times up to the author's death in 1790, the *Theory* reflects Smith's dissatisfaction with the existing state of moral philosophy. The task that Smith sets himself is to provide a systematic account of human moral experience, and the result is perhaps the finest account of moral psychology produced by any British thinker. Its success lies in its subtlety and constant reference to actual examples of everyday moral judgment. Smith's aim is to provide an account of moral experience that is more satisfactory than previous attempts on the grounds that it can account more accurately for how we actually experience moral judgment. Mandeville is inadequate because his focus on self-interest fails to provide a satisfactory account of benevolence while his account of virtue and vice is unnecessarily rigorous. Hutcheson fails because he relies on a non-evident cognitive faculty of the moral sense driven by an unrealistic

---

[2] Hutcheson 2004: 125. [3] Bentham 1948a: 36. [4] Smith 1976b, henceforth *TMS*.

claim about universal benevolence, rather than focussing on extant sentimental reactions and admitting the virtue of some purely self-regarding
behaviour. Hume's account of moral judgment, as we noted, gives too
prominent a place to utility, with Smith arguing that utility may help to
account for the evolution of institutions of justice, but does not accurately
reflect the psychology of actual moral judgments. An accurate account of
moral experience will be able to explain the place of self-interest, benevolence
and utility rather than reducing its explanation to any one of these principles.
In Part VII of *TMS* Smith goes through each of the ancient and modern
schools of moral philosophy and demonstrates how each fails to capture
some important aspect of judgment – by implication suggesting that the
account in Books I–VI provides a superior explanatory account of human
moral experience.

Like Hutcheson and Hume, Smith rejects moral rationalism and grounds
his theory in the notion of moral sentiment and, in particular, in the fact that
sociable humans are capable of fellow-feeling. From this he develops his
technical notion of sympathy. Smithian sympathy refers to the capacity to
experience fellow feeling with any sentiment of another person. It is the
product of the imagination entering into the situation of others and assessing
the emotional response that occurs. Perhaps even more significant is that for
Smith our drive towards imaginative sympathy is so basic to our nature that it
does not depend on the agent observed feeling anything. Indeed we can
sympathise with the dead by imagining what we would lose were we, like
them, incapable of further life.

Smith argues that when we find ourselves in sympathy with others we gain
a sense of pleasure. This sense of pleasure from mutual sympathy applies to
all cases where we are able to enter into the feelings of others. That is to say
that sympathetic pleasure occurs when any fellow feeling is generated; the
sympathetic pleasure does not depend on the original feeling being pleasurable, but rather on the coincidence taking place. It is the desire for this mutual
sympathy, itself the basis of humanity's natural sociability, that is the motivation to moral conduct. Beliefs about good and evil, right and wrong, are the
product of the experience of moral judgment that actual agents have undertaken in actual social settings. Since humans are aware that they find pleasure
in mutual sympathy and that others experience the same feelings, we are led
to take this into account in our display of emotion. The result is that a
spectator, who is able to enter into our situation imaginatively, will be able to
reproduce the basis of our reaction, but this reproduction will necessarily be
of a weaker intensity than that experienced by the 'person principally

concerned'.[5] The result is that the person principally concerned will, through self-command, seek to control his emotional response and reduce its pitch to a level closer to that of the spectator. Once this has taken place we see the development of a notion of propriety – of approval of a reaction as suitable.

Moral judgment is the assessment of the appropriateness of an agent's reactions. Society, as Smith famously says, is a 'mirror'[6] and we are only able to become morally reflective beings because we are able to take account of the reaction of other agents to our behaviour. We assess the merit or demerit of an individual's behaviour by imaginatively comparing what we would do were we them with what they actually do. As a part of this we assess them as individuals – we judge them and so part of our assessment is our imaginative reconstruction of their motives. If we approve of their action we praise them, if we disapprove we blame them. But here we meet another key feature of Smith's account – because our assessment is in a large part emotional, we also enter into the situation of those we judge on an emotional as well as an imaginative level. That is to say that when we approve we also feel well disposed to the individual, and when we disapprove we feel resentment towards that individual – and this resentment is compounded if we are moved to feel bad for those affected by their actions. Smith uses this as the basis of his account of punishment. The desire to punish is the result of 'sympathetic indignation'[7] on behalf of those affected by an action that we disapprove of. Smith's account allows for this process to involve sophisticated imaginative judgments. Chief among these are assessments of merit, assessing the extent to which we believe an agent to have intended or to be responsible for the outcomes of his actions. The account is a sentimental retributivism that places the urge to judge, the desire to punish and, unusually, to reward, at the heart of moral experience.

This process is affected by two contingent features. First, the pre-existing relationship that we have with those who observe us: if the agent is known to us, and is partial to us, they will be willing to allow us greater licence in our emotional displays. Second, the partial spectator may be more intimately aware of us and so capable of accessing greater knowledge of our situation which may in turn lead to a more accurate imaginative sympathy. In both of these cases Smith invokes the idea of 'circles of sympathy'[8] whereby knowledge and emotional attachment lead us to concern ourselves to a greater degree with the fortunes of those closer to us. However, we are also subject to the judgments of impartial spectators, of individuals who are less familiar

[5] Ibid., 10. [6] Ibid., 110. [7] Ibid., 76. [8] Forman Barzilai 2010.

with our lives and who are thus less inclined to emotional approval. In this situation we retain the desire for the approval of others and the sympathetic pleasure that it would produce, but conduct an imaginative reflection where we imagine what an impartial spectator would think of our behaviour. This allows us to screen out bias and personal proclivity and exercise the virtue of self-command. Once we have learned to do this we become habituated to thinking in this fashion and develop what Smith calls the 'man within',[9] the impartial spectator who exists in our own mind. This figure provides us with a number of advantages when it comes to moral judgment. First, it allows us to judge our actions before we act and to consider whether an impartial spectator would consider them to be appropriate. Second, it allows us to judge our own action with a greater degree of knowledge of our feelings, thought processes and motives than would be available to an external spectator. The result of this is the next step in Smith's account.

We approve or disapprove of the behaviour of others to the extent that we find it worthy of praise or blame, but with the introduction of the internalised impartial spectator we also come to assess our own action as praiseworthy or blameworthy. Smith uses this as a device to move his account of conscience beyond mere conventionalism. Up to this point one might worry that Smith had provided us with a descriptive account of socialisation that gave the philosopher no further content to moral experience than whatever is absorbed from the common practices of the society that we find ourselves in. The impartial spectator allows us to judge our own actions and motives and to deem them praiseworthy even if no praise is forthcoming, and to assess both our own true motives and the propriety of the judgment of actual external spectators. This allows us, if necessary, to make the difficult choice of rejecting the judgment of our peers. And while we may pay a price for this in terms of ostracism, it forms a part of how Smith accounts for changes in moral attitudes. They change through time as first some, and then others, reject the current consensus and come to approve of new forms of behaviour. It is worth reiterating at this point that this process remains one of sentimental imaginative reflection and is not, in Smith's view, a process of 'reasoning'.

Moral rules are the habituated norms of behaviour that arise from the process of socialisation that is itself characterised by imaginative, sentimental reflection. Smith was clearly aware that this account left him open to the potential charge of relativism, and while he accepted that there would be a

---

[9] Smith 1976b: 130.

variety of moral belief systems and that they could, to a large degree, be moulded by the economic circumstances of a society, he did not regard this as problematic. He has two main reasons for this. First, he believed that there was a universal human nature and that diversity of moral belief was a result of its adaptation to particular circumstances. He also believed that societies of a similar stage of social and economic development would experience similar issues which demanded a moral reaction, and so the ground was set for there to be a kind of comparative ethics to run alongside his comparative jurisprudence. Different types of society have moral codes with different emphases and a descriptive account of moral psychology that cannot accommodate this fact is bound to fail. Second, Smith argued that there were certain institutions and beliefs that were essential to the existence of any society – chiefly the protection of property and person. This represented the question of justice for Smith and when examined through comparative social science it would provide us with an account of the basis of political morality. The other elements of moral experience were capable of less certain assessment than justice and so these virtues were better understood on the level of individual judgment, where greater nicety could be introduced and allow the process of sympathetic interaction to provide appropriate judgments of propriety. Hence Smith distinguishes between justice and benevolence. Following the traditional jurisprudential distinction he views justice as enforceable through the actions of government because we feel sympathetic indignation at injustice, while benevolence attracts our approbation, but not the same degree of resentment at its absence.

As we noted above Smith does not share Hume's view of the centrality of utility to the development of moral beliefs. Hume famously argued that justice was a result of the gradual acceptance of the utility, understood more generally as 'usefulness' rather than in the strict hedonic sense that we will see Bentham deploy, of political stability followed by the development of sympathy with the public good.[10] Smith rejects this view. His ground for this is again based in empirical observation: we disapprove of injustice before we assess the utility of promoting justice. For Smith utility is an 'after-thought'[11] – it is a device that philosophers use to explain social practices after the fact, it is not part of the cognitive process of the actors who initiate and then habituate the beliefs. Likewise Smith argues that the desire to punish injustice comes before any assessment of the utility of the punishment. He believes that his account is a more accurate psychological picture of the 'conjectural history' of moral

---

[10] Hume 1976: 499–500.   [11] Smith 1976b: 20.

experience. So though utility can play a part in our moral experience, the part that it plays is in the considerations of philosophers rather than in the thought process of agents. This is an important point to grasp, as many assume that Smith's argument in the *Wealth of Nations* encourages a morality grounded in self-interest and utility calculation. But nothing could be further from the truth. Smith acknowledges that self-interest is a powerful motive in human life and argues that, when properly bounded by a sympathetically generated moral code, it forms itself into the useful virtue of prudence. Utility does reappear in Smith's thought though. As Campbell and Ross have pointed out, Smith appeals to utility when he makes contributions to policy debates. This leads them to view him as a 'contemplative' or 'system' utilitarian, where he is comfortable in appealing to utility in philosophical abstraction so long as we are aware that it cannot provide as satisfactory an account of the psychology of actual moral judgment as that provided by sympathy.[12]

BENTHAM

In his critical assessment John Stuart Mill provided a frank opinion of Bentham's skills. He 'was not a great philosopher', but was instead the 'great questioner of things' or the 'great subversive' who coupled this critical faculty with an 'essentially practical mind'.[13] In contrast to Smith's attempt to analyse and absorb the lessons of past moral philosophers, Bentham singularly refused to engage with alternative philosophical approaches and was largely dismissive of alternatives to his own. Of his published works those most widely read during his lifetime and most often read by philosophers are *The Fragment on Government* (1776), *An Introduction to the Principles of Morals and Legislation* (1780/1789), *In Defence of Usury* (1787) and *Anarchical Fallacies* (1796/1834).

In the *Fragment* Bentham rejected the widely influential jurisprudence of William Blackstone. Blackstone argued, in his *Commentaries on the Laws of England* (1767), that the British Constitution was a historically evolved balance between the best points of monarchy, aristocracy and democracy. Reform was dangerous as it threatened to unbalance the constitution. The common law was based on precedent, and as such looked backwards for justification to the wisdom of past judges. Bentham's jurisprudence concerned itself with attacking what he saw as the mystical origins and unsystematic nature of

---

[12] Campbell and Ross 1981.   [13] Mill 1974: 2–5.

eighteenth-century English law. His aim was to introduce clarity through codification, but behind this lay a larger project to create a scientific jurisprudence that would guide reform. In this connection he became particularly concerned with the use of clear language and strictly defined concepts in order to purge the law of ambiguity. Through his theory of 'fictions' Bentham sought to break down many of the traditional terms of legal discourse (such as rights, authority, power) into the implicit presuppositions that form the concept. Through this analysis the language of jurisprudence is purged of rhetoric and ambivalence.

The basis of this scientific jurisprudence was to be a consequentialist ethics and the systematic deployment of psychological hedonism as a guide to both legislation and penal policy. Part of his critique in the *Principles* is directed at the social contract theory which Blackstone drew from Locke, but it was in *Anarchical Fallacies* that Bentham developed the attack on natural rights that is still discussed today. For Bentham there are no natural rights. Rights are legal fictions which only have existence within the bounds of a legal order. Natural rights theories are incoherent and meaningless, and they represent little more than the preferences of the speaker dressed in rhetoric to stifle dissent. Natural and imprescriptible rights are 'Nonsense on Stilts'[14] and have no place in the determinations of judges. Determining the nature and extent of rights is a political exercise in Bentham's view and depends upon a Sovereign legal authority providing the terminology to be used within its jurisdiction.

Bentham applied the same argument to all pre-existing attempts to engage in normative moral philosophy.[15] Arguments that appeal to the moral sense, common sense, natural rights, right reason, divine will, and so forth are exercises in rhetorical dogma. They are little more than attempts to support one's favoured position in a language designed to place one's opponents at a disadvantage. This, in Bentham's view, is a most unsatisfactory way to undertake moral reasoning in a scientific age. It was this refusal to countenance sloppiness in conceptual language that underpinned his philosophical and jurisprudential criticism.

Bentham famously opened the *Principles* by declaring that:

> Nature has placed mankind under the governance of two sovereign masters, pain and pleasure. It is for them alone to point out what we ought to do, as well as to determine what we shall do. On the one hand the standard of right and wrong, on the other the chain of causes and effects, are fastened to their throne.[16]

---

[14] Bentham 2001: 405.   [15] Bentham 1948b: 140–3.   [16] Ibid., 125.

From this he argued that the words 'right' and 'wrong' are only truly meaningful if they are used in accordance with the Utilitarian principle: whatever increases the net surplus of pleasure over pain is right and whatever decreases it is wrong. For Bentham utility was both the normative standard and the psychological motivation providing him with his guiding idea, the greatest happiness principle: 'it is the greatest happiness of the greatest number that is the measure of right and wrong'.[17] Bentham's apparent blindness to other aspects of moral motivation or other potential considerations in moral judgment led Mill and many after him to regard Bentham as a peculiarly 'one-eyed' philosopher.[18] However, recent textual analysis by, among others, David Lyons (1991) and Frederick Rosen (2006) has highlighted how Bentham's more trenchant statements of the greatest happiness principle as the basis of ethics are actually quite carefully qualified in notes and surrounding passages. For example, he allows that there are many secondary principles that we pursue and there are many more sophisticated motives to action. However his key point was that these motives and principles are essentially incommensurable without the utility principle. Thus we find him promoting the greatest happiness principle as a common denominator which will allow systematic moral debate. Similarly, the purpose of jurisprudence is to provide rules and channels that direct individuals to forms of behaviour that promote the greatest happiness for the greatest number. But even here, the greatest happiness principle should not be expected to be formally undertaken 'previously to every moral judgement, or to every legislation or judicial operation'.[19]

Instead Bentham saw himself as engaged in a project of systematic reform of the jurisprudence and politics of Britain and by accepting the greatest happiness principle as an organisational principle he was able, so he thought, to provide an objective external standard that could both settle disputes about the law and guide the implementation of policy. Moreover, the universality of the greatest happiness principle paved the way for a universal jurisprudence that would allow theoretical assessment of all existing legal systems. In the ordinary account of Bentham's position he set out how to weigh the consequences of an action, and thereby decide whether it is right or wrong. We must, he says, take account of the pleasures and pains of everyone affected by the action, and this is to be done on an equal basis. Each person affected must be considered and then the effect on their level of happiness included in the calculation. But far from this being an implausibly crude moral psychology, it is rather the basis of a far more complex attempt to think about human behaviour in consequentialist terms.

---

[17] Bentham 1948a: 3.   [18] Mill 1974: 17.   [19] Bentham 1948b: 117.

When Bentham appears in undergraduate moral philosophy courses it is often as a foil for J.S. Mill's discussion of higher and lower pleasures in *Utilitarianism*. The passage most often cited is Bentham's assertion that: 'quantity of pleasure being equal, pushpin is as good as poetry'.[20] But the apparent philistinism of this observation belies Bentham's attempts to produce a nuanced measure of utility. Even if we lay aside the fact that the example is drawn from aesthetics rather than jurisprudence, we find that Bentham was alive to the difficulties of hedonic calculus. In the *Principles* Bentham devotes Chapters IV and V to the categorisation of types of pleasure and pain and their measurement, and makes the case for a quantitative analysis. His discussion of the elements of happiness in terms of Intensity, Duration, Certainty/Uncertainty, Propinquity/Remoteness, Fecundity (marginal utility), Purity, and Extent was intended to provide us with a means of comparing the shared characteristics of all pleasures. Thus the statement 'quantity of pleasure being equal' assumes that both pushpin and poetry have been similarly quantified according to these principles. The problem was not so much that Bentham was arguing that all pleasures were equal; it was rather his democratic view that individuals were the best judge of their own pleasures. As he puts it in his case against Smith's usury restrictions: 'no simplicity, short of absolute idiotism, can cause the individual to make a more groundless judgment, than the legislator ... would have made for him'.[21]

In Bentham's later political thought democracy ensures that government passes laws in the interests of all and reduces the danger of corruption. The governors must be dependent on the people to ensure that they act in their interest. Bentham combines this with the view that freedom of choice is justified on the grounds that each individual is best placed to decide what makes them happy. Thus Mill's true response to Bentham on pushpin and poetry does not really lie in the oft cited argument about a dissatisfied Socrates being preferable to a satisfied fool and the soft elitism of the introduction of higher and lower qualities of pleasure in *Utilitarianism*, but rather in the harder paternalism of his *Considerations on Representative Government*, where an educated elite are given extra political influence. And here Mill is closer to Bentham than it would appear at first glance, as Bentham was well aware that legislation required the wisdom of the educated and experienced.

---

[20] Mill 1974: 36.   [21] Bentham 1952–3: 140.

Bentham's elements of pleasure and pain were to form part of the felicific calculus that would allow government to design a legal order that would promote the happiness of society understood as the sum of the happiness of its individual members through four subsidiary ends of security, subsistence, abundance and equality. This, in Bentham's view, was the only justification for government: 'The business of government is to promote the happiness of the society, by punishing and rewarding.'[22] The *Principles* takes this as the basis for an analysis of what matters ought to be the province of the law and how the penal system ought to respond to them. All punishment involves unpleasantness and can only be admitted to exclude a greater evil. The balance of pleasure and pain provides a guide for appropriate punishment. Similarly there are cases which are 'unmeet' for punishment: where the act does not affect others or where punishment will not deter future acts and so causes greater harm.[23] This famously led Bentham to an interest in prison reform and to the design of the Panopticon, a 'scientific' prison designed to both punish and reform inmates through fear of punishment.

This does return us to one of the deeper philosophical worries about Bentham's account. The initial introduction of the greatest happiness principle in the *Principles* would appear to leave Bentham, like Mill, open to the charge of committing a naturalistic fallacy, but as we have seen he views this as largely beside the point – it simply is the case that the generalisation of how we behave (hedonic egoism) happens to fit with the only plausible philosophical denominator that will allow meaningful moral argument (ethical utilitarianism). More difficult is explaining the link between the two: why should hedonically egoistic individuals direct their behaviour in line with the greatest happiness principle? Without an account of moral sentiment or sympathy like that we find in Smith (Bentham discusses these and dismisses them as too weak to work), there would appear to be a missing link in the basic structure of his theory. One solution would be that Bentham is operating with some sort of crude identification of interest argument where the interests of individuals and the public magically cohere. But this is clearly not the case given his focus on deliberate legislation. Nor can it be the case that he is denying the possibility of public spirited political action, as he himself spent a large part of his life engaged in this. Instead what we have is an account of

---

[22] Bentham 1948b: 189.
[23] It is also worth noting that Bentham spends a great deal of the *Principles* discussing intention, guilt, blame and liability in such a way as to mitigate the common charge that consequentialist jurisprudence leaves open the punishment of the innocent.

the generation of a political system of representative democracy that ensures that the political incentives and accountability of legislators directs them to create laws that channel individual behaviour in a direction that promotes the greatest happiness for the greatest number.

To crystallise our discussion we can consider the very different approaches to jurisprudence adopted by Smith and Bentham and what that reveals about their respective attitudes to the relationship between philosophy and public policy. Smith's account traces the desire to punish to sentimentally generated resentment within a system of socially evolved norms of behaviour. In line with his descriptive approach to moral psychology, Smith's jurisprudence is historical and centres on the conceptual analysis of the development of basic legal notions in specific cultural and economic settings. His attitude to reform is gradualist, grounded no doubt in his belief that law, like morality, evolves along with the societies in which it exists. Reform should be careful, gradual and in response to problems that arise with existing regulations. For Bentham, sympathy cannot be an adequate basis for jurisprudence. As he notes, sympathetic resentment tends to 'err on the side of severity'[24] and invite harsh punishment for trivial offences. It provides no reliable principle of analysis upon which to construct a rational legal code. Punishment, in his view, can only reasonably be assessed in light of utility calculations. Sympathy leaves too much room for individual whim and ingrained prejudice in deciding how to make use of punishment. Reform, for Bentham, involved the assessment of existing legal orders in comparison with his rationally constructed codification grounded on the greatest happiness principle. This was the only solid basis for a scientific jurisprudence.

We began by noting that both Smith and Bentham have a somewhat uneasy place in the canon of moral philosophy, but they are becoming increasingly influential in the link between public policy and philosophy. Bentham's utilitarianism is enjoying something of a revival via the impact on public policy of the 'happiness studies' of Layard and others.[25] Smith, on the other hand, is slowly being restored to his place in the history of philosophy by the increasing interest in moral psychology and by the interest in his concept of the impartial spectator seen in the work of Stephen Darwall, Gilbert Harman and Amartya Sen. Both Smith and Bentham deserve to be taken more seriously by philosophers.

[24] Bentham 1948b: 143. [25] Layard 2005.

BIBLIOGRAPHY

An asterisk denotes secondary literature especially suitable for further reading.

Bentham, J. 1948a. 'Fragment on Government', in W. Harrison (ed.), *A Fragment on Government and An Introduction to the Principles of Morals and Legislation*, Oxford, Basil Blackwell, pp. 1–112.

Bentham, J. 1948b. 'An Introduction to the Principles of Morals and Legislation', in W. Harrison (ed.), *A Fragment on Government and An Introduction to the Principles of Morals and Legislation*, Oxford, Basil Blackwell, pp. 113–435.

Bentham, J. 1952–3. 'Defence of Usury', in W. Stark (ed.), *Jeremy Bentham's Economic Writings*, 3 vols. London, George Allen & Unwin, vol. 1.

Bentham, J. 2001. 'Anarchical Fallacies', in R. Harrison (ed.), *Bentham: Selected Writings on Utilitarianism*, Ware, Wordsworth Editions, pp. 381–459.

Campbell, T.D. and Ross, I.S. 1981. 'The Utilitarianism of Adam Smith's Policy Advice', *Journal of the History of Ideas*, 42.1, 73–92.

Forman Barzilai, F. 2010. *Adam Smith and the Circles of Sympathy: Cosmopolitanism and Moral Theory*, Cambridge University Press.

Hume, D. 1976. *A Treatise of Human Nature*, L.A. Selby-Bigge (ed.), P.H. Nidditch (rev.), Oxford, Clarendon Press.

Hutcheson, F. 2004. *An Inquiry into the Original of Our Ideas of Beauty and Virtue*, W. Leidhold (ed.), Indianapolis, IN, Liberty Fund.

Layard, R. 2005. *Happiness: Lessons from a New Science*, Harmondsworth, Penguin.

Lyons, D. 1991. *In the Interests of the Governed: A Study in Bentham's Philosophy of Utility and Law*, Oxford, Clarendon Press.*

Mill, J.S. 1974. 'Bentham', in B. Parekh (ed.), *Jeremy Bentham: Ten Critical Essays*, London, Frank Cass, pp. 1–40.

Phillipson, N. 2010. *Adam Smith: An Enlightened Life*, London, Allen Lane.*

Rosen, F. 2006. *Classical Utilitarianism from Hume to Mill*, London, Routledge.

Schofield, P. 2009. *Utility and Democracy: The Political Thought of Jeremy Bentham*, Oxford University Press.*

Smith, A. 1976a. *An Inquiry into the Nature and Causes of the Wealth of Nations*, R.H. Campbell & A.S. Skinner (eds.), 2 vols., Oxford University Press, vol. 1.

Smith, A. 1976b. *The Theory of Moral Sentiments*, D.D. Raphael & A.L. Macfie (eds.), Oxford University Press.

28

Rousseau

SUSAN MELD SHELL

INTRODUCTION

Rousseau famously criticized all philosophic "systems," though he also insisted on the systematic coherence of his own thinking, for all of its apparent paradoxes.[1] His leading principle – that man is naturally good and made wicked by society – challenged both the Christian dogma of original sin and the facile cynicism of figures like Voltaire; and it set in motion an intellectual and moral revolution whose force is arguably not yet fully spent.

More than any thinker preceding him, Rousseau placed human freedom at the center of his concerns. "Man," as he famously stated, "is born free" although he is also "everywhere in chains."[2] Freedom is in the first instance the active principle that we feel within ourselves in sensing our own existence.[3] All of Rousseau's moral and political projects can be profitably read as so many experiments in recovering this primal sentiment in social settings that continually place it in jeopardy. Among those experiments, his treatment of moral conscience plays a crucial role by providing a universal standard by which more partial, purely local solutions treated in the *Social Contract* can themselves be measured. This universal moral standard, which is especially prominent in such works as *Emile*, would exercise a profound influence on Kant and later German thinkers.

Rousseau accepted Hobbes's assumption that men are naturally a-social, and that they are driven by self-love. At the same time, he rejected Hobbes's

[1] Compare *Rousseau, Judge of Jean-Jacques, OC* 1: 932; Rousseau 1990: 212–13; and *Letter to Beaumont, OC* 4: 928; Rousseau 2001: 163. (All citations to Rousseau's text list the volume and page number of the Gallimard *Œuvres Complètes* edition (abbreviated to *OC*), followed in most cases by a reference to the English translation.)

[2] *Social Contract, OC* 3: 351; Rousseau 2012: 164.

[3] For a fuller discussion of Rousseau's understanding of "existence" see Cooper 1999.

conclusion that the natural human condition was one of conflict and war. In seeking to return to the state of nature, Hobbes, in Rousseau's famous formulation, had failed to arrive there: he attributed to man's nature a mutual hostility that was in fact the product of society.[4] Natural man, at least in his most primitive state, would have needed little, Rousseau countered, and would have desired no more than he could provide for on his own. Far from being "nasty, brutish and short," man's "solitary" life would not even have been "poor," if poverty is taken to imply unhappiness.[5]

For thinkers like Hobbes and Locke, man is distinguished from other animals not by reason, whose characteristic (or "highest") activity is contemplation, but rather by a certain "freedom" to defer present for the sake of future gratification (to borrow Locke's language),[6] and thus use reason to secure himself. Rousseau observed the inherent ambiguity – not to say irrationality – of reason thus construed.[7] In thus striving to secure himself had man not given up more than he gained? Had he not replaced a primitive contentment that was his natural birthright with an illusory good whose pursuit had actually led to real and growing misery?

In thus questioning the "goodness" of reason so understood, i.e., as the servant of the desire for comfort and security, Rousseau did not return to the traditional understanding of reason, which he rejected no less than Hobbes and Locke. Instead, he sought to reorient the mind by directing it toward a freedom more fundamental, and unambiguously desirable, than that connected with the pursuit of an imaginary idea of happiness. In place of the single drive for self-preservation he distinguished a primary passion of self-love (*amour de soi*) and accompanying sentiment of one's existence, prior to reason itself, and a secondary and derivative self-love that involves comparison with others (*amour propre*).

The sentiment of existence is not only inherently sweet; it is also expressive of a primary, active spontaneity whose enjoyment requires nothing further. *Amour propre*, which is aroused under conditions of social dependence, on the other hand is rooted in the human tendency to love those we think wish to help us and to hate those who we think wish to harm us.[8] In its distorted or "enflamed" form, *amour propre* leads us to demand that others prefer us to themselves, a desire that it is impossible to satisfy, and that gives

---

[4] *Discourse on Inequality, OC* 3: 132; Rousseau 1997: 132.
[5] *Discourse on Inequality, OC* 3: 139–40, 160; Rousseau 1997: 139, 157.
[6] Locke 1694 2: xxi, 47.   [7] *Discourse on Inequality, OC* 3: 156; Rousseau 1997: 153.
[8] *Emile, OC* 4: 492; Rousseau 2010: 363. As a "modification" of *amour de soi, amour propre* is not entirely opposed to it. For an alternative view, see Neuhouser 2008: 235.

rise to all the miseries and vices of society that Hobbes blamed on human nature proper.

A final preliminary point bears noting. The "goodness" of nature, for Rousseau, refers mainly to the goodness of our beginnings rather than to any natural "end" or "perfection" to which human nature, on an older view, was thought to point. Though man is "perfectible," how far that perfection can reach remains unknown or indeterminate.[9]

The meaning of "perfectibility," a term evidently coined by Rousseau himself, remains contentious among scholars. Some associate it with an "almost infinite malleability" or changeability;[10] while others see it as a sign of underlying continuities with "neo-Platonism."[11] Still others (including Kant) have treated it as an invitation to free self-completion, or to return to natural plenitude in a way that engages all the faculties, which in the rude state of nature remain merely latent. However one understands the term, it seems undeniable that Rousseau took his primary bearings not from a presumed knowledge of man's highest nature (as with Aristotle), but from the sentiment of existence, along with certain formal and dynamic principles of order to which that sentiment lends access.[12]

The term "sentiment of existence" owes something to the usage of Pascal and Malebranche, for whom it reflects the direct activity of God on or within the human soul. More metaphysically modest, or skeptical, than his predecessors, Rousseau leaves open the question as to the ultimate source of this sentiment. Indeed, a key practical advantage of his account is its apparent compatibility with a variety of metaphysical systems.[13] What distinguishes sentiment in Rousseau's meaning from merely passive sense or sensitivity is the peculiar sort of activity (or living force), and related principle of individuation, to which it bears immediate witness. An organized body is a peculiar sort of "whole," whose parts or members come together (*convenir*)[14] in such a way that they serve as one another's ends and means (as Kant will later put it).[15] Where Hobbes had treated "active" and "passive" power as reciprocal

---

[9] *Discourse on Inequality*, OC 3: 142; Rousseau 1997: 141.
[10] See, for example, Strauss 1953: 271.
[11] See, for example, Gouhier 1970 and Williams 2007.
[12] *Emile*, OC 4: 242, 305, 253; Rousseau 2010: 158, 211, 167.
[13] *Discourse on Inequality*, OC 3: 142; Rousseau 1997: 141.
[14] On "*convenir*" (to suit) and "*convenance*" (suitability) as terms of art in Rousseau, see Guénard 2004. Unlike the Stoic *convenentia*, *convenance* is apprehended by sentiment, rather than requiring knowledge of man's "essence" or natural perfection.
[15] Kant, *Critique of Judgment*, Section 66 [1913, vol. 5: 376].

expressions, both implicated on the same level in the communication of motion from one body (the active power) to another (the passive power), Rousseau's "sentiment of existence" expresses activity of another, higher order: a principle of organic individuation and related power of self-affection. "Living" entails an active joy beyond the fleeting pleasures that accompany the passive satisfaction of our bodily needs. The disposition to and emergence of (in man at least) the sentiment of one's *own* existence (as in the "idea, or better, sentiment, of *moi*")[16] reflects a potentially higher state of organization than that exemplified by simpler forms of life; at the same time, it also opens up the possibility of new, potentially deforming, complications.

THE IDEA OF "A GENERAL SOCIETY OF THE HUMAN RACE"

The idea of an organic whole implicit in the sentiment of existence also provides Rousseau with his primary model of the "true" social body, which in turn gives rise to the idea of a universal moral order that both resembles and differs from that held up as models by his Enlightenment predecessors.[17] A particularly revealing discussion occurs in the "Geneva Manuscript," where it serves as a corrective to the claim of Diderot (following Pufendorf) that there is a "general society of the human race" to whose moral authority one can rationally appeal.[18] Rousseau states in reply:

> The word "human race" [*genre humain*] offers the mind [*esprit*] nothing but a purely collective idea which does not suppose any real union among the individuals that constitute it: add, if you like, this supposition; conceive the human species as a moral person having, along with a common sentiment of existence, which gives it individuality and constitutes it one, a universal turning wheel [*mobile*] that makes each part act for an end that is general and

[16] Cf. Brunet and Guillarme 2010.

[17] *On the Social Contract; or Essay about the Form of the Republic*, the "*Geneva Manuscript*," an early version of the published *Social Contract*, was written around the time Rousseau was completing *Emile*. Alternative sub-titles included *Essay on the Constitution of the State, Essay on the Formation of the Political Body*, and *Essay on the Formation of the State*. In his earlier essay on *Political Economy*, Rousseau credits Diderot for the "great and luminous principle" that the body politic is a moral being directed by the general will. For a fuller account of Rousseau's complex intellectual and personal relations with Denis Diderot, see Masters 1968, Cranston 1991, and Damrosch 2005.

[18] See Diderot's essay on "Natural Right" in the *Encyclopédie*; Diderot's general defense of the position of modern jurists such as Pufendorf was intended as a response to Rousseau's *Discourse on the Origin of Inequality*.

relative to [the] all. Let us conceive that this common sentiment is that of humanity and that the natural law is the active principle of the entire machine. Then let us observe what results from the constitution of man in his relations with his like; and, altogether contrary to what we have supposed, we will find that the progress of society, in awakening personal interest, stifles humanity in the hearts, and that notions of [the] natural law, which one would have rather to call the law of reason, only begin to develop themselves when the anterior development of the passions render all its precepts impotent. By this one sees that the presumed social treaty [*traité*] dictated by nature is a true chimera; since the conditions for it are always unknown or impracticable and one must necessarily either be ignorant of them or violate them.[19]

Diderot's notion of a general society of mankind is a "true chimera," because the reason necessary to apprehend its laws could not develop in society without the prior destruction of the sentiments needed for their execution. Diderot cannot adequately respond to the "violent reasoner" (whom Diderot loosely models on Rousseau himself), who has neither a rational nor sentimental motive to be just.

But Rousseau does not leave matters here. If such a "general society" were actually to exist, he goes on to say, "somewhere other than in the systems of the philosophers,"

it would be. . . a moral being that had qualities proper and distinct from that of the particular beings that constituted it, a little like chemical compositions that have properties that it in no way take from any of the mixtures that compose it. There would be a universal language that nature would teach all men, and that would be the first instrument of their mutual communication: there would be a sort of common sensorium that would serve for the correspondence of all the parts; the public good or harm would not only be the sum of particular goods and harms as in a simple aggregation, but would reside in a liaison that united them, it would be greater than that sum, and far from the public felicity being established from the happiness of the particulars, it would be this that was the source.[20]

Were it to exist, in other words, such a society would resemble those chemical compounds whose effects differ in kind from the effects of their components taken in isolation. If such a social organism could indeed be formed, it would involve a comparable transformation of the effects of the

[19] *Geneva Manuscript, OC* 3: 283–4; Rousseau 1978: 159. (Both this and the passage quoted below are cancelled in the original version.)
[20] *Geneva Manuscript, OC* 3: 284; Rousseau 1978: 159–60.

self-love we naturally owe ourselves without attempting, *per impossibile*, to change its fundamental constitution. In order to teach a "violent reasoner" what "interest [he has] in being just" one should not try to deny self-love; instead, on the basis of "new associations" fashioned to correct the defect of the old, one should teach him "to enlarge upon his being and his felicity by sharing them with others":

> Let him see in a better constitution of things the value [*prix*] of good actions, and the punishment of bad ones, and the sweet harmony of justice and happiness. Let us enlighten his reason with new insights and his heart with new feelings ... And if my zeal does not blind me ... let us not doubt that, given a strong soul and an upright mind [*sens droit*], reason that led this enemy of the human race astray would lead him back to humanity.[21]

Rousseau here sketches out, in a few brief strokes, the series of experiments he will perform on a larger canvass in *Emile*, which traces Emile's journey from the uncorrupted self-love of early childhood to a devotion to justice that coincides with his maturity, in an effort to show how far one might go in reconciling "man" and "citizen," i.e., in overcoming a seemingly irreducible tension between virtue and self-love or happiness.

EMILE: ROUSSEAU'S MORAL LABORATORY

In *Emile* (1763), or "On Education," Rousseau undertakes to show what the social "chemistry"[22] alluded to in the above passage might accomplish under ideal conditions consistent with the human condition broadly understood.[23] To the extent that that experiment succeeds, Rousseau will have proven that the contradictions to which modern men especially are prone are surmountable in principle, at least for an individual who is carefully raised. Such an individual would be at once a "man of nature" and the virtual citizen of a universal republic, existing only in speech, whose laws "are written in the

---

[21] *Geneva Manuscript*, OC 3: 288–9; Rousseau 1978: 162–3.

[22] For a searching analysis of Rousseau's own early studies of chemistry, see Kelly 2016. On the chemical analogy as it pertains to the formation of the general will, see Bernardi and Bensaude-Vincent 2013: 69–72; and Bernardi 2006: 49–75, 125–50. Adam Smith appears to appropriate the metaphor in his own review of Rousseau's *Discourse on Inequality* in the *Edinburgh Review*, as quoted in Rasmussen 2006: 631.

[23] Virtue, in Rousseau's view, is most likely to flourish in small, homogeneous societies that "denature" man. But such societies are unlikely, he thought, to arise in a post-Christian era, and, in any case, raise moral difficulties of their own, given their often harsh conduct toward foreigners.

depth of the heart by conscience and reason."[24] To the extent that this effort falls short, it will at least show the limit beyond which human nature cannot go. Either way, unlike Diderot's "true chimera," Rousseau's fiction is a useful one, because it lays down a mark that can be productively approximated as circumstances permit rather than eliciting futile and ultimately self-destructive expectations that exacerbate those contradictions rather than relieving them.

Emile rewrites the history of human decline, by reversing or otherwise reordering the fateful steps by which the rosy era, that Rousseau elsewhere calls "the happiest and best" for man,[25] was lost. Emile's "romance," as Rousseau puts it, "ought to have been the history of [our] species."[26] Under the most primitive conditions, under which each could satisfy his own needs, men had more reason to pity others (on the few occasions it was warranted) than to harm them. As conditions changed, and men grew more dependent on one another for the satisfaction of their needs, they began to seek the esteem of others – at first with compensating new delights (including ideas of merit and beauty) – but culminating in the desire, fatal to that primitive contentment, that others love us more than they love themselves. And it is this desire, *amour propre* in its simplest form, that is responsible on Rousseau's account for all mankind's subsequent unhappiness and wickedness.

But *amour propre* – or self-love in relation to others – has its positive uses, above all with respect to morality. The educator's task is not to stifle *amour propre*, but to hold it back until Emile's mind and body are sufficiently developed for him to join the moral order without giving up his native strength and self-sufficiency.

In the *Discourse on Inequality*, this moment coincides with the so-called "golden age,"[27] in which sexual preference, ideas of merit and beauty, and violence and vengeance appear almost simultaneously:

> [Men and women] grow accustomed to ... make comparisons; imperceptibly they acquire ideas of merit and of beauty which produce sentiments of preference ... Everyone began to look at everyone else and to wish to be looked at himself and public esteem acquired a price ... From these first

[24] *Emile, OC* 4: 858; Rousseau 2010: 667.
[25] *Discourse on Inequality, OC* 3: 171; Rousseau 1997: 167; cf. *Emile, OC* 4: 859; Rousseau 2010: 668.
[26] *Emile, OC* 4: 777; Rousseau 2010: 599.
[27] Rousseau calls this age a "just mean" between primitive indolence and the "petulant *amour propre*" of our current state, "the happiest and most long lasting era" and "the best for man." *Discourse on Inequality, OC* 3: 171; Rousseau 1997: 167.

preferences arose vanity and contempt on the one hand, shame and envy on the other; and the fermentation caused by these new leavens eventually produced the compounds fatal to happiness and innocence.[28]

Recapitulating and drawing on the "fermentation" that characterized the "youth of the species," Books Four and Five of *Emile* improve upon the golden age, rendering a formerly "cruel and malignant" *amour propre* "humane and gentle,"[29] and retailing the moral chemistry that would be required to transform self-love without undermining or otherwise betraying its primary tendency.[30] The wicked man, who is "delighted that everyone act justly with the exception of himself," has instrumental reason on his side, Rousseau writes in words echoing the *Geneva Manuscript*:

> [Nevertheless,] when the strength of an expansive soul makes me identify myself with my fellow, and I feel that I am, so to speak, in him, it is in order not to suffer that I do not want him to suffer. I am interested in him for love of myself and the reason for the [Golden Rule] is in nature itself, which inspires in me the desire of my wellbeing in whatever place I sense my existence . . . Love of men derived from love of self is the principle of human justice.[31]

The steps by which this transformation comes about are left obscure, however, at crucial points, it being not Rousseau's business to "produce treatises on metaphysics and morals." Instead, he merely "marks out the order and the progress of our sentiments" in "relation to our constitution," leaving it to others "to *perhaps* demonstrate" what he only "indicates."[32]

Rousseau's reticence is nowhere more noticeable than when it becomes time, finally, to deal with the religious education through which Emile is at last to find "his true interest in being good," all previous efforts in this direction being, as it would appear, merely provisional. Instead, Rousseau recounts his own youthful encounter with an obscure Savoyard priest whose earlier disgrace had precipitated a crisis of faith, yielding a new religion of "sincerity" based on the authority of conscience, or the "inner sentiment."[33] That moral sentiment, in the Vicar's view, is the expression of a "higher"

---

[28] *Discourse on Inequality, OC* 3: 169–70; Rousseau 1997: 165–6.
[29] *Emile, OC* 4: 523; Rousseau 2010: 389.
[30] Emile's spirits are to be "purified," in other words, without being either "denatured," like the citizen of Sparta, or turned into "*marc* without vigor" (*OC* 4: 343, 250; Rousseau 2010: 241, 165). ("*Marc*" is a term for the residue left behind when fruit is distilled.)
[31] *Emile, OC* 4: 523n; Rousseau 2010: 389n.
[32] *Emile, OC* 4: 523–4; Rousseau 2010: 389 (emphasis added).
[33] *Emile, OC* 4: 599; Rousseau 2010: 452.

self-love, or *amour de soi*, as distinguished from the lower self-love associated with our attachment to the body and its pleasures from which death promises to free us. In support of this view he adopts three "articles of faith" endorsed by sentiment and not opposed by reason: namely 1) that a will moves the universe and animates nature; 2) that this will is intelligent and good; and 3) that man is free and animated by an immaterial substance.[34]

ROUSSEAU'S AMBIGUOUS DUALISM

Amour de soi, on this account, is a complex sentiment, divided between a spiritual self and one rooted in the body. It may be rash, however, to assume that the Vicar's speech is a completely accurate representation of Rousseau's own deepest thoughts.[35] The Vicar's dualism is partly rooted in his own abiding sense of moral failure,[36] leading to a longing on his part to be freed from the temptations of the body.[37] Rousseau's own position on the tension between conscience and self-love seems considerably more nuanced, especially when he is speaking in his own name.[38]

[34] Many of the Vicar's claims, including the moral primacy of good intentions, the infallibility of conscience, and the practical or moral basis of religious faith, would exercise a decisive influence on Kant.

[35] For alternative views on this question, compare Gouhier 1970 and Williams 2007 with Melzer 1990 and Marks 2006. It is striking that Rousseau explicitly excludes fear of death from the most primitive human condition, a moment that is partly repeated in his own rapturous experience in awakening from unconsciousness, as recounted in the *Reveries* (*OC* 1: 1005–7). Most strongly dualistic readings of Rousseau draw extensively on the letters to Beaumont and to Franquières. Critics of such readings point to the peculiar audience of these two letters, and to Rousseau's defense elsewhere of benevolent deception (*Reveries, OC* 1: 1024–35). On the awakening scene, see also Kelly 2012.

[36] *Emile, OC* 4: 604; Rousseau 2010: 457.

[37] *Emile, OC* 4: 603; Rousseau 2010: 456. Although self-divided, the virtuous man, unlike the merely good man, can take credit for his goodness. Rousseau never claims to have himself been virtuous. He does, however, claim to be happy. On the complexity of Rousseau's understanding of conscience, appeals to the "sublime science of simple souls" notwithstanding, see Grace 2013; cf. Rousseau, *Discourse on the Arts and Sciences, OC* 3: 30; Rousseau 1997: 28.

[38] Whereas the Vicar is "sure" that matter "cannot think," Rousseau adds in a note that in order "either to accept or reject" the idea of sensitive or thinking matter "one would have to begin by understanding it," which he has not done. *Emile, OC* 4: 584n, 551; Rousseau 2010: 440, 412; see also *Moral Letters, OC* 4: 1098; Rousseau 2007: 86.

This ambiguity is echoed in Rousseau's later description of Emile's own ascent from a goodness grounded in self-love to moral virtue proper, without passing through the purgatory of self-reproach to which the Vicar seems to be condemned. Having found it "simple" to "rise from the study of nature to the quest for its author," the tutor finds new ways of speaking to Emile's still innocent heart.

> It is only then that he finds his true interest in being good, in doing good far from the sight of men and being forced by the laws, in being just between God and himself, in fulfilling his duty, even at the expense of his life, and in carrying virtue in his heart. He does this not only for the love of order, to which each of us always prefers love of self, but for love of the author of his being – a love which is confounded with the same love of self – in order to enjoy at last that durable happiness which the repose of a good conscience and the contemplation of this supreme being promise him in the other life after he has spent this one well. Abandon this, and I no longer see anything but injustice, hypocrisy among men. Private interest, which in case of conflict necessarily prevails over everything, teaches everyone to adorn vice with the mask of virtue. Let all other men do what is good for me at their expense; let everything be related to me alone; let all mankind, if need be, die in suffering and poverty to spare me a moment of pain or hunger. This is the inner language of every unbeliever who reasons.[39]

If conscience, in other words, is an "expanded" version of *amour de soi*, moral virtue requires *amour propre*, of which it is a peculiarly benign modification. Man's natural "goodness" suffices to secure a feeling of "humanity"; the latter also enlists our desire to "count" for something, both to ourselves, and in the eyes of a just God. The heart that can bear witness to its own virtue before God no longer seeks to satisfy its need for "recognition" at the expense of others. At the same time, without a belief in a just God, and an afterlife in which virtue is rewarded, virtue, Rousseau says, "seems impossible."[40]

The education of Emile represents Rousseau's most explicit and complete response to the Christian dogma of original sin. It is also his most extended answer to the "violent reasoner" depicted in the *Geneva Manuscript*. Emile's heart has opened him to "raptures" of which the violent reasoner knows nothing. And Emile's *amour propre*, trained to take satisfaction only in esteem that is truly merited, not only leads him to esteem himself without seeking that esteem from other men; it also rewards him with the promise of enduring happiness, rather than, as with corrupted souls, tormenting both himself and others. His morally tempered heart is open to the life-enhancing

---

[39] *Emile, OC* 4: 636; Rousseau 2010: 482.   [40] Rousseau 1974: 128–9.

joys of love and friendship without relinquishing its native independence from the opinions and esteem of others. Accepting no authority external to itself, it treats others as it would be treated, and thereby instantiates, without compulsion, the basic moral teachings of the Gospel.

But the tutor's effort to restrain Emile's temperament and arouse his reason so that man might *"as much as possible* always be one"[41] suggests that his success, in this regard, remains imperfect. Emile, too, is a divided being, albeit one in which the "gap" between his physical and moral nature has been narrowed to the greatest possible extent.[42]

It is thus especially striking that Rousseau ends Book Four by briefly leaving Emile aside, to provide a sketch of his own moral taste, one that is surprisingly Epicurean in tone.[43]

This alternative answer to the "violent reasoner" – one that places fewer strains upon man's "wholeness" than that suggested by the examples of the Vicar or (even) Emile – will re-emerge in Rousseau's final work, the *Reveries of a Solitary Walker*, in which he lays aside the moral hopes, and related indignation, that had previously disturbed his happiness. On this alternative view, the most satisfying response to the human condition lies neither in moral virtue as promulgated by Rousseau's Vicar, nor in the reconstitution of society on a roughly Spartan model, but in reflection and reverie undertaken in solitude.[44]

That "trans-moral" perspective is already anticipated in Rousseau's earlier *Moral Letters*, which present the moral life less as an end in itself than as a stepping stone toward the higher goal of securing human happiness through self-awareness.[45]

In the same work, Rousseau draws a striking distinction between reason and mere reasoning:

> The art of reasoning [*raisonner*] is not reason at all; often it is its abuse. Reason [*Raison*] is the faculty of ordering all the faculties of our soul suitably [*convenablement*] to the nature of things and their relations with us. Reasoning [*raisonnement*] is the art of comparing known truths in order to compose from them other truths that one did not know and which this art makes us discover. But it does not at all teach us to know these primitive truths which

---

[41] *Emile, OC* 4: 635; Rousseau 2010: 482.   [42] *Emile, OC* 4: 551; Rousseau 2010: 412.

[43] *Emile, OC* 4: 683, 687–8; Rousseau 2010: 522, 526.

[44] See, for example, *Letters to Malesherbes, OC* 1: 1140–1; Rousseau 2007: 156.

[45] *Moral Letters, OC* 4: 1112; Rousseau 2007: 96; see also *Emile, OC* 4: 601; Rousseau 2010: 454.

serve as elements of all the others, and if we put in their place our opinions, our passions, and our prejudices, far from enlightening us it blinds us.[46]

"Reason," as distinguished from "reasoning," one might tentatively conclude, is the intellectual faculty that Rousseau's moral philosophy especially seeks to engage. But the character of reason is not spelled out explicitly, either in the *Moral Letters* or elsewhere in the published writings.

Rousseau's moral philosophy offers a perplexing mixture of seemingly contradictory assertions, expressed with a rhetorical force and poetic charm that are unequalled among modern moral philosophers. He sought to replace the two chief moral intellectual rivals of his time – materialist atheism and traditional religious orthodoxy – with a new moral and religious teaching that took its primary bearings from a novel understanding of human freedom as life-activity. The effect, he hoped, would be both more humanly satisfying than the former and less sanguinary and intolerant than the latter. Not surprisingly, he left behind a complex and in many ways divided philosophic legacy, which inspired such diverse figures as Kant, Fichte, Hegel, and more recently, John Rawls and Jürgen Habermas. On the one hand, his moral resolution of the problem of *amour propre* anticipated both the Kantian principle of autonomy and the Hegelian "dialectic of recognition" and accompanying philosophy of history.[47] The unreservedly egalitarian orientation of most contemporary moral theory, including its attachment to the idea of (equal) human dignity, owes a significant intellectual debt to this aspect of Rousseau's moral thought. On the other hand, Rousseau's late writings suggest that an alternative philosophic trajectory, devoted to a solitary quest for happiness through self-recognition or self-knowledge (and taken up by later figures such as Goethe) may represent his own deepest thoughts.

BIBLIOGRAPHY

An asterisk denotes secondary literature especially suitable for further reading.

Bernardi, B. 2006, *La fabrique des concepts: Recherches sur l'invention conceptuelle chez Rousseau*. Paris: Honoré Champion.

Bernardi, B. and B. Bensaude-Vincent 2013, "The Presence of Sciences in Rousseau's Trajectory and Works," in *The Challenge of Rousseau*, ed. Eve Grace and Christopher Kelly. Cambridge University Press, 59–75.

[46] *Moral Letters, OC* 4: 1090; Rousseau 2007: 80.
[47] For a recent interpretation along these lines, see Neuhouser 2008.

Brunet, M. and B. Guillarme 2010, "The Subject and its Body: Love of Oneself and Freedom in the Thought of Rousseau," in *Rousseau and Freedom*, ed. C. McDonald and S. Hoffmann. Cambridge University Press, 216–28.

Cooper, L. 1999, *Rousseau, Nature, and the Problem of the Good Life*. University Park, PA: Pennsylvania State University Press.

Cranston, M. 1991, *The Noble Savage: Jean-Jacques Rousseau 1754–1762*. University of Chicago Press.

Damrosch, L. 2005, *Jean-Jacques Rousseau*. Boston, MA and New York: Houghton Mifflin.

Gauthier, D. 2006, *Rousseau: The Sentiment of Existence*. Cambridge University Press.

Gouhier, H. 1970, *Les méditations métaphysiques de Jean-Jacques Rousseau*. Paris: Vrin.

Grace, E. 2013, "Built on Sand: Moral Law in Rousseau's *Second Discourse*," in *The Challenge of Rousseau*, ed. Eve Grace and Christopher Kelly. Cambridge University Press, 168–93.

Guénard, F. 2004, *Rousseau et le travail de la convenance*. Paris: Honoré Champion.

Kant, Immanuel. 1913, *Kritik der Urteilskraft, Kants gesammelte Schriften*, ed. Royal Prussian Academy of Sciences. Berlin: Georg Reimer.

Kelly, C. 2012, "On the Naturalness of the Sentiment of Justice," *L'Esprit Créateur* 52: 68–80.

Kelly, C. 2016, "Rousseau's Chemical Apprenticeship," in *Rousseau and the Dilemmas of Modernity*, ed. Mark Hulliung. New Brunswick, NJ and London: Transaction, 3–28.

Locke, John. 1694, *An Essay Concerning Humane Understanding*. London: Th. Dring and S. Manship.

Marks, J. 2006, "The Divine Instinct? Rousseau and Conscience," *Review of Politics* 68: 564–85.

Masters, R. 1968, *The Political Philosophy of Jean-Jacques Rousseau*. Princeton University Press.*

Melzer, A.M. 1990, *The Natural Goodness of Man: On the System of Rousseau's Thought*. University of Chicago Press.

Neuhouser, F. 2008, *Rousseau's Theodicy of Self-Love*. Oxford University Press.

Rasmussen, D. 2006, "Rousseau's 'Philosophical Chemistry' and the Foundations of Adam Smith's Thought," *History of Political Thought* 27, 620–41.

Riley, P. 1986, *The General Will before Rousseau: The Transformation of the Divine into the Civic*. Princeton University Press.

Rousseau, J.-Jacques 1954–, *Œuvres Complètes*, vols. 1–5. Paris: Gallimard.

Rousseau, J.-Jacques 1974, *Lettres Philosophiques*, ed. H. Gouhier. Paris: Vrin.

Rousseau, J.-Jacques 1978, *On the Social Contract, with Geneva Manuscript and Political Economy*, ed. R.D. Masters. New York: St. Martin's Press.

Rousseau, J.-Jacques 1990, *Rousseau Judge of Jean-Jacques: Dialogues, The Collected Writings of Rousseau*, ed. R.D. Masters and C. Kelly. Hanover, NH: University Press of New England.

Rousseau, J.-Jacques 1997, *The Discourses and Other Early Political Writings*, ed. Victor Gourevitch. Cambridge University Press.

Rousseau, J.-Jacques 2001, *Letter to Beaumont, Letters Written from the Mountain, and Related Writings*, ed. C. Kelly and Eve Grace. Hanover, NH: Dartmouth College Press.

Rousseau, J.-Jacques 2007, *Rousseau on Philosophy, Morality, and Religion*, ed. C. Kelly. Hanover, NH: Dartmouth College Press.

Rousseau, J.-Jacques 2010, *Emile or on Education, The Collected Writings of Rousseau*, trans. Christopher Kelly and Allan Bloom. Hanover, NH: Dartmouth College Press.

Rousseau, J.-Jacques 2012, *The Major Political Writings*, ed. J.C. Scott. University of Chicago Press.

Shell, S.M. 2013, "Stalking *Puer Robustus*: Hobbes and Rousseau on the Origins of Human Malice," in *The Challenge of Rousseau*, ed. E. Grace and K. Kelly. Cambridge University Press, 271–94.

Strauss, L. 1953, *Natural Right and History*. University of Chicago Press.

Williams, D.L. 2007, *Rousseau's Platonic Enlightenment*. University Park, PA: Pennsylvania State University Press.

29

Rationalism and Perfectionism

STEFANO BACIN

Rationalist accounts of morality played a central role in eighteenth-century moral philosophy. This applies especially to Britain and Germany, where new views, like Hutcheson's, Hume's or Kant's, entered the stage in reaction to the traditional rationalist positions. Although the debates in the English- and German-speaking areas developed largely independently, in both of them the rationalist views shared some fundamental theses. Both British and German rationalists of the eighteenth century regarded reason as the main moral faculty, insofar as reason is the cognitive power allowing human beings to discover within reality the sources of moral demands. Both British and German rationalists possessed a realistic account of the normative force of moral demands, as they held that its ultimate grounds lie in reality. All these thinkers rejected the attempt to explain moral obligation through positive commands, issued by a divine or human legislator. In spite of these shared points, there are, however, some important differences between British and German rational-isms in the eighteenth century, which will be highlighted in the following.

MORAL RATIONALISM AND MORAL REALISM: SAMUEL CLARKE, WOLLASTON, BALGUY

Between the end of the seventeenth and the beginning of the eighteenth century, the rejection of Hobbes's view and of law-centred voluntarist accounts of morals in general led to a new wave of realist accounts of morality. Along with Shaftesbury's *Inquiry Concerning Virtue and Merit* (1699), Samuel Clarke's second set of Boyle lectures (*A Discourse Concerning the Unchangeable Obligations of Natural Religion, and the Truth and Certainty of the Christian Revelation*, 1706) is the most important attempt of this kind at the

Please see the list of abbreviations at the end of the chapter. I have modernized the spelling of the sources.

outset of the eighteenth century. Clarke (1675–1726) aimed at an explanation of moral obligation that both accounts for its necessity and secures its accord with, on the one hand, Christian religion and, on the other, the new scientific image of the world. The most comprehensive statement of his views on morality provided in the *Discourse Concerning the Unchangeable Obligations of Natural Religion* is closely connected with the discussion of the main issues of philosophical theology presented in the first set of lectures (published as *A Discourse Concerning the Being and Attributes of God*, 1705).

Clarke shares with Cudworth and Shaftesbury a broadly Platonic background. However, the position that he develops is different from theirs in important respects. Unlike Shaftesbury, Clarke does not think that moral distinctions are harmonious proportions in actions and character traits perceived through affections. Clarke does hold that moral distinctions are rooted in the nature of things, but conceives of them as relations holding between elements of the world. The nature of things gives the foundation for the authority of moral demands, but their obligating character is determined by the relations between circumstances and agents. Clarke maintains that "[t]here is a Fitness or Suitableness of certain Circumstances to certain Persons, and an Unsuitableness of others; founded in the nature of things, and the Qualifications of Persons." It is, thus, not directly from the nature of things, but "from the different relations of different Persons one to another" that "there necessarily arises a fitness or unfitness of certain manners of Behaviour of some Persons towards others" (*SCW*, 2: 608). In particular circumstances, it is simply fitting to "so deal with every Man, as in like circumstances we could reasonably expect he should deal with Us" (*SCW*, 2: 619), and that we "endeavour to promote in general, to the utmost of our power, the welfare and happiness of all men" (*SCW*, 2: 621). The ways in which we ought to do so are examined by Clarke according to the traditional distinction between obligations towards God, others, and oneself (cf. *SCW*, 2: 619ff).

Unlike Cudworth, Clarke does not rely on the assumption of the intrinsic teleological character of the nature of things. (Cudworth's *Treatise on Eternal and Immutable Morality* would appear only later, in 1731.) Through his often unclear talk of "fitness," Clarke emphasizes that moral distinctions not only have a foundation in reality, or in the "reason of things," but are evident to the mind. He thereby stresses the epistemological character of moral realism in a way that profoundly influenced the discussions which followed.[1] Applying an already familiar analogy, Clarke holds that the relations of fitness or unfitness are somewhat like mathematical relations, and are as evident as

---

[1] See Irwin 2008: 378f.

they are (cf. *SCW*, 2: 609, 613f).[2] He maintains, therefore, that reason is the faculty of the soul granting access to moral obligations: "The indispensable necessity of all the great and moral Obligations of Natural Religion" is "in general deducible even demonstrably, by a Chain of clear and undeniable reasoning" (*SCW*, 2: 598).

In spite of the evidence of moral fitnesses and the analogy with mathematical truths, however, freedom makes an essential difference between theoretical assent and practical determination: as Clarke remarks, "Assent to a plain speculative Truth, is not in a Man's power to withhold; but to Act according to the plain Right and Reason of things, this he may, by the natural Liberty of his Will, forbear" (*SCW*, 2: 613).[3] If moral truths are ignored and consequently not put into practice, this happens not because of epistemic difficulties, but because of moral shortcomings, that is, "corruption of Manners, or perverseness of Spirit" (*SCW*, 2: 609), or because of the willingness to be persuaded by the bad philosophy of those "who had in earnest asserted and attempted to prove, that there is no natural and unalterable difference between Good and Evil" (*SCW*, 2: 609; cf. 614). In fact, moral cognition is accessible to "any Man of ordinary capacity, and unbiassed judgment" (*SCW*, 2: 609).

Clarke holds it to be equally evident that the obligatory force of the law of nature is eternal and therefore wholly independent of any reward or punishment: "the view of particular Rewards or Punishments, which is only an after-consideration, and does not at all alter the nature of Things, cannot be the original cause of the Obligation of the Law" (*SCW*, 2: 627f). In fact,

> these eternal and necessary differences of things make it fit and reasonable for Creatures so to act; they cause it to be their Duty, or lay an Obligation upon them, so to do; even separate from the consideration of these Rules being the positive Will or Command of God; and also antecedent to any respect or regard, expectation or apprehension, of any particular private and personal Advantage or Disadvantage. (*SCW*, 2: 608)

Taking the Platonic side on Euthyphro's problem, Clarke thus holds that the immutable law based in the nature of things "is commanded by God because 'tis Holy and Good" (*SCW*, 2: 627). God, "who has no Superior to direct him [. . .] yet constantly obliges himself to govern the World by" the same "eternal Reason of Things" wherein all obligations lie (*SCW*, 2: 614). Therefore, moral obligations belong to natural religion not because they

---

[2] On the analogy between morals and mathematics in eighteenth-century rationalism, see Gill 2007.

[3] On Clarke's conception of freedom, see Harris 2005: 46f.

depend on God's command, but because they are rooted in the perfect order of things created by God's perfect nature (cf. *SCW*, 2: 549). In virtue of the same "Reason of Things" human understanding, finite and corrupt, needs God's assistance and revelation.

Some of the main points of Clarke's view were developed in different terms by William Wollaston (1659–1724) in *The Religion of Nature Delineated* (*RND*; 1st edn 1722/1724). Wollaston emphasizes the epistemological character of moral realism by expressing the centrality of relations between actions and circumstances in the vocabulary of propositions.[4] In his formulation the law of nature demands "That every intelligent, active, and free being should so behave himself, as by no act to contradict truth; or, that he should treat every thing as being what it is" (*RND*, 18). Since "[t]ruth is but a conformity to nature" (*RND*, 9), an action can thus express a truth or contradict it, if it corresponds to the circumstances or not. Its value (or "significancy," as Wollaston puts it) can be assessed with regard to its conformity to the nature of things, governed by eternal axioms. In these terms, Wollaston believed, the nature of moral demands should become clearer than through referring to "fitnesses of things."

On the other hand, Clarke's views were attacked by writers maintaining a theological voluntarist conception, such as John Clarke in *The Foundation of Morality in Theory and Practice* (1726). However, the debate's main focus gradually shifted in a different direction, as writers defending Clarke's view opposed Hutcheson's sentimentalism, thereby making the contrast between rationalism and sentimentalism the centre of the discussion. While at the beginning of the century Clarke had taken his adversaries to be Hobbes, deists, and voluntarists, the epistemological issue now became predominant. Gilbert Burnet (1690–1726) engaged the views put forward in Hutcheson's *Inquiry into the Original of Our Ideas of Beauty and Virtue* in an important exchange of letters with Hutcheson (*BL*, 1735), which prompted Hutcheson to clarify aspects of his view in the *Illustrations on the Moral Sense*. Burnet, explicitly following Clarke and Wollaston, formulated several of the critical remarks taken up by later opponents of moral sentimentalism.[5] Analogously, Burnet argues that Hutcheson has "rested satisfied with the bare Description of Moral Good and Evil, by the Effects the Apprehension of them work in us" (*BL*, vi). In fact, feelings result from the cognition of moral truths through reason. On the contrary, Burnet maintains that while affection can merely be

---

[4] On Wollaston's view of morals, see Tweyman 1976 and Tilley 2012.
[5] On the Burnet–Hutcheson debate see Gill 2006, ch. 12.

physically good, moral goodness is only predicated on free actions, and consists in appropriateness to the power of an agent as such (cf. *BL*, 79).

Along similar lines, John Balguy (1686–1748) addressed Hutcheson's view in his *Foundation of Moral Goodness* (1728; *A Second Part, with Responses by an Advocate of Sentimentalism*, 1729). If virtue should consist in benevolent affections "depending upon Instincts," as Balguy takes Hutcheson to say, then morality would be "of an arbitrary and positive Nature" (*FMG*, 8). The sentimentalist view is thereby reduced to a variant of arbitrarism, analogous to voluntarism. Against such a view, Balguy reaffirms that "virtue, or moral goodness, is the conformity of our moral actions to the reasons of things" (*FMG*, 28; cf. 55). If virtue does not consist in affections, these are not to be expunged from moral life, but they are merely derivative, as effects of the evidence of moral truths. Therefore, Balguy rejects Hutcheson's distinction between exciting and justifying reasons (cf. *FMG*, 41f). On Balguy's view, an affection for goodness is not "planted in the mind," but only produced by the perception of goodness (cf. *FMG*, 53f). Accordingly, obligation as "a state of the mind" is a function of our understanding, which provides "some motive, some inducement, some reason, that is fit to influence and incline the will, and prevail with it to choose and act accordingly" (*FMG2*, 14; cf. *LT*, 6ff).

MORAL RATIONALISM RESTATED: PRICE

The union of moral realism and moral rationalism reached a higher level of complexity in Richard Price's *Review of the Principal Questions in Morals* (*RPQ*, 1758). Price (1723–1791) takes over the core of earlier moral realism, maintaining the independent reality of moral distinctions, but at the same time puts forward a more systematic version of moral rationalism which is rich in original distinctions and new arguments.[6] Price pursues further Balguy's attack on sentimentalism and is also influenced by Cudworth's anti-voluntarist view of "eternal and immutable" morality.

The epistemological aspect of the dispute against the sentimentalists is particularly conspicuous, as Price begins his argument with a thorough critique of Locke's epistemology, which he regards as the philosophical premise of the sentimentalist account of moral concepts. In the Platonic view that he advocates, on the contrary, reason is capable of generating new ideas through intuition. Price thus maintains that the concepts of right and

---

[6] The most recent examination of Price's view is in Irwin 2008: 714–53. For more detailed studies on Price's moral view, see Hudson 1970 and Allegri 2005.

wrong belong to notions that are not derived from the senses, but originate from rational intuition. Otherwise it would be impossible to explain the intrinsic necessity of moral truths, namely that moral concepts are immutable notions that "denote what actions are. Now whatever any thing is, that it is, not by will, or decree, or power, but by nature and necessity" (*RPQ*, 50). Accounts built on the demands of self-love and on God's commands are not able to explain this fundamental feature of morality, since they ultimately construe moral features as belonging to our responses to actions. In fact, Price argues that the moral qualities themselves belong to actions and, more specifically, that they are to be understood as irreducible properties: "Were not this true, it would be palpably absurd in any case to ask, whether it is right to obey a command, or wrong to disobey it; and the propositions, obeying a command is right, or producing happiness is right, would be most trifling, as expressing no more than obeying a command, is obeying a command, or producing happiness, is producing happiness" (*RPQ*, 16f; cf. 43). Much of the attention devoted to Price's thought in the twentieth century focused on this point, which is regarded as an anticipation of Moore's "open-question" argument. Price's argument is even more general than Moore's, as it concerns not only "good," but all fundamental moral notions, such as "right," "wrong," and "obligation." Remarkably, his anti-reductionism leads Price to apply the same argument also to the naturalist accounts of Wollaston and of other followers of Clarke, when he observes that expressions like "acting suitably to the nature of things [. . .]; conformity to truth; [. . .] congruity and incongruity between actions and relations [. . .] are of no use, and have little meaning, if considered as intended to define virtue; for they evidently presuppose it" (*RPQ*, 125).[7]

Price rejects not only voluntarist accounts of moral obligation, but also Hutcheson's psychological account of obligation. Unlike Balguy, Price insists on the impossibility of defining basic moral concepts through non-moral notions in order to argue that obligation cannot be understood merely as the state of mind arising from the perception of a reason to act, but lies in fact in the rightness of action itself (cf. *RPQ*, 105, 114). The perception of the rightness of an action gives a reason to act accordingly, thereby providing the agent with a motive. Like Balguy, Price insists that the feelings motivating one to act are merely effects of the intellectual apprehension of moral demands. A "perception of the understanding" is connected with a "feeling of the heart" (*RPQ*, 62). The derivative nature of the emotional aspect of moral choice, however, is not

---

[7] On the differences between Price's view and naturalistic versions of rationalism see Irwin 2008: 730ff.

merely causal. Price holds that "[r]eason is [. . .] the natural and authoritative guide of a rational being" (RPQ, 109).

Such formulations show that, if he often draws on Cudworth's views, Price is also strongly influenced by Butler on significant points, as he himself stresses on the very first page of the Review. The most important of them is probably the rejection of Hutcheson's reduction of virtue to benevolence. Price pushes this line of thought further, arguing for a more complex picture of the content of moral demands. Several aspects of virtue are self-evident: gratitude, veracity, beneficence, justice, along with our duty to God and our duties to ourselves, are all equally perceived as obligatory. Price recognizes that this view of virtue entails that there can be conflicts between obligations stemming from different "heads of virtue." However, these conflicts can be resolved, at least in principle, and depend not on intrinsic features of morality, but on the limits of the human grasp of moral matters. The insistence on the plurality of the aspects of virtue is another element of Price's view that received attention in the twentieth century, when it was associated with W.D. Ross's conception of prima facie duties. Unlike Ross and other normative pluralists, though, Price at the same time strongly maintains the necessary unity of virtue, arguing that the different "heads of virtue [. . .] should be considered as only different modifications and views of one original, all-governing law" (RPQ, 165).

PERFECTIONIST MORAL REALISM AGAINST
THEOLOGICAL VOLUNTARISM: WOLFF

In the German philosophical discussion of the same decades another version of moral rationalism took centre stage. Its most significant and influential champion was Christian Wolff (1679–1754), who developed very extensively some of Leibniz's ideas in moral philosophy. Wolff's early contact with Leibniz, which led to an extensive exchange of letters, was crucial for his thought in general and for his moral philosophy in particular. Leibniz's critical remarks against voluntarist accounts of morality prompted Wolff to reject Pufendorf's position, which had influenced him up till then. Drawing on Leibniz's ideas, Wolff developed at great length a naturalist conception of morality, first in the German exposition of his system (1710–1725), and then in the much more detailed Latin version (1728–1754).[8]

---

[8] The most comprehensive study of Wolff's thought, which also analyzes his moral philosophy at length, is Campo 1980. For more recent studies see Schwaiger 1995 and Schröer 1988.

Leibniz, however, did not inspire Wolff's own project of a "universal practical philosophy" (*philosophia practica universalis*). In fact, Wolff first made contact with Leibniz by sending him an early draft. After a first outline was published in 1703, Wolff developed the project extensively in his subsequent works, always regarding it as one of his most significant contributions to philosophy in general.[9] Drawing on the early modern debates on the method of philosophy, Wolff held that practical philosophy would have been capable of achieving certainty only if based on a preliminary inquiry of the fundamental elements of practical life. Universal practical philosophy should be a general theory of praxis, providing the proper foundation for the three special practical sciences of ethics, politics, and economics. Wolff does not understand universal practical philosophy as a mere systematic introduction to the substantive parts of the system, though, but rather as an inquiry into the nature of the will that directs free actions towards their fitting end.[10] Through an empirical theory of the will, practical philosophy can be effective and achieve its essential aim of directing the conduct of human beings.[11] One of the most important points of Wolff's theory of the will is his psychological account of obligation: "To obligate someone to do or omit something is only to connect a motive of willing or not willing to it" (*DE*, § 8; 335).[12] Wolff thereby develops at greater length a view rather close to Balguy's.

In Wolff's view, the fundamental normative concept is perfection, which he understands primarily in metaphysical terms as "concordance of the manifold" (*DM*, § 152), equating it with what the Scholastics called "transcendental goodness" (cf. *PPO*, § 503). In the practical domain, perfection consists in the coherence of actions towards the best possible realization of human nature and its essential ends (cf. *PPU1*, § 9). Wolff formulates the "law of nature" accordingly as follows: "Do what makes you and your condition, or that of others, more perfect; omit what makes it less perfect" (*DE*, § 15; 336). Since Wolff maintains that the morality of actions depends on the perfection that they can bring about, his account is decidedly consequentialist. Good is thus "what makes ourselves and our condition more perfect" (*DM*, § 422; cf. *DE*, § 3). The bindingness of the law of nature has natural grounds. Wolff

---

[9] *PPU1* and *PPU2*.

[10] Cf. *PPU1*, § 3: "universal practical philosophy is the affective practical science of directing free actions through the most general rules [*scientia affectiva practica dirigendi actiones liberas per regulas generalissimas*]."

[11] On Wolff's idea of a universal practical philosophy, see Schwaiger 2005.

[12] Page references following *DE* clause numbers are to the translation in Schneewind 2003.

holds that moral obligation cannot arise from the threat of sanctions or from the command of a superior. The law of nature is binding in virtue of a "natural obligation" since "nature has connected motives with men's inherently good and bad actions," "because the good and bad that we meet in actions are the ground of willing or not willing them" (DE, § 9; 335).

Assessing the morality of actions requires an empirical investigation of their effects: "if one will judge whether actions are good or evil, one must research what alterations in our internal condition of body and soul as well as in our external condition they carry in their train, and thereby attend to whether the altered condition is concordant with the essence and nature of the human being, that is, of the body and the soul, and with the preceding condition, or is contradictory to it" (DE, § 4; 335). While Wolff initially insisted on the constitutive connection between perfection and the essential nature of things, his understanding of the demand of perfection comes increasingly close to eudaimonism, as is especially apparent in the Latin works. If the genuine moral motive is the goodness of actions (cf. PPU2, § 369), happiness is ultimately what really motivates us to act according to the natural law (cf. PPU2, §§ 326, 328).[13] Elaborating on the foundation given in universal practical philosophy, Wolff provides a very extensive treatment of ethical duties, especially in the five-volume Philosophia moralis (PM, 1750–1753), which discusses in great detail specific issues of the obligations towards the self, God, and others. The content of the particular duties consists in their contribution to the agent's own perfection, or to the perfection of others.

The faculty that teaches the law of nature is reason, which Wolff understands as "the capacity to have insight into the interconnection of truths" (DM, § 368). Yet Wolff stresses the epistemological character of his view less than do Clarke and his followers. Since Wolff, like Leibniz, sees no divide between sensible and intellectual cognition, his view does not entail any strong opposition to empiricist accounts of morality. In fact, as he stresses the necessity of a "marriage of reason and experience" in every domain, Wolff emphasizes that moral life needs not only intellectual insight, but also sensible and experiential cognition. Furthermore, Wolff holds that an important role in morality is played by pleasure, which, following Leibniz, he understands as the mind's response to the cognition of perfection.

Following Leibniz, Wolff rejects voluntarism, but at the same time stresses the harmony between natural law and creation, natural obligation and divine obligation. As creator of the whole of reality, God is the author of the law of

---

[13] On perfection and happiness in Wolff's moral philosophy, see Schwaiger 1995.

nature (cf. *PPU1*, § 273), according to Wolff, who also denies that sanctions are necessary to moral obligation (cf. *DE*, § 35). Yet the cognition of the content of morality does not require Christian revelation, but merely insight into the nature of things. Applying this general thesis, Wolff maintains in his lecture on *The Practical Philosophy of the Chinese* (*PPC*, given in 1721) that the wisdom of Confucius shows that Christian revelation is not needed to have access to the criteria of moral virtue.[14] As he later clarifies, however, full-fledged virtue can be reached only through the teachings of the Christian religion.[15]

While the most significant opponents of the British rationalists were the advocates of the new moral sentimentalism, Wolff's adversaries were mainly inspired by religious orthodoxy. His appreciation of Confucius's practical philosophy in the lecture of 1721 attracted such hostile attention that the Prussian government sent him into exile. The opposition was, however, not only academic, religious, and political, but also philosophical. Wolff's leading philosophical opponent was a theologian close to the traditional Lutheran party, Christian August Crusius (1715–1775). In his main work on ethics, the *Instructions for a Reasonable Life* (*Anweisung, vernünftig zu leben*, AVL, 1744), Crusius developed a divine command account of morals, presenting core ideas of Lutheranism in a philosophically updated form.[16] Responding to a traditional objection against voluntarism, Crusius observes that defending such a view does not amount to making the good arbitrary, because "the will of God, in which the highest laws of nature have their ground, is not a free but a necessary will" (*AVL*, § 173; 579).[17] Crusius formulates the general moral rule as follows: "Do what is in accordance with the perfection of God and your relations to him and further what accords with the essential perfection of human nature, and omit the opposite" (*AVL*, § 137; 576). The formulation is influenced by Crusius's adversary Wolff, but at the same time shows up the main difference between the two accounts. The morally relevant perfection that sets the normative standard to which human agents have to conform, for Crusius, is God's. Therefore, "morally good [. . .] is what is in accordance with the moral designs of God, that is, those that he wills to have forwarded through the reason and free wills of created minds or, to put it otherwise, the morally good is what agrees with his laws" (*AVL*, § 26; 570). Accordingly, "the love of God above all things is the main virtue from which all others must

---

[14] On this text see Louden 2003.   [15] See Albrecht 1992.

[16] The only book-length treatment of Crusius's moral philosophy is Benden 1972. For a concise presentation, see Schneewind 1998: 445–56.

[17] Page references following *AVL* clause numbers are to the translation in Schneewind 2003.

flow" (*AVL*, § 240; 582). Moral obligation arises from human beings' dependence on God (cf. *AVL*, §§ 133, 194), which is fully independent of the representation of sanctions.

Crusius states, however, that the general moral rule is found *a posteriori* to summarize the content of ethical duties, or of "most of them, at least" (*AVL*, § 137; 576). The foundation of morals is given not with a rule, but with the fact of human beings' dependence on God together with their immediate awareness of it. This fundamental bond expresses itself in human nature through the "drive of conscience" (*Gewissenstrieb*), which Crusius understands as a "fundamental drive to recognize a divine moral law" (*AVL*, § 132) and, with that, "universal obligations [. . .] by which we have to abide out of obedience" (*AVL*, § 133). For Crusius, reason can be helpful in providing an inferential knowledge of moral demands, but is not the faculty responsible for moral cognition and action. Conscience plays this role, enabling every human being to easily judge of moral matters through "a natural sensation of what is right and proper" (*AVL*, § 368), thereby teaching us what our duties are, without referring to any rule. The crucial feature of conscience, however, is in Crusius's view not a strictly epistemological primacy, but a direct connection to God's will. As Crusius remarks, "one should not confuse conscience with consciousness in general or with the awareness of the perfection or imperfection of one's actions in general." In fact, "the German word *Gewissen* does not express what in the good Latin writers is called *conscientia*, but what is called *religio*" (*AVL*, § 132; cf. 574), namely, a fundamental bond with God.

Crusius devotes much attention not only to the divine will, but also to the finite will of the addressees of God's command. He bases his moral philosophy on a preliminary inquiry into the natural features of the will, which he calls "thelematology" (i.e. the doctrine of will and choice). A central role in this inquiry has the idea that the human will is moved by three fundamental drives or impulses (*Triebe*). Besides the crucial drive of conscience, which represents Crusius's key to the foundation of moral obligation in finite beings, Crusius isolates a drive to the perfection of oneself (*AVL*, § 111) and a drive consisting in "the urge for union with objects in which we perceive perfection"(*AVL*, § 122; 574).

In the disputes with the adversaries of Wolff's rationalism, some Wolffians tried to overcome the limits of Wolff's own view. The most original among them is probably Alexander Gottlieb Baumgarten (1714–1762), who proposes significant changes to the official Wolffian position.[18] If some of Wolff's

---

[18] On Baumgarten see Schwaiger 2011.

adversaries had pointed out that his view amounted to mere eudaimonism, Baumgarten strongly downplays the moral significance of happiness and does not take over Wolff's idea of the continuity between perfection and happiness. Baumgarten focuses, instead, on perfection alone, trying to clarify its moral significance through a distinction between perfection as a means and perfection as an end (cf. *IP*, § 43; *EP*, § 10). Furthermore, Baumgarten is closer to Wolff in understanding obligation as deriving from "overriding impulsive causes" (cf. *IP*, §§ 12–16). In Baumgarten's account, however, the concept of obligation acquires a much more important role, as it is understood as unifying the whole practical sphere: practical philosophy is the "science of the obligations of man to be known without faith" (*IP*, § 1), and ethics specifically deals with internal obligations (cf. *EP*, § 1). Finally, moral obligation does not rest on the normative authority of nature itself, as Wolff maintained. In fact, Baumgarten holds that moral demands can be fully obligatory only by virtue of God's rational will (cf. *IP*, § 69). His rationalism is thus significantly qualified by the explicit rejection of Grotius's "impossible hypothesis" that the law of nature and moral obligation would hold even if God would not exist (cf. *IP*, § 71).

In spite of its opponents, Wolff's rationalism maintained its primacy in German moral philosophy during most of the eighteenth century, probably because of its capacity to accommodate different developments. Unlike the views of Clarke and his followers, Wolff's rationalism did not entail an uncompromising opposition to sentimentalism. In fact, several Wolffians took over Leibniz's and Wolff's acknowledgment of the role of pleasure in the determination of the will, drawing on the underlying idea of a continuity of the different grades of representation ranging from the sensible to the intellectual. A case in point is Moses Mendelssohn (1729–1786).[19] More generally, the idea of a universal practical philosophy was regarded by many as being to some degree independent of Wolff's perfectionism. Even an empiricist in the wake of Locke and common-sense philosophy such as Johann Georg Heinrich Feder (1740–1821) stated repeatedly the great importance of Wolff's innovation in providing moral philosophy with a proper foundation through a preliminary inquiry of that kind.[20] In Feder's view, however, that project must be developed focusing on the two fundamental drives, self-love and sympathy. The Wolffian project, while explicitly appreciated, was thereby adapted to a view of morality closer to Hutcheson's and Smith's, where the normative reference to perfection thus no longer had a role in the account of moral life.

---

[19] See Kuehn 1987: 42f.   [20] See e.g. Feder 1779–1793, vol. 1: 19f.

ABBREVIATIONS

AVL   *Anweisung vernünftig zu leben*, Crusius 1969

BL   *Letters Between the Late Mr. Gilbert Burnet, and Mr. Hutchinson [sic], Concerning the True Foundation of Virtue or Moral Goodness*, Burnet 1735

DE   *Deutsche Ethik, Vernünfftige Gedancken von der Menschen Thun und Lassen zur Beförderung ihrer Glückseligkeit*, Wolff 1996

DM   *Deutsche Metaphysik, Vernünfftige Gedancken von Gott, der Welt und der Seele des Menschen, auch allen Dingen überhaupt, den Liebhabern der Wahrheit mitgetheilt*, Wolff 1983

EP   *Ethica philosophica*, Baumgarten 1969

FMG   *The Foundation of Moral Goodness*, Balguy 1728

FMG2   *The Second Part of the Foundation of Moral Goodness*, Balguy 1733a

IP   *Initia philosophiae practicae primae*, Baumgarten 1760

LT   *The Law of Truth Or, the Obligations of Reason Essential to All Religion*, Balguy 1733b

PM   *Philosophia moralis sive ethica*, Wolff 1970

PPC   *Rede über die praktische Philosophie der Chinesen*, Wolff 1985

PPO   *Philosophia prima sive ontologia methodo scientifica pertractata qua omnis cognitionis humanae principia continentur*, Wolff 1962

PPU1   *Philosophia practica universalis, methodo scientifica pertractata, Pars prior . . .*, Wolff 1971

PPU2   *Philosophia practica universalis, methodo scientifica pertractata, Pars posterior . . .*, Wolff 1979

RND   *The Religion of Nature Delineated*, Wollaston 1738

RPQ   *A Review of the Principal Questions in Morals*, Price 1974

SCW   *The Works of Samuel Clarke*, Clarke 1738

BIBLIOGRAPHY

An asterisk denotes secondary literature especially suitable for further reading.

Albrecht, M., 1992, "Die Tugend und die Chinesen. Antworten von Christian Wolff auf die Frage nach dem Verhältnis zwischen Religion und Moral," in Sonia Carboncini and Luigi Cataldi Madonna (eds.), *Nuovi studi sul pensiero di Christian Wolff*, Hildesheim *et al.*, Olms, 239–62.

Allegri, F., 2005, *Le radici storiche dell'etica analitica. Richard Price e il fondamento della virtù*, Milan, Franco Angeli.

Balguy, J., 1728, *The Foundation of Moral Goodness*, London.

Balguy, J., 1733a, *The Second Part of the Foundation of Moral Goodness*, 2nd edn, London (1st edn, 1729).

Balguy, J., 1733b, *The Law of Truth: Or, the Obligations of Reason Essential to All Religion*, London.

Baumgarten A.G., 1760, *Initia philosophiae practicae primae*, Halae Magdeburgicae [Halle an der Saale].

Baumgarten A.G., 1969, *Ethica philosophica*, Hildesheim, Olms (reprint of 3rd edn, Halle, 1763 [1st edn 1740]).

Beiser, F., 1996, *The Sovereignty of Reason*, Princeton University Press.

Benden, M., 1972, *Christian August Crusius: Wille und Verstand als Prinzipien des Handelns*, Bonn, Bouvier.

Burnet G., 1735, *Letters Between the Late Mr. Gilbert Burnet, and Mr. Hutchinson [sic], Concerning the True Foundation of Virtue or Moral Goodness*. Formerly Published in the London Journal, London.

Campo, M., 1980, *Il razionalismo precritico di Cristiano Wolff*, Hildesheim *et al.*, Olms (reprint of Milan, 1939 edn).

Clarke, S., 1738, *The Works of Samuel Clarke*, 4 vols., London.

Crusius, Ch.A., 1969, *Anweisung vernünftig zu leben*, Hildesheim *et al.*, Olms (reprint of Leipzig, 1744 edn).

Feder, J.G.H., 1779–1793, *Untersuchungen über den menschlichen Willen*, 4 vols., Göttingen and Lemgo, Meyer (reprint, Brussels, Culture et Civilisation, 1968).

Gill, M., 2006, *The British Moralists on Human Nature and the Birth of Secular Ethics*, Cambridge University Press.

Gill, M., 2007, "Moral Rationalism vs. Moral Sentimentalism: Is Morality More Like Math or Beauty?," *Philosophy Compass* 2, 16–30.

Harris, J., 2005, *Of Liberty and Necessity: The Free Will Debate in Eighteenth-Century British Philosophy*, Oxford, Clarendon Press.

Hudson, W.D., 1970, *Reason and Right: A Critical Examination of Richard Price's Moral Philosophy*, London, Macmillan.

Irwin, T., 2008, *The Development of Ethics*, vol. 2: *Suárez to Rousseau*, Oxford University Press.*

Kuehn, M., 1987, *Scottish Common Sense in Germany, 1768–1800*, Kingston, Montreal, McGill-Queen's University Press.

Louden, R.B., 2003, "'What Does Heaven Say?': Christian Wolff and Western Interpretations of Confucian Ethics," in Bryan W. Van Norden (ed.), *Confucius and the Analects. New Essays*, Oxford University Press, 73–93.

Price, R., 1974, *A Review of the Principal Questions in Morals*, ed. D.D. Raphael, Oxford University Press, (1758, 3rd edn. 1787).

Schneewind, J.B., 1998, *The Invention of Autonomy: A History of Modern Moral Philosophy*, Cambridge University Press.*

Schneewind, J.B. (ed.), 2003, *Moral Philosophy from Montaigne to Kant*, Cambridge University Press.

Schröer, Chr., 1988, *Naturbegriff und Moralbegründung. Die Grundlegung der Ethik bei Christian Wolff und deren Kritik durch Immanuel Kant*, Stuttgart, Kohlhammer.

Schwaiger, C., 1995, *Das Problem des Glücks im Denken Christian Wolffs. Eine quellen-, begriffs- und entwicklungsgeschichtliche Studie zu Schlüsselbegriffen seiner Ethik*, Stuttgart, Bad Cannstatt, Frommann-Holzboog.*

Schwaiger, C., 2005, "Christian Wolffs 'Philosophia practica universalis'. Zu ursprünglichem Gehalt und späterer Gestalt einer neuen Grundlagendisziplin," in Luigi Cataldi Madonna (ed.), *Macht und Bescheidenheit der Vernunft. Beiträge zur Philosophie Christian Wolffs*, Hildesheim *et al.*, Olms, 219–33.

Schwaiger, C., 2011, *Alexander Gottlieb Baumgarten – ein intellektuelles Porträt. Studien zur Metaphysik und Ethik von Kants Leitautor*, Stuttgart, Bad Cannstatt, Frommann-Holzboog.

Tilley, J., 2012, "The Problem of Inconsistency in Wollaston's Moral Theory," *History of Philosophy Quarterly* 29, 265–80.

Tweyman, S., 1976, "Truth, Happiness and Obligation: The Moral Philosophy of William Wollaston," *Philosophy* 51, 35–46.

Wolff, Chr., 1962, *Philosophia prima sive ontologia methodo scientifica pertractata qua omnis cognitionis humanae principia continentur*, ed. Jean École, Hildesheim *et al.*, Olms (reprint of Frankfurt, 1730 edn [2nd edn. 1736]).

Wolff, Chr., 1970, *Philosophia moralis sive ethica*, Hildesheim *et al.*, Olms (reprint of Halle, 1750–1753 [5 vols.] edn).

Wolff, Chr., 1971, *Philosophia practica universalis, methodo scientifica pertractata, Pars prior, theoriam complectens, qua omnis actionum humanarum differentia, omnisque juris ac obligationum omnium, principia, a priori demonstrantur*, Hildesheim *et al.*, Olms (reprint of Francofurti et Lipsiae [Frankfurt and Leipzig], 1738 edn).

Wolff, Chr., 1979, *Philosophia practica universalis, methodo scientifica pertractata, Pars posterior, praxin complectens, qua omnis praxeos moralis principia inconcussa ex ipsa animae humanae natura a priori demonstrantur*, Hildesheim *et al.*, Olms (reprint of Francofurti et Lipsiae [Frankfurt and Leipzig], 1739 edn).

Wolff, Chr., 1983, *Vernünfftige Gedancken von Gott, der Welt und der Seele des Menschen, auch allen Dingen überhaupt, den Liebhabern der Wahrheit mitgetheilet*, Hildesheim, Olms (reprint of Halle, 1751 [4th] edn [1st edn 1719]).

Wolff, Chr., 1985, *Oratio de Sinarum philosophia practica*, Latin text with German translation: *Rede über die praktische Philosophie der Chinesen*, ed. M. Albrecht, Hamburg, Meiner (reprint of Francofurti ad Moenum [Frankfurt am Main], 1726 edn).

Wolff, Chr., 1996, *Vernünfftige Gedancken von der Menschen Thun und Lassen zur Beförderung ihrer Glückseligkeit*, ed. H.W. Arndt, Hildesheim *et al.*, Olms (reprint of Frankfurt and Leipzig, 1733 [4th] edn [1st edn 1720]).

Wollaston, W., 1738, *The Religion of Nature Delineated*, London (1st edn 1722/1724).

30

Kant

JENS TIMMERMANN

Kant's writings contain some of the most powerful and influential ideas in the history of moral philosophy.[1] They centre on the notion of human beings as persons endowed with pure practical reason, possessing dignity, in charge of their own affairs. Kant's philosophical approach, however, is paradoxical. On the one hand, he sets out to find a secure foundation for ordinary moral judgement, the correctness of which he never calls into doubt. Philosophy is not needed to know what one ought to do. As in the natural law tradition, ordinary agents have access to moral truths through reason. In this respect he was no revisionist. On the other hand, he claims that his own ethics of autonomy is the only theory that can provide this foundation. He dismisses all other theories as making, implicitly or explicitly, the same mistake of looking for the source of normativity outside the human will. Moreover, while theory is not needed to determine good and bad, right and wrong, the right kind of theory will ultimately help us to improve morals by strengthening respect for the moral law.

TWO KINDS OF FINAL END

Human beings actively pursue ends by taking the means they consider appropriate. Means derive their value from the value attributed to the end the agent has in mind. When I turn the handle of my grinder the end I seek to realize is ground coffee. But ground beans are not the final end. They are ingredients needed for a cup of coffee, which in turn is a means to my enjoyment. Some ends – ground coffee, even a good cup of coffee – thus

---

[1] Kant's writings are cited with reference to volume and page numbers of the standard edition, edited under the auspices of the Berlin (previously Royal Prussian) Academy of Sciences. Abbreviations used for individual works: G = *Groundwork of the Metaphysics of Morals*; KpV = *Critique of Practical Reason*; MdS = *The Metaphysics of Morals*.

become means when they are realized. But in all action there must be an end for the sake of which means are ultimately taken. Without such an end acting would be pointless. What, then, is the final end of human action? Kant assumes that there are two competing final ends: morally good activity and an agent's own happiness.

The desire for happiness seeks to influence human action first. But happiness, though universally valued as an end, is not unconditionally good. It is good only if impartial reason approves, i.e. if the agent deserves to be happy, if the agent is a person with a morally good will. By contrast, the happiness of the vicious has no objective value. As the opening sentence of Kant's *Groundwork* of 1785 states, '[i]t is impossible to think of anything at all in the world, or indeed even beyond it, that could be taken to be good without limitation, except a *good will*' (G 4: 393). There is thus a sharp divide between what initially we feel we would like to do and what on reflection we judge we ought to do. The desire for happiness, though legitimate, must take second place.[2]

The notion of conditional value is not as peculiar as it may seem. It is, for instance, recognizable in ordinary judgement about the value of competitive activity. Any competitive runner wants to win the race, just as any human agent wants to be happy. However, desire does not make the end good (i.e. objectively – not just subjectively – worth having). An honest runner will say that victory is worth having only if the race is fair, just as an honest agent will judge that happiness is worth having only if it is not attained at the expense of impartial morality. Of course, victory, like happiness, is always attractive, and it is often tempting to violate honest judgement. But it is still bad if a runner wins the race because he manages to trip up a rival with impunity. He does not deserve to win. In the same way reason disapproves of the flourishing of those who recklessly put their own happiness first.[3]

Kant occasionally formulates his theses about the value of virtue and happiness in the traditional language of the 'highest good'. In one obvious sense morality or virtue is the highest good – it is the supreme and only unconditional good upon which the value of any other good thing depends.

---

[2] See Korsgaard 1983 for a classic discussion of Kant's two types of goodness.
[3] The idea that only a morally good will is unconditionally good has another remarkable consequence: Morally impermissible actions are not just worse than moral actions in the judgement of reason, they lack goodness altogether. Moral commands are not simply 'overriding' when they conflict with inclination. Non-moral objective value is undermined by moral impossibility. An immoral option, no matter how attractive or pleasant, is not good.

But, as we have already seen, moral goodness is not the only ultimate good – that would be the stark thesis of Stoicism, criticized by Kant in the second *Critique* as unrealistic and inhumane (KpV 5: 126–7). We can enhance the goodness of the morally good will by adding the other non-instrumentally good thing, the happiness of a good person. We then arrive – most explicitly in the *Critique of Practical Reason* – at the notion of the 'highest good' in the sense of the *complete* good: the sum of everything that is good as an end (KpV 5: 110–11).[4]

THE GOOD WILL IN PRACTICE

Intuitions about value are only the starting point of Kant's inquiry in the *Groundwork*. The leading question of the first section is: What makes morally good willing good?

What makes instrumentally good action valuable is obvious: it brings about the intended end. We know that the value of the good will must be different in kind. It does not depend on the consequences. It is self-contained. What, then, is the principle of morally good willing? On his way to providing an answer to this question, Kant discusses four examples that sparked controversy as soon as the *Groundwork* was published.

The first is that of a shopkeeper who reliably sells goods at a fixed price even to inexperienced customers, not because he is honest but because he deems behaving honestly to be in his own overall interest (G 4: 397). In Kant's terminology, he acts *in accordance* with duty but not *from* duty. While his actions superficially comply with moral norms, they are determined by self-interest, not by a moral disposition. The shopkeeper wrongs no one, but the fact remains that his actions are amoral. That is why the example is set aside. It is no use to Kant in his search for the supreme moral principle.

The other three examples – most famously that of the 'philanthropist' (G 4: 398–9) – are devised to isolate actions that *are* determined by moral considerations. This is done by stipulating away any inclination recommending the action required by morality, and in some cases by assuming that morality and inclination are in tension. Consider someone who is generally inclined to help others. He helps them because he enjoys it. According to Kant, the philanthropist acts less strategically, but his actions merely accord with duty, just like those of the shopkeeper. Such actions lack moral value because they rely upon sympathetic

---

[4] For a recent comprehensive discussion of the doctrine of the highest good in Kant see Moran 2012.

sentiment. Kant is assuming that action from inclination is done for the sake of the desire effect. It is – at best – instrumentally good. So, action from inclination can never be good in the special, self-contained way in which moral action is meant to be good. Without sympathy the person in Kant's example would not help. But moral action cannot be contingent like that. There must be something else in him that can be active independently: the will to help when help is needed, not just when it accords with feeling.[5]

So, for an action to be directly determined by morality it must be done not for the sake of some ulterior end but simply from duty or – what comes to the same thing – from *respect* for the moral law. This law is the law of the good will: only to act on subjective principles or 'maxims' that can be willed as applying universally. The derivation of this formulation is riddled with difficulties, but the basic idea is that the form of law – its universality – is the only consideration left to determine the will if all considerations tied to specific ends we are inclined to pursue are excluded. The principle of the good will, Kant argues, is implicitly at work in ordinary moral judgement. It was the philosopher's task to make it explicit.[6]

THE CATEGORICAL IMPERATIVE, AND HOW IT WORKS

The principle of the good human will is called the 'categorical imperative':

> There is [...] only a single categorical imperative, and it is this: *act only according to that maxim through which you can at the same time will that it become a universal law.* (G 4:421)

What does this mean? Kant distinguishes two types of command of practical reason: 'hypothetical' and 'categorical' imperatives. Hypothetical imperatives are authoritative for us on condition that we want to achieve something, that we want to realize an end. While still valid in the abstract, they have no normative force for us if we do not.[7] To return to the above example,

---

[5] Note that Kant is not saying what many readers take him to say, namely that we should be unsympathetic. Acts of beneficence should not be *determined* by sympathy. For a helpful and influential discussion of these matters see Baron 1995.

[6] On the face of it, then, the law is primary and the notion of moral value depends on it. Some scholars argue that a further value – e.g. rationality or freedom – is required in turn to ground the law (e.g. Wood 1999, Herman 1993 and Guyer 2007). Others contend that this is not the case (see, most prominently, Sensen 2011).

[7] There are two types of hypothetical imperative, depending on the kind of end pursued. There are 'prudential' imperatives that teach us how to advance our own happiness, and 'technical' imperatives that tell us how to achieve just any end we

the command 'Turn the handle!' applies to coffee drinkers only. It has no purchase on tea drinkers (unless, of course, they want to make a cup of coffee for someone else). A categorical imperative, by contrast, commands unconditionally, telling us to do something regardless of whether or not we want to do it.

Kant argues that it is an essential element of our ordinary conception of morality that the spirit of a moral command can only be captured as a categorical imperative. Moral commands cannot depend on what I am inclined to do. The fact that I would like to make a promise I intend not to keep does not make fraudulent promising any more permissible, and its impermissibility cannot be grounded in the fact that the act may have disagreeable consequences. Moreover, there are no non-moral commands that are categorical in this sense. Prudential imperatives are conditional on our desire to be happy – a desire that can be taken for granted in the case of finite beings like ourselves, but which still provides the basis for pursuing many different purposes we think we will enjoy. So, again, all action ultimately relates to either of two practical spheres: one's own happiness or morality.

Kant is extraordinarily optimistic about the potency of his formula of the categorical imperative:

> Here it would be easy to show how, with this compass in hand, it is very well informed in all cases that occur, to distinguish what is good, what is evil, what conforms with duty or is contrary to it, if – without in the least teaching it anything new – one only, as Socrates did, makes it aware of its own principle; and that there is thus no need of science and philosophy to know what one has to do in order to be honest and good, indeed even to be wise and virtuous.
>
> (G 4: 404)

So, can Kant's universalization test produce determinate duties? If so, how? This is, once again, a highly controversial issue. Ever since the publication of the *Groundwork* Kant's critics have been arguing that Kant's formula is empty in that it cannot yield positive results (a criticism popularized by G.W.F. Hegel), or at any rate the right results.[8]

---

intend to realize (e.g. to dissect a line, to make a cup of coffee). Both require knowledge of the nature of things, e.g. knowledge of causal connections. Prudential imperatives face the further challenge that we often lack a clear sense of what our various interest are and how they are best served long term (cf. G 4: 418).

[8] See Wood 1999: 97–110 for a thorough discussion of the danger of 'false positives' and 'false negatives'.

In coming to understand Kant's formal procedure we must bear in mind that it is not meant to operate in a volitional vacuum. The maxim put to the test is suggested by inclination: You scrutinize the principle you would be acting on were you to do what you would like to do.[9] Consider Kant's favourite example: You would like to extract yourself from a difficult financial situation by making a promise you do not intend to keep, say to repay a loan in a week's time.[10] The promise is necessary as a means. Without it the money will not be forthcoming. If you decide to make this promise the principle of your action will be: when I am in a tight spot I will make a fraudulent promise to escape. The decisive question is whether it is possible for you to will this maxim as a universal law, i.e. a law applying consistently to all agents just like you at all times. Kant's answer is that you cannot. The universality of the maxim would undermine the institution of promising, and without this institution you would be unable to make a *fraudulent* promise. You would be unable to obtain the money because there would be no such institution for you to take advantage of.

This example shows how a purely formal thought experiment can produce concrete results when an agent is inclined to act immorally. Moreover, it sheds light on several important features of Kant's moral theory.

First, what makes practical reason reject the maxim is the fact that it generates a contradiction when universalized – not, as in certain versions of rule consequentialism, that the universal adoption of a policy would cause disvalue.[11] It is true, we have to imagine the consequences of the universalized maxim. But consequences as such do not determine moral status. The decisive question is whether the universalized maxim can *consistently* be willed by the agent. Universality is an attribute of reason; and reason abhors contradictions. Kant thus rejects David Hume's thesis that reason is subservient to the passions (inclinations) twice over. Applied to a possible principle of human action, pure reason can determine its moral status. Furthermore, moral judgement by itself provides a motive we can always act on if we so choose: respect for the moral law.

[9] The procedure does not directly concern specific actions. In a sense, Kant does not believe that there are individual actions in isolation. All action springs from maxims, adopted explicitly or implicitly and subject to rational revision, which jointly form our character. Because maxims can be revised in the light of moral reflection human action is free.

[10] Again, inclination is the essential point of departure. If we were never tempted to make a false promise a duty not to promise falsely would be superfluous.

[11] There are several different ways of understanding this contradiction: see Korsgaard 1985.

Second, immoral action is easily recognizable as a violation of an egalitarian or republican Enlightenment ideal. Someone who acts on a maxim impossible to will as a universal law is making an exception for the sake of his own perceived interests. He is arrogating to himself the status of being special because he is acting as if he were justified in doing something others – his equals – cannot be allowed to do.[12]

Third, the example shows how the principle of Kantian ethics is a tool to curb the natural inconsiderateness of human beings. We initially deliberate to satisfy our own inclinations. As the example of the philanthropist shows, some of them are kind and other-regarding – they are not selfish in the narrow sense of the word. Still, all inclinations are of the same kind. Morality does not as such feature when we think about what we would like to do. In prudential deliberation we seek to realize inclinations most efficiently across the board, and this is the starting point of agency. But it would be a mistake to conclude, as critics from Arthur Schopenhauer to John Rawls and Ernst Tugendhat have done, that the categorical imperative is a principle of refined selfishness, or that its reliance on natural selfishness as a starting point undermines its moral credibility. The categorical imperative restrains selfishness by making it turn on itself. When we realize that we cannot will a proposed maxim as a universal law we have to abandon it and proceed in the opposite fashion even if that is likely to leave us worse off.[13]

KANT'S SYSTEM OF DUTIES

The general categorical imperative produces individual categorical imperatives when applied to maxims suggested by inclination. In the *Groundwork*, Kant generates four duty types by combining two different dichotomies: strict (perfect) duty vs. wide (imperfect) duty and duty to self vs. duty to others (cf. G 4: 421–4). Not to throw away one's life is a strict duty to oneself;[14]

---

[12] The derivation from the categorical imperative of duties to oneself does not involve universalization across all agents. A different story – about privileging the present self at the expense of temporal universality – will have to be told to substantiate them.

[13] The duty of beneficence provides another good example. I cannot will universalized indifference because such a maxim would deprive me of vital assistance along with all others. But that does not make the categorical imperative a principle of selfishness. I have an obligation to help even if I never profit in return. That is precisely why the imperative is categorical.

[14] Duties to oneself play a crucial part in Kant's moral system. The idea sits uneasily with modern ethics, which tends to focus on our relationships with others. See Denis 2001.

not to make fraudulent promises a strict duty to others. To develop one's talents is a wide duty to oneself; to be helpful a wide duty to others. The categorical imperative generates these duties in different ways. Duty to others depends on timeless universality across agents. Duty to self relies on temporal universality only.[15] A maxim that violates strict duty cannot be *thought* as a universal law: it is inconceivable that you obtain a loan by means of a false promise in a world in which promising is impossible. A maxim that violates wide duty cannot be *willed* as a universal law: as a vulnerable human being, you cannot want a world in which, as a matter of principle, people are indifferent to others' needs. It is the characteristic mark of strict duties (paradigmatically negative duties of omission) that they enjoy lexical priority over wide duties (positive duties to adopt and pursue certain ends). They bind the will directly, just by virtue of their form, not through ends that are to be pursued, and that is why they are absolute. For example, there is no obligation to help if it can only be done by violating strict duty. This may seem unduly rigorous, but there can be little doubt that it was Kant's considered view.

The fourfold classification of the *Groundwork* has its limitations. Kant himself notes that it is provisional, using categories borrowed from the natural law tradition, and promises to provide his own system at a later date (G 4: 421 fn).[16] It is, for instance, questionable whether the fourfold scheme can accommodate all duties. There may be the need for an intermediate category between (negative) perfect and (positive) imperfect duties, e.g. a fairly strict positive duty to honour a promise once it has been made. Moreover, even if we accept the lexical priority of perfect duty, Kant's contention that duties cannot conflict – explicit in *The Metaphysics of Morals* (at MdS 6: 224) – still depends on the alleged negative nature of strict duties (assuming that we can comply with all negative duties simultaneously) and on the enigmatic idea that wide duties – when they apply – issue insufficient obligating reasons, which fall short of obligation proper.[17] If we make these assumptions, Kant's assertion that conflicts of duties or obligations are impossible makes good sense. General duties cannot conflict if the system itself is internally consistent. Concrete obligations cannot conflict because there can only ever be at most one obligation – any consideration defeated would be an insufficient reason.

---

[15] The stipulation that the law apply at all times is important; see Glasgow 2003.
[16] It is not clear whether Kant makes good his promise in the *Metaphysics of Morals* of 1797.
[17] See Timmermann 2013.

Moreover, the fourfold classification does not make explicit the distinction between (juridical) duties of right and (ethical) duties of virtue, which informs the structure of the late *Metaphysics of Morals*. Duties of right must be a subset of all perfect duties. If we put to one side the question whether Kant came to believe in duties of right to oneself, they are those strict duties to others that individuals can claim by right, and that the state should enforce, e.g. by means of the public threat of punishment. Note that this threat must be in place when the crime is committed; only then is it plausible to say that the criminal has brought the punishment upon himself by willingly violating a public warning. Punishment is illegitimate without an existing law. So, the state does not punish criminals because they are evil; it punishes criminals because they have broken a public law. Also, the threat must be proportionate, neither excessive nor unduly lenient. There is thus a sharp distinction between three elements: the public threat as a deterrent, the principle of proportionality (*ius talionis*) used to determine the sentencing guideline, and individual acts of punishment according to law. This makes Kant defy the conventional categories of being either a retributivist or a deterrence theorist.[18]

It is significant that there are duties of virtue as well as duties of right. Modern critics of the 'morality system' tend to assume that duty prescribes specific actions, the omission of which merits blame.[19] But Kant's system of duties is more subtle. The failure to observe juridical duties merits blame, whereas the failure to enact ethical duties deserves disapproval in the much weaker sense that praise is inappropriate.[20] Someone who decides not to help someone at a significant cost to himself is not a bad person who deserves to be blamed. But he is not a particularly good person either. He is not as good as he ought to be. Kant thus combines – not always happily – the concept of obligation from the natural law tradition with notions like character, merit and gratitude that we tend to associate with virtue ethics.[21]

---

[18] On Kant's theory of punishment see Sharon Byrd's seminal article (Byrd 1989).

[19] The most prominent exponent of this tradition is Williams 1985.

[20] It is possible to comply with juridical duties from respect for the law, but from the point of view of the state motive is irrelevant. Mere conformity with law (or 'legality') is sufficient. Also, there is no merit in the mere act of not violating duties of right, and those whose rights are respected need not be grateful. There is, however, merit in virtue.

[21] Moral philosophy comprises both ethics and the philosophy of law (or 'right'), but it is disputed whether juridical duties depend on ethics for their authority, and whether the principle of right (a principle of equal external freedom) can be derived

MORAL STATUS: PERSONS, ANIMALS, GOD

Kant operates with an unequivocal ontological distinction between entities that possess moral standing (persons, ends in themselves) and those that do not (things, mere means). What separates them is the radical moral freedom of self-determination – the freedom to obey the moral law regardless of one's natural tendencies[22] – that only persons possess. They are exempt from and elevated above the causal nexus of the world of nature. The dichotomy has its attractions as well as its drawbacks. On the positive side, the class of moral agents is de facto identical with the class of moral patients. All duties are duties to a person, oneself or another. All persons are bound by the same moral law. They enjoy an essential equality.[23] Kant's theory thus exemplifies the egalitarian spirit of the Enlightenment. On the negative side, all entities that lack personhood lack moral standing entirely. As the bar is set very high,[24] the class of mere things comprises not just inanimate objects and plants but also non-human animals.[25]

Kant briefly discusses our moral relationship with animals in the *Metaphysics of Morals* (MdS 6: 443). In principle, they can serve as means for our own human purposes. So his recommendation to treat them kindly may come as a surprise. Torturous physical experiments are expressly forbidden. We should kill them painlessly (if we must). The services of an old horse may even merit a sense of gratitude. Still, if we ought to treat animals well it is not for their sake, but because treating them badly would brutalize us, violating a duty we bear to ourselves. Responsibilities that may appear to be duties *to* animals are actually, on closer inspection, duties to ourselves *with regard to* animals. Many of Kant's modern readers find this result disturbing.

---

from the categorical imperative of the *Groundwork*. For two attempts to defend the independence of ethics from the sphere of law see Willaschek 2002 and Wood 2002.

[22] A desire can determine the will of a human being only insofar as he has made it his principle to act accordingly, in Kantian terms: insofar as he has 'incorporated' it into his 'maxim'. This idea – the 'incorporation thesis' – is explored in detail in Allison 1990.

[23] Persons need not be human beings. The categorical imperative applies to us as *rational* beings endowed with a certain kind of will. It is just that to date human beings are the only kind of person we are acquainted with.

[24] Note that it is the capacity for moral agency that distinguishes persons from things. If there were non-moral rational beings they would lack moral standing like animals or any other 'thing'.

[25] I set aside the question of the moral status of human beings that appear to lack moral capacities.

Kant also rejects the idea that there are duties to God, as traditionally conceived within the natural law tradition (MdS 6: 443–4). Samuel Pufendorf devised three classes of duties, depending on their object: oneself, others and God. Kant retains the first and the second, but he abandons the third. He conceives of God as a person who, as the head of an ideal moral commonwealth, is bound by the same moral law as other moral agents, and in that sense he is regarded as a member of the moral community.[26] Still, there is no empirical evidence for the existence of God, and we cannot interact with him in the way required for there to be duties to him. It was one of the most important findings of the *Critique of Pure Reason* that we cannot even demonstrate his existence. The appropriate attitude to God is religious belief or faith, founded on moral conviction.[27] We should, however, view all moral duties as endorsed by God, a thought that frail human beings will find uplifting and inspiring. Religion generally is founded on morality and it serves to improve the moral character of human agents. Revelation has no independent standing – it is legitimate only insofar as it can be put to good moral use. As the title of Kant's 1793 treatise on the subject indicates, religion must operate within the boundaries set by mere reason.

VARIANTS OF THE CATEGORICAL IMPERATIVE

The categorical imperative can be expressed in several different ways, emphasizing different aspects of the moral law. The second section of the *Groundwork* contains three permutations.

The first is similar to the general formulation of the categorical imperative discussed in the section above, but it imports the idea of nature as a system, so the question you ought to ask yourself is whether the maxim of an action could become a universal law *of nature* (cf. G 4: 421). The examples according to the fourfold classification of duty mentioned above are discussed in the context of this variant of the 'formula of the law of nature'. It is more than likely that Kant took this formulation to preserve the grain of truth contained in the Stoic injunction to live in accordance with nature, which was popular with eighteenth-century German rationalists like Christian Wolff and Alexander Gottlieb Baumgarten.

---

[26] If not in quite the same way: God's will is perfect, he cannot fail to do what is morally good. That is why the moral law is descriptive of his actions and does not address him as a categorical imperative.

[27] Similarly, moral conviction leads to the justified belief that there is an immortal soul, which the first *Critique* had also placed beyond human cognition.

The second variant revolves around the proper objects of moral concern. The fundamental idea is that persons – oneself as well as others – do not deserve to be treated like things. We must treat humanity always as an end in itself, never merely as a means (cf. G 4: 429). The second condition is the condition of strict duty: when you obtain a loan by means of a false promise you use the other person as you would use a thing. The first condition is the general condition of duty, and the only condition that applies in cases of wide duty: when you fail to help a friend in need you do not treat him just as a means to your purposes, but you fail to respect his status as a fellow person, as an 'end'. Kant uses the same four examples as illustrations of this variant formulation, which is often called the 'formula of humanity'.

The third variant combines the idea of systematicity of the first variant and the notion of persons as ends in themselves of the second: the standard by which to judge our maxims is the question whether we can will them as laws in an ideal moral commonwealth, called a 'kingdom' or 'realm' of ends (cf. G 4: 432–3). We are subject to the law by virtue of being equal members of it; and only those maxims qualify that are independent of inclination, that the agent's practical reason itself actually endorses. That is why the third variant is not just the formula of the 'kingdom of ends' but also a 'formula of autonomy'.

The relation between the formulations of the categorical imperative is a highly contentious issue.[28] It is reminiscent of the mystery posed by the Christian doctrine of the Trinity. On the one hand, Kant makes it abundantly clear that there is only one categorical imperative. On the other, the one moral imperative exists in three distinct manifestations. It is, however, clear that different formulations serve different purposes. For better or worse, Kant seems to trust formal universalization more when it comes to decision making, whereas humanity and autonomy are more likely to inspire moral agents to act morally. Reformulating the categorical imperative in those terms helps us to make morality more intuitive and to secure access for the moral law to the human will (G 4: 436–7).

In the *Groundwork*, Kant strongly suggests that education based on the right kind of ethical theory is the only method that will lead to moral progress (see G 4: 411 fn). Moral education as advocated by educationalists to date was not sufficiently pure. The remedy is a metaphysics of morals, a pure

---

[28] This is something of an understatement because the number and nature of the various formulations is itself contentious. Compare Paton 1946, Wood 1999, Guyer 2007, Timmermann 2007 and Allison 2011 on this topic.

representation of the autonomy and august dignity of the human will, which will inspire respect. The *Critique of Practical Reason* devotes a whole chapter to the way pure judgement can affect sensibility. Things are less clear in the later *Metaphysics of Morals*, where we find several reflections on the anthropological preconditions of morality that might appear to be in tension with the purity demanded by the *Groundwork*.

AUTONOMY

The categorical imperative serves to determine what we should do. But why are its prescriptions binding? Kant rejects any source that originates outside the human will. The reason is the following. For the will to be determined by an external object[29] there must be a connection between the object and will, an inclination to bring this object about, so the practical law is determined by the object. Kant calls this 'heteronomy'. But, as we saw above, making willing conditional upon inclination does not adequately reflect the nature of morality. Moral commands must be unconditional; and acting on inclination, for the sake of a desired object, renders the *action* instrumentally good only, which directly contradicts the most fundamental assumption of Kant's ethical thought. Kant concludes that the only source of a law that can bind the will unconditionally is the will itself, our own practical reason (G 4: 434, cf. G 4: 440–1). We are subject only to laws that we impose upon ourselves. This is autonomy.[30]

As we have already seen, the principle of autonomous legislation can also serve as a reformulation of the categorical imperative. But the autonomy–heteronomy divide serves another useful function: it can be used to classify ethical theories, depending on whether the theory in question is, implicitly or explicitly, committed to the autonomy of the will (i.e., whether the theory can account for the categorical nature of moral commands). In other words, all theories other than Kant's own are dismissed under the heading of 'heteronomy' because they one and all, more or less crudely, make the same mistake of locating the source of obligation outside the human will, rendering impossible a will that is good in itself.

[29] A condition sanctioned by God's will or by society, even the value of happiness.
[30] There is nothing arbitrary or voluntarist about these laws – they are objective, but the source of their bindingness is to be sought in the human will. On Kant's conception of autonomy – as opposed to modern, often more subjectivist notions – see Hill 1992 and O'Neill 2003.

THE JUSTIFICATION OF MORALITY

One of the most difficult subjects in Kant's moral philosophy concerns the question of how we can be sure that morality is real. This is a worry not so much because of the dangers of deep-rooted egoism or amoralism. Kant thought that, when exposed to examples of virtuous conduct, even (as he puts it in the *Groundwork*) the 'most hardened scoundrel' cannot but acknowledge the authority of the moral law (G 4: 454–5). The problem is rather that scientific experience challenges the validity of moral commands. Free moral choices as such are invisible to both observers and agents. The moral value of virtuous action does not emerge. Like all action, it is to be explained within the framework of empirical psychology. But, if Kant is right, we must assume that human action is *not* wholly determined by the laws of cause and effect, which cannot account for the unconditional nature of the categorical imperative. A command of reason to do what – if necessary – defies inclination would be illusory in a purely naturalistic world.

This worry is taken very seriously in the *Groundwork*. There is a clear division of labour between the first two sections of the book, which give an account of what morality is by stating its principle and its variant formulations with philosophical precision, and the final section, in which Kant tries to defuse sceptical objections by showing how morality, understood in those terms, is possible.[31] By way of preparation he devises a vicious circle which the core of the 'deduction' will help us escape (G 4: 446–50). There is, first, an argument from freedom to the moral law: we are subject to the moral law by virtue of our freedom because freedom from natural causes leaves self-determination (autonomy) as the only option. There is also, second, a straightforward argument from actually being subject to moral commands to being free. If our argumentative resources were limited to these two moves we would lack any independent support for the thesis that we are bound by moral laws. We would be in a position similar to someone who tries to show that there is a God by citing the Bible as evidence and who, when challenged regarding its authority, argues that the Bible derives its authority from God. Kant seeks to escape the circle of freedom and morality by showing that we conceive of ourselves not just as members of the world of experience; as beings capable of devising concepts of pure reason or 'ideas',

---

[31] Kant assumes that giving a correct account of what we take something to be is one task, dispelling legitimate concerns to show that there is such a thing is another. Giving a correct account of the nature of God, a bachelor or a unicorn is distinct from proving that God, bachelors or unicorns exist.

we emancipate ourselves from that world to transport ourselves into a superior 'intelligible' world, which is the source of the moral law as it applies to our will (G 4: 452–4).

A few years later, in the *Critique of Practical Reason*, Kant changes his tune. The thought that morality might be unrealistic is no longer a cause for concern. Consciousness of being legitimately bound by the moral law is now dubbed a 'fact of reason' (KpV 5: 31).[32] This fact is deemed indubitably certain. If so, any attempt to persuade ourselves of its impossibility must be futile. Our commitment to morality is even used to deduce the reality of freewill, declared to lie outside the realm of theoretical cognition in the *Critique of Pure Reason*. We are thus justified in assuming, from the first-person point of view of the moral agent, what we were unable to grasp from the third-person point of view of the theorist: that we are endowed with a will that is free (KpV 5: 47).

BIBLIOGRAPHY

An asterisk denotes secondary literature especially suitable for further reading.

Allison, Henry E. 1990. *Kant's Theory of Freedom*. Cambridge University Press.
Allison, Henry E. 2011. *Kant's Groundwork for the Metaphysics of Morals: A Commentary*. Oxford University Press.
Baron, Marcia 1995. *Kantian Ethics Almost Without Apology*. Ithaca, NY, and London: Cornell University Press.*
Byrd, Sharon 1989. 'Kant's Theory of Punishment: Deterrence in Its Threat, Retribution in Its Execution'. *Law and Philosophy* 8: 151–200.
Denis, Lara 2001. *Moral Self-Regard: Duties to Oneself in Kant's Moral Theory*. New York: Garland Publishing.
Glasgow, Joshua 2003. 'Expanding the Limits of Universalization: Kant's Duties and Kantian Moral Deliberation'. *Canadian Journal of Philosophy* 33: 23–48.
Guyer, Paul 2007. *Kant's Groundwork for the Metaphysics of Morals: A Reader's Guide*. London: Continuum.*
Herman, Barbara 1993. 'Leaving Deontology Behind'. In *The Practice of Moral Judgment*, 208–40. Cambridge, MA, and London: Harvard University Press.
Hill, Thomas E. 1992. 'The Kantian Conception of Autonomy'. In *Dignity and Practical Reason in Kant's Moral Theory*: 76–96. Ithaca, NY, and London: Cornell University Press.*
Kleingeld, Pauline 2010. 'Moral Consciousness and the "Fact of Reason"'. In Andrews Reath & Jens Timmermann (eds.), *Kant's Critique of Practical Reason: A Critical Guide*. Cambridge University Press.

---

[32] For a recent discussion of the 'fact of reason' and Kant's argumentative strategy see Kleingeld 2010.

Korsgaard, Christine M. 1983. 'Two Distinctions in Goodness'. *Philosophical Review* 92: 169–95.

Korsgaard, Christine M. 1985. 'Kant's Formula of Universal Law'. *Pacific Philosophical Quarterly* 66: 24–47.

Moran, Kate A. 2012. *Community and Progress in Kant's Moral Philosophy*. Washington, DC: The Catholic University of America Press.

O'Neill, Onora 2003. 'Autonomy: The Emperor's New Clothes'. *Aristotelian Society Supplementary Volume* 77: 1–21.

Paton, H.J. 1946. *The Categorical Imperative: A Study in Kant's Moral Philosophy*. London: Hutchinson.*

Sensen, Oliver 2011. *Kant on Human Dignity*. Berlin and Boston: De Gruyter.

Timmermann, Jens 2007. *Kant's 'Groundwork of the Metaphysics of Morals': A Commentary*. Cambridge University Press.*

Timmermann, Jens 2013. 'Kantian Dilemmas? Moral Conflict in Kant's Ethical Theory'. *Archiv für Geschichte der Philosophie* 95: 36–64.

Willaschek, Marcus 2002. 'Which Imperatives for Right? On the Prescriptivity of Juridical Laws in Kant's "Metaphysics of Morals"'. In Mark Timmons (ed.), *Kant's 'Metaphysics of Morals': Interpretative Essays*, 65–87. Oxford University Press.

Williams, Bernard 1985. *Ethics and the Limits of Philosophy*. London: Fontana Press.

Wood, Allen W. 1999. *Kant's Ethical Thought*. Cambridge University Press.*

Wood, Allen W. 2002. 'The Final Form of Kant's Practical Philosophy'. In Mark Timmons (ed.), *Kant's 'Metaphysics of Morals': Interpretative Essays*, 1–21. Oxford University Press.

31

Fichte

ALLEN WOOD

Fichte is a major voice in modern moral and political philosophy, fully the equal, in depth and importance, to Kant, Hegel, Marx or Nietzsche. Few modern social thinkers have been as radical in their starting point or their conclusions; none at all has also been so seminal in influence. No social thinker of comparable power or historical importance in any tradition whatever is now so seldom read or discussed. The traditional neglect of Fichte's moral and political thought thus has serious consequences for our understanding of where our own ideas and problems originated (see Wood 1991 and 2016).

Fichte's entire philosophy was animated by moral and political concerns. His views on right and ethics, which are often innovative and sometimes extreme, were passionately held. Fichte's conversion to Kant's critical philosophy around 1790 was above all a conversion to the Kantian moral outlook, its conception of human dignity as rooted in freedom and the moral vocation of human beings as rational agents. The decisive period in Fichte's development, moreover, the Jena years of 1795–1800, were dominated by the production of his chief ethical writings: *Foundations of Natural Right* (1796–1797) and *System of Ethics* (1798).

It is customary to think of Fichte – and he thought of himself – as a follower of Kant. But he is an odd sort of follower, in that Fichte's chief works on ethics, right and religion each appeared about a year *before* the corresponding work by Kant on the same topic. Compared to Kant's, Fichte's ethical theory focuses attention more strongly on the relation of moral personality to individual identity, and even more systematically on the place of the individual moral agent in a living community with others.

Writings by Fichte are cited according to the following abbreviations: GA, *J.G. Fichte-Gesamtausgabe* (1962-) (cited by part/volume: page number or, in the case of letters in vol. 3, by letter number); SW, *Fichtes Sämmtliche Werke* (1970) (cited by volume: page number).

Fichte

THE "I," RECOGNITION AND THE RELATION OF RIGHT

Every act of awareness, Fichte maintains, involves an awareness of the I. "No object comes to consciousness except under the condition that I am aware of myself, the conscious subject" (GA I/4: 274–5). The activity that is the I is originally unconscious, but it becomes conscious of itself, first as an intellectual *intuition*, and secondly as reflective self-consciousness that forms a *concept* of the I. In pre-reflective activity the I "posits itself absolutely"; but in consciousness it "reiterates this positing" (GA I/2: 408, SW 1: 276; GA I/4: 212–13). "If it is to be an I, it must also posit itself as self-posited" (GA I/2: 408, SW 1: 274). Regarding intuitive self-consciousness, Fichte seems to have in mind what Sartre was later to call the "pre-reflective" or "non-positional" self-consciousness we have even when our attention is focused on objects entirely distinct from the self.[1] For Fichte what is crucial about this awareness is not only its ubiquity and certainty, but even more that it is an awareness of my *activity*. In every thought "you directly note activity and freedom in this thinking, in this transition from thinking the I to thinking the table, the walls, etc. Your thinking is for you an *acting*" (SW 1: 522, GA I/4: 271–2).

The condition for reflective self-awareness, or forming a conception of oneself as an I, is that the I as activity is opposed and limited by the not-I. In part this means: opposed and limited by a material world, but it also means: opposed and limited by other I's. An I cannot conceive itself at all unless it conceives itself as one of a plurality: "The consciousness of individuality is necessarily accompanied by another consciousness, that of a *thou*, and is possible only on this condition" (GA I/4: 229, SW 1: 476); "No thou, no I" (GA I/2: 337, SW 1: 189). Fichte's argument for this in the *Foundations of Natural Right* is based on the idea that the I must act on a not-I and be checked by that same not-I in one and the same moment. From this he derives the conclusion that the I must *itself* limit its own action based on a *concept* of limitation from outside: this concept he calls a "summons" (*Aufforderung*). But the external source of a *concept* of action can be thought only as another I, who issues the summons. Therefore, the I is possible only on the condition that it conceives of another I, which summons it to act, and to limit its actions, in certain ways (GA I/3: 342–7, SW 3: 29–37).

To understand another as a rational being issuing such a summons, and to display such understanding in action, is to "recognize" (*anerkennen*) the other (GA I/3: 353, SW 3: 44). Since every free being necessarily wills to make use of

[1] Sartre 1978: 11–15.

411

its freedom, the basic demand I necessarily make on every other free being is that it should limit its action in such a way that I am allowed a sphere for the exercise of my freedom (GA I/3: 357–8, SW 3: 52). Fichte argues that for this reason I must assume that others will recognize me, but since I cannot expect others to do so unless I treat them as rational beings, I am bound by mere logical consistency (and prior to any moral requirement) to recognize all others and treat them accordingly (GA I/3: 349–56, SW 3: 41–7). Recognition grounds the "relation of right": "I must in all cases recognize the free being outside me as such, i.e. limit my freedom through the concept of the possibility of its freedom" (GA I/3: 358, SW 3: 52). By the principle of right each free being is to have an external sphere for the exercise of its freedom, and others are to limit their freedom accordingly. This external sphere begins at the point of origin of one's action on the external world itself. Because human beings are free, their modes of activity are endlessly perfectible and adaptable (GA I/3: 377–9, SW 3: 71–2).

More immediately, it is the foundation of "original rights" (*Urrechte*), that is, those not based on any positive laws, but serve as the basis of any conceivable community of free beings (GA I/3: 390, 403–10, SW 3: 85, 111–19). Original rights are fundamentally only two: the inviolability of the body, and the right to act freely on the external world (GA I/3: 409, SW 3: 118). Fichte insists that property rights are entirely derivative from – and exhaustively analyzable into – rights to non-interference with one's *actions* (GA I/3: 415–23, SW 3: 93–100). Thus he says that, properly speaking, persons stand in relations of right only to other persons, never to non-rational things (GA I/3: 360, SW 3: 55). Fichte even goes so far as to deny that there is any right of property, literally speaking, to the substance of things, or to land (GA I/3: 428–9, SW 3: 401).

POLITICAL PHILOSOPHY

Fichte maintains that the recognition of others, including treatment of them in accordance with their original rights, does not require any moral principle as its rational basis. It also does not necessarily provide us with a reason for respecting the rights of others in practice, or for expecting others to respect ours (GA I/3: 384–5, SW 3: 86–7). The actualization of a community of rational beings must therefore depend on an external force capable of coercing rational beings to observe its laws. Each of us, he argues, has a "right of coercion" – but no satisfactory community can come about in this way, since that community requires that each have a guarantee *in advance* that others will subject themselves to the principle of right (GA I/3: 395, SW 3: 100). This, in turn, is possible only if all equally subject themselves unconditionally to the judgment of another party, transferring to it their power as well (GA I/3: 396, SW 3: 101). This power must erect a "law of coercion" bringing it about whenever someone attempts to violate these laws, the opposite of what it intends should happen, so that such intentions annihilate themselves (GA I/3: 426, SW 3: 142).

The common governmental power which is to make possible a relation of right between people can be consistent with their freedom only if it is the result of their mutual consent. Consequently, Fichte argues, the state must be founded on an express declaration establishing a will common to all members of a state, that is, a "civil–political contract" (*Staatsbürgervertrag*) (GA I/3: 432–4, SW 3: 152–3). Fichte argues for the necessity of a series of such contracts as transcendental conditions for the possibility of a relation of right – which, in turn, as we have seen, is regarded as a condition for the possibility of a relation of community or mutual recognition between free beings.

The first condition of a relation of right between persons is therefore an agreed determination of the limits of their respective external spheres of action. This agreement Fichte calls the "property contract" (GA I/4: 8–9, SW 3: 196). It confers no right unless each has reason to believe that everyone's property rights will be coercively enforced by all. Hence it presupposes an agreement that all will unite their strength in protecting the property of each. This second agreement is the "protection contract" (GA I/4: 9–11, SW 3: 197–9). But the bindingness of any contract on me is conditional on the fulfilment by the other parties of their obligation. This condition can be met, Fichte argues, only if each person enters into an agreement not with another, or even with all the others, taken severally, but with a real whole made up of all united together (GA I/4: 13–14, SW 3: 201–4). The agreement through which such an organic whole is established Fichte names the "unification contract" (GA I/4: 15, SW 3: 204); and the civil–political contract is concluded between each individual and this whole, in the form of a "subjection contract" (GA I/4: 18, SW 3: 206).

Fichte follows Rousseau in distinguishing the government from the law it administers. Unlike Rousseau, he does not understand this as a separation of the legislative power from the governing power. On the contrary, all law is understood merely as the application of a fundamental law or constitution. Since the constitution must be a law freely accepted by everyone bound by it, its adoption must be unanimous, not merely by a majority vote (GA I/3: 443, SW 3: 195). Those who cannot consent to it must emigrate, and find a place on earth where they can consent to enter into relations of right with others (GA I/4: 163, SW 3: 384).

Fichte believes in an undivided governmental power, but he equally insists that the government (especially in its executive function) must be accountable to the law. Unlike Kant, he did not regard the rights of the people against the government as real but in principle unenforceable. Instead, he proposes what is his most innovative political idea: that of the "ephorate." This term, meaning "overseers" (in Greek, επι + οραω) was applied to a Spartan political institution, but Fichte insists that what he means is entirely different and that the closest ancient analogue to what he has in mind were the Roman tribunes of the people (GA I/3: 449n, SW 3: 171). The ephors are to remain entirely independent of the government and their persons are inviolable (GA I/3: 451–3, SW 3: 177–8). Their only power is to be that of suspending the existing government and of calling for a convention of the people for the purpose of trying the government on its indictment (GA I/3: 449–50, SW 3: 172–3). The final judge is always the people: "Only against a higher power can there be rebellion. But what on earth is higher than the people? It could rebel only against itself, which is absurd" (GA I/3: 456–7, SW 3: 182).

Fichte appears to deny that any existing political order is truly consented to by those living under it. The existing political regime is therefore at best a *Notstaat*, an emergency state which we accept only provisionally and on the condition that it tends to progress toward legitimacy. "Any constitution of the state is in accord with right which does not make it impossible to progress toward something better . . . Only that constitution is completely contrary to right which has the end of preserving everything as it presently is" (GA I/5: 313–14, SW 4: 361). It is not hard to understand why Fichte was notoriously accused of Jacobin political views.

ECONOMIC JUSTICE

All property, according to Fichte, depends on the property contract, through which people apportion their respective external spheres for free action. The purpose of entering into this contract is to acquire a sufficient external sphere to perpetuate one's free activity in the future, that is, to satisfy one's external needs (GA I/4: 21, SW 3: 213–14). Fichte infers that only they are parties to the property contract who thereby acquire some property; but not only that – they must have enough property that they can live independently by what they own (GA I/4: 8–9, 20–2, SW 3: 195, 212–15). The state's fundamental responsibility for protecting the private property of every citizen therefore charges the state with the duty of distributing property in such a way that no individual falls into destitution. Conversely, every citizen must have an occupation, which is known to the state and which the state can guarantee as a sufficient means of livelihood (GA I/4: 23, SW 3: 214).

> All property rights are grounded on the contract of all with all which says this: We all retain this on the condition that we allow you what is yours. Thus as soon as someone cannot live from his labor, that which is absolutely his is not being allowed him, and regarding him the contract is cancelled completely, and he is not bound by right to recognize the property of any other human being. (GA I/4: 22, SW 3: 213)

THE I AS PRACTICAL PRINCIPLE

In Fichte's transcendental use of the term, "I" refers not to a thing but to an *activity*. This means that it is a doing we are engaged in; in other words, it is not only an action which *is done*, but an action which is *to be done*, or which *should be done*. "I" is therefore not so much a conception of what I am as of what I ought to be (see Wood 1999). This conception of the I requires that a "concept" (regarded as a norm for action) should precede every conception of what the I is. Fichte therefore insists that the I must, in a certain sense, be before it is anything, or exist before it has a nature. Fichte never actually uses the verbal formulation "existence precedes essence," but his doctrine of human freedom is evidently the source of the one championed by Sartre in *Being and Nothingness*.

In every awareness of the "I," I find myself active in the objective world counterposited to the I (GA I/2: 393–5, SW 1: 257–60). In other words, the I "finds itself" only as "willing" (GA I/5: 37, SW 4: 18). If reflecting is a "centripetal" activity, in which the I "returns into itself," willing by contrast is a "centrifugal" activity, which seeks to posit the I, to expand its domain in the not-I. Taken by itself, it would *abolish* the not-I (GA I/2: 401, SW 1: 270). But since this would be to abolish the condition for the possibility of the I itself, this activity must be regarded as a "causality which is not a causality" – or in other words, a "striving" that is "infinite" in the sense that it has no determinate end or point of satisfaction (GA I/2: 397, SW 1: 262). Fichte locates this insatiable striving in the organic body which, in reciprocal interaction with the external world, is a condition of the I's possibility. Consciousness of this indeterminate striving is "longing" (*Sehnen*), but any determinate form it assumes is called "desire" and the immediate sensuous experience of such a desire is called a "drive" (GA I/5: 118–23, SW 4: 109–15). Desire in general is directed outward at objects. Its general form is to seek to abolish their independence, yet not by destroying them but rather by making them conform to the I, or to its "practical concepts" of what they ought to be, assigning to each object its "final end" (GA I/2: 396, SW 1: 261; I/3: 31–2, SW 6: 299; I/5: 158–60, SW 4: 152–3).

Desire for Fichte takes two forms: One "natural" or *particular*, involving feelings produced by sensuous encounter with specific objects and aiming at determinate ends, the other "pure" or *ideal*, aiming at the absolute freedom or self-sufficiency of the I: this pure drive is a "tendency to self-activity for the sake of self-activity" (GA I/5: 45, SW 4: 28). If self-legislation is for Kant an essential capacity of the free and rational self, for Fichte the striving for absolute self-activity is the condition for there to be an I at all. I can regard myself as an I only to the extent that I understand myself in terms of the task of absolute self-activity. Inclinations for Kant are a contingent addition (or encumbrance) to the freedom of a rational being, falling outside its self-legislation. For Fichte, however, empirical desires are only so many limited manifestations of the I's fundamental tendency to freedom. In their partiality and objective passivity they may constitute a resistance to the moral impulse, but at bottom they are manifestations of it, hence in their totality they cannot be opposed to it. It is only in the harmony of the pure and natural drives that determinate moral action is to be found.

Any concept of myself as a free being is always essentially a *normative* conception: I must conceive of myself as subject to rational *demands*, so that certain free activities are conceived as proper to me, and others excluded as not truly mine – not in the sense that I *can't* perform them, but rather in the sense that I *ought* not, because if I do so I am not being my authentic self or living up to what I am. The I which is *formally* free, in always having the ability to do otherwise than it does, achieves freedom in a different sense, *material* freedom, by actions that bring its empirical I into harmony with what I truly am, the pure or ideal or absolute I (GA I/5: 132, 140, SW 4: 135, 139; I/3: 30, SW 6: 297; I/2: 399, SW 1: 264–5; see Neuhouser, 1990, ch. 4 and Tugendhat 1986: 132–3).

The key to material freedom lies in the I's intersubjectvity. The I needs others in order to determine itself, even its demand to be in unity with others in order to acquire its own unity as a condition for its own determinacy. The argument Fichte most often presents is *genetic* in character, based on the conditions under which there can *come to be* an I with a determinate practical or normative concept of itself (Philonenko 1984: 46). I can learn to apply a normative conception to myself, in other words, to make demands on myself, only through "the imitation of an activity present at hand" (GA I/5: 200). This original relation to the demands of others Fichte calls "education" (*Bildung*) (GA

I/3: 348). Fichte also argues that as a rational being, the I is rational – or rather, as Fichte prefers to say, it is reason itself. But reason is one, that is, all rational beings necessarily have the same final end and will freely according to the same principles (GA I/3: 40, SW 6: 310). Only on this condition can we reconcile the freedom of every I with the impulse of every I to make the external world conform to itself (GA I/5: 208–10, SW 4: 234–6). That is, however individuals may differ, each I must fulfil its vocation or determinacy in a way that is in fundamental harmony with others (GA I/3: 38, SW 6: 305–6). Thus "the final and highest end of society is the complete unity and unanimity of all its members" (GA I/3: 40, SW 6: 310). The quest for individual identity is a quest for rational norms by which to live, and these, Fichte holds, are knowable only through communication with others, which consists in mutual activity and passivity, affecting others and being affected by them (GA I/3: 3–39, SW 6: 306–7; I/5: 209–12, SW 4: 235–8). The true vocation (*Bestimmung*) of human beings within society is therefore "unification," or the endless approximation to unanimity and equality (GA I/3: 40, SW 6: 310–11). Fichte holds that the true human society will be attained only when people freely act on the same principles because, through a process of communication, they have reached rational agreement on these principles. A society based on authority or coercion is therefore not merely imperfect, it is less than human (GA I/3: 37, SW 6: 307). The state, which is founded on coercion, is thus "a means for establishing the perfect society," but "like all human institutions which are mere means, the state aims at abolishing itself. *The goal of all government is to make government superfluous*" (GA I/3: 36, SW 6: 306). In the end, therefore, "the state will be abolished, as a legislative and coercive power" (GA I/5: 226–7, SW 4: 253).

MORAL SYSTEMATICS AND MORAL EPISTEMOLOGY

In Chapter 3, Section 2 of the *System of Ethics*, Fichte develops a transcendental theory of duties, analogous to Kant's Doctrine of Virtue. He divides duties into "conditioned" (to oneself) and "unconditioned" (to others), and into "general" (applying equally to everyone) and "particular" (applying to people in virtue of their social estate or profession). In developing a theory of "particular" duties, Fichte anticipates Hegel's conception of "ethical life," in which duties are seen as a function of one's "particularity" and one's role in a rational social structure. He anatomizes the economy of the state, and considers also such estates as that of clergy, scholars and artists, emphasizing the morally uplifting (and socially progressive) function of all these social roles, when they are properly performed.

Duties are considered from this transcendental standpoint, however, solely for philosophical purposes. Fichte does not think that moral reasoning begins with a general moral principle, such as Kant's formula of universal law. Here again Fichte anticipates Hegel, arguing that this principle is "purely heuristic"; the principle is practically empty and no determinate duties are derivable from it (GA I/5: 212, SW 4: 234). This point is usually seen as a *criticism* of Kantian ethics. For Fichte, however, it has no tendency at all to discredit Kantian ethics; it is merely an observation about the structure of the theory. It means that the fundamental principle of morality is wholly formal: *"Always act according to the best conviction of your duty, or Act according to your conscience"* (GA I/5: 146, SW 4: 156). The applicability of the principle, and then its application to conscientious actions, is to be deduced separately. The content of conscience or moral conviction is the result of a *theoretical* inquiry, which we are always duty-bound to carry out (GA I/5: 152–64, SW 4: 157–63). The most general criterion for this conviction is coherence with the system of an individual's convictions, but individual convictions attain to certainty when we feel a harmony between the empirical I and the absolute or ideal I which is its criterion (GA I/5: 155–61, SW 4: 163–7).

The ideal I must be determinate. That is, it must project a determinate series of actions as those that ought to be done, or as duties. Fichte rejects Kant's position that there are imperfect duties, and latitude or "play-room" (*Spielraum*) allowing for merely permissible actions or morally meritorious actions whose omission would not be morally wrong: "The moral law, according to the above proofs, leaves no play-room: under its dominion there are no indifferent actions; in every situation of my life I either ought or ought not" (GA I/5: 237, SW 4: 264). At any given time, in the temporal manifold of possible acts, "absolutely only one (a determinate part of the manifold) accords with duty; everything else is contrary to duty" (GA I/5: 190, SW 4: 195). (Compare Kant: "That human being can be called 'fantastically virtuous' who allows nothing to be *morally indifferent* (*adiaphora*) and strews all his steps with duties, as with man-traps ... Fantastic virtue is a micrology which, were it admitted to the doctrine of virtue, would turn the government of virtue into tyranny.")[2] Equally strict for Fichte are the *motivational* demands of morality. Since the unity of the I depends above all on acting from the drive to wholeness, to free determinacy, the very identity of the I is threatened when action proceeds from isolated feelings or empirical desires. Thus contrary to Kant, Fichte maintains that even benevolent deeds, when done from motives other than pure respect

[2] Kant 1798/1991: 6: 409.

for the moral law, are, insofar as their motivation is concerned, wrong and blameworthy. Even the person who acts from sympathy, compassion or love of humanity acts "legally, but absolutely not morally, on the contrary, *to that extent* against morality" (GA I/5: 144–5, SW 4: 154).

Yet in view of the fact that morality is only an expression of our own absolute freedom, Fichte's view may be looked at in a different and less threatening way. Rather than seeing Fichte as a ferocious rigorist, who thinks morality should swoop in from outside and take over our lives, we might see Fichtean morality as the way for us to be true to our authentic selves in every one of our actions. In fact, Fichte was the founder of the existentialist idea, found in Kierkegaard, Heidegger and Sartre, that each of us can and should let our autonomy inform every action, feeling and motivation. For Fichte, morality does not consist in our reason dictating to the rest of our nature, but rather in achieving the rational unity and harmony of all aspects of our nature.

BIBLIOGRAPHY

An asterisk denotes secondary literature especially suitable for further reading.

Fichte, J.G. (1962–) *J.G. Fichte-Gesamtausgabe*, ed. Reinhard Lauth and Hans Gliwitzky. Stuttgart, Bad Cannstatt: Friedrich Frommann.

Fichte, J.G. (1970) *Fichtes Sämmtliche Werke*, ed. I.H. Fichte. Berlin: DeGruyter.

Fichte, J.G. (1988). *Fichte: Early Writings*, ed. Daniel Breazeale. Ithaca: Cornell University Press.

Fichte, J.G. (2000) *Foundations of Natural Right* [1796], ed. F. Neuhouser, trans. Michael Baur. Cambridge University Press.

Fichte, J.G. (2006) *System of Ethics* [1798], trans. D. Breazeale and G. Zöller. Cambridge University Press.

Fichte, J.G. (2010) *Attempt at a Critique of All Revelation* [1792], ed. A. Wood, trans. G. Green. Cambridge University Press.

James, David (2011) *Fichte's Social and Political Philosophy: Property and Virtue*. Cambridge University Press.

Kant, Immanuel (1798/1991) *Metaphysik der Sitten*. Akademie Ausgabe. Berlin: DeGruyter. (Translated by Mary Gregor, *The Metaphysics of Morals*, Cambridge University Press).

Neuhouser, Frederick (1990) *Fichte's Theory of Subjectivity*. Cambridge University Press.

Philonenko, Alexis (1984) *L'Œuvre de Fichte*. Paris: Vrin.

Sartre, Jean-Paul (1978) *Being and Nothingness*, trans. Hazel Barnes. New York: Simon and Schuster.

Tugendhat, Ernst (1986) *Self-Consciousness and Self-Determination*, trans. Paul Stern. Cambridge, MA: MIT Press.

Verweyen, Hansjürgen (1975) *Recht und Sittlichkeit in J.G. Fichtes Gesellschaftslehre*. Freiburg: Alber.

Wood, Allen (1991) "Fichte's Philosophical Revolution," *Philosophical Topics* 19/2, pp. 1–28.

Wood, Allen (1999) "The I as Principle of Practical Philosophy," in S. Sedgwick (ed.), *The Reception of Kant's Critical Philosophy: Fichte, Schelling, and Hegel*. Cambridge University Press.

Wood, Allen (2006) "Fichte's Intersubjective I," *Inquiry*, vol. 49, No. 1, Special issue "Kant to Hegel," edited by Songsuk Susan Hahn (February), pp. 62–79.

Wood, Allen (2016) *Fichte's Ethical Thought*. Oxford University Press.*

32

Hegel

DUDLEY KNOWLES

G.W.F. Hegel is widely recognized as the last great metaphysician, articulating an ambitious programme of absolute idealism which has found few supporters. His work in ethics, by contrast, has been more influential both as a source and a foil for subsequent philosophers. Hegelian ethics was developed and refined by the British Idealist philosophers, notably T.H. Green, F.H. Bradley, D.G. Ritchie and Bernard Bosanquet.[1] Many of Hegel's insights have been rediscovered in recent years by the ranks of communitarian social philosophers, notably Charles Taylor (a notable Hegel scholar), and Michael Sandel. Equally, Hegel is celebrated as the target of radical critique in the work of Karl Marx and the critical theorists of the Frankfurt School.

Hegel thought hard about – and wrote about – ethics in its broadest sense throughout his intellectual career. His early theological works were driven by a concern for social improvement and for finding a place for religion as a vehicle of cultural reform. In Jena he published his critical (1802–3) essay on Natural Law (*On the Scientific Ways of Treating Natural Law, Its Place in Practical Philosophy, and Its Relation to the Positive Sciences of Law*), introducing sharp criticisms of 'individualist' systems of normative ethics, notably Kantian ethics and social contract theories of the state. In the magnificent (1807) *Phenomenology of Spirit* (henceforth *Phenomenology*) he would elaborate the related concepts of spirit, mutual recognition and freedom.[2] Hegel's ethics and political philosophy are sketched in the 'Objective Mind' section of the (1817) *Encyclopaedia of the Philosophical Sciences*[3] and then in much greater detail in successive drafts of the *Elements of the Philosophy of Right* (henceforth *PR*),[4] his fullest and most carefully articulated text in ethical

---

[1] For a useful introductory anthology of their writings, see Boucher 1997.
[2] *Phenomenology of Spirit*: cited at paragraph (¶) numbers as given in the Miller translation: Hegel 1977.
[3] Translated as Hegel 2007, *Philosophy of Mind*.
[4] *Elements of the Philosophy of Right* [PR]: cited at section (§) numbers from Hegel 1991.

theory, first published in 1821 as a handbook to accompany lectures. Additional material on ethics can be found in the *Lectures on the Philosophy of World History* and the *Lectures on the History of Philosophy* (both published after his death). We need to investigate what makes this body of work so distinctive.

CONSERVATIVE ETHICS

In modern times it has become standard practice to conceive of ethics as *normative* ethics, the study of how putative ethical rules or principles might be grounded or validated. Much of *applied* ethics has been constructed as attempts to discern whether specific policies might be challenged or vindicated using the apparatus of utilitarian, Kantian or human rights versions of normative ethics. For many, the favoured methodology has been: first, defend some basic account of normative ethics; secondly, apply the normative ethics in an evaluation of candidate projects or principles, using it as a generative or testing instrument. This simplified story is complicated by the inclusion of virtue ethics and Rawlsian reflective equilibrium, both of which grant some credence to currently admirable character traits or strongly entrenched ethical intuitions. But it is rare to find a moral philosopher who disowns any attempt to state how things ought to be and restricts himself to describing and explaining how things are in the moral world he observes.

Yet this is Hegel's explicit project in the *Philosophy of Right*: 'The *truth* concerning *right, ethics and the state* is at any rate *as old* as its *exposition and promulgation* in *public laws and in public morality and religion*' (*PR* Preface, p. 11). Further in the Preface to *PR*, he sharply (even contemptuously) attacks both those who believe it is 'the essential task of a philosophy of the state to invent and propound *yet another theory*' (p. 12) and those subjectivist sceptics who insist that 'the *truth itself cannot be known*, but that truth consists in what *wells up from each individual's heart, emotion, and enthusiasm*' (p. 15). Hegel encapsulated this perspective in his famous *Doppelsatz* (or double dictum) towards the end of the Preface (p. 20):

> What is rational is actual;
> and what is actual is rational.[5]

---

[5] This *Doppelsatz* is notorious. Seemingly an endorsement of all the actual institutions of Prussia in 1820–1, it generated immediate and widespread hostility towards Hegel. See Pinkard 2000: 457–61 for details. Interpretation of it can be difficult and complex. See Knowles 2002: 67–77 and, most impressively, Stern 2006.

This amounts to ethical conservativism – the grant of an ethically probative status to the moral world one inhabits, with its distinctive laws, public morality, and religious prescriptions.

For many, and not only the targets that Hegel singled out for criticism in the Preface of *PR*, this is shocking, seemingly abandoning any prospect of a critical approach to the moral beliefs and ethical institutions of one's community. To make matters worse, for many readers the charge that Hegel was a methodological conservative in ethics was further supported (and inflamed) by the thought that he was a political conservative, not to say reactionary. It has been argued that some of the substantial descriptions of the rational state which are found in the *Philosophy of Right* were intended to accommodate the authoritarian monarchist forces in Prussia at the time of its publication. These heavily conservative elements in Hegel's ethical thought have been identified as just cause for strong attacks on his work at the time of its composition and by critics ever since.

Conservatism of this stripe is not a novel ethical position, but it is rare. In its favour, and this is not a trivial point, it does justice to the great tenacity with which folks hold on to the deep moral convictions they find themselves saddled with as they go about their daily business. Notice however that, although conservatism as a methodological position eschews normative ethics as a testing or generative instrument, it will often stress the importance of giving an explanation of the moral world it endorses. It will find some sense in it. In Hegel's terms it will seek 'to comprehend and portray the state as an inherently rational entity'[6] (*PR* Preface, p. 21).

Hegel is in good philosophical company hereabouts. Amongst others, Aristotle places great credence in the opinions of the many and the wise, the collected wisdom of the community. This is his source material for a careful enquiry into the principles and practices which underlie the good life. In modern times, Hume accepted the institutions and practices of modern society as both constituting justice and articulating the hard-learned wisdom of humankind in its various tribes concerning how best to promote utility, the well-being of the general run of persons to whom the various rules apply. Even J.S. Mill, for many a normative philosopher *par excellence*, was keen to assert that 'during all that time ["the whole past duration of the human species"] mankind has been

---

[6] By 'the state' Hegel intends us to understand the 'rational state', the whole system of norms that binds citizens – public morality and religious precepts as well as the rule of law. This obviously includes the 'political proper state' (*PR* §267).

learning by experience the tendencies of actions'.[7] The implication is that, absent conspicuous exceptions, everyday morality with its injunctions against e.g. theft and murder can be trusted to instruct us how to behave.

Whereas the key explanatory concept for Hume (and Mill, of course) was utility, for Hegel it was freedom. Human history, in his terms the history of spirit, has bequeathed to us institutions and principles which permit mankind to be free.[8] In the *Philosophy of Right* he will display his comprehension of the rational state as a structure of freedom. Although he sees this task as fundamentally explanatory, the key concept of freedom is evidently normatively charged. The gap between the 'ought-to-be' and the 'is', between normative and conservative ethics, turns out to be narrower than is suggested by the prospectus Hegel gives of his methodology in the Preface. What exactly does it mean to say that the rational state, with all its constituent institutions, practices and rules, is a structure of freedom?

FREEDOM

First, we should note a metaphysical implication. In Hegel's system the study of ethics, social and political philosophy is the study of 'objective mind'. Hegel is an absolute idealist, which is to say, at its simplest, that the world is ultimately constituted by reason. This is an exotic metaphysical thesis, but it is not unprecedented and it is not absurd. Idealism in social philosophy (of the kind that Marx aimed to turn 'on its head' as stated in the 1872 Preface to *Capital*) is an altogether more robust thesis. It claims that social institutions such as families, firms, trades unions, legal systems, states and their governments are structures of mind (or Spirit – *Geist* is Hegel's term). The social world is a system of Objective Mind (as against Subjective Mind, exemplified in the mental life of individuals), constituted by such mental entities as intentions, expectations, decisions, beliefs, values, moral rules, conventions and laws. These are all constructions of will and since 'the will is free ... the system of right is the realm of actualized freedom' (*PR* §4).

Hegel explains the freedom of the will in the 'Introduction' to the *Philosophy of Right*. The argument is complex and intricate in detail.[9] The

[7] Mill 1863: Ch.2.
[8] The standard text supporting this claim is Hegel's *Lectures on the Philosophy of History*, translated as *The Philosophy of History*, Hegel 1956. See also Hegel 1975 for the 'Introduction' to the *Philosophy of History*.
[9] For a reading of the detail, see Knowles (2002: 23–62).

upshot is a theory of positive freedom: we act freely when we disengage ourselves from the press of desires and review the possibilities of action in light of a conception of ourselves which is both the product of the history of spirit as it has developed in our communities and normatively potent, engaging our values and desires as free agents.

The social world is a structure of freedom because it fully actualizes the free will. The free will combines two elements, (i) the (universal) power of abstracting any (particular) determinate content of the will (as when one holds back from acting to satisfy a desire and considers whether this is the sort of thing one ought to be doing) (*PR* §5) and (ii) some (particular) desire which one seeks to satisfy (*PR* §6), into (iii) a synthesis of universality and particularity when one finally decides to act (say, to satisfy this particular desire rather than that) (*PR* §7). So free agency combines the Hobbesian element of acting from desire and the Kantian element of distancing oneself from otherwise determining forces. Bluntly, on Hegel's account, one acts freely when he acts to satisfy desires which he has independently validated.

How is this achieved? The basic idea is that a person acts freely when he acts in accordance with values (social rules, laws or norms) that are endorsed as rational. Suppose Alan desires the plum that he sees dangling from the tree. He realizes that the plum and the tree from which it hangs belong to Bob, who owns it and thereby has rights of exclusive possession and use of it. Alan accepts rules of private property, believing, like Hegel, that these are necessary for persons to be free. He therefore acts freely when he restrains himself from picking the plum. In the opposite case, if Alan had judged (correctly) that this was a wild plum tree and that its fruit belonged to no one, he would have been acting freely had he picked it to eat. In both cases we have examples of free agency.

More generally we should note that free agency, whilst manifest in the conduct of individuals, is necessarily a social achievement. This was explicit in the famous 'Master–Slave' passages of the *Phenomenology*, where Hegel demonstrates the failure of all strategies which seek to attain the freedom of one person or a limited group at the expense of the submission or domination of others.[10] Individuals enjoy freedom only within social institutions which permit mutual recognition – in 'the unity of independent consciousnesses [who] enjoy perfect freedom and independence: "I" that is "We" and "We"

---

[10] See Hegel, *Phenomenology* B. Self-Consciousness, IV. The Truth of Self-Certainty, A. Independence and Dependence of Self-Consciousness: Lordship and Bondage, ¶¶ 178–98. For commentary, see Stern 2002: 71–85.

that is "I"' (Hegel, *Phenomenology*, ¶ 177). We shall need to put some flesh on the bones of this concept: of social structures which permit mutual recognition amongst citizens who enjoy perfect freedom and independence; and we find the fully fleshed out materials in the *Philosophy of Right*.

THE ARGUMENT OF THE PHILOSOPHY OF RIGHT

The values which are engaged when agents act freely are encoded in structures of social norms. How are these (correct or valid) norms to be identified? Hegel's quite distinctive story explains that they are constitutive of conceptions of the self with which modern agents have learned to identify. Allen Wood dubs this a *self-actualization* theory.[11] It specifies that agents are free when their actions are guided by a nested series of normative systems, within each of which there is a range of self-descriptions which agents recognize and endorse, and thus apply to themselves and their fellow citizens. Modern agents therefore identify themselves as persons (i.e. bearers of rights), moral subjects striving to act conscientiously, family members, economic agents belonging to a variety of social classes, subject to the rule of law and acting in association with others in the corporations to which they belong as members, and finally as patriotic citizens of a political state with several possible constitutional roles. Each of these identifications is ethically potent in that they demand subscription to characteristic ethical norms. This is a conservative ethic insofar as the moral norms which direct the behaviour of free persons are the norms which are actualized by or embedded within the communities they inhabit, and it is ultimately the historically formed community – Hegel's rational state – with which persons identify which gives them their ethical life. I portray this nested series of ethical domains, together with their associated and normatively potent self-descriptions, in Figure 1.

In the sketch of the fully actualized modern self that follows we shall trace the elements of it as these are presented in the *Philosophy of Right*, moving outwards from the centre of the concentric circles in the diagram. This outwards movement is *dialectical* in two senses: first and most straightforwardly, we move from the simplest conception we have of ourself – the atomistic person – to the most complex and fully articulated – the citizen of the rational state – as the prior, simpler, conceptions are revealed as

---

[11] Wood 1999: 17–35.

Normative Domains

Self-ascriptions

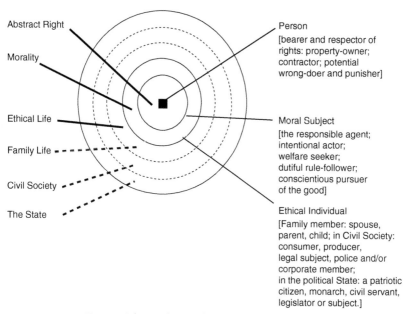

Abstract Right

Morality

Ethical Life

Family Life

Civil Society

The State

Person
[bearer and respector of
rights: property-owner;
contractor; potential
wrong-doer and punisher]

Moral Subject
[the responsible agent;
intentional actor;
welfare seeker;
dutiful rule-follower;
conscientious pursuer
of the good]

Ethical Individual
[Family member: spouse,
parent, child; in Civil Society:
consumer, producer,
legal subject, police and/or
corporate member;
in the political State: a patriotic
citizen, monarch, civil servant,
legislator or subject.]

Figure 1 The Modern Self in Hegel's Rational State

incomplete or contradictory ethical structures. This is a reasonable expository practice.

Secondly, the movement is dialectical in that it reveals what Hegel believes to be the 'logic of the concept'. It recapitulates the dialectical sequence of universality (Abstract Right) and particularity (Morality) being subsumed in individuality (Ethical Life). Since I do not find this logical process convincing (one could argue just as plausibly that Morality is a structure of universality and that Abstract Right is a structure of particularity) and since Hegel himself contravenes it (for example in his discussion of the constitutional monarchy), I shall ignore it in what follows.

ABSTRACT RIGHT

Thus in *PR* Part 1, 'Abstract Right', we see ourselves and others as 'persons', a technical term denoting the discrete atomic units of agency who are bearers of rights, making claims of right against others and recognizing the reciprocal claims on themselves that other persons make in turn. This is a primitive ethic of individual rights, an up-dated version of the morality of natural rights that was developed in the fifteenth and sixteenth centuries, although Hegel traces it to Roman antecedents. Seeing ourselves as persons, we make claims of right to personal integrity, individual conscience and religious faith, and, most important, private property. These rights are fully *actual* only when they are enforced, and this requirement prompted Hegel to advance a distinctive retributive conception of punishment as the legitimate enforcement of these rights. Modern persons, Hegel insists, are ineluctably individualists, separate persons to use Rawls's term, both claimants to and governed by a regime of rights which operate as side-constraints in the fashion described by Robert Nozick in *Anarchy, State, and Utopia*[12] (*pace* the modern communitarian who says such a person is a fiction). But Hegel differs from this style of contemporary liberalism in insisting that this minimal self-ascription cannot represent the whole truth about our moral personality, not least because it is unable to determine appropriate measures of just punishment.

MORALITY

We are persons, but we are also moral subjects. In the Morality chapter that follows (*Moralität:* capitalized in my usage because Hegel employs it as a technical term) Hegel examines the possibility that our understanding of ourselves as moral subjects might itself furnish the repertoire of moral principles and particular moral judgements that Abstract Right cannot provide. This, of course, was Kant's project and throughout this chapter Hegel stalks Kant, gathering insights concerning the nature of human agency but finally rejecting Kant's moral psychology (with its dichotomy of duty and inclination) and Kant's normative ethics (with its employment of the Categorical Imperative as the definitive test of any proposed moral principle).[13] So, Hegel concludes, 'from this point of view, no immanent theory of duties is possible' (PR §135). This, in essence, is the famous

[12] Nozick 1974.
[13] The criticism of Kant in the Morality chapter of PR is a sketchy summary of the criticisms of Kant to be found in Hegel's earlier works, notably the *Natural Law* essay and the *Phenomenology*. Some elements of this criticism are original, but some are not, deriving from the strongly critical reaction to Kant's ethics as the various works were published.

'emptiness' challenge to Kantian ethics.[14] The categorical imperative cannot serve as either a testing method or a generative algorithm because examples show that it gets things wrong, yielding both false positives when it legitimates evidently wrongful behaviour by rigging the maxims to be tested and false negatives when it rejects principles that are either worthy or morally innocuous. If the Kantian account is supplemented by the claims of conscience or some other subjectivist strategy, these projects are undermined by the fact of typical human fallibility. The most (subjectively) conscientious agents can get things disastrously wrong and do appalling evil.

It would be a mistake to dismiss Hegel's critique of Morality as entirely negative. A crucial insight which he endorses is the '*right of the subjective will* [which] is that whatever it is to recognize as valid should be *perceived* by it *as good*' (PR §132). If we take this as the claim that neither priests nor princes can just dictate to us how we should behave (as Kant equally insisted), that norms of conduct should be understood and endorsed by all those to whom they apply, we can see Hegel as accepting a crucial thesis of modern ethical liberalism in its broadest sense. It is a matter of very great dispute how far Hegel himself respects this important right in the details of the argument to follow. It is also important that one recognizes that this right is entirely formal. It does not tell us what the good is. It does not deliver 'an immanent theory of duties'. For that we have to investigate Ethical Life (*Sittlichkeit*), Hegel's distinctive name for the actual norms of the Rational State, i.e. the moral community he inhabits.

ETHICAL LIFE

F.H. Bradley's coinage, 'My Station and Its Duties', gives a clear sense to the difficult term 'Ethical Life'. Our duties are furnished by our ethical location (our station in life) in communities of sentiment fashioned throughout history which have passed the test of time. If this sounds like subjection rather than freedom, Hegel emphasizes that the opposite is the case. 'A binding duty can appear as a *limitation* ... the individual however finds his *liberation* in duty' (PR §149). Our duties do not constrain us, like a ball and chain; rather they make us free in two familiar and intuitive ways: first, we find our natural desires and immediate emotional responses are tamed and controlled when we understand and endorse the requirements put on us by

---

[14] This famous 'challenge' has been widely discussed. For a good discussion, see Wood 1999: 97–107.

our duties; we are not enslaved by our desires. Secondly, we grasp that the institutions of ethical life, family, civil society and state, enable us to realize personal capacities that would otherwise fail to find an adequate expression.

Human persons have a distinctive capacity for love and a long-term commitment towards others. Hegel tells us that the uniquely satisfactory means of exercising this capacity in the modern world is found in the nuclear family where family members, as parents, children or siblings, love each other and recognize appropriate duties of care. Nowadays many would regard this position as controversial. That is often because of the dated and ethically unacceptable view of the role of women (as when he compares them to plants and tells us that 'when women are in charge of government, the state is in danger' (PR §166A)), which taints his view of marriage. And many would reject the explicit restriction of marriage to heterosexual relationships. Nonetheless and despite the obvious challenges there is much truth to Hegel's account of the ways in which domesticity contributes to human freedom. Hegel's writings are a good target for feminists and others, but a narrow focus on what are nowadays diagnosed as errors will miss the nuances of his position.

Civil Society is the second element of ethical life. It is a curiously abstracted construction, gathering together the major non-political institutions of the modern state. Hegel explains how economic, legal and administrative structures enable 'concrete persons' (chiefly male family members) to promote their freedom by satisfying the particular self-interest of themselves and their families. In the course of this achievement, 'the principle of particularity passes over into *universality*' (PR §186) as individuals form strategic links with others to achieve common goals, and these links in turn are transformed into a genuinely general will. Guided mainly by the writings of British economists, notably Smith and Ricardo, Hegel developed strong and interesting views on how the emergent capitalism of his day is a liberating force, how the ever more productive forces released by rapid industrialization enable humans to satisfy their increasingly sophisticated needs, and how social classes form in the different areas (agricultural, business and bureaucratic) of economic life. It is an odd feature of Marx's writing that he never discusses directly Hegel's published views on economic life.

The administration of law protects the citizens' rights, enforces contracts, and corrects the deficiencies of state of nature punishment systems, as these were explained in Abstract Right. Two further elements of Civil Society are the 'Police', all those social agencies designed to provide regulative and infrastructural support to the system of production and exchange, including public education services, and the 'Corporations' – a strange confection of mediaeval guilds, employers' associations and trades unions. All these institutions serve the passing-over of particularity into universality as individuals associate together to serve their particular purposes more efficiently. But one problem of modern social life obdurately resists solution. Hegel portrays poverty as a deforming scar on the face of modern civilization caused not only by idleness and stupidity but, more deeply and problematically, by the structural problems of market capitalism when, for example, markets collapse or technological change makes ancient skills redundant. At this point the state is evidently necessary to fashion remedies. He mentions redistributive taxation, compulsory work schemes, and even colonization as policy alternatives, but shows little enthusiasm for them, and (oddly, given the severity of the problem of poverty as he describes it) he does not take the issue further when he moves on to discuss the state, the final element of ethical life.

THE STATE

By the 'Rational State', we are to understand the modern system of social freedom which wraps up in a harmonious construction all the normative systems encountered in the modern world. Thus the Rational State is the integration of the ethical demands of personal rights, moral subjectivity, family life, civil society and the political institutions of the state. These domains make ethical demands which are harmonious in the sense that individuals can recognize and respect moral rules which derive from all these sources without finding themselves in circumstances of tragic conflict wherein rules conflict and the complex identity of the modern self is torn apart. If there are conflicts they will be resolved by ordering principles, most conspicuously by obeying the laws of the state. Since the State is Rational there will be no modern Antigones, no moral rebels. (If, by contrast, there turned out to be irresolvable conflicts, then this existent state would not be rational. The conflicts would ensure that it would go under, as an imperfect episode in the progress towards the actual Rational State.)

I paraphrase *PR* §260: 'The state is the actuality of concrete freedom. As members of it, persons should be able to develop all their capacities and satisfy all the interests they have as individuals, as family members and as members of civil society. But they should not and do not live as private persons alone. They recognize their universality, their ties with others. And these ties bind them to serve a common purpose, a universal end which they freely acknowledge as they perform the duties incumbent on them in their particular stations in life, as determined ultimately by the state.'

A different sense of the term 'state' denotes the 'political state proper' or the 'strictly political state' (PR §267). This is a political system with a constitution that Hegel describes in some detail. The strictly political state, as Hegel describes it, is a ramshackle, bodged edifice. (I insist that this is not a crassly anachronistic judgement; there were discussions of philosophical principle of which Hegel was well aware that could have been shaped into a radical critique of the institutions he endorses – as Marx sharply pointed out.)[15] Hegel's presentation of the constitution disobeys the logical principles (of universality synthesized with particularity into an individual unity) which he himself advanced as constituting the rational structure of all reality. At its head is a monarchy which has a symbolic personal role, dotting the 'i's and crossing the 't's (PR §280A), yet also turns out to have formidable and decisive political powers. The second element of the constitution is the executive, a civil service owing allegiance to the monarch who appoints the senior ministers. The third element is the legislative power. This includes the monarch and the executive, which closely oversee the operations of the two further constituent structures: two Estates (roughly assemblies): one a collection of wealthy landowners, the other appointed from the corporations (and not elected by universal suffrage).

It is a very good question whether these dismal political structures respect the right of the subjective will, as explained above, in the case of the ordinary run of citizens who exercise no active political powers and who will be hard put to understand the rationale behind the political structures which govern them, as explained by Hegel. The obedience of the patriotic citizen may not be blind – it will be informed by a free press, for example (PR §§ 314–20) – but Hegel believes that public opinion should be despised as much as it is respected.

As one state amongst others, states may find themselves at war, which 'should not be regarded as an absolute evil' (PR §324) since good may come of it. It may quicken otherwise dormant and degenerating sentiments of patriotism. Some have found Hegel's views on war abhorrent. Others insist that once a fully nuanced account is given, this should be acceptable to sophisticated non-pacifists. Hegel ends the *Philosophy of Right* by locating the Rational State in the space of International Law (of which he gives a Hobbesian account as consisting of non-mandatory rules and agreements which states

---

[15] Marx 1970.

should try to keep so long as their own interests are not compromised), and in the time of World History, which he summarizes in the concluding half-a-dozen pages.

I have presented Hegel as a methodological conservative. We cannot tell the world how it ought to be; we are locked into the ethical world we inhabit and seek to comprehend. We comprehend it only in retrospect, with a philosophically informed hindsight:

> When philosophy paints its grey in grey, then has a shape of life grown old.
> By philosophy's grey in grey it cannot be rejuvenated but only understood.
> The owl of Minerva spreads its wings only with the falling of the dusk.
>
> (*PR* Preface, p. 13)[16]

We can bracket the problem of how far Hegel is committed to political conservatism in the *Philosophy of Right*. But we should address the question of how much of modern ethical liberalism is embedded in his doctrines. In this context, there are three important points that we should note.

First, we should recognize that Hegel's style of conservatism does not bar all change. It is the *actual* world that furnishes our moral duties, and this actual world is constitutively rational. The *real* world that we encounter in all its detail may not fully articulate its rational underpinnings – indeed, in specific respects it may violate them. So there is space for critical work to be done – philosophical as well as politically activist – in reconfiguring our ethical habitat. This is the task of *immanent critique*: that of ensuring that the ethical world measures up to its moral credentials. Sensible, ethically-directed change can be managed by constructive reform of the Rational State.

Secondly, we should recognize that the grounding principles of liberalism – centrally the right of the subjective will, but also notable human rights, as well as associated concrete political freedoms (freedom of conscience and worship, freedom of the press, freedom to find one's own career path, amongst many others) – are all entrenched *within* Hegel's Rational State. They are not moral luxuries or indulgencies, they cannot be rejected; they are as much a feature of the modern political world as Hegel (mistakenly) takes a constitutional monarchy to be. In these respects Hegel is a liberal, but this

---

[16] I quote the elegant Knox translation: Hegel 1952. For an explanation of the image of philosophy painting its grey in grey, see Knowles 2002: 70, 78–82, 346 n.3.

should not be a surprise. The methodological conservative endorses principles as he finds them and liberal principles are central to modern ethics.

Thirdly, we should recall that the central explanatory concept of the *Philosophy of Right* is freedom. There are many critical questions the reader can target at the detail of Hegel's ethical settlement:

Is Hegel right to dismiss all varieties of social contract theories as individualistic and prescriptive, because he believes them to be historically false?

How far does the crucial political sentiment of patriotism, which holds the state together as love unites the family, occlude a properly critical spirit on the part of citizens?

How far does the education of citizens, in which religion has an important part to play, undermine their rational independence?

It is a measure of Hegel's greatness that the probing reader will not find simple answers to sceptical challenges such as these (although I would support all of them). And even where it is obvious that Hegel's descriptions-cum-prescriptions for the Rational State are desperately out of date, the intelligent scholar may well find modern equivalencies for the institutions which Hegel falsely believed to be a permanent feature of the ethical and political landscape.

BIBLIOGRAPHY

An asterisk denotes secondary literature especially suitable for further reading.

Boucher, David (ed.) 1997. *The British Idealists.* Cambridge University Press

Hegel G.W.F. 1952. *Hegel's Philosophy of Right*, trans. T.M. Knox. Oxford University Press

Hegel, G.W.F. 1956 (first pub. 1837). *Lectures on the Philosophy of History*, trans. as *The Philosophy of History* by J. Sibree. New York: Dover

Hegel, G.W.F. 1975 (first pub. 1840). *Lectures on the Philosophy of History: Introduction*, trans. H.B. Nisbet. Cambridge University Press

Hegel, G.W.F. 1977 (first pub. 1807). *Hegel's Phenomenology of Spirit*, trans. A.V. Miller. Oxford University Press

Hegel, G.W.F. 1991 (first pub. 1821). *Elements of the Philosophy of Right*, ed. Allen W. Wood, trans. H.B. Nisbet. Cambridge University Press

Hegel, G.W.F. 1999 (first pub. 1802–1803). 'On the Scientific Ways of Treating Natural Law, on its Place in Practical Philosophy, and its Relation to the Positive Sciences of Right', in G.W.F. Hegel, *Political Writings*, ed. L. Dickey and H.B. Nisbet, trans. H.B. Nisbet. Cambridge University Press, pp. 102–80

Hegel, G.W.F. 2007. *Philosophy of Mind (Encyclopaedia of the Philosophical Sciences*, Part 3, §§ 377–577, first pub. 1817; 3rd edn, 1830), trans. W. Wallace and A.V. Miller, revised with introduction and commentary by Michael Inwood. Oxford University Press

Knowles, Dudley 2002. *Hegel and the Philosophy of Right*. London: Routledge

Marx, K. 1970. *Critique of Hegel's 'Philosophy of Right'* ed. J. O'Malley. Cambridge University Press

Mill, J.S. 1863. *Utilitarianism*. London: Parker, Son and Bourn

Nozick, Robert 1974. *Anarchy, State, and Utopia*. New York: Basic Books

Pinkard, Terry 2000. *Hegel: A Biography*. Cambridge University Press

Stern, Robert 2002. *Hegel and the Phenomenology of Spirit*. Abingdon: Routledge*

Stern, Robert 2006. 'Hegel's *Doppelsatz*: A Neutral Reading', *Journal of the History of Philosophy* 44: 235–66

Wood, Allen W. 1999. *Kant's Ethical Thought*. Cambridge University Press*

33

Mill

CHRISTOPHER MACLEOD

MILL AND THE NINETEENTH CENTURY

The spirit of Mill's philosophy is, first and foremost, one of naturalism. For the purposes here, we can understand the basic thrust of Mill's naturalism as a commitment to two connected claims. Firstly, that man is wholly part of nature: humans are objects broadly continuous with other simpler objects which we encounter in experience and which are subject to natural laws. Secondly, all of our knowledge of the world must come through empirical observation: there can, in effect, be no substantial knowledge that is gained *a priori*. The claims are distinct, but clearly related. The guiding thought is that *if* man is merely a part of nature, no transmission of information about some part of nature can occur *except* by causal chains leading from those external events to ourselves – which is to say by way of sense perception.[1]

Mill's commitment to naturalism makes him an invigorating philosophic companion for twenty-first century readers – but we should not lose sight of the historical context in which he wrote. Mill was the most influential English-language philosopher of the nineteenth century, and his work in epistemology, metaphysics, political theory, and moral philosophy reflects characteristically nineteenth-century concerns. The period in which Mill's general outlook was crystallised was one asking searching questions about how to move beyond the legacy of the European Enlightenment, and how to respond to the rise of democratic social structures. Much of Mill's moral philosophy, which shall be the focus of this chapter, can be seen to engage with these issues.

To the generation active in the early nineteenth century, Enlightenment optimism had been significantly tempered by the chaos of post-Revolutionary France. The breakdown of traditional modes of authority seemed to usher in an age of individualism and materialism, corrosive of

---

[1] See Skorupski 1998 for discussion of the relation of Mill's naturalism to the various aspects of his philosophy.

any meaningful ethical life. A ready explanation was offered. The Enlightenment had been committed to the unrestricted use of free critique: no doctrine was sacrosanct, and every principle was asked to justify itself on the basis on evidence. This thoroughgoing commitment to criticism, however, seemed to undermine the possibility of any agreement upon or attachment to substantive moral doctrines, ending in a sceptical reliance of each individual on his own preference. The Enlightenment was, in this sense, seen as a *negative* moment, in need of supplementation.

Mill shares this view: the eighteenth century is characterised by him as an age which is dominated by thinkers who saw 'what was not true, not what was'. 'To tear away, was indeed all that these philosophers, for the most part, aimed at: they had no conception that anything else was needful.'[2] The problem for the nineteenth century was how to fill the void left by the Enlightenment and overcome scepticism without reverting to dogmatism. As Frederick Beiser puts it: 'how is it possible to educate the public about the principles of morality, politics, and taste when reason casts nothing but doubt upon them?'[3]

This anxiety is deeply connected to the issues of alienation and disenchantment that came sharply into focus during the period. During the famous 'mental crisis', Mill felt closely the disaffection that could be caused by seeing oneself as a manufactured individual of the modern era. Mill's extraordinary education by his father and Bentham in preparation for leadership of the philosophical radicals had left him unable to feel and identify with goals not properly his *own*. To Mill, as to many during the early period of the nineteenth century, the modern world seemed to threaten to mechanise the individual, to make him passive in the process of having his desires determined by forces beyond his control. The question of how the individual could feel at home in an artificial world loomed large.

These are romantic questions, and Mill engaged seriously with the answers the romantics offered. Romanticism has often been characterised in philosophy as an attempt to in some sense reverse the Enlightenment – as a retreat from reason towards aestheticism, irrationalism or mysticism.[4] If it were only this, Mill would have had little time for thinkers such as Wordsworth,

[2] Mill, *Coleridge*, 10: 131–2, 139. References to Mill are taken from 1963–1991, citing volume and page. See also Mill, *Bentham*, 10: 80, Mill, *Spirit of the Age*, 22: 230–3.
[3] Beiser 2003: 47.
[4] See, for example, Berlin 2000 for an account of romanticism as a 'violent onslaught upon the premises of the Enlightenment' (p. 7).

Coleridge, Carlyle, and Goethe, whom he held in high esteem.[5] In fact, the romantics sought not to dethrone reason, but rather to stress the use of the imagination in the discovery, teaching, and sustaining of truth. Recent scholarship has stressed the broad continuity between the objectives of the Enlightenment and romantic periods. 'If the romantics were the critics of the *Aufklärung*, they were also its disciples', Beiser notes.[6]

The romantics sought to steady the powers of reason by deepening the input of the imagination in supporting ethical ideals, and to show that man need not be seen as a passive recipient of desires and opinions, but could attain a degree of autonomy over his character. Mill's work reflects this influence, being infused with nineteenth-century desire for active engagement with the world, spontaneity of character and self-direction, and the full development of man in all his faculties. He did not, however, agree with the philosophic premises of the romantics. Often, these were post-Kantian in orientation, and this was an aspect of romanticism he could never accept.

The empiricists of the eighteenth century were correct in their philosophical starting point, but their boyish enthusiasm for progress led them to overlook the genuine problems modernity presented.[7] The romantic tradition understood these issues all too well, grappled with some of the deepest issues of ethical life in a profound and imaginative way, but was intellectually undisciplined. Both sides in the 'fight between the nineteenth century and the eighteenth' had seen 'one side of the truth'.[8] '[W]hoever could master the premises and combine the methods of both, would possess the entire English philosophy of their age.'[9] This, then, was Mill's project: to integrate nineteenth-century insights and aspirations into the philosophical framework of naturalism. He expresses this well when claiming that 'out of my mechanical premises, I elicit *dynamical* conclusions'.[10]

---

[5] I name only four of the most prominent romantics cited in the *Autobiography* (see Mill, *Autobiography* 1: 149ff). Mill also knew works of other key thinkers of the romantic period, however. See Macleod 2011: 1–6.

[6] Beiser 2003: 44.

[7] 'Boyish' is in fact Mill's term. Mill describes Bentham thus: 'He knew no dejection, no heaviness of heart. He never felt life a sore and a weary burthen. He was a boy to the last' (Mill, *Bentham*, 10: 92). The claim that the eighteenth century was characterised by an innocence to the coming effects of modernisation was of course popular sentiment. 'Bliss was it in that dawn to be alive, But to be young was very heaven!' (Wordsworth 1970: 196).

[8] Mill, *Autobiography*, 1: 169–71.   [9] Mill, *Coleridge*, 10: 121.

[10] Mill, Letter to Carlyle, 12: 181.

HIGHER PLEASURES AND FREEDOM

Bentham's theory of value is hedonistic, holding that the only ultimate bearers of value are occurrences of pleasure, and that the only ultimate bearers of disvalue are occurrences of pain. His theory, moreover, assumes that instances of value are well ordered, and in a manner that maps directly on to quantity of pleasure. Pleasure, that is to say, comes in various quantities, and more pleasure is always to be preferred to less.

All that matters in terms of value, according to this theory, is the *amount* of pleasure generated: 'quantity of pleasure being equal, pushpin is as good as poetry'.[11] The *type* of pleasure experienced, for Bentham, was of no matter. Many critics had found this characterisation of value objectionable, implying that the goal of life was a mundane state of satisfaction.

> [S]uch a theory of life excites in many minds, and among them in some of the most estimable in feeling and purpose, inveterate dislike. To suppose that life has (as they express it) no higher end than pleasure – no better and nobler object of pursuit – they designate as utterly mean and grovelling; as a doctrine worthy only of swine[.][12]

Such a conception of value was said to 'represent human nature in a degrading light',[13] and confirmed the suspicion of many nineteenth-century thinkers that modern social structures bred mediocrity and undermined the possibility of high ideals. Mill had sympathy for these criticisms. His solution, however, was to point out that this was not a result of treating pleasure as the sole bearer of value. Rather, the problem lay in Bentham's assumption that ordering of values takes place solely on the basis of quantity of pleasure generated. 'It would be absurd', Mill writes, 'that while, in estimating all other things, quality is considered as well as quantity, the estimation of pleasures should be supposed to depend on quantity alone'.[14]

Mill rejects the claim that value correlates to quantity of pleasure, and that such a simple algorithmic decision procedure can specify which states of affairs are most valuable. Instead, Mill claims that some experiences are more valuable on the basis that the pleasure involved is of a higher quality.

> If I am asked, what I mean by difference of quality in pleasures, or what makes one pleasure more valuable than another, merely as a pleasure, except its being greater in amount, there is but one possible answer. Of two pleasures, if there be one to which all or almost all who have

[11] Mill, *Bentham*, 10: 113. [12] Mill, *Utilitarianism*, 10: 210. [13] Ibid. [14] Ibid., 211.

experience of both give a decided preference [. . .] that is the more desirable pleasure.[15]

This claim is a purely formal one about value ordering – that there can exist pleasures p_h and p_l, such that p_h is more valuable than p_l, even where p_l is present in an equal or greater quantity. Some commentators have claimed that Mill holds that *any* quantity of a higher pleasure is more valuable than *any* quantity of a lower pleasure on the basis of the following passage:[16]

> If one of the two [pleasures] is, by those who are competently acquainted with both, placed so far above the other that they prefer it [. . .] and would not resign it for any quantity of the other pleasure which their nature is capable of, we are justified in ascribing to the preferred enjoyment a superiority in quality[.][17]

This interpretation, though, has implications too implausible to attribute to Mill. As Miller asks: 'How, for instance, could ten minutes of one person's pleasurably reading philosophy possibly be worth more than all of the physical sexual pleasure to be experienced by humanity over the next 1,000 years?'[18] In fact, Mill does not make this claim: in the passage cited, he only registers a *sufficient* condition for considering one pleasure of a higher quality to another – not a *necessary* condition.[19]

In reality, Mill gives very little indication as to how to weigh quality against quantity of pleasure – he simply does not speak to the specifics of how varying quantities of pleasures at varying qualities are to be reconciled against one another. Indeed, given the vast array of different *sorts* of pleasure human beings are capable of experiencing, there may well be no formula to derive a ranking. This is not to say that there *is* no ranking between them. Rather, given the choice between five units of the pleasure of art appreciation and fifty units of the pleasure of gentle dozing, it may be that there is no decision procedure to determine the optimal choice, except practising careful judgment, in dialogue with other competent judges.[20]

---

[15] Ibid. [16] See Riley 1993 and 2003. [17] Mill, *Utilitarianism*, 10: 211.

[18] Miller 2014. The assumption that the pleasure of reading philosophy is qualitatively higher than that of sex is a substantive one, though the point generalises easily.

[19] See Saunders 2011.

[20] Note, of course, that the verdict that x is more valuable than y by competent judges need not be taken to *constitute* x's status as more valuable, even if this is the only manner by which to discover this status. Most interpreters take it that Mill holds that the competent judges *track* the value of pleasure. See, however, Millgram 2000 for a contrasting view.

On a question which is the best worth having of two pleasures, or which of two modes of existence is the most grateful to the feelings, apart from its moral attributes and from its consequences, the judgment of those who are qualified by knowledge of both, or, if they differ, that of the majority among them, must be admitted as final.[21]

It has sometimes been claimed that by incorporating qualitative concerns, Mill abandons hedonism as a theory of value.[22] It should be obvious from the exposition offered here that this is not so. Mill's denial that the ordering of values takes place solely on the basis of quantity of pleasure generated does not imply that anything *other* than pleasure is valuable. Rather, it implies that quality can be a feature which in part determines the ranking of exactly the same pleasurable experiences that all other hedonists value.

None of what has so far been said addresses the substantive issue of which *sorts* of pleasures are of higher quality than others. Commentators have been quick to accuse Mill of prudishness on the basis of his apparent privileging of pleasures of the mind. Certainly, he uses Socrates as an example of one who is capable of higher pleasures 'of the intellect, of the feelings and imagination, and of the moral sentiments'.[23] But Mill's doctrine need not be read as restrictively intellectualist: if Socrates is chosen on this occasion, Pericles is the choice in *On Liberty*.[24] The sustained contrast Mill appeals to is not between intellectual pleasures and physical pleasures, but rather between the pleasures which involve distinctively human capacities and those that do not.

Such pleasures certainly do include those that might ordinarily be thought of as physical. The pleasure I receive from carelessly swinging on my chair does not represent the same quality of pleasure as that enjoyed by someone executing a carefully mastered complicated gymnastic manoeuvre – but both tasks are certainly physical. The pleasure generated by eating popcorn in the cinema is not the same sort of pleasure as someone appreciating fine cuisine, but terming the latter an 'intellectual' pleasure would misrepresent the experience entirely. The relevant distinction seems to be one of *activity*, and, in this sense, speaks to the nineteenth-century concerns outlined above. Certain pleasures – and this may be a characteristic of the animal pleasures – are enjoyed passively. The gap is perhaps best understood as that between being *given* pleasure *by* certain experiences, and *taking* pleasure *in* experiences. The former involves a receptive stance to the world. The latter requires a concerted activity – *doing*, with an engaged awareness of what one is doing.

[21] Mill, *Utilitarianism*, 10: 213. [22] See, for example, Moore 1993: 130–2.
[23] Mill, *Utilitarianism*, 10: 211. [24] Mill, *On Liberty*, 18: 266.

This focus on activity is connected to the arguments offered in *On Liberty*. As is well known, *On Liberty* argues for the preservation of a sphere of liberty for the individual, inside which his conduct should remain free from coercive interference. Freedom, to the previous generation of philosophical radicals, was argued for on the basis that it would allow individuals to better satisfy their pre-existent desires: illiberal modes of government were criticised on the grounds that they led to the unnecessary frustration of interests of a large section of the population. Mill preserves this argument, but incorporates it into a broader case for freedom, which becomes a mechanism not just for *pursuing* one's interests and desires, but for the *development* of one's interests and desires.

Freedom is important to Mill primarily because it allows room for self-development: for the formation of interests and desires that are genuinely one's own. 'He who lets the world, or his own portion of it, choose his plan of life for him, has no need of any other faculty than the ape-like one of imitation.'[25] Such a life, passively received, would not involve genuine identification with one's own experiences. A situation in which each took their model of life from the prevailing consensus would be one in which lives were lived in a manner 'inert and torpid, instead of active and energetic'.[26] Such lives do not allow for the possibility of experiencing higher pleasures.

In the climate of conformity, human character is quashed. Individuals 'become incapable of any strong wishes or native pleasures, and are generally without either opinions or feelings of home growth, or properly their own'.[27] Such, Mill thinks, was the mistaken ideal of Calvinism, which sought to root out, rather than cultivate, the seeds of human nature. In place of such self-abnegation and alienation, Mill advocates a 'Greek ideal of self-development'.[28] He encourages the fostering of 'spontaneity' and 'individuality', the full and unimpeded exploration of the individual's own nature.[29] Consistently with his overall naturalistic approach, this argument for freedom is an anthropological one, based not on 'abstract right', but on considerations about the conditions under which human beings at a certain stage of development thrive, and are most truly happy.[30]

THE 'PROOF' AND MORALITY

We have so far dealt with the content of Mill's axiology – what things he thinks are valuable. Mill's attempt to demonstrate this axiology in Chapter 4 of *Utilitarianism* has been the subject of much controversy. His 'proof of the

---

[25] Ibid., 262. [26] Ibid. [27] Ibid., 265. [28] Ibid., 266. [29] Ibid., 264. [30] Ibid., 234.

principle of utility' takes place by way of three subclaims. Mill means to show that:

(a) happiness is desirable as an ultimate end,
(b) nothing but happiness is desirable as an ultimate end, and
(c) each person's happiness is equally desirable.

Mill indicates that '[b]y happiness is intended pleasure, and the absence of pain'.[31] As such, by demonstrating the truth of these three subclaims, he will have shown impartialistic hedonism to be true.

Though much has been made of the argument for (a), Mill assumes it relatively uncontroversial. True to his naturalism, which allows no appeal to sources other than ordinary experience and observation, Mill argues that the best and only possible evidence that something is desirable is that people do desire it.

> The only proof capable of being given that an object is visible, is that people actually see it. The only proof that a sound is audible, is that people hear it: and so of the other sources of our experience. In like manner, I apprehend, the sole evidence it is possible to produce that anything is desirable, is that people do actually desire it.[32]

The analogy he presents in the first two sentences of this passage is clearly not a good one, and this is the root of the accusation that Mill commits the naturalistic fallacy.[33] The fact that something can be seen or heard *means* that it is visible or audible, and there is no such *a priori* link between what is desired and the desirable. But this does not at all undermine Mill's basic argument, which is merely that something's being desired serves as evidence ('[c]onsiderations [...] capable of determining the intellect'[34]) for its desirability.

Every agent, Mill suggests, under 'practised self-consciousness and self-observation',[35] is forced to admit that they *do* desire happiness for its own sake, at least amongst other things. This is an anthropological reality that cannot fail to have a bearing on our view of ethics. In the absence of under-mining arguments, the fact that observed agents *do* universally exhibit a primitive desire for happiness serves as overwhelming evidence for its desir-ability. Mill refuses to take scepticism about this natural tendency seriously without compelling evidence – in just the same way that he treats our natural

---

[31] Mill, *Utilitarianism*, 10: 210. [32] Ibid., 234.
[33] See Moore 1993: 117–26 for the classic statement of this criticism.
[34] Mill, *Utilitarianism*, 10: 208. [35] Ibid.

tendency to believe inductive generalisations as trustworthy in the absence of undermining reasons.[36]

Mill's basic strategy in arguing for (b) is to show that other candidates to be added to our axiology are desired either as *means* to happiness, or as a *part of happiness*. The claim that many apparently desirable things are not so, being desired only as means, is an uncontentious and familiar move. Mill's talk of *parts* of happiness is more obscure. Mill holds that certain objects desired originally as means to happiness can become so psychologically intertwined as to be inseparable from happiness – we would, that is to say, be caused a net-loss of happiness to be without them.

Mill offers the example of virtue. 'Virtue, according to the utilitarian conception, is a good of this description. There was no original desire of it, or motive to it, save its conduciveness to pleasure, and especially to protection from pain. But through the association thus formed, it may be felt a good in itself, and desired as such with as great intensity as any other good.'[37] There is counterfactual dependence of the desirability of virtue on its conduciveness to pleasure – had virtue not been conducive to pleasure, it would not have been desired. This is not to say that it is desired only as a means, 'as a psychological fact' – but it does undermine any claim it has to being ultimately desirable.[38] Such, Mill argues, is the origin of all we desire as an end, other than happiness.

Mill spends very little time at all on (c). He argues for it thus: 'each person's happiness is a good to that person, and the general happiness, therefore a good to the aggregate of all persons'.[39] In one respect, Mill is here simply confirming his methodological individualism by stating that the good of a group can be nothing other than the good of its members. But the claim is clearly deeper than that. Mill's view of value is at root impersonal: to say that something is good-for-*x* is to say that it is a good *simpliciter*, held by *x*. The supposition that 'equal amounts of happiness are equally desirable, whether felt by the same or by different persons'[40] is clearly contentious, however: one might well insist that adding to the happiness of the content or undeserving is *not* to add to the general good at the same level as adding to the happiness of the discontent or deserving.

---

[36] See Macleod 2013. Mill does not seek to supplant everyday morality with a set of abstractly deduced norms, but rather to sharpen moral reasoning that is in any case present: 'If the end which the utilitarian doctrine proposes to itself were not, in theory and in practice, acknowledged to be an end, nothing could ever convince any person that it was so' (Mill, *Utilitarianism*, 10: 234). This stance, I have argued, is instructively similar to Kant's use of 'Common Human Reason'. See Macleod 2014.

[37] Mill, *Utilitarianism*, 10: 236.   [38] Ibid., 235.   [39] Ibid., 234.   [40] Ibid., 258n.

It is important to note that the claims made so far concern *axiology*. They concern what states of affairs are valuable – which outcomes are *good*. These axiological claims are, in themselves, silent on the question of *rightness* – a point which is easy to miss. While some accounts of the rightness of an action might suggest that an action is morally right if and only if it brings about the highest amount of value in the world possible, Mill's does not. Maximising utilitarianism is a coherent moral stance – and when, for instance, Mill writes that 'actions are right in proportion as they tend to promote happiness, wrong as they tend to produce the reverse of happiness',[41] he does seem to suggest that this is his view. But other, more careful, statements clearly show that this is not his considered position.

We are not morally obliged, Mill thinks, to bring about the *best* outcome: there are many circumstances in which, though a high-level self-sacrifice might optimise happiness in the world, this is nevertheless not morally required. It is a mistake to think 'that whatever is not a duty is a sin. [...] There is a standard of altruism to which all should be required to come up, and a degree beyond it which is not obligatory, but meritorious.'[42] The question arises, then, of Mill's standard of *moral rightness*, and its relation to his *theory of value*. The clues are given in Chapter 5 of *Utilitarianism*, and in *System* 6: xii. In Chapter 5 of *Utilitarianism*, Mill clearly links the notion of *morality* to that of *punishment*.

> We do not call anything wrong, unless we mean to imply that a person ought to be punished in some way or other for doing it; if not by law, by the opinion of his fellow-creatures; if not by opinion, by the reproaches of his own conscience. This seems the real turning point of the distinction between morality and simple expediency.[43]

An act or omission might cause a net-loss in terms of happiness, but if it is not something that an individual ought to be punished for, 'it is not a case of moral obligation'.[44] The conceptual connection of morality to punishment of course opens up the question of how the appropriateness of punishment can be spelt out without any prior appeal to morality, and how this view of morality fits together with Mill's overall theory of value.

We must note first of all that morality is, for Mill, only *one* domain of practical reason. Bentham is in error in 'treating the *moral* view of actions and characters, which is unquestionably the first and most important mode of looking at them, as if it were the sole one'.[45] The axiology that Mill articulates

---

[41] Ibid., 210. [42] Mill, *Auguste Comte*, 10: 337. [43] Mill, *Utilitarianism*, 10: 246.
[44] Ibid., 10: 246. [45] Mill, *Bentham*, 10: 112. See also Mill, *Auguste Comte*, 10: 336.

in Chapter 2 and demonstrates in Chapter 4 of *Utilitarianism* grounds practical reason – the 'Art of Life', as Mill puts it – as a whole. The Art of Life has three departments: 'Morality, Prudence or Policy, and Aesthetics; the Right, the Expedient, and the Beautiful or Noble'.[46] There are norms of prudence: an action is *prudent* simply to the extent that it maximises a person's individual utility, which can of course be in part a function of others' utility. There are aesthetic norms: an action is *beautiful* to the extent that it is admired, and excites aesthetic pleasure in its contemplation. Moral norms play a role in guiding and evaluating action, but so do norms of aesthetics and prudence: these too are structured to promote the general happiness, and as such provide reasons for action.[47] An action is *morally obligatory* if its non-performance should be subject to punishment, by law, opinion or conscience. But, Mill is clear, the notion of the propriety of punishment is tied up with the sentiment of *blame*: we think punishment appropriate only in such circumstances as we feel an agent blame-worthy for their conduct.[48]

Like judgments of beauty and prudence, then, our judgments about moral wrongs are constrained by anthropological facts about how we experience and react to the actions of ourselves and others. Such dispositions are of course malleable over time – and part of the project of reforming our ethical lives is learning to respond to actions in terms of sympathy, admiration and blame where we have not previously. Mill recommends that art, poetry and religion be marshalled in the service of advancing and entrenching such sentiments – helping us to identify with our norms, and solidifying their place within our common lives.[49] What sorts of reform would be desirable is itself an important question, and one to be determined by appealing to happiness, as the overarching end of life.

[46] Mill, *System*, 8: 949.
[47] See Loizides 2013: 133–40 for discussion of the various ways in which the distinction between the prudence, morality, and beauty of actions has been read by commentators.
[48] Mill, *Utilitarianism*, 10: 246. See Jacobson 2008, for discussion of this sentimentalist constraint within Mill's account of morality.
[49] See, for instance, Mill, *Utilitarianism*, 10: 232; Mill, Letter to Carlyle, 12: 113.

Mill

BIBLIOGRAPHY

An asterisk denotes secondary literature especially suitable for further reading.

Beiser, F., 2003. *The Romantic Imperative: the Concept of Early German Romanticism* (Cambridge, MA: Harvard University Press)

Berlin, I., 2000. *The Roots of Romanticism* (London: Pimlico)

Crisp, R., 1997. *Mill On Utilitarianism* (London: Routledge)

Donner, W., 1991. *The Liberal Self: John Stuart Mill's Moral and Political Philosophy* (Ithaca, NY: Cornell University Press)*

Jacobson, D., 2008. 'Utilitarianism without Consequentialism: The Case of John Stuart Mill', *Philosophical Review*, 117, 159–91

Loizides, A., 2013. *John Stuart Mill's Platonic Heritage: Happiness Through Character* (Plymouth, Lexington Books)

Macleod, C., 2011. 'John Stuart Mill and Romanticism', unpublished PhD thesis, University of St Andrews

Macleod, C., 2013. 'Mill, Intuitions and Normativity', *Utilitas*, 25, 46–65

Macleod, C., 2014. 'Mill on the Epistemology of Reasons: a Comparison with Kant', in A. Loizides, *Mill's A System of Logic: Critical Appraisals* (London: Routledge)

Mill, J.S., 1963–1991. *The Collected Works of John Stuart Mill*, edited by J.M. Robson (London and Toronto: University of Toronto Press and Routledge)

Miller, D.E., 2010. *J.S. Mill* (London: Polity)*

Miller, D.E., 2014. 'John Stuart Mill's Moral, Social, and Political Philosophy', in W. Mander (ed.), *Oxford Handbook of British Philosophy in the Nineteenth Century* (Oxford University Press)

Millgram, E., 2000. 'Mill's "Proof" of the Principle of Utility', *Ethics*, 100, 282–310

Moore, G.E., 1993. *Principia Ethica* (Cambridge University Press)

Riley, J., 1993. 'On Qualities and Quantities of Pleasure', *Utilitas*, 5, 291–300

Riley, J., 2003. 'Interpreting Mill's Qualitative Hedonism', *Philosophical Quarterly*, 53, 410–18

Saunders, B., 2011. 'Reinterpreting the Qualitative Hedonism Advanced by J.S. Mill', *Journal of Value Inquiry*, 45, 187–201

Skorupski, J., 1989. *John Stuart Mill* (London: Routledge)*

Skorupski, J., 1998. 'The Fortunes of Liberal Naturalism', in J. Skorupski, *The Cambridge Companion to John Stuart Mill* (Cambridge University Press), pp. 1–34.

Wordsworth, W., 1970. *The Prelude: the 1805 Text* (Oxford University Press)

34

Schopenhauer

ALISTAIR WELCHMAN

Arthur Schopenhauer (1788–1860) was broadly a Kantian transcendental idealist, notable for his belief that Kant's thing-in-itself is 'will' (WWR1: 124).[1] The term 'will' however is not limited to intentional action, which is an appearance or representation. The thing-in-itself is striving subtracted from the forms of representation, without an ultimate goal. This underlies Schopenhauer's pessimism: striving is experienced as suffering; and each of us is, in-ourselves, an endless striving. Still Schopenhauer is not without all hope: art can free us briefly from the will; moral actions relieve suffering; and the saintly few may succeed in renouncing the will altogether.

These concerns – with suffering, meaning, asceticism and renunciation – are already problems in moral philosophy in a wide sense. But Schopenhauer also has a moral philosophy in the 'narrower' sense (WWR2: 589) that addresses issues such as freedom of the will, moral responsibility, the proper criterion for right action, moral motivation, the moral significance of animals, and the virtues and vices. Indeed Schopenhauer makes a distinctive and quite contemporary contribution to virtue theory, advocating compassion (*Mitleid*) as the source of all human virtues.

DETERMINISM

In his 1839 *On the Freedom of the Will*, Schopenhauer makes a strong case for determinism (OF: 75). He believes that prescription is futile and hence claims not to have any moral philosophy in the usual sense of the term: that is, he eschews a normative role for philosophy, where it could 'become practical, guide action, shape character' (WWR1: 297). Philosophy, he claims, 'can never do more than interpret and explain' what there is (WWR1: 298).

---

[1] References to Schopenhauer's works will be to the abbreviations given at the end of this chapter.

When Marx claims that philosophers have only tried to interpret the world, he is virtually quoting Schopenhauer.

Schopenhauer gives two rationales for determinism, one a priori and the other a posteriori. The a priori argument follows Kant's Second Analogy: the concept of causation is a priori because it makes experience possible (OF: 50). A free action would be an effect without a cause. But this would violate the conditions of experience and be an 'inexplicable miracle' (OF: 66).

In the a posteriori argument, Schopenhauer differentiates various forms of the principle of sufficient reason (*Grund*) – broadly kinds of ground/consequent or causal relations – and demonstrates the *de facto* commitment of various branches of science to this principle, thus raising the likelihood that it holds of human actions too. This adds little substance to the a priori argument, but he does gives an account of how the principle of sufficient reason works in the case of intentional action. Animals act only on immediately present perceptual motives, while human beings can also act on a different 'class of representations', that of 'abstract concepts, thoughts'. In contrast to Kant, such rational determination of the will is still, for Schopenhauer, strictly subordinated to the principle of sufficient reason: 'all motives are causes, and all causality brings necessity with it' (OF: 57). Every type of cause is necessarily connected to its effect as if by a 'wire'. The 'sole advantage' accruing to human beings is 'the length of the conducting wire' that connects cause to effect (OF: 58).

Typically, Schopenhauer uses this distinction to offer a diagnosis of the tendency to believe we are free: we misunderstand the increase in the range of possible motives available to us for the possibility that we can will different things; and the epistemic challenge of figuring out what motivates other people's actions is misunderstood as demonstrating that they are not acting on motives at all, but acting freely.

Determinism, and the consequent requirement for philosophy to have a 'contemplative' attitude (WWR1: 297), are not mere intellectual doctrines for Schopenhauer; instead he regards belief in freedom of the will as essentially childish. We (certainly we philosophers) should grow up and recognize that we are not free (WWR1: 298, BM: 243). In the *Freedom* essay, he claims that determinism is so important that it 'is really a touchstone by which one can distinguish . . . deep thinking minds' (OF: 78).

This is not Schopenhauer's last word on freedom, for he thinks there is a genuine and important sense in which empirical determinism fails to account for moral responsibility. But first, a brief summary of the rest of Schopenhauer's moral philosophy is in order.

CRITIQUE OF KANT

Schopenhauer's critique of Kant takes up almost a third of the text of his second major treatise on moral philosophy, *On the Basis of Morality*, and he regards his own views as 'only half intelligible' if not situated in relation to Kant (BM: 122). At the bottom of Schopenhauer's objections is another diagnostic claim. He thinks morality has entered a crisis. Traditionally morality had been based in theology; but that grounding came loose, in part because Kant's critique destroyed the 'foundations of *speculative theology*' (BM: 119). Kant however does not succeed in freeing himself entirely from theological presuppositions, and his moral philosophy is a kind of compromise formation. As Schopenhauer puts it, Kant's work is a 'mere dressing up of theological morals' (BM: 181), and this inability to let theology go underlies the objections Schopenhauer makes to Kant.

The primary symptom of vestigial theology in Kant's ethics is its law-like, prescriptive, 'imperative' (BM: 125ff) form, i.e. its denial of Schopenhauer's purely descriptive notion of ethics: Schopenhauer's critique of freedom of the will dovetails with his critique of Kant. The fact that Kant writes in archaic Lutheran German 'thou shalt [*du sollt*] not lie' is a giveaway for Schopenhauer that Kant is rationalizing the Mosaic Decalogue. At the very least, Schopenhauer claims, the view that ethics must take an imperative form 'ought not to be assumed as existing without proof' (BM: 126), though really his rejection of prescriptive ethics is much stronger, not only because of his commitment to a descriptive stance, but also because god cannot be coherently eliminated from this residually theological form: an imperative makes sense 'only in relation to threatened punishment or promised reward', and hence is hypothetical (BM: 128): a *categorical* imperative is contradictory.

Schopenhauer uses a similarly structured incoherence argument several times, but one example stands out: duty is a relational notion, conceptually connected with a context, like the relation between 'master and servant, superior and subordinate, regime and subject' (BM: 129). Schopenhauer objects vehemently to this aspect of theological morality: on that view every morally worthy act must be *commanded*: 'What a slave-morality', Schopenhauer exclaims, continuing 'I assert with confidence that . . . what opens the hand of the beneficent agent . . . can never be anything other than slavish *fear of gods*, never mind whether he entitles his fetish "categorical imperative"' (BM: 137). Here Schopenhauer anticipates, and inspires, Nietzsche's critique of Christian morality.

Many elements of Schopenhauer's Kant critique resonate with similar critiques in the twentieth century motivated by the resurgence of virtue

ethics. The accusation that deontological ethics is a rationalization of theological ethics anticipates Anscombe and the claim that there are only
hypothetical imperatives anticipates Foot.[2] But more striking still is the
similarity between Schopenhauer's criticism of the motivational inadequacy
of Kant's theory, and Michael Stocker's indictment.[3] In fact, the invective
against Kantian ethics as a 'slave morality' is directly tied to a Stocker-type
objection: we must, on Kant's view, be 'commanded' to do the right thing
because actions motivated by inclination lack moral worth. This is
Schopenhauer's outraged reaction:

> Worth of character is to commence only when someone, without sympathy
> of the heart, cold and indifferent to the sufferings of others, and *not properly
> born to be a philanthropist*, nevertheless displays beneficence merely for the
> sake of tiresome *duty*. This assertion . . . outrages genuine moral feeling, [it is
> an] apotheosis of unkindness. (BM: 136–7)

And this is the very context in which Schopenhauer inveighs against Kant's
residual theism: the quotation is the continuation of the passage on 'slave
morality'. Thus the various strands of Schopenhauer's critique are knotted
together: Kant's theism represents a failure to think through the consequences of Kant's own critique of speculative theology; it is 'slavish' (as
Nietzsche will go on to argue more thoroughly); and it is also inconsistent
with the exercise of the virtues: morally worthy actions spring from compassion, not from a grudging sense of duty. And, since Schopenhauer identifies
commandment with normativity in general, his Kant critique also dovetails
with his determinism and purely descriptive ethics.

EGOISM, COMPASSION AND MALICE

In fact, another strand of Schopenhauer's critique of Kant also emerges from
Schopenhauer's commitment to empirical determinism: his rejection of
Kant's view that reason is a sufficient moral incentive. In part this criticism
is grounded in Schopenhauer's general scepticism about the strength and
ultimate significance of human reason:

> [f]or the most part, cognition always remains subordinated to the service of
> the will, as it in fact developed in this service, and indeed sprang from the will
> like the head springs from the trunk of the body. (WWR1: 200)

---

[2] Anscombe 1958; Foot 1972. [3] Stocker 1976.

Reason is merely a passive storehouse for experience: it is like the 'borrowed light of the moon' as opposed to perception's 'direct light of the sun' (WWR1: 57). But reason is not simply too weak a force to overcome the will. For Kant rational determination of the will depends on the postulation of (at least possible) intelligible causes. But this is impossible for Schopenhauer: all causes are empirical. So reason cannot be practical.

If the category of morally worthy actions is not to be empty, there must be some empirical incentive for moral actions. Identifying this incentive is Schopenhauer's 'modest path' in ethics (BM: 189). After his blistering critique of Kant, Schopenhauer's *criterion of an action of moral worth* is still more or less Kantian: concern for the well-being of the other in '[t]he absence of all egoistic motivation' (BM: 197). For Schopenhauer, the task of moral philosophy is to give an empirical explanation for altruistic actions.

Making the minimal assumptions of a distinction between (a) one's own interests ('weal and woe') and those of others and (b) a positive and a negative valorization of these interests, Schopenhauer has a matrix of four possible incentives for human action: furthering one's own interests, or those of others; or frustrating the interests of others, or even of oneself. The desire to frustrate others (*Bosheit* or maliciousness) is theoretically disinterested, and grounds Schopenhauer's account of evil, but cannot be a moral incentive. So morally worthy actions must originate in a disinterested concern for the welfare of others.

It is not obvious that any actions do in fact fall into this category, a claim that Schopenhauer equates with moral scepticism (BM: 181ff). Certainly Schopenhauer is aware of the power of egoism. It is the practical corollary of the asymmetry between our awareness of our selves and of others: we experience the external world, including others, only indirectly, as representation; but we are aware of our own selves directly as willing, striving beings. So others appear to me as mere representation; they are, in the first instance, just façades with no inner life. Such a viewpoint is of course wrong, Schopenhauer thinks, for at the level of the thing-in-itself everything is an expression of the same non-individuated will. But the empirical viewpoint is the natural one, and its practical expression is egoism:

> Egoism is colossal: it towers above the world. For if the choice were given to any individual between his own destruction and that of the world, I do not need to say where it would land in the great majority. (BM: 190)

Widespread egoism is consistent with people *appearing* to perform morally worthy acts: it would be a 'great and very juvenile error' Schopenhauer remarks, 'if one believed that all [the externally] just and legal actions of human beings were of moral origin' (BM: 182). As a result, Schopenhauer has a Hobbesian view of the state, which is required to provide a series of counter-incentives against the egoistic 'war of all against all', incentives that cow us into at least the semblance of moral order (BM: 192).

The primacy of the will over reason makes Schopenhauer sensitive to self-deception as well as the deception of others:

> *Hope* makes us regard what we desire, and *fear* what we are afraid of, as being probable and near, and both magnify their object . . . *Love* and *hatred* entirely falsify our judgment; in our enemies we see nothing but shortcomings, in our favourites nothing but merits and good points, and even their defects seem amiable to us. (WWR2: 216–17)

How then can Schopenhauer show that morally worthy actions are indeed possible? He regards it as an 'empirical' (BM: 189) issue, citing examples (BM: 106). In fact Schopenhauer does offer an argument: although altruistic actions may be questionable, they are nevertheless grounded in a quite familiar experience, that of *compassion* (BM: 200).

Schopenhauer argues that the conditions of representational experience (space, time and causality) are also the conditions of individuation. It follows that the will in itself is not individuated. Thus, at the most basic metaphysical level things are 'one' or at least non-multiple. The virtuous person

> sees through the *principium individuationis* [principle of individuation] . . . [and] *makes less of a distinction than is usually made between himself and others.*
> (WWR1: 397, 399)

This metaphysical analysis is not very popular, and is open to internal objections as well. For if I am identical with others, then my incentive looks egoist.

Schopenhauer mentions a different account of identification in his discussion of Urbaldo Cassina, author of a 1788 treatise on compassion. Cassina argues that compassion is an *imaginative* identification of oneself with the other: we 'sub-stitute ourselves in place of the sufferer and then, in our imagination, take ourselves to be suffering *his* pains in *our* person' (BM: 203). This is less metaphy-sically problematic, but it does not solve the other difficulty, which rests on the notion of identification itself. In fact Schopenhauer rejects Cassina's view on rather acute phenomenological grounds: we do not confuse our selves with the other, as the Cassina view requires; 'it remains clear and present to us at every single moment that he is the sufferer, not *us*: and it is precisely *in his* person, not in ours, that we feel the pain' (BM: 203). Here my experience of your suffering is irreducible either to first personal projections or third personal description.[4]

However it is explained, compassion is the basis of morality for Schopenhauer: it is the incentive in altruistic actions. This alone makes Schopenhauer a virtue theorist because a compassionate character is both necessary and sufficient for morally worthy actions. Schopenhauer is also interested in other virtues, in particular 'justice [*Gerechtigkeit*] and loving kindness [*Menschenliebe*]' (BM: 192), but tries to 'derive' them from compassion (BM: 201).

Schopenhauer expresses the content of his moral theory in an admirably pithy slogan: 'harm no one; rather help everyone as much as you can' (BM: 140), the first part corresponding to justice, and the second to loving kindness. The distinction is close to the Kantian distinction between duties of right and duties of virtue or beneficence (WWR1: 398, BM: 204).

Although most moral wrong stems from the vice of egoism, Schopenhauer also has an account of genuinely malicious, evil or 'devilish' actions, those that are motivated by a disinterested desire to harm, even to the detriment of the agent's own interests (WWR1: 359, BM: 192f). Schopenhauer opposes the vice of malice to the virtue of loving kindness (as he opposes the vice of egoism to the virtue of justice): in loving kindness, I see the suffering of the other, and compassion motivates me to come to their aid; in maliciousness, I see the happiness of the other and envy motivates me to eliminate it; or I see the suffering of the other and Schadenfreude motivates me to heighten it in cruelty (BM: 193f). Schopenhauer's psychology of vice is acute, and his indictment of humanity is at its most pathetic when he discovers this same devilish malice in such commonplace occurrences as teasing and practical jokes (P2: 195–6).

This diabolism is the only thing that separates humans from animals. Suffering is the only bad for Schopenhauer, and animal suffering is qualitatively identical to human suffering. So our responsibility not to harm extends to animals. Indeed Schopenhauer regards the Kantian view that animals have no moral status as 'outrageous and revolting', a *reductio* of Kant's moral

---

[4] The disagreement between Cassina and Schopenhauer here on the nature of compassion anticipates contemporary cognitive scientific accounts of 'empathy', which divide between psychological 'simulation' theories and phenomenologically inflected direct perception (Zahavi 2008).

philosophy (BM: 161). Moreover, since compassion, the basis of morality, doesn't involve reason, animals can even be (unconscious) moral actors (BM: 206).

Schopenhauer is an excellent moral psychologist and a sensitive, informed interpreter of human virtue and vice; and it is in his analyses especially of compassion, but also of loving kindness and the extent of self-deception in egoism, that he is at his best, rather than in the systematic presentation of a theory of morality.

RESPONSIBILITY, PESSIMISM AND ASCETICISM

The *Freedom* essay shows the impossibility of inferring that we are free from the fact that we think we are free. So it is surprising that at the end of that same essay Schopenhauer accepts at face value our 'wholly clear and sure feeling of responsibility for what we do' (OF: 105), and even more surprising that he endorses the standard view that responsibility presupposes freedom (OF: 106).

Individual actions cannot be evaluated morally because they are the inevitable product of character and circumstance. Instead evaluation targets the *character* that is revealed by someone's actions. Such views are common among virtue theorists from Aristotle to the present day. However they do not seem to help answer the question of how we can be responsible or free, since it seems prima facie less plausible that we should be responsible for and freely choose our characters than that we are responsible for our individual actions. The problem is especially acute for Schopenhauer because he regards character as 'inborn and unalterable' (OF: 106, 68f).

Here Schopenhauer appeals to Kant: the content of my character is fixed like any other phenomenon, caught in the causal nexus; but in itself my will is no longer determined, for it is no longer subordinated to the principle of sufficient reason. The will in itself is free. Schopenhauer here adopts the vocabulary of Kant in distinguishing between my empirical character and my intelligible character, which is the non-temporal ground of the former. My empirical character is the result of a free but non-temporal deed. Because the deed is non-temporal it has, as it were, always already happened (so that its effect, my character, appears phenomenally as 'inborn and unalterable'); but because it is still my free act, I am responsible for my character, its effect.

Schopenhauer outlines a suggestive moral phenomenology: we some-times do have to take responsibility for elements of our character that are 'inborn and unalterable'. In particular he has a singular account of conscience:

we feel its bite not because we could have done otherwise (for, according to Schopenhauer we could not have); but rather because of an agonized recognition that our action really does reveal what we are.

Still the view raises a large number of problems: the notion of a nontemporal act is problematic; the act itself appears to be criterionless; the notion of self-choice appears incoherent; and Schopenhauer helps himself to a notion of individuation at the level of the thing-in-itself to which he is not entitled. One recent suggestion has been simply to drop the requirement that responsibility entails freedom and read Schopenhauer as claiming that we are sometimes responsible for things that we did not choose.[5]

Perhaps this account of responsibility is a harsh doctrine; but it pales by comparison with Schopenhauer's signature pessimism. Schopenhauer is a hedonist: pleasure and pain are the only intrinsic values, and pessimism is the view that life is of no overall value in this sense, that its pains outweigh its pleasures. Although Schopenhauer often gives a posteriori evidence that people very often do not get what they want, and are unhappy as a result, he also argues that we are unhappy *even if we do get what we want*.

The argument rests on two claims: (1) we *are* will, so that we can never stop willing; (2) willing is an intrinsically painful state, at least to some degree (WWR1: 335–6, 219f). Although (1) follows straightforwardly from Schopenhauer's metaphysics, he also provides phenomenological evidence for it in the familiar experience of achieving some aim that one has been striving at, and finding almost at once that another aim demands satisfaction. Schopenhauer argues for (2) by claiming that when one wills an object, one must lack the object, and that lack is painful. Schopenhauer seems to realize that the conjunction of (1) and (2) does not entail the pessimistic conclusion that conscious life is painful – I could experience a series of episodes of willing, each of whose successful conclusions yielded more satisfaction than the willing itself caused pain. So Schopenhauer goes on to claim that pleasure or satisfaction is nothing more than the elimination of the pain of willing, not anything positive in itself (WWR1: 345f). Thus the hedonistic balance of conscious existence consists only of negative or null entries, so that 'it would be better for us not to exist' (WWR2: 605).[6]

---

[5] Janaway 2012.

[6] Just to cap the argument off, Schopenhauer also claims that the absence of will is experienced negatively as boredom or languor (WWR1: 189, 338). Schopenhauer's analysis of boredom bears comparison with Baudelaire and Heidegger.

Schopenhauer's pessimism has been extremely influential, especially on Nietzsche's conception of nihilism. Similarly, the negative understanding of pleasure is taken up essentially unchanged by Freud. But most commentators have found his arguments unconvincing. Nietzsche proposes two of the most famous objections: that willing itself, striving to attain a goal, may be experienced positively as a kind of pleasure,[7] and the famous denial of hedonism – pain is not an objection to life.[8]

Morality – compassion – takes the edge off Schopenhauer's pessimism, but the most valuable kind of life involves denial of the will. This idea is frankly religious, and shows that, like Kierkegaard, Schopenhauer does not think that ethical values are ultimate.

Denial of the will and compassion are based on a similar metaphysical insight, but denial of the will extends the insight: where the compassionate person distinguishes 'less' between self and other, denial of the will is predicated on a complete dismantling of the distinction between self and other; similarly, where the compassionate person is equipped to see and react appropriately to at least some suffering, resignation depends on seeing that the world as a whole *is* suffering. This precipitates a dramatic change: it acts as a 'tranquillizer' on the will, 'turning' it away from life in 'renunciation', 'resignation' and ultimately 'complete will-lessness' (WWR1: 406), a state that Schopenhauer describes in religious terms as both saintly and akin to Buddhist nirvana (WWR1: 383).

Schopenhauer's account looks paradoxical, for I cannot consistently will not to will: the higher order willing defeats the lower order non-willings. But for Schopenhauer only suicide is self-defeating (WWR1: 425ff) while the will cannot (despite Schopenhauer's sometimes inconsistent use of language) be denied intentionally: Schopenhauer identifies denial as 'the *effect of divine grace*, which comes to us as if from outside, without any effort on our part' (WWR1: 433). What this solution gains in resolving the paradox, it loses in religious mystery.

These broader ethical issues help to situate Schopenhauer's moral philosophy, in part by highlighting his own understanding of its limits: we are responsible without being free; and at the most basic axiological level, conscious existence lacks any overall value, so that the best, most knowing, response to life is not ultimately ethical at all, but to renounce it – or to let it be renounced in you. These views had a deep impact on Nietzsche's conception of the ascetic ideal.

[7] Soll 2012: 304.   [8] Nietzsche 1888: 124.

ABBREVIATIONS

BM	Schopenhauer 1841b ("On the Basis of Morality")
OF	Schopenhauer 1841a ("On the Freedom of the Will")
P2	Schopenhauer 1851 (*Parerga and Paralipomina*, vol. 2)
WWR1	Schopenhauer 1818 (*The World as Will and Representation*, vol. 1)
WWR2	Schopenhauer 1844 (*The World as Will and Representation*, vol. 2)

BIBLIOGRAPHY

An asterisk denotes secondary literature especially suitable for further reading.

Anscombe, Elizabeth 1958 'Modern Moral Philosophy', *Philosophy*, 33: 1–19

Foot, Philippa 1972 'Morality as a System of Hypothetical Imperatives', *The Philosophical Review*, 81 No. 3 (July): 305–16

Janaway, Christopher 2012 'Necessity, Responsibility and Character: Schopenhauer on Freedom of the Will', *Kantian Review*, 17: 431–57

Nietzsche, Friedrich 1888 [2005]. *Ecce Homo* in *The Anti-Christ, Ecce Homo, Twilight of the Idols*, ed. Aaron Ridley and Judith Norman, trans. Judith Norman. Cambridge University Press

Schopenhauer, Arthur 1818 [2010]. *The World as Will and Representation*, vol. 1, trans. and ed. Judith Norman, Alistair Welchman and Christopher Janaway. Cambridge University Press

Schopenhauer, Arthur 1841a [2009]. 'On the Freedom of the Will', in *The Two Fundamental Problems of Ethics*, ed. and trans. Christopher Janaway. Cambridge University Press

Schopenhauer, Arthur 1841b [2009]. 'On the Basis of Morality', in *The Two Fundamental Problems of Ethics*, ed. and trans. Christopher Janaway. Cambridge University Press

Schopenhauer, Arthur 1844. *The World as Will and Representation*, vol. 2, trans. E.J.F. Payne. New York: Dover

Schopenhauer, Arthur 1851 [2015]. *Parerga and Paralipomina*, vol. 2, trans. Adrian Del Caro, ed. Christopher Janaway and Adrian Del Caro. Cambridge University Press

Soll, Ivan 2012. 'Schopenhauer on the Inevitability of Unhappiness', in Bart Vandenabeele (ed.), *A Companion to Schopenhauer*. Oxford: Blackwell, pp. 300–13

Stocker, Michael 1976. 'The Schizophrenia of Modern Ethical Theories', *The Journal of Philosophy*, 73: 453–66

Wicks, Robert 2008. *Schopenhauer*. Oxford: Blackwell*

Zahavi, Dan 2008. 'Simulation, Projection, and Empathy', *Consciousness and Cognition*, 17: 514–22

Introductory treatments of Kierkegaard's thought are best prefaced with a warning to the reader: scholars disagree about even the most fundamental aspects of Kierkegaard's thought, so any such summary – whether it be of Kierkegaard's ethics, metaphysics, epistemology, or just about any other topic – will be controversial. It is a fascinating feature of the Kierkegaardian corpus that it has elicited such a vast array of interpretations in its readers, and there seem to be two primary and interrelated reasons for it, especially in regard to Kierkegaard's views on ethics. The first is that Kierkegaard employed a number of interesting and complex literary methods – including extensive use of pseudonyms, the Socratic method, and something he called "indirect communication" – all aimed at the goal of edifying, rather than merely informing, his readers. The second is that we find in Kierkegaard's writings numerous approaches to ethics that are not obviously compatible with one another. The following essay will introduce some of the most important of these ethical views, first saying a word about the importance of properly understanding Kierkegaard's methods in interpreting the texts, then offering a possible explanation of what Kierkegaard hoped to achieve in presenting these opposing views in his writings, and finally developing the major contours of Kierkegaard's own, explicitly Christian ethic.

THE ETHICS OF THE "LOWER" PSEUDONYMS: *EITHER/ OR* AND *FEAR AND TREMBLING*

Kierkegaard's ethic often has been the subject of vehement criticism, but what has been labeled "Kierkegaard's ethic" is in fact an array of views comprised of (1) the views represented and/or discussed by various Kierkegaardian pseudonyms, (2) Kierkegaard's own Christian ethic, presented primarily in *Works of Love* and other non-pseudonymous writings, and (3) caricatures of Kierkegaard's view. (1) and (3) are often closely connected. The pseudonymous authorship presents unique challenges to interpretation that many readers – especially first-time or occasional readers of Kierkegaard – underestimate or ignore altogether.

In general, it is not safe to assume that the views expressed by the pseudonyms are shared by Kierkegaard himself, or that the arguments developed pseudonymously are ones that Kierkegaard would endorse. Use of pseudonymity in Kierkegaard's writings often (though, as we will see, not always) indicates an intent on Kierkegaard's part to distance himself from the views expressed in the book. The ethical views most often confused with Kierkegaard's own are those of Judge William, a character in *Either/Or* who writes an extensive defense of an ethical way of life to a friend committed to an opposing, aesthetic approach to life, and Johannes de Silentio, the pseudonymous author of *Fear and Trembling*, who discusses the ethical status of the patriarch Abraham, venerated in Genesis as the father of faith for his willingness to obey God's command to sacrifice his son Isaac.

The ethics endorsed by Judge William and discussed by Johannes de Silentio are in many ways very similar; both are likely some version of Hegelian *Sittlichkeit*, though the Judge's ethic may be more Kantian in certain respects.[1] Both are representatives of views that fall within what Kierkegaard calls the ethical stage (or sphere) of existence – a form of existence whose fundamental commitments and orientation Kierkegaard himself does not endorse. The outlook that characterizes the ethical sphere is a commitment to *immanence*: a commitment to grounding ethics in human capacities and activities. Sometimes this is put in the language of universalizability;[2] other times it is put in the language of social norms.[3] The important point here is that ethics of this type are not religious in Kierkegaard's sense of the term, and – as I will argue later – Kierkegaard's own ethic is a thoroughly religious ethic. Reading these works in isolation from the rest of the corpus thus tends to produce a distorted view of Kierkegaard's own understanding of ethics.

The religious sphere of existence takes as its point of departure an absolute commitment to God, which is transformative of one's view of ethics. Whereas ethics within the ethical sphere is grounded in immanence and characterized by

---

[1] For an analysis of the Kantian elements of Judge William's ethic, as well as an argument that "... the ethics Kierkegaard has in mind in *Fear and Trembling* is significantly Kantian," see Green 1992: 86–109. For an argument that it is crucial that "the ethical" in Johannes's discussion be understood as *Sittlichkeit* rather than Kantian ethics, see Westphal 1987: 76–7.

[2] Kierkegaard 1983: 54–5.

[3] As in the discussion of the three tragic heroes – Jephthah, Agamemnon, and Brutus – in Kierkegaard 1983: 57–9.

transparency to other persons,[4] ethics within the religious sphere is grounded in transcendence (the authority of God) and characterized by transparency before God (self-knowledge and obedience).[5] The differences between the two spheres explain why Johannes de Silentio must wrestle so hard with the question of the ethical status of Abraham's willingness to sacrifice Isaac. From the perspective of the ethical sphere Abraham's act is unethical: it is an act neither universalizable nor objectively defensible to others. But from the perspective of the religious sphere his act is righteous, because it is an act of obedience to God's expressed will. The key to reconciling these seemingly conflicting views is that "the ethical," as Johannes is using the term, refers specifically to the ethics of immanence rather than to right action, broadly construed. Thus an action can be both right and "unethical," in Johannes's sense of the term. This makes it clear that Kierkegaard's own Christian ethic is not identical to "the ethical" of *Fear and Trembling*.

A major source of confusion for many readers on this point is created by Johannes's talk of a "teleological suspension of the ethical." Many readers take Johannes (and Kierkegaard himself) to be advocating the view that, in the religious sphere, one must be ready to do something immoral if God commands it. In such a case, one suspends a commitment to morality for the sake of obeying God. This reading of *Fear and Trembling* is mistaken, however. A teleological suspension of the ethical occurs when God commands one to perform an action that is not universalizable or defensible according to the accepted norms of one's society. Such an action might be indefensible on purely secular grounds, but to one who accepts the fundamental commitments that characterize religious existence, obedience to God in such cases is still the *right* thing to do.

Another common mistake in reading Kierkegaard stems from misunderstanding what the pseudonymity of the texts is meant to convey or accomplish. Some have taken the message of *Either/Or* to be that ethics must be based on a "radical choice" – i.e., that ethics has no grounding beyond an individual's subjective choice to employ ethical categories in personal decision-making – which is why Kierkegaard juxtaposes the incommensurate worldviews of the aesthete and Judge William without offering any resolution of the conflict in the book.[6] This reading not only attributes to Kierkegaard a highly problematic view,[7] it fails to

---

[4] See, for example, Kierkegaard 1983: 82: "The ethical as such is the universal; as the universal it is in turn the disclosed."

[5] See, for example, Kierkegaard 1990: 104–5.   [6] See MacIntyre 1981: 38–42.

[7] MacIntyre has no trouble pointing out the "deep internal inconsistency" to be found in the view he ascribes to Kierkegaard "between its concept of radical choice and its concept of the ethical." He writes, "the doctrine of *Enten–Eller* [*Either/Or*] is plainly to the effect that the principles which depict the ethical way of life are to be adopted for no

account for the reasons Kierkegaard himself gives to explain his use of pseudonymity.[8] Kierkegaard's intended purpose in all his works is the edification of the reader, and he often judged the use of pseudonymity to be necessary to accomplish this goal.[9] In presenting ethical and aesthetic forms of existence from first-person perspectives in *Either/Or*, Kierkegaard invites the reader to consider each form of existence by way of seeing each from the inside, so to speak. The structure of the book is intended not to privilege either perspective, and thereby to force the reader to judge for herself two things: first, which approach characterizes her own life, and second, which approach constitutes a life well lived.

This is not to say that Kierkegaard regards each form of existence as objectively equally valid. One of his later pseudonyms remarks that aesthetic existence is clearly "perdition" and chides the reader who would need the aesthetic characters of *Either/Or* to meet ruinous ends to see this.[10] The remark seems to express

reason, but for a choice that lies beyond reason, just because it is the choice of what is to count for us as a reason. Yet the ethical is to have authority over us. But how can that which we adopt for no reason have any authority over us? The contradiction in Kierkegaard's doctrine is plain" (MacIntyre 1981: 41). The problem with this argument is that it is a straw man. Not only does Kierkegaard not advocate this approach to ethics, he actually develops this same critique of radical choice that MacIntyre levels against him, both in his published writings (Kierkegaard 1980: 69) and in an important journal entry in which the objection is made against Kant (Kierkegaard 1976, journal entry no. 188, [*Pap.* X² A 396] *n.d.*, 1850; journal references are to an English translation and the Danish edition). What these passages in Kierkegaard's writings demonstrate is that MacIntyre's critique of "Kierkegaard's ethics" is actually one of Kierkegaard's own critiques of the ethics of immanence given in different forms by Kant, Hegel, and a host of other Enlightenment thinkers: a moral law grounded in immanence fails to be binding because those whom the law is supposed to bind retain the power to repeal it. On this point, see Evans 1998: 27.

8 See especially "The Point of View for My Work As an Author: A Report to History," in Kierkegaard 1998. Kierkegaard's journals are also an invaluable source of insight on this issue.

9 Tietjen 2013.

10 The pseudonym here is Johannes Climacus, who will be discussed later in this essay. He writes, "A reader who needs the trustworthiness of a severe lecture or an unfortunate outcome (for example, madness, suicide, poverty, etc.) in order to see that a standpoint is in error still sees nothing and is merely deluding himself, and to behave that way as an author is to write effeminately for childish readers. Take a character like Johannes the Seducer. The person who needs him to become insane or shoot himself in order to see that his standpoint is perdition does not actually see it but deludes himself into thinking that he does. In other words, the person who comprehends it comprehends it as soon as the Seducer opens his mouth; in every word he hears the ruination and the judgment upon him" (Kierkegaard 1992: 296–7).

Kierkegaard's own view as well. He hopes his readers will see clearly what is wrong with aesthetic existence when it is presented in its pure form, but he thinks there can be no shortcut to this insight. It would not do simply to *tell* the reader that aesthetic existence is perdition; the *seeing for oneself* is essential to edification. There is no way to communicate these kinds of truths directly in a way that brings about significant change in the reader, which is why an indirect method must be employed.

The purpose of the pseudonymity in *Fear and Trembling* seems to be somewhat different. Here Kierkegaard intends to demonstrate that obedience to God can put one in diametrical opposition to the accepted moral standards of one's culture and society, and thus genuine Christianity is not identical to 'Christendom', the term Kierkegaard uses to denote the cultural phenomenon in which one is considered a Christian merely by being born into a certain society and adopting its practices and norms. Kierkegaard wants his readers to understand that being a good person according to prevailing social standards does not make one a Christian, and he tries to communicate this by presenting the problem of Abraham though the eyes of one who does not himself have faith but who tries to comprehend faith from the outside. This is the perspective of Johannes de Silentio, the messenger who does not himself fully understand the message he bears.[11] The intent of *Fear and Trembling* is to raise a dilemma for those readers who profess to be Christian but who have traded genuine Christianity for the mock-up of Christendom. It does so with a simple question: Was Abraham's willingness to sacrifice Isaac morally defensible or not? If not, then Abraham cannot rightly be considered the father of faith. But if so, then there must be a standard of morality that is higher than the immanent ethics of cultural norms. At the foundation of Christian ethics lies an implicit refutation of Christendom, and Kierkegaard's aim is to open the eyes of his readers to this fact.[12]

THE ETHICS OF THE "HIGHER" PSEUDONYMS:
CONCLUDING UNSCIENTIFIC POSTSCRIPT AND *SICKNESS UNTO DEATH*

Thus far, we have seen in Kierkegaard's writings a discussion in which ethical existence is contrasted with aesthetic existence (*Either/Or*) and a discussion in

[11] See Evans 2009: 101–2.
[12] For more on "the ethical" in *Fear and Trembling*, see Outka 1973, Evans 1981, Evans 2004: 61–84, and Evans 2006.

which ethical existence is contrasted with religious existence (*Fear and Trembling*). Yet another approach to ethics is found in what is considered by many to be Kierkegaard's greatest work, *Concluding Unscientific Postscript to "Philosophical Fragments."* Once more, the work is pseudonymous – the title page lists Johannes Climacus as the author, and S. Kierkegaard as the editor – but the purpose of the pseudonymity is different yet again. The inclusion of Kierkegaard's name on the title page of this work and its companion, *Philosophical Fragments*, is the first clue that Kierkegaard does not intend the same degree of distance from this pseudonym as he does from the pseudonyms of earlier works. There is independent textual evidence to demonstrate that Kierkegaard is in agreement with many of the views expressed by Climacus. In these texts we are thus drawing closer to the ethical views of Kierkegaard himself.

Here we find ethics as the point of departure for the religious sphere of existence. The approach of Climacus is best viewed as being within the ancient tradition of virtue ethics, with its emphasis on the necessity of one's acquiring a virtuous character in order to live a good life.[13] The acquisition of the virtues is part, but not all, of what Climacus is referring to when he speaks of "becoming a self" – a central and recurring theme in the Kierkegaardian corpus. For Climacus, ethics is not fundamentally a matter of discerning right principles of action, but rather a task: the task of becoming the individual self one ought to be. This is the meaning of the famous – and very often misunderstood – claim from *Postscript* that "truth is subjectivity."[14] It is not a claim about truth in general,[15] and it is not the claim that personal beliefs are made true by their being believed strongly or with passionate conviction, as is often assumed. It is rather a claim about the right and wrong ways that one can be related to the deepest truths about human existence. Mere intellectual assent to such truths, without any corresponding attempt to appropriate or live one's life in accordance with them, is "untruth," failure to live authentically. A "true" life is one that at least approximately instantiates a certain ideal: the ideal for human existence, as given by our nature.[16] Both

---

[13] See Roberts 1998 and Evans and Roberts 2013.

[14] See Kierkegaard 1992: ch. 2, "Subjective Truth, Inwardness; Truth is Subjectivity," pp. 189–251.

[15] Kierkegaard 1992: 199, footnote. For more on this point, see Evans 2009: 57–61.

[16] As Evans puts it, "If there is an ideal for human life, a model that humans should aspire to realize, I see no reason why a human life that approximates that ideal should not be described as true, just as a proposition that approximates the way things are is appropriately described as true ... It is even possible, I think, that the whole discussion of 'truth as subjectivity' is an attempt to make sense of the claim

Climacus and Kierkegaard reject the idea that "existence precedes essence," the idea that humans have no eternal, pre-ordained, or divinely determined nature prior to existing; if acceptance of this idea is what it is to be an existentialist, as Sartre later claimed,[17] then neither is an existentialist. For Climacus (and Kierkegaard), to live well is to achieve one's potential for selfhood, both in its universal aspect (becoming the right *kind* of person) and in its individual aspect (becoming the *particular* person one ought to be).

In contrast to the Cartesian view in which selfhood is essentially a matter of being an isolated mental substance, Climacus thinks of selfhood as a process that occurs in a social context. We are shaped by our relations to others, and the most important social relation of all is one's relation to God. Climacus assumes that, as our Creator, God has the authority to make demands of us, and the most fundamental of these is the demand to become the individual self that God intends one to become; each of us is commanded to "become oneself." Thus ethics, properly pursued, is the point of departure for the religious life.

In *The Sickness unto Death*, the theme of becoming a self is further developed by way of an exploration of the connection between ethics and soteriology (theory of salvation) – or, perhaps more accurately, the connection between sin and damnation. The pseudonymous author of the text, Anti-Climacus, bears an even closer connection to Kierkegaard than Climacus. In fact, there is textual evidence that Kierkegaard endorses Anti-Climacus's views without reservation and added the pseudonym only because he (Kierkegaard) considered himself personally unworthy to present the Christian requirement in its pure ideality given his failure to express it in his own life.[18]

In its most general form, *Sickness unto Death* is a taxonomy and development of the ways that the task of selfhood can become derailed, with

attributed to Jesus in the Gospel of John: 'I am the way, and the truth, and the life'" (Evans 2009: 62).

[17] Sartre 1957; see especially pp. 16–22.

[18] Kierkegaard 1978, journal entry no. 6446, (*Pap.* X[1] A 548). Kierkegaard writes the following in his journals regarding his relation to these later pseudonyms: "Johannes Climacus and Anti-Climacus have several things in common; but the difference is that whereas Johannes Climacus places himself so low that he even says that he himself is not a Christian, one seems to be able to detect in Anti-Climacus that he considers himself to be a Christian on an extraordinarily high level . . . I would place myself higher than Johannes Climacus, lower than Anti-Climacus" (Kierkegaard 1978, journal entry no. 6443, [*Pap.* X[1] A 517]).

disastrous results. As mentioned above, selfhood is achieved in relation to others, but it is also a process in which one "relates oneself to oneself," and the condition in which the self becomes misrelated to itself, Anti-Climacus tells us, is despair. The notion of relating oneself to oneself is complex, but the basic idea is twofold: first, that a human self is a "synthesis" of opposing features – physical and spiritual, temporal and eternal, determined and free, etc. – that stand in a certain relation to each other and which must be brought into balance, and second, that personal development requires an ongoing introspection in which one relates the person one is presently (the actual self) to the person one desires to become (the ideal self), which is necessary if the task of becoming a self is to be undertaken deliberately and in freedom. Despair is essentially a matter of failing to be what a human being *ought* to be, given the kind of beings we are by nature,[19] a condition that results either from the parts of the synthesis (the self) failing to be in proper relation to one another, or from the self's failing to be in proper relation to "the power that established it" – i.e., God.[20]

Without some understanding of what it is to be a human self, such misrelation is inevitable, because the process of becoming a self never gets off the ground; such persons are shaped entirely by the causal and social forces acting on them, blown by every changing wind of their circumstances. To lack any deep constancy in one's character is to fail to be a self (a point Judge William develops at great length in *Either/Or*). This is one form of despair, and Anti-Climacus suggests that it is the most common form: the despair of ignorance, in which one fails to become an authentic self without even being conscious of the fact that one's condition is one of despair.

In the "higher" forms of despair, in which there is greater consciousness of what it is to be a self and more intentionality in one's life choices, the defining relation is the self's relation to God. Here the misrelation is either a matter of weakness – understanding what is required for authentic selfhood but failing to will it – or defiance – willing to be the self of one's own choosing, in opposition to what God calls one to be. All three forms of despair – in ignorance, in weakness, and in defiance – are sin, *hamartia*, missing the mark in the most fundamental way, in one's life as a whole. They are ways that people fail to become what God calls them to be, and consequently fail to

[19] Recall the point above about Kierkegaard's rejection of existentialism.
[20] The phrase comes from Anti-Climacus's definition of faith: "the formula for the state in which there is no despair at all: in relating itself to itself and in willing to be itself, the self rests transparently in the power that established it" (Kierkegaard 1980: 131).

achieve selfhood in a way that would allow them to be in communion with God in eternity.[21] Ethics for Anti-Climacus is not simply a matter of an earthly life well lived; it is a task of literally infinite consequence, a matter not just of life and death, but eternal life and eternal death.

KIERKEGAARD'S ETHIC IN *WORKS OF LOVE*

Building upon this foundational idea of becoming a self in relation to God, we turn now to *Works of Love*, Kierkegaard's most important and developed work of ethics.[22] Here we find Kierkegaard writing in his own name, and the concerns we faced with the pseudonymous works about whether the views are those of Kierkegaard himself can be set aside. *Works of Love* is a multi-faceted but sustained discussion of the foundation of Christian ethics: the divine command to love God and to love our neighbors as ourselves. It is an agapeistic ethic in that the love commanded of us is not one of the "natural" loves that we find in parental affection, friendship, and romantic relationships, but rather the kind of love that Jesus displays: a self-sacrificing love that wills the good of the other, even at great personal cost.

The foundational features of the Kierkegaardian ethic are twofold: first, its emphasis on human indebtedness to God, our Creator who loves us and wills our highest good, and second, its emphasis on divine requirements, given primarily in the form of divine commands that are revealed in conscience and in special revelation and directed toward the highest good of both ourselves and our neighbors. Kierkegaard places great emphasis on the "shall" of the love command. We are obligated to love our neighbors because God commands it, and the command is authoritative for us because we belong to God as "bond servants." We begin with an infinite debt to God,[23] and each of us "infinitely and unconditionally owes everything" to Him,[24] including unconditional obedience, love, and worship.

In many ways, Kierkegaard's view is close to those of contemporary divine command theorists.[25] Like these thinkers, Kierkegaard assumes both that God's commands are sufficient to impose moral obligations[26] and that divine

---

[21] See Manis 2016.
[22] Kierkegaard 1995. It should be noted that the texts are being discussed slightly out of chronological order at this point: *Works of Love* was published in 1847; *The Sickness unto Death* was written in 1848 and published in 1849.
[23] Kierkegaard 1995: 102.   [24] Ibid., 103.
[25] See Evans and Roberts 2013, especially pp. 214–23.
[26] Kierkegaard 1995: 20. For further defense of this claim, see Evans 2004: 123.

love is crucial to the authority that God's commands have for us. God's commands are directed toward individual and collective human flourishing, not arbitrarily issued by God without reason.[27] More specifically, God issues commands, both to individuals and to groups, which guide persons toward the achievement of authentic selfhood. Thus, for Kierkegaard, the task of becoming a self is achieved only in relation to – in fact, in absolute dependence upon – God.

Unlike most divine command thinkers, however, Kierkegaard places great emphasis on the debt that free creatures owe to God, perhaps even seeing this as the very foundation and essence of moral obligations.[28] God's requirements of us can be conceived as ways that He "calls in" part of our debt. A divine requirement takes a general, infinite debt and gives it a specific, local content: we are directed to "forward" our repayment to God by serving other people, at which point we become morally obligated to our neighbors.[29] In this way, all of our duties to other created beings are grounded in and derived from our infinite debt to God.

Kierkegaard expresses this hierarchical status of our relationship to God and other people in the (in)famous "middle term" thesis of *Works of Love*:

> *Worldly wisdom is of the opinion that love is a relationship between persons; Christianity teaches that love is a relationship between: a person – God – a person, that is, that God is the middle term ... To love God is to love oneself truly; to help another person to love God is to love another person; to be helped by another person to love God is to be loved.*[30]

---

[27] Prior to developments of divine command theory in the late twentieth century, it was common for critics to object that the theory renders God's commands completely arbitrary. If goodness and badness are determined by God's commands, then God has no *reason* to command one action (say, loving the neighbor) rather than another (say, torturing the neighbor).

[28] See Manis 2009.

[29] As Kierkegaard puts it, "If you want to show that your life is intended to serve God, then let it serve people, yet continually with the thought of God. God does not have a share in existence in such a way that he demands his share for himself; he demands everything, but as you bring it to him you immediately receive, if I may put it this way, a notice designating where it should be forwarded, because God demands nothing for himself, although he demands everything from you" (Kierkegaard 1995: 161). I have here altered the translation slightly so that several words or phrases accord with the Hongs' earlier translation of *Works of Love* (1962: 159). All other references to *Works of Love* are from the Hongs' 1995 translation.

[30] Kierkegaard 1995: 106–7; italics in original.

It is hard to overemphasize the importance of this claim for Kierkegaard's ethic.[31] But by itself, it is easy to misunderstand the claim that *what it is* to love the neighbor is to help the neighbor love God. Critics have alleged that it reveals the Kierkegaardian ethic to be without any concrete content, that Kierkegaard divorces ethics from the task of meeting any of the real needs of one's neighbors such as feeding the hungry, healing the sick, etc.[32] But this is not at all what Kierkegaard has in mind. The "middle term" thesis is properly understood only within the broader context of Kierkegaard's thought: specifically, his view that the ethical task is the task of becoming a self, which in turn is ultimately aimed at the human telos of communion with God, the highest good possible for human beings. On Kierkegaard's view, the purpose of the Love Commandment is to facilitate each person's achieving this end. We are creatures made in the divine image, the image of the One who is love, and it is only in loving – loving God and loving our neighbors – that we become what we are meant to be. By helping the neighbor to love God, which in turn requires the neighbor to love other people, one aids the neighbor in attaining what is most valuable – indeed what makes life ultimately worth living – and thereby helps the neighbor to flourish as a human being.

None of this is to deny that we must strive to meet the concrete needs of our neighbors wherever we can. One cannot help the neighbor to become a self before God while neglecting the neighbor's most basic physical needs. But our duty to the neighbor is not fully discharged with the fulfilling of these needs. The Kierkegaardian ethic requires more of us, not less. Beyond meeting our neighbors' physical, psychological, and emotional needs, we must attend to what they need spiritually, for without doing so we neglect their very deepest needs and thereby fail to love them truly.

It is important to note that for Kierkegaard the achievement of the human telos is, in one respect, a highly individual project, and in another, an essentially communal project. The communal aspect of achieving selfhood has already been noted. What all of us are commanded to do, most

---

[31] Kierkegaard himself certainly tries to emphasize it, both by placing it in italics and by repeating it numerous times; see 1995: 106–7, 114, 121, and 130.

[32] One prominent critic, Knud Ejler Løgstrup, goes so far as to claim that the Kierkegaardian ethic in *Works of Love* ultimately amounts to "a brilliantly thought out system of safeguards against being forced into a close relationship with other people" (1997: 232). For an excellent discussion of the most important objections to Kierkegaard's ethic in *Works of Love*, see Ferreira 2001. Ferreira's response to this objection from Løgstrup is found on pp. 76–83.

fundamentally, is to love, and it is by loving that we actualize our full potential and become what God intends us to be. By issuing the command to love the neighbor, God has made everyone's task of striving toward human fulfillment interconnected: one achieves one's end by helping others achieve theirs. But while the task of loving God and the neighbor is universal, the content of this task is highly specific – determined, in large part, by each person's individual calling. I must become the person God intends *me* to be, but my duty to my neighbor is to help her become the person God intends *her* to be. To "become oneself" is, most fundamentally, a matter of becoming the self that God intends one to be. One achieves this through obedience to God's commands, some of which are issued only to certain people – and perhaps, in some cases, only to a single individual. Thus, God's commands may in some cases be tailored to an individual to facilitate her achieving the unique end that is proper for her and her alone.

BIBLIOGRAPHY

An asterisk denotes secondary literature especially suitable for further reading.

Evans, C. Stephen 1981, "Is the Concept of an Absolute Duty Toward God Morally Unintelligible?," in Robert Perkins (ed.), *Kierkegaard's Fear and Trembling: Critical Appraisals* (Tuscaloosa, AL: University of Alabama Press), 141–51.
Evans, C. Stephen 1998, "Authority and Transcendence in *Works of Love*," in Niels Jørgen Cappelørn and Hermann Deuser (eds.), *Kierkegaard Studies 1998* (Berlin: de Gruyter), 23–40.
Evans, C. Stephen 2004, *Kierkegaard's Ethic of Love: Divine Commands and Moral Obligations* (Oxford University Press).
Evans, C. Stephen 2006, "Introduction," in Søren Kierkegaard, *Fear and Trembling*, ed. C. Stephen Evans and Sylvia Walsh, trans. Sylvia Walsh (Cambridge University Press), vi–xxxv.
Evans, C. Stephen 2009, *Kierkegaard: An Introduction* (Oxford University Press).
Evans, Stephen C. and Roberts, Robert C. 2013, "Ethics," in John Lippitt and George Pattison (eds.), *The Oxford Handbook of Kierkegaard* (Oxford University Press), 211–29.
Ferreira, M. Jamie 2001, *Love's Grateful Striving: A Commentary on Kierkegaard's* Works of Love (Oxford University Press).*
Green, Ronald M. 1992, *Kierkegaard and Kant: The Hidden Debt* (Albany, NY: State University of New York Press).
Kierkegaard, Søren 1962, *Works of Love*, ed. and trans. Howard V. Hong and Edna H. Hong (London and Glasgow: Collins).
Kierkegaard, Søren 1976, *Journals and Papers* – Volume 1: A–E, ed. and trans. Howard V. Hong and Edna H. Hong assisted by Gregor Malantschuk (Indiana University Press).
Kierkegaard, Søren 1978, *Journals and Papers – Volume 6: Autobiographical, Part Two, 1848–1855*, ed. and trans. Howard V. Hong and Edna H. Hong assisted by Gregor Malantschuk (Indiana University Press).

Kierkegaard, Søren 1980, *The Sickness unto Death*, ed. and trans. Howard V. Hong and Edna H. Hong (Princeton University Press).

Kierkegaard, Søren 1983, *Fear and Trembling*, ed. and trans. Howard V. Hong and Edna H. Hong (Princeton University Press).

Kierkegaard, Søren 1990, *For Self-Examination / Judge for Yourself!*, ed. and trans. Howard V. Hong and Edna H. Hong (Princeton University Press).

Kierkegaard, Søren 1992, *Concluding Unscientific Postscript to* Philosophical Fragments, ed. and trans. Howard V. Hong and Edna H. Hong (Princeton University Press).

Kierkegaard, Søren 1995, *Works of Love*, ed. and trans. Howard V. Hong and Edna H. Hong (Princeton University Press).

Kierkegaard, Søren 1998, *The Point of View*, ed. and trans. Howard V. Hong and Edna H. Hong (Princeton University Press).

Løgstrup, Knud Ejler 1997, "Settling Accounts with Kierkegaard's *Works of Love*," in Hans Fink and Alasdair MacIntyre (eds.), *The Ethical Demand* (University of Notre Dame Press), 218–64.

MacIntyre, Alasdair 1981, *After Virtue: A Study in Moral Theory* (University of Notre Dame Press).

Manis, R. Zachary 2009, "Foundations for a Kierkegaardian Account of Moral Obligation," *Southwest Philosophy Review*, 25/1, 71–81.

Manis, R. Zachary 2016, "'Eternity Will Nail Him to Himself': The Logic of Damnation in Kierkegaard's *The Sickness unto Death*," *Religious Studies*, 52/3, 287–314.

Outka, Gene 1973, "Religious and Moral Duty: Notes on *Fear and Trembling*," in Gene Outka and John P. Reeder, Jr. (eds.), *Religion and Morality: A Collection of Essays* (Garden City, NY: Anchor Press/Doubleday), 204–54.

Roberts, Robert C. 1998, "Existence, Emotion, and Virtue: Classical Themes in Kierkegaard," in Alastair Hannay (ed.), *The Cambridge Companion to Kierkegaard* (Cambridge University Press), 177–206.

Sartre, Jean-Paul 1957, "Existentialism," in *Existentialism and Human Emotions* (New York: Philosophical Library), 11–55.

Tietjen, Mark A. 2013. *Kierkegaard, Communication, and Virtue: Authorship as Edification* (Bloomington, IN: Indiana University Press).

Westphal, Merold 1987, "Abraham and Hegel," in *Kierkegaard's Critique of Reason and Society* (University Park, PA: The Pennsylvania State University Press), 61–84.

Westphal, Merold 1996 *Becoming a Self: A Reading of Kierkegaard's* Concluding Unscientific Postscript (West Lafayette, IN: Purdue University Press).*

36

American Transcendentalism

RUSSELL B. GOODMAN

Ralph Waldo Emerson (1803–1882) is at the center of American Transcendentalism, historically and intellectually. In 1836, he and another Harvard Divinity School graduate, Frederic Henry Hedge, began what became known as the Transcendental Club, responding to what Hedge called the "rigid, cautious, circumspect, conservative *tang* in the very air of Cambridge which no one, who has resided there for any considerable time, can escape."[1] The club included George Ripley, who founded the experimental community of Brook Farm; Bronson Alcott, who established the controversial Temple School in Boston; and, in subsequent years, Margaret Fuller (1810–1850), Henry David Thoreau (1817–1862), and others. After the furor over Emerson's Divinity School Address of 1838 (where he spoke of a church that proceeded "as if God were dead" (CW 1: 84)), the club established their own journal, *The Dial*, edited by Fuller and then Emerson.[2] Fuller's "The Great Lawsuit" (1843) (the core of *Woman in the Nineteenth Century* (1845)) appeared in *The Dial*, along with prose and poetry by Emerson, Alcott's "Orphic Sayings," Thoreau's "The Natural History of Massachusetts," and, after Emerson became editor, translations of Chinese, Indian, and Persian classics.[3] There is no one essence to Transcendentalism, and standard anthologies consider as many as thirty writers. Here we focus on three principal figures: Emerson, Thoreau, and Fuller.

---

[1] Richardson 1995: 245.

[2] References in the text to Emerson's *Collected Works* are indicated by CW followed by volume and page number; to Thoreau's *Walden* by W, "Resistance to Civil Government" by R, "Slavery in Massachusetts" by S; and to Fuller's "Great Lawsuit" by G.

[3] For an intellectual history of Transcendentalism, see Packer 2007. For more on the philosophies of Emerson and Thoreau, see Goodman 2015.

EMERSON

Emerson looks out over the movement in its heyday in "The Transcendentalist" (1842). He observes that because of their emphasis on individuality there "can be no Transcendentalist *party*," and he distances himself from the movement by characterizing its members in the third person. "They are lonely," he writes: "They cannot gossip with you, and they do not wish, as they are sincere and religious, to gratify any mere curiosity which you may entertain" (CW 1: 208). Nevertheless, their isolation serves a desire for a reformed society: "it is really a wish to be met . . . to find society . . ., which prompts them to shun what is called society" (CW 1: 210). In this way they are much like Emerson himself, who wrote a year earlier that "a greater self-reliance must work a revolution in all the offices and relations of men; in their religion; in their education; in their pursuits; their modes of living; their association; in their property; in their speculative views" (CW 2: 44).

Emerson traces the term "Transcendentalism" to the anti-skeptical ideal-ism of Kant, who showed "that there was a very important class of ideas, or imperative forms, which did not come by experience, but through which experience was acquired; . . . and he denominated them Transcendental forms" (CW 1: 206–7). Kant and his followers, as conveyed by Samuel Taylor Coleridge, James Marsh, Germaine de Staël, and others, taught the Transcendentalists the basic lesson that the mind is not a passive recipient of the world's impressions, but a powerful instrument of its own in knowledge, morality, poetry, and religion. Rousseau, Herder, Wordsworth, and other romantics taught them the parallel lesson that the deepest access to nature lies through the self.[4] As Emerson puts the point in "The American Scholar" (1838): "the ancient precept, 'Know thyself,' and the modern precept, 'Study nature,' become at last one maxim" (CW 1: 55).

Knowing oneself is no easy task, but it is possible for everyone, and Emerson urges each reader of "Self-Reliance" to "learn to detect and watch that gleam of light which flashes across his mind from within, more than the luster of the firmament of bards and sages" (CW 2: 27). He portrays spontaneous, original judgments about the world in the image of "boys who are sure of a dinner, and would disdain as much as a lord to do or say aught to conciliate one." (Emerson characteristically blends the lord with the child, the aristocratic with the romantic.) These boys deliver "independent, irresponsible" judgments on the people and events they see, "in the swift, summary way of boys, as good, bad,

---

[4] Cf. Taylor 1989: 369–72.

interesting, silly, eloquent, troublesome . . ." The "nonchalance" of these boys, Emerson writes, "is the healthy attitude of human nature" (CW 2: 29).

Emerson offers a genealogical picture of the virtues in "Circles" (1841), where he states: "There is no virtue which is final; all are initial." Virtues are like civilizations, religious rites, or "rules of an art." They serve certain purposes, have their strengths and limitations; and they come and go: "The terror of reform is the discovery that we must cast away our virtues, or what we have always esteemed such, into the same pit that has consumed our grosser vices . . . The virtues of society are vices of the saint" (CW 2: 187). The virtues of society that Emerson wishes to discard – virtues of the "herd" and the "mass" (CW 1: 65) – include the idolization of books and figures of the past, the routines of a worn-out religion or a low friendship, the respect paid to clothing and other symbols of status, and the "forced smile which we put on in company where we do not feel at ease in answer to conversation which does not interest us" (CW 2: 32).

Many of our so-called virtues, Emerson argues, are really "penances" or apologies for our failures to act – for "our daily non-appearance on parade" as he puts it, using a military metaphor for an existential condition (CW 2: 31). We lack existential courage: "Man is timid and apologetic; he is no longer upright; he dares not say 'I think,' 'I am,' but quotes some saint or sage." Emerson here quotes a sage, Descartes,[5] but his point is to play on the necessity of *stating* "I think" for it to be necessarily true. Unlike "2+2=4," "I am" or "I exist" are not necessary truths – for one thing, because unstated by anyone they have no referent. When Emerson says that we dare not say "I think, I am," he is conceiving of human existence as something that requires courage or daring and that must be claimed, stated, or undertaken. In this sense, Emerson thinks that most people, most of the time, *don't exist*.[6]

Although Emerson's heroes are great and noble beings, like the "boys who would disdain as much as a lord" to placate anyone, Emerson argues that such nobility is available to everyone – if only in "the few real hours of life" (CW 1: 90). Sometimes he figures our greatness as an inner "gleam of light" for which we are to search, sometimes as a direction in which we move with ease when all other ways are blocked: "Each man has his own vocation . . . He is like a ship in a river; he runs against obstructions on every side but one;

---

[5] See Cavell 2003b.
[6] Emerson's contemporary Søren Kierkegaard similarly writes that "[e]xistence . . . is a striving," and that people "forget" that they are existing individuals (Kierkegaard 1968: 84, 109).

on that side all obstruction is taken away, and he sweeps serenely over a deepening channel into an infinite sea" (CW 2: 82).

Friendship can come this way, easily and naturally: "a brother or sister by nature, comes to us so softly and easily, so nearly and intimately ... that we feel as if some one was gone, instead of another having come ..." (CW 2: 87). But Emerson's ideal friendship also includes titanic struggles between powerful equals, who spur each other to greater efforts and greater deeds:

> That great defying eye, that scornful beauty of his mien and action, do not pique yourself on reducing, but rather fortify and enhance ... Guard him as thy counterpart. Let him be to thee forever a sort of beautiful enemy, untameable, devoutly revered, and not a trivial conveniency to be soon outgrown and cast aside. (CW 2: 123–4)[7]

Friends so conceived need a break from each other, time to settle and gather themselves. They should "meet each morning, as from foreign countries, and spending the day together should depart, as into foreign countries" (CW 3: 81). The search for such friendships may require departures from old friends: "A man's growth is seen in the successive choirs of his friends ... Men cease to interest us when we find their limitations" (CW 2: 182).

Emerson's essays present a series of oppositions – one / many, flux / stability, conformity / originality, society / solitude, immigrancy / domesticity – and many of them consider whether and how it is possible to reconcile, or find a middle way between, these oppositions. Sometimes this seems possible, as in "Montaigne; or the Skeptic" (1851), where the skeptic occupies "the middle ground" between the "abstractionist" and the "materialist" (CW 4: 88). "Self-Reliance" also offers a reconciliation between society and solitude in the thought that solitude is a human condition that the great person always retains: "it is easy in the world to live after the world's opinion" and "easy in solitude to live after our own [but] the great man is he who in the midst of the crowd keeps with perfect sweetness the independence of solitude" (CW 2: 31).

More often, the conditions of human experience make such harmony impossible. "Life is a train of moods, like a string of beads," Emerson writes in "Experience," "and each shows only what lies in its focus" (CW 3: 30).[8] Moods come with their own tissue of beliefs: they "do not believe in each other" (CW 2: 182). How then are we to conduct ourselves in a world of shifting moods and outlooks? In "Experience," Emerson speaks of skating

---

[7] For the anticipations of Nietzsche here see Goodman 2010.

[8] Such statements are the basis for Cavell's claim that "Experience" presents "an epistemology of moods" (Cavell 2003a: 11).

over the surfaces of life and "finding the journey's end in every step of the road" (CW 3: 35). But he also learns to "accept the clangor and jangle of contrary tendencies" (CW 3: 36).

THOREAU

Thoreau's *Walden, or Life in the Woods* (1854) was first drafted during his twenty-six months living in a cabin he built near Walden Pond, on land recently purchased by Emerson. The book considers the true necessities of human life, concluding that we sacrifice the chance "to adventure on life now" in the quest for luxuries and "superfluities" (W: 15). Thoreau builds not only a cabin, but a little republic, with a farm, visitors, books, and above all, nature in the forms of birds, fish, pines, water, ice, and weather. From his vantage point by the pond he observes that "the mass of men lead lives of quiet desperation" (W: 8).

Thoreau argues that we are slave drivers of ourselves, that our virtues and lifestyles resemble the self-inflicted torments of "Bramins sitting exposed to four fires and looking in the face of the sun; or hanging suspended, with their heads downward, over flames ..." (W: 4). The book's long first chapter considers the economic forms these torments take. People work most of their lives to pay the debt on their large farms and houses, and they labor to support their animals as much as their animals labor to support them. By his "experiment" living in his cabin at Walden Pond, his careful accounting of his receipts and expenditures, and his shift of orientation to the fundamental "cost of a thing," one's "life" (W: 31), Thoreau aims both to open up for his readers the range of their own human possibilities and the false necessities under which they labor. In describing the life he seeks, he alludes to the "ancient philosophers, Chinese, Hindoo, Persian, and Greek" who attained an impartial view of life from a condition that "*we* should call voluntary poverty." Philosophy so conceived is a way of life: "There are nowadays professors of philosophy, but not philosophers. Yet it is admirable to profess because it was once admirable to live. To be a philosopher is not merely to have subtle thoughts, nor even to found a school, but so to love wisdom as to live according to its dictates, a life of simplicity, independence, magnanimity, and trust" (W: 14–15).

Thoreau grows beans and other vegetables on a small plot, and finds that he can support himself by working about six weeks a year. He is not saying everyone should do so, nor even that he will live this way for the rest of his life, but he thinks we should consider adjusting our priorities in view of the unnecessary labor in which we engage. He seeks "to improve the nick of time" as he spends his days reading, writing, walking, talking, and attending to the variety and changes of nature. He is, he writes, a "self-appointed inspector of snow-storms and rain-storms" (W: 18).

Thoreau finds wealth in not owning things. He walks and sits on his neighbor's farm, eats its wild apples, and imagines how he would lay it out into fields and woodlots, were he to buy it. Then he lets it be: "for a man is rich in proportion to the number of things which he can afford to let alone" (W: 81–2).

As for society, Thoreau reports that he had more visitors in the cabin than when he lived in town, and that he particularly enjoys the company of children, hunters, and fishermen. But the cabin is obviously a place where he is alone most of the time, and his chapter on "Solitude" is a meditation on the subject. "I have a great deal of company in my house," he writes, "especially in the morning, when nobody calls" (W: 137). He loves to be alone in a certain way, most of the time:

> I find it wholesome to be alone the greater part of the time. To be in company, even with the best, is soon wearisome and dissipating. I love to be alone. I never found the companion that was so companionable as solitude. We are for the most part more lonely when we go abroad among men than when we stay in our chambers.   (W: 135)

When he is alone, Thoreau finds a "certain doubleness" in himself that allows him to "stand aloof from actions and their consequences ... We are not wholly involved in Nature. I may be either the driftwood in the stream, or Indra in the sky looking down on it" (W: 134–5).

Thoreau's concern with nature as a source of wisdom and comfort is part of the romantic movement that includes Rousseau, Wordsworth and, most immediately, Emerson. Emerson observes in *Nature* (1836) that: "few adult persons can see nature" (CW 1: 9). But he adds: "In the woods we return to reason and faith" (CW 1: 10). Thoreau's experiments in the woods lead him to a new intimacy with the natural world that begins on a day when he wonders whether he might not need humanity closer by:

> In the midst of a gentle rain, I was suddenly sensible of such sweet and beneficent society in Nature, in the very pattering of the drops, and in every sound and sight around my house, an infinite and unaccountable friendliness all at once like an atmosphere sustaining me, as made the fancied advantages of human neighborhood insignificant, and I have never thought of them since.   (W: 131–2)

This is the Thoreau who bathes in the pond every morning as a "religious exercise" (W: 88), hears the ice crack on a winter night, watches "the spring come in" (W: 302), and – though he does not spend much time describing this activity – writes *Walden*.[9]

Thoreau's quest for a philosophical life led him to leave the town of Concord, and then to leave Walden Pond. "It is remarkable," he observes, "how easily and insensibly we fall into a particular route, and make a beaten track for ourselves." At the pond, it was less than a week "before my feet wore a path from my door to the pond-side; and though it is five or six years since I trod it, it is still quite distinct" (W: 323). You can get into a rut anywhere, and Thoreau, like Emerson, finds unsettlement and abandonment as important in human life as settling, building, and domesticity.

Thoreau's "Civil Disobedience" is the most important political statement written by any of the Transcendentalists. It was provoked by Thoreau's arrest in 1846 for six years' non-payment of his poll tax, as he came into town to pick up a repaired shoe (R: 78, 83). His night in jail and subsequent release showed him the familiar town from another angle, revealed the "half-witted" nature of the state's actions and led him to develop his theory of "resistance to civil government" – the title under which his address was first published (R: 315–21). There is power in the individual, Thoreau asserts, but also power in numbers: "If a thousand men were not to pay their tax-bills this year, that would not be a violent and bloody measure, as it would be to pay them, and enable the State to commit violence and shed innocent blood. This is, in fact, the definition of a peaceable revolution, if any such is possible" (R: 76). In the case of an "unjust war" like the US invasion of Mexico, Thoreau holds, one must become "a counter-friction to stop the machine" (R: 73–4).

Like Alcott, Emerson, and many others, Thoreau became even more exercised after Congress passed the Fugitive Slave Law in 1850. His "Slavery in Massachusetts" (1854) considers the absurdity of the Massachusetts justice system "trying a MAN, to find out if he is not really a SLAVE" (S: 92). In the case of Anthony Burns, an escaped slave living and working in Boston: "The whole military force of the State is at the service of a Mr. Suttle, a slaveholder from Virginia, to enable him to catch a man whom he calls his property; but not a soldier is offered to save a citizen of Massachusetts from being kidnapped!" (S: 94).[10] Ten years before the outbreak of the Civil War, the peaceable Thoreau writes that thoughts of violence towards the state haunt him, even in his withdrawal amidst "the beauty of nature":

[9] See Richardson 1986: 183.   [10] See von Frank 1999.

Who can be serene in a country where both the rulers and the ruled are without principle? The remembrance of my country spoils my walk. My thoughts are murder to the State, and involuntarily go plotting against her. (S: 108)

FULLER

Talking to Margaret Fuller, Emerson wrote, was "like being set in a large place. You stretch your limbs & dilate to your utmost size."[11] She was a prodigy, the daughter of a Massachusetts congressman educated by tutors at home in classical languages and literature, and later in Spanish, French, German, and Italian. Exercising "her peculiar powers of intrusion and caress,"[12] she became friends with several of the Harvard-educated transcendentalists.

People paid to hear Fuller talk, or rather, as she insisted, to talk with her. She organized a series of "Conversations" for Boston women beginning in 1839. (Her fee, about two-thirds of what Emerson charged for his lectures, was her primary means of support.) Drawing on her knowledge of Greek and Latin literature, she conducted sessions on Venus, Cupid and Psyche, Minerva, and the intellectual differences between men and women.[13] She required that her students not simply listen to her, but that they "communicate what was in their mind."[14] In doing so, she was in accord with Emerson's idea that everyone has something original to say and do.

Fuller published a long essay on Goethe in *The Dial* in 1841, a successful travel narrative, *Summer on the Lakes* (1843), and a series of dispatches for Horace Greeley's *New York Tribune*, but her major work is *Woman in the Nineteenth Century* (1845), which first appeared in *The Dial* as: "The Great Lawsuit. Man versus Men. Woman versus Women" (1843). The original title emphasizes her point that both men and women suffer in the current arrangements of the sexes, where the ideal man and the ideal woman are at odds with their lower or degraded selves. She writes: "What woman needs is not as a woman to act or rule, but as a nature to grow, as an intellect to discern, as a soul to live freely, and unimpeded to unfold such powers as were given her when we left our common home" (G: 394). Her work on women is not just about women then, but about human possibility.

---

[11] Emerson 1939, 2: 32. [12] Packer 2007: 113. [13] See Marshall 2013: 137–41. [14] Ibid., 134.

Like Emerson and Thoreau, Fuller calls for periods of withdrawal from a society whose members are in various states of "distraction" and "imbecility," and a return only after "the renovating fountains" of individuality have risen up. Such alternations of solitude and engagement are essential, she holds, for that form of society known as marriage: "Union is only possible to those who are units" (G: 419). Most marriages, she observes, are forms of "degradation" in which "the woman belongs to the man, instead of forming a whole with him" (G: 422).

Fuller develops a gendered philosophical psychology, maintaining that masculinity and femininity pass into one another, that there is "no wholly masculine man, no purely feminine woman" (G: 418). The romantic poet Percy Bysshe Shelley, for example, "shared the feminine development, and unlike many, knew it." Shelley "abhorred blood and heat, and, by his system and his song, tended to reinstate a plant-like gentleness in the development of energy" (G: 417). Turning to classical mythology, Fuller writes that "Man partakes of the feminine in the Apollo, woman of the Masculine as Minerva" (G: 419). But there are differences: the feminine genius is "electrical" and "intuitive," the male more inclined to "classification" (G: 418).

Fuller does more than develop a gendered psychology. She speaks as a woman, for women, in a developing tradition that includes the abolitionist Angelina Grimké, Mary Wollstonecraft, and the writer George Sand, all of whom she mentions (G: 415–16). "Ye cannot believe it, men," Fuller writes, "but the only reason why women ever assume what is more appropriate to you, is because you prevent them from finding out what is fit for themselves" (G: 402). Like Emerson and Thoreau, she looks forward: to social reform, to a changed relation to the universe at large, and to what Emerson calls the "unattained but attainable self" (CW 2: 5).

BIBLIOGRAPHY

An asterisk denotes secondary literature especially suitable for further reading.

Cavell, Stanley 2003a. "Thinking of Emerson," in David Justin Hodge (ed.), *Emerson's Transcendental Etudes*. Stanford University Press, pp. 10–19.
Cavell, Stanley 2003b. "Being Odd, Getting Even," in David Justin Hodge (ed.), *Emerson's Transcendental Etudes*. Stanford University Press, pp. 83–109.
Emerson, Ralph Waldo 1939. *The Letters of Ralph Waldo Emerson*, ed. Ralph L. Rusk. New York and London: Columbia University Press.
Emerson, Ralph Waldo 1971. *The Collected Works of Ralph Waldo Emerson*, ed. Alfred R. Ferguson, Jean Ferguson Carr, *et al.* Cambridge, MA: Harvard University Press.

Fuller, Margaret 2000. "The Great Lawsuit. Man versus Men. Woman versus Women," in Myerson 2000, pp. 383–427.

Goodman, Russell B. 2010. "Emerson and Skepticism: A Reading of Friendship," in John T. Lysaker and William Rossi (eds.), *Emerson and Thoreau: Figures of Friendship*. Bloomington, IN: Indiana University Press, pp. 70–85.

Goodman, Russell B. 2015. *American Philosophy before Pragmatism*. Oxford University Press.

Kierkegaard, Søren 1968. *Concluding Unscientific Postscript*, trans. David F. Swenson and Walter Lowrie. Princeton University Press.

Marshall, Megan 2013. *Margaret Fuller: A New American Life*. Boston and New York: Houghton Mifflin Harcourt.

Myerson, Joel (ed.) 2000. *Transcendentalism: A Reader*. Oxford University Press.

Packer, Barbara L. 2007. *The Transcendentalists*. Athens, GA: University of Georgia Press.*

Richardson, Robert D., Jr. 1986. *Henry Thoreau: A Life of the Mind*. Berkeley, CA: University of California Press.

Richardson, Robert D., Jr. 1995. *Emerson: The Mind on Fire*. Berkeley, CA: University of California Press.*

Taylor, Charles 1989. *Sources of the Self: The Making of Modern Identity*. Cambridge, MA: Harvard University Press.

Thoreau, Henry David 1973a. "Resistance to Civil Government," in *Reform Papers (The Writings of Henry D. Thoreau)*, ed. Wendell Glick. Princeton University Press, pp. 63–90.

Thoreau, Henry David 1973b. "Slavery in Massachusetts," in *Reform Papers (The Writings of Henry D. Thoreau)*, ed. Wendell Glick. Princeton University Press, pp. 91–109.

Thoreau, Henry David 1989. *Walden, or Life in the Woods (The Writings of Henry D. Thoreau)*, ed. J. Lyndon Shanley. Princeton University Press.

Von Frank, Albert J. 1999. *The Trials of Anthony Burns: Freedom and Slavery in Emerson's Boston*. Cambridge, MA: Harvard University Press.

37

Nietzsche

LAWRENCE HATAB

Nietzsche's place in the history of moral philosophy might seem unusual because of his seeming rejection of morality, even to the point of advocating a kind of "immoralism." Nevertheless his writings offer significant contributions to moral philosophy, and this has been gaining recognition over the last few decades. In one respect Nietzsche's entire philosophy is about values, in the broadest sense of finding meaning and worth in life. He proclaims that human beings are essentially "esteemers" (Z I, On a Thousand and One Goals), whose principal function is creating values and shaping the meaning of existence. Nietzsche's philosophical agenda turns on what *kind* of values are created and how they measure up to natural life, which must include the carnal, dynamic character of earthly existence with its full array of passions, drives, conflicts, vicissitudes, and destructive elements. Nietzsche's charge against the moral tradition is that in the main its values have been antithetical to earthly life – because of commitments to frameworks of being that govern forces of becoming and conceptions of reason and spirit that supersede animal nature. Nietzsche sees his task as the diagnosis and critique of any such life-negating values and the promotion of new values that can be "faithful to the earth" (Z I, Prologue, 3).

Nietzsche's examination of values is not restricted to ethical domains because it reaches into every area of culture and thought – which can be gathered by considering his famous declaration of the death of God (GS 125), which is delivered in the voice of a "madman." The audience is not religious believers, but nonbelievers who are chastised for not facing the consequences of God's demise. Since God is the ultimate symbol of supernatural transcendence, his death is to be welcomed but its impact concerns a lot more than

Nietzsche's works are cited according to the abbreviations listed at the end of this chapter. References are to text sections unless otherwise indicated; references to *KSA* are to volume and page number.

482

religious belief. In the modern secular world God is no longer the mandated core of intellectual pursuits. Yet historically the notion of God had been the warrant for all sorts of cultural constructs in moral, political, philosophical, even scientific domains, all of which harbored a *devaluation* of natural conditions of becoming and carnal life. From Plato through to the Enlightenment a divine mind had been the ultimate foundation of origins and truth, thus justifying the governance of more natural forces. With the eclipse of God, however, any and all inferences from theological grounds must come undone (*TI* Skirmishes, 5). Even though divinity is no longer an intellectual requirement, the modern world still has confidence in the "shadows" of God (*GS* 108), in supposedly secular and worldly constructs – in ethics, politics, science, etc. – that have nevertheless lost their historical warrant. The modern world therefore faces the specter of nihilism, the abnegation of value, meaning, and intelligibility, unless the world can be rethought in terms faithful to natural life.

A central concept in Nietzsche's "naturalized" philosophy is will to power (see *BGE* 36), which is meant to gather the sense of life energies that had been suppressed in the Western tradition. Will to power names any movement wherein an aspect of life seeks to overcome some counterforce or resistance; yet it entails more than simply the achievements of particular life forms because it names the force field of conflicting conditions within which a form of life finds its meaning in overcoming something (see *KSA* 13: 37–8, 258, 270–1). Resisting forces therefore are constitutive of meaning, which is why any attempt to override conflict and becoming is implicitly nihilistic. Will to power is also not restricted to natural violence or brute control because it includes cultural formations of meaning that are constituted by overcoming other cultural counterforces (see *GM* II, 12) – so that, for example, the founding of Christianity and even the promotion of pacifism would count as instances of will to power (see *KSA* 13: 52). This cultural dynamic of will to power figures prominently in Nietzsche's "genealogical" analysis of moral valuation.

Genealogy in Nietzsche's hands is a quasi-historical examination of life conditions that have spawned human values, and it is meant to disturb any confidence that presumed norms have fixed foundations, whether in traditional theological terms or in modern secularized models of social utility or rational subjectivity. According to Nietzsche, the contingency of modern moral thinking is shown in its derivation from pre-modern Judeo-Christian sources, which were not the wholesale discovery of morality per se but the promotion of one kind of valuation that aimed to overcome another, more original set of moral values. This historical scenario is gathered in Nietzsche's account of slave morality and master morality. He stipulates that hierarchical domination was a standard condition in early human societies (*BGE* 257), and stratified status brings different modes of valuation depending on the lived circumstances of ruling or being ruled (*BGE* 260). Master and slave morality are distinguished by two sets of estimation: good and bad in master morality, good and evil in slave morality. Ruling types assess what is good in terms of their condition of manifest strength in the world. They experience pleasure in their victories and exaltation in their prominence over weaker types. Characteristics such as courage, aggression, and command that generate overt power are deemed "good," while weaker traits such as cowardice, humility, and dependence are deemed "bad." Good and bad here are not universals. What is good is such only for the master; what is bad in the slave type arouses contempt in the master, but not condemnation because sub-ordination is constitutive of the master's sense of goodness, of superiority in the social order.

Slave morality is a reversal of master morality. What the master deems bad is called good by the slave; and what is good for the master is called "evil." The difference between "bad" and "evil" is important for Nietzsche because the former coexists with the good, while the latter must be utterly annulled if the good is to endure. The latter valuation stems from the existential circumstance of the slave type, whose immediate condition is powerlessness and subservience. In effect the slave lacks any agency and so masterly power cannot coexist with the slave's interests; it must be eliminable. The only resolution of the slave's predicament is to find "virtue" in passive subser-vience, which will be rewarded in an imagined rectification where divine justice liquidates evil (*GM* I, 10 and 14). This is where power for the slave type finds a place in psychological hopes for eventual victory (*GM* I, 15). Here Nietzsche is redescribing Judeo-Christian ideals – where justice and love supplant worldly forms of power – as simply a disguised aim for power dressed up in a theological script.

In the slave mentality elements of life that involve opposition, strife, destruction, danger, and overt power are evil and merit eradication. Yet for the master mentality a world without such elements would neutralize the very conditions of goodness in life. Slave morality must also posit its virtues (e.g., humility, selflessness, peacefulness) as the measure for all human beings if its interests are to be served. Nietzsche asserts that a universalization of such values is unwarranted and stems from a resentment of worldly strength by weaker types (*GM* I, 10) rather than any self-affirming accomplishment in life. Finally, the universalization of slave values went hand in hand with seeking the *conversion* of master types and their choosing to live in a different manner from that afforded by their worldly station. Accordingly slave morality introduced the idea of *free will* as a precondition for moral judgment and reform, but which Nietzsche claims is not exhibited in the natural order (*GM* I, 13–14).

The master–slave analysis establishes important elements of Nietzsche's philosophical agenda. Master morality is more attuned to natural life forces and overtly indicative of will to power. Slave morality is more alienated from life and exhibits a *covert* form of will to power in seeking to overcome master morality. The larger question for Nietzsche here is the capacity or incapacity to affirm life, with all its negative limits, conflicts, and dangers. He is aiming to disturb and critique long-standing values associated with universality, equality, harmony, selflessness, and the like – seemingly positive notions that Nietzsche wants to say are connivances of negative dispositions (fear of danger, hatred of suffering, resentment of superiority) and ultimately a sign of "ascetic" disaffection with natural life.

It is important not to miss the ambiguities in Nietzsche's genealogical account. The slave mentality is not utterly dismissed because it served the needs of certain types and also engendered a cultivating force in human history. The original master scenario was largely the brute world of physical achievement and was relatively crude, coarse, and "unsymbolical" (*GM* I, 16). When outward action is thwarted or blocked, life energies – as will to power – turn inward (*GM* II, 16), thus opening up imaginative capacities to conceive possibilities beyond the brute conditions of life. Such internalization is the precondition for cultural creativity and achievement in sophisticated domains such as art, religion, philosophy, and science – and Nietzsche was throughout his career a philosopher of culture. The inward turn allows *depth* and turns the human being into "an *interesting animal*" (*GM* I, 6). The lack of external power is no dead end because "the history of mankind would be far too stupid a thing if it had not had the intelligence of the powerless injected into it" (*GM* I, 7). Such cultural forces are simply a redirected instance of will to power (see *BGE* 51; *GM* I, 15) and indeed an advance over brute nature.

From Nietzsche's perspective the problem with modes of culture succeeding master morality is not that they came to pass or served no purpose; rather, they did not see themselves as dispositional responses to natural life forces but as grounded in transcendent or strictly rational sources, as something different from maneuvers of power. Beyond such pretense is also a matter of self-consumption. Any belief system that aims to supersede natural conditions of power relations undermines the very conditions of its own historical emergence, as an aim to overcome some counterforce. From this perspective Nietzsche thinks he has good reason to challenge the life-negating undertones in traditional thought.

Nevertheless the slave mentality opened up cultural pathways of will to power beyond erstwhile crude beginnings. And the capacity for innovative divergence from established conditions marks the higher creative types that Nietzsche celebrates as engines of culture. This accounts for his analysis moving beyond the original master–slave relationship and positing the possibility of blending the two forces. Higher cultures exhibit mediations between master and slave tendencies (GM I, 16), and the two energies can even coexist within a single individual (BGE 260). The original tension between masterly power and slavish subordination is reconfigured in more advanced cultures as the tension between innovative divergence and conformity, which Nietzsche calls "herd morality." Now the "evil" that threatens people is creative disruption that "wants to conquer, to overthrow the old boundary stones and pieties" (GS 4). Innovators now become the new object of resentment, the new "criminals" and perpetrators of "war" (see Z Old and New Tablets, 26; TI Skirmishes, 45; BGE 230; and GS 283). But since cultural creativity arises out of the internalization of power withdrawn from brute physical power, the master–slave distinction in the end is far from a separation of two discrete forces; it constitutes elevated modes of culture creation.

A central insight is operating in Nietzsche's analysis: Any development of culture out of natural conditions and any innovation out of established conditions entail a dynamic of discomfort, resistance, and overcoming – in other words, a conflict with counter-conditions. Nietzsche alerts us to the danger of converting this tension into a polarization of good and evil, an eliminative project that undermines the very conditions of cultural production and that alienates humanity from the natural energies of life. Affirmation of life therefore involves contending with otherness without seeking to annul it, since conflicted relations constitute self-development and cultural development.

The second essay of GM takes up an important historical development following the early master–slave scenario. Original slavish hopes for power could only be imagined in religious stories of divine judgment. The worldly success of Christianity in European history helped supplant pagan forces (which exhibited aristocratic values) and gave slave morality institutional power. Ultimately Christian norms became the prevailing guidelines for moral development, culminating in modern secular conceptions of rational "self-determination." In this regard Nietzsche traces how moral constraints began as socially enforced regulations and evolved into internalized self-regulation. The modern notion of moral responsibility grew out of a long history of cultural preconditions. Nietzsche notes that responsibility for past and future actions requires the power of memory, which had to be "bred" into human beings because of the more original force of forgetting (GM II, 1–2). Memory was first encouraged through brutal forms of public punishment (GM II, 3–5), which would sear into the mind a deterrent force. With the growing prominence of slave values, which extol passive inhibitions over assertive dominance, there developed a transition from the external power of social cruelty to the internalized "cruelty" of suppressing natural energies – which created the force of moral "conscience" (GM II, 3). Nietzsche is here trying to sketch the ways in which individual moral responsibility took shape in European culture, which is important because the original lack of agency in slave morality was repaired when individual responsibility came to be cultivated and reinforced by modern social and political developments that neutralized vestiges of master morality in aristocratic regimes and that valorized egalitarian ideals of self-determination. Nietzsche's challenge to moral philosophy amounts to this: Standard ethical frameworks are revealed to be historically contingent and traceable to life-averse dispositions. Natural forces of becoming, differentiation, and conflict were opposed in slave morality, which over time spawned comparable ideals that stress universal, utilitarian, and rationalized moral principles, and that likewise suppress life energies.

It would be fitting now to sketch some of the ways in which Nietzsche's analysis specifically targets familiar moral theories. But first it must be established that Nietzsche's critique of traditional values is not a wholesale repudiation of moral discourse. We have seen that his genealogical narrative is not simply an account of slave morality's displacement of master morality because the master–slave dynamic can still exhibit productive permutations. In the Genealogy of Morality he asks if the conflict between master and slave values has come to an end or if there are still possibilities of it being furthered after the ascension of slave morality (GM I, 17). He closes with an indication of his own posture on the question of morality, his own interest in retrieving some elements of master morality as a correction for the dominance of slave morality. He addresses this matter with the following assumption:

that it has been sufficiently clear for some time what I *want*, what I actually want with that dangerous slogan which is written on the spine of my last book, *Beyond Good and Evil* ... at least this does *not* mean "Beyond Good and Bad."

Nietzsche not only grants historical importance to the good–bad distinction in noble morality, he also considers this distinction to be a workable alternative to the good–evil distinction for his own thinking on morality, his own recommendations for a moral sense that can overcome traditional versions of slave morality.

One Nietzschean criticism of modern moral theories – particularly the utilitarian and Kantian models – is that their theories are not reinventing the ethical wheel, but rather offering a rational *reconstruction* of familiar values, to sidestep mere custom and religious allegiance and provide a reflective model that can secure these values with a rational consensus. Utilitarianism provided a reconstruction of common notions of happiness and the balancing of different goods. Kant reconfigured traditional notions of freedom, responsibility, and moral commands. Nietzsche questions the exclusive status of both traditional values and their rational reconstruction. Moral philosophers aimed to *ground* a morality that was accepted as "given" and thereby simply expressed an erudite *faith* in established morality (*BGE* 186).

Compared with utilitarian and Kantian morality, one would think that Nietzsche might find favor with moral egoism, especially given his deconstruction of selflessness as a slavish maneuver to neutralize stronger types. There are indeed elements of egoism that appeal to Nietzsche; nevertheless, caution is called for here. Moral egoism has usually been cast as a universal model for all selves. Yet Nietzsche rejects the universal application of egoism because it offends his insistence on different levels of worth among human types. The value of selfishness is measured by the value of the one who has it: it can be very great or worthless and contemptible, in terms of whether it represents an ascending or descending form of life. If individuals are of the ascending type, "their value is in fact extraordinary," and they deserve special consideration – not for their own sake but "for the sake of life as a whole, which through them takes a step *further*" (*TI* Skirmishes, 33). Nietzsche favors *exceptional* individuals, creator types who advance human culture. His objection to universal egoism on behalf of rank compares with objections from other quarters about the dangers of excess in egoistic liberation, but not for the same reasons:

> Excess is a reproach only against those with no right to it; and almost all the passions have been brought into ill repute on account of those who were not sufficiently strong to employ them. (*KSA* 12: 283)

He claims that without "spiritual greatness, independence ought not to be allowed, it causes mischief" (*KSA* 11: 277). Nietzsche advocates freedom *for* creative work and not simply freedom *from* constraint or an unbridled satisfaction of desires (Z I, On the Creator). That is why the restraints of normalization are affirmed by Nietzsche for most people: "My philosophy aims at an ordering of rank: not an individualistic morality. The ideas of the herd should rule in the herd – but not reach out beyond it" (*KSA* 12: 280).

Regarding utilitarianism, Nietzsche rebukes the notion that morality can be sufficiently explained in terms of happiness and the beneficial consequences of group interests. What is missing is the historical awareness of an earlier aristocratic morality and its different sense of valuation. In this context Nietzsche can say that utilitarianism is simply the formalization of slavish constraints on strong individuals. He does say that the "happiness of the greatest number" is useful as a measure of common interests, but not as a universal conception of the good, because this would be detrimental for "higher men" (*BGE* 228). More pointedly, Nietzsche takes aim at the fundamental principle of utilitarianism when he declares that happiness – conceived as the maximization of well-being and the minimization of ill-being – is antithetical to the exercise of creative power (*BGE* 225). Since creativity is disruptive of the existing order and risky for the innovator, it would not likely get off the ground if happiness were the criterion.

Regarding Kant's moral theory, beyond targeting its universalization of values, Nietzsche's most fundamental criticism takes aim at the Kantian model of an autonomous rational agent, whose discipline requires internalized "cruelty" toward natural impulses. Since moral worth, for Kant, can never be grounded in natural inclinations, since moral duty can only come to light when natural impulses run against it, then genuine moral worth always runs counter to natural life in some basic way, thus requiring a disciplined stand "against ourselves" in this sense. Accordingly, genuine morality in Kant cannot become settled in the self as a natural expression of desire that could even be experienced as pleasurable (as it would be for Aristotle). Such a self-inflicted struggle against nature is precisely what Nietzsche called ascetic cruelty, and so Kant can fit the bill (see *GM* II, 6). In an early text (*D* 339) Nietzsche even talks of a duty toward the rights of others that "ceases to be a burden" and "becomes a pleasurable inclination," unlike the Kantian demand "that duty must *always* be something of a burden ... that it never become habit and custom" – which is a "concealed remnant of ascetic cruelty." Nietzsche's charge of asceticism highlights both the psychological and intellectual demands of Kant's moral philosophy, in that universality is purchased at the expense of natural conditions of life; indeed the binary opposition between duty and lived experience guarantees that a reconciliation of the two spheres can never be attained.

It is noteworthy that Kant's promotion of an abstract universal right can stand against possible abuses in egoism and utilitarianism. Universal consistency provides an effective tactic in ruling out injustice without appeal to human dispositions. Respect for persons on *rational* grounds is well illustrated in the example of slavery, which easily fails the categorical imperative test: I cannot will the universal enslavement of human beings because that would rule out the very institution of slavery; if everyone were a slave then no one could be master. Yet Nietzsche aims to intercept such an argument in his analysis of master and slave morality. Master morality ruled out any universal standpoint or attribution of value, and it justified subjugation by actual outcomes of power over others. The tactic of positing universal enslavement would be met with bemusement. Nietzsche would not deny the power that universalization has achieved in history, but he would deny the universality of universalization. Rational moral principles are an inheritance of *one kind* of moral perspective, which was built from dissatisfaction with another moral perspective animated by more natural hierarchies. It seems clear that any moral viewpoint would involve some kind of expanded horizon beyond brute immediacy. Nietzsche's question would be: Why does an expanded horizon have to achieve universality to be truly moral? Why is moral particularity unacceptable? What do claims about a categorical imperative tell us about the people who make them (*BGE* 187)? The urge toward universality, for Nietzsche, is akin to slave morality's need for relief from a natural economy of differing forces.

For much of the twentieth century, moral philosophy was primarily engaged in debates between deontological and consequentialist theories. Then virtue ethics came on the scene, in part as a revival of an Aristotelian orientation. Virtue ethics is not based on rules and principles that guide actions; it focuses on character traits and dispositions at the heart of human actions, capacities that are needed to lead a good life. If any moral tradition can fit well with Nietzsche's approach it would be virtue ethics, which has been recognized in the literature. There are several reasons: the emphasis in virtue ethics on self-development, on character traits rather than mere social configurations and consequences; and especially the de-emphasis on formal principles and demonstrative reason in favor of a self-manifesting moral compass that would not require governing constraints in order to lead a good life. Nietzsche's overall preference for "noble" over "slavish" traits can bear on this question. Consider the following aristocratic slant on virtue:

One should defend virtue from the preachers of virtue: they are its worst enemies. For they teach virtue as an ideal *for everyone*; they take from virtue ... its aristocratic charm ... Virtue has all the instincts of the average man against it: it is unprofitable, imprudent, it isolates; it is related to passion and not very accessible to reason. (*KSA* 12: 517)

Nietzsche on occasion specifically affirms certain virtues that can apply to ethics. In *Daybreak* he names "the good four": honesty, bravery, magnanimity, and courtesy (*D* 556). In *Beyond Good and Evil* he names another set of virtues: courage, insight, solitude, and fellow-feeling (*BGE* 284).

In general virtue ethics is the most appropriate traditional model applicable to Nietzsche, but some hesitation is still called for. In *Beyond Good and Evil* (*BGE* 216) Nietzsche warns against the attribution of familiar moral words to the new values and possibilities he is promoting. These new horizons require a modesty and concealed goodness, which "forbids the mouth from using solemn words and virtue formulas." In *Beyond Good and Evil* (*BGE* 230) he says the same about "moral baubles and beads" such as honesty, love of wisdom, and even the "heroism" of truth-seeking. This is the section where Nietzsche directly names his naturalistic project: "to translate humanity back into nature," and nature does not support the elevation of humanity to some special higher status. That is why Nietzsche is suspicious of high-blown moral words, because such "verbal pageantry" is too much "human vanity."

What kind of moral philosophy can be located in Nietzsche's writings? He seems to posit different kinds of moral valuation in order to overcome the *exclusive* character of herd morality, which suppresses what he calls a "higher morality" (*BGE* 202), higher in the sense that it accords more with natural life forces and instincts, rather than anti-natural tendencies in traditional norms (*TI* Anti-nature, 5). Creative forces are what Nietzsche especially wants to esteem because they further life, but they come into conflict with normalized values that reflect conformity, stability, and normalization. When Nietzsche calls himself an immoralist it is really rhetorical hyperbole, and even there he associates it with an eclectic taste for the significance of all kinds of valuation, even the anti-natural sort (*TI* Anti-nature, 6). There is room for the values Nietzsche puts in question, but not as binary exclusions that rule out entirely what is disvalued. Nietzsche's genealogical challenge to certain norms is meant not to erase them but selectively situate them within certain aspects of life (*KSA* 12: 160–1). Nor is it meant to simply reverse a standard value and call for its opposite; as Nietzsche puts it in the context of religion, refuting God does not mean we are left with the devil (*BGE* 37).

It would be a mistake to interpret Nietzsche's texts as a call for suspending traditional moral prescriptions against killing, stealing, lying, abuse, violence, and so on; nowhere can we find blanket recommendations for such behaviors. Rather, Nietzsche wants to contextualize and problematize traditional values to undermine their isolation from earthly conditions of finitude, their pretense of purity, universality, and stability.

> It goes without saying that I do not deny – unless I am a fool – that many actions called unethical ought to be avoided and resisted, or that many called ethical ought to be done and encouraged – but I think they should be encouraged and avoided *for reasons other than hitherto*. We have to *learn to think differently* . . . (D 103)

Nietzsche's destabilization of traditional *belief systems* need not imply a renunciation of certain values operating in those systems. Indeed there may be hidden resources in Nietzsche's critique that can open up these values in a more existentially meaningful way. There are passages in Nietzsche's texts that suggest as much: One might uncover a deeper sense of morality by denying it and unsettling its assumptions and comfortable acceptance (GS 292); and overcoming moral prejudices in one's culture must include reorientation within it (GS 380).

The deconstruction of "good and evil" is concerned not with denying normative judgments but with supplanting the polar opposition of the good and the non-good. Such categorical segregation generates a number of mistakes and distortions in moral understanding: It encourages a hyper-confidence in the rectitude of one's sense of the good and the malignancy of otherness (which can instigate exclusion, oppression, or worse); it conceals the essential *ambiguity* in values, that no value is "pure" or immune from complicity with harmful effects; there are times when something deemed wrong can be worthy (see KSA 12: 477), in that what might seem cruel can be a proper challenge, or what is dangerous can produce good results.

If we consider Nietzsche's preference for the good–bad distinction over the good–evil distinction, we can conclude that moral distinctions and judgments regarding good and bad are possible in the light of Nietzsche's thinking, and even preferable to the distortions that follow from isolating the good from the non-good construed as evil. One and the same action can be called "evil" or "bad." In both cases there is a moral judgment, but the second term is favored from a Nietzschean perspective because it allows for the ambiguities and correlations that adhere to normative judgments. With the relational structure of good and bad, there can be no overarching principle of unambiguous moral purity, or judgments without remainder or regret, or hopes for the complete rectification of tensions within the moral field. What is lost here? Certain values or simply a certain way of interpreting these values?

We can make some headway by distinguishing the following: 1) moral commitments, decisions, and judgments that indicate particular estimations of better and worse ways of living, that reflect particular decisions about a normative affirmation or denial in an ethical context; 2) moral theories, formulas, and metaphysical foundations that have served to ground and guarantee moral judgments, which in effect decide the issue *for* us – we only have to conform our decisions to such measures to be in the right; 3) moral universalism and perfectionism, which suggest some transformed condition wherein normative differences and conflicts can be resolved or overcome in the light of a secure concept of the good; and 4) moral judgments that involve a condemnation of that which stands on the other side of the good – which tends toward practices of exclusion and demonization. I think that items 2, 3, and 4 can be targets of a Nietzschean critique; but the first item can be sustained, indeed it can be called an ethical version of the "groundless" creative posture championed by Nietzsche, as a moral move in life without guarantees. If I need theoretical assurance that feeding a hungry person is the right thing to do, or if I feel helpless in the face of indifference without a rational argument against it, Nietzsche might deem this a sign of slavish weakness or question whether my life is really empowered by my values.

ABBREVIATIONS

Cited numbers refer to text sections unless otherwise indicated; references to *KSA* are to volume and page number.

BGE *Beyond Good and Evil*, trans. Judith Norman (Cambridge University Press, 2002).
D *Daybreak*, trans. R.J. Hollingdale (Cambridge University Press, 1982).
GM *On the Genealogy of Morality*, ed. Keith Ansell-Pearson, trans. Carol Diethe (Cambridge University Press, 2007).
GS *The Gay Science*, trans. Josephine Nauckhoff (Cambridge University Press, 2001).
KSA *Sämtliche Werke: Kritische Studienausgabe*, ed. G. Colli and M. Montinari (Berlin: Walter de Gruyter, 1967).

TI   *Twilight of the Idols*, in *The Anti-Christ, Ecce Homo, Twilight of the Idols, and Other Writings*, trans. Judith Norman (Cambridge University Press, 2005).

Z   *Thus Spoke Zarathustra*, trans. Adrian Del Caro (Cambridge University Press, 2006).

BIBLIOGRAPHY

An asterisk denotes secondary literature especially suitable for further reading.

Acampora, Christa Davis, ed. 2006, *Nietzsche's* On the Genealogy of Morals: *Critical Essays*. Lanham, MD: Rowman & Littlefield.

Acampora, Christa Davis and Ansell Pearson, Keith, eds. 2011, *Nietzsche's* Beyond Good and Evil: *A Reader's Guide*. London: Bloomsbury.

Hatab, Lawrence 2008, *Nietzsche's* On the Genealogy of Morality: *An Introduction*. Cambridge University Press.

Hunt, Lester 1991, *Nietzsche and the Origin of Virtue*. London: Routledge.

Leiter, Brian and Sinhababu, Neil, eds. 2009, *Nietzsche and Morality*. Oxford University Press.*

May, Simon, ed. 2011, *Nietzsche's* On the Genealogy of Morality: *A Critical Guide*, Cambridge University Press.

Schacht, Richard, ed. 1994, *Nietzsche, Genealogy, Morality: Essays on Nietzsche's* Genealogy of Morals. Berkeley, CA: University of California Press.

Slote, Michael 1998, "Nietzsche and Virtue Ethics." *International Studies in Philosophy* 30/3, pp. 23–7.

Swanton, Christine 1998, "Outline of a Nietzschean Virtue Ethics." *International Studies in Philosophy* 30/3, pp. 29–38.

38

Marxism

JEFFREY REIMAN

Marxism has made three major contributions to recent moral philosophy.[1] The first is to stimulate a deep and wide-ranging discussion of the moral status of capitalism,[2] provoked by the attempt to determine whether the Marxian critique of capitalism is a moral critique and, if so, upon what moral ideal the critique is based. The second is to require moral philosophers to confront the problem of ideology. The third is to put on the table a vision of the good human life that is an alternative to the individualistic and egoistic view of human beings' good typical of modern capitalist societies. I shall take up the problem of the moral status of the Marxian critique of capitalism in the first section, and the problem of the ideological status of morality in the second. I close, in the third section, with a brief statement of Marx's view of the good human life.

MORALITY AND THE MARXIAN CRITIQUE OF CAPITALISM

Much recent discussion by Marxist moral philosophers has focused on determining whether Marx condemned capitalism, and called for its replacement by socialism or communism, on moral grounds. And if so, did Marx think that the appropriate moral grounds were those of justice, or of some other moral ideal?

The question whether the Marxist critique of capitalism is based on moral grounds is answered negatively by those who think that Marxism is simply a

---

[1] This essay draws on the following previously published writings of mine on the topic of Marx and moral philosophy: Reiman 1987a, 1991, 2012, 2013. Note that I generally assume here that readers know the basics of Marx's theory. For a brief summary, see Reiman 1987b, especially 34–9.

[2] "Moral" is used here in the standard sense, with no particular contrast to "ethical" implied.

science of history that aims to predict the necessary and inevitable breakdown of capitalism (with private ownership of means of production by a few) and its transformation, via revolution, first into socialism (state ownership of means of production), and eventually into communism (direct worker ownership of means of production).

But Marxism is not merely a scientific account of capitalism or of history; it is also an invitation to engage in practical activity aimed at replacing capitalism with communism. Such practical activity makes sense only if there is some norm implying the appropriateness of action aimed at the demise of capitalism and the establishment of communism. But is such a norm a *moral* norm? Not all norms are moral norms. Ideal body weight, high marks in school, health, efficiency, and cleanliness are examples of non-moral norms. Allen Wood contends that Marx saw nothing morally wrong with capitalism, and condemned it because it gives rise to non-moral evils: it cripples human creativity and engenders alienation and servitude.[3] However, since moral systems often take human flourishing (including both creativity and sociability) and liberation from servitude as moral goods, there is no definitive reason to deny that Marx's criticisms here are moral (whether or not he saw them that way).

Wood was among the first of recent philosophers to deny that Marx condemned capitalism as unjust. Wood supports this claim with a variety of quotes from Marx, perhaps the most impressive being the following from *Capital*: "that . . . the value which its [the worker's labor-power] use during one day creates is double what he [the capitalist] pays for that use . . . is, without doubt, a good piece of luck for the buyer, but by no means an injustice to the seller."[4] Note that it is precisely this difference between what the capitalist pays for the worker's labor, and what the capitalist gets from that labor, that enables Marx to claim that capitalist profit is based on unpaid labor.

Wood also points out that, in the *Critique of the Gotha Program*, Marx characterizes notions like that of "fair distribution" as "obsolete verbal rubbish" and "ideological . . . humbug so common among the democrats and French Socialists."[5] Also in *Gotha*, Marx contends that rights invariably take people in a one-sided fashion (my right to my wage is based on viewing me as worker and nothing else, such as, husband, father, etc.) and, since people are different in their various facets, this one-sidedness means that rights give effect to inequality (when a childless worker and a worker with several children receive equal wages for equal work, the former is effectively

---

[3] Wood 1981: 43; see also Wood 1972, 1979.   [4] Marx 1967a: 194.   [5] Marx 1974b: 347–8.

made richer than the latter). On such grounds, Marx maintains that the worker's equal right to an amount of goods that took as much labor to produce as he has performed (which Marx puts forth as the imperfect distributive standard of the first stage of communism, generally called "socialism") is a right "of inequality, just like any other right," and he goes on to assert that the final stage of communism will be governed by the principle "From each according to his ability, to each according to his needs."[6]

Wood takes this latter principle as not concerned with equality or with rights, and thus not a principle of justice at all.[7] This is implausible, however, considering that Marx moves from the socialist distributive standard to the communist standard precisely because the socialist standard leads to inequality.

The late G.A. Cohen responded to Wood's argument by pointing out that there are passages in Marx's writings where he characterizes the very same extraction of unpaid surplus labor that we saw him earlier calling "no injustice" to the worker as "theft of another's labour-time."[8] Writes Cohen: "since, as Wood will agree, Marx did not think that by capitalist criteria the capitalist steals, and since he did think he steals, he must have meant that he steals in some appropriately non-relativist sense. And since to steal is, in general, wrongly to take what rightly belongs to another, to steal is to commit an injustice, and a system which is 'based on theft' is based on injustice." Cohen then concludes "that anyone who thinks capitalism is robbery must be treated as someone who thinks capitalism is unjust, even if he does not realize that he thinks it is." Given that Marx sometimes denies that capitalism is unjust, Cohen concludes: "at least sometimes, Marx mistakenly thought that Marx did not believe that capitalism was unjust."[9]

Another writer who denies that Marx's critique of capitalism is based on justice is Robert Tucker.[10] Tucker contends that Marx's moral ideal is embodied in communism, and communism is an ideal *beyond justice*. Justice, contends Tucker, is an ideal for resolving conflicts of interest between individuals. Rights generally limit what one person can do to another ("your right to swing your fist ends where my nose begins"), or they give one person a claim on another's action (rights to education or welfare, for example) whether or not that other wants so to act. Accordingly, the ideal of justice assumes that people stand in antagonistic rather than cooperative relations to one another. Communism, by contrast, is held to be an ideal of communal

---

[6] Marx, 1974b: 347.   [7] Wood 1979: 292; cf. Reiman 1983: 157–9.
[8] Cohen 1983b: 443; Marx 1974c: 705.   [9] Cohen 1983b: 444.   [10] Tucker 1970: 42–53.

solidarity in which antagonistic relations have been overcome, and people do not require justice or rights to get what they want or need. Taking justice as the highest ideal for society, then, does ideological work for capitalism by conveying the notion that human conflict is inevitable, and thus proposals for eliminating antagonistic social relations are unrealistic.

But one can hold *both* that we should eliminate antagonistic social relations *and* that things should be distributed justly among people. Consider this analogy: That members of happy families need not insist on their rights, or even think about them, does not imply that they do not, or should not, have those rights. On this analogy, the elimination of antagonistic social relations, or of conflict generally, has the effect that people's claims for justice are satisfied easily, so easily in fact that people need not press those claims. They may not even have to think about justice. Then, the sign that people in capitalism are in antagonistic relations is not that people *have* rights, but that they must *insist* on their rights, even *fight* for them at law or in the streets. That communism has overcome antagonistic relations will be known, not by the fact that rights have been transcended, but by the fact that people's rights are satisfied so easily and spontaneously that people never need to appeal to justice, maybe never even need to think about it. On this view, the belief that communism is *beyond justice* is a mistake that results from taking the fact that justice will not be noticed when antagonistic relations are eliminated, for the absence of justice. Then communism is just, not beyond justice.

Another version of the argument that Marx's moral ideal is beyond justice is Allen Buchanan's claim that for Marx the chief evil of capitalism is *alienation*.[11] Primarily in his early writings, especially "The Economic and Philosophical Manuscripts of 1844," Marx speaks of capitalism as estranging the worker from his product (the product is not only owned by another, but adds to the other's power over the worker), estranging the worker from his labor (rather than a spontaneous and free expression of his creative powers, his labor is a task shaped and imposed on him by the capitalist as the price of his living at all), estranging the worker from his fellow human beings (worker and capitalist stand in hostile relations, and workers themselves become adversaries as they compete for jobs).[12]

Marx surely thought that capitalism was alienating in these ways. However, there are several reasons for doubting that this is Marx's core criticism of capitalism. First of all, after his early writings, Marx rarely speaks of alienation. Talk of alienation is largely retired by Marx after the 1840s. After

[11] Buchanan 1982: 36–49. [12] Marx 1975: 322ff.

that, it shows up in the *Grundrisse* which, however, Marx chose not to publish. Moreover, since alienation happens not only between workers and capitalists, but among workers themselves and among capitalists themselves, focus on alienation blurs the centrality of the class relation to the Marxian critique. Likewise, because alienation pervades capitalist society, this focus undermines the Marxian emphasis on production. By contrast, when Marx tells us that labor in capitalism is coercive (because capitalists control the means of earning a living, and thus workers have little choice but to work for capitalists), or that wage-workers are slaves (because forced to work in part without pay), these evils directly characterize the capitalist class relation and its system of production. Then, the alienation that coercion and slavery no doubt breed is a symptom of this core evil, not its essence.[13]

George Brenkert emphasizes that the products alienated from the worker stand against him as fetters on his freedom, and puts this idea forward as an alternative to the view that Marx condemned capitalism as unjust.[14] But this is a false opposition: protection of freedom is commonly part of the ideal of justice.

Among those who think that Marx condemned capitalism because it is unjust is John Rawls. Rawls holds that Marx believed that justice included a right of all to access to the means of production, which is obviously violated by private ownership of the means of production by a small number of capitalists.[15] Rawls also contends that, rather than transcending principles of justice, the standard "From each according to his ability, to each according to his need" is a principle of justice affirming everyone's equal right to self-realization.[16]

The best known of recent Marxist philosophers to defend the view that Marxism condemns capitalism as unjust is G.A. Cohen. I have already mentioned Cohen's argument for holding that this was Marx's view (even if Marx was mistaken about what Marx believed). But Cohen also argues that injustice is a necessary presupposition of the Marxian condemnation of capitalist exploitation. Cohen contends that, even if owning the means of production enables the capitalist to force the worker to work longer than the amount of labor-time the worker gets back in his wage, this won't count as exploitation *if the capitalist is justly entitled to own the means of production*.[17] In that case, the capitalist acts within his rights when he allows the worker to use the means of production in return for the worker's excess labor-time, and no charge of exploitation can be sustained.[18]

---

[13] See Reiman 1987a.   [14] Brenkert 1981.   [15] Rawls 2007: 354.   [16] Rawls 2007: 343.
[17] Cohen 1983a: 316; see also Roemer 1982 and 1985; Buchanan 1987; Reiman 1987a.
[18] Cohen 1983b: 445.

This argument seems basically sound. Exploitation is a morally-freighted term. It should only be used about an extraction of labor that is in some sense wrong. Otherwise, we will have to call it exploitation if we force criminals to work as punishment. Given that behaviors just like exploitation (e.g., forcing prisoners to labor for the state) are not exploitative though they have its consequences, then exploitation must be wrong because it's exploitation, not because of its effects. The wrong must be in the extraction of labor itself, and since the extraction is a kind of taking of something by one person from another, the wrong seems to be theft, and thus injustice.

The problem with Cohen's position, however, is that he takes the injustice of exploitation to be a distributive injustice – an injustice in the distribution of property. But Marx primarily criticizes capitalism for its coerciveness, for enslaving workers – not merely for robbing workers of surplus value, but for forcing them to produce that surplus. On these grounds, I hold that Marx primarily criticizes capitalism in light of a conception of *social* justice that does not aim at some ideal distribution of things. It aims, rather, at an ideal social relation in which human beings stand to one another as "equal sovereigns" – each equally free to direct his own destiny, and to participate in directing the destiny he shares with others.

This ideal social relation resonates with Marx's famous call that the "life-process of society, which is based on the process of material production" be "treated as production by freely associated men, and ... consciously regulated by them in accordance with a settled plan."[19] And it supports the idea that Marx condemned capitalism for its injustice and recommended communism because of its justice. Protection of equal freedom (or liberty) is central to all modern conceptions of justice. For example, Rawls's first principle of justice is one that guarantees each person the greatest possible set of liberties compatible with the same for all. Thus, one could accept Brenkert's view that Marx condemned capitalism because of its coerciveness and still hold that Marx opposed capitalism because it was unjust. And, versus Cohen, its injustice would not be primarily distributive.

IDEOLOGY AND THE MARXIAN CRITIQUE OF MORALITY

Marx believed that ideology is part of how exploitative societies, such as capitalism, continue to exist. Ideology protects exploitative societies by *mis*-representing them as morally acceptable. Ideology is not primarily conscious

[19] Marx 1967a: 80.

lies or propaganda because it is widely believed, even by the ruling class. For Marx, ideology is a reflection in ideal and idealizing terms of the material conditions in the society. "The ruling ideas are nothing more than the ideal expression of the dominant material relationships, the dominant material relationships grasped as ideas."[20] Ideology works because the moral ideals in terms of which we judge a society (such as capitalism) arise from that society as an idealized version of what is actually there. When we judge what is actually in capitalism against these ideals, capitalism will naturally approximate those ideals and thus appear to be good and justified.

Consider the moral ideal of *liberalism*. Liberalism is the belief that freedom – effectively defined by John Stuart Mill, in *On Liberty*, as absence of physical interference with people's actions – is the most important moral value in terms of which societies are to be judged. So defined, capitalism appears free and thus morally justified. As we have seen, for Marx, this appearance is in an important sense false. The appearance of freedom arises from the fact that, for Marx, the force in capitalism is not physical interference, but the leverage that owners of means of production have over non-owners. To understand how liberal ideology works, then, we need to understand how its conception of freedom as absence of physical interference arises from the way that capitalism actually is.

Capitalism *is* free in the sense that the sale of labor-power and other commodities occurs with both parties to any transaction prohibited from using violence to get the other to come to terms. This is clearest in "the sphere of exchange," of which Marx wrote that "There alone rule[s] Freedom ... because both buyer and seller of a commodity, say of labour-power, are constrained only by their own free will."[21]

Since physical coercion is the most vivid threat to freedom, and since it is one that people experience or fear from childhood on, it is normal to see capitalist trades or exchanges as free. Moreover, since such free exchanges initiate employment in capitalism – the worker's employment begins with an agreement to exchange work for wages, an agreement that the capitalist cannot legally force upon the worker – it is as natural to see free exchanges as the basis for all capitalist relations, as it is to see the earth as the fixed ground against which the sun rises. Thus, it becomes natural for members of capitalist societies to view capitalism generally as free.

Furthermore, since capitalism requires freedom – in the sense of absence of overt violence – in exchange, capitalism survives only if exchange relationships are normally free in this sense. Members of capitalist societies will naturally

[20] Marx and Engels 1978: 64.   [21] Marx 1967a: 176.

come to see such freedom as the (at first, statistical) norm, and overt violence as something "abnormal," to be resisted or corrected. As people come to expect it, the statistical norm is subtly transformed into a moral norm, and people will naturally assume that the freedom they value morally is the absence of overt violence.

This gives us the main elements of a Marxian account of liberalism. With its characteristic definition of freedom as *freedom from* physical impediment or harm, the moral ideal of liberalism is "read off" the face of capitalist exchange. And then the ideological alchemy works directly: Since members of capitalist societies get their conception of freedom from capitalism, without recognizing its source, they naturally find that capitalism approximates their ideal.

In addition to liberalism, the major contemporary moral doctrines are Kantianism, social contractarianism, and utilitarianism. In the remainder of this section, I shall suggest how each might be viewed as embodying a moral ideal that is *read off the face of capitalist exchange*, with the effect that each such doctrine is congenitally biased in capitalism's favor. For ease of identification, I shall number the paragraphs in which each of the three moral doctrines is taken up.

1. Kantianism takes the autonomous person – distinguished by her capacity to subject her behavior to her rational will – as the keystone of its moral teaching. Moral rules are those principles that autonomous persons could consistently will to be applied universally to all persons. Murder is immoral because a person cannot consistently will that all human beings have the right to kill their fellows at their discretion, since that would require that the person will that others have the right to kill her, which conflicts with her own will to stay alive and to pursue her purposes. The idea that morality is equivalent to the principles that all persons could freely will is an idealization of capitalist exchanges, since, as Marx says of the agreement reached in capitalist exchange, it "is but the form in which they give expression to their common will."[22]

What's more, since Kant's notion of rational will is of a will that is independent of material obstacles and inclinations, emphasis on it has the effect of discounting the effects of material inequality on the relative power and thus real freedom of individuals. Kant saw that accumulation of property could lead to significant inequality such that "the welfare of one very much

---

[22] Marx 1967a: 176.

depends on the will of another (that of the poor on the rich), [and thus] one must obey ... while the other commands, one must serve (as laborer) while the other pays."[23] This too reflects capitalist exchange, since exchangers treat each other as equal in their freedom to dispose of what they own – accordingly, their freedom is "equal" in spite of even vast differences in what they happen to own. This supports capitalism by inclining us to believe that, in the morally important respects, the owner of nothing but labor-power is equal in freedom to the owner of factories with whom he enters into contractual agreement.

Generalized to cover such issues as just punishment, Kant's view naturally treats the criminal's economic deprivation as irrelevant to his freedom to commit crime and thus to his deservingness of punishment. In an article on "Capital Punishment," in the *New York Daily Tribune* of February 18, 1853, Marx commented that "there is only one theory of punishment which recognizes human dignity in the abstract, and that is the theory of Kant," but he went on to add that this theory:

> has but given a transcendental sanction to the rules of existing society. Is it not a delusion to substitute for the real individual with his real motives, with multifarious social circumstances pressing upon him, the abstraction of "free will"?[24]

2. Social contractarianism, in its classical form, is the view that the principles of justice for societies are those that it would be rational for all human beings to agree to in a "state of nature." In the state of nature, human beings lack political institutions to resolve conflicts between them. People are taken as self-interested and self-aggrandizing, and thus naturally prone to conflict with their fellows. Accordingly, it is rational for them to agree to some set of political institutions that would keep conflicts from bursting into open warfare. Moreover, since people are self-interested and self-aggrandizing, they find it in their interest to have some system of private property such that each is able to own the products of his own efforts. Consequently, classical contractarians – Hobbes and Locke – ended up justifying a state that protects people against violence, and an economy based on the capitalist right to private property.

Where did the classical contractarians get their notion that human beings in a natural setting are self-interested and self-aggrandizing? Marx held that capitalist societies are divided into public and private realms: the state characterized by shared laws and equal rights, and civil society marked by

---

[23] Kant 1983: 73.   [24] Marx 1959: 487.

competitive pursuit of personal gain, and unequal success in that pursuit. People in capitalist societies are equal citizens in the state, and unequal egoistic individuals in civil society. Of this distinction, Marx writes in *On the Jewish Question*, "man as he is a member of civil society is taken to be the real man, man as distinct from citizen, since he is man in his sensuous, individual and immediate existence, whereas political man is simply abstract, artificial man."[25] What the classical contractarians took as man in the natural condition is man as he appears in civil society, that is, as an egoistic participant in capitalist economic exchanges.[26] If the social contract reads its conception of human nature off the face of capitalism, it is no surprise that the economy that social contractarians find ideally suited to human nature is capitalism.

3. Classical utilitarianism takes the satisfaction of people's desires to be the measure of goodness, and thus it views arrangements which maximize the aggregate satisfaction of all people's desires as morally good and just. There are several ways in which this doctrine reflects aspects of capitalist exchange. Utilitarianism's view of human motivation is that each person pursues what increases his or her satisfaction. This view comes of taking human beings as they function in exchange as one's model of human nature, since free people will only exchange if they think they are made better off by what they get compared to what they give for it. Furthermore, utilitarianism assumes that all human behaviors – no matter how unique or particular – can be translated into a common measure: satisfaction or "utility." This is what occurs in exchange, where unique and particular human productive endeavors are resolved into a common currency: money. In the *German Ideology*, Marx and Engels wrote,

> The apparent stupidity of merging all the manifold relations of people in the *one* relation of usefulness ... arises from the fact that, in modern bourgeois society, all relations are subordinated in practice to the one abstract monetary-commercial relation ... [T]hese relations are supposed ... to be the expression and manifestation of some third relation introduced in their place, the relation of utility ...[27]

To utilitarianism has been added the idea that interpersonal comparisons between different people's satisfactions are impossible.[28] Individuals can know what gives them satisfaction, but no one can know if one person's satisfaction is equal to, or more or less than, another's satisfaction. This

---

[25] Marx 1975: 234. [26] See Macpherson 1962. [27] Marx and Engels 1978: 109, 110. [28] See Rawls 1999: 282–5.

implies that we cannot know that redistributing from the wealthy to the poor will increase overall utility. The loss to the wealthy might cause them more dissatisfaction than the satisfaction created by giving some of their wealth to the poor. So utilitarianism cannot be used to justify redistribution of wealth.

That the main theories and ideals of modern moral philosophy can be seen to reproduce features of capitalism, particularly capitalist exchange, must make us suspicious of the popularity of these theories and ideals. Have they been so widely accepted because of their inherent appeal, or because they subtly remind us of the relations around us that we have taken to be normal – in all senses of that term? And what of the particular moral principles that emerge from these approaches? Do they subtly reinforce our allegiance to the capitalist system? Do they promote the interests of capitalists at the expense of workers while pretending to be disinterested?

If moral beliefs serve the interests of some at the expense of others, their moral status is dubious. If morality functions ideologically then it stops being morality. Consequently, moral philosophy cannot establish the moral credentials of any putative moral principle without adequately defending it against the suspicion that it is ideology. Thus, Marxism forces the problem of ideology onto the agenda of moral philosophy.

MARX'S VISION OF THE GOOD HUMAN LIFE

Karl Marx did not provide a systematic analysis of the moral good.[29] He did, however, have a moral vision – a view of the good human life – that has proven quite influential. We can get to this vision by considering what Marx took to be evils of capitalist society and projecting from them to what he thought a good human society would be like. From our analysis to this point, we can see that Marx identified three evils of capitalism: it is unjust in that it coerces workers to work without pay; it alienates people from their fellows, from their work, and from nature; and, finally, it is shrouded with ideology that keeps people from seeing the true nature of their society.

Marx imagined that the coercive nature of capitalism would be ended in two stages, a socialist stage in which workers owned the means of production via the state, and a communist stage in which workers directly owned the means of production. In these forms, workers would no longer be forced to work for capitalists, though they might be forced to work by necessity. Marx thought that technology would reduce necessary work to a minimum.

[29] Kamenka 1969: 2.

But only with communism is full freedom achieved. Under communism, distribution is governed by the principle: "From each according to his ability, to each according to his needs" which frees workers because it severs the tie between labor and reward.[30] Since labor is no longer the price of (earning a) living, workers are no longer forced to work: "the full and free development of every individual forms the ruling principle."[31] Since no one owns the means of production privately, no one gains profit in the form of uncompensated labor. The injustice of capitalism is cured. Then, there is no need for ideology, and society "strip[s] off its mystical veil."[32]

In this condition, people are no longer alienated from their labor or from the nature upon which they work: "labour has become not only a means of life but life's prime want."[33] People labor for the love of creative activity, for the pleasure of self-expression, and for the rich social life their labor sustains. Since workers no longer have to compete with each other to get what they need, they are no longer alienated from one another. Rather, their natural sociability flourishes and people cooperate freely.

Here then we see the outlines of Marx's vision of the good human life: a social existence in which human beings live and work cooperatively with their fellows, see their society accurately, and labor freely for their own satisfaction and self-expression, at home in their bodies and in the natural world.

BIBLIOGRAPHY

An asterisk denotes secondary literature especially suitable for further reading.

Bottomore, Tom, ed. (1983) "Morals," in *A Dictionary of Marxist Thought*, Cambridge, Mass.: Harvard University Press, pp. 341–2.*

Brenkert, G.G. (1981) "Marx's Critique of Utilitarianism," in Nielsen and Patten 1981: 193–220.

Buchanan, Allen E. (1982) *Marx and Justice: The Radical Critique of Liberalism*, Totowa, N.J.: Rowman and Littlefield.

Buchanan, Allen E. (1987) "Marx, Morality, and History: An Assessment of Recent Analytical Work on Marx," *Ethics* 98, no. 1, pp. 104–36.

Cohen, G.A. (1979) "The Labour Theory of Value and the Concept of Exploitation," *Philosophy and Public Affairs* 8, no. 4, pp. 338–60.

Cohen, G.A. (1981) "Freedom, Justice and Capitalism," *New Left Review*, no. 126, pp. 3–16.

Cohen, G.A. (1983a) "More on Exploitation and the Labour Theory of Value," *Inquiry* 26, no. 3, pp. 309–31.

Cohen, G.A. (1983b) "Review of Allen Wood's *Karl Marx*," *Mind* 92, no. 367, pp. 440–5.

[30] Marx 1978: 531.   [31] Marx 1967a: 592.   [32] Marx 1967a: 80.   [33] Marx 1978: 531.

Cohen, M., Nagel, T., and Scanlon, T., eds. (1980) *Marx, Justice, and History*, Princeton University Press.

Engels, Friedrich (1967) "Socialism, Utopian and Scientific," *Engels: Selected Writings*, ed. W. Henderson, Harmondsworth and London: Penguin Books, pp. 185–225.

Geras, Norman (1985) "The Controversy about Marx and Justice," *New Left Review*, no. 150, pp. 47–85.*

Godelier, Maurice (1977) "Structure and Contradiction in *Capital*," in *Ideology in Social Science: Readings in Critical Social Theory*, ed. Robin Blackburn, London: Fontana, pp. 334–68.

Husami, Ziyad I. (1978) "Marx on Distributive Justice," *Philosophy and Public Affairs* 8, no. 1, pp. 27–64.

Kamenka, Eugene (1969) *Marxism and Ethics*, London: Macmillan.

Kant, Immanuel (1983) "On the Proverb: That May Be True in Theory, But Is of No Practical Use," in *Perpetual Peace and Other Essays*, Indianapolis, Ind.: Hackett Publishing Company.

Macpherson, C.B. (1962) *The Political Theory of Possessive Individualism: Hobbes to Locke*, Oxford University Press.

Marx, Karl (1959) "Capital Punishment," in L.S. Feuer, ed., *Marx and Engels: Basic Writings on Politics and Philosophy*, Garden City, N.Y.: Doubleday Anchor.

Marx, Karl (1967a) *Capital*, vol. 1, trans. Samuel Moore and Edward Aveling, New York: International Publishers.

Marx, Karl (1967b) *Capital*, vol. 3, New York: International Publishers.

Marx, Karl (1974a) *Political Writings*, vol. 1: *The Revolutions of 1848*, ed. David Fernbach, "Marx Library," New York: Random House/Vintage and Monthly Review; Harmondsworth and London: Penguin Books and New Left Review, 1973.

Marx, Karl (1974b) *Political Writings*, vol. 3: *The First International and After*, ed. David Fernbach, "Marx Library," New York: Random House/Vintage and Monthly Review; Harmondsworth and London: Penguin Books and New Left Review.

Marx, Karl (1974c) *Grundrisse*, trans. Martin Nicolaus, "Marx Library," New York: Random House/Vintage and Monthly Review; Harmondsworth and London: Penguin Books and New Left Review.

Marx, Karl (1975) *Early Writings*, trans. Rodney Livingstone and Gregor Benton, "Marx Library," New York: Random House/Vintage and Monthly Review; Harmondsworth and London: Penguin Books and New Left Review.

Marx, Karl (1978) *The Marx–Engels Reader*, ed. Robert C. Tucker, New York: Norton.

Marx, Karl, and Engels, Friedrich (1978) *The German Ideology*, Part One with selections from Parts Two and Three, ed. C.J. Arthur, New York: International Publishers.

Mill, John Stuart (1978) *On Liberty*, Indianapolis, Ind.: Hackett Publishing Company.

Nielsen, K., and Patten, S., eds. (1981) *Marx and Morality, Canadian Journal of Philosophy*, supplemental vol. 7.

Pashukanis, Evgeny B. (1978) *Law and Marxism: A General Theory*, trans. Barbara Einhorn, London: Ink Links.

Paul, E., Miller, F., Paul, J., and Ahrens, J., eds. (1986) *Marxism and Liberalism*, Oxford: Blackwell.

Pennock, J., and Chapman, J., eds. (1983) *Marxism: Nomos XXVI*, New York University Press.

Rawls, John (1999) *A Theory of Justice*, revised edn, Cambridge, Mass.: Harvard University Press.

Rawls, John (2007) *Lectures on the History of Political Philosophy*, Cambridge, Mass.: Harvard University Press.

Reiman, Jeffrey (1983) "The Labor Theory of the Difference Principle," *Philosophy and Public Affairs* 12, no. 2, pp. 133–59.

Reiman, Jeffrey (1987a) "Exploitation, Force, and the Moral Assessment of Capitalism: Thoughts on Roemer and Cohen," *Philosophy and Public Affairs* 16, no. 1, pp. 3–41.

Reiman, Jeffrey (1987b) "The Marxian Critique of Criminal Justice," *Criminal Justice Ethics* 6, no. 1, pp. 30–50.*

Reiman, Jeffrey (1991) "Moral Philosophy: The Critique of Capitalism and the Problem of Ideology," in T. Carver (ed.), *Cambridge Companion to Marx*, New York: Cambridge University Press, pp. 143–67.

Reiman, Jeffrey (2012) *As Free and as Just as Possible: The Theory of Marxian Liberalism*, Boston, Mass.: Wiley-Blackwell.

Reiman, Jeffrey (2013) "Marx, Karl," in Hugh Lafollette (ed.), *The International Encyclopedia of Ethics*, Boston, Mass.: Wiley-Blackwell, pp. 3117–23.

Roemer, John (1982) "Property Relations vs. Surplus Value in Marxian Exploitation," *Philosophy and Public Affairs* 11, no. 4, pp. 281–313.

Roemer, John (1985) "Should Marxists Be Interested in Exploitation?," *Philosophy and Public Affairs* 14, no. 1, pp. 30–65.

Tucker, Robert C. (1970) *The Marxian Revolutionary Idea*, New York: W.W. Norton

Wood, Allen W. (1972) "The Marxian Critique of Justice," *Philosophy and Public Affairs* 1, no. 3, pp. 244–82.*

Wood, Allen W. (1979) "Marx on Right and Justice: A Reply to Husami," *Philosophy and Public Affairs* 8, no. 3, pp. 267–95.

Wood, Allen W. (1981) *Karl Marx*, London: Routledge and Kegan Paul.

39

Sidgwick

KATARZYNA DE LAZARI-RADEK

HENRY SIDGWICK AND *THE METHODS OF ETHICS*

John Rawls wrote that Henry Sidgwick's (1838–1900) *The Methods of Ethics* is "the first truly academic work in moral philosophy which undertakes to provide a systematic comparative study of moral conceptions." The book, first published in 1874 and revised six times, was an important step in developing meta-ethics, the field of philosophy that became so popular in the twentieth century and remains so up to this day. The author's aim in *The Methods* was to present and compare the different ways of reasoning that we use when we need to decide what we ought to do. He explained that he undertook this task not to develop one "harmonious system" but rather to "afford aid towards the construction of such a system." Although he did not want the book to be a defence of one particular method of reasoning, by the end of the treatise it is not hard to see that Sidgwick inclines towards utilitarianism.

These ways of reasoning are called by Sidgwick "methods." He defines a method as "any rational procedure by which we determine what individual human beings 'ought' – or what it is 'right' for them – to do, or to seek to realize by voluntary action" (ME: 1).[1] Though his starting point in looking for such methods is "the common sense of mankind," he does not see his role as a philosopher in just describing the common thought but rather in systematizing it and, most importantly, in ensuring that it produces internally consistent conclusions. If our reasoning produces conclusions that are inconsistent, a philosopher should revise them. According to Sidgwick it is "a fundamental postulate of Ethics, that so far as two methods conflict, one or other of them must be modified or rejected" (ME: 6). He discusses three

---

[1] References in brackets in the text are to Sidgwick 1907, *The Methods of Ethics*.

methods: egoism, which states that we ought to aim at our own goꝺ intuitionism, which prescribes following certain rules regardless of theiɩ consequences, and utilitarianism, which claims we ought to aim at the good of all.

In the introduction to *On What Matters*, Derek Parfit writes that "Sidgwick's book contains the largest number of true and important claims."[2] What might they be? Here are a number of most important claims that Sidgwick viewed as justifiable.

REASON AND ETHICAL JUDGMENT

In Chapter 3 of Book 1 on "Ethical Judgments" Sidgwick opposes Hume's claim that moral judgments are statements about feelings of approbation or aversion.

> [T]he ordinary moral . . . judgments which, in the case of all or most minds, have some – though often an inadequate – influence on volition, cannot legitimately be interpreted as judgments respecting the present or future existence of human feelings or any facts of the sensible world. (ME: 25)

Sidgwick is an objectivist who believes that reason is not a "slave to the passions" but rather a guide which presents objectively true moral judgments about what we ought to do. Sidgwick is ready to accept that the feeling of approbation, which we may call "moral sentiment," may accompany moral judgments but considers it absurd to say that the proposition "Truth ought to be spoken" expresses only the existence of the feeling of approbation of truthspeaking in me. If we utter the sentence with a belief that truth should be spoken, then we are convinced that truthspeaking is *really* right (ME: 27). Sidgwick might have added that in such a case we are ready to present reasons for that. If however we believe that such propositions are only expressions of feelings, then even if two people have apparently contradictory ethical propositions they can do nothing else but accept that they have different feelings about it, in which case they cannot really be contradicting each other. Further on, Sidgwick says that a moral judgment is "a possible object of knowledge" and knowledge cannot be contradictory – if something is true, it must be true for all the people under the same circumstances (ME: 33).

---

[2] Parfit 2011: xxxiii.

According to Sidgwick moral judgments have motivating force in rational beings to undertake the right action – knowing the truth of a moral judgment provides an impulse or motive for action. This view again is contrary to Hume, who claims that only desires can move us to act. Sidgwick is ready to accept, however, that human beings as such are not fully rational – in practice we are often guided not only by our reason but also by our desires or passions, which sometimes may overpower reason. Therefore, he is ready to accept other motives, such as a feeling of love or appreciation, if only they lead to the right action.

In the above quote Sidgwick says that moral judgments describe neither our feelings, nor any other physical or psychological facts of the world. He rejects those theories that refer to nature or our natural dispositions, feelings, abilities, etc. in order to decide what we should do. The terms that we use in moral judgments are of a special, non-natural kind. He explains this in another place, where he anticipates Moore's rejection of the naturalistic fallacy:

> [T]he fundamental notion represented by the word "ought" or "right," which such judgments contain expressly or by implication, being essentially different from all notions representing facts of physical or psychical experience.
> (ME: 25)

THE FAILURE OF COMMON SENSE MORALITY

Sidgwick is looking for self-evident moral judgments that could be treated as axioms and that could serve as guidelines for action. It is believed, he says, that common sense morality is able to present us with such axioms. He devotes most of Book 3 to a close look at different common sense rules that correspond to virtues such as: wisdom, self-control, benevolence, justice, good faith, veracity, prudence, and purity. He examines whether common sense can present us with self-evident principles. He concludes:

> [P]hilosophers have too easily been led to satisfy themselves with ethical formulae which implicitly accept the morality of Common Sense en bloc, ignoring its defects.
> (ME: 374)

Some of these defects are as follows. At first glance those rules seem self-evident and clear but when we try to use them in particular cases, under different circumstances, we notice that they are not precise enough and we are unable to learn what the right action is from this particular principle. The terms used in those rules are not clear either. Take the example of truthful-ness. Most of us would agree that we should tell the truth and avoid lying but when we think of specific cases, this agreement collapses. Must we tell the truth to a person who will use it to hurt us? Can a lawyer, in defending his client, intentionally create false beliefs in the jury? Is it incompatible with truthfulness to take part in religious ceremonies that require us to utter words that we believe to be literally false? Common sense morality does not say that truthfulness is an absolute rule that should be obeyed always by all means, but it also does not make it clear when exactly we are allowed to break it. From the examples of common sense agreeing with lying to small children or gravely ill patients, Sidgwick draws a conclusion that it is a "benevolent deception" which is permitted in some cases. In other words, common sense has to refer to a distinct principle of utility in order to be a guide to action. If so, the principle of telling the truth is not an independent principle and cannot be an axiom. Apart from a decision problem, there is another problem with explaining what the virtue of veracity consists of. For example, common sense cannot give a clear answer whether it is a form of deception if, when keeping a secret is important for the wellbeing of society, we say something that is not really a lie but is intended to lead our inter-locutor to form false beliefs.

SELF-EVIDENT PRINCIPLES

If common sense morality cannot present us with self-evident moral judg-ments, how are we supposed to reach them? How will we know that a principle is really self-evident? Sidgwick presents four conditions that a self-evident proposition has to meet.

> The terms of the proposition must be clear and precise. (ME: 338)

> The self-evidence of the proposition must be ascertained by careful reflection.
> (ME: 339)

> The propositions accepted as self-evident must be mutually consistent. (ME: 341)

> To the extent that other equally competent judges deny the truth of a proposition that I hold, my own confidence in the truth of that proposition should be reduced, and if I have no more reason to suspect that the other judges are mistaken than I have to suspect that I am mistaken, this should lead me, at least temporarily, to "a state of neutrality."
> (paraphrased from ME: 341–2)

After giving these conditions, Sidgwick presents his own remedy in the shape of three axioms that he takes to be self-evident.

> It cannot be right for A to treat B in a manner in which it would be wrong for B to treat A, merely on the ground that they are two different individuals, and without there being any difference between the natures or circumstances of the two which can be stated as a reasonable ground for difference of treatment.
> (ME: 380)

This is what Sidgwick calls the principle of justice, which requires that rules should be applied impartially as far as mere difference of persons is concerned. It does not however yet tell us what this thing that should be done impartially is. He does that in the next two principles.

> Hereafter *as such* is to be regarded neither less nor more than Now.
> (ME: 381)

This is the principle of prudence, which comes from his concern that we should aim at our own good "on the whole" and not only parts of it. The principle encourages us to give equal consideration to all moments of our own existence. It does not say that under certain circumstances we should not prefer a present good to a future good – it may be that the present good is more certain than the future one or it may happen that a week some time in the future may be more important to us than a week now, because we expect that our abilities to enjoy it will increase during the interim. It does not let us say, however, that one week is more important than another *simply* because it is nearer or further away in time. The principle as such does not imply egoism but Sidgwick does treat it as part of the basis for the method of egoism.

Sidgwick reaches the third of his axioms by pointing out that just as we can talk about the good on the whole of an individual person, summing up parts of the good in his life, we can also talk about universal good as a sum of particular goods of all individuals. In this way we reach a further self-evident principle:

> ... the good of any one individual is of no more importance, from the point of view (if I may say so) of the Universe, than the good of any other; unless, that is, there are special grounds for believing that more good is likely to be realised in the one case than in the other.
> (ME: 382)

Sidgwick then makes a further claim:

> And it is evident to me that as a rational being I am bound to aim at good generally, – so far as it is attainable by my efforts, – not merely at a particular part of it.
> (ME: 382)

From these two rational intuitions, Sidgwick deduces the principle of benevolence:[3]

> ... each one is morally bound to regard the good of any other individual as much as his own, except in so far as he judges it to be less, when impartially viewed, or less certainly knowable or attainable by him.   (ME: 382)

The principle of benevolence orders us to aim at the good of all people impartially and for Sidgwick it is the basis for utilitarianism.

EGOISM

None of the principles that Sidgwick has now enumerated orders us to aim at our own good directly. He does, however, make it completely clear from the start of his book that he believes this is what we should do. He summarizes his point in the following quote:

> I hold with Butler that "one's own happiness is a manifest obligation" independently of one's relation to other men.   (ME: 386)

As we shall see toward the end of this section, acceptance of egoism as part of morality will lead him to a most difficult problem in ethics.

THE GOOD: HAPPINESS AS PLEASURE

The method of egoism as well as the method of utilitarianism talk about promotion of the good. What is this good then? Sidgwick answers this question in two steps: in Book 1, he is concerned with the conceptual question of what we mean by the term "good," and in Book 3 he is occupied with the substantive question of what the good is. In Book 1, he rejects Hobbes' view that: "whatsoever is the object of any man's Desire, that it is which he for his part calleth Good, and the object of his aversion, Evil."[4] The good cannot be linked just with what we desire because we sometimes desire things that are on the whole bad for us – like revenge, when we know that reconciliation would be better for us. If good cannot be understood in terms

---

[3] Note that this principle is not an axiom in the strict sense because it is deduced from the above two self-evident intuitions. Nevertheless, Sidgwick refers to it as an axiom.

[4] Hobbes 1985: 120. (Sidgwick slightly misquotes Hobbes. The original reads: "whatsoever is the object of any man's appetite or desire, that is it which he for his part calleth good; and the object of his hate and aversion, evil ... ")

of what we actually desire, then maybe it can be defined by what we *would* desire if we knew all the consequences of all possible choices? Again, Sidgwick is unsatisfied with such an idea. Such a notion of "good" is in a sense an idealized notion, because no one ever does have such fully informed desires. Nevertheless, it is a notion that refers only to facts about the world and "does not introduce any judgment of value, fundamentally distinct from judgments relating to existence." Sidgwick thinks, however, that the common sense notion of a person's good on the whole includes in it some kind of judgment of value, rather than of fact, and even a "dictate of reason" – to be specific, a rational dictate to aim at my "good on the whole." Finally he reaches the conclusion that:

> "Ultimate good on the whole" . . . must be taken to mean what as a rational being I should desire and seek to realise. . . (ME: 112)

What is this thing that as a rational person I should aim at? Sidgwick takes only two possibilities into account: it is either happiness or perfection. When discussing perfection as an ultimate end of our actions he defines it in several possible ways and discusses each option: living virtuously, being virtuous, having a good will, or possessing "other talents, gifts and graces" such as rationality, the pursuit of knowledge, or caring for others. He rejects all these options, concluding that none of them is good or valuable in itself but rather is promoted as a means to "desirable conscious life" (ME: 395). Not all of consciousness is desirable, as it includes both pain and pleasure, and what is painful is not desirable. Sidgwick says that if all life were "as little desirable" as some parts of his own experiences have been then the preservation of life would be "unmitigatedly bad." If we regard the preservation of life as generally good, it is because we regard human life as having, on average, a positive balance of happiness. The "mere existence of human organisms, even if prolonged to eternity," does not appear to Sidgwick in any way desirable. So it is not even conscious life as such that is ultimately good but only life that is accompanied by consciousness that is "on the whole desirable." In conclusion he states:

> Ultimate Good can only be conceived as Desirable Consciousness.
> (ME: 398)

What is a desirable state of consciousness is happiness, understood as pleasure. Sidgwick defines pleasure as "a feeling which, when experienced by intelligent beings, is at least implicitly apprehended as desirable or . . . preferable" (ME: 127). Thus Sidgwick supports hedonism.

INTUITIONISTIC JUSTIFICATION

Hedonism is often associated with a naturalistic justification. It is enough to recall Mill's statement that "No reason can be given why the general happiness is desirable, except that each person, so far as he believes it to be attainable, desires his own happiness ... we have not only all the proof which the case admits of, but all which it is possible to require, that happiness is a good."[5] As we saw earlier, Sidgwick rejects naturalism and naturalistic justification. According to him, the first principles, whether they refer to what is right or to what is good, cannot be drawn from experience; they are rational, self-evident intuitions, independent from what we desire, want or aim at.

> If Hedonism claims to give authoritative guidance, this can only be in virtue of the principle that pleasure is the only reasonable ultimate end of human action: and this principle cannot be known by induction from experience.
>
> (ME: 98)

THE DUALISM OF PRACTICAL REASON

Now we shall return to Sidgwick's methods and their principles. The method of egoism with its principle of prudence tells us to aim at our own happiness on the whole, taking all parts of our conscious life into account. The method of intuitionism with its principle of justice orders us to treat everyone equally under the same or similar circumstances. Because the principle does not say anything about what is the thing that we should do impartially, and the part of intuitionism which states rules, that is the common sense morality, collapses and cannot serve as a guide to conduct, utilitarianism can take over the method of intuitionism and fill it with its own content. Thus utilitarianism will tell us to aim at the good of all in an impartial manner and the conflict between intuitionism and utilitarianism no longer exists.

We are still left however with the first method – the method of egoism. For Sidgwick this leads to the most profound problem of ethics, which he calls the dualism of practical reason:

> ... even if a man admits the self-evidence of the principle of Rational Benevolence, he may still hold that his own happiness is an end which it is irrational for him to sacrifice to any other; and that therefore a harmony between the maxim of Prudence and the maxim of Rational Benevolence

[5] Mill 1961: 438–9.

must be somehow demonstrated, if morality is to be made completely
rational. (ME: 498)

In short, this means that our reason presents us with two, sometimes
conflicting reasons. Utilitarianism can often embrace egoism, as my experiencing pleasure adds to the total sum of the pleasures of everyone. But there
will be cases where, by aiming at the greater good of all, I need to sacrifice my
own pleasure. This conflict is deeply troubling for Sidgwick. He mentions at
the beginning of his book that a basic postulate of reason is that if two reasons
conflict one of them or both must be wrong. At the end of his book, Sidgwick
is unable to say which of the methods is "righter." This made him finish the
first edition of *The Methods* with the word "failure." And although he changed
the concluding paragraphs in later editions, it is still obvious that Sidgwick
could not find any solution to what he thought was the most serious problem
for ethics: reason may not be a perfect guide to our moral actions.

OBLIGATIONS TO THE POOR, ANIMALS, POPULATION ISSUES, AND ESOTERIC MORALITY

Apart from the issues that constitute the core argument of *The Methods* and
can be seen as the most important of Sidgwick's claims, there are dozens of
smaller issues that are of great interest. Sidgwick lays the ground for discussions of such practical topics as obligations to the poor, the ethical treatment
of animals, population issues and the requirement for transparency in ethics.

Sidgwick supports utilitarianism and its demands but is aware that the
theory "is more plausibly charged with setting up too high a standard of
unselfishness and making exaggerated demands on human nature" (ME: 87).
Common sense morality allows for a special set of obligations that we have
towards those close to us. Utilitarianism, at least in theory, does require that
we treat everyone in a similar way, for it aims at achieving the greatest
possible general good. Sidgwick tries to deal with the problem by agreeing
that "the practical application of this theoretical impartiality of Utilitarianism
is limited by several important considerations" (ME: 431). Generally, we will
achieve better utilitarian results if we are close to and supportive towards
those that we know and care for. This does not mean, however, that we do
not have obligations towards strangers if we are able to help them effectively.

Like his philosophical predecessors Bentham and Mill, Sidgwick thought
that our moral consideration should extend to "all the beings capable of
pleasure and pain whose feelings are affected by our conduct." If our

obligation is to aim at universal good then, he thought, it is "arbitrary and unreasonable to exclude from the end ... any pleasure of any sentient being" (ME: 414). Some may respond that to include non-human animals in the ethical circle means it will be even more difficult to calculate pleasure and pain on the whole. But Sidgwick responds that unless we do not care about animals *at all*, we will have to face the problem of calculations anyway.

Even if we limited these calculations only to other human beings, it would still be not clear who exactly we should take into account. Do we have any duties towards future generations? Do we have those duties if the happiness of future people conflicts with the happiness of people who are living now? Sidgwick refers to time impartiality again: "the time at which a man exists cannot affect the value of his happiness from a universal point of view" (ME: 414). Hence "the interests of posterity must concern a Utilitarian as much as those of his contemporaries, except in so far as the effect of his actions on posterity – and even the existence of human beings to be affected – must necessarily be more uncertain" (ME: 414).

Sidgwick seems to be the first to notice that our choices may affect not only the amount of happiness future people experience, but also the number of those future people. Is it good to increase the size of the future population? It seems to the author of *The Methods* that "supposing the average happiness enjoyed remains undiminished, Utilitarianism directs us to make the number enjoying it as great as possible." At this point Sidgwick notices a further ethical issue that arises: what should we do if "we foresee as possible that an increase in numbers will be accompanied by a decrease in average happiness"? Sidgwick does not hesitate to face the problem; he explains:

> ... if we take Utilitarianism to prescribe, as the ultimate end of action, happiness on the whole, and not any individual's happiness, unless considered as an element of the whole, it would follow that, if the additional population enjoy on the whole positive happiness, we ought to weigh the amount of happiness gained by the extra number against the amount lost by the remainder. So that, strictly conceived, the point up to which, on Utilitarian principles, population ought to be encouraged to increase, is not that at which average happiness is the greatest possible, – as appears to be often assumed by political economists of the school of Malthus – but that at which the product formed by multiplying the number of persons living into the amount of average happiness reaches its maximum.   (ME: 415–16)

It is usually assumed that morality is a public system and that everyone should know what it requires; what is moral should be done openly and there is no reason to keep it secret. Sidgwick challenges this view, for he holds that ethics is not about the right public system but rather about reasons for action that each individual has in the situation that she is in. On these grounds he defends what he calls "esoteric morality":

> it may be right to do and privately recommend, under certain circumstances, what it would not be right to advocate openly; it may be right to teach openly to one set of persons what it would be wrong to teach to others; it may be conceivably right to do, if it can be done with comparative secrecy, what it would be wrong to do in the face of the world; and even, if perfect secrecy can be reasonably expected, what it would be wrong to recommend by private advice or example. (ME: 489)

This perspective is an implication of the normative view we now call "act-utilitarianism."

SIDGWICK AND CONTEMPORARY ETHICS

It is hard to overestimate Sidgwick's role for current Anglophone ethics. He influenced some of the greatest philosophers of the twentieth century in creating their own theories, both his opponents, like G.E.M. Anscombe and John Rawls, and his supporters, like Derek Parfit and Peter Singer.

Most of the issues that Sidgwick raised in *The Methods* had been discussed long before him and none of them has in any way now become outdated. What Sidgwick introduced to twentieth-century philosophy, however, was a comparative approach of discussing them, which now has become standard, at least in analytical philosophy. Discussion over the question whether ethical judgments can be objectively true became especially interesting when in 1936 Alfred Ayer rejected the cognitive status of moral propositions and gave rise to a whole group of non-cognitive approaches towards ethics. Simon Blackburn and Allan Gibbard are now leading a forceful discussion with a most important supporter of objectivism: Derek Parfit. An exciting philosophical discussion exists on the role of moral intuitions in our ethical deliberation, as well as on their validity. Intuitionism seems to have had a revival in philosophy because of Phillip Stratton-Lake, Jonathan Dancy, and Robert Audi. In the field of utilitarianism, the idea that it is happiness, and not simply the satisfaction of our desires, that we should aim at is receiving the renewed attention it deserves. Discussion of this issue is led now by Roger Crisp, Daniel Haybron, Fred Feldman, and Neil Sinhababu.

One of the most challenging discussions in ethics is on rationality and reasons in egoism and morality. There are those, like David Gauthier or David Brink, who try to reconcile egoistic and moral reasons by showing that what we do for others in a public system of morality will pay us back in one way or the other. Derek Parfit, however, does not believe that you can reach such harmony at all times. Though we always have sufficient reasons to act morally, it may often happen that at the same time we also have sufficient reasons to act egoistically. Moral reasons may not always be overriding reasons. Parfit may have overcome Sidgwick's dualism in some cases (as he believes, unlike Sidgwick, that at least sometimes moral reasons are over-riding, and not only sufficient) but he may not have gone far enough. Even if only sometimes I have sufficient reasons to act in both directions – egoistically or morally – will morality matter, if every time I choose to act egoistically?

Finally, discussion of such practical problems as our obligations to aid the poor, animal rights, or population issues are being carried out by a myriad of thinkers, including the most prominent modern utilitarians: Peter Singer and Derek Parfit.

BIBLIOGRAPHY

An asterisk denotes secondary literature especially suitable for further reading.

Hobbes, Thomas 1985. *Leviathan*. London, Penguin Books.
Lazari-Radek, de, Katarzyna and Singer, Peter 2014. *The Point of View of the Universe*. Oxford University Press.*
Mill, John Stuart 1961. *Utilitarianism*. New York, Dolphin Books.
Parfit, Derek 2011. *On What Matters*. Oxford University Press.
Phillips, David 2011. *Sidgwickian Ethics*. Oxford University Press.*
Schultz, Bart 2004. *Henry Sidgwick: Eye of the Universe*. Cambridge University Press.*
Sidgwick, Henry 1907. *The Methods of Ethics*. 7th edn, London, Macmillan.

40

Pragmatism

CHERYL MISAK

Pragmatists are empiricists and naturalists – the founders of the tradition were heavily influenced by Alexander Bain, August Comte, and Charles Darwin.[1] They require our beliefs and our philosophical theories to be linked to experience and they seek non-metaphysical, non-supernatural, explanations. But pragmatists reject any naturalism that gives ontological priority to matter or physicality – they want to consider whether value, generality, chance, etc. might be part of the natural world. That is, they are holists, taking their view to encompass all of science, logic, mathematics, art, religion, ethics, and politics. Unlike most of their fellow empiricists, they fence off no realm of inquiry from the principles they set out. The question of whether ethics[2] falls under our cognitive scope has thus engaged the pragmatists from the beginning. John Dewey sums it up nicely: The pragmatist 'has at least tried to face, and not to dodge, the question of how it is that moral and scientific "knowledge" can both hold of one and the same world' (*MW* 4: 132; 1908).[3]

C.S. PEIRCE: ETHICS AND INQUIRY

Here is Peirce, one of the founders of pragmatism, expressing the core sentiment of the tradition:

[1] This chapter provides a whirlwind tour through one theme in my *The American Pragmatists* (Misak 2013).

[2] I will use 'moral' and 'ethical' interchangeably.

[3] All citations of John Dewey refer to his *Collected Works*. *The Early Works of John Dewey, 1882–1898* (Dewey 1967–1972), are cited as '*EW* n: m; year', where n is the volume number, m the page number, and the year that of the quoted text. *The Middle Works of John Dewey, 1899–1924* (Dewey 1976–1983), are cited as '*MW* n: m; year', where n is the volume number, m the page number, and the year that of the quoted text. *The Later Works of John Dewey, 1925–1953* (Dewey 1981–1990), are cited as '*LW* n: m; year', where n is the volume number, m the page number, and the year that of the quoted text.

> ... there is but one state of mind from which you can 'set out', namely, the very state of mind in which you actually find yourself at the time you do 'set out' – a state in which you are laden with an immense mass of cognition already formed, of which you cannot divest yourself if you would ... Do you call it doubting to write down on a piece of paper that you doubt? If so, doubt has nothing to do with any serious business ... (CP 5: 416; 1905)[4]

Our body of background beliefs is susceptible to doubt on a piecemeal basis, so long as that doubt is prompted by 'some positive reason' (CP 5: 51; 1903) – a surprising or recalcitrant experience. The inquirer has a fallible background of belief that is not in fact in doubt. Only against such a background can a belief be put into doubt and a new belief adopted. Inquiry 'is not standing upon the bedrock of fact. It is walking upon a bog, and can only say, this ground seems to hold for the present. Here I will stay till it begins to give way' (CP 5: 589; 1898). When it gives way, the ground merely shifts, rather than opens up underneath us. We can doubt one belief and inquire, but we cannot doubt all of our beliefs and inquire. The inquirer, Peirce says, 'is under a compulsion to believe just what he does believe ... as time goes on, the man's belief usually changes in a manner which he cannot resist ... this force which changes a man's belief in spite of any effort of his may be, in all cases, called a *gain of experience*' (MS 1342, p. 2, undated).

Peirce argues against 'transcendental' accounts of truth, such as the correspondence theory, on which a true belief is one that mirrors the believer-independent world (CP 5: 572; 1901). Such views of truth are 'vagabond thoughts that tramp the public roads without any human habitation' (CP 8: 112; 1900). They make truth the subject of empty metaphysics. For the very idea of the believer-independent world, and the items within it to which beliefs or sentences might correspond, seems graspable only if we could somehow step outside our corpus of belief, our practices, or that with which we have 'dealings'. Peirce argues, rather, that a true belief is one that would withstand doubt, were we to inquire as far as we fruitfully could into the matter. A true belief is such that, no matter how much further we

---

[4] If a passage occurs in the new *Writings of Charles S. Peirce: Chronological Edition* (Peirce 1982), I cite that source as 'W n: m; year', where n is the volume, m the page number, and the year that of the quoted text. If it is not in the *Writings*, but in the older *Collected Papers* (Peirce 1931–1958), the citation is '*CP* n: m; year', where n is the volume number, m the paragraph number, and the year that of the quoted text. If it is available in none of these collections, then I cite the manuscript number in the microfilm edition of Peirce's papers, as MS n, where n is the manuscript number in the Houghton Library, Harvard University.

were to investigate and debate, it would not be overturned by recalcitrant experience and argument. On Peirce's view, we aim at beliefs that would be forever stable – we aim at getting the best beliefs we can. Hence we must adopt a method of inquiry that pays close attention to experience and be alert to when experience interferes with a belief. The question then arises whether we can make sense of beliefs about what is right or wrong, just or unjust, as being the best they can.

Peirce did not think much about ethics and politics, but I have argued in *Truth, Politics, Morality: Pragmatism and Deliberation* that he gives us the seeds for an excellent account of how we might aim at truth or at getting things right in deliberation about these subject matters.[5] Peirce suggests that when politicians disagree the dispute usually has 'some other object than the ascertainment of scientific truth' (*CP* 4: 34; 1893). We would now say that 'it's just political' – that is, these deliberations are aimed at something instrumental, like getting re-elected. He also tells us that in inquiry about ethics, deliberators often might be justifiably hesitant to revise their beliefs. But sometimes in these kinds of inquiries, truth *is* at stake and sometimes change of belief *is* justified: 'Like any other field, more than any other [morality] needs improvement, advance ... But morality, doctrinaire con-servatist that it is, destroys its own vitality by resisting change, and positively insisting, This is eternally right: That is eternally wrong' (*CP* 2: 198; 1902). Ethical judgments, Peirce thinks, should be brought into the field of inquiry. They are revisable in light of experience: 'just as reasoning springs from experience, so the development of sentiment arises from the soul's Inward and Outward Experiences' (*CP* 1: 648; 1898). For Peirce, experience is simply that which is compelling, surprising, or upsetting of a settled belief. We then scrutinize these brute compulsions and bring them under the scope of reasoning. Experience might have a different character in different domains. Peirce spends much time on how it is in mathematics – there we feel the force of experience when we manipulate diagrams or proofs. He also thinks that we can perform thought experiments. The experience that is relevant for ethics might also not come directly via our sensory apparatus, but if we are surprised by it, it is experience nonetheless.

Notice the 'we' in Peirce's account of truth. He argues that truth is a matter for the community of inquirers – not for this or that individual inquirer. He says: 'logicality inexorably requires that our interests shall *not* be limited. They must not stop at our own fate, but must embrace the whole

[5] Misak 2000.

community' (*W* 3: 284; 1878). Inquiry and rationality are matters of getting your beliefs in line with the *best* experience, evidence, and reasons, not just your own. Logic is rooted in a 'social principle', for investigation into what is true is not a private interest but an interest 'as wide as the community can turn out to be' (*CP* 5: 357; 1868). Here we find, in 1868, the first pragmatist articulation of the idea that truth and inquiry must be a democratic, community project.

WILLIAM JAMES: EXPERIENCE AND VALUE

A second founder of pragmatism, William James, is even more committed to considering *all* forms of experience – to 'sportsmanlike fair play in science' (*WWJ* [1891]: 9).[6] He even took seriously experiences under the influence of drugs and alcohol, as well as those in religious trances. That was going far too far for Peirce. But in this much Peirce and James agree: inquiry into value, James says, deals with 'life answering to life' (*WWJ* [1891]: 149). The 'sense for abstract justice', the 'passion for music', the 'feeling of the inward dignity of certain spiritual attitudes, as peace, serenity, simplicity, veracity', and the aversion to 'querulousness, anxiety, egoistic fussiness' are 'quite inexplicable except by an innate preference' (*WWJ* [1891]: 143). 'Purely inward forces are . . . at work here', and constitute a kind of evidence in morals not available to the standard empiricist (*WWJ* [1891]: 144). A question immediately arises about how we might tell whether a given experience or feeling (the deliverances of conscience, say) should be granted weight in ethical deliberation. While the classical pragmatists did not give very strong answers to this question, the reader might turn to C.I. Lewis and to Misak (2008b) for an account of how we can make sense of veridical experiences in ethics and how ethical experiences can be scrutinized and evaluated.

James argues, with Peirce, that society may be seen as a long-running experiment aimed at identifying the best kind of conduct. Its conventions thus deserve respect. Our background beliefs capture the experience of generations. James thinks that 'ethical science is just like physical science, and instead of being deducible all at once from abstract principles, must simply bide its time, and be ready to revise its conclusions from day to day' (*WWJ* [1891]: 157). Here he sounds rather like Rawls:

---

[6] All citations of William James refer to his *Works* (James 1975–1988), cited as *WWJ*, are of the form (*WWJ* [year]: m), where the year is the original date of publication, and m is the page number.

The course of history is nothing but the story of men's struggles from generation to generation to find the more and more inclusive order. *Invent some manner* of realizing your own ideals which will also satisfy the alien demands – that and only that is the path of peace! Following this path, society has shaken itself into one sort of relative equilibrium after another by a series of social discoveries quite analogous to those of science.

(*WWJ* [1891]: 155–6)

Experiments have shown us, for instance, that 'slavery, private warfare and liberty to kill, judicial torture and arbitrary royal power have slowly succumbed to actually aroused complaints'. They have succumbed to experience. But 'there is nothing final in any actually given equilibrium of human ideals' – we must keep inquiry and deliberation going (*WWJ* [1891]: 156). We can have progress and even revolution in matters of value. But in the meantime, we must go on our current well-grounded beliefs: 'it would be folly quite as great, in most of us, to strike out independently and to aim at originality in ethics as in physics' (*WWJ* [1891]: 157).

The pressing question for pragmatism is as follows: how can we make sense of our standards of rationality, truth, and value as genuinely binding while recognizing that they are profoundly human phenomena? How do normativity and authority arise from within a world of human experience and practice? James does not give us entirely satisfactory answers. He tends towards saying that whatever is good for me to believe – whatever works for me – is what I should take to be true, and indeed, that is what is true. He says: 'Any idea upon which we can ride . . . any idea that will carry us prosperously from any one part of our experience to any other part, linking things satisfactorily, working securely, simplifying, saving labor, is . . . true *instrumentally*' (*WWJ* [1907]: 34). 'Satisfactorily', for James, 'means more satisfactorily to ourselves, and individuals will emphasize their points of satisfaction differently. To a certain degree, therefore, everything here is plastic' (*WWJ* [1907]: 35). Sometimes he puts his position as follows: 'True ideas are those that we can assimilate, validate, corroborate and verify';[7] 'truth *happens* to an idea' (*WWJ* [1907]: 97).

This is the brand of pragmatism that attracted the scorn of Russell and Moore on one side of the Atlantic, and of countless others on the home front. It seemed at times to live on in Dewey and was resurrected by Richard Rorty in the 1970s. Pragmatism, however, would have been better off taking its direction from Peirce and C.I. Lewis. James was right to call himself a radical empiricist, but he was too radical.

---

[7] Emphasis in original omitted.

JOHN DEWEY AND THE QUESTION OF VALIDITY

John Dewey was devoted to breaking down the dichotomy between fact and value. Like Peirce and James, he wants to offer a 'unified theory of inquiry' – a single way of thinking about how we resolve problematic situations in science, ethics, politics, and law (*LW* 12: 102; 1938).

He begins with the Peircean epistemology: inquirers try to resolve doubt in favor of better, well-settled, belief. They aim to transform a doubtful or problematic situation into one in which 'confusion and uncertainty' are resolved (*MW* 14: 144; 1922). Dewey expands on Peirce's nascent idea that democracy walks hand in hand with inquiry. Democracy is the use of the experimental method to solve practical problems; it is an application of 'cooperative intelligence' or inquiry (*LW* 13: 187; 1939).

Dewey sees that there are differences between ethics and science. Unlike science, ethics involves voluntary conduct or behavior that manifests the agent's character (*MW* 5: 188; 1908). A moral problem or situation is thus: 'Which shall he decide for and why? The appeal is to himself; what does *he* really think the desirable end? What makes the supreme appeal to him? What sort of an agent, a person, shall he be? This is the question finally at stake in any genuinely moral situation: what shall the agent *be?*' (*MW* 5: 194; 1908). Choices about what to do or what to value are choices that make up our very selves.

The problem of validity presses in on Dewey as well. How am I to make sense of the ideas of accuracy, error, getting a better belief, and making a mistake, if the aim of moral inquiry is to construct my self? The difficulties do not go away when Dewey links the self to the community. For it is not clear how he has anything to say to those who think that the height of self-realization is to forge a homogenous community by eliminating 'the other' or all who are different. A community, that is, might well exclude any who would question a current ideal of self-realization or who would question dominant cultural norms. Must we say that whatever a community thinks right, is right? Morton White, a fellow-pragmatist whose career overlapped with Dewey's, charged him with making Mill's mistake – conflating what is desirable with what is desired.[8]

Dewey felt the force of this problem, although he never managed to solve it.[9] But when he gets down to an examination of how inquiry works in ethics, the insights for moral philosophy flow in a steady stream. For instance,

---

[8] White 1996: 230ff.   [9] See Richardson 1995; Misak 2013.

Dewey follows Peirce in taking thought experimentation to be crucial, especially in ethical inquiry. In ethics, experiment

> is a process of tentative action: we 'try on' one or another of the ends; imagining ourselves actually doing them, going, indeed, in this make-believe action just as far as we can without actually doing them. In fact, we often find ourselves carried over the line here; the hold which a given impulse gets upon us while we are 'trying it on' passes into overt act without us having consciously intended it. (*EW* 4: 251; 1894)

Dewey thinks that we can learn something in thought experimentation. We can learn something about ourselves, about how we react to certain moral scenarios, and, if we try on other people's shoes, we can learn something about how those others might react. As Elizabeth Anderson puts it, Dewey argues that we propose potential solutions to the ethical problems that confront us; we try to predict the consequences of those solutions; and we ask whether our reactions to those consequences would be positive or negative.[10] Once a solution has withstood the challenge of testing in thought experiment or experiment in the imagination, we can go with it in real life.

While this is no neat and tidy solution to the validity problem faced by the pragmatist, who unlinks what is right from the spurious anchor of certainty, it takes us a considerable distance to *understanding* validity in the moral domain. Ethical judgment is bound up with human wants, needs, and culture. It is only to be expected that what we find when we examine possibilities in thought experiments is our reactions to things – our feeling that x is desirable, loathsome, etc. It is also only to be expected that those reactions will not be uniform across inquirers; across communities; and across times. It is not appropriate to look for fully determinate answers in an area of inquiry such as ethics – an area of inquiry in which the subject matter is tied to human needs and in which many issues are not answerable without a residue of regret that one could not act on other competing but legitimate concerns.

As Alan Ryan puts it, at the heart of Dewey's view is that our moral judgment is just that: *judgment*.[11] We consider, reflect, experiment, get more information, and scrutinize our desires. We ask whether what we desire really is desirable. We open up the gap between the two. The problem of adjudication or validity now exists in a more manageable form. We still do not have a good philosophical account of how an individual might examine and revise her own desires and still be wrong. But we do have the following insight: being genuinely engaged in the effort of improving one's ethical

---

[10] Anderson 1993. [11] Ryan 1995: 337.

beliefs is surely an important part of the battle. In its finest form, Dewey's view is that we do not know what we value or what is valuable until we engage in democratic inquiry.

C.I. LEWIS: KNOWLEDGE AND VALUATION

C.I. Lewis is one of the most under-rated and misunderstood of the pragmatists. He did not, as philosophical lore would have it, uphold the Myth of Given[12] – the idea that something certain or indubitable is given to us in experience. But his extraordinarily promising pragmatist theory of ethics has left hardly a trace on the contemporary philosophical consciousness.

Lewis argues that we experience value in more or less the same way we experience a thing's being green or hard. 'Value judgments are a form of empirical cognition, directed upon facts as obdurate and compelling as those which must determine the correctness of any other kind of knowledge' (*AK* [1946]: 407).[13] Something compels, or impinges upon, us. When we make a judgment or form a belief about that which impinges upon us, what was given to us flies away (*LCP* [1923]: 231). The mystic and the intuitionist might be 'outraged' at this view, as it stands against anyone who would see us 'sinking ourselves in the presentation itself and putting thought to sleep' (*LCP* [1923]: 406). But if we are to have any knowledge at all of value, then, just as with any kind of experience, we must bring to immediate presentations of value our network of thought structures.

Lewis recoils from the emotivist branch of empiricist ethics. He thinks that 'one of the strangest aberrations ever to visit the mind of man' is the idea that value-predictions are not true or false matters of fact, but are merely expressions of emotion (*AK* [1946]: 365–6, 399; *LCP* [1934]: 259). We would now call his opponent a non-cognitivist in ethics and there are more sophisticated versions than the one Lewis was concerned with. Nonetheless, emotivism, he thinks, implies that 'one belief would be as good as another'. It results in 'both moral and practical cynicism' and makes action 'pointless' (*AK* [1946]: 366). If it were not better to be right than wrong in what one believes, why

---

[12] See Dayton 1995; Hookway 2008; Misak 2013 for corrective accounts.

[13] If a passage occurs in C.I. Lewis' *Collected Papers* (1970) I cite that source as (*LCP* [year]: m), where year is the original date of publication and m is the page number of the quoted text in the modern edition. If a passage occurs instead in Lewis' *An Analysis of Knowledge and Evaluation* (1946), the citation is (*AK* [year]: m), where year is again the original date of publication and m is the page number of the quoted text in the modern edition.

bother about your belief or your grounds for it? If our observations of value did not have any connection whatsoever to 'the objective value-properties of things, then it would be totally impossible for us to learn from experience how to improve our lot in life'. Lewis, more than any of his fellow pragmatists, save Peirce, is determined to address the problem of validity. He wants to set out a 'naturalistic' conception of values on which human beings are the judges of what is right and wrong, but which does not entail that 'the evaluations which the fool makes in his folly are on a par with those of the sage in his wisdom'. Human beings 'stand in need of all that can be learned from the experience of life in this natural world' (*AK* [1946]: 398–9).

Underlying Lewis' account of ethics is the pragmatist idea that we need to be able to apply or verify a meaningful expression in action – either physical or imaginative (*AK* [1946]: 134–5). But we do not aim at the false grail of certainty when we verify a hypothesis. What we need to do is to say what would be further evidence for or against the hypothesis in question (*AK* [1946]: 136–7).

He distinguishes three kinds of value predication. First we have expressive statements of the sort 'This is good', said at the table, where the speaker intends merely to express her immediate impression about the food, not to make a statement that is verifiable by others. This is 'apparent value' or 'felt goodness' or a sense that something is 'prized' (*AK* [1946]: 374, 398). This kind of value judgment is the data for the other two kinds of value statements. 'Without the experience of felt value and disvalue, evaluations in general would have no meaning' (*AK* [1946]: 375). Here we see the makings of a distinction in Lewis' thought between what seems to me to be good and what is good. Expressive statements about what seems to me to be good are not subject to error. They are only true or false in the sense that we can tell lies about what we experience. They do not fall into the category of knowledge. There is a distinction to be made between what is prized, on the one hand, and what is judged or 'appraised' on the other.

The second kind of value predication consists of evaluations that are verifiable by the course of experience. Although we can never verify these (or any other kind of empirical judgment) with certainty, some of them are 'terminating judgments' (*AK* [1946]: 375). We predict a course of experience and that prediction is decisively, but fallibly, verified or falsified. We set a test and it is passed or not passed. These statements are predictions that a course of action will be good or bad, or will cause enjoyment or pain. We have here 'a form of empirical knowledge, not fundamentally different in what determines their truth or falsity, and what determines their validity and justification, from other kinds of empirical knowledge'. The validity of these judgments 'will be disclosed in experience'. If we judge falsely, that can have 'devastating consequences' (*AK* [1946]: xi). Sometimes these terminating judgments are easily and decisively verified – if my aim is to get pleasure and I predict that doing *A* will bring me pleasure, verifying my prediction might be a relatively straightforward matter. But if my purpose 'is to make the world safe for democracy', that will not be easily verifiable (*AK* [1946]: 368–9). No limited set of experiences is going to be sufficient to exhaust the empirical significance of predictions about that.

The third kind of evaluative judgment also falls under our cognitive scope. We often evaluate things, actions, and states of affairs as good or bad – we attribute a value to them, just as we attribute the property of red, say, to an object. These evaluations are diverse and complex, but they are also subject to verification – this time in 'non-terminating' experiences. They cannot be decisively verified: further experience might always turn out to be relevant (*AK* [1946]: 365, 375f). They are never more than probable. But we might have so much to go on that they are 'practically certain' (*AK* [1946]: 376). Examples include statements in normative ethics, such as 'Torture is odious' or 'It is right to help others' (*LCP* [1940]: 111; *LCP* [1941]: 166). These are not unverifiable expressions of desires, but verifiable judgments that continue to be responsive to experience, even if we are pretty sure we have them right.

It is clear that Lewis is gripped by the question of validity or of making sense of how we can get right and wrong answers. What is valuable is not equivalent to what is immediately perceived as valuable by this or that person. Lewis notes that he might get enormous satisfaction from a cartoon on his desk, but he can nonetheless see that it is a trivial, not very valuable, matter (*AK* [1946]: 381). And the goodness of a good object is not dependent upon its being experienced by someone (*AK* [1946]: 388). Following Peirce, Lewis moves to subjunctive conditionals to articulate his position. Something may be beautiful even if no human were ever to behold it. What is important is how 'it *would be* beheld if it ever *should be* beheld under conditions favorable to realization in full of the potentialities for such delight which are resident in the thing' (*AK* [1946]: 389). Nonetheless, it is a 'peculiarity' of value judgments that 'expressive meaning' (what is felt to be valuable) drives 'objective meaning' (what is in fact valuable).

Moreover, someone can discover that something is of value without actually experiencing it for himself. Lewis gives the following example: he might come to believe that his neighbor is a good musician through his rendition of difficult passages, even though the music leaves him cold. One might add that one can learn something about the moral rightness or wrongness of a practice by reading first-person reports of those who have been subject to the practice, by listening to the argument on either side, and so on.[14] For Lewis, value ascriptions are subjective in the sense that they are driven by how human beings would experience a thing or an act. But they are not subjective in the sense that if I or we value A, then A is valuable.

Naturalist or pragmatist conceptions of value must also cope with the fact that value judgments are likely to encounter 'more variation from person to person' and more variation for an individual from one time to another. Our very likes and dislikes also seem particularly sensitive to our own attitudes – to 'how one goes out to meet' objects and situations (AK [1946]: 418). Lewis is of the view that these facts merely distinguish value judgments from sensory judgments by degree, rather than by kind. All data are influenced by 'internal' and interpretative factors. In other kinds of empirical matters, we simply do not look as often to these factors as explanations for why our judgments diverge. We tend to look rather to differences in the external set-up (AK [1946]: 422–3). Indeed, we tend to emphasize divergence of belief in ethics because it is important for us to do so. It is vital to note the disagreements of others when we diverge about whether, for instance, assisted dying is permissible, whereas it is less important with garden-variety judgments of greenness or hardness (AK [1946]: 419).

Lewis, it should by now be clear, builds validity into his account of value by showing us how the notions of disagreement, error, and getting things right play a vital role in our ethical deliberation. He identifies ways we can be mistaken about our value judgments and speaks to how we can learn from experience so that we improve our value judgments. I can be mistaken about my felt judgments – I might mistakenly think that my experiencing A as valuable on one occasion means that I will experience it as valuable on every occasion. Or I might be wrong in inferring that because I take A to be good, others will also take it to be good. That is, my experiencing A as valuable need not be connected to A's really being valuable. It may be connected, rather, to my 'personal make-up or personal history or personal attitude on this occasion' (AK [1946]: 416).

What about those whose idea of the good life is inconsistent with the ideas of others? What of those whose aim is to ensure substantive homogeneity in a population, by genocidal means? Lewis' attempt at

---

[14] See Misak 2008b.

answering such questions is to say that we have to hope, if there is to be any chance of improvement in our lives, that there is enough commonality in the experience of value so that inquiry will converge upon the right answer:

> if there were a complete absence of community in our value-findings on given occasions, or if communities of value-apprehension in the presence of the same object should be mere matters of chance, then no one could, with the best will in the world, learn how to do anybody else any good – or for that matter, how to do him harm. (*AK* [1946]: 423–4)

This is a critically important theme in Lewis' work. It is the (naturalized) Kantian strain in the brand of pragmatism he shares with Peirce.[15] The very practices of assertion and of acting with intent require that we hold ourselves up to standards and norms:

> To act, to live, in human terms, is necessarily to be subject to imperatives; to recognize norms ... To repudiate normative significances and imperatives in general, would be to dissolve away all seriousness of action and intent, leaving only an undirected floating down the stream of time; and as a consequence to dissolve all significance of thought and discourse into universal blah. Those who would be serious and circumspect and cogent in what they think, and yet tell us that there are no valid norms or binding imperatives, are hopelessly confused, and inconsistent with their own attitude of assertion.
> (*AK* [1946]: 481)

Lewis thinks that two imperatives we are bound by are the following: 'Be consistent, in valuation and in thought and action; Be concerned about yourself in future and on the whole.' We need to abide by these requirements if we are to make sense of the life we live. The abandonment of standards is barely conceivable, and even if we could do it, we would be crippled in our attempt at making sense of a human life. We can only repudiate these norms if we are willing to repudiate all norms and the distinction between validity and invalidity itself. And we can't do that while remaining the kinds of beings we are and think it important to be (*AK* [1946]: 483–4). This is the naturalized Kantian pragmatist position of Lewis and Peirce. It has been rather lost in the literature and we would do well to re-discover it.

---

[15] Peirce and Lewis also have affinities with contemporary neo-Kantians such as Korsgaard; see Korsgaard 1996.

BIBLIOGRAPHY

An asterisk denotes secondary literature especially suitable for further reading.

Anderson, Elizabeth 1993. *Value in Ethics and Economics*. Cambridge, MA: Harvard University Press.

Dayton, Eric 1995. 'C.I. Lewis and the Given', *Transactions of the Charles S. Peirce Society*, 31/2: 254–87.

Dewey, John 1967–1972. [1882–1898]. *The Early Works of John Dewey, 1882–1898*. Ed. Jo Ann Boydston. Carbondale, IL: Southern Illinois University Press.

Dewey, John 1971 [1894]. 'The Study of Ethics: A Syllabus', in *The Early Works of John Dewey, 1882–1898*, vol. 4: *1893–1894, Essays, The Study of Ethics*. Ed. Jo Ann Boydston. Carbondale, IL: Southern Illinois University Press, 221–362.

Dewey, John 1976–1983 [1899–1924]. *The Middle Works of John Dewey, 1899–1924*. Ed. Jo Ann Boydston. Carbondale, IL: Southern Illinois University Press.

Dewey, John 1977 [1908]. 'Does Reality Possess Practical Character', in *The Middle Works of John Dewey, 1899–1924*, vol. 4: *1907–1909, Essays, Moral Principles in Education*. Ed. Jo Ann Boydston. Carbondale, IL: Southern Illinois University Press, 125–42.

Dewey, John 1980 [1916]. 'Organization in American Education', in *The Middle Works of John Dewey, 1899–1924*, vol. 10. *1916–1917, Essays*. Ed. Jo Ann Boydston. Carbondale, IL: Southern Illinois University Press, 397–411.

Dewey, John 1981–1990 [1925–1953]. *The Later Works of John Dewey 1925–1953*. Ed. Jo Ann Boydston. Carbondale, IL: Southern Illinois University Press.

Dewey, John 1983 [1922]. *Human Nature and Conduct. The Middle Works of John Dewey, 1899–1924*, vol. 14. Ed. Jo Ann Boydston. Carbondale, IL: Southern Illinois University Press.

Dewey, John 1986 [1938]. *Logic: The Theory of Inquiry. The Later Works of John Dewey 1925–1953*, vol. 12. Ed. Jo Ann Boydston. Carbondale, IL: Southern Illinois University Press.

Dewey, John 1988 [1939]. *Freedom and Culture*, in *The Later Works of John Dewey, 1925–1953*, vol. 13: *1938–1939, Essays, Experience and Education, Freedom and Culture, and Theory of Valuation*. Ed. Jo Ann Boydston. Carbondale, IL: Southern Illinois University Press, 63–188.

Dewey, John and J.H. Tufts 1978 [1908]. *Ethics. The Middle Works of John Dewey 1899–1924*, vol. 5. Ed. Jo Ann Boydston. Carbondale, IL: Southern Illinois University Press.

Hookway, Christopher 2008. 'Pragmatism and the Given: C.I. Lewis, Quine, and Peirce', in Misak 2008a: 269–89.

James, William [1891a]. 'The Moral Philosopher and the Moral Life', in James (1975–1988), vol. 6: *The Will to Believe and Other Essays in Popular Philosophy*, 141–62.

James, William [1891b]. 'Preface', in James (1975–1988), vol. 6: *The Will to Believe and Other Essays in Popular Philosophy*, 5–10.

James, William [1907]. *Pragmatism: A New Name for Some Old Ways of Thinking*, vol. 1 of James (1975–1988).

James, William 1975–1988. *The Works of William James*. 19 vols. Ed. F.H. Burkhard, F. Bowers, and I.K. Skrupskelis. Cambridge, MA: Harvard University Press.

Korsgaard, Christine 1996. *The Sources of Normativity*, Cambridge University Press.

Lewis, Clarence Irving [1923]. 'A Pragmatic Conception of the A Priori', in Lewis 1970: 231–9.

Lewis, Clarence Irving [1934]. 'Experience and Meaning', in Lewis 1970: 258–76.

Lewis, Clarence Irving [1940]. 'Logical Positivism and Pragmatism', in Lewis 1970: 92–112.

Lewis, Clarence Irving [1941]. 'The Objectivity of Value Judgments', in Lewis 1970: 162–74.

Lewis, Clarence Irving [1946]. *An Analysis of Knowledge and Evaluation* (1971). La Salle, IL: Open Court.

Lewis, Clarence Irving 1970. *Collected Papers*. Ed. John D. Goheen and John L. Mothershead, Jr. Stanford University Press.

Misak, Cheryl 2000. *Truth, Politics, Morality: Pragmatism and Deliberation*. London and New York: Routledge.

Misak, Cheryl 2008a. *The Oxford Handbook of American Philosophy*. Oxford University Press.

Misak, Cheryl 2008b. 'Experience, Narrative, and Ethical Deliberation', *Ethics*, 118: 614–32.

Misak, Cheryl 2013. *The American Pragmatists*. Oxford University Press.*

Peirce, Charles Sanders (1931–1958). *Collected Papers of Charles Sanders Peirce*. Ed. C. Hartshorne and P. Weiss (vols. 1–6), A. Burks (vols. 7 and 8). Cambridge, MA: Belknap Press.

Peirce, Charles Sanders (1982–) [1900–]. *The Writings of Charles S. Peirce: A Chronological Edition*. Ed. E. Moore. Bloomington, IN: Indiana University Press.

Peirce, Charles Sanders (n.d.). Charles S. Peirce Papers, Houghton Library, Harvard University.

Richardson, Henry 1995. 'Beyond Good and Right: Toward a Constructive Ethical Pragmatism', *Philosophy and Public Affairs*, 24/2: 108–41.

Ryan, Alan 1995. *John Dewey and the High Tide of American Liberalism*. New York: W.W. Norton.

Talisse, Robert 2007. *A Pragmatist Philosophy of Democracy*. London: Routledge.

Talisse, Robert 2009. *Democracy and Moral Conflict*. Cambridge University Press.

White, Morton 1996. 'Desire and Desirability: A Rejoinder to a Posthumous Reply by John Dewey', *Journal of Philosophy*, 93/5: 229–42.

41

British Idealism

ROBERT STERN

In his recent magnum opus on the history of ethics, Terence Irwin gives the thought of the British Idealists, and particularly T.H. Green and F.H. Bradley, an unusually prominent role, as in many ways representing the high-point of moral philosophy in modern times. This is surprising, because most contemporary ethicists have probably never read their work, and would certainly hesitate to rank them above figures such as J.S. Mill, Henry Sidgwick, G.E. Moore and John Rawls, for example. However, when one realizes where Irwin's own concerns lie, then this is less surprising. For Irwin is interested in the Aristotelian tradition within ethics, and its subsequent development, and thus how it has fared in relation to its critics, of whom perhaps none is more prominent than Kant. Irwin believes, however, that much of this Kantian critique is misplaced, and that in fact when properly developed, Kant's own thinking turns out to need some appeal to Aristotelian insights, and thus that these apparently divergent traditions can be brought together, to the mutual benefit of each.[1]

However, if Irwin's approach does the British Idealists the great favour of rescuing them from historical obscurity, it also immediately highlights what may be seen as problematic with their views: namely, that by attempting to combine Aristotelianism with Kantianism, they end up with an incoherent position that can only be dialectically unstable. Clearly, then, even if Irwin is right about what the British Idealists were trying to achieve, their impact can only prove to be lasting if they managed to succeed, and so create some sort of genuine synthesis rather than an inconsistent ethical system.

In this chapter, therefore, I want to use Irwin's suggestion as the background to my account of the British Idealists, and to explore it further. I will claim that Irwin's way of locating them within the history of ethics is indeed

---

[1] Cf. Irwin 2007: 5. The main discussion of Green and Bradley can be found in Irwin 2009, in chs. 85 and 84 respectively.

helpful, while also allowing us to bring out the difficulties in their position. Broadly speaking, I will argue, this position can be understood as a form of 'post-Kantian perfectionism':[2] that is, an ethics that is based on claims about how the moral life relates to human self-realization, while at the same time taking into account Kant's well-known critique of any such view. After Kant, it may have appeared that such perfectionism was a 'dead duck'; the interest of Green and Bradley, however, is that they self-consciously attempt to show how this response was premature, while nonetheless taking such Kantian concerns seriously. The result, therefore, is a new take on this traditional ethical position, which in their hands is reshaped in unexpected ways.

I will begin by sketching the Kantian critique of perfectionism, before examining how Green and Bradley[3] responded in different ways to that critique, in their attempts to revive what they took to be valuable in the approach that Kant had attempted to surpass.

THE KANTIAN CRITIQUE OF PERFECTIONISM

The core ideas behind the approach that Kant took himself to be attacking are helpfully captured in Irwin's summary of Aristotle's position:

> [Aristotle] defends an account of the human good as happiness (*eudaimonia*), consisting in the fulfilment of human nature, expressed in the various human virtues. His position is teleological, in so far as it seeks the best guide for action in an ultimate end, eudaimonist, in so far as it identifies the ultimate end with happiness, and naturalist, in so far as it identifies virtue and happiness in a life that fulfils the nature and capacities of rational human nature.[4]

While a position of this sort can be called eudaimonist, it can also be called perfectionist, because it takes such happiness to consist in the development of our distinctive capacities, rather than simply pleasure or desire-satisfaction. On the other hand, it may be distinguished from a more narrow form of perfectionism, which takes this development to be a good in itself, rather than as an aspect of the well-being of the individual.

---

[2] I borrow this helpful phrase from Douglas Moggach: see e.g. Moggach 2011.

[3] In what follows, I will be focusing just on Green and Bradley, as these are by common consent the most significant ethicists in the British Idealist tradition. For discussion of other figures such as Edward Caird and Henry Jones, see Mander 2011. Mander 2016 also offers an insightful systematic discussion of this ethical tradition.

[4] Irwin 2007: 4.

Within the ethical thinking of his time, and when combined with certain theological themes concerning the purposes of God's creation, this outlook may be taken to be the dominant viewpoint of Kant's contemporaries, where its most influential spokesperson was Christian Wolff. Thus, when Kant came to propose that the much sought-after 'supreme principle of morality' should be 'to never proceed except in such a way *that I could also will that my maxim could become universal law*',[5] one prominent alternative candidate amongst others that he sought to discredit was the perfectionist principle: 'Seek perfection as much as you can.' Consequently, when Kant sets out to distinguish his account of the supreme principle of morality from all those so far put forward, perfectionism is one of the options he rejects, for several related reasons: it is heteronomous; it collapses morality into a system of merely hypothetical imperatives; it makes morality empirical rather than a priori; it puts the good prior to the right; and it is unable to provide any contentful guidance on how we should act. Let us briefly consider each of these points in turn.

According to Kant, all prior attempts to arrive at a supreme principle of morality, including those made by the perfectionist, are misguided because they are based on a heteronomous conception of the will: namely, that the ends of the will are set by desire or inclination, to which reason then determines the means. The consequence, however, is that 'the will does not give itself the law, but the object by its relation to the will gives the law to it',[6] and thus autonomy is undermined as reason becomes the slave of the passions. Thus, in the case of perfectionism, Kant argues that the link between perfection and well-being is foundational, where it is then the desire for the latter that is seen to motivate agents in following the principle of perfecting themselves, given the satisfactions that acting in accordance with it will bring. The result, however, is to make practical reason subservient to desire, in a heteronomous manner. Moreover, as a consequence of this connection between perfectionism and well-being, Kant argues, the perfectionist can only treat the imperatives of morality as hypothetical and not categorical: that is, they hold only because we have a sufficiently strong inclination towards the end of happiness to which perfecting ourselves and our capacities is the means. Furthermore, the position is a consequentialist and hence empirical one, for the rightness of an act is determined by how far it increases perfection, and this can be

---

[5] Kant 2012 4: 402. References to the work of Kant use the pagination of the Akademie edition, which is given in the margins of the translations cited in this chapter and most others.

[6] Kant 2012 4: 441.

determined only on the basis of experience, whereas for Kant moral judgements should be possible a priori.[7]

As well as these mistakes, Kant also accuses perfectionism of making a fundamental but tempting methodological error in conducting its inquiry into the supreme principle of morality: namely, of starting from a conception of what is good, and from that trying to arrive at an account of the moral law, whereas for Kant we must proceed the other way round if we are not to be led into error. For, Kant argues, if we try to conceive of the good unconstrained by some prior conception of the moral law, we will inevitably think of the good in terms of happiness and pleasure, and thus end up with the sort of heteronomous and hypothetical view of morality that one finds in perfectionism, amongst other moral systems.[8] Kant allows that perhaps the perfectionist might respond to a worry of this sort by accepting Kant's point and so holding that attributes are not perfections because they make us happy, but because they make us morally good; but then, Kant argues, the perfectionist principle is an empty one, because we now need to know what it is to be morally good before we can assess which attributes to cultivate and which capacities to realize, so the position is hopelessly circular, and cannot help us decide how to act.[9]

We have therefore seen the problems that Kant raised for the perfectionist tradition, which may seem to leave it fatally damaged. Nonetheless, of course, Kant's own position is far from unproblematic, so that once this became apparent, it was perhaps inevitable that the attempt would be made to see if in fact these two approaches can be brought together somehow to the mutual advantage of both, rather than being set at odds with one another. As Irwin has argued, the British Idealists may be seen as adopting this strategy, and thus as developing perfectionism in a post-Kantian form, which takes aspects of Kant's critique on board, and modifies the position accordingly, thereby giving it a new lease of life.

TWO FORMS OF PERFECTIONISM: CAPACITY-BASED AND HOLISTIC

Before we turn to the discussion of the work of Green and Bradley, however, it is useful to draw out a distinction within the perfectionist approach which

---

[7] For helpful further discussion of some of these themes, see Guyer 2011.
[8] Kant 1996 5: 58; cf. also 5: 64–5.
[9] Cf. Kant 2012 4: 443: '[Perfectionism] has an unavoidable propensity to revolve around in a circle, and covertly to presuppose the morality it is supposed to explain.'

(I will claim) underlies an important difference in their respective approaches, and thus in the way that each tries to deal with the Kantian challenge. This is the distinction between a perfectionism which sees the ideal self as one that has fully developed its capacities or capabilities, and a perfectionism which sees the ideal self as a unified or harmonious whole.

This difference may be traced back to the origins of this tradition in Plato and in Aristotle. Thus, for Plato, goodness is taken to be a proper balance or order among parts in a holistic manner,[10] whilst for Aristotle the focus is more on how far certain potentialities or capacities are realized and successfully developed. In general, it might be argued, Aristotle's approach is the predominant one, and can be found for example in Aquinas when he contrasts the imperfection of potentiality with the perfection of actuality.[11] However, Plato's outlook also remains embedded in the perfectionist tradition. Thus, for example, while his position also contains Aristotelian elements, Wolff argues that 'The harmony [*Zusammenstimmung*] of the manifold constitutes the perfection of things',[12] so that the perfection of the will consists in 'the harmony of all and every volition with one another, none running contrary to the rest'.[13]

Now of course, both forms of perfectionism can easily be put together, in the thought that in order to realize our capacities, we must do so in a harmonious manner, without each being at odds with the others; or, it could be argued that some capacities can only themselves be properly actualized in a unified and coherent way. This convergence between the two views explains why they are often run together and the difference is not usually highlighted or held to be significant. Nonetheless, they are still conceptually distinct; and, I will now suggest, when it comes to Green and Bradley, they do indeed come apart, under the pressure of finding an adequate perfectionist response to Kant's critique.

GREEN'S CAPACITY-BASED PERFECTIONISM

In his *Prolegomena to Ethics*, Green prefaces his theory of morality with an important discussion of the will in Book 2. He starts by offering an account of

---

[10] Cf. Kraut 1992: 322: '[T]he goodness of Forms consists in the fact that they possess a kind of harmony, balance, or proportion; and their superiority to all other things consists in the fact that the kind of order they possess gives them a higher degree of harmony than any other type of object.' In support of this reading, Kraut cites *Philebus* 23c–d and 64d–e.

[11] Aquinas 1920: 1–2 question 3 article 2.

[12] Wolff 1751: §152. Cf. Baumgarten 1779: §94.   [13] Wolff 1751: §907.

action, where he argues that what guides the will is not some specific want or desire, but a conception of the agent's own greatest good – hence, he claims, the agent in acting aims at 'self-satisfaction'.[14] For Green, therefore, when it comes to making a choice, there is no selection between competing desires made by the will; rather, the choice is made in determining which of the desires, if satisfied, would constitute the agent's greatest good, and on the basis of this decision the will then comes to act, with the other desires having been silenced.[15]

Green recognizes, however, that this picture leaves an important question unanswered when it comes to ethics: namely, what is it that distinguishes a morally good will from a morally bad one? Of course, on some accounts, this difference is marked by a distinction between the good agent who has no concern for their own well-being, and a bad one who is so concerned: but Green cannot take this option, given his account of action outlined above where such self-concern is present in *all* agents – so where does the difference lie? Green's answer is that the difference comes from the different conceptions of self-satisfaction that agents can have, and thus in 'the character of that in which self-satisfaction is sought, ranging from sensual pleasure to the fulfilment of a vocation conceived as given by God'.[16] Green's position depends, therefore, on making out some grounds on which to distinguish good and bad conceptions of self-satisfaction that might be held by different agents, where this explains the basis on which we might make a moral distinction between them.

For Green, then, the difference between the good and the bad person lies in his or her different conceptions of where and in what manner he or she can find self-satisfaction, and what this consists in.[17] But Green recognizes a difficulty: namely, that there is a circle here, as we seem to have to already know what moral goodness consists in before we can characterize an agent as moral and thus what the self-satisfaction of such an agent will involve; and on the other hand, if we do already know what such moral goodness amounts to, we wouldn't have to characterize it as what brings satisfaction to the moral agent, but must be able to grasp it independently in a prior manner, or not at all.[18] Faced with this difficulty, Green refers back to the metaphysical theorizing that he had developed in Book 1 of the *Prolegomena*, before he turned to the will and ethics as such, which argued that the world is the realization of a self-developing eternal mind;[19] and from this, he thinks we are

---

[14] Cf. Green 2003: §95.   [15] Cf. ibid., §104 and §§145–6.   [16] Ibid., §154.
[17] Cf. ibid., §171.   [18] Cf. ibid., §172.   [19] Cf. ibid., §67.

entitled to infer that what leads to the fulfilling of our capacities and thus our self-satisfaction is also what is morally good, and vice versa.[20]

We have seen, then, that Green holds that the good agent aims at the realization of his or her capacities, where he now argues that this 'will keep before him an object, which he presents to himself as absolutely desirable, but which is other than any particular object of desire'.[21] In the case of such particular objects, he will take these to have value only in so far as they satisfy some desire of his; but in the case of his self-realization, '[i]t will be an interest as in an object conceived to be of unconditional value; one of which the value does not depend on any desire that the individual may at any time feel for it or for anything else, or on any pleasure that, either in its pursuit or in its attainment or as its result, he may experience'.[22] In other words, Green claims that while the agent may see the value of everything else in terms of his wants and their attendant pleasures, he does not see the realization of his capacities in this way, as these constitute the end against which such wants and pleasures are themselves measured.[23]

However, we still have the problem of specifying what this unconditional good of self-realization consists in, where if we say that it is what the good will is directed towards, we will just be 'moving in a circle', because we have no independent conception of the good will, while the complete realization of human capacities has not yet been achieved.[24] Nonetheless, Green thinks, we can turn to the history of ethics to provide us with an important clue, where the key here (he argues) has been the central 'moral ideal' of the common good, in which individuals find their good to be bound up with that of others. At an earlier stage, in Greek ethics, these 'others' just comprised one's immediate community or polis; but in Christian ethics, this is widened to include all individuals. As a result of this conception of self-realization, Green argues that the distinction between 'benevolence' and 'self-love', and thus Sidgwick's famous 'dualism of practical reason', collapses and is shown to be a 'fiction',[25] insofar as no clear distinction can be drawn between the good of the individual and that of the society of which he or she is part, as the former good depends on the latter. Green therefore writes that '[t]he opposition of self and others does not enter into the consideration of a well-being so constituted'.[26] Thus, Green argues, the agent will come to treat others not

[20] Cf. ibid., §181.   [21] Ibid., §193.   [22] Ibid.   [23] Cf. ibid., §193.   [24] Cf. ibid., §194.
[25] Ibid., §232.
[26] Ibid., §235. Cf. also §232: 'His own permanent well-being he thus necessarily presents for himself as a social well-being.'

merely as means, but also as ends, in so far as he will be 'living for an object common to himself and all rational beings and consisting in the perfection of the rational nature', not just in himself but also in others.[27]

Finally, in Book 4 Green considers how far his account can help in providing us with guidance for conduct. Here he admits that superficially, at least, a theory like utilitarianism may appear to be in a better position, in seeming to give us a more concrete criterion of right action. On the other hand, he argues, in practice the calculation of consequences in utilitarian terms is in fact virtually impossible, while the very search for a simple solution to cases of moral perplexity is itself wrong-headed. Thus, Green argues, while it may not be easy to use perfection to tell us how to act, it is perhaps no worse than any other moral theory is or should be.

Taken as whole, therefore, it is easy to see why Green's student D.G. Ritchie should have characterized his view as having 'corrected Kant by Aristotle and Aristotle by Kant';[28] for, while returning to something like Aristotle's eudaimonism, this also takes a 'post-Kantian' form, and is importantly shaped by Kant's critique of the perfectionist tradition. So, in response to the charge of heteronomy, Green argues that our conception of the good is not merely set for us by desires and their satisfaction in a subjectivist manner, but involves the use of reason to determine where our proper self-satisfaction lies.[29] Thus, he argues, moral requirements can be based on the good of self-realization but still be categorical imperatives, as this goodness is independent of contingent inclinations and interests.[30] Green also shows himself to be sensitive to Kantian concerns regarding the priority of the moral law over the good, where the claim is that we must use the former to determine the latter; Green responds to this concern by using the history of ethics as a guide to the nature of self-realization, and so does not first try to offer an account of the good that does not take the principles of morality into account. Moreover, Green tries to deal with Kant's objection that the criterion of perfection is circular or morally empty – or at least, he argues that it is no more so than Kant's own criterion of universalizability, or the utilitarian criterion of the greatest happiness of the greatest number. At the same time, Green may claim to have 'corrected Kant by Aristotle', in offering a theory of action and motivation that gives a more central and plausible role to the conative side of the self, and hence shows how some of Kant's notorious dichotomies can be overcome, for example between duty and inclination, reason and desire.

---

[27] Green 1911: §118.   [28] Ritchie 1891: 139.   [29] But cf. Skorupski 2006: 57–8.
[30] Cf. Green 2003: §193.

Finally, the sense in which Green is a 'post-Kantian perfectionist' may be underlined by the way in which he connects self-realization not only with flourishing but also with freedom as a form of autonomy, in a way that gives a distinctively Kantian slant to his perfectionism.

At the same time, however, Green's way of trying to accommodate Kant's concerns may seem to reveal the weakness of his capacity-based view of perfectionism. For example, he is required to appeal to a 'divine principle' to justify his claim that we will find proper self-realization in a morally good end and vice versa, which then allows him to use the history of ethics as a guide to what human self-realization involves. This enables him to avoid the essentialist or biologistic claims of the Aristotelian regarding what our capacities consist in that then need to be exercised in order to attain flourishing; but he does so at the price of having to rely on his idealist metaphysics. Moreover, the Kantian may object to Green's attempt to show how, by starting off with a concern for our own self-realization, we will end up with a concern for that of others, based on his claim that an individual's good requires him or her to promote a common good, i.e. a good in which others also share. There are two worries here. First, the bridge Green tries to build from the individual's good to the common good may seem shaky, for it seems plausible to argue (as Sidgwick does, for example)[31] that my self-realization, conceived of as the development of my capacities, will not always mean that it is best served through contributing to the good of others; or at least, Green's account of what self-realization involves seems too vague to assert this connection with any great confidence,[32] where it could plausibly be argued that some aspects of my good require not co-operation with others, but competition against them. Second, even if this connection could be assumed, the Kantian may still argue that while on Green's picture there is a categorical imperative to realize in me a certain kind of character, and while that character may be one that takes an interest in the good of others as well as myself, nonetheless ultimately this interest is still not properly impartial, as my reason to have this attitude is that I will then have the right conception of my own good, in a way that ultimately concerns the benefits it brings to me in terms of self-satisfaction, and so is egoistic and not properly ethical.[33] In this way, Kant may think, his claims about morality as involving an impartial concern with the significance of others are still not properly accommodated within Green's perfectionism, and his attempts to revive Aristotelianism in this post-Kantian form have failed.

[31] Cf. Sidgwick 1902: 47–8 and 64.   [32] Ibid., pp. 55–6.
[33] Cf. Dewey 1873: 51. Cf. also Prichard 1928: 43.

We will now consider Bradley's approach, which involves a rather different view of the perfectionist position, in a way that may allow us to see how some of these concerns might be addressed.

In the second 'essay' or chapter of *Ethical Studies*,[34] Bradley appears to show himself to be sensitive to some of the concerns that have been raised above regarding Green's position, and to echo Kantian worries over the attempt to offer a perfectionist answer to the question of 'why should I be moral?' For, Bradley observes (in ways that came to be associated with H.A. Prichard some decades later),[35] unless this is itself a moral question (in which case the answer is obvious), it will make being moral into the means to a non-moral end, as concerning the interests of the individual, where 'to take virtue as a mere means to an ulterior end is in direct antagonism to the voice of the moral consciousness'.[36] Bradley may thus seem to be more alert than Green to the dangers of approaching morality in a perfectionist spirit, and hoping to find in it a response to the question of 'why be moral?'.

However, despite this, Bradley still thinks that the question can be given *some* meaning that will not lead us astray: for instead of asking if some prior end gives us a sufficient reason or motive to be moral, we can still ask what the *relation* is between acting morally and achieving our ultimate end qua human being and thus our good, even when we do not think of the former as the means to the latter, where the question then becomes: 'Is morality the same as the end for man, so that the two are convertible; or is morality one side, or aspect, or element of some end which is larger than itself? Is it the whole end from all points of view, or is it one view of the whole?'[37] Now, to answer *this* question, of course, requires us to specify what 'the end for man' is, which Bradley says is *self-realization*. He admits at once, however, that it is hard for him to prove this claim, as to do so would require 'something like a system of metaphysics',[38] which he cannot hope to provide here; nonetheless, he thinks it can be made plausible if we think about the nature of action, where again like Green he emphasizes that on a variety of different accounts, actions only occur if and when we 'feel ourselves asserted or affirmed in them',[39] and so take ourselves to realize ourselves in so acting.

[34] Bradley 1927. [35] Prichard 1912. [36] Bradley 1927: 61. [37] Ibid., 64. [38] Ibid., 65.
[39] Ibid., 68.

At this point, therefore, Bradley thinks he is entitled to ask about the relation between morality and self-realization;[40] but now of course he needs to tell us something about self-realization and what this amount to. It is here that his holistic perfectionism begins to emerge, where he argues that what the individual is trying to realize cannot be a 'mere one' or a 'mere many', but rather a 'one in many, or a many in one' – namely, 'the self as a whole, which is not merely the sum of its parts, nor yet some other particular beside them'. Thus Bradley asks rhetorically, 'must we not say that to realize self is always to realize a whole, and that the question in morals is to find the true whole, realizing which will practically realize the true self?'[41] This, then, gives the focus for the rest of *Ethical Studies*, as we can now ask, of various ethical systems, whether on their accounts morality as they conceive it would coincide with self-realization taken in this way, and thus how it would relate to 'the end for man'.

On this basis, therefore, Bradley argues that a morality of 'pleasure for pleasure's sake' or of 'duty for duty's sake' (which roughly correspond to utilitarianism and Kantianism respectively) cannot be satisfactory, as in neither can the self realize itself as a whole, given that each position takes a one-sided view of this totality: the former views the self as a collection of particular interests, while the latter views it as a pure will operating at an abstractly universal level standing above all such differentiation.[42] Moving in a dialectical manner, Bradley then introduces a third option of 'my station and its duties', that seems to resolve the one-sided opposition between these earlier alternatives, and thus arrive at a moral outlook that can do justice to the unity-in-difference of the self, by balancing the plurality of particularity with the oneness of universality.

What this requires, Bradley argues, is that morality comes from the ethical life of the community, in which there is room for both particularity and universality, as the individual carries out the specific and concrete social role that he or she occupies, while that role fits into a wider and more universal totality of which the individual is a part.[43] Earlier in *Ethical Studies*, Bradley had adapted a saying of Goethe's to write: 'You can not be a whole, *unless* you join a whole',[44] where it is thus in the unity of the community with its ethics of 'my station and its duties' that the self can be realized in this holistic sense.

---

[40] Cf. Ibid., 214 and 228.   [41] Ibid., 68–9.   [42] Ibid., 142.

[43] The influence of the Hegelian notion of *Sittlichkeit* is clearly very strong at this point in the text.

[44] Bradley 1927: 79.

However, despite arguing with considerable rhetorical force for this position,[45] Bradley also recognizes its limitations, including the worry that the individual may live within an imperfect state and so find no self-realization in ethical life, or may find such self-realization elsewhere, outside the moral life of the community altogether, for example in scientific inquiry or aesthetic production. Thus, in his search for a view of morality that coincides more fully with self-realization, Bradley moves to what he calls 'ideal morality', where the moral is seen as including more than the social relations of 'my station and its duties', and so as involving both demands that may be made on us beyond those required by any actual society, and also the kinds of duties to oneself that make the life of the artist or theorist moral in this broader sense.[46] Once broadened in this way, Bradley observes, it may be tempting to answer his original question in the affirmative.[47]

However, despite this seemingly optimistic result of his inquiries so far, Bradley still raises a difficulty: for morality, he thinks, involves what *ought* to be, not what *is*, and this always incorporates a gap between our actual existence and our full and final self-realization, so that for morality to make sense at all, the two can never coincide completely.[48] It is this tension, Bradley holds, that in thinking about self-realization takes us beyond morality altogether, and into religion, where *Ethical Studies* closes.

Before it does so, however, Bradley interposes a chapter on 'Selfishness and Self-Sacrifice', in which inter alia he considers how far a theory like his might be accused of doing away with morality and reducing it to self-interest, in so far as he holds that 'there is self-realization in all action; witness the feeling of pleasure'.[49] He argues, however, that while pleasure does indeed come from self-realization, this does not make pleasure the motive for the action, or our reason for it, and the same is true of self-realization itself; he therefore rejects the charge of selfishness that might be raised against his perfectionist ethics.[50]

We can again see, therefore, how far Bradley's form of perfectionism attempts to offer a 'post-Kantian' variant on this tradition, in aiming to respond to or avoid Kant's criticisms of this position in ethics. Bradley in a sense concedes a good deal of ground to those criticisms, for example by

---

[45] Bradley admits 'perhaps we have heated ourselves a little' in presenting the outlook of 'my station and its duties' (ibid., 202).

[46] Cf. ibid., 222–3. Green also raised this kind of case as a concern for his social ethics, but did not develop a response to it: see Green 2003: §§289–90.

[47] Cf. Bradley 1927: 228.　　[48] Ibid., 234–5.　　[49] Ibid., 84.

[50] Cf. ibid., 62 note. Green makes a similar point: see Green 2003: §158.

allowing that perfectionism cannot and should not provide an answer to the moral sceptic, or set itself up as offering guidance as a 'supreme principle of morality'. On the other hand, he argues that the former goal is inappropriate, while we can still intelligibly ask questions regarding the relation between morality and self-realization, and whether in acting morally we *do* realize ourselves, even while allowing that we do not act morally *in order to do so* in an instrumental fashion; and as regards the latter, Bradley argues that this is also not the business of moral theory, and that Kant himself is no more successful than other moralists in providing us with such a 'supreme principle'.[51] In this sense, his strategy is more sophisticated than Green's, who is generally not so self-conscious about the limitations of his project, and the justifications for such limitations.

Equally, perhaps, Bradley's holistic perfectionism helps him avoid the difficulties that Green had in having to employ his metaphysics to show why the capacities we have can best be realized in the moral life. Bradley's answer, by contrast, depends on his account of the structure of the will and its possible harmony,[52] rather than appealing to the 'divine principle' in man to ensure that self-realization and morality will coincide. While of course not without its problems, this would seem to give perfectionism a basis that is likeliest to be persuasive to the contemporary mind, and thus, of the two idealist thinkers, to offer us the more powerful insight into a perfectionism that takes this post-Kantian form. At the very least, it should now perhaps be clear that, as a result of the Kantian critique, perfectionism came to take two rather different forms in the hands of its idealist proponents, so what had formerly been inseparable aspects of this tradition – the capacity view and the holistic view – here come apart, with Green emphasizing one aspect, and Bradley the other.

BIBLIOGRAPHY

An asterisk denotes secondary literature especially suitable for further reading.

Aquinas, Thomas 1920. *Summa Theologica*. London: Burns Oates and Washbourne
Baumgarten, Alexander 1779. *Metaphysica*, 7th edn, reprinted Hildesheim: Olms, 1962
Bradley, F.H. 1927. *Ethical Studies*, 2nd edn. Oxford University Press
Brink, David O. 2003. *Perfectionism and the Common Good: Themes from the Philosophy of T.H. Green*, Oxford University Press*

---

[51] Cf. Bradley 1927: 193.   [52] Cf. ibid., 71–3.

Candlish, Stewart 1978. 'Bradley on My Station and Its Duties', *Australasian Journal of Philosophy*, 56, 155–70*

Dewey, John 1873. 'Self-Realization as the Moral Ideal', reprinted in *The Early Works of John Dewey, 1882–1898, vol. 4: 1893–1894, Early Essays and The Study of Ethics*, edited by Jo Ann Boydston. Carbondale, IL: Southern Illinois University Press, 2008

Green, T.H. 1911. *Lectures on the Philosophy of Kant, in Works of Thomas Hill Green*, edited by R.L. Nettleship, vol. 2. New York: Longman, Green & Co.

Green, T.H. 2003. *Prolegomena to Ethics*, edited by David O. Brink. Oxford University Press

Guyer, Paul 2011. 'Kantian Perfectionism', in Lawrence Jost and Julian Wuerth (eds.) *Perfecting Virtue*. Cambridge University Press, pp. 194–214

Irwin, Terence 2007. *The Development of Ethics*, vol. 1. Oxford University Press

Irwin, Terence 2009. *The Development of Ethics*, vol. 3. Oxford University Press

Kant, Immanuel 1996. *Critique of Practical Reason, in Practical Philosophy*, translated and edited by Mary J. Gregor. Cambridge University Press

Kant, Immanuel 2012. *Groundwork of the Metaphysics of Morals*, translated and edited by Mary Gregor and Jens Timmermann. Cambridge University Press

Kraut, Richard 1992. 'In Defense of Justice in Plato's *Republic*', in Richard Kraut (ed.), *The Cambridge Companion to Plato*. Cambridge University Press, pp. 311–37

Mander, W.J. 2011. *British Idealism: A History*. Oxford University Press

Mander, W.J. 2016. *Idealist Ethics*. Oxford University Press*

Moggach, Douglas 2011. 'Post-Kantian Perfectionism', in Douglas Moggach (ed.), *Politics, Religion, and Art: Hegelian Debates*. Evanston, Ill.: Northwestern University Press, pp. 179–202

Prichard, H.A. 1912. 'Does Moral Philosophy Rest on a Mistake?', reprinted in *Moral Writings*, edited by Jim MacAdam. Oxford University Press, 2002, pp. 7–20

Prichard, H.A. 1928. 'Duty and Interest', reprinted in *Moral Writings*, edited by Jim MacAdam. Oxford University Press, 2002, pp. 21–49

Ritchie, D.G. 1891. *The Principles of State Interference*. London: Swan Sonnenschein

Sidgwick, Henry 1902. *Lectures on the Ethics of T.H. Green, Mr Herbert Spencer, and J. Martineau*. London: Macmillan

Skorupksi, John 2006. 'Green and the Idealist Conception of a Person's Good', in Maria Dimova-Cookson and W.J. Mander (eds.), *T.H. Green: Ethics, Metaphysics, and Political Philosophy*. Oxford University Press, pp. 47–75

Wolff, Christian 1751. *Vernünfftige Gedancken von Gott, der Welt und der Seele des Menschen*, reprinted in *Gesammelte Werke*, ed. Ch. A. Corr. Hildesheim: Olms, 2009

42

Ethical Intuitionism

PHILIP STRATTON-LAKE

Ethical intuitionism is a movement in ethics that dates back to the early eighteenth century. It includes Ralph Cudworth, Samuel Clark, John Balguy, Richard Price, Henry Sidgwick, G.E. Moore, H.A. Prichard, W.D. Ross and A. C. Ewing. Not everyone would include Sidgwick and Moore as intuitionists, and both of them at times describe their view in opposition to intuitionism. This is because they were both consequentialists, and so denied the view held by most intuitionists that there is an irreducible number of basic moral principles. But I think both Sidgwick and Moore share enough in common with the other philosophers listed to be included amongst the intuitionists. In particular they both endorse the intuitionist epistemology according to which basic moral truths are self-evident, and the non-naturalist moral realism that is distinctive of ethical intuitionists. But their cases remind us that there is no clear cut-off point between intuitionism and other schools of moral thought.

SAMUEL CLARKE

Samuel Clarke was the most significant of the first generation of intuitionists. In opposition to Hobbes, whom he regarded as claiming that morality is simply the result of a contract, Clarke maintained that there are certain eternal and necessary relations of fittingness between certain personal relations and certain acts. He writes:

> from the different relations of different persons one to another, there necessarily arises a fitness or unfitness of certain manners of behaviour of some persons towards others.　　　　　　　　　　　　　(DNR 192)[1]

Certain relations, he maintains, are of a nature to make certain actions fit to be done, and these necessary relations of fittingness give rise to immutable

---

[1] Clarke 1991 [1706], *Discourse of Natural Religion*, cited as *DNR*.

laws that cannot be the outcome of any agreement or act of will by us. Indeed, even the will of God cannot give rise to these laws. For Clarke, we are not required to act in certain ways because God commands that we do. Rather God commands that we do certain acts because of their moral nature, a nature that is independent of his will.

Because morality is based on a strictly universal and necessary system of laws, it cannot be the upshot of any agreement. Indeed, Clarke raises a number of serious objections to Hobbes's view by showing that his own thesis presupposes obligations prior to the original contract if that contract is to bind us. For instance he argues that Hobbes's view that morality stems from an agreement can only work if there is a prior moral requirement to abide by our agreements. He also points out that if the destruction of mankind is such an evil that it is fit and reasonable that men enter into a compact to avoid it,

> then it was manifestly a thing unfit and unreasonable in itself that men should all destroy one another. And if so, then for the same reason it was also unfit and unreasonable, antecedent to all compacts, that any man should destroy another arbitrarily and without any provocation, or at any time when it was not absolutely and immediately necessary for the preservation of himself. (DNR 195)

But this contradicts Hobbes's view that nothing is in itself good or evil, just or unjust, prior to compact and positive law.

Clarke was more systematic than many pluralist intuitionists, and tries to impose some unity on the plurality of basic duties, rather than just list the principles of common sense. First he divides the laws of duty into three kinds: duties to God, duties to others, and duties to oneself. The duty to God is to honour and worship him, and is grounded in the relation of his infinite superiority to us.

Duties to others are divided into those of equity and love. The duty of love is one of impartial benevolence. Clarke offers different formulations of the duty of equity. Sometimes he describes this duty with reference to how we *desire* others to treat us (see e.g. DNR 208), and represents this principle as a version of the golden rule. But at other times he makes no reference to desire in describing this duty, as when he characterises it as the requirement that 'we so deal with every Man, as in like circumstances we could reasonably expect he should deal with Us' (DNR 207). This is not a point about how we want others to treat us, but rather one about how we might reasonably expect them to treat others. So this formulation does not seem to be a version of the golden rule. It is rather a point about the universality and impartiality of moral requirements.

Finally there is the duty to oneself of self-preservation (*DNR* 211). Clarke seems to include the duties of prudence and temperance under this general duty. The duty of self-preservation is grounded in the relation of creation to creator. Since we do not decide when and why we are brought into this world, it is not for us to decide when we will leave it, according to Clarke.

Clarke regards the three branches of duty mentioned above as the basic ones from which all others may be derived (*DNR* 212). So although Clarke was a pluralist about basic duties, and so rejected the idea that all duty could be grounded in a single principle, he was nonetheless engaged in the foundationalist project of determining which duties are basic, and which derived, and presumably wanted to reduce the number of basic duties to the minimum necessary to cover all of our obligations.

The systematisation of the deliverances of ordinary moral consciousness that Clarke and later intuitionists offers has epistemological and normative implications. It is only the most fundamental moral principles that intuitionists claim are self-evident. The most fundamental moral principles must, they think, be self-evident if we have any moral knowledge at all. Our belief in derivative moral principles is justified by our knowledge of the more basic principles that ground them. So unless we are justified in believing the more basic grounding principles we will not be justified in believing the derivative ones. Clearly this process must come to an end at some point, and this will be when we have reached the most fundamental moral principle (or at least one of them). The most fundamental principles will be those that explain and justify our belief in other moral principles, but are not themselves grounded in some other moral principle. Since our knowledge of the most fundamental moral principles cannot be justified on the basis of our knowledge of some other moral principle, then either these principles are in some way self-justifying or there is no justification for believing them. If there is no justification for believing the most fundamental moral principles, then we will have no moral knowledge, as the derivative principles that are grounded in them will also be unjustified. So if we have any moral knowledge, or justified moral beliefs, the basic moral principles must be self-evident.

Clarke had no doubt that basic principles of duty are self-evident and so need no argument for them (*DNR* 203–4). By 'self-evident' he seemed to mean that these propositions are such that an adequate understanding of them compels belief (*DNR* 206). This understanding was shared by other intuitionists, but seems too strong. For it would imply that disagreement about such basic principles implies lack of understanding, and it is difficult to accept that philosophers who deny putative self-evident moral truths lack an adequate understanding of what they deny. It is better, therefore, to regard self-evident truths as those that can justify, rather than compel, belief if adequately understood.[2]

Certain normative implications follow from the systematisation of ordinary moral thought. If derivative duties are grounded in more basic principles, then they will apply only when these more basic duties apply. If, for example, the duty not to lie is grounded in the duty not to break an implicit promise to tell the truth or not to harm others, then if my lie neither breaks an implicit promise nor harms anyone, as for instance in certain games, it will not be wrong. This is because the wrongness of lying is grounded in, and is thus conditional on, these other principles. Since basic moral duties do not acquire their normative force from some other duty, they will not be conditional upon the (contingent) applicability of these other duties. Transgressing basic duties will, therefore, always be wrong. Consequently, basic, unconditional, moral principles will be universally binding, whereas derivative, conditional, principles will not. No doubt this is why Clarke thought that the basic duties express universal and immutable relations of fittingness.

RICHARD PRICE

Price accepted most of what Clarke said about morality. He accepted that there are certain basic duties grounded in personal relations, that these duties are objective in the sense that they are grounded in the nature of things rather than in our constitution or in any contract made by us. He also accepted that basic propositions expressing basic duties are self-evident, and so need only be understood to gain assent (PQM 187).[3]

Where Price adds to Clarke's intuitionism is in his account of our moral ideas, or concepts. He was concerned to argue against the sentimentalist view that moral feelings are merely caused in us by the perception of certain acts (PQM 133). His view is that these ideas are the result of the intellect's intuition of real features of actions, of rightness and wrongness. Indeed, in so far as these ideas are simple they must be given directly to the mind by apprehension (PQM 141), as we cannot fabricate simple ideas.

This last point shows that it is important for Price to argue that moral ideas, such as good, bad, right and wrong, are simple, for his view that these ideas correspond to real properties in the object depends on this view. He argues for the simplicity, or indefinability, of moral concepts using what may

---

[2] See Audi 1996.
[3] Price 1991 [1758], *A Review of the Principal Questions in Morals*, cited as PQM.

be regarded as an early version of Moore's 'open-question argument' (see below). Any definition of right in terms of, say, producing happiness, cannot be correct, Price maintains, for if such a definition were correct then the substantive evaluative judgement that producing happiness is right would be converted into the empty tautology that producing happiness is producing happiness. Since the former but not the latter is an evaluative judgement, the former cannot be the same as the latter. Since this would apply to all definitions of moral terms, Price argues, moral terms must be simple and indefinable. They cannot be constructed from other ideas we have, but must be the immediate perception of real features of acts.

Price also filled out some of the details of Clarke's epistemology. Price distinguishes between three grounds of knowledge or belief. The first is immediate consciousness or feeling, by which he means the mind's awareness of its own existence and mental states (*PQM* 159). The second is intuition, which includes the 'mind's survey of its own ideas, and the relations between them, and the notice it takes of what is or is not true and false, consistent and inconsistent, possible and impossible in the nature of things' (*PQM* 159). The third ground of belief he lists is argumentation, or deduction (*PQM* 160). The first is immediate apprehension by sense; the second immediate apprehension by the understanding; and the third is truths grasped by arguing *from* what is immediately apprehended.

It is in the second way that we apprehend self-evident truths. Price claims that self-evident truths are 'incapable of proof' (*PQM* 160),[4] and many intuitionists endorse this view, but this is a mistake. The fact that a self-evident proposition can be known immediately does not mean that it cannot be known in some other, mediate, way, and so does not entail that it could not be known by means of some proof or argument. The point is simply that one does not need such an argument to know self-evident propositions. But that something is not needed does not show that it cannot be had.

HENRY SIDGWICK

Sidgwick rejected the pluralist, common sense, normative theory of Clarke and Price, and argued for a certain form of consequentialism. But although

---

[4] Although he does allow that such propositions admit of clarification, and that they may be illustrated 'by an advantageous representation of them, or by being viewed in particular lights' (*PQM* 159). Whether it is possible to spell out the distinction between an 'advantageous representation' of such propositions and an argument for them is something I leave undecided here.

Sidgwick rejected earlier intuitionists' pluralism, he endorsed their moral epistemology. Indeed, he developed this by listing a number of criteria for testing whether some proposition is self-evident. Such propositions must be:

1. clear and distinct
2. ascertained by careful reflection
3. consistent with other self-evident truths
4. attract general consensus (*ME* 338).[5]

If some apparent self-evident proposition does not have all of these features then we should reduce our confidence that it is a genuine self-evident proposition. Sidgwick rejected many of the principles Clarke and Price endorsed as he felt that those principles did not meet his criteria, or stood in need of justification. But Sidgwick did not reject all self-evident moral principles. He accepted Clarke's principle of equity and universal benevolence as self-evident (*ME* 379, 382). He also maintained that it is self-evident that we ought to aim at our own good on the whole, where 'good on the whole' involves treating future benefits to ourselves as we would treat equal present benefits.

The principle of equity, he maintains, is something that all moral theories must acknowledge. They will differ with regard to when and why it will be right to treat someone in a certain way, but must accept that the same considerations that make it right for me to treat you in a certain way will make it right for you to treat me in the same way (all other things being equal). We may, then, regard this as a formal principle, rather than a substantive principle telling us *what* we ought to do.

This leaves the principles of rational egoism and universal benevolence. It may seem from this that Sidgwick is after all a pluralist, albeit a pluralist with only two basic principles. But it is not clear that his principle of rational egoism is a moral principle, and if that is right then only the principle of beneficence is a moral principle. So although he lists two substantive (plus one formal) self-evident principles, he believes that there is only one basic *moral* principle.

Since Sidgwick identifies my good and the good of others with happiness, and understands happiness to be simply pleasure and the absence of pain, rational egoism will involve producing as much net pleasure for oneself as one can, and universal benevolence will involve producing as much net pleasure in the world as is possible (*ME* 402). But in both cases this goal is

[5] Sidgwick 1967 [1874], *Methods of Ethics*, cited as *ME*.

best achieved indirectly. What he means by this is that we are much more likely to live a pleasant life and produce pleasure in general if we aim at things other than pleasure, such as virtue, truth, freedom, beauty, etc. for their own sake (*ME* 405). So his consequentialism requires non-consequentialist motivations and goals. But what justifies these motivations and goals is the consequentialist principle of maximising good.

It is a striking feature of Sidgwick's principles that they do not pass his own tests for self-evidence. For instance the principle of rational egoism and universal benevolence will often conflict, and in such cases it looks like Sidgwick is committed to saying that I ought to do both the benevolent act and the self-interested act. So it looks like these two principles fail the third test of consistency. Also the principle of impartial benevolence is very controversial. Many philosophers think that it fails to recognise the moral significance of certain personal relations. Since this principle is controversial it seems it fails the fourth test of consensus.

G.E. MOORE

G.E. Moore was greatly influenced by Sidgwick, and agreed with him that we ought always to produce as much good as possible, and that the best way to do that was indirectly, by deliberating in accordance with common sense principles. But Moore differed from Sidgwick in several important ways. First, he was pluralistic about the good that is to be promoted. Pleasure will figure in many of those goods, but is not itself of any great intrinsic value, according to Moore, and is certainly not the sole good. Amongst the many diverse goods Moore held that the admiring contemplation of beauty and pleasures of social intercourse were by far the most important (*PE* 237).[6]

A further way in which Moore differed from Sidgwick is that in his *Principia* he argued that 'right' *means* 'maximises good' (*PE* 196). So he thought that consequentialism was true by definition. This is quite a surprising thing for Moore to say given that he devoted considerable energy, in his *Principia Ethica*, to arguing that 'good' is indefinable, and the arguments he uses in support of this view about good apply equally well to right. Moore later came to see the unsustainability of analytic consequentialism, and in his later work (*Ethics*) maintained that this principle expresses a synthetic truth.

There is something like the open-question argument in Sidgwick, but Moore placed much greater emphasis on this, and on the conclusion that is

---

[6] Moore 1993 [1903], *Principia Ethica*, cited as *PE*.

supposed to follow from it – that the fundamental moral notion of 'good' cannot be defined in terms of concepts of the empirical sciences. The open-question argument is, then, supposed to show that naturalists commit what Moore calls the naturalistic fallacy – the fallacy of thinking that goodness is a natural property.

His argument rests on the idea of an open question. A question is open if it is significant and thus is a real question for someone who understands the concepts used. This is contrasted to a closed question, which is one that betrays a lack of understanding of the concepts used if it is thought to be significant. So for example, the question 'x has red fur, but is it a fox?' is an open question, but the question 'x is a vixen, but is it a fox?' is closed. The latter is closed because 'vixen' means 'female fox', so the question asks 'x is a female fox, but is x a fox?'

Moore held that if 'good' (G) could be defined in terms of some natural property (N), then the question 'x is N, but is it G?' would be closed. It follows that if it is open, then the definition is false. Moore then applied this argument to naturalistic definitions of 'good'. Suppose someone proposes that to be good is just to be pleasant. We can test this definition by asking whether the question 'x is pleasant, but is it good?' is open or not. Prima facie this question is open – it is a perfectly sensible question, which betrays no misunderstanding of the concepts used. If that is right then this definition is false. Moore held that all naturalistic definitions of good would fail the open-question argument, and so concluded that good is a *sui generis* concept.

Another distinctive feature of Moore's intuitionism is his doctrine of organic unities. According to this doctrine the intrinsic value of a complex whole may not be the sum of the intrinsic value of its constituent parts. For example, pleasure is intrinsically good, but its presence can make the whole of which it is a part worse rather than better. If someone is suffering, that is a bad thing. But if someone takes pleasure in their suffering, that makes things worse rather than better, even though pleasure is a good thing. Similarly, although suffering is intrinsically bad, the addition of suffering can sometimes make the world a better place. This is the case when a criminal is punished for his wrong-doing, according to Moore. That the criminal is made to suffer makes things better rather than worse, even though suffering is a bad thing.

H.A. PRICHARD

Prichard opposed the influence of Sidgwick and Moore by arguing that the right can never be derived from the good. He argued for this view by claiming that there are three possible ways in which the right can be grounded in the good, and that all three fail.

The first is to ground rightness in the agent's own good. This is ethical egoism. Prichard dismisses this quickly on two grounds. First he takes it as a common fact about everyday life that self-interest and morality can conflict, so the latter cannot be grounded in the former. The ethical egoist might see this as a conflict between short-term and long-term self-interest, but that is not very plausible, as morality may require one to sacrifice one's own life for the greater good. It cannot be said that complying with morality in such cases promotes the agent's long-term interests.

His second argument is that ethical egoism conflates hypothetical imperatives with categorical ones. If some act promotes the individual's good, then that individual ought to do that act. But the 'ought' in question is only hypothetical, Prichard maintains, and he understands this to mean that this act is necessary to get what you want. But moral 'oughts' are categorical rather than hypothetical. We ought to do obligatory acts regardless of what we want. So, he says, seeing that some act will promote our own good can get us to want to do it, but cannot instil a sense of obligation to do it. Since it is obligations that need to be explained, the egoist fails to answer this question with his explanation.

The second attempt to ground the right in the good is to ground rightness in the instrumental goodness of the act – which is what consequentialism does. Prichard objects to this attempt with reference to counter-examples. If utilitarianism were true then we should create as much happiness as we can. It does not, however, matter whose happiness we promote. But, Prichard objects, it often does matter. For instance, if I could save either a stranger or my father, then it is clear that I ought to benefit my father, even though I would produce as much good if I saved the stranger.

But Prichard does not rely simply on the force of counter-examples. He also argues that the attempt to derive the right from the good involves a fallacy of equivocation. The consequentialist claims that we are obligated to do certain acts because those acts produce the best outcome. But, Prichard claims, one can only derive an 'ought' from another 'ought', so an 'ought' is needed in one of the premises. The only way the consequentialist can meet this requirement is by claiming that the good ought to exist.[7] One could then argue that what is best most ought to exist, and conclude that we ought to do the acts that would make it the case that the best state of affairs does exist.

---

[7] Prichard 2002b [1912], 9–10.

The equivocation in this argument is that the 'ought' in the conclusion is the 'ought' of obligation, but the sense in which the good ought to exist is not the 'ought' of obligation. To suppose that it was would involve the absurdity of supposing that obligations can apply to states as well as actions. Since the 'ought' in the consequentialist premise is not the same as the 'ought' in the conclusion, this is not a valid argument for consequentialism. This anti-consequentialist argument has had little influence on intuitionist thought, and it is not clear that Prichard thought it was a strong argument, as he does not repeat it. If it does work against consequentialism, it would seem to work against Prichard's own view, as he thought that certain personal relationships were sufficient to ground obligations. Since a personal relationship is not an 'ought', it looks like Prichard himself tries to derive 'oughts' from 'is's.

The third attempt to derive the right from the good is Kantian in style. According to this view, the reason why we ought to do certain acts is that those acts are intrinsically good. Prichard starts his objection to this view by claiming that acts by themselves, when abstracted from their motives, have no intrinsic value. It is only if we think of the motive as a part of the act that an act can have intrinsic value, for all of its value would stem from its motive – either the motive of duty, or some intrinsically good desire, such as love of benevolence. If that is right, then if we ought to do certain acts because they are intrinsically good, then we ought not only to do certain acts, but to do them from good motives. But, Prichard objects, we are only ever required to do certain acts; never to do them from certain motives. If, for example, I promise to repay what you have lent me, then I have done the right thing if I repay you, regardless of motive. You could not object that I have failed to do the right thing because I did not repay you from an intrinsically good motive.

This argument has some force with duties of fidelity, since what it is we are required to do is determined by what we have promised, and we tend only to promise to do certain acts, rather than act from certain motives. But Prichard's view is less compelling in relation to other duties. For instance, sometimes I ought to be kind, but it is unclear that I could comply with this duty regardless of motive. If I helped someone from some selfish, or spiteful, motive, it seems as though I have failed to act kindly, and so failed to do the right act. The same is true of duties of gratitude. It is not clear that I have complied with this duty if I act from some ulterior motive, or from spite.

In general Prichard maintained that all we can do if we come to doubt whether some act is our duty is to get the situation clearly in mind, and come to see by reflection that the state we are in in relation to the proposition that our duty is to do a certain act is one of knowing rather than believing. If it were believing that would imply uncertainty and the need for an argument. Knowing does not involve such uncertainty and does not need an argument in support of what is known. This is just seen directly. Once this is recognised, Prichard thinks, we will see that the goal of moral philosophy of providing some criterion by which we can check our moral beliefs is a mistake.

W.D. ROSS

Ross was persuaded by Prichard's arguments against the attempt to derive the right from the good, and so was content to repeat them in the opening chapters of *The Right and the Good*.[8] He rejected Moore's consequentialism, but accepted a great deal of what Moore had to say about the good, although he thought that the doctrine of organic unities was not very significant.

Ross's own contribution to intuitionism, and to moral philosophy in general, was to introduce the idea of a prima facie duty. Ross distinguished between duty proper and prima facie duty. Duty proper is what we ought to do all things considered, whereas prima facie duties pick out features of acts that count for or against doing them. The idea is that the various competing prima facie duties determine what our duty proper is. So, for instance, that we have promised to meet a friend generates a prima facie duty to do that, and the fact that we can help someone generates a prima facie duty of beneficence. Sometimes these prima facie duties will conflict. In such cases the weightier prima facie duty determines our duty proper. So if the prima facie duty of beneficence is weightier than the prima facie duty of fidelity, then our duty proper, what we ought to do all things considered, is to help the person. Our act will be prima face wrong in the respect that it transgresses the prima facie duty of fidelity, but it will not be wrong. Rather, in such circumstances the right thing to do is to help rather than keep our promise. That the prima facie duty of beneficence can sometimes outweigh that of fidelity does not mean that it always will. Sometimes the help we can give to someone is not very significant, and the promise is quite weighty. In such cases it is likely that our duty proper is to keep our promise.

No prima facie duty is such that it always wins out in a conflict with another prima facie duty. So there can be no strictly universal principles of duty proper. There are however strictly universal principles of prima facie duty. It may not always be right to help someone in distress, but the fact that

[8] Ross 2002 [1930].

one would be helping always counts in favour of one's act, and that one would fail to help someone always counts against it. Similarly, it is not always right to keep one's promises, but the fact that one would be keeping one's promise always counts in favour of one's act, and that one would be breaking a promise always counts against.

Ross maintained there is an irreducible plurality of basic prima facie duties. He started with a provisional list of seven, but reduces these to five basic duties – fidelity, gratitude, reparation, promoting the good, and non-maleficence. Ross claims that all of our duties can be derived from these five principles. For instance, the duty of honesty is derived from the prima facie duty of fidelity to an implicit promise to use language to express our opinion, and the prima facie duty of non-maleficence.

It is not clear, however, that Ross's list does cover everything. For instance it is not clear how the duties of parents to their children are explained with reference to Ross's list. The prima facie duty to promote the good doesn't help, as that would not explain why we have a special responsibility for our own children, rather than for children in general. Similarly it is unclear whether the special responsibility we have to our friends can be explained by Ross's list of prima facie duties. So it may be that Ross has to add more basic prima facie duties to his list to explain all the duties we have.

Ross is, arguably, the last of the great classical ethical intuitionists. After Ross intuitionism fell into disrepute. Many philosophers found its non-naturalist realism and rationalist epistemology hard to accept, while others found the sort of normative theory offered by Ross empty and unsystematic. This lack of sympathy to intuitionist thought lasted for much of the twentieth century, but by the 1990s philosophers such as Dancy, Audi and Shafer-Landau started to defend various aspects of intuitionist thought. It is now regarded as a serious position in both meta-ethics and normative ethics.

BIBLIOGRAPHY

An asterisk denotes secondary literature especially suitable for further reading.

Audi, R. (1996) 'Intuitionism, Pluralism, and the Foundations of Ethics', in Sinnott-Armstrong, W. and Timmons, M. (eds.), *Moral Knowledge?* New York: Oxford University Press.
Audi, R. (1998) 'Moderate Intuitionism and the Epistemology of Moral Judgment', *Ethical Theory and Moral Practice* 1 (1): 15–44.
Audi, R. (1999) 'Self-Evidence', *Philosophical Perspectives* 13: 205–28.
Audi, R. (2004) *The Good in the Right: A Theory of Intuition and Intrinsic Value.* Princeton University Press.

Clarke, S. (1991) [1706] *Discourse of Natural Religion*, in Raphael, D.D. (ed.), *The British Moralists 1650–1800*, vol. 1. Indianapolis, IN: Hackett, pp. 191–225.

Cook Wilson, J. (1926) *Statement and Inference: With Other Philosophical Papers*. Farquarson, A.S.L. (ed.), Oxford: Clarendon Press.

Cudworth, R. (1969) [1731] *A Treatise Concerning Eternal Immutable Morality*, in Raphael, D. D. (ed.), *The British Moralists 1650–1800*, vol. 1. Indianapolis, IN: Hackett, pp. 103–34.

Ewing, A.C. (1947) *The Definition of Good*. London: Routledge.

Moore, G.E. (1993) [1903] *Principia Ethica*. Baldwin, T. (ed.), Cambridge University Press.

Portmore, D.W. (2003) 'Position-Relative Consequentialism, Agent-Centered Options, and Supererogation', *Ethics* 113 (2): 303–32.

Price, Richard (1991) [1758] *A Review of the Principal Questions in Morals*, in Raphael, D.D. (ed.), *The British Moralists 1650–1800*, vol. 2. Indianapolis, IN: Hackett, pp. 131–98.

Prichard, H.A. (2002a) 'What is the Basis of Moral Obligation?', in *Moral Writings*. McAdam, J. (ed.), Oxford: Clarendon Press, pp. 1–6.

Prichard, H.A. (2002b) [1912] 'Does Moral Philosophy Rest on a Mistake?', in *Moral Writings*. McAdam, J. (ed.), Oxford: Clarendon Press, pp. 7–20.

Ross, W.D. (1927) 'The Basis of Objective Judgements in Ethics', *International Journal of Ethics* 37: 113–27.

Ross, W.D. (2002) [1930] *The Right and the Good*. Stratton-Lake, P. (ed.), Oxford: Clarendon Press.

Shaver, R. (2011) 'The Birth of Deontology', in Hurka, T. (ed.), *Underivative Duty: British Moral Philosophers from Sidgwick to Ewing*. Oxford University Press, pp. 126–45.

Sidgwick, H. (1967) [1874] *The Methods of Ethics*, 7th edn. London: Macmillan.

Sturgeon, N. (2002) 'Ethical Intuitionism and Ethical Naturalism', in Stratton-Lake, P. (ed.), *Ethical Intuitionism: Re-evaluations*. Oxford University Press, pp. 184–211.*

Warnock, M. (1968) *Ethics since 1900*. Oxford University Press.

Wiggins, D. (1976) 'Truth, Invention, and the Meaning of Life', *Proceedings of the British Academy* 62: 331–78.

Williams, B. (1995) 'What Does Intuitionism Imply?', in *Making Sense of Humanity and Other Philosophical Papers 1982–1993*. Cambridge University Press.*

43

Husserl and Phenomenological Ethics

NICOLAS DE WARREN

Husserlian phenomenology is widely recognized for its enduring philosophical contributions. "Intentionality," "the life-world," "the lived-body" and other notions have long been absorbed into contemporary thought, even as Husserl's project remains a matter of contention. Lesser known is the originality of Husserl's phenomenological approach to ethics, even though Husserl's ethical thought followed as well as shaped his phenomenological enterprise from its beginning. As with other aspects of his thinking, Husserl never arrived at a definitive statement of his ethics. His voluminous manuscripts and lecture courses on ethics present a work in progress marked by insight, transformation, and promise, much of which still remains undeveloped today.

As Husserl declares in "Philosophy as Rigorous Science," the genuine aim of philosophy is to become a "rigorous science" that would satisfy the "theoretical need" for a fundamental clarification of how knowledge is possible and "render possible from an ethical-religious point of view a life by pure rational norms."[1] Phenomenological philosophy is intrinsically an ethical project in its aim to provide a foundation for knowledge, ethical values, and the norms of practical ends. As Husserl formulated in 1906: "In the first place, let me state the general task that I must realize for myself, if I am ever to call myself a philosopher. I mean a critique of reason. A critique of logical and practical reason, above all a critique of valuing reason (*der wertenden Vernunft*)" (Hua 24: 445).[2]

My thanks to Ullrich Melle and the editors of this volume for comments on an earlier version of this essay.

[1] Husserl 1965: 71.

[2] "Hua" refers to Husserliana, the standard German collection of Husserl's works published by Martinus Nijhoff and its successors, Kluwer and Springer. References are to volume and page. "HuaMat" refers to the Materialien volumes – non-critical editions – published in the Husserliana series.

BRENTANO'S REFORM OF ETHICS

Husserl's remark that "without Brentano, I would not have written a word of philosophy" holds equally well for his work on ethics.[3] The importance of ethics for Brentano has long been over-shadowed by his more influential study of consciousness and his acclaimed introduction of "intentional relation" and "inner perception" as distinguishing marks of the mental. Brentano, however, expressly conceived of his "psychology without a soul" as leading to a reform of ethics. As he writes: "How many evils might be remedied by the correct psychological diagnosis or by the knowledge of the laws by which a mental state can be modified?"[4] Less visible from his published writings, this ethical promise occupied a central place in his teaching, public lectures, and unpublished reflections.[5]

The significance of Brentano's ethical thought was not lost on his contemporaries. As G.E. Moore acknowledges in his review of *The Origin of Our Knowledge of Right and Wrong*:[6] "This is a far better discussion of the most fundamental principles of Ethics than any others with which I am acquainted. Brentano himself is fully conscious that he has made a very great advance in the theory of Ethics [. . .] and his confidence both in the originality and in the value of his own work is completely justified."[7] As Brentano himself declares: "I have attempted to determine the principles of our knowledge of ethics upon the basis of new analyses and in a way quite different from what has been done before."[8] These "new analyses" refer to Brentano's descriptive analysis of his threefold classification of mental phenomena into presentation (*Vorstellung*), judgment, and the emotions of loving and hating (a third class combining willing and feeling). Each of these intentional relations aims at a

---

[3] For the purpose of this essay, I shall restrict my discussion to Brentano's ethical thought during the 1870s–1890s – the starting point for Husserl.

[4] Brentano 1973a: 31.   [5] See Brentano's essays (1926 and 1929); see also Gubser 2009.

[6] Brentano's *Vom Ursprung sittlicher Erkenntnis* (1889) was translated into English by Cecil Hague as *The Origin of the Knowledge of Right and Wrong* (London: Constable & Co, 1902). A later translation was undertaken as *The Origin of Our Knowledge of Right and Wrong* on the basis of Oskar Kraus' 1921 edition. Brentano's notes for his lectures on practical philosophy at the University of Vienna from 1876 to 1894 were posthumously published as *Grundlegung und Aufbau der Ethik*, ed. F. Mayer-Hildebrand (Bern: A. Francke, 1952), and translated into English as *The Foundation and Construction of Ethics*, trans. E. Schneewind (London: Routledge & Kegan Paul, 1973).

[7] Moore 1903: 115. Moore did not discover the English translation of Brentano's work until he had completed his *Principia Ethica* (published in 1903).

[8] Brentano 2009: x.

particular kind of perfection: the Beautiful, the True, and the Good. For Brentano, the presentation of an object as well as its affirmation in judgment can be accompanied by an emotional stance of value that renders the object as either "good" (worthy of love) or "evil" (worthy of hate). The highest perfection of love, the exalted feeling on the basis of which Brentano establishes his ethics, is the highest good, or end, most worthy of love that rises above self-interest, pleasure, and utility.

Brentano understands ethics as the "practical discipline that teaches us about the highest end and the choosing of the means to achieve it."[9] Brentano's ethical thought is accordingly guided by three aims: to establish an ethical principle of the highest good; to uncover the origin of our knowledge of good and evil; to develop a system of practical norms. For the highest practical good, Brentano proposes the principle, "Choose the best among the ends which are attainable."[10] Contrary to Mill, maximizing happiness is not *always* the highest end, since Brentano stipulates that one should strive to realize the best end among possible (i.e., reasonably attainable) ends; the best is that end most preferable within a range of other ends. Contrary to Kant, the highest end is not a formal demand of practical reason, but based on a right kind of emotional apprehension, or "rightness of striving (*Erstreben*)," which establishes the "rightness of the end" (*die Richtigkeit des Zweckes*). The highest good is ultimately God and the "Ideal of all Ideals" is the "unity of all Truth, Goodness, and Beauty" that promises "blessedness" for whomever beholds this threefold unity. Yet, the highest good is not identical with the highest *practical* good, which, instead, is that end most worthy of love that one must (and *can*) strive to realize: the greatest amount of good within the widest sphere of influence extending beyond the individual to embrace family, nation, and, indeed, all of humanity. As Brentano formulates this principle of summation (*Summierungsprinzip*): "To further the good throughout this great whole so far as possible – this is clearly the correct end in life, and all our actions should be centered around it."[11]

Brentano's originality consists in locating the origin of "good" (and its contrary, "evil") in experiences of love and hate. As Brentano argues, "this

[9] Brentano 1973b: 5; 88.
[10] Brentano 2009: 12. "Wähle das Beste unter dem Erreichbaren!"
[11] Ibid., 40. Brentano's normative ethics – omitted here from consideration – develops a system of practical principles by which, in any given situation, we are able to choose the right end of action. For a discussion of Brentano's normative ethics, highly influenced by Mill's utilitarianism, and its situational account of practical principles, see McAlister 1982: 128ff.

concept [*the good*], like all our others, has its origin in certain intuitive presentations," and such presentations are characterized as an intentional relation to an object.[12] Descriptive psychology offers a subjective foundation for objective moral values and normative principles of conduct. While Brentano accepts Hume's argument that moral distinctions are grounded in feelings (and not in cognition), he insists that ethical values and norms cannot be reduced to their mental apprehension as feelings. For Brentano, an object is *intrinsically* good if and only if the love (and hence: striving) relating to it is "correct" or "proper" (*richtig*); love is experienced as "correct" or "proper" in an intentional relation to the intrinsic goodness, or worthiness, of an object.[13] As Brentano claims, "we call a thing *true* when the affirmation relation to it is correct. We call a thing *good* when the love relating to it is correct. In the broadest sense of the term, the good is that which is worthy of love, that which can be loved with a love that is correct."[14] Brentano thus proposes an analogy between judgments and feelings: whereas judgment intends the existence or non-existence of objects, feeling intends the "goodness" or "worthiness" of the object. In this manner, Brentano establishes a parallelism between a correspondence theory of truth as *adaequatio rei et intellectus* and a correspondence theory of ethical knowing as *adaequatio rei et amoris*.[15]

HUSSERL'S ETHICS BEFORE WORLD WAR I

Husserl's phenomenological ethics prior to the First World War is largely conceived as a development of Brentano's ethical reform. As with his mentor, Husserl considers his own phenomenological ethics as reconciling the question of whether ethical values and imperatives have their origin in reason or feeling.[16] Husserl accepts the desiderata of discovering a foundation for ethical knowledge and practical norms of action by way of what Husserl proposes as the new disciplines of "formal axiology" and "formal theory of praxis (*Praktik*)."[17] In both instances, Husserl seeks to establish the a priori laws of values and action (means and ends) as analogous to the a priori laws of

---

[12] Brentano 2009: 15.
[13] See Chisholm 1966 for a reconstruction of Brentano's axioms of love.
[14] Brentano 2009: 18.   [15] McAlister 1982: 86.
[16] In his 1920/1924 lecture course "Einleitung in die Ethik," Husserl critically discusses the moral theories of Cudworth, Clarke, Shaftesbury, Butler, Hume, and Kant (Hua 37: 125–237).
[17] As Husserl announces in his 1914 lecture course "Vorlesungen über Grundfragen der Ethik und Wertlehre," both of these new disciplines, intended to formulate the

formal logic. Husserl further envisions a practical discipline of prescriptive norms for ethical action, a description of the material content of ethical imperatives, and a rank ordering of values (and rational preferences). Husserl follows a methodological approach based on "new analyses" of consciousness, albeit in the form of his own essential ("eidetic") analysis of intentionality. Husserl's investigations follow four trajectories: analysis of "noetic acts" of consciousness (valuing, willing); analysis of the rationality of valuing and willing; analysis of the ontological status of values; analysis of ethical theories within modern philosophy.

With the publication of the *Logical Investigations*, Husserl began to define his phenomenological project as a systematic critique of reason in its three domains (epistemological, axiological, and practical) corresponding to three kinds of intentionality: acts of judging grounded in perception, acts of valuation (feeling) (*Gefühlsakte* or *Fühlen*), and acts of volition (*Willensakte* or *Wollen*).[18] Cognitive judgments apprehend intentional objects and/or states-of-affairs as either "true" or "false"; valuing apprehends the value of intentional objects; and willing intends the means and ends of an action (structured as choice, fiat for acting, and sustaining volition).

Although accepting Brentano's analogy between judgment and feeling, Husserl, however, breaks with him in two regards. First: in light of the distinction between "objectifying" and "non-objectifying" consciousness, Husserl only considers perception (and judgment) as "objectifying," whereas valuing and feeling are "non-objectifying" acts of consciousness, and hence dependent on an underlying perceptual act for their objectification (Hua 28: 68). Husserl thus blends "cognitivist" and "non-cognitivist" elements: willing in view of an end is founded on the feeling-apprehension of a value (I act for the sake of X on the basis of apprehending its value Y), which, in turn, is founded on an act of perception (I apprehend an object as possessing value Y on the basis of perceiving that object); it is only to the underlying perceptual apprehension that values and willing owe their respective intentional reference (Hua 19/1: 404).[19] As Husserl writes, cognitive acts "illuminate" (*hineinleuchten*) otherwise "blind" and "mute" acts of valuing and willing. Value-feelings are blind without judgments, while ethical judgments are empty without affective intuition of ethical values. Second: Husserl undoes Brentano's unification of

formal principles of "correct feeling" and "correct willing," have "never previously existed in the philosophical tradition" (Hua 37: 4).

[18] Feeling and willing belong together under the heading of *Gemüt*.
[19] See also *Logical Investigations*, §10 (Husserl 2001) and *Ideen* I, § 95 (Husserl 1976).

feeling and willing into one single intentional relation. Husserl's distinction between felt values and willing thus opens a broad field of investigation into moral motivation and the relationship (as well as tension) among the force of values, the traction of the will, and the weight of cognitive judgment.

During the years 1902–1913, Husserl struggled with the considerable challenges raised by his approach to ethics. In his lecture courses and manuscripts, he appears torn between two *analogies* for the experience of value: either as akin to perceptual properties of an object, for which Husserl coined the term *Wertnehmen*, or as akin to what Husserl calls "doxic characters," or modalities of belief ("probable," "certain," etc.), for which Husserl patterned the experience of value on a form of "position-taking" (*Stellungnahme*). Husserl equally struggles with his conception of the stacked foundation of perception, feeling, and willing, and begins to explore a more "interwoven" relationship (Hua 28: 72). Valuing/feeling and willing still possess an a priori form of reason, yet Husserl begins to weaken his claim that valuing reason and practical reason are *founded* on theoretical reason. Husserl does not, however, endorse Max Scheler's view, for whom cognition is *based* on an a priori order of "value-being" (*Wertsein*) and corresponding acts of love and hate.[20] Values as well as (proper) ends of action can be verified in the corresponding evidence of intuitive presentations. Yet, the ontological status of values (and proper ends) remained elusive for Husserl as it depended in part on how to construe value-experiences as either an intuitive apprehension (*Wertnehmen*) *or* a "position-taking" (*Stellungnahme*).[21] In his 1914 lecture course, for example, Husserl considers feeling and willing as different "position-takings." On this view, the "positing" of an object as valuable is seen as analogous to the positing of an object as "existing" in a judgment; differences among "position-takings" correspond to different "modalities of being." On such a view, different "noetic" acts of valuing would correspond to different "doxic characteristics" of the intentional ("noematic") object, for example, how an object appears as "probable," "questionable," etc. On the alternative view of value-experiences as *Wertnehmung* ("value apprehension"), the value of an object is akin to a perceptual property that is apprehended in a feeling. Truth-claims about values can therefore be adjudicated with appeal to how the object appears *through* corresponding feelings.

---

[20] See Scheler 1973.

[21] Husserl's efforts to think-through by phenomenological means the analogy between knowing, feeling, and willing would prove inconclusive – as Husserl himself realized. See Melle 1988.

Husserl further modifies Brentano's ethical principle into: "the best attainable within the entire practical sphere is not merely the best comparatively speaking, but rather the sole practical good" (Hua 28: 221).[22] Husserl thus places a greater emphasis on the future of practical possibilities: willing aims in an intentional manner at its own practical possibilities within the circumscribed situation of acting and must determine within this field of possible action the highest, or best, end within a range of attainable ends. Husserl's basic ethical principle has the outward form of a categorical imperative, yet critically depends on the material a priori (and apprehension) of values. As Husserl writes: "Were there no material a priori [...] then the concept of objective value would have no support, and consequently there would be no support for the idea of an objectively pre-established preferability and for the idea of a 'best'" (Hua 28: 139).

THE RENEWAL OF HUSSERL'S ETHICS AFTER WORLD WAR I

The Great War provoked a dramatic transformation in Husserl's ethical thought as well as in his vision of the historical imperative and cultural mission of transcendental phenomenology. As with the many twists and turns in Husserl's thinking, this change within his ethical thought provided an occasion for a deepening of central insights from his earlier writings.[23]

The transformation of Husserl's thinking steered his ethical investigations away from a *primary* concern with axiology and theory of praxis as "regional ontologies" to a transcendental concern with the conditions of possibility for an ethical life and moral obligation. At the center of this new orientation is the theme of "self-constitution" as the project of "absolute (self)-responsibility" towards ethical values. This concern with the self-constitution of ethical life was substantially influenced by Husserl's reading of Fichte's ethical

---

[22] See also Husserl's formulation: "Sei ein wahrer Mensch; führe ein Leben, das du durchgängig einsichtig rechtfertigen kannst, ein Leben aus praktischer Vernunft" ("Be a true human being; lead a life which you can thoroughly justify through insight, a life according to practical reason") (Hua 27: 36).

[23] Husserl continued to nurture quietly his interest in the a priori and eidetic structures of cognition, valuing, and willing well into the late 1920s. As late as 1928, Husserl intended to write a systematic eidetic psychology. The manuscripts for this planned work, *Studien zur Struktur des Bewußtseins*, are currently in preparation for publication in the Husserliana by my colleague Ullrich Melle at the Husserl Archives.

writings during the calamitous years of the war,[24] although the influence of Max Scheler's concept of the person is also not to be discounted (despite Husserl's own scathing view of Scheler) nor the Catholic-inspired phenomenological ethics of Dietrich von Hildebrand and Edith Stein, and the resonance of Brentano's notions of blessedness and love.[25] Fichte was equally a catalyst for integrating the idea of God into Husserl's ethical thought.[26]

This pull away from Brentano is first registered with the notions of renewal and responsibility, formulated in essays for the Japanese journal *The Kaizo* in 1923–1924 under the title *Renewal of Humanity and Culture.*[27] As Husserl now understands: "Renewal of man, renewal of both the single person and the community is the chief theme of ethics. Ethical life is essentially and consciously inspired by the idea of renewal; it is a life willfully led and formed by this idea" (Hua 27: 20). This emphasis on renewal underpins a conception of ethical life as a project of self-responsibility that becomes mirrored in Husserl's conception of history and the idea of Europe as an "absolute obligation" and "vocation." In *The Crisis of European Sciences*, Husserl's call for a fundamental reflection (*Besinnung*) on the *telos* and meaning of European history is cast as an ethical call for responsibility and renewal of the "spiritual" and scientific vocation of European culture and humanity. Husserl's ethics of renewal seeks to "harmonize" an ethics of the individual with an ethics of the social. As Husserl states: "a fully developed ethics of the individual necessarily leads to an ethics of community (*Gemeinschaftsethik*)" (HuaMat 9: 172). Husserl's envisioned ethics of community reflects the constitutive function of inter-subjectivity for his

---

[24] See Husserl's 1917 lectures, "Fichtes Menschheitsideal (Drei Vorlesungen 1917)," Hua 25: 267–92.

[25] In a letter to Pickard Bell (8 September 1921), Husserl writes: "Ferner die neukatholische Bewegung mit dem Heer der Convertiten, deren großer Stern Max Scheler ist – leider ebenfalls ein Genie der Pose, ein im innersten unechter Profet; und leider will er die katholische kirchliche Philosophie dadurch reformieren, dass er sie statt auf Aristoteles auf Phänomenologie gründet" ("Moreover, the New Catholic movement with its army of converts, whose great star is Max Scheler – unfortunately he is genius at posing, in his innermost being an inauthentic prophet; and regrettably he wants to reform Catholic Church philosophy by grounding it in Aristotle rather than in phenomenology"): Husserl 1994: 25.

[26] See Husserl's letter to Adolf Grimme (6 August 1918): "I have become even more aware that the religious prospects that phenomenology has opened for me display surprisingly close connections to Fichte's later theology [. . .] Naturally, there are many obscure comments and much Fichtean violence, but also beautiful intuitions" (Husserl 1994: 81–2).

[27] Hua 27: 3–42.

transcendental phenomenology and the idea of a community as a "person of higher order," as well as a strong interest in social ontology, cultural types, and so-called "we-intentionality."[28] Yet, Husserl's ethical thought also reaches towards a phenomenological metaphysics of "facticity." As Husserl writes: "The intrinsically first being, the being that precedes and bears every worldly objectivity, is transcendental inter-subjectivity: the universe of monads, which effects its communion in various forms. But, within the de facto monadic sphere and (as an ideal possibility) within every conceivable monadic sphere, occur *all the problems of accidental facticity* [*zufälligen Faktizität*], *of death, of fate*, of the possibility of a *'genuine'* human life demanded as 'meaningful' in a particular sense [. . .] We can say that they are the *ethico-religious* problems, but stated in the realm where everything that can have a possible sense for us must be stated."[29]

Husserl's ethics of renewal centers on the generating axis of love. As Husserl reflects: "If we prefer according to our best knowledge and conscience of the best of what is attainable, we have acted ethically, then and only then our will is absolutely right."[30] The new thought here is to conceive of "the best" through an individual's affective conscience and (self)-knowledge of her vocation in view of "absolute values" grounded in love. Of this differentiation between an ethics of reason and an ethics of love (the latter exclusively developed in Husserl's private and unpublished research manuscripts), one example recurs in Husserl's meditations. The example might have originally stemmed from his student Dietrich von Hildebrand, yet its tragic resonance must surely have played a role in its enduring poignancy.[31] As Husserl reflects:

> Should the mother first deliberate and make considerations of the highest possible good? This whole ethics of the highest practical good such as it was

---

[28] For an overview, see the lecture "Soziale Ethik" (1919) in HuaMat 9: 169–80. For representative insights of Husserl's social ethics, see the texts "Gemeingeist I" (1921) and "Gemeingeist II" (1921/1922) in Hua 14: 164–83; 192–204. See Hart 1992 and Perreau 2013.

[29] Husserl 1999: 156. As Husserl warns: "Finally, lest any misunderstanding arise, I would point out that, as already stated, phenomenology indeed *excludes every naive metaphysics* that operates with absurd things in themselves, but *does not exclude metaphysics as such*. It does not do violence to the problem-motives that inwardly drive the old tradition [. . .]" (p. 156). For reasons of space, I shall omit discussion of Husserl's treatment of death, birth, and other "generative" themes from his ethical reflections in the 1930s.

[30] Husserl 2014: 391.

[31] Von Hildebrand 1916: 126–251. Husserl's youngest son Wolfgang was killed at Verdun in 1916. News of his son's death was received on his wife Malvine's birthday. She thereafter refused to celebrate her own birthday again.

derived from Brentano and taken over by me in its essential traits cannot be the last word. Essential determinations are needed! Vocation and inner calling cannot be done justice in this way. There exists an unconditional "you ought and must" that addresses itself to the person and that is not subject to a rational justification and does not depend for its legitimate obligation (*rechtmässige Bindung*) on such a justification for the one who experiences this absolute affection. This affection (*Affektion*) precedes all rational explanation even where such an explanation is possible.[32]

While objective values are characteristics of objects apprehended in *Wertnehmung*, absolute affections of love *constitute* the ethical person in her responsibility towards her vocation (*Berufung*) in response to absolute values of love.

In this example of the mother's love for her child, the child possesses "objective" and "subjective" ethical value: objective value comparable with other children falling under the scope of justice and fairness; absolute, subjective value incomparable with the children of others. The absolute value of a mother's love for her child springs from and constitutes the mother as a person; it defines her calling (*Ruf*) to be an ethical person. This absolute value cannot be absorbed into other values, but can only be related to other values, including other absolute values, through the incomparable measure of *sacrifice*. As Husserl remarks: "An individual value is not simply a value in general, that is, under the tacit condition that a greater value is not in question, a value whose practical feasibility would absorb the lower value in question. Rather, an individual value, a value which exclusively concerns the individuality of the person and the individuality of what is valued, can by no means be absorbed, but only sacrificed."[33] An inverse relation between absorption and sacrifice implicitly structures this original dimension to Husserl's ethical renewal. Conflict between absolute values requires the sacrifice of one value for the other, and, in such sacrifice, the person herself, as the realization of an absolute value, becomes herself sacrificed, as in the example of a mother's sacrifice *for* her son and *to* the absolute value of her love.

With this turn to a phenomenology of love and absolute values, Husserl offers a *transcendental* account of moral obligation and its underpinning affective "material" values in conjunction with the constitution of the self as an ethical project. As Husserl argues in his criticism of Kant's notion of respect for the moral law, the pure (or ethical) will must be motivated by the

---

[32] Husserl 2014: 179.   [33] Husserl 2014: 252.

affection of an absolute value, yet pure affection is itself insufficient to generate the ethical force of moral obligation. The affectivity of love must be formed through an activity of self-determination, or autonomy, as the project of an individual's deliberate self-constitution. The affective ground of moral obligation is therefore twofold: the ethical person becomes freely bound to herself in being bound to an absolute value, for which she assumes absolute responsibility in assuming her own ethical vocation, or "person." As Husserl further argues, a mother's love originates as a "drive" that becomes re-configured into "social" and "ethical" love. In itself, the drive (love) towards the child, as the subject of care and affection, is neither "ethical" nor "social." It is only through an I–Thou relationship (*Ich–Du-Beziehung*) that a person becomes fully constituted such that the mother and child form a primordial "community" (*Gemeinschaft*): the mother, in her love for her child, establishes an "inner" relationship with her child (and likewise the child with her mother).[34]

This affective and social dimension of love is not yet fully fledged ethical love as *moral obligation*. The trajectory towards the ethical must progress through an awakening of the person to her own genuine vocation, requiring an attitude towards one's life as a whole akin to a *transcendental reduction* (Hua 27: 39). Self-constitution requires the performance of an "ethical epoché" and critical self-renewal by which we are awoken to our genuine vocation and ideal ethical self, and through which we come to regard our lives as an *infinite task*. The person is thus called *to* genuine existence as a responsibility towards the "voice of conscience of the absolute ought."[35] The "absolute ought" of affection is not "the best" among attainable ends, not even a preference among possibilities, but a vocation that singularizes the ethical striving and self-constitution of the person. In Husserl's words: "I am who I am and the individual particularity shows itself in that I, as who I am, love exactly as I love, that precisely this calls me and not that."[36] A mother's

---

[34] As Husserl writes: "Self-awareness of oneself as a person is only gained in a relationship to a Thou (*Du*)" Hua 14: 170. See also Hua 14: 175: "The origin of personality resides in empathy and in further emerging social acts. It is not sufficient for personality that the subject becomes aware of itself as the pole of its own acts. Personality is first constituted when the subject enters in social relations with other subjects, through which the subject becomes objective in praxis [...]."

[35] Husserl 2014: 379.

[36] Husserl continues: "There is an unconditioned 'You ought and must,' which is addressed to the person and which for the one experiencing this absolute affection is not submitted to a rational foundation nor is it dependent on an appropriate

absolute love for her child is conative, affective, and cognitive; in its ethical realization as an "absolute ought," it shapes the mother's ethical project as a singular universal.[37] A genuine human life must "give itself over" (hingeben) to absolute values of love, which thereby become "realized" through the fulfillment of an ethical person's vocation.[38] Brentano's "principle of summation" is here re-fashioned in an original and transcendental manner: to strive for an ethical existence entails the employment of my life for the realization of absolute (and *pure* in the phenomenological sense of "non-worldly") values *in the world* so to broaden my own life into the broadest realization of values. The ethical person strives to become a gift of values; likewise, an ethical community emerges as "the wealth of all through the realization of absolute values" (*der Reichtum aller bei Realisierung von absoluten Werten*). Failure to heed this call, or better: this being-addressed (*Angesprochen-sein*), whether at the individual or collective level (i.e. Europe), means to "damage" oneself: "to go against this [*absolute*] value is to be untrue, to lose oneself, to betray one's true 'I,'" and thus to live a life in untruth as one's own "absolute practical contradiction."[39] Genuine existence requires an orientation towards *life*-in-truth, not a being-towards-death.

Husserl's manuscripts on ethics during the 1930s reveal an untiring effort to resolve the apparently paradoxical relation between reason and love. As Husserl acknowledges: "Among the persons in my environment, my child is the 'closest' to me, and therein is contained an irrationality of the absolute 'ought.'"[40] Faced with the "irrationality" of a singularized ethical imperative of absolute love, Husserl sketches a two-pronged strategy for the reconciliation of love and reason. The ethical self is continually exposed to the demand

---

connection with such a foundation. This affection goes in advance of all rational analysis, even when such is possible" (Husserl 2014: 355).

[37] Husserl writes: "Die Kinder sind Kinder dieser Mutter nicht als objektive Tatsachen, sondern [*sie sind*] für sie in ihrer Individualität Werte und *zurückbezogen* auf die Individualität der Mutter" ("The children are the children of this mother not as objective facts, but [*they are*] values for her in their individuality and *referred back* to the individuality of the mother") (added emphasis) (Husserl 2014: 465).

[38] Husserl 2014: 412: "Das echte Ich liebt, ist liebend hingegeben seinem echten Ziel und seine Sorge ist liebende Sorge. Das echte Leben ist durchaus Leben in der Liebe. Das völlig damit gleichbedeutende heißt leben in dem absoluten Sollen." ("The genuine ego loves, is given lovingly to its genuine goal and its concern is loving concern. Genuine life is absolutely life through love. This is equivalent in meaning to living under the absolute ought.")

[39] Husserl 2014: 356.   [40] Husserl 2014: 383.

of justification from others. Each person in her ethical striving and self-constitution is answerable to others in being answerable to themselves (as paradigmatically with the instance of the mother and child) for the affective sway of absolute values in their lives. This inter-subjective "harmonization" of the reasons for our ethical projects is further implicated in the rational self-scrutiny demanded by the renewed performance of the ethical epoché without which each person would not become awoken to their own idealized self-conception. Husserl further seeks a solution to the harmonization of love and reason with a nuanced appropriation of Kant's notion of God as a rational idea in speaking of a necessary "reason of faith" (or rational faith: *Vernunftglaube*) in God as the ideal unity for the "harmonization" of irrational bindings of absolute love. Importantly, God is an *Idea*, not a person, but an Idea that offers a regulative Idea for the teleological convergence – and hence progress – for humanity's various strivings for self-perfection and ethical self-constitution. As a regulative Idea that conditions the infinite task of self-constitution, the *telos* of ethical life is to attain blessedness and the life of "saint" or, in other words, a self-fulfillment of one's ethical calling *without remainder* through a synthesis of identification between the empirical self and the idealized form of one's genuine vocation (Hua 37: 342).[41] In this manner, as Husserl confessed towards the end of life, "Human existence is nothing other than a way to God. I attempted to attain this goal without theological proof, methods or support, namely, I attempted to reach God without attaining God."[42]

BIBLIOGRAPHY

An asterisk denotes secondary literature especially suitable for further reading.

Brentano, Franz 1926. *Die Vier Phasen der Philosophie*. Leipzig: Meiner.
Brentano, Franz 1929. *Über die Zukunft der Philosophie*. Leipzig: Meiner.
Brentano, Franz 1973a. *Psychology from an Empirical Standpoint*, trans. Antos Rancurello, D. Terrell and L. McAlister. London: Routledge.
Brentano, Franz 1973b. *The Foundation and Construction of Ethics*, trans. E. Schneewind. London: Routledge.

[41] See also Hua 35: 44: "A blessed total life as such would be a unified life in which all its intentions and all its striving would play itself out in the form of pure filled intentions."

[42] Jaegerschmid 1981: 56: "Das Leben des Menschen ist nichts anderes als ein Weg zu Gott. Ich versuche, dieses Ziel ohne theologische Beweise, Methoden und Stützpunkte zu erreichen, nämlich zu Gott ohne Gott zu gelangen."

Brentano, Franz 2009. *The Origin of our Knowledge of Right and Wrong*, trans. R. Chisholm and E. Schneewind. London: Routledge.

Chisholm, Roderick 1966. "Brentano's Theory of Correct Emotion," *Revue internationale de philosophie*, 20: 395–415.

Drummond, John 1995. "Moral Objectivity: Husserl's Sentiments of the Understanding," *Husserl Studies*, 12: 165–83.*

Gubser, Michael 2009. "Franz Brentano's Ethics of Social Renewal," *The Philosophical Forum*, 40 (3): 339–66.

Hart, James 1992. *The Person and the Common Life*. Kluwer: Dordrecht.

Hildebrand, Dietrich von 1916. *Die Idee der sittlichen Handlung, Jahrbuch für Philosophie und phänomenologische Forschung*, vol. 3, pp. 126–251.

Housset, Emmanuel 2010. *Husserl et l'idée de dieu*. Paris: Les Éditions du Cerf.

Husserl, Edmund 1965. "Philosophy as a Rigorous Science," trans. Quentin Lauer, in: *Phenomenology and the Crisis of Philosophy*. New York: Harper and Row, pp. 71–147.

Husserl, Edmund 1973. *Zur Phänomenologie der Intersubjektivität (1921–1928)*, ed. I. Kern. The Hague: Martinus Nijhoff. Husserliana 14.

Husserl, Edmund 1976. *Ideen zu einer reinen Phänomenologie und phänomenologischen Philosophie. Erstes Buch: Allgemeine Einführung in die reine Phänomenologie*, ed. K. Schuhmann. The Hague: Martinus Nijhoff. Husserliana 3/1.

Husserl, Edmund 1985. *Einleitung in die Logik und Erkenntnistheorie, Vorlesungen 1906/07*, ed. Ullrich Melle. The Hague: Martinus Nijhoff. Husserliana 24.

Husserl, Edmund 1987. *Aufsätze und Vorträge (1911–1921)*, ed. T. Nenon and H.R. Sepp. The Hague: Martinus Nijhoff. Husserliana 25.

Husserl, Edmund 1988. *Vorlesungen über Ethik und Wertlehre (1908–1914)*, ed. U. Melle. Dordrecht: Kluwer. Husserliana 28.

Husserl, Edmund 1989. *Aufsätze und Vorträge (1922–1937)*, ed. T. Nenon and H.R. Sepp. The Hague: Martinus Nijhoff. Husserliana 27.

Husserl, Edmund 1994. *Briefwechsel*, vol. 3, ed. Karl Schuhmann. The Hague: Kluwer.

Husserl, Edmund 1999. *Cartesian Meditations*, trans. D. Cairns. Dordrecht: Kluwer.

Husserl, Edmund 2001. *Logical Investigations*, vols. 1 and 2, trans. J.N. Findlay with a new preface by Michael Dummett, ed. with a new introduction by Dermot Moran. London: Routledge.

Husserl, Edmund 2002. *Einleitung in die Philosophie. Vorlesungen 1922/23*, ed. Berndt Goossens. Dordrecht: Kluwer. Husserliana 35.

Husserl, Edmund 2004. *Einleitung in die Ethik. Vorlesungen Sommersemester 1920 und 1924*, ed. H. Peucker. Dordrecht: Kluwer. Husserliana 37.

Husserl, Edmund 2012. *Einleitung in die Philosophie. Vorlesungen 1916–1920*, ed. H. Jacobs. Dordrecht: Springer Verlag. Husserliana Materialien 9.

Husserl, Edmund 2014. *Grenzprobleme der Phänomenologie*, ed. Rocus Sowa and Thomas Vongehr. Dordrecht: Springer Verlag.

Jaegerschmid, Adelgundis 1981. "Gespräche mit Edmund Husserl 1931–1936," *Stimmen der Zeit*, 199: 48–58.

Loidolt, Sophie 2009. "Husserl and the Fact of Practical Reason – The Phenomenological Claims Towards a Philosophical Ethics," *Santalka. Filosofia*, 17, 3: 50–61.*

McAlister, Linda 1982. *The Development of Franz Brentano's Ethics*. Amsterdam: Rodopi.

Melle, Ullrich 1988. "Zu Brentanos und Husserls Ethikansatz: Die Analogie zwischen den Vernunftarten," *Brentano Studien*, 1: 109–20.

Melle, Ullrich 1991. "The Development of Husserl's Ethics," *Études phénoménologiques*, 13–14: 115–35.*

Melle, Ullrich 2002. "Edmund Husserl: From Reason to Love," in: *Phenomenological Approaches to Moral Philosophy*, ed. J. Drummond and L. Embree. The Hague: Kluwer, pp. 229–48.*

Moore, G.E. 1903. "Review of Franz Brentano's *The Origin of the Knowledge of Right and Wrong*," *International Journal of Ethics*, 14 (October): 115–23.

Perreau, Laurent 2013. *Le monde social selon Husserl*. Dordrecht: Springer Verlag.

Roth, Alois 1960. *Edmund Husserls ethische Untersuchungen*. The Hague: Martinus Nijhoff.

Scheler, Max 1973. *Formalism in Ethics and Non-Formal Ethics of Values*, trans. M. Frings and R. Funk. Evanston, IL: Northwestern University Press.

44

Ethics in Freudian and Post-Freudian Psychoanalysis

EDWARD HARCOURT

INTRODUCTION: PSYCHOANALYSIS AS AN ETHICAL INQUIRY

Few would doubt that ethics and psychoanalysis make contact at *some* point: 'What are the proper limits of confidentiality?' is a question psychoanalysts need to think about in relation to their patients, and it is an ethical question. But it is a question accountants and doctors need to think about too, and yet the aims of accountancy and medical practice and the bodies of theory that underpin them are not, or are only marginally, ethical. It's perhaps because Freud presented himself, sometimes at least, as a medical doctor ('psychoanalysis is a procedure for the medical treatment of neurotic patients', *SE* 15: 15; *SE* 12: 115)[1] that it has been possible for so long – and notwithstanding a succession of dissenting voices[2] – to get away with the view that, professional ethics apart, there's nothing much in psychoanalysis to interest the moral philosopher.[3] Another reason is that Freud presented the body of theory underlying psychoanalytic therapy as natural science (*SE* 12: 168) while Anglo-American philosophy, unimpressed by *that* claim, has tended to dismiss psychoanalysis altogether, with the result that those philosophers – including the moral philosophers – who might have found something of interest in psychoanalysis untouched by the question of its scientific status have not on the whole bothered to go looking.

Be that as it may, much of psychoanalytic theory not only is of interest to moral philosophy but is moral philosophy. Plato and Aristotle – albeit in different

---

[1] All references to Freud's works, in the form [volume number: page number], are to *The Standard Edition of the Complete Psychological Works of Sigmund Freud*, 1953–1964 (*SE*).

[2] Rieff 1959/1979; De Sousa 1982; Wollheim 1984, 1987; Lear 1990; Wallwork 1991; Cottingham 1998; Blass 2001, 2003.

[3] Hartmann 1960: 20.

ways – argued for a tight relationship between virtue, what they called 'mental health', and the good life for human beings,[4] and Aristotle especially set these ideas in a developmental perspective. To possess virtue as they conceived it is also to be mentally healthy, in the sense of the parts or faculties of the mind – reason, appetite and so on – bearing the right relation to one another; mental health so understood is the best condition of life for the human being whose life it is; and virtue, mental health and well being are all realized together by the fullest possible development of the capacities which are by nature distinctively our own. Whether or not it is what Plato and Aristotle had in mind, contemporary 'virtue ethics' has seen in this cluster of ideas the hope of resolving the antinomy between morality and self-interest:[5] since it's obvious why it's in my interest to pursue mental health if mental health spells well-being, it follows that if moral virtue is mental health, it's in my interest also to pursue moral virtue. This kind of optimism raises a number of questions: is the scope of human beings' self-interest so narrow that it only ever includes states of themselves? If so, do morality and well-being after all pull in opposite directions; or – a developmental descendant of the same question – can the right relationship between our various faculties of mind develop without our possessing moral virtue or, worse still, only if we don't possess it? But, if all that is so, how are we to explain the fact that we comply with moral requirements as widely as we do? These questions are clearly central to moral philosophy. Less widely recognized is the fact that they are also central to psychoanalysis; indeed, though there's obviously more to psychoanalysis than just its answers to these questions, the various schools of Freudian and post-Freudian psychoanalysis and psychody-namic psychotherapy ('psychoanalysis' for short) divide according to their rival – optimistic and less optimistic – answers to them. Psychoanalysis is thus one of the most culturally visible twentieth- and twenty-first-century continuators of a central Platonic–Aristotelian line of ethical inquiry.

VIRTUE AND WELL-BEING, LOVERS AND STRANGERS

Probably the most salient answer to these questions from within psychoanalysis is what I'll call 'Freudian pessimism', a conjunction of two pessimistic views. The first of these is that our natural endowments on the one hand and, on the other, civilization – including morality – make conflicting demands on us, so the characteristics necessary for social living require an inevitable sacrifice in well-being, and perhaps also in mental health. This pessimism can come in an

---

[4] Plato 1961: 55 [444], Aristotle 1984: 1843–4 [IX.4].   [5] Sidgwick 1907/1962: 508.

uncritical or at least a resigned version (the claims of morality are genuine, or if not genuine at least inescapable), but also a radical one (the claims of morality are not genuine – the only genuine claims being the claims of desire – and are also escapable).[6] Secondly comes an equally pessimistic view of the scope of self-interest: each person by nature seeks only a state of themselves. The two varieties of pessimism are apparently logically independent of one another: even if the scope of self-interest were not so narrow, so we were for example disposed to identify our own good with the good of certain particular others, it looks as if the demands of civilization would still be liable to conflict with those of well-being (and perhaps mental health), because the former are (to some extent) impartial and the latter partial. Each form of pessimism also goes with a picture of the proper development of our faculties of mind that is relatively independent of morality or sociability, and of the psychological mechanisms of conscience or self-regulation (which harness selfish energies and turn them against ourselves, a further recipe for unhappiness).

Alongside 'Freudian pessimism', however, the literature of post-Freudian psychoanalysis also contains a family of more optimistic answers, with an account of self-regulation to match: as long as 'conscience' meets the standards for mental health,[7] it needn't make us unhappy. J.C. Flugel, writing in the 1940s, saw in mental health as conceived by psychoanalysis the possibility of a 'smooth coalescence of wish and duty'.[8] But it is rare to find psychoanalysts with a wholly uncritical conception of virtue or excellence of character arguing for a fit between these and mental health and well-being. Psychoanalytic conceptions of the proper development of our natures tend to assume that what's *unquestionably* of value is mental health, once again understood as the right relation between rational and non-rational parts of the mind. There is room for difference over how that relation is to be understood (for example as dominating or as more co-operative),[9] and how it is to be further specified – the notions of individuation,[10] separation–individuation,[11] autonomy,[12] the depressive position,[13] integration,[14] and self-realization[15] are all to be found.[16]

[6] Lacan 1986: 362; Marcuse 1956/1987: 272.   [7] Money-Kyrle 1952: 233.
[8] Flugel 1945/1973: 252.   [9] Harcourt 2015: 613 n. 37.
[10] Loewald 1978: 14; Lear 1990: 21.   [11] Mahler 1986: 222.
[12] Mitchell 1988: 134; Holmes 2011: *passim.*
[13] Klein 1946/1988: 14–16; Spillius 1994; Waddell 1998: 6–13.
[14] Klein 1946/1988: 324–6; Hinshelwood 1997: 155–6.
[15] Horney 1950/1991: 15–16; Meissner 2003: 21. Horney's writing has a strikingly Aristotelian flavour.
[16] Eagle 1984: 185; Harcourt, in press.

But any one of these ideals may be invoked as the standard by means of which to identify the *real* virtues or excellences of character, as distinct from mere 'superego moralism'.[17] The list of real excellences may thus differ considerably from a familiar Christian or post-Christian catalogue, though the result of applying the standard may also be to confirm a familiar virtue as such: as it might be, marital fidelity.[18] But however revisionist this mental-health-based picture, it is also optimistic in the sense that the real excellences (whatever they are) are assumed not only to be sufficient for mental health and well-being but also – in contrast to some versions of the radical pessimism described above – to include a set of recognizably social virtues and thus to fulfil the 'demands of civilization'.[19] Indeed it is possible that they are *too* optimistic in this respect. Post-Freudian accounts of psychological development typically give pride of place to our capacity to form relationships with particular others – as Hans Loewald put it, 'a human being's becoming a person . . . is [a matter of the] development of our love-life'.[20] To justify post-Freudian optimism, therefore, an account is needed of how *this* development connects with the dispositions to do right by strangers generally assumed to be necessary for social living.

The equivalence of the pessimistic with the Freudian and the optimistic with the post-Freudian, however, should not be assumed: not only are there post-Freudian pessimists, but these rival answers to my Platonic–Aristotelian menu of questions have inspired rival interpretations of Freud. Thus we can distinguish – at least – 'loyalist' readings of Freud which ascribe pessimism to him while also seeking to justify it;[21] more or less anti-Freudian versions of psychoanalysis which advocate the optimistic view against the pessimism they find in Freud;[22] and 'revisionist' readings of Freud which advocate the optimistic view and find it in Freud, albeit sometimes in a mixed form.[23] Since it's not possible in a short space to explore the full variety even of 'optimistic' post-Freudian positions, my focus here will be chiefly on Freud. I shall trace the roots of 'Freudian pessimism' in his work, and, by assessing the prospects for an 'optimistic' reply to it within Freud himself, thereby also keep an eye on the way these rival interpretations of Freud reflect disagreements in ethics between later schools of psychoanalytic thinking.

---

[17] Fromm 1947; Hartmann 1960: 51; Erikson 1964: 113; Wallwork 1991: 225.
[18] Holmes 1997: 338. [19] Sagan 1988: 164. [20] Loewald 1978: 32.
[21] Abel 1989: *passim*; cf. Wollheim 1984: 204–5. [22] Suttie 1963; Sagan 1988.
[23] Dilman 1983, Abramson 1984, Lear 1990, Wallwork 1991.

FREUD AND 'FREUDIAN PESSIMISM'

The sources of 'Freudian pessimism' within Freud lie in his theory of instinct, which is basic to his theory of motivation generally. Within this theory, two ideas are especially important: (i) the relationship between the 'pleasure principle' and the 'reality principle', and (ii) Freud's conception of the aims of an instinct.

For most of his career, Freud held that 'the principle which governs all mental processes . . . [has] the purpose of reducing to nothing, or at least of keeping as low as possible, the sums of [instinctual] excitation flowing in upon it' (*SE* 19: 255) – what he called the 'pleasure principle'. But since the basic mechanism of satisfying an instinct is, in Freud's view, to 'hallucinate' its satisfaction (*SE* 12: 219 n.1), no organism governed by the unmodified pleasure principle could survive for long unaided (*SE* 17: 159). So the pleasure principle comes to be supplemented by the 'reality principle', more properly the capacity to press knowledge of reality – including social reality – into the service of the pleasure principle, and so to make survival consistent with as much instinctual satisfaction as possible. Though Freud also believed that healthy psychological development involves a transformation in the focus of sexuality, ending in 'full genitality' (*SE* 11: 45), the proper adjustment of the pleasure principle to the reality principle is arguably the closest equivalent – in *this* phase of his theory: compare the later 'where Id was, there Ego shall be' (*SE* 22: 80) – to the right relationship among our faculties of mind in which, on the Platonic–Aristotelian view, mental health consists. The big question, however, is how much satisfaction this development allows. If submitting to the demands of reality in the interests of survival inevitably leaves some instincts unsatisfied, the pessimistic view – that there's an irresoluble tension between the demands of civilization and what we are constrained by our natures to aim at – is vindicated, and the characteristics required for civilized living (whether genuine virtues or virtues in name only) are in tension with well-being or 'happiness' (*SE* 21: 70). Moreover, neurosis and psychosis are different forms of maladjustment to reality caused by incapacity to deal with frustration (*SE* 12: 218; 14: 93; 19: 185; 21: 87), so the demands of civilization may also be in tension with mental health. But they needn't be: by 'transforming [neurotic] misery into ordinary unhappiness' (*SE* 2: 305), psychoanalysis can apparently restore mental health, though without any gain in well-being.

So far we have focused on the idea that thanks to the modification of the pleasure principle by the reality principle, instincts may be frustrated. The second source of 'Freudian pessimism' is if anything more deeply pessimistic, because it goes to what we would accomplish if our instincts were satisfied: that is, it concerns the *ends* with which our nature equips us. It might be protested that talk of ends is out of place here, because talk of ends goes with desires and Freud's instincts – because they're features of the subpersonal 'operation of the mental apparatus' (*SE* 21: 70; cp. *SE* 14: 120) – are not desires. But his *examples* of things we pursue allegedly under the pressure of instinct – be it sexual activity or work or artistic creation – *sound* like things desired: how could work be the object of mere appetite, still less the effect of a subpersonal automatism? So what's the 'aim' of an instinct? Two answers are especially prominent: first, that instincts aim at pleasure understood as an experience of some kind (*SE* 21: 70), and secondly that they aim at their own extinction (*SE* 7: 168; 14: 122).[24] But given that the 'process' of an instinct's seeking extinction is described as the 'programme of the *pleasure-principle*' (*SE* 21: 70; my italics), and Freud frequently identifies pleasure with the diminution of the originating stimulus (*SE* 5: 598), it seems reasonable to identify the instinct's aim with pleasure. When the reality principle comes on the scene, human beings are supplied with a great many more 'objects' than they had before, but the 'aim' remains the same: translating, the route to pleasure becomes more circuitous, but everything that's desired is nonetheless desired as a means to pleasure ('the object … is the thing … through which the instinct is able to achieve its aim', *SE* 14: 122). This makes Freud – like Mill, to whose team of original German translators Freud belonged[25] – what might be called a 'hedonist plus': a hedonist because he thinks that whatever is desired is desired because it is pleasant, plus the further twist that pleasure is viewed as an independently characterizable effect of which things done for its sake are the causes. Without the twist, playing a game for pleasure could be an *instance* of doing something for its own sake; with the twist, anything *apparently* done for its own sake – from the baby playing at the breast to the creation of a work of art – is in fact done simply as the means to a state of oneself (as Freud thought, a sensory state, 'the experiencing of strong feelings of pleasure', *SE* 21: 70);[26] or, if Freud sees this as a genuinely distinct answer, as a means to the extinction of the painful state of wanting to do it (*SE* 21: 70). To be sure, this view of human purposes yields a pessimistic view of life if this one universal desire is always partially frustrated, but the picture scarcely cheers up if we imagine it fulfilled, and it is not clear on Freud's assumptions

---

[24] Cf. Schopenhauer 1883: 253–4; Russell 1921: Lecture III, *passim.*   [25] Molnar 2002: 112.

[26] Cp. Korsgaard 1996: 251–2.

why what he describes as 'the crudest, but also the most effective method of influencing [our own organism]', namely 'the chemical one – intoxication' (*SE* 21: 78) is not – given its ready availability *within* the constraints of civilization – more widely preferred to the more roundabout alternatives.

This pessimistic reading of Freud is complicated, however – though not in the end ruled out – by three factors. The first two are his theory of 'sublimation' and his sexual liberalism, which I deal with in the next section; the third is his late-career 'dual instinct' theory, which deserves a section to itself.

SUBLIMATION AND SEXUAL FREEDOM

The most common fate to befall instincts which cannot be satisfied is, in Freud's view, repression. But he also speaks – less often – of a second mechanism, sublimation. The crucial difference between them lies not in the actions in which repressed or, alternatively, sublimated instincts express themselves – the actions may be the same – but in the fact that under repression the aim of the instinct is unchanged, whereas under sublimation it is transformed. Since – in the case of sexual instinct or libido, at least, with which Freud is chiefly preoccupied – its aim is discharge in sexual activity (*SE* 3: 108), a repressed or 'aim-inhibited' instinct which discharges itself in – say – work or in morally motivated self-denial must be at least in part frustrated. (Thus society 'has tightened the moral standard to the greatest possible degree, and . . . forced its members into a yet greater estrangement from their instinctual disposition', *SE* 14: 284; cp. *SE* 14: 93.) With a sublimated instinct, however, this is not so. The theory of sublimation promises therefore to bring Freud closer to an 'optimistic' Platonic–Aristotelian position: through civilization we acquire *second* natures (Freud's *transformed* instinctual aims) which civilization itself provides – sometimes – the opportunity to satisfy in full. As he says, though 'generally speaking our civilization is built upon the suppression of instincts', it's in 'the capacity to exchange [the] original sexual aim [of an instinct] for another one, which is no longer sexual' (*SE* 9: 186) but 'has a higher social or ethical valuation' (*SE* 18: 256) that sublimation's 'value for civilization' lies (*SE* 9: 187).

One problem with relying in this way on the notion of sublimation is that, as Freud emphasizes, the capacity for sublimation varies greatly from individual to individual: *most* people aren't capable of very much at all and – crucially – of less than is needed to enable them 'to comply with the demands of civilization' (*SE* 9: 191).[27] If such people – the majority – 'wish to be more noble-minded than

---

[27] Cp. Hale 1971: 122.

their constitution allows', they will 'fall victim to neurosis'; 'they would have been more healthy if it could have been possible for them to be less good' (*SE* 9: 191). Freud thus rejects – at least as far as the majority are concerned – any Platonic equation of mental health with moral goodness, though becoming more healthy may require the virtues of courage and truthfulness.[28]

To leave matters there, however, would be to ignore an important first-order ethical strand in Freud's thinking, his sexual liberalism (*SE* 3: 278).[29] 'We may well raise the question whether our "civilized" sexual morality is worth the sacrifice which it imposes on us' (*SE* 9: 204; *SE* 16: 434). So even if the civilization of late nineteenth- and early twentieth-century Europe and – in Freud's view, far worse – the USA exacted a heavy toll in frustration, might there not be *a* civilization with sexual mores so liberal that any instincts not sublimated could be satisfied rather than repressed? Freud hints that there might be: psychoanalysts are indeed 'not able to compensate our neurotic patients for giving up their neurotic illness', but this 'reinforces our determination to change other social factors [e.g. the prohibition on extra-marital sexual relations] so that men and women shall no longer be forced into hopeless situations'.[30]

So did Freud chart a way out of 'Freudian pessimism' in sexual liberalization for the many plus sublimation for the few? To be sure, Freud contrasts 'strong natures who openly oppose the demands of civilization' with 'well-behaved weaklings' (*SE* 9: 192, 197; cp. *SE* 14: 284), wavering on whether this flouting of the 'demands of civilization' is *actually* bad ('[psycho]analysis makes for integration, but … not of itself … for goodness')[31] or whether – as some subsequent psychoanalytic thinkers asserted unequivocally[32] – at least some of the characteristics civilization demands are not genuinely good. But be that as it may, why under sexual liberalization shouldn't the many achieve the satisfaction now available only to those 'strong natures' able to run the gauntlet of (deserved or undeserved) social disapprobation?

Part of the difficulty in assessing this way out lies in pinning down Freud's notion of the sexual.[33] Sexual liberalization is presumably a remedy only for distinctively sexual frustration, so the more there is to instinct beyond the sexual – or the more implausibly inclusive Freud's notion of the sexual – the less sexual liberalization alone seems able to help. That is perhaps why we often find Freud denying that liberalizing sexual mores is enough to do away with the tension between civilization and instinct. 'Civilization … presupposes

---

[28] Ibid., 171; cp. Rieff 1959/1979: 315. [29] Hale 1971: 189. [30] Ibid., 1971: 91.
[31] Ibid., 1971: 188. [32] Erikson 1964: 113. [33] De Sousa 1982: 152.

precisely the non-satisfaction of powerful instincts' (*SE* 21: 97). More pessimistically still, he speaks of

> the instinctual repression upon which is based *all* that is most precious in human civilization. The repressed instinct never ceases to strive for complete satisfaction. . . . No substitutive or reactive formations *and no sublimations* will suffice to remove the repressed instinct's persisting tension   (*SE* 18: 42; my italics).

But there's another difficulty with the way out I've suggested. Even if sublimation were enough to deal with all the instincts sexual liberalization cannot, the notion of sublimation is theoretically weak. Though Freud can see clearly which problem would be solved if there were such a thing, the 'mechanism' of sublimation (a 'special process', *SE* 14: 94) is drastically underspecified, as Freud himself confesses (*SE* 14: 95; 21: 79): it 'has a special quality which we shall one day be able to characterize in metaphysical terms'.[34] At best it labels the thought that the 'problem of civilization' has a solution; at worst, it labels a solution that's inconsistent with other central theses in Freud's theory of mind, notably the fact that it is essential to an instinct that its aim is unalterable (*SE* 14: 122; cp. *SE* 11: 54). If that's so, sublimation as explained above is impossible; conversely, if sublimation *is* possible, it's not clear how much remains of Freud's theory of instinct, the centrepiece of his theory of motivation (*SE* 14: 122).[35]

'PESSIMISM' AFTER THE DUAL INSTINCT THEORY

Ascribing 'Freudian pessimism' to Freud is further complicated by the appearance, late in Freud's career, of the 'dual instinct theory'. Suppose we think of the theory, provisionally, as the view that there is at least one instinct or group of instincts that, contrary to Freud's earlier position, is not subject to the pleasure principle. If that's so, and one source of 'Freudian pessimism' is the universality of the pleasure principle, isn't this another and perhaps better way out?

The dual instinct theory – whose two instincts are Eros and the death instinct – is hard to interpret. Since sex looms large in Freud's original theory of instinct and 'Eros' is the Greek for 'sexual love', it looks as if the *new* instinct must be the death instinct. But when one looks at what Eros and the death instinct *do* rather than at their names, it becomes apparent that the

---

[34] Hale 1971: 190.   [35] De Sousa 1982: 152.

newcomer is Eros.[36] For the death instinct is a kind of principle of entropy (tending 'towards the restoration of an earlier state of things . . . the aim of all life is death' (*SE* 18: 37–8)), and it is libido (on the earlier theory) that seeks its own extinction (*SE* 7: 168; 14: 122; 19: 255). Eros on the other hand does no such thing, striving rather 'to combine organic substances into ever larger unities' (*SE* 18: 43). But if the dual instinct theory is effectively a rethinking of sexuality as (constructive) Eros rather than as (entropic) libido, what is the death instinct itself? Freud's problematic answer is 'aggression' or 'destruction' (*SE* 22: 209), problematic because the loud bangs associated with both do not *seem* like matter simply returning to a state of quiescence. The 'dual instinct theory' may, then, introduce *two* newcomers, Eros *and* aggression.

Be that as it may, if the 'sexual instincts' are now theorized as 'part of Eros' (*SE* 18: 60 n. 1), and indeed 'the part of Eros which is directed towards objects' (ibid.), there now seems to be an instinct in Freud's theoretical repertoire that plays the same fundamental role in his theory as libido, but which doesn't commit him to what I have called 'hedonism plus' as a theory of the ends of human action. Some of the best of psychoanalytic thought has taken off from the observation that human beings seek relatedness to others for its own sake, not as a means to something else (a sensory state of themselves not excluded), from the word go – our 'germinal capacity for social interaction'.[37] This observation has been seen as a reason to reject Freud, but on the reading now in view, Freud himself is the first 'object relations' theorist. Moreover though there's no reason to think that Eros itself *couldn't* be frustrated given the demands of civilization, since one of the things civilization demands is human association and the virtues necessary for that (for example the ability to keep agreements once they're no longer advantageous) then, since the *aim* of Eros is precisely 'to combine organic substances' (including people), frustration – even without appeal to a mysterious mechanism of sublimation – looks less like a guaranteed feature of social existence than under the old Freudian theory. So one and the same developmental trajectory seems to fit both mental health – the proper development of our own capacities – and the social virtues.

Finally, we can see in the dual instinct theory a more clearly articulated Freudian answer to another question of central concern to moral philosophy, namely 'what psychological resources explain compliance with moral requirements?' – a question which, given that moral requirements are in fact widely

---

[36] Lear 1998.
[37] Bowlby 1988: 7; cp. Fairbairn 1952: 82; Lomas 1973: 67; Winnicott 1975: 163.

complied with, needs an answer all the more urgently the more compliance is said to be at odds with human instinct. While Freud's focus was solely on libido, his answer to the source of compliance seems to be simply 'the reality principle', that is, the need to inhibit at least the immediate satisfaction of instinct in order to survive. This is a good answer to the question why humans should bother (say) to plant potatoes if the unmodified 'programme of the pleasure principle' is to hallucinate eating potatoes. But it is not a good answer to the question why humans should bother to plant their own potatoes rather than stealing someone else's, and yet they frequently do. The dual instinct theory has a better answer: there is now another instinct, aggression, which once harnessed by an internal agency – the superego (*SE* 22: 110) – inhibits the expression of instinct, including its own expression. One is reminded of Hume's solution to essentially the same problem: 'There is no passion, there-fore, capable of controlling the interested affection, but the very affection itself, by an alteration of its direction ... [I]tself alone restrains it'.[38]

However, proposals to conjure compliance with moral requirements out of the personal ties to which we are independently inclined[39] always encounter the same problem: because morality is impartial, we owe compliance with moral requirements to more people than those to whom we are personally related (whether as lovers, friends, or confederates of whatever sort) and the proposal seems to have no resources to fill that gap. Now it may be that psychoanalysis has the resources to explain the origin of *impartial* moral dispositions without an inevitable residue of frustration.[40] But it is not a possibility clearly seen by Freud. Indeed Freud himself raises, ahead of time, the very problem I have raised with his followers' attempt to press the dual instinct theory into the service of an optimistic way out of 'Freudian pessimism'. Eros 'binds in love among a loving pair', but civilization's demands are impartial: 'we derive the antithesis between civilization and sexuality from the circumstance that sexual love is a relation between two individuals ... whereas civilization depends on rela-tions between a considerable number of individuals' (*SE* 21: 108). 'Love thy neighbour' is still treated – as on the earlier theory – as an 'ideal demand' (*SE* 21: 109; cp. *SE* 14: 93, 'the formation of an ideal would be the conditioning factor in repression'). If Freud also says that the purpose of Eros is to 'combine single human individuals ... into one great unity, the unity of mankind' (*SE* 21: 107), this isn't an answer to the problem (and Freud needn't be interpreted as saying it is): a universal community which Eros may construct in future cannot explain our compliance with impartial requirements here and now.

---

[38] Hume 1975: III.2.ii.   [39] Flugel 1945/1973: 242; Sagan 1988: 194.   [40] Britton 1998: 42.

Moreover, the presence of aggression in the theory appears to introduce fresh grounds for thinking civilization spells frustration: 'Restriction of the individual's aggressiveness is the first and perhaps the severest sacrifice which society demands of him' (*SE* 22: 109). Even though at least some of society's restrictions, including the injunction to love one's neighbour, stem from the harnessing of aggression to form the superego (*SE* 22: 110; 21: 138), 'the ego does not feel happy in being thus sacrificed to the needs of society, in having to submit to the destructive trends of aggressiveness *which it would have been happy to employ ... against others*' (*SE* 22: 110; my italics). In other words, the conflict between civilization and aggression mirrors the conflict, on the earlier theory, between civilization and libido. Indeed Freud sometimes says that both Eros *and* aggression are subject to the pleasure principle (*SE* 23: 116, 148), so perhaps he did not go 'beyond the pleasure principle' after all, but only expanded his view of the instincts that are subject to it. If that's so, then the position of sublimation within the theory (*SE* 23: 155) remains the same: if Freud can explain what it is, then civilization may not spell frustration because it is capable of transforming our instincts as well as merely inhibiting them. If he can't, the message is the same under the dual instinct theory as before: civilization inevitably requires the repression of untransformed instincts, so the superego is stationed in our psyche 'like a garrison ... in regions inclined to rebellion' (*SE* 22: 110). He describes 'ethics' as a 'therapeutic attempt ... to get rid of the ... constitutional inclination of human beings to be aggressive towards one another' (*SE* 21: 142) – therapeutic because it attempts to find satisfactions in complying with superego demands to compensate for the frustrations. But Freud seems to incline to the Thrasymachean conclusion that 'anyone who follows such a precept [as "love thy neighbour as thyself"] in present-day civilization only puts himself at a disadvantage vis-à-vis the person who disregards it' (*SE* 21: 143). As regards the interest of psychoanalysis for moral philosophy, however, the fundamental question is not about the interpretation of Freud but whether, between its various manifestations, psychoanalysis has the resources to provide a critical but also a credible account of human excellence.

BIBLIOGRAPHY

An asterisk denotes secondary literature especially suitable for further reading.

Abel, Donald C. 1989. *Freud on Instinct and Morality*. Albany, NY: State University of New York Press.
Abramson, Jeffrey B. 1984. *Liberation and Its Limits*. London and New York: Free Press.

Aristotle 1984. *Nicomachean Ethics*, in J. Barnes (ed.), *Complete Works of Aristotle*, vol. 2. The Revised Oxford Translation (Bollingen online edn). Princeton University Press, pp. 1729–1867.

Blass, Rachel 2001. 'On the Ethical and Evaluative Nature of Developmental Models in Psychoanalysis', *The Psychoanalytic Study of the Child* 56, pp. 193–218.

Blass, Rachel 2003. 'On Ethical Issues at the Foundation of the Debate over the Goals of Psychoanalysis', *International Journal of Psychoanalysis* 84, pp. 929–43.

Bowlby, John 1988. 'Caring for Children', in *A Secure Base*. London: Routledge, pp. 1–21.

Britton, Ronald 1998. 'Subjectivity, Objectivity and Triangular Space', in *Belief and Imagination*. London: Routledge, pp. 41–58.*

Cottingham, John 1998. *Philosophy and the Good Life*. Cambridge University Press.

De Sousa, R. 1982. 'Norms and the Normal', in R. Wollheim and J. Hopkins (eds.), *Philosophical Essays on Freud*. Cambridge University Press, pp. 139–62.*

Dilman, Ilham 1983. *Freud and Human Nature*. Oxford: Blackwell.

Eagle, Morris 1984. *Recent Developments in Psychoanalysis*. Cambridge, MA: Harvard University Press.

Erikson, Erik 1964. 'Human Strength and the Cycle of Generations', in *Insight and Responsibility*. London: Faber, pp. 109–58.

Fairbairn, W.R.D. 1952. *Psychoanalytic Studies of the Personality*. London: Tavistock Publications.

Flugel, J.C. 1945/1973. *Man, Morals and Society*. London: Duckworth.

Freud, Sigmund 1953–1964. *The Standard Edition of the Complete Psychological Works of Sigmund Freud*, ed. J. Strachey *et al.* 24 vols. London: Hogarth Press/Institute of Psychoanalysis.*

Fromm, Erich 1947. *Man for Himself*. Greenwich, CT: Fawcett.

Hale, Nathan G., Jr. 1971. *James Jackson Putnam and Psychoanalysis: Letters between Putnam and Sigmund Freud and Others*. Cambridge, MA: Harvard University Press.

Harcourt, Edward 2015. 'The Place of Psychoanalysis in the History of Ethics', *Journal of Moral Philosophy* 12 (5), pp. 598–618.

Harcourt, Edward In press. 'Madness, Badness, and Immaturity: Some Conceptual Issues in Psychoanalysis and Psychotherapy', *Philosophy, Psychiatry and Psychology*.

Hartmann, Heinz 1960. *Psychoanalysis and Moral Values*. New York: International Universities Press.

Hinshelwood, R.D. 1997. *Therapy or Coercion?* London: Karnac.

Holmes, Jeremy 1997. 'Values in Psychotherapy', *Australian and New Zealand Journal of Psychiatry* 31:3, pp. 331–9.

Holmes, Jeremy 2011. *Exploring in Security*. London and New York: Routledge.

Horney, Karen 1950/1991. *Neurosis and Human Growth*. New York: Norton.

Hume, David 1975. *A Treatise of Human Nature*, ed. L. Selby-Bigge. Oxford University Press.

Klein, Melanie 1946/1988. 'Notes on Some Schizoid Mechanisms', with 'Explanatory Notes' by Edna O'Shaughnessy, in *Envy and Gratitude*. London: Virago Press, pp. 1–25, 324–6.*

Korsgaard, Christine 1996. 'Two Distinctions in Goodness', in *Creating the Kingdom of Ends*. Cambridge University Press, pp. 249–74.

Lacan, Jacques 1986. *Le séminaire VII: l'éthique de la psychanalyse*. Paris: Éditions du Seuil.

Lear, Jonathan 1990. *Love and its Place in Nature*. London: Faber.*

Lear, Jonathan 1998. 'The Introduction of Eros', in *Open Minded*. Cambridge, MA and London: Harvard University Press, pp. 123–47.

Loewald, Hans W. 1978. *Psychoanalysis and the History of the Individual*. New Haven, CT, and London: Yale University Press.*

Lomas, Peter 1973. *True and False Experience*. London: Allen Lane.

Mahler, Margaret 1986. 'On the First Three Subphases of the Separation–Individuation Process', in P. Buckley (ed.), *Essential Papers on Object Relations*. New York and London: New York University Press, pp. 222–31.

Marcuse, Herbert 1956/1987. *Eros and Civilization*. London: Routledge.

Meissner, W.W. 2003. *The Ethical Dimension of Psychoanalysis*. Albany, NY: State University of New York Press.

Mitchell, Stephen 1988. *Relational Concepts in Psychoanalysis*. Cambridge, MA: Harvard University Press.*

Molnar, Michael 2002. 'John Stuart Mill Translated by Sigmund Freud', in F. Geerardyn and G. van de Vijver (eds.), *The Pre-Psychoanalytic Writings of Sigmund Freud*. London: Karnac, pp. 112–23.

Money-Kyrle, R.E. 1952. 'Psycho-Analysis and Ethics', *International Journal of Psychoanalysis* 33, pp. 225–34.

Plato 1961. *Republic* in Plato, *The Collected Dialogues*, ed. E. Hamilton and H. Cairns. Bollingen Foundation. Princeton University Press.

Rieff, Philip 1959/1979. *Freud: The Mind of the Moralist*, 3rd edn. Chicago, IL and London: University of Chicago Press.

Russell, Bertrand 1921. *The Analysis of Mind*. London: Routledge.

Sagan, Eli 1988. *Freud, Women and Morality*. New York: Basic Books.

Schopenhauer, Arthur 1883. *The World as Will and Idea*. London: Trübner.

Sidgwick, Henry (1907/1962). *The Methods of Ethics*. 7th edn. London: Macmillan.

Spillius, Elizabeth Bott 1994. 'Developments in Kleinian Thought: Overview and Personal View', *Psychoanalytic Inquiry* 14:3, pp. 324–64.

Suttie, Ian 1963. *The Origins of Love and Hate*. Harmondsworth: Penguin.*

Waddell, Margot 1998. *Inside Lives*. London: Duckworth.*

Wallwork, Ernest 1991. *Psychoanalysis and Ethics*. New Haven, CT, and London: Yale University Press.

Winnicott, D.W. 1975. *Through Paediatrics to Psycho-Analysis*. London: Hogarth Press/ Institute of Psychoanalysis.

Wollheim, Richard 1984. The Thread of Life. New Haven, CT, and London: Yale University Press.

Wollheim, Richard 1987. 'Bradley and the British School of Psychoanalysis', in *The Mind and Its Depths*. New Haven, CT, and London: Yale University Press, pp. 39–63.

45

Noncognitivism: From the Vienna Circle to the Present Day

JOHN ERIKSSON

How should we understand the nature of moral thought and talk?[1] This is one of the central questions in meta-ethics and responses fall into two main categories. According to cognitivism, moral statements express beliefs that purport to represent moral properties and can be true or false. Noncognitivism, on the other hand, can be understood as the denial of cognitivism and the theses associated with it, i.e., as denying that moral statements express beliefs that can be true or false. More broadly, noncognitivism is associated with a set of negative theses regarding metaphysics, epistemology, philosophy of language and mind. In particular, theses to the effect that there are no moral facts, that there is no moral knowledge, and that moral thought and talk is non-representational. A problem with characterizing noncognitivism as a set of distinct negative theses is that not all philosophers associated with the noncognitivist tradition adhere to them all.[2] A different way to approach noncognitivism is therefore as a distinct tradition running from emotivism through prescriptivism to expressivism. In what follows these two ways of understanding noncognitivism will be pursued side by side. By examining the noncognitivist tradition running from the Vienna Circle to the present day the reader will become acquainted with the views, theses and motivations associated with it.

THE EARLY DAYS

A natural starting point for an inquiry into noncognitivism is A.J. Ayer's version advanced in *Language, Truth and Logic* (1936). Not only is this one of

[1] The terms "moral" and "ethical" are used interchangeably for the simple reason that different philosophers in the noncognitivist tradition have used them thus.

[2] It should be noted that "cognitivism" is equally difficult to define. For instance, it is not the case that all cognitivists affirm all the theses mentioned. Error-theorists, for example, claim that moral thought and talk purport to describe moral properties, but argue that moral properties don't exist. Hence, moral statements are systematically false.

the earliest statement of noncognitivism, but it also nicely illustrates the main associated theses and fits well into the view that noncognitivism emerges from a critique of the intuitionism propounded by H.A. Prichard (1912), W.D. Ross (1930), and, in particular, G.E. Moore (1903). Moore thought that the history of moral philosophy was guilty of committing what he called the naturalistic fallacy, i.e., trying to define "goodness" in natural terms, e.g., pleasure, something desired by the speaker, commanded by God or the like. Moore famously argued for this by wielding the open-question argument. The idea behind this argument is that a proper definition entails that some-one who understands it cannot intelligibly ask whether M (the *analysandum*) is S (the *analysans*). For example, if one understands the concept "square" the question "This is a plane figure with four equal straight sides and four right angles, but is it a square?" is closed. By contrast, "This is good, but is it pleasant?" appears open. Indeed, Moore argued that regardless of what naturalistic definition is proposed, the question will remain open. This led Moore to the view that the term "goodness" is unanalyzable and denotes a simple non-natural property.[3]

Ayer agreed that the term "goodness" is unanalyzable on Moorean grounds. Hence, naturalism was not an option. However, neither was Moore's intuitionism. In order to understand the ground for his rejection of Moore's intuitionism we must consider the influence of the Vienna Circle and Logical Positivism on Ayer's thinking. The Vienna Circle was a group of philosophers, including Rudolf Carnap, Otto Neurath and Moritz Schlick, with a firm commitment to empiricism. A central doctrine of the group is what is known as the verification criterion.[4] A statement is literally significant provided that that it is empirically verifiable. For example, a proposition is (weakly) verifiable "if it is possible for experience to render it probable."[5] The alternative is that the statement is analytic (true by definition). Since no naturalistic definition is feasible, moral statements are not analytic. However, given how Moore and other intuitionists understood statements of value,

---

[3] Moore 1903: 110–11. Note that Moore thought that "moral rightness" and "moral obligation" are complex notions – "rightness," for instance, means that it will produce more goodness, which in turn is indefinable. For an early critical discussion of Moore's argument see Frankena 1939.

[4] The criterion was partly inspired by remarks made by Wittgenstein in *Tractatus*, where negative remarks about ethics also can be found. "It is clear that ethics cannot be put into words. Ethics is transcendental. (Ethics and aesthetics are one and the same)" (Wittgenstein 1922, 6: 421).

[5] Ayer 1936: 18.

Ayer thought it was clear that they are not verifiable. Intuition is not a scientific method of verification and it gives us no way of adjudicating between different intuitions. Consequently, "a mere appeal to intuition is worthless as a test of a proposition's validity."[6] But why is it that moral statements cannot be defined in naturalistic terms or be empirically verified? According to Ayer, the reason is that moral terms are "mere pseudo-concepts" that lack literal significance.

> The presence of an ethical symbol in a proposition adds nothing to its factual content. Thus if I say to someone, "You acted wrongly in stealing that money," I am not stating anything more than if I had simply said, "You stole that money." In adding that this action is wrong I am not making any further statement about it. I am simply evincing my moral disapproval of it. It is as if I had said, "You stole that money," in a peculiar tone of horror, or written with the addition of some special exclamation marks. The tone, or the exclamation marks, adds nothing to the literal meaning of the sentence. It merely serves to show that the expression of it is attended by certain feelings in the speaker.[7]

Ayer's statement illustrates the main negative theses associated with non-cognitivism. Metaphysically, there are no moral facts. Epistemologically, there is no moral knowledge. Semantically, moral statements do not purport to represent moral reality and therefore cannot be true or false. Ayer does not say much about moral thinking, but it is clear that it is not a species of belief. Despite Ayer's negative remarks he actually anticipates one of the central claims associated with contemporary expressivism when he claims that "we may define the meaning of the various ethical words in terms of both the different feelings they are ordinarily taken to express, and also the different responses which they are calculated to provoke."[8]

Given the Vienna Circle's commitment to the verification criterion it should not be very surprising to find noncognitivist views among its members. Carnap (1935), for instance, claimed that "most moral philosophers have been deceived into thinking that a value statement is really an assertive proposition ... But actually a value statement is nothing else than a command in a misleading grammatical form."[9] However, although Ayer and some of the members of the Vienna Circle advanced noncognitivist ideas, moral philosophy or meta-ethics was not one of their primary interests. In

---

[6] Ibid., 106. Urmson therefore declares that noncognitivism in the guise of emotivism arose from epistemological despair (1968: 19).
[7] Ayer 1936: 107.   [8] Ibid., 108.   [9] Carnap 1935: 24–5.

fact, Ayer's reason for considering value statements is in the context of addressing an objection to the verification criterion (see e.g. 1936, beginning of Chapter VI).

On the other side of the Atlantic, Charles Stevenson advanced a form of emotivism in "The emotive meaning of ethical terms" (1937), which is elaborated in *Ethics and Language* (1944). In contrast to Ayer, moral philosophy or meta-ethics was of central interest to Stevenson. Like Ayer, however, Stevenson was also concerned with problems facing naturalist analyses of moral terms. In particular, focus is on so-called interest theories (a term Stevenson gets from R.B. Perry) where "This is good" means "desired by me" or "approved of by most people" – views Stevenson attributes to Hobbes and Hume respectively (the latter view is also attributed to Perry).

Part of Stevenson's reason for objecting to interest theories is that they run into the kind of problems considered above in relation to the open-question argument. An analysis of "good," as Stevenson puts it, "must not be discoverable solely through the scientific method." However, Stevenson also adds two further requirements that have played major roles in subsequent arguments for noncognitivism. First, "'goodness' must be a topic for intelligent disagreement" and second, "it must be 'magnetic,'" i.e., it must explain how "[a] person who recognizes X to be 'good' must ipso facto acquire a stronger tendency to act in its favour than he otherwise would have had"[10] (these arguments are treated in more detail below). No (pure) interest theory satisfies all these requirements, but, Stevenson argues, a kind of interest theory does.

> Traditional interest theories hold that ethical statements are descriptive of the existing states and interests [. . .]. Doubtless there is always some element of description in ethical judgments, but this is by no means all. Their major use is not to indicate facts but to create an influence. Instead of merely describing people's interest they change or intensify them. They recommend an interest in an object rather than state that the interest already exists.[11]

Stevenson, by contrast to Ayer, thus claims that ethical judgments are indeed descriptive. However, they do not merely function to communicate beliefs or describe. Instead, their major function is to create an influence. This function is explained by the emotive meaning of ethical terms. "The emotive meaning of a word is the power that the word acquires, on account of its history in emotional situations, to evoke or directly express attitudes, as distinct from describing or designating them."[12]

---

[10] Stevenson 1937: 18.   [11] Ibid., 16.   [12] Ibid., 32.

The source of Stevenson's "emotive meaning" is C.K. Ogden and I.A. Richards' *The Meaning of 'Meaning'* (1923) and a proper presentation of emotivism is not complete without a brief account of their view. In this work Ogden and Richards actually present an emotive theory of moral terms. "This peculiar ethical use of 'good' is, we suggest, a purely emotive use. When so used, the word has no symbolic function. . . . it serves only as an emotive sign expressing our attitude . . . and perhaps evoking similar attitudes in other persons, or inciting them to action of one kind or another."[13] Like Ayer and Stevenson, this statement is partly motivated by the open-question argument and problems with intuitionism.

It seems plausible that Ogden and Richards' "emotive meaning" played an important role in the early development of emotivism.[14] However, their positive view is arguably not motivated by a commitment to logical positivism. Instead, the origin of their view can be traced to another continental source, viz., Franz Brentano.[15] Ethics is, according to Brentano, concerned with correct emotions (love and hate). An emotion is correct when it is adequate to its object. Anton Marty, one of Brentano's students, can be read as making semantics out of Brentano's psychology and a linguistic sign Marty called "ein Emotiv" is plausibly the origin of Ogden and Richards' "emotive meaning." Brentano is also arguably the source of Stevenson's concept of interest or emotion with the polarity of "for" and "against," a concept he acquired through Perry's *General Theory of Value* (1926). In fact, noncognitivist views arose in different places at the beginning of the twentieth century.[16] This may, of course, be a coincidence. However, it may also be argued that Brentano's heritage, via various other philosophers, is an important source of inspiration. Given the latter view, it seems rather plausible that Ayer and Stevenson's respective views have quite different historical backgrounds. Stevenson's view is "grounded in the psychology of Brentano and Perry

[13] Ogden and Richards 1923: 125.
[14] Ayer (1984) admits having read Ogden and Richards' book before writing *Language, Truth and Logic*, but that the "plagiarism" was unconscious.
[15] This draws on Satris (1987).
[16] See, e.g., Axel Hägerström's inaugural lecture "On the Truth of Moral Propositions" (1911) made accessible to the English-speaking world in the early 1950s by C.D. Broad's translation. Broad (1933–4) also attributes a noncognitivist view to A.S. Duncan Jones. Urmson (1968) claims that the use of the "boo-hurrah theory of ethics" derives from the examples used to illustrate Jones' view, e.g., that "This is good" may be equivalent to "That's an act of self-sacrifice. Hurrah!" See also Russell (1935).

and not in the main" – as for Ayer – "an ethical work developed in reaction to Moore's *Principia Ethica*."[17]

One of the main virtues of Stevenson's view is its intuitive accommodation of both the descriptive and practical dimensions of moral language. Throughout his work, he offers a number of different analyses meant to shed light on this dual function. To a first approximation, "This is good" means "I approve of this – do so as well." In *Ethics and Language* (1944), a second pattern of analysis is advanced. According to it, "'This is good' has the meaning of 'This has qualities or relations X, Y, Z ...,' except that 'good' has as well a laudatory emotive meaning which permits it to express the speaker's approval, and tends to evoke the approval of the hearer."[18] In the retrospective comments of *Facts and Value* (1963), finally, Stevenson considers deleting the autobiographical element and suggests that "X is good" means "Let us approve of X."[19] Stevenson never thought that these suggestions provided adequate analyses of the meaning of moral terms. Rather, they (or at least the two first) serve to illustrate the idea that moral thought and talk are not merely a matter of description, but also have an action-guiding function. Moral language is conceived of as an instrument devised for adjusting human interests (this theme is elaborated in, e.g., Gibbard (1990) where it is argued that moral language is essential for co-operation).

Ayer and Stevenson are the main emotivists in the noncognitivist lineage. The next major development we find is R.M. Hare's *The Language of Morals* of 1952, where a different account of moral language is presented. Hare was critical of the emotivists' attempt to shed light on the meaning of moral language in terms of expression of attitudes. Instead, Hare argued that moral language is best accounted for as a sort of prescriptive language. To say that someone is a good person, for example, is to commend that person. This is essential to understand the evaluative meaning of a value statement. However, Hare also argued, like Stevenson, that value statements involve a descriptive component. Commendations require grounds. It always makes sense to ask someone who claims that a person is good why the target agent is good. The answer to this question depends on the speaker's standard. For instance, a person may commend someone in virtue of the target agent having certain good-making characteristics X, Y, Z (compare Stevenson's second pattern). These characteristics, in turn, are important to understand the descriptive meaning of a value statement. As Hare writes, "[t]o know the descriptive meaning is to know by what standard the speaker is judging."[20]

---

[17] Satris 1987: 126.   [18] Stevenson 1944: 207.   [19] Ibid., 214.   [20] Hare 1952: 146.

He also claimed that the descriptive meaning of a value statement is secondary whereas the evaluative meaning is primary. Hare's reason for thinking this is twofold. First, the evaluative meaning of "good" or "right" is constant whereas the descriptive meaning isn't. Second, the evaluative force of "good" and "right" can be used to change their descriptive meaning.[21]

Moreover, value statements do not merely apply to the situation at hand, but are covertly universal. Commending an agent in virtue of certain good-making characteristics commits the judger to commend other people if they possess the same (or relevantly similar) property. This has to do with the supervenience of the evaluative on the non-evaluative. It is impossible for there to be a difference in evaluative matters (between two persons, situations or the like) without there being a difference in descriptive matters, e.g., motives, consequences or the like. "[T]his impossibility is a logical one, stemming from the way in which, and the purposes for which, we use these words."[22] Because of the "covert" universality of moral statements, Hare's position is also known as "universal prescriptivism."

CONTEMPORARY VIEWS

Ayer, Stevenson and Hare all in different ways influence the development of the next stage of noncognitivism: expressivism. Here the main proponents are Simon Blackburn (1984, 1993, 1998) and Allan Gibbard (1990, 2003). Gibbard explicates expressivism as a distinctive approach to meaning: "to explain the meaning of a term, explain what state of mind the term can be used to express."[23] This explication requires the addressing of (at least) two questions. First, how should the expression relation be understood? It may be understood as a causal, intentional, conventional or more technical notion.[24] A suggestion made popular by Schroeder (2008) is that a sentence expresses the state of mind that makes it semantically appropriate to use. The next question is what state of mind moral sentences express (or what makes them semantically appropriate to use). The central idea among expressivists is still that the relevant state of mind isn't a belief that purports to represent or describe some kind of moral reality, but a state of mind with a different direction of fit, i.e., something more like approval or disapproval.

However, a potential problem for expressivism is that moral disapproval must be distinguished from other kinds of disapproval, e.g., aesthetic or

[21] Ibid., 118–19.   [22] Ibid., 153.   [23] Gibbard 2003: 7.
[24] See Schroeder 2008 for discussion.

gustatory (a.k.a. the moral attitude problem). Blackburn does not think that a strict definition of the attitude involved can be given.[25] Gibbard, by contrast, tries to be more specific. In *Wise Choices, Apt Feelings* (1990), he advances a psychological theory of moral judgments and judgments of rationality. In fact, moral judgments are about the rationality of certain sentiments, viz., guilt and anger. To judge that an act is morally wrong is to judge it rational for the perpetrator to feel guilt and for other people to be angry with him or her. However, to judge that it is rational is not to attribute any property, but to accept a system of norms. This is the kind of state of mind that a moral sentence functions to express. In *Thinking How to Live* (2003), Gibbard's view is slightly different. Moral sentences are said to express plans or planning states.

One of the central theses of noncognitivism is that moral thought and talk is radically different from descriptive thought and talk. However, moral thought and talk behaves pretty much like descriptive thought and talk. For example, we talk as if moral statements can be true or false, that moral terms denote moral facts that are mind-independent, that people have moral beliefs and that we can be wrong about moral matters. This seems decisively odd if moral thought and talk is a matter of attitudes, as noncognitivists think.

Part of the contemporary expressivist aim is to "explain, and justify, the realistic-seeming nature of our talk of evaluations"[26] without abandoning the expressivist framework. Blackburn calls this project quasi-realism. The aim is to show that the realistic-seeming nature is compatible with expressivism. For instance, Blackburn (1984) makes use of higher-order attitudes in order to explain why we think and talk as we do. In his later work he relies more on so-called minimalist notions of "truth," "properties," "facts," and "beliefs" and "propositions." Minimalism about truth (as an illustration) is the view that all there is to understand the truth predicate is to understand instances of the following schema: the proposition that p is true if and only if p (see Horwich 1990). According to minimalism, truth is not a substantive property. Saying "Stealing is wrong is true," on this picture, just amounts to saying "Stealing is wrong." Moreover, once "truth" is accounted for it seems that facts come along, since saying that it is a fact that stealing is wrong amounts to no more than saying that it is true. Blackburn develops this theme.[27] In his early work,

---

[25] Blackburn 1998: 13–14.   [26] Blackburn 1984: 180.

[27] Blackburn (1993, 1998). A potential problem with quasi-realism and the appeal to minimalism is that it makes it difficult to see what the differences between expressivism and more realist accounts of moral thought and talk amount to. See Dreier (2004) for discussion.

Gibbard denies that moral statements can be either true or false. In his more recent work, however, he is more open to minimalism.[28] Terry Horgan and Mark Timmons (2006) also defend a view in this family, which they call "cognitivist expressivism." According to this view, moral judgments are genuine beliefs, but lack descriptive content.

One difference between Ayer, Blackburn and Gibbard, on the one hand, and Stevenson and Hare, on the other, is that the former think that a moral statement does not express a belief or has descriptive meaning. These views are versions of *pure* expressivism. The latter views are, by contrast, impure. Recently, Michael Ridge (2006) has advanced an influential theory in the spirit of the latter, which he calls "ecumenical expressivism." Moral statements, on this view, express both beliefs and desires.[29] The latest addition of views in the expressivist family is "relational expressivism." Rather than that moral statements express a pair of attitudes, it is claimed that they express relational states (Schroeder 2013; Toppinen 2013; Ridge 2014). As this recent development shows, expressivism is constantly being refined in different ways and relational expressivism is not likely to be the last step in the evolution of noncognitivist or expressivist ideas.

CENTRAL MOTIVATIONS

As this brief historical survey illustrates, there are both similarities and differences between noncognitivist views. However, the central motivations are more uniform. We have already become familiar with one of the main arguments, viz., Moore's open-question argument. This, together with the apparent implausibility of non-naturalism, once "seemed to force anyone to noncognitivism, even kicking and screaming."[30] Those days are long gone, but the apparent difference between facts and values is still a consideration that makes noncognitivism attractive. Normative terms generally seem to be different from ordinary descriptive terms. As Gibbard writes, "the normative involves a kind of endorsement – an endorsement that any descriptive analysis treats inadequately."[31] Along with the traditional metaphysical and epistemological considerations, this still makes some kind of noncognitivism

---

[28] See also Stevenson (1963: 214–18).
[29] Ridge conceives of his view as part of the noncognitivist tradition. See Schroeder (2009) for discussion of other hybrid options. See also Eriksson (2009) for a hybrid theory inspired by Hare.
[30] Darwall *et al.* (1992): 144.   [31] Gibbard 1990: 33.

attractive.[32] It should be noted that these considerations also suggest that noncognitivism or expressivism cannot, for better or worse, be confined to the moral domain. In fact, it has recently become popular to examine extensions to other domains, e.g., epistemology, truth, epistemic modality and so on.

Stevenson, recall, also claimed that an adequate analysis of "good" is expected to comply with two additional requirements: (1) "'goodness' must be a topic for intelligent disagreement"; (2) it must be "magnetic."[33] Arguments based on these requirements have played important roles in meta-ethics and will, in reverse order, be briefly presented below.

Stevenson's second requirement is the idea that "[a] person who recognizes X to be 'good' must ipso facto acquire a stronger tendency to act in its favour than he otherwise would have had."[34] Similarly, Hare claims that the most reliable way of finding out what a person's moral principles are is to study his or her behavior.[35] For instance, if someone claims that one ought to donate to charity, but when given the opportunity displays complete indifference to the cause, we are likely to doubt his or her sincerity. The underlying observation here is that there is an intimate connection between an agent's values and motivation.

A common argument for noncognitivism based on this observation draws inspiration from David Hume's *Treatise* (1739–1740). Hume claimed that reason is inert, i.e., that it cannot influence our actions and affections. Only our passions have this ability. However, Hume also observed that an agent's moral opinions have an influence on his or her actions and affections, which seems to suggest that they must belong to our passions rather than reason.[36] In modern parlance, the argument relies on two premises. The first is what is commonly referred to as "motivational internalism," which is usually understood as the thesis that there is a necessary connection between moral judgments and motivation. The second premise is the Humean theory of motivation, i.e., the thesis that beliefs do not motivate, only desires do. From these two premises it seems to follow that moral judgments aren't beliefs. Hence, they must be desires.

That noncognitivism easily explains why motivational internalism is true is often presented as one of the major attractions of such a view. However, it is also frequently invoked as an argument against such theses. In virtue of

---

[32] Although these considerations for a long time discouraged any defense of nonnaturalism, this is no longer the case. See e.g. Enoch (2011) and Parfit (2011).

[33] Stevenson 1937: 18.   [34] Ibid.   [35] Hare 1952: 1.   [36] Hume 1739–1740: 3.1.1.6.

identifying moral judgments with emotions, commendations or the like, critics argue, noncognitivism rules out the conceivability of agents who judge that an act is right or wrong in a certain situation, but who are wholly indifferent in the relevant circumstances. Such agents are clearly possible, critics argue (Boyd 1988 and Brink 1989). However, noncognitivism cannot account for them and is in this respect seriously flawed. One response is simply to deny that such agents are conceivable. Perhaps the best interpretation of such agents is that they use moral terms in an "inverted commas" sense, e.g., meaning that so-and-so is approved of by the majority of the agent's circle or the like.[37] Another response is to weaken the connection between moral judgments and motivation.[38] However, weakening the connection between moral judgments and motivation also weakens the traditional argument for noncognitivism. Nevertheless, one may still think that the apparent action-guiding function is a feature of moral thought and talk that makes noncognitivism more plausible than rival views.[39]

Stevenson's third requirement concerns moral disagreement. For example, if Jack judges that stealing is wrong and Jill judges that stealing is right, then they are, intuitively, disagreeing. According to cognitivists, in order for Jack and Jill to disagree they must express inconsistent beliefs. However, suppose that Jack and Jill judge by completely different standards. Jack is a utilitarian. Jill is a virtue ethicist. This, in turn, makes it plausible to think that the descriptive meaning of their respective uses of the terms will differ. This is what Hare's famous example involving cannibals and missionaries purports to show.[40] In this case, there is no apparent disagreement in belief. If moral disagreement is exhausted by disagreement in belief, then Jack and Jill will not really disagree.

However, possible disagreements are arguably not exhausted by disagreement in belief. Stevenson famously distinguished between disagreement in beliefs and disagreement in attitude. The latter is illustrated by a number of different examples. Bill and Berta are going out to eat. Bill suggests an Italian place, but Berta expresses her aversion to Italian food and suggests that they eat Thai. In this example they seem to disagree about where to eat. However,

---

[37] Hare 1952: 124–6, 164–5.
[38] See, e.g., Blackburn 1998, Gibbard 1993, Björnsson 2002 and Eriksson 2014 for discussion.
[39] The relevance of internalism to noncognitivism (and in meta-ethics more generally) continues to be debated. See Björklund *et al.* (2012) for a brief overview of the recent debate and theses.
[40] Hare 1952. See also Horgan and Timmons 1992a and 1992b.

it seems that they could agree completely in belief (i.e., on all factual matters). Instead, "the disagreement springs [. . .] from divergent preferences [. . .] and will end when they both wish to go to the same place."[41]

Stevenson gives a number of slightly different explications of disagreement in attitude, but most importantly it occurs when two people have opposing attitudes that cannot be simultaneously satisfied. How does this play into the hands of noncognitivism? Given the considerations advanced above, it seems that Jack and Jill do not disagree in belief. On noncognitivist premises, on the other hand, moral statements are not used to (merely) express belief, but (also) to express attitudes, e.g., approval or disapproval. Given such a view, Jack and Jill give voice to (or accept) attitudes that cannot be satisfied simultaneously. Hence, the disagreement is explained in terms of disagreement in attitude.[42]

Considerations based on the open-question argument, the practicality of moral thought and talk and the ability to account for disagreement even in the absence of disagreement in belief continue to attract philosophers to noncognitivism. However, noncognitivism is also problematic for a number of reasons. We will end by briefly considering the most influential objection: the Frege–Geach problem.

The name of the problem derives from Peter Geach (who attributes the point to Frege), whose presentation has been most influential.[43] The target of Geach's argument was primarily a view like Hare's, according to which we should understand the meaning of a moral sentence in terms of the speech act of commending. The argument, however, applies to noncognitivism more generally. Noncognitivism seems well suited to explain simple contexts.

---

[41] Stevenson 1944: 3.

[42] See also Gibbard 2003. For discussion regarding the Stevensonian conception of "disagreement" and how "disagreement" should be understood, see Ridge (2013, 2014) and Eriksson (2016). For a thorough examination of various arguments from disagreement and the relevance to the debate, see Tersman 2006. Ayer, interestingly, claimed that "one really never does dispute about questions about value" (1936: 110). A "moral disagreement" is not really a disagreement about value but a disagreement in belief or question of fact.

[43] Searle 1962 independently advanced a similar argument against Hare's view. Historically, it may be argued that Ross (1939: 33–4) was the first to formulate the problem.

(1) Stealing is wrong.

Saying (1) could be interpreted as functioning to express disapproval of stealing. Geach's simple observation, however, was that in more complex contexts no speech act of the relevant kind is performed.

(2) If stealing is wrong, then getting little brother to steal is wrong.

Saying (2), by contrast to (1), does not seem to express any disapproval. For instance, whereas it seems semantically inappropriate to say (1) unless you have the relevant attitude, this is not the case for (2). The upshot of this is that "wrong" seems to be ambiguous – it seems to mean different things in (1) and (2). Moreover (1) and (2) seem to logically entail

(3) Getting little brother to steal is wrong.

However, if "wrong" has different meaning in (1) and (2), then the argument isn't valid. It commits the fallacy of equivocation.

This is, in brief, the classic Frege–Geach problem. Philosophers in the noncognitivist tradition have offered a number of different purported solutions to it. Hare (1952, 1970) considers the possibility of a logic concerning imperatives. Blackburn (1984) advanced a logic of attitudes according to which sentences like (2) express higher-order attitudes, e.g., disapproval of certain combination of attitudes. For instance, (2) expresses disapproval of disapproval of stealing without also disapproving of getting little brother to steal. Accepting the attitudes involved in (1), (2) and (3), Blackburn then argues, amounts to a kind of incoherence that explains the inconsistency of (1), (2) and (3), which in turn explains the validity of the argument. This suggestion has been the target of much criticism. Hale (1993), for instance, argues that it conflates logical validity with mere pragmatic validity.[44] More recent accounts try to avoid such problems and appeal to commitments incurred upon accepting a state of mind. Blackburn (1998) argues that accepting (2) amounts to "tying oneself to a tree." For instance, accepting "if p then q" is to commit oneself to the combination "either not-p or q."[45] Gibbard (1990, 2003) advances a similar view. Accepting a state of mind rules out accepting certain other states of mind (Gibbard 2003). These accounts aim to explain the sense in which different combinations of states of minds (and sentences expressing those states of mind) are genuinely inconsistent.

---

[44] See also van Roojen 1996 and Schueler 1988.   [45] Blackburn 1998: 72.

Although the Frege–Geach problem is associated with conditional sentences it is much broader. A related problem concerns negated contexts (Unwin 1999, 2001; Schroeder 2008). A sentence and its negation are inconsistent.

(4) Stealing is not wrong.

(4) is the negation of (1) and they should therefore come out as inconsistent. Given that approval of stealing and disapproval of stealing cannot simultaneously be satisfied it may be argued that we have an explanation of why this is the case. However, negation can also be inserted in (1) as follows.

(5) Not stealing is wrong.

Intuitively, (4) means that stealing is permissible and (5) that stealing is obligatory. The problem is that it is difficult to see how noncognitivists can explain these different interpretations without positing a new attitude, e.g., tolerance. Noncognitivist analyses have too little internal structure.[46] This leads to problems explaining why (4) (tolerance of stealing) is inconsistent with (1) (disapproval of stealing). In addition to conditionals and negations, noncognitivists must provide a story about the mental states expressed in contexts like the following.

(6) Is stealing wrong?
(7) I wish that stealing were wrong.
(8) Stealing is wrong and grass is green.

Noncognitivism still has to provide some way of accounting for the semantics of more complex constructions containing moral language.

BIBLIOGRAPHY

An asterisk denotes secondary literature especially suitable for further reading.

Ayer, A.J. 1936. *Language, Truth and Logic*, 2nd edn. London: Victor Gollancz.
Ayer, A.J. 1984. *Freedom, Morality and Other Essays*. Oxford University Press.
Björklund, F., Björnsson, G., Eriksson, J., Francén Olinder, R., and Strandberg, C. 2012. "Recent Work: Motivational Internalism," *Analysis* 72: 124–37.
Björnsson, G. 2002. "How Emotivism Survives Immoralists, Irrationality, and Depression," *Southern Journal of Philosophy* 40: 327–44.

[46] A different problem also allegedly having to do with the structural features of the relevant noncognitive attitude is the problem of accounting for certitude, importance and robustness. See Smith (2002).

Björnsson, G., and McPherson, T. 2014. "Moral Attitudes for Non-Cognitivists: Solving the Specification Problem," *Mind* 123: 1–38.★

Blackburn, S. 1971. "Moral Realism," reprinted in Blackburn 1993: 111–29.

Blackburn, S. 1984. *Spreading the Word: Groundings in the Philosophy of Language*. Oxford University Press.

Blackburn, S. 1988. "Attitudes and Contents," reprinted in Blackburn 1993: 182–97.

Blackburn, S. 1993. *Essays in Quasi-Realism*. New York: Oxford University Press.

Blackburn, S. 1998. *Ruling Passions: A Theory of Practical Reasoning*. Oxford University Press.

Boyd, R. 1988. "How to Be a Moral Realist," in G. Sayre-McCord (ed.), *Essays on Moral Realism*. Ithaca, NY: Cornell University Press, pp. 181–228.

Brink, D.O. 1989. *Moral Realism and the Foundations of Ethics*. New York: Cambridge University Press.

Broad, C.D. 1933–4. "Is 'Goodness' a Name of a Simple Non-natural Quality?" *Proceedings of the Aristotelian Society* 34: 249–68.

Carnap, R. 1935. *Philosophy and Logical Syntax*. London: Kegan Paul.

Darwall, S., Gibbard, A., and Railton, P. 1992. "Toward Fin de Siècle Ethics: Some Trends," *Philosophical Review* 101: 115–89.★

Dreier, J. 2004. "Meta-Ethics and the Problem of Creeping Minimalism," *Philosophical Perspectives* 18 (Ethics): 23–44.

Enoch, D. 2011. *Taking Morality Seriously: A Defense of Robust Realism*. Oxford University Press.

Eriksson, J. 2009. "Homage to Hare: Ecumenism and the Frege–Geach Problem," *Ethics* 120: 8–35.

Eriksson, J. 2014. "Elaborating Expressivism: Moral Judgments, Desires and Motivation," *Ethical Theory and Moral Practice* 17: 243–67.

Eriksson, J. 2016. "Expressivism, Attitudinal Complexity and Two Senses of Disagreement in Attitude," *Erkenntnis* 81: 775–94.

Frankena, W.K. 1939. "The Naturalistic Fallacy," *Mind* 48: 464–77.

Geach, P. 1960. "Ascriptivism," *Philosophical Review* 69: 221–25.

Geach, P. 1965. "Assertion," *Philosophical Review* 74: 449–65.

Gibbard, A. 1990. *Wise Choices, Apt Feelings*. Cambridge, MA: Harvard University Press.

Gibbard, A. 1993. "Reply to Sinnot-Armstrong," *Philosophical Studies* 69: 315–28.

Gibbard, A. 2003. *Thinking How to Live*. Cambridge, MA: Harvard University Press.

Hägerström, A. 1911. "On the Truth of Moral Propositions," in *Philosophy and Religion*, London: George Allen and Unwin, 1964, pp. 77–96.

Hale, B. 1993. "Can there Be a Logic of Attitudes?" in J. Haldane and C. Wright (eds.), *Reality, Representation, and Projection*. New York: Oxford University Press, pp. 337–63.

Hale, B. 2002. "Can Arboreal Knotwork Help Blackburn Out of Frege's Abyss?" *Philosophy and Phenomenological Research* 65: 144–9.

Hare, R.M. 1952. *The Language of Morals*. Oxford University Press.

Hare, R.M. 1970. "Meaning and Speech Acts," *Philosophical Review* 79: 3–24.

Horgan, T., and Timmons, M. 1992a. "Troubles for New Wave Moral Semantics: The 'Open Question Argument' Revived," *Philosophical Papers* 21: 153–75.

Horgan, T., and Timmons, M. 1992b. "Troubles on Moral Twin Earth: Moral Queerness Revived," *Syntheses* 92: 224–60.

Horgan, T., and Timmons, M. 2006. "Cognitivist Expressivism," in T. Horgan and M. Timmons (eds.), *Metaethics after Moore*. Oxford University Press, pp. 255–98.

Horwich, P. 1990. *Truth*. Oxford: Blackwell.

Hume, D. 1739–1740. *A Treatise of Human Nature*, ed. D.F. Norton and M.J. Norton. Oxford University Press, 2000.

Moore, G.E. 1903. *Principia Ethica*, ed. T. Baldwin. Cambridge University Press, 1993.

Ogden, C.K., and Richards, I.A. 1923. *The Meaning of Meaning: A Study of the Influence of Language upon Thought and of the Science of Symbolism*. London: Routledge and Kegan Paul.

Parfit, D. 2011. *On What Matters*. Oxford University Press.

Perry, R.B. 1926. *General Theory of Value: Its Meaning and Basic Principles Construed in Terms of Interest*. New York: Longmans, Green and Co.

Prichard, H.A. 1912. "Does Moral Philosophy Rest on a Mistake?" *Mind* 81: 21–37.

Ridge, M. 2006. "Ecumenical Expressivism: Finessing Frege," *Ethics* 116: 302–37.

Ridge, M. 2013. "Disagreement," *Philosophy and Phenomenological Research* 86: 41–63.

Ridge, M. 2014. *Impassioned Belief*. Oxford University Press.

Ross, W.D. 1930. *The Right and the Good*. Oxford: Clarendon Press.

Ross, W.D. 1939. *Foundations of Ethics*. Oxford University Press.

Russell, B. 1935. *Religion and Science*. New York: Oxford University Press.

Satris, S. 1987. *Ethical Emotivism*. Dordrecht: Martinus Nijhoff.

Schroeder, M. 2008. *Being For: Evaluating the Semantic Program of Expressivism*. Oxford University Press.

Schroeder, M. 2009. "Hybrid Expressivism: Virtues and Vices," *Ethics* 119: 257–309.

Schroeder, M. 2010. *Noncognitivism in Ethics*. London: Routledge.*

Schroeder, M. 2013. "Tempered Expressivism," in R. Shafer-Landau, ed., *Oxford Studies in Metaethics*, vol. 8, Oxford University Press, pp. 283–314.

Schueler, G.F. 1988. "Modus Ponens and Moral Realism," *Ethics* 98: 492–500.

Searle, J.R. 1962. "Meaning and Speech Acts," *Philosophical Review* 71: 423–32.

Smith, M. 2002. "Evaluation, Uncertainty, and Motivation," *Ethical Theory and Moral Practice* 5: 305–320.

Stevenson, C.L. 1937. "The Emotive Meaning of Ethical Terms," reprinted in Stevenson 1963: 10–31.

Stevenson, C.L. 1944. *Ethics and Language*. New Haven, CT: Yale University Press.

Stevenson, C.L. 1963. *Facts and Values: Studies in Ethical Analysis*. New Haven, CT: Yale University Press.

Tersman, F. 2006. *Moral Disagreement*. Cambridge University Press.

Toppinen, T. 2013. "Believing in Expressivism," in R. Shafer-Landau, ed., *Oxford Studies in Metaethics*, vol. 8, Oxford University Press, pp. 253–82.

Unwin, N. 1999. "Quasi-Realism, Negation and the Frege–Geach Problem," *Philosophical Quarterly* 49: 337–52.

Unwin, N. 2001. "Norms and Negation: A Problem for Gibbard's Logic," *Philosophical Quarterly* 51: 60–75.

Urmson, J.O. 1968. *The Emotive Theory of Ethics*. London: Hutchinson.

van Roojen, M. 1996. "Expressivism and Irrationality," *Philosophical Review* 105: 311–35.

van Roojen, M. 2015. *Metaethics: A Contemporary Introduction*. London: Routledge.*

Wittgenstein, L. 1922. *Tractatus Logico-Philosophicus*. London: Routledge.

46

The Frankfurt School

FRED RUSH

The Frankfurt School comprises a group of thinkers who collected themselves around the Institute for Social Research, established in Frankfurt in 1923. The most important philosophers belonging to the School were Max Horkheimer (1895–1973), Herbert Marcuse (1898–1979), and Theodor Adorno (1903–1969). Jürgen Habermas (b. 1929) is also often associated with the School. Among contemporary philosophers whose work falls within the general concerns of the School are, e.g., Seyla Benhabib (b. 1950), Axel Honneth (b. 1949), and Christoph Menke (b. 1958). The designation 'Frankfurt School' gained currency after the return of Adorno and Horkheimer to Germany from exile in the United States during World War II. Prior to that, the Frankfurt thinkers preferred to describe themselves as 'critical theorists'.

'Critical theory' is a social-scientific concept for the Frankfurt philosophers; however, they denied that criticism constituted a proprietary methodology. Broadly construed, criticism consists in a historically-informed amalgam of social theory and philosophy that forms a platform for views on a wide range of topics in value theory and social epistemology, including ethics. But any consideration of the 'ethics' of the Frankfurt School must reckon with a rather uncomfortable fact: that it is questionable whether critical theory in principle can embrace moral philosophy or ethics. The point can be brought out by considering two main intellectual sources of the School. Marx, for one, excoriated 'ethical theory' on grounds that it is the smug, self-satisfied expression of the class interests of those who are 'on top', which seeps imperceptibly 'down' into the self-conception of those 'below', a form of alienation on the part of both those who have and those who have not. Freud as well questioned the notion of a pure form of subjectivity that often constitutes the core of autonomy-based ethical theory, preferring instead to explain that very idea as an expression of repressed desire. Of course, critical theory is not merely the sum of its intellectual predecessors, nor do Marx and Freud stand as that sum. Still, it is not in the least beside the point to be alert to the possibility that a properly 'critical' outlook rules out a positive relation to 'ethics' in traditional philosophical senses of the term.

CONCEPTUAL BACKGROUND

From their earliest writings Horkheimer, Marcuse, and Adorno regarded modern Western forms of society as increasingly self-enclosed and inimical to individual freedom. The most proximate cause for and expression of this state of affairs is capitalism, which critical theory treats as much broader than a strictly economic phenomenon. The main influences on the School in this regard are the sociologist Max Weber's analysis of rationalization and the philosopher Georg Lukács' account of reification.

Marx held that capitalist modes of production inherently subvert present demands for freedom and that this undermining is caused in important part by pathological protocols of belief- and desire-formation instilled by social-psychological structures secreted by capitalism. Even where some critical distance can be established from capitalism by virtue of the impact of unlivable work conditions capitalism adapts to such critique by exuding fake revolutionary ideals or entertainments. The early Frankfurt School held that Marx was too sanguine in his view that the worsening of material work conditions by itself will drive revolutionary intent. Weber and Lukács offer correctives. Although the critical theorists reject the neo-Kantian Weber's half-hearted 'ethics of accommodation' as a merely pessimistic *faute de mieux*, they accept his account of the development of rationalization in modern society as properly realistic and theoretically salient. Weber saw secularization in the modern world give rise to a conception of reason that fails to substitute for outmoded theological constraints new ones intrinsic to rationality. Reason is reduced in its basic conception to an *apparatus* that does not generate basic ends intrinsically but rather operates on ends given to it. Weber held this tendency to be fully institutionalized across modern, 'bureaucratic' European society but, for all its detrimental aspects, he regards the institutionalization as an improvement over prior forms of social authority. This resignation was too accommodating for Horkheimer, Marcuse, and Adorno, and for a counterweight they turn to a form of Marxism that pressed harder on the issues of ideology. Lukács' collection *History and Class Consciousness* (1923) provided a spur.[1] Lukács argued that

---

[1] As influential as this text was for the development of the social theory of early critical theory, it must take second place to Lukács' own *Theory of the Novel* (1916 / 20), which had the status of a cult object for the Frankfurt philosophers (and for others of their generation).

'reification', a term he lifts from Marx's analysis of the fetishism of capital and reformulates, was a primary device in the maintenance and extension of capitalism, one that affects basic cognitive and conative capacities of agents, rendering them dis-unified or, in the standard terms of Marxist thought, 'alienated'. Lukács marshals the more Hegelian resources of what he reconstructs to be Marx's early thought, seeing in it resources for explaining the deep psychological effects of capitalism that have made it much more difficult to extirpate than Marx had believed. Objects of reification are ideas or their products; reification is essentially an 'interpretative function' that takes those objects as 'values' and produces an understanding of the objects as *not* based in ideas, i.e. as 'natural' in the sense of wholly given antecedent to thought. Because of this, social structures (e.g. the economy) are treated as invariant and self-sealing, not subject to human intervention at their basic levels. Reification is a socially-inculcated category error that is difficult to correct on account of the inferential halo-effect provided by the 'totality' of social belief. Because so many other implicit beliefs prop up reification, coming to reject it requires massive total cognitive readjustment.

Horkheimer and Adorno's views on what they call 'instrumental reason' are a composite of this Weber–Lukács line and Freud. Freud's account of the unconscious allows the Frankfurt philosophers to view instrumental reasoning as infiltrating the primary cognitive and conative structures so deeply that the needed correction is a matter of strict and incessant critical scrutiny of every reason that self-presents as non-instrumental. In the post-Idealist context, reason is no longer conceived of as being pre-adapted to discern ethical world-order. Reason is rather a subjective faculty only problematically associated with the ideal of objectivity. The sense in which values can be 'objective' in this modern historical context is borrowed from canons of objectivity native to a scientific, observational regard for nature (*CT* 188–243/*KT* 521–76; *ER* 3–57).[2] Reason is treated reductively as the capacity for detached investigation. Connected with this, recto to verso, are views of freedom qua freedom *from* nature. Because the modern conception evacuates value out of nature, being good is no longer a matter of being caused in the right way; rather, it involves freedom from causation but modeled in ways that betray a continuing dependence on instrumental reasoning, i.e. freedom as a radically non-natural form of *causation*.

In light of this state of affairs, the Frankfurt thinkers hold that there are two possibilities. One can be a stalwart 'positivist' and argue that instrumental

[2] Abbreviations are explained at the end of the chapter.

reason either is the only kind of reason or that it is the basic kind of reason. On this view, the only goods that reason can secure are those typically associated with the operations of 'theoretical reason' traditionally understood: the validity and soundness of arguments concerning the good, whether particular conceptions of the good are internally coherent or cogent, etc. It cannot establish the truth of what is taken to be the specification of the good as it figures in such arguments or conceptions. In part, critical theory finds the positivist attitude toward reason salutary, for it clears away the dead wood of esoteric appeals to supernatural reason without turning back to ancient conceptions of naturalism. But the critical theorists deny both that reason can be identified with instrumental rationality and that all appeal to value is irrational.

Reason can also be 'critical'. While critical reason cannot establish intrinsic goods as ends, it can operate reflexively to criticize from within any purported conception of the good. The critical theorist treats societies as wholes, i.e. entities whose internal structure is holistically concentrated around a conception of final ends or goods. This conception is, except in the rare instances in which the social fabric is about to undergo massive alteration, largely implicit. And, as implicit, the conception guides the social formation relative to a given society obliquely. The critical theorist must trace those indirect connections and in doing so reconstitutes theoretically at a much more explicit level the systematic concentration on that conception of the good. The barriers of entry to such an endeavor are higher than social scientists often think; such critique must be immanent, undertaken with no initial conceptual resources not also available to those holding the views under analysis (*CT* 224ff / *KT* 556ff; *N* 147f / *KG* 115f). When critique has reconstructed the whole nature of the society in question, that result must be such that it is available to the social group for reflection on its own true commitments. This does not in itself require the society to regard itself as in need of change; critical theory cannot postulate some rational measure ulterior to the deliverances of 'critique' against which failure to change might be measured. Critical reason is, as Adorno emphasizes, 'negative' in its dialectical import: it can only set before society the degree to which society lives up to the implicit standards it sets for itself.

DIALECTIC OF ENLIGHTENMENT

Perhaps the key component of the Frankfurt School analysis of the critical potential of moral philosophy up to the late 1960s is its deep-seated suspicion

of *idealization*, or what Horkheimer and others following him call 'transfiguration'. Oppressive social formations maintain themselves in part by holding out hopes for over-idealized consolations for present inequities. The
critical theorists view the history of European thought as much more deeply
implicated in the cognitive structures that lead up to transfiguration than
could be made evident by merely tracing them back to origins in, say,
Christianity. In *Dialectic of Enlightenment* (DE; 1944/1947), Horkheimer and
Adorno attempt to show that, contrary to the self-conceptions of enlightenment in modern Europe which take it to be an antidote to myth, superstition, and irrationality, enlightenment is dependent for its content on myth
(and myth for its content on enlightenment). Horkheimer and Adorno argue
that 'myth' and 'enlightenment', as those concepts figure in modern thought
as antipodes, are commonly rooted in much more primitive human responsiveness to the world. It is Horkheimer and Adorno's thesis that, in this case,
myth and enlightenment are still conceptually intertwined to such an extent
that thinking of them as completely separate phenomena is a grave error (see
DE 25ff/*AGS* 3: 49ff). Human beings are weak in many ways, confronted by a
world that is hostile, unpredictable, and fearsome. This is the basic human
condition, not merely fear of this or that, but rather fear as a general form of
receptivity to the world. Reflection permits two main responses to fear. The
first of these is to allay fear by immersing oneself and becoming more like
what is feared. Drawing on early work of Walter Benjamin, Horkheimer and
Adorno call this 'mimesis' (the theme of mimesis remains a crucial component in all of Adorno's work) (*DE* 148–51/*AGS* 3: 205–8; *AT* 53–4/*AGS* 7: 86–7).[3]
The second response is more recognizably reflective: to attempt to control
what is fearsome by 'subsuming', i.e. categorizing, it. The sought control is
established by reducing the thing to its 'identity' as determined by its role in a
scheme of human making, thereby rendering it an *object* to which predicates
can attach, making the thing less experientially volatile. Conceptions of
enlightenment that exclude a mythic component are falsely triumphal; they
are frantic, delusional, and totalitarian expressions of a particular dialectical
imbalance of myth–enlightenment dyad.

One particularly dangerous aspect of uncritical enlightenment is that, in its
tendency to extend its deracinated and over-intellectualized conception of
rationality to the world as a whole without exception, it threatens to destroy
the understanding of anything as singular. Adorno, especially in later works,
goes so far as to claim that general thought, even predication itself, is

---

[3] See Früchtl 1986 for an excellent treatment.

ideological 'identity thinking'. With a bit of charity, his claim may be interpreted as one involving a tendency on the part of general (i.e. conceptual)
thought towards overgeneralization and, thus, toward uniformity. (Adorno's
posthumously published *Aesthetic Theory* (1998) is devoted to the project of
preserving as much singularity across the domain of art as is consistent with
conditions of dialectical discursivity.) This has particularly detrimental effects
on modern conceptions of individuality. The standard modern concept of an
individual, as it would figure in most ethical theories, is both atomic and
abstract. According to this conception, an individual is nothing but an
instance of a type and individuality the particular way the type is instantiated.
The type in question is determined holistically by the system in which it
figures: the type is 'pre-social and atomic' and the system in this case is liberal
democratic / capitalist. This submerges singularity in typicality and skews the
idea of how individuals might be related in groups. Modern concepts of
individuality are, in this way, at the same time generic and asocial. The
reverse of this situation in the Frankfurt estimation, what Horkheimer calls
'irrationalism' (*BPSS* 151–61 / *KT* 200–12) or what he and Adorno mean by the
term 'fascism', is an attempt to overcome individuality by immersing oneself
in a purportedly pre-conceptual collective.[4] This strand, which critical theory
ascribes especially to developments in twentieth-century phenomenology, is
often put forward as an antidote to overbearing enlightenment rationality,
but it is likewise un-dialectic – this time on the mythic side.

'FALSE LIFE' AND ETHICS AFTER AUSCHWITZ

Perhaps in response to Habermas' claim that the thought of the early
Frankfurt School fails to establish a positive ethical theory, there has been a
good deal of attention paid to the question of whether things are quite so
bleak for the first generation of the School. The principal figure here is, again,
Adorno.

The question that drives Adorno, given his tendency to view moral issues as
arising within the greater ambit of social and political concern, is whether one
can live an ethically good life in a social and political world that is severely
compromised in terms of the freedom. He encapsulates his view of the
prospects in his dictum that 'es gibt kein richtiges Leben im falschen' (*MM*
38–9 / *AGS* 4: 42–3), and that is as good a place as any to begin discussing what

---

[4] See Hammer 2005: 49–71 for a particularly good examination of Adorno's understanding of fascism.

one might take to be Adorno's more 'positive' ethical views. The statement, like many of Adorno's dicta, is not meant to be univocal in meaning; rather, it is written in order to prompt in its reader an operation of 'wit' that holds together two mutually reinforcing orders of meaning where different emphasis given to one dimension compared to the other will give a different overall experience on the part of the reader *as* the reader. The main weight of the dictum depends on construal of the word 'falsch'. The German adjective can mean 'false' in the abstract sense of 'not being the case' or 'not true'. But the English word 'false' hits a bit harder than the more ordinary German use of the word to mean simply 'wrong'. This more commonplace usage forms the better contrast with 'richtig', i.e. 'right', 'correct', or 'proper' (one would expect 'wahr' otherwise). Notwithstanding this more ordinary meaning, Adorno wishes to keep the more formal meaning of 'falsch' on hand, under the surface as it were. Seeing why he would want to do this requires a bit of syntactical gerrymandering. At first blush it seems clear that the adjective is attributive, modifying 'Leben'. But because adjectives are declined in German it is possible to place them at lexical distance from the nouns they modify, as Adorno has done here. In so doing, Adorno implies another construction. Because it is separated from 'Leben' the adjective seems to be in predicate position. As written though, it cannot be, for then the elided preposition and determinate article are stranded. But the hint of predicative structure suggests another thought. If 'falsch' *were* capitalized in the phrase 'im Falschen', the dictum might be taken to assert a domain of 'the False' in which living rightly is impossible. This conveys a very strong sense of the pervasiveness of falsity in life – not just a false or wrong way of living or acting but an ontological realm of 'false-life', in which all that there is, is false as a matter of structure. And, in turn, this presses on the reader Adorno's view that, in a very real sense, false-life is not life at all; it is the opposite to, or absence of, life.[5]

This view – that there are practically fundamental and theoretically pre-moral structures in the world that are massively deformed in ways that undermine whatever good might be done – follows from the early Frankfurt School inheritance and development of the ideas of rationalization and reification as they are combined in and supplemented by the account of instrumental reasoning. Adorno need not hold the self-stultifying view that the structural 'pathologies' of instrumental reasoning are so deeply seated in

---

[5] Cf. a *Stichwort* that came to Adorno in a dream: 'The townsfolk are faithful only if the dogs are fierce' (*Nur wenn die Hunde scharf sind, sind die Einwohner treu*), T 84 (entry for 27 November 1967).

human ethical responsiveness as to irremediably corrupt it. But he does regard with great skepticism views presented under the mantle of 'ethics'; they are quite likely to be substitutes for freedom and not paths to it. Put in the argot of early critical theory, such theories are 'traditional', overgeneralizing, and unsuited to capturing what is ethically salient under the pluralistic conditions of the modern world. They often make a fool's bargain with instrumental conceptions of reason borrowed from science (e.g. consequentialism), notions of lawfulness lifted just as instrumentally from the same sources (e.g. deontology), or devolve into instrumental reason's dialectical mate, myth (e.g. virtue ethics).

There have been two main tactics deployed to tease out of Adorno a more directive approach. The first of these cleaves to an analog of Adorno's claim that 'after Auschwitz it is barbaric to write a poem' ('nach Auschwitz ein Gedicht zu schreiben, ist barbarisch . . .' (*AA* 146–62/*AGS* 10.1: 11–30; see also *AA* 19–33/*AGS* 10.2: 674–90). Transferring this idea to ethics places a burden on ethical theories not to be merely 'lyrical' enterprises that direct attention away from the degree to which freedom is compromised in social reality. Such a theory is no better than religion, merely *il materasso contro la pallottola*. The Frankfurt School treats fascism as a logical extension of the dialectically joined dyad of myth–enlightenment, and thus as bound up with instrumental thought in its own way. The Frankfurt School heaped scorn on accounts of Nazism that interpreted its foundations as essentially discontinuous with modern rationality. This approach to the roots of the Shoah allows the Frankfurt theorists to elevate Auschwitz to a negative ideal against which to measure purported ethical standpoints without losing in the bargain fealty to the proscription in critical theory against transfiguring ideals. Auschwitz expresses a possible form of modern rationality and expresses it to the highest degree possible. On that basis, one may invoke Auschwitz as exemplary of a form of rationality that must never happen again. But Auschwitz was (and still is, in Adorno's estimation) *actual* and precisely *not* a mere ideal rule, constructed by extrapolation from what might happen.

So, even though Adorno does say that avoiding the barbarism of fascism, especially in its German strain, takes the form of a 'new categorical imperative' (*ND* 365/*AGS* 6: 358), it is exceedingly important not to read that injunction flatly. It is true that, when it comes to issues of moral philosophy, Adorno focuses attention squarely on Kant, often seemingly at the expense of figures like Hegel, Nietzsche, and Freud, who would seem to have more in common with Adorno's own views on ethical questions. And this focus is not remotely exclusively negative, i.e. the focus is not expressive of an

overarching evil that lurks inside Kantian virtue. In a way, Adorno admires
what he takes to be Kant's unflinching moral rigorism because it expresses
with greatest possible clarity the contradiction at the heart of moral experience. Moral demands are inherently universal in their sought application;
they are demanding because their source and structure is general. But what it
is to be a modern moral subject is not captured by that generality, in fact the
generality suppresses the singularity of moral impetus in one (*ND* 260–1; *AGS*
6: 252–3). And the idea that there is a single overarching moral precept or test
for precepts is the most suppressing of all. The experience of moral subjectivity for Adorno is shot through with this tension or 'contradiction'. So, for
all of its power as a litmus test for the wages of being moral under conditions
of modernity, in the final analysis Kant is part of the problem and not its
solution. Adorno is decidedly *not* recommending a new form of deontology
orbiting around a refurbished statement of the highest duty or its effect on
action. One has to appreciate the irony; what Adorno is proposing here is a
co-optation of the sort of authority that ethical imperatives are meant to
convey and directing it back to whatever contributes to Auschwitz, Kant
included.[6] This involves in essence juxtaposition of two conceptions of
utopia. The first is negative and to be avoided: the false idea of a heaven on
earth, of a world transmuted by means of idealism. This is more than just a
fake utopia; it is a dystopia that suborns Auschwitz. The second idea of
utopia, to be embraced by strictly distinguishing it from the first, is one in
which the social and ethical imagination is rooted in criticism of the cardinal
atrocities of history and insists upon the understanding required never to
repeat their like. What 'their like' amounts to is of course no easy matter to
discern, and one will get nowhere with appeals to rules in this activity.
Categorical or not, Auschwitz is not an imperative in the standard ethical
sense. It is rather a 'call' or a 'summons' to treat an event as *exemplary*, a focal
point for continued meditation on what might go 'wrong' next.

Yet another line in the reception of Adorno's thought is to infer from his
analysis of the origins and development of reason in the interaction of
mimesis and predictive control an account of immediate, non-instrumental
thought that has positive moral content. The suggestion here is that there is a
form of non-dominated, non-conceptual thought that might provide the basis
for a better ethical regard. One variant of this line ascribes to Adorno the

[6] Cf. the equivalence asserted by Horkheimer and Adorno between certain background assumptions concerning the highest operation of reason in Kant's ethics and
Sade (*DE* 71–6/*AGS* 3: 108–16).

position that some special experiences – usually aesthetic – can afford this freedom directly, if fleetingly. Another has it that Adorno endorses something like a 'regulative' function for the *idea* of such a state or activity, and idea of a state one can only approximate.[7] Both versions characteristically feature the idea of the ineffable, of a radically immersive experience in which epistemic and perhaps even ontological divisions between subjectivity and objectivity are no longer in play. There are very good philosophical reasons for holding the idea of the ineffable at arm's length, and many of these militate against ascribing to Adorno any role for the ineffable. It is easy to see that any direct version of the role of the ineffable in Adorno's thought is unsupportable (see *ND* 18/*AGS* 6: 21). Adorno would hold such thought to be impossible, since he conceives of the basic constituent of thought to be a tension between (1) a drive to never-completed immediacy (mimesis) and (2) a drive to never-completed distanced contemplation. Both drives must be present in any experience. Moreover, Adorno, for one, held that attraction to the idea that the ineffable could play a role in free thought is a decisive step toward the combination of positivism and magical thought that contribute to fascism. The second, more indirect notion – that the idea of the ineffable must operate as a regulative ideal – may seem more plausible as an interpretation of Adorno, but it is not. True, Adorno's philosophy of art does feature prominently the idea that art works are freedom inducing if they successfully operate at the ever-shrinking margin of what is not stereotypical and already commodified. Art that attacks the accepted confines of experience *eo ipso* strains categories and can give a glimpse of what is (not yet) categorized. The main thought here – and it is important for Adorno's account of freedom – is that vigilance must be exercised at every turn when one is confronted with accounts of what it is possible to experience. But this is, again, not a point about a kind of experience that is *unalterably* subconscious or sub-doxastic. It is rather an idea of resistance within experience to any claim as to its proper borders. It is, moreover, not a claim even

---

[7] Cf. Bernstein 2001: 437–50. Bernstein's view is more 'dialectical', arguing that the fragile conditions of unity governing modern art works spell a notion of ethical life as a provisional equilibrium between the implicit demands for universality in moral regard and the damage those demands inflict on one's singular subjectivity as a basis for moral impulse. It is not clear to me that the specious idea of ineffability *need* play a role in this view, if it does for Bernstein. In essence, it seems that Bernstein accepts that under conditions of modernity, ethical life is conflicted moral life and that one must just live with that fact – a kind of tragic Kantianism. I suggest below an alternative, more 'negative' approach.

that experience has its limits; it is rather the claim that such limits cannot be preordained. No one needs the cant of 'the ineffable' to make these points on Adorno's behalf.

It is fair to say then that Adorno never published a 'positive' moral theory. *Minima Moralia* (1978) and *Negative Dialectics* (1973) offer both critiques of standard moral philosophy and diagnoses of the ethical corruptions of modern life, but nothing amounting to a comprehensive ethics. And the doctrines of posthumously published *Aesthetic Theory* (1998) are not as fertile a source for ethics as proponents of ineffability might regard it nor is it Adorno's substitute for ethics, as Habermas sometimes charges. One must, I think, for now be satisfied with some clues Adorno leaves in his lectures on 'problems of moral philosophy'. The lectures are bookmarked by *Minima Moralia*'s dictum concerning false life or living in 'the False' (*ANS* IV.10: 9, 262). At the conclusion of the lectures Adorno offers a tentative assessment of how to live rightly in the teeth of the wrong (ibid., 261–2; see also ibid., IV.13: 366). The suggestion is slightly less Weberian in its teeth-grinding resolution; the ontological structure of morality is contradiction and it is wrong to see that as a deficiency. For Adorno contradiction (not logical contradiction, but dialectical contradiction) can be a proper, irresolvable structure of the world. The best one can do is to keep the structure active in and integral to thought by constant criticism of anything that presents itself as a resolution of the contradiction. What does this mean for questions of what one should do in concrete contexts? As did Hegel and Marx, Adorno is not very prescriptive; it is not the business of philosophers to legislate results or forecast the future. Cases of blatant inhumanity are not inherently difficult to spot; what is hard is not to argue away their significance once one has spotted them. For that, there is criticism.

MARCUSE, HABERMAS, AND THE REJECTION OF 'NEGATIVITY'

Critical theory up to the end of the 1960s has a bifurcated relationship with utopian political and moral thought. On the one hand, the practice of critical theory is explicitly directed against many forms of utopian thought – those that stem from religious or capitalist forms of life that promise dispensation in forms that leave in place material and social-psychological inequality and lack of freedom. Not only are such utopias 'false' in the sense that the goods that they proffer are illusory, they are false forms of reason. On the other hand, the emphasis placed in critical theory on the ability to freely exercise social and political imagination to conceive of at least general outlines of how life might be different, if only in juxtaposition with the status quo, contains a clearly utopian component. Marcuse's early essays, in particular, highlight this aspect of critical theory.

Beginning in the late 1960s two thinkers associated with the Frankfurt School come to deny the merely negative potential for critical thought. The first of these is Marcuse. Although his *Eros and Civilization* (1955) is a portent in some ways of his later thought, he breaks with the proscription against positive critical thought, first, with the publication of *One-Dimensional Man* (1964) and then, definitively, with *An Essay on Liberation* (1969). Marcuse remained in California after Horkheimer and Adorno had reinstalled themselves in Frankfurt (in fact, Marcuse had not been close to them for a number of years) and was quite positively impressed by the student movement. It was for him a true counterculture, which is to say a form of social life that was both non-repressed and that possessed a new institutional structure. It could form the basis, in his estimation, for a new set of political imperatives (*L* 22–48; see also *FL* 62–82). Marcuse never came to an adequate specification of what these might be (leaving that up to the students); neither did the students, as it turned out.

A bit less tranquilly optimistic is the work of Habermas. Critical theory has been called a Kantian form of Marxism, and that does not seem wrong so long as one specifies in what way 'Kantian' and in what form 'Marxism'. It is very important to be circumspect when one uses this catch-phrase so as to not over-assimilate the Frankfurt School to Kant. Notwithstanding this, forging substantial links to transcendental philosophy is Habermas' main impetus from the 1980s onwards. In particular, he embraces the view that transcendental argumentation is both forced upon the critical theorist and efficacious. Habermas' numerous early works from the 1960s to the early 1970s – from *Structural Transformation of the Public Sphere* (1962) to *Legitimization Problems in Late Capitalism* (1973) – show a marked interest in two intersecting issues: (1) the co-optation of the rationality of discourse by that of instrumentality and (2) the historical and social character of 'the public sphere'. This was work, like Marcuse's, that was responsive to unrest on the Left, although Habermas does not credit, as did Marcuse, the idea that a radical breakdown in communication between the status quo and radical thought could be productive. Even in this early work Habermas is set on understanding what normative potential there might still be for discussion between adverse ethical and political parties. Also unlike Marcuse, and Adorno by implication, Habermas did not excoriate technological forms of understanding, so long as they might be reasonably cordoned off from the domain of discourse. This embrace of the technological control of nature, in particular, marks Habermas as more in line with classical Marxism than the critical theorists of the prior generation. *Knowledge and Human Interests* (1968) is in many ways the systematization of these early views, arguing for a crosscutting classification of 'interests' to analyze the various forms of rationality and to preserve a critical function for reason. It is at this point that Habermas begins writing that rational discourse must be both reconstructed and normative along 'quasi-transcendental' lines. *The Theory of Communicative Action* (1981) is a massive reconsideration of Habermas' prior thought in terms of speech act theory and the action theory of Talcott Parsons. Habermas never endorses the metaphysics that underpins Kant's transcendental idealism, but the 'communicative action theory' he develops in the 1980s and 1990s that provides a platform from which to mount his so-called 'discourse ethics' a bit later has become for many almost synonymous with recent Frankfurt School philosophy.

The primary aim of Habermas' theory of communicative action is to reconstruct necessary conditions on rationality in the 'non-strategic' (viz. non-instrumental) realm in terms of the practical knowledge required on the part of an individual in order to count as a full agent in the intersubjective process of rational exchange. This is provided by an assumption of 'mutual understanding' (*Verständigung*), that is, that rationality is a coordination exercise that is from the outset geared to reaching accord (*TCA* 1: 94–102/ *TkH* 1: 141–51; see also *FN* 119/*FG* 152). Habermas does pay lip service to immanent critique in this enterprise – in the form of trying to understand another's 'rationality claim' from the inside out, as it were. But the over-arching impetus of 'action' in this sense is to agree, and this will constrain interpretations.

Although Habermas does not emphasize the matter as he does in later works, the theory of communicative action departs from core earlier Frankfurt School views in its fledgling attempt to argue for a universal basis for rationality. This departure is much more patent in Habermas' expressly ethical work that builds on the theory of communicative action, what he terms 'discourse ethics'. Habermas presents ethics of this sort as a specification of a set of more general claims having to do with practical reason. Habermas starts out with the sensible view that different aims for argumentation will eventuate in different formal structures of argumentation. Ethical argumentation involves unconditional obligation in his view (Habermas seems to take this to be an analytic truth). As such, ethical discourse as rational exchange has to base itself in an invariant ground, and it is just here that Habermas tacks toward Kantianism. Unlike Kant, Habermas' account of practical reason – and by implication – ethical discourse is non-metaphysical and is dialogical. What Habermas calls the 'discourse principle' (*MCCA* 66, 121–2 / *MBkH* 75–6, 132–3) presents the justification of moral claims as based in mutual rational acceptability by all under optimal conditions of rationality. The reliance on optimality is already transcendental and idealizing, but the further principle, which must constrain ethical discourse, is even more in this vein: the so-called 'universalization principle' (*MCCA* 63–5, 86f / *MBkH* 73–6, 96f) which states that optimal conditions are 'without coercion' and embeds in the Kantian idea of individual autonomous rational agents, whose rational interests must be 'satisfied' across the board in order for discourse to be truly ethical. Again, the reference to ideal structures such as non-coercion, as well as the invocation of stable, autonomous entities as the requisite agents of ethical concern, would be far too optimistic and 'traditional' by Horkheimer and Adorno's lights.[8] And the contrast with even Marcuse's later and more affirmative position on ethics must not be missed. Habermas' theory of communicative action and his discourse theory allow for a plurality of types of discourse each with their own form of rationality. But each is driven by idealizations internal to them, and there is very little overlap one to the other. Aesthetic matters, for instance, unlike in Marcuse (*TCA* 1: 10 / *TkH* 1: 28; cf. *AD* 54–69), do not interfere with ethical standing. Of course Habermas realizes this and would not count it as a deficiency in his view; after all what he calls the 'colonization' of one realm of discourse by another is just what causes instrumental reasoning. But one might think that it is one thing to acknowledge the potential for ill in virtue of such encroachment and quite another to erect an ideal system of policing the borders. However one comes down on the question, Habermas' views take him away from his critical theory roots, something that he fully intends.

ABBREVIATIONS

AA   *Can One Live after Auschwitz?* (Adorno 2003)
AD   *The Aesthetic Dimension* (Marcuse 1978)
AGS   *Gesammelte Schriften* (Adorno 1970ff)
ANS   *Nachgelassenen Schriften* (Adorno 2001f)
AT   *Aesthetic Theory* (Adorno 1998)

[8] See Geuss 1981: 66–7 and Bernstein 1995: 214f for critiques that are, as it were, delivered from the earlier Frankfurt School perspective.

BPSS   *Between Philosophy and Social Science* (Horkheimer 1995)
CT   *Critical Theory* (Horkheimer 1975)
DE   *Dialectic of Enlightenment* (Adorno 2002)
ER   *Eclipse of Reason* (Horkheimer 1974)
FG   *Faktizität und Geltung* (Habermas 1992)
FL   *Five Lectures* (Marcuse 1970)
FN   *Between Facts and Norms* (Habermas 1998)
KG   *Kultur und Gesellschaft* (Marcuse 1965)
KT   *Kritische Theorie* (Horkheimer 1968)
L   *An Essay on Liberation* (Marcuse 1969)
MBkH   *Moralbewußtsein und kommunikatives Handeln* (Habermas 1983)
MCCA   *Moral Consciousness and Communicative Action* (Habermas 1991)
MM   *Minima Moralia* (Adorno 1978)
N   *Negations* (Marcuse 1968)
ND   *Negative Dialectics* (Adorno 1973)
T   *Traumprotokolle* (Adorno 2005)
TCA   *Theory of Communicative Action* (Habermas 1984)
TkH   *Theorie des kommunikativen Handelns* (Habermas 1981)

BIBLIOGRAPHY

An asterisk denotes secondary literature especially suitable for further reading.

Adorno, Theodor W., 1970ff. *Gesammelte Schriften*, ed. Rolf Tiedemann (Frankfurt am Main: Suhrkamp).
Adorno, Theodor W., 1973. *Negative Dialectics*, trans. E.B. Ashton (London: Routledge). (NB: This translation is notoriously inadequate and must be used with caution.)
Adorno, Theodor W., 1978. *Minima Moralia*, trans. E.F.N. Jephcott (New York and London: Verso).
Adorno, Theodor W., 1998. *Aesthetic Theory*, trans. R. Hullot-Kentor (Minneapolis, MN: University of Minnesota Press).
Adorno, Theodor W., 2001f. *Nachgelassenen Schriften*, ed. Theodor-Adorno-Archiv (Frankfurt am Main: Suhrkamp).
Adorno, Theodor W., 2002. *Dialectic of Enlightenment* (with Max Horkheimer), ed. Gunzelin Schmidt, trans. Edmund Jephcott (Stanford University Press).
Adorno, Theodor W., 2003. *Can One Live after Auschwitz?*, ed. R. Tiedemann, trans. R. Livingstone *et al.* (Stanford University Press).
Adorno, Theodor W., 2005. *Traumprotokolle* (Frankfurt am Main: Suhrkamp).
Bernstein, J.M., 1995. *Recovering Ethical Life: Jürgen Habermas and the Future of Critical Theory* (London: Routledge).
Bernstein, J.M., 2001. *Adorno: Disenchantment and Ethics* (Cambridge University Press).

Früchtl, Josef, 1986. *Mimesis. Konstellation eines Zentralbegriffs bei Adorno* (Würzburg: Königshaus and Neumann).

Geuss, Raymond, 1981. *The Idea of a Critical Theory* (Cambridge University Press).*

Habermas, Jürgen, 1962. *Strukturwandel der Öffentlichkeit. Untersuchungen zu einer Kategorie der bürgerlichen Gesellschaft* (Neuwied and Berlin: Luchterhand), trans. Thomas Burger and Frederick Lawrence as *The Structural Transformation of the Public Sphere: An Inquiry into a Category of Bourgeois Society* (Cambridge, MA: MIT Press, 1989).

Habermas, Jürgen, 1968. *Erkenntnis und Interesse* (Frankfurt am Main: Suhrkamp), trans. Jeremy J. Shapiro as *Knowledge and Human Interests* (Boston, MA: Beacon Press, 1971).

Habermas, Jürgen, 1973. *Legitimationsprobleme im Spätkapitalismus* (Frankfurt am Main: Suhrkamp), trans. Thomas McCarthy as *Legitimation Crisis* (Boston, MA: Beacon Press, 1975).

Habermas, Jürgen, 1981. *Theorie des kommunikativen Handelns*, vol. 1 (Frankfurt am Main: Suhrkamp).

Habermas, Jürgen, 1983. *Moralbewußtsein und kommunikatives Handeln* (Frankfurt am Main: Suhrkamp).

Habermas, Jürgen, 1984. *Theory of Communicative Action*, vol. 1, trans. T. McCarthy (Boston, MA: Beacon Press). (Translation of Habermas 1981.)

Habermas, Jürgen, 1991. *Moral Consciousness and Communicative Action*, trans. C. Lenhardt and S.W. Nicholsen (Cambridge, MA: MIT Press). (Translation of Habermas 1983.)

Habermas, Jürgen, 1992. *Faktizität und Geltung* (Frankfurt am Main: Suhrkamp).

Habermas, Jürgen, 1998. *Between Facts and Norms*, trans. W. Rehg (Cambridge, MA: MIT Press). (Translation of Habermas 1992.)

Hammer, Espen, 2005. *Adorno and the Political* (London: Routledge).

Horkheimer, Max, 1968. *Kritische Theorie* (Frankfurt am Main: Fischer).

Horkheimer, Max, 1974. *Eclipse of Reason* (New York: Continuum).

Horkheimer, Max, 1975. *Critical Theory*, trans. M. O'Connell (New York: Continuum). (Partial translation of Horkheimer 1968.)

Horkheimer, Max, 1995. *Between Philosophy and Social Science*, trans. G.F. Hunter, M. Kramer, and J. Torpey (Cambridge, MA: MIT Press). (Partial translation of Horkheimer 1968.)

Lukács, Georg, 1916/20. *The Theory of the Novel*, trans. A. Bostock (London: Merlin, 1971).

Lukács, Georg, 1923. *History and Class Consciousness: Studies in Marxist Dialectics*, trans. Rodney Livingstone (Cambridge, MA: MIT Press, 1971).

Marcuse, Herbert, 1955. *Eros and Civilization: A Philosophical Inquiry into Freud* (Boston, MA: Beacon Press).

Marcuse, Herbert, 1964. *One-Dimensional Man: Studies in the Ideology of Advanced Industrial Society* (Boston, MA: Beacon Press).

Marcuse, Herbert, 1965. *Kultur und Gesellschaft* (Frankfurt am Main: Suhrkamp).

Marcuse, Herbert, 1968. *Negations*, trans. J. Shapiro (Boston, MA: Beacon Press). (Partial translation of Marcuse 1965 and other works.)

Marcuse, Herbert, 1969. *An Essay on Liberation* (Boston, MA: Beacon Press).

Marcuse, Herbert, 1970. *Five Lectures* (Boston, MA: Beacon Press).

Marcuse, Herbert, 1978. *The Aesthetic Dimension* (Boston, MA: Beacon Press).

Theunissen, Michael, 1983. 'Negativität bei Adorno', in L. von Friedeburg and J. Habermas (eds.), *Adorno-Konferenz 1983* (Frankfurt am Main: Suhrkamp), pp. 41–65.

47

Heidegger

SACHA GOLOB

There are three obstacles to any discussion of the relationship between Heidegger's philosophy and ethics. First, Heidegger's views and preoccupations alter considerably over the course of his work. There is no consensus over the exact degree of change or continuity, but it is clear that a number of these shifts, for example over the status of human agency, have considerable ethical implications. Second, Heidegger rarely engages directly with the familiar ethical or moral debates of the philosophical canon. For example, both *Sein und Zeit* (SZ)[1] and the works that would have completed its missing third Division, works such as his monograph on Kant (Ga3), and the 1927 lecture course *The Basic Problems of Phenomenology* (Ga24), place enormous emphasis on the flaws present in earlier metaphysics or philosophies of language or of the self. But there is no discussion of what one might think of as staple ethical questions: for example, the choice between rationalist or empiricist meta-ethics, or between consequentialist or deontological theories. The fundamental reason for this is Heidegger's belief that his own concerns are explanatorily prior to such debates (Ga26: 236–7). By extension, he regards the key works of ethical and moral philosophy as either of secondary importance, or as not really about ethics or morals at all: for example, Ga24, when discussing Kant, states bluntly that '"Metaphysics of Morals" means the ontology of human existence' (Ga24: 195). Essentially his view is that, before one can address ethics, construed as the question of how we ought to live, one needs to get clear on ontology, on the question of what we are. However, as I will show, the relationship between Heideggerian ontology and ethics is more complex than that simple gloss suggests. Third, the very phrase 'Heidegger's ethics' raises a twofold problem in a way that does not similarly occur with any other figure in this volume. The reason for this is his links, personal and institutional, to both National Socialism and to

---

[1] Abbreviations are explained at the end of the chapter.

anti-Semitism. The recent publication of the *Schwarze Hefte* exemplifies this issue: these notebooks interweave rambling metaphysical ruminations with a clearly anti-Semitic rhetoric no less repulsive for the fact that it avoids the biological racism of the Nazis (see, for example, Ga95: 97; Ga96: 243 or Ga96: 261–2). In this short chapter, I will take what will doubtless be a controversial approach to this third issue. It seems to me unsurprising, although no less disgusting for that, that Heidegger himself was anti-Semitic, or that he shared many of the anti-modernist prejudices often found with such anti-Semitism among his demographic group. The interesting question is rather: what are the connections between his philosophy and such views? To what degree do aspects of his work support them or perhaps, most extremely, even follow from them? Yet to answer this question, one needs to begin by understanding what exactly his philosophical commitments were, specifically his 'ethical' commitments. The purpose of this chapter is to address that question.[2]

As the citations for the *Schwarze Hefte* indicate, Heidegger left behind an enormous quantity of work. The *Gesamtausgabe* currently runs to 102 volumes: all of these are complex texts, and many are extremely lengthy. For that reason, what I provide here is, at best, a snapshot of some of the key issues, arguments, and assumptions underlying this dimension of Heidegger's thought.

AUTHENTICITY AND EXISTENTIALISM

Sein und Zeit, often regarded as Heidegger's masterpiece, is a complex fusion of Kantian, existentialist, theological and Aristotelian themes. In the current context, the place to start is with the second half of the text, where Heidegger presents two distinct pictures of 'Dasein', a term we can take, at least provisionally, as referring to human beings as he conceives them.[3]

On the one hand, Dasein is typically 'inauthentic' (*uneigentlich*) and dominated by '*das Man*': I translate this as 'the one', to be read as in phrases such as 'one does not do that'. The basic idea is that Dasein is particularly vulnerable to simply taking over as 'quasi-natural "givens"' the assumptions, practices, and ideals of the society in which it is socialised (SZ: 115).[4] Heidegger sees this tendency as an inevitable side effect of the necessary process of sustaining a

---

[2] For those interested, I discuss the '*Schwarze Hefte*' and Heidegger's politics specifically in Golob forthcoming.

[3] There are passages in which Heidegger introduces a third 'undifferentiated' mode (for example, SZ: 53, 232): unfortunately, space prohibits treatment of this here (see Golob 2014: 214–24 for discussion).

[4] Crowell 2007: 326.

common 'world' a world which provides the context for any action (SZ: 129, 299). However, to succumb to it, to live inauthentically, is to fail in several senses: (i) Epistemically: 'the one' is unconsciously oriented towards evaluating and performing acts in terms of their social salience. This can include appearing socially appropriate, solidifying one's self-identity, or taking a predictably rebellious stance on existing mores (SZ: 174–5). As Heidegger sees it, these all contrast with discourse and action motivated by and oriented around a genuine engagement with the truth of a particular topic (SZ: 168–9). (ii) Normatively: by tacitly deferring to an existing social framework, Dasein fails to take responsibility for itself. Heidegger here replays a classic Enlightenment theme: there is a strong temptation to exist in a tranquil-lised unquestioning state, in which the individual need never take personal responsibility for the principles that underlie her life (SZ: 126–7, 175, 322). (iii) Ontologically: insofar as Dasein fails to recognise the historical con-tingency of any particular set of social norms and practices it fails to recognise its own nature as 'thrown' (SZ: 144).

On the other hand, Heidegger presents what is clearly his preferred alterna-tive: authenticity (*Eigentlichkeit*). Authentic agents, like all Dasein, operate against the backdrop of a common social world (SZ: 299). However, they are distinctive in that they live in a manner which recognises the fundamental facts about their own being, in particular their finitude: for example, they recognise both the contingency of social norms and the absence of any transcendental alternative (SZ: 391). As Taylor Carman neatly puts it, all value is understood as 'worldly through and through, embedded in the contingencies of historical tradition and social life'.[5] To frame the point in Kantian terms, the authentic agent is aware that there are no categorical imperatives to be found either in the precepts and practices of particular societies, or in some set of a priori facts about the self. According to Heidegger this realisation is both prompted and dramatised by moods such as anxiety in which Dasein experiences the world as a whole as lacking any normative significance: to continue the Kantian analogy, it is exposed simply as a chain of hypothetical imperatives which can thus be simultaneously suspended (SZ: 187–8, 343). One sees here Heidegger's use of paradigmatically existentialist themes, such as the 'limit experiences' of alienation, anxiety and death, to advance what are essentially claims about normativity.[6]

---

[5] Carman 2003: 307.

[6] As I see it, 'death' in SZ refers similarly not to a biological event, but to a distinctive fact about the normative space within which Dasein operates: see Golob 2014: 223–4. For an overview of the debate see Thomson 2013.

From an ethical perspective, these remarks raise several questions, which I will take in turn.

First, is authenticity an ethical ideal? One striking point is that Heidegger presents authenticity as the single universal 'demand' (*Zumutung*) on Dasein (Ga29/30: 246–8). The sketch above thus needs an immediate modification: the sole obligation binding merely on Dasein *qua* Dasein is to recognise the absence of any other such obligations. This is an ethical demand in at least a broad sense: it identifies a privileged way of life such that we would be obliged to give up certain other projects or practices if they were found to conflict with it (for example, because they were likely to bring Dasein under the influence of 'the one'). I thus agree with Lee Braver when he talks of 'an ethical dimension' to authenticity's 'existential imperative'.[7] However, the second order nature of authenticity – it is effectively an awareness of the limits and topology of the space of reasons – means that it is hard to see how it itself could enjoin or forbid any very specific first-order course of action (one could, for example, presumably be an authentic torturer). Heidegger clearly further believes that agents who are authentic will thereby possess a distinctive capacity for phronetic choice, for immediately discerning, in a quasi-perceptual manner, what needs to be done given the complex contours of each specific situation (SZ: 264, 384; Ga19: 163–4; Ga24: 407–8). But it is not obvious why this should be. An awareness of supposedly meta-normative facts about the contingency of social practices is neither necessary nor sufficient for making good decisions in any plausible sense of good. It is not necessary because there may be situations where an agent's unwillingness to reflect on and question certain beliefs is precisely what allows them to endure intense physical or social pressure, and yet nevertheless take the right course. It is not sufficient, as Heidegger's own political choices make clear. Hubert Dreyfus suggests an interesting reading when he notes, drawing on SZ: 391, that authentic agents, since they do not unreservedly identify with any practice, are more able to let unsuccessful projects go.[8] Undoubtedly, a willingness to cut one's losses is a useful thing. But we still lack any explanation as to why authentic agents would be not just more ready to do this but, crucially, ready to do it at the right time. In sum, it seems plausible that Heidegger himself regarded authenticity as an ethical ideal in at least a broad sense.[9] It is also true that he took this ideal to have implications for an agent's

---

[7] Braver 2014: 24.   [8] Dreyfus 1991: 326.

[9] For a defence of this in relation to the existing secondary literature, see Golob 2014: 241–5.

ability to act appropriately at the first order; but his argument for that is unconvincing.

The second issue is why Heidegger takes authenticity to be such a desirable goal: crudely, what reason do I have to be authentic? One answer would be to cite the supposed benefits of authenticity with respect to first-order decisions. But, as noted, that seems the weakest part of Heidegger's position. Heidegger himself tends to present the issue in perfectionist terms. Authentic Dasein fully realises its own essence: it 'becomes "essentially" Dasein in that authentic existence' (SZ: 323). Elsewhere, he talks in terms of the full realisation or liberation of Dasein. The one unavoidable demand on us is:

> [T]o liberate the humanity in man, i.e. the essence of man, *to let the Dasein in him become essential.*[10]   (Ga29/30: 246–8, cf. 254–5; original emphasis)

As with anxiety, Heidegger again appeals to specific experiential states in support of this view. For example, the 'call of conscience' is analysed not as a warning against any specific misdeeds, but rather as a disturbing awareness of Dasein's true nature, a call from itself to itself, making visible the fact that Dasein is not 'at home' in the world, that none of the projects which it pursues have any necessary connection to it (SZ: 187–8, 273–6). One distinctive feature of Heidegger's work, though, is that perfectionism is not the endpoint of his argument. He often suggests that such perfectionism is important precisely because it makes possible a further activity: namely philosophy. The suggestion is that only insofar as the philosopher herself is authentic will she understand Dasein well enough to 'coin the appropriate existential concepts' (SZ: 316, 178; Ga26: 22). The result is a vision of philosophy as fundamentally bound up with a personal revelation and commitment:

> What philosophy deals with only manifests itself at all within and from out of a transformation of human Dasein.   (Ga29/30: 423)

This move may appear puzzling: why support the perfectionist demand for a full realisation of one's own essence by arguing that it is necessary for philosophy, an activity participated in by only a handful of the population? The answer is that Heidegger views all human action as tacit philosophising: in SZ's terms, all human action assumes an understanding of the being of entities, and philosophy

[10] As Heidegger's work progresses this basic perfectionism is spun in terms of a full realisation of our relationship with being itself: thus the *Beiträge* glosses '*Da-sein*' as the possibility of 'future being human' (*des künftigen Menschseins*), a possibility to be attained insofar we come to understand ourselves as 'guardians' of being (Ga65: 297).

simply makes such understanding explicit (SZ: 324, 363; Ga25: 24–6). Thus 'to be a human means already to philosophise' (Ga27: 3). The norm of authenticity is thus ultimately grounded in the practice of philosophy as fundamental ontology; as we will see, this tendency to reform ethical questions as ontological ones also plays a central role in Heidegger's later writings.

FREEDOM AND THE HISTORY OF BEING

I want now to turn to a second theme, one that forms a transition point between Heidegger's earlier and later writings: freedom. From the vantage point of SZ, Heidegger's stance on freedom may seem a largely pessimistic one. As Béatrice Han-Pile observes:

> Dasein is often pictured in *Being and Time* as anything but free: it 'ensnares itself' (267), is 'lost' (264), 'alienated' (178) and needs to be 'liberated' (264, 303).[11]

I introduced the possibility of liberation, understood in terms of authenticity, in the previous section. During the years following SZ, Heidegger frequently combines a Kantian discourse focussed on autonomy and self-responsibility with this perfectionist framework. The 1930 lecture course *The Essence of Human Freedom* (Ga31), for example, concludes that:

> Practical freedom as autonomy is self-responsibility, which is the essence of the personality of the human being, the authentic essence, the humanity of man. (Ga31: 296)

During the decades after SZ, however, freedom comes to play two further, central roles in Heidegger's thought: its importance is such that he is ultimately willing to identify it as prior even to being and time (Ga31: 134).

First, during the late 1920s and early 1930s, Heidegger increasingly appeals to an interplay between freedom and a capacity to act on the basis of reasons. On the one hand, it is Dasein's freedom which initially explains its ability to take on obligations or recognise laws: freedom is thus a necessary condition on any ethics, or indeed any rationally guided activity. For example, when discussing the normativity of logic, Heidegger raises the following question:

> How must that entity who is subject to such laws, Dasein itself, be con-stituted so as to be able to be thus governed by laws? How 'is' Dasein according to its essence so that such an obligation can arise? (Ga26: 24)

---

[11] Han-Pile 2013: 291.

His immediate answer is that:

> Obligation and being governed by law in themselves presuppose freedom as the basis for their own possibility. Only what exists as free could be at all bound by an obligatory lawfulness. Freedom alone can be the source of obligation. (Ga26: 25)

On the other hand, it is because Dasein is able to recognise and act on the basis of reasons that its behaviour cannot be analysed in purely causal terms, and so is immune to the traditional arguments of hard determinism. As Heidegger sees it, Dasein necessarily experiences the world as structured in terms of norms or grounds, where 'grounding something means making possible the why-question in general' (Ga9: 168/64). Furthermore, any causal story about human behaviour is explanatorily derivative since it is possible only in virtue of the interpretative capacities of Dasein, for example its ability to construct scientific theories (Ga31: 303).

One can raise several concerns about these aspects of Heidegger's work. It is not so much that he articulates some independently graspable notion of freedom which is then used to illuminate our capacity to recognise norms; rather, his actual practice tends simply to be to use 'freedom' as another name for Dasein's understanding of being, albeit one that stresses its normative dimension (Ga34: 60; Ga9: 190/86; Ga54: 213). Furthermore, the attempt to demonstrate the derivative status of causal explanation trades off an obvious ambiguity: the fact that our *theories* about causation depend upon our rational capacities clearly does not rule out the possibility that those capacities are themselves susceptible to an entirely causal explanation. One underlying problem here is that Heidegger regards any real engagement with a naturalistic determinism as illegitimate: indeed, he holds that even to define human freedom in opposition to natural causality is a mistake, 'for when something is defined by distinguishing it from something else, the latter plays a determinative role in the definition' (Ga31: 210).

Second, during the later 1930s and the 1940s, Heidegger starts to place particular emphasis on the limitations on human agency. This marks a key moment in the series of developments in his work known as the 'turn' (*Kehre*), and it has exercised an enormous influence on structuralist and post-structuralist trends in French philosophy, an influence amplified by a concurrent backlash against Sartrean radical freedom. Heidegger analyses history as a series of shifting metaphysical frameworks, of different ways of conceiving being: for example, as that which is immediately and unchangingly present, that which is created by God, or that which appears as a resource for our technological manipulation of nature. Each epoch can be thought of, to borrow a Foucauldian phrase, as a historical a priori; and Heidegger at times suggests that our agency is sufficiently determined by these frameworks that we have little option but to play them out.

> No human calculation or activity, in and of itself, can bring about a turn in the present world's condition: one reason for this is the fact that the whole of man's activity has been stamped by this world condition, and has come under its power. How then should he ever become master of it? (Ga4: 195)

This comes close to a metaphysical determinism: as I will now discuss, this question of the scope of agency, of how we can or should respond to being, is central to his later discussions of technology and of thought.[12]

TECHNOLOGY, THINKING AND THANKING

The recurrent discussions of technology in Heidegger's post-war work are of obvious interest for anyone seeking to construct a Heideggerian ethics. Heidegger argues that modern technology is problematic in a way in which its medieval counterpart, say, was not: the hydroelectric plant on the Rhine differs in essence, rather than merely in scale and sophistication, from earlier attempts to tame and utilise the river, such as wooden bridges (Ga7: 16). Underlying this claim is the belief that 'modern technology' is distinguished by a fundamental change in attitude, one that supposedly began with Descartes: entities are viewed as either resources for, or obstacles to, our manipulation of the natural world. In this sense, modern technology exemplifies a standpoint in which we 'reduce everything down to man' (Ga11: 43). Post-Galilean science both supports and results from this shift insofar as it supposedly identifies that which is with that which is measurable, quantifiable and controllable; Heidegger thus sees such science not primarily as an empirically warranted theory, but rather as a projection of a specific interpretative framework and set of standards which then, unsurprisingly, finds its own evidential confirmation (Ga41: 92–4).

Heidegger's writings on technology have a certain easy resonance with contemporary environmentalism which shares his disgust at a view of 'the earth as a coal mining district, the soil as a mineral deposit' (Ga 7: 15). He also anticipates the concern that a technologised obsession with productivity will

---

[12] I say 'comes close' owing to the presence of the qualifier 'in and of itself' in his remark in the previous quotation.

ultimately subordinate the very beings, human agents, whose wishes it supposedly serves.

> The current talk about human resources ... gives evidence of this. The forester who, in the wood, measures the felled timber and to all appearances walks the same forest path in the same way as did his grandfather is today commanded by profit-making in the lumber industry, whether he knows it or not. He is made subordinate to the demand for cellulose, which for its part is demanded by the need for paper, which is then delivered to newspapers and illustrated magazines. (Ga7: 18–19)

Heidegger sees these developments as linked to two deeper metaphysical trends. In one sense they constitute the 'acme of the subjectivism of man' (Ga5: 111). This is both because of the identification of value with human needs, and because of the links between technology and what Heidegger calls 'representation' (Vorstellen) or the 'world picture' (Weltbild): essentially, a view of being as that which can be grasped, pictured, and manipulated by us (Ga5: 89). The details of his position here are deeply unclear, but he often suggests that this subjectivism articulates biases in philosophy first entrenched by Plato's appeal to ideas (Ga40: 197/144; Ga40: 207/151).[13] However, Heidegger nevertheless denies, for the reasons introduced in the previous section, that these changes are ultimately explicable in terms of human agency. When we make sense of the world in this way, locating it within what he calls an 'enframing' (Ge-stell), it is because we are ourselves subject to the changing dynamics in the history of being, where that is understood not primarily as a story about how humanity has interpreted being, but rather as one about how being has revealed itself to us (Ga7: 19). As he puts it bluntly 'modern technology ... is no merely human doing' (Ga7: 20).

How should we assess this position from an ethical perspective? There are, I think, two related points to be made.

First, there is the issue of agency. Heidegger goes beyond a conventional historicism on which the scope for contemporary action is limited by the assumptions and practices we have taken over from earlier periods, and by the perhaps unforeseen and unintended implications of earlier actions. This is because, as he sees it, the explanatorily primary driver of historical change is not human agency at all – be it past or present – but rather shifts in the way in which being discloses itself to us. Yet there is no clear analysis of what this means, and there is an obvious danger of hypostatising being into

---

[13] For discussion of this aspect of that deeply complex relationship see Golob 2014: 123–35.

a quasi-mystical agent, what Thomas J. Sheehan rightly satirised under the label 'big being'.[14] Furthermore, the minimisation of agency here may seem to entail a stark break between Heidegger and a recognisably ethical project. This is Raymond Geuss's view, for example:

> Heidegger's own analysis does result in what he calls a 'demand' ('*Forderung*'), the demand for a new experience of Being, but this is not a moral or ethical demand ... it does not result from common sense or traditional forms of philosophic thinking, it is not anything that could conceivably be in the power of any individual (or group of individuals) to do or not do, etc.[15]

I think matters are more complex, though. Heidegger does indeed identify various practices as required, and it seems that there are certain actions, such as his own writing, which he conceives at least as a good means of fostering these. The privileged class of actions is effectively ways of responding to being: thinking it, giving thanks for it, and watching over it (Ga9: 303/105; Ga7: 32).[16] The result, prima facie, is an ethics of a type, albeit one with a highly unusual conception of the good life. As Heidegger puts it himself, 'humanism is opposed because it does not set the humanity of the human being high enough' (Ga9: 330/161). This is because the true basis for our dignity is an ability to respond appropriately to being, to serve as the 'shepherd of being'.

> The human being is the shepherd of being. Human beings lose nothing in this 'less'; rather, they gain in that they attain the truth of being. They gain the essential poverty of the shepherd, whose dignity consists in being called by being itself into the preservation of being's truth.   (Ga9: 342/172)

This brings me to the second point: Heidegger's concern over technology is fundamentally different from that of modern environmentalists. For him the problem is not primarily that technological and economic practices are damaging the natural world, where 'damage' is measured in terms of pollution, loss of habitat, loss of wilderness, or species extinction. Rather, the problem is that building a hydroelectric plant on the Rhine crudely forces being into a particular conceptual framework, the *Ge-stell*: as Lee Braver comments, 'pollution isn't the problem with technology; our distorted

---

[14] Sheehan 2001: 8.   [15] Geuss 2005: 59.

[16] Heidegger takes his point to be supported by the fact that the German names for many of these acts are linked etymologically: for example *denken* (to think) and *danken* (to thank).

relation to being is what we should be concerned about'.[17] In the 'Letter on Humanism', Heidegger puts the point in terms of dwelling: responding to being is the way in which we dwell in the world, and this question of dwelling is prior to either ethics or ontology (Ga9: 357/188). However, it is clear that the bias is very much towards the ontological: no content is ever given to the idea of an appropriate response to being other than one which follows the contours of being itself, and thus 'gets it right' ontologically. In this sense, as I suggested with respect to his early work in the first section, Heidegger's philosophy ultimately remains deeply theoretical in its outlook. Since he assumes that 'to exist means to philosophise' (Ga27: 214), it is perhaps unsurprising that he ultimately analyses the question of how we should live in terms of a correct or incorrect understanding of being. Indeed, one can see the ramifications of this assumption throughout his work. Consider, for example, the absurd insistence that the 'Greeks are the utterly apolitical people' (Ga54: 142): the problem here is that he simply reduces the *polis* to the openness within which being appears and thus recasts it, and the debates about value that occur within it, in purely ontological terms (Ga54: 133).

I have argued that Heidegger's work, both 'early' and 'late', supports a displacement of the ethical by the ontological. I want to end with one of the consequences of this displacement. Whilst Heidegger's anti-humanism supposedly grants us a higher 'dignity' as shepherds of being, he offers no real account of what this dignity would amount to: for example, what political or market actions might it enjoin or forbid?[18] At the level of the theory itself there is, at best, a disturbing vacuum here. In Heidegger's own case, this vacuum was all too easily filled with the metaphysical anti-Semitism of the *Schwarze Hefte*.

> The question of the role of world Jewry is not a racial question, but the metaphysical question about the kind of humanity that, without any restraints, can take over the uprooting of all beings from being as its world-historical 'task'.　　　　　　　　　　　　　　　　　　(Ga96: 243)

The relation between a philosophical doctrine or school, and the way in which its ideas and rhetoric function in a given political context, will always be a complex one: consider, for example, the history of the journal *Kant-Studien* during the Nazi period.[19] Yet the ease with which Heidegger's occlusion of

---

[17] Braver 2014: 147.

[18] Doubtless, Heidegger would regard this demand for some kind of policy outcome as just another symptom of the technological viewpoint.

[19] For a detailed treatment, see Leaman and Simon 1994.

ethics as an independent discipline meshes with the idiocy just cited is simultaneously jolting and utterly predictable.

ABBREVIATIONS

References are to the *Gesamtausgabe* edition (Ga, Frankfurt: Klostermann), with the exception of SZ where I use the standard text (Tübingen: Max Niemeyer, 1957). The paginations of these German editions are displayed marginally in almost all translations. In the case of Ga9 and Ga40, I also follow the standard practice of listing the pagination of the original edition after that of the *Gesamtausgabe* text. With respect to translations, I have endeavoured to stay close to the Macquarrie and Robinson version of SZ on the grounds that it is by far the best known. In the case of Heidegger's other works, I have typically consulted, but often modified, existent translations: these are listed below.

Ga3   *Kant und das Problem der Metaphysik* (1998); *Kant and the Problem of Metaphysics*, trans. R. Taft (Bloomington, IN: Indiana University Press, 1997)

Ga4   *Erläuterungen zu Hölderlins Dichtung* (2012)

Ga5   *Holzwege* (1997)

Ga7   *Vorträge und Aufsätze* (2000)

Ga9   *Wegmarken* (1976); *Pathmarks*, ed. and trans. W. McNeill (Cambridge University Press, 1998)

Ga11   *Identität und Differenz* (2006)

Ga19   *Platon: Sophistes* (1992); *Plato's Sophist*, trans. R. Rojcewicz and A. Schuwer (Bloomington, IN: Indiana University Press, 1997)

Ga24   *Die Grundprobleme der Phänomenologie* (1997); *Basic Problems of Phenomenology*, trans. A. Hofstadter (Bloomington, IN: Indiana University Press, 1982)

Ga25   *Phänomenologische Interpretation von Kants Kritik...* (1995)

Ga26   *Metaphysische Anfangsgründe der Logik im Ausgang von Leibniz* (1978); *The Metaphysical Foundations of Logic*, trans. M. Heim (Bloomington, IN: Indiana University Press, 1984)

Ga27   *Einleitung in die Philosophie* (1996)

Ga29/30 *Die Grundbegriffe der Metaphysik* (1983); *The Fundamental Concepts of Metaphysics*, trans. W. McNeill and N. Walker (Bloomington, IN: Indiana University Press, 1995).

| Ga31 | *Vom Wesen der menschlichen Freiheit.* (1982); *The Essence of Human Freedom*, trans. T. Sadler (London: Continuum, 2002) |

Ga31   *Vom Wesen der menschlichen Freiheit.* (1982); *The Essence of Human Freedom*, trans. T. Sadler (London: Continuum, 2002)

Ga34   *Vom Wesen der Wahrheit. Zu Platons Höhlengleichnis und Theätet* (1988); *The Essence of Truth*, trans. T. Sadler (London: Continuum, 2002)

Ga40   *Einführung in die Metaphysik* (1983); *Introduction to Metaphysics*, trans. R. Polt (New Haven, CT: Yale University Press, 2000)

Ga41   *Die Frage nach dem Ding* (1984)

Ga54   *Parmenides* (1982); *Parmenides*, trans. R. Rojcewicz and A. Schuwer (Bloomington, IN: Indiana University Press, 1992)

Ga65   *Beiträge zur Philosophie (Vom Ereignis)* (1989)

Ga94   *Überlegungen II–VI (Schwarze Hefte 1931–1938)* (2014)

Ga95   *Überlegungen VII–XI (Schwarze Hefte 1938/39)* (2014)

Ga96   *Überlegungen XII–XV (Schwarze Hefte 1939–1941)* (2014)

SZ   *Sein und Zeit* (Tübingen: Niemeyer, 1957); *Being and Time*, trans. J. Macquarrie and E. Robinson (New York: Harper & Row, 1962)

BIBLIOGRAPHY

An asterisk denotes secondary literature especially suitable for further reading.

Braver, L. (2014), *Heidegger: Thinking of Being*. Cambridge: Polity.*

Carman, T. (2003), *Heidegger's Analytic*. Cambridge University Press.

Crowell, S. (2007), 'Sorge or Selbstbewußtsein?', *European Journal of Philosophy*, 15: 315–33.

Dreyfus, H. (1991), *Being-in-the-World*. Cambridge, MA: MIT Press.

Geuss, R. (2005), *Outside Ethics*. Princeton University Press.

Golob, S. (2014), *Heidegger on Concepts, Freedom and Normativity*. Cambridge University Press.

Golob, S. (forthcoming), 'Heidegger and The Occlusion of the Political: *Schwarze Hefte* Bd. 1', in Espinet, D., Figal, G., Keiling, T., and Mirkovic, N. (eds.), *Geschichte, Politik and Ideologie*. Tübingen: Mohr Siebeck.

Han-Pile, B. (2013), 'Freedom and the Choice to Choose Oneself in Being and Time', in Wrathall, M. (ed.), *The Cambridge Companion to Heidegger's Being and Time*. Cambridge University Press, pp. 291–319.

Leaman, G. and Simon, G. (1994), 'Die Kant-Studien im Dritten Reich', *Kant Studien*, 85: 443–69.

Sheehan, T. (2001), 'A Paradigm Shift in Heidegger Research', *Continental Philosophy Review*, 32: 183–202.

Thomson, I.D. (2013), 'Death and Demise in *Being and Time*', in Wrathall, M.A. (ed.), *The Cambridge Companion to Heidegger's* Being and Time. Cambridge University Press, pp. 260–90.

48

Sartre

SEBASTIAN GARDNER

Sartre's claim to have founded a humanistic ethics of freedom has met with considerable opposition.[1] Though viewed sympathetically by a small minority of commentators,[2] the majority verdict has been that Sartre's ethical rhetoric, his assertion of human freedom as a supreme value, deflates on examination and leaves behind a radical subjectivism indistinguishable from moral nihilism. On the standard construal, Sartre allows nothing to figure as a ground of value save the individual's bare consciousness of their own power of self-determination, and in consequence the Sartrean subject is required to make a rationally ungrounded choice in favour of some or other arbitrary value, commitment to which is unconditional yet can be maintained only through sheer force of will.[3] Sartre may then be regarded as exemplary of the predicament of late modern ethics, committed to the infinite value of the individual but without any theological or other supporting context for this

I am grateful to Sarah Richmond for helpful comments on an earlier draft.

[1] I do not follow any strict systematic distinction in my usage of "ethical" and "moral," but generally intend the former to have broader scope and the latter to refer to ethical values that have taken determinate imperatival shape.

[2] Typically these commentators are sensitive to Sartre's continuity with Kant: see esp. Baiasu 2011. For further general discussion of Sartre's ethics, see Anderson 1979 and 1993, Baldwin 1986, Bell 1989, Detmer 1988, Flynn 1984, McBride 1991, chs. 1–2, Poellner 2012, and Simont 1992.

[3] Exemplifying this assessment, in the earliest anglophone literature on Sartre, see Alfred Stern's short and straightforward discussion in Stern 1953, chs. 10–11; Stern's association of Sartre with Nietzsche is characteristic. Alvin Plantinga gives the standard grounds for dissatisfaction with Sartre's ethical claims in Plantinga 1958: 245–50. While analytic philosophers have been prominent in attacking Sartre's ethics, commentators in this camp share a variety of orientations and can be found in Sartre's earliest reception: see, e.g., Marcel 1948 and Lefebvre 2003, both from 1946.

doctrine,[4] or alternatively, as an object-lesson in the impossibility of upholding a broadly Kantian view of the centrality of individual freedom to morality without the accompanying apparatus of Kant's pure practical reason and metaphysics of the intelligible.

If this judgement is correct, then a cruel irony afflicts Sartre's philosophical project as a whole, which aims precisely to steer phenomenology in an ethical direction. From his earliest writings, which broach particular topics in theoretical philosophy on account of their perceived practical implications,[5] Sartre regarded philosophical enquiry as addressing the question of how one should lead one's life, paralleling his treatment in literature of the vicissitudes of human aspiration.

Various circumstantial facts help to explain the predominantly negative reception of Sartre's ethics, above all, the absence of any single published text in which his position receives the kind of detailed exposition and defence with which the phenomenological ontology of *Being and Nothingness* is equipped.[6] The chief obstacle to a correct appreciation of Sartre's contribution to moral thought, however, lies in the failure to recognize the nature of the strategy he employs, which is of a kind not currently favoured or even regarded as viable.

[4] See MacIntyre 1981, ch. 3. MacIntyre's approach to Sartre from the standpoint of analytic meta-ethics is representative of much earlier commentary; see, e.g., Danto 1975, ch. 5.

[5] See *The Transcendence of the Ego* (TE), Conclusion; *Sketch for a Theory of the Emotions* (Sartre 1971), *passim*, and *The Imaginary* (Sartre 2004a), ch. 4. Abbreviations are explained at the end of the chapter.

[6] The chief writings of Sartre's relevant to his ethical theory are as follows. The key sections in *Being and Nothingness* (BN) are the treatment of value in Part 2, Chapter 1, Section III (BN 84–95), and Section II of the Conclusion, on "ethical implications" (BN 625–8). Sartre's main published statement of his ethics is – *faute de mieux*, since it was intended only as a synoptic reply to critics – the short and widely read *Existentialism is a Humanism* (EH), a lecture from 1945. Simone de Beauvoir's *Pyrrhus and Cineas* (2004), ch. 3, pp. 77–150, and *The Ethics of Ambiguity* (1996) may be regarded, up to a point, as an amplified statement of Sartre's ethical outlook at this period. So too may Jeanson 1980, which has Sartre's own stamp of approval: see Part 3, Chapter 3, "Moral Perspectives." The subsequent development of Sartre's ideas on ethics can be followed in the posthumously published *Notebooks for an Ethics* (NE) from 1947–1948. All of this comprises what has come to be known as Sartre's "first ethics." The "second ethics," in which Sartre affirms ethical consciousness as a force within history, belongs to the period 1962–1965. Concerning the unpublished material which comprises it, see Stone and Bowman 1986 and 1991. A short extract from Sartre's Rome lecture notes is translated as "Determinism and Freedom."

Sartre's ethics are grounded in a theoretical, indeed a metaphysical account, not simply of human beings but of Being as such and in general. These metaphysics are moreover highly revisionary, and fiercely anti-naturalistic.

Even before the virtues of those metaphysics are considered, this will hardly recommend Sartre to contemporary moral philosophers. In response it may be pointed out that Sartre does not stand alone: two other modern thinkers have, like Sartre, supposed that what is essential to ethical thinking is an unobscured perception of the nature of reality and appreciation of its highly uncommonsensical character, namely Spinoza and Schopenhauer.[7] But in any case, and this is the crucial point, if we want to understand what Sartre is attempting to do, then it is necessary that we understand his argument in these terms.

Sartre's ethical theory may be viewed as a drama in three acts. As will be seen, the analogy is appropriate, for narrative structure is integral to the way that Sartre understands moral epistemology. The first act clears the ground, dispelling illusion but leaving the individual in a contradictory situation, subject to both the necessity, and the apparent impossibility, of positing value. The second shows that the affirmation of human freedom provides the unique means of exiting from these contradictory demands. The third, which presented Sartre with the greatest difficulty and occupied the bulk of his attention after 1945, concerns the task of translating the affirmation of freedom into concrete practical terms in our actual social and historical situation.

PURGATION: METAPHYSICAL INSIGHT

The phenomenological ontology of *Being and Nothingness* rules out directly various longstanding and widely endorsed conceptions of morality and moral knowledge. Two metaphysical claims above all are decisive for Sartre's rejection of a swathe of familiar positions, including hedonistic consequentialism, sentimentalist accounts such as Hume's, and all forms of moral realism: first, the impossibility of given reality's containing any ground for value; second, the impossibility of the self's containing any determinate content capable of sustaining value in a way that withstands critical examination.

Sartre holds that consciousness involves, at the most fundamental level and as a condition for its existence, the setting into opposition of two utterly

---

[7] Heidegger is also a contender for inclusion, though uncertainty surrounds his endorsement of the notion of moral value.

heterogeneous forms of being, which he famously calls being-for-itself and being-in-itself, the latter characterized negatively by its indifference to all of the features which are constitutive of the for-itself, including normativity and end-directedness. A phenomenological-style transcendental argument is offered for this thesis, the implication of which is that whatever features of the world figure objectually in consciousness as having an evaluative or normative character must be traced back to the subject. Sartre has thus taken seriously the Kantian lesson that moral theory cannot begin with supposed apprehensions, whether empirical perceptions or rational intuitions, of the Good.[8] It is noteworthy that Sartre, following Max Scheler and going beyond Kant, accepts nonetheless that our phenomenology is axiologically rich, saturated with normativity;[9] the question is what exactly within subjectivity provides its source. And once Sartre's full analysis of the structures of subjectivity – which occupies Part 2 of *Being and Nothingness* – has been completed, we are brought to recognize that the ground of the subject's apprehension of value can only be *choice*, more precisely, the reflexive, self-chosen and self-constituting *project* of the individual for-itself, which stands above all efficient causality, natural or supernatural.

It may be asked what justifies the transition from a *subjective* ground for value, a weak claim that many modern ethical theories would of course accept, to its identification with *choice*, construed in Sartre's transcendental, non-naturalistic manner. Here Sartre's second claim is crucial. Application of Sartre's dualist ontological insight to ourselves yields the radical result that any conceptualization of our minds or personalities which involves a commitment to the existence of abiding and efficacious mental entities, conceived as existing objectively beyond or outside acts of consciousness, is guilty of hypostatization. The mind, Sartre argues, can have no intentional, representational or qualitative "content," and can enjoy no "states" or "dispositions." Sartre does not doubt that we, in our ordinary experience of the world, accord reality to such entities – they are not mere philosophical fictions or inventions of psychological science, nor are they confined to the third-person standpoint. Philosophy and psychology may aggravate our tendency to postulate such entities, but they have their ultimate source in introspection, as ordinarily understood, in the reflective endeavour to grasp how one truly is, to *know* what one truly feels, thinks, desires, etc. There is, therefore, an entire ontological

---

[8] The Good, or value, is not what *has being* but what is *beyond being* and yet *has-to-be*, through *us*: see BN 38 and NE 555–7.

[9] E.g. TE 19, and BN 38–9.

stratum affirmed in the common-sense image of the world – "the psychic" or "Psyche," as it is termed in *Being and Nothingness* – which Sartre relegates to a species of fiction.[10] This fiction is not arbitrary but necessitated by the original teleology of the for-itself, its "fundamental project," which is to become in-itself-for-itself or *causa sui*, to exist as a self-grounding entity, in which freedom and nature are one. This unachievable end is served originally by degrading consciousness to the immobile condition of the psychic. Such metaphysically false self-representation is mobilized in the primary forms of bad faith, where the human subject loses itself in images of congealed selfhood, binding itself practically by means of a fictive self-identity, disavowing its freedom and approximating, in its experience and understanding of itself, to being-in-itself.

The implications of Sartre's revisionary metaphysics of mind for ethical theory are plain. If none of the qualities standardly attributed to persons and appealed to in action explanation – states of belief, desire, and emotion; character traits and qualities of personality – can be accorded reality, then the dispositions in terms of which virtue theory understands morality, and the affective cum conative states that provide the foundation for anti-realist and other Humean meta-ethical outlooks, are swept away.[11]

CONVERSION: AFFIRMATION OF FREEDOM

Fundamental though it may be, Sartre believes that it is possible, in a complex and qualified sense, to suspend the original project of seeking assimilation to the in-itself, and that the rational development of the for-itself – as it cycles through the various forms of bad faith and becomes aware of their futility – requires this "radical conversion." In what Sartre calls "pure," "purifying," or "nonaccessory" reflection, the subject repudiates the fictive substratum of the "psychic" and withdraws their commitment to whatever concrete projects sub-serve the fundamental project.[12]

---

[10] *BN* 158–70.   [11] See *EH* 32–3.

[12] Radical conversion involves, as it may be put, recognition of the impossibility of happiness. It is referred to in *BN* 412, 464, 475–6, and throughout the *Notebooks*, e.g., *NE* 49, 102, 281, 406–7, 471–84, 506–7. Sartre describes it succinctly at *NE* 470: "Conversion: nonaccessory reflection. Its motive: the impossibility of recovering oneself. The meaning of conversion: rejection of alienation." Concerning pure reflection, see *BN* 155, 158–60, 199, and *NE* 12, 473–82, 560; the idea is first formulated in *TE* 28, in connection with Husserl's *epoché*. Authenticity figures in *BN* almost exclusively as a category of Heidegger's and is employed only once by Sartre

The initial result of this suspension is not extinction of the drive to attain the condition of being-in-itself-for-itself[13] but merely a dissociation from it sufficient to shake its absolute hold over us. Nor is it simple cessation of will. Sartre gives in *Being and Nothingness* a transcendental account of the possibility of value from which it follows that value is constitutive of both self-consciousness and our very being-in-the-world – it is what precipitates consciousness' transcendence of itself out into the world and gives it an orientation towards the future, allowing the cogito to escape mere instantaneity.[14] Since our essential mode of being is teleological, the resignation recommended by Schopenhauer as the route to salvation is not genuinely thinkable.

The imperative to locate value thus remains in force, and if we now ask what way forward is available for the enlightened Sartrean subject, it is clear that identification with some contingent desire, entity, or ideal – patriotism, the Church, the Party – is not an intelligible option, any more than, for Kant, pure practical reason can resolve itself into inclination. Nothing that merely happens to be in the world, or that I happen to locate in my psyche, can exert authority at the transcendental level.

Because the necessity of valuing does not entail logically the availability of rationally acceptable values, thus far it remains possible that the Sartrean subject will grind to a halt, its practical and theoretical aspects at odds with one another. But as should be evident from the way in which Sartre has structured the development of the for-itself – as an axiological *via negativa* – there is one remaining candidate, namely human freedom itself, and once its candidacy is recognized, affirmation of freedom cannot fail to follow.[15] Here it is crucial to recognize that when freedom advances to occupy the vacant axiological spot, no discursive justification – no conceptual linkage of freedom with the Good – is either offered by Sartre, or needed: affirmation of freedom proceeds directly from grasping correctly one's metaphysical nature

---

himself (at *BN* 70, where it is defined as the self-recovery of corrupted being), but becomes part of Sartre's own philosophical vocabulary in *Existentialism is a Humanism* and the *Notebooks* (see, e.g., *NE* 474–82).

[13] *NE* 37: "The converted man cannot suppress the pursuit of Being through conversion." See also *NE* 473.

[14] See *BN* 84–95.

[15] Recognition of the necessity of *affirming* freedom is barely distinct, if at all, from insight into its *necessity*, i.e. our being "condemned" to be free, a constant refrain in Sartre's writings.

and situation.[16] This reflexive turn gives the for-itself a kind of formal completeness, something akin to the self-coincidence of the in-itself which it has renounced, yet is not undertaken for that reason: the negative motive, of escaping the contradiction of having to value and yet finding everything but freedom ineligible, suffices to force through the affirmation of freedom.[17]

The passages in which Sartre may appear most candidly subjectivist[18] should therefore not be read as meta-ethical analyses, as if Sartre were clumsily attempting to formulate the doctrines of emotivism or prescriptivism, nor as implying that Sartre supposes values to be chosen in the ordinary sense of a choice of furniture coverings. Sartre's concern, when he talks of the "unjustifiability" of commitments, is to correct the *mode* of our consciousness of value in such a way that the sustaining role of our freedom in axiological consciousness becomes phenomenologically manifest: Sartre seeks to modify the *way in which* we hold values, in order that it should display correctly, make visible, their only possible motivation. It is helpful to regard Sartre in Kantian terms as asserting the *transcendental ideality* of value *per se, contra* the tendency of natural consciousness to handle values in reflection as if they had transcendental reality, the "spirit of seriousness,"[19] as Sartre calls it; Sartre considers that this transcendental ideality must be explicit in the phenomenology of valuing.[20]

It may seem that further work needs to be done if Sartre is to arrive at an ethical destination: commitment to the value of *my* freedom must be shown

---

[16] Strictly, in so far as the "grasping" is no mere theoretical cognition, the two are identical. The ontological novelty which is involved in *affirming* freedom, as opposed to simply *being* free and knowing oneself as such in a merely abstract discursive manner, consists in the appearance of a new *demand*, freedom having become the object of reflective thetic consciousness (see BN 94–5). In Hegelian terms, freedom has become "conscious of itself." Sartre makes it very clear that this presupposes metaphysical insight at the deepest level: "the original structure of authentic existence [...] is indissolvably linked to the consciousness of Being as a fixed explosion" (NE 493–4).

[17] Grounding ethics directly on metaphysical facts, without intervening justificatory practical argumentation, is the explicit strategy of Schopenhauer's *On the Basis of Morality*, and implicitly that of Spinoza in Part 4 of the *Ethics*.

[18] E.g., BN 464–5.   [19] BN 626.

[20] Sartre in one place suggests that the tendency to reify values – to regard them as transcendentally real – derives not originally from the hypostatizing motive of the fundamental project, but from the fact that their origin lies in *pre*-reflective consciousness, which can only posit values out in the world, in objectual form: see NE 559. The fundamental project merely ratifies this transcendental illusion of the natural attitude.

to lead to affirmation of the *other*'s freedom. But again it would be a mistake to regard this as a logical gulf which needs to be bridged by argumentative means, for once again we find that the negative work of purgation has covered the distance. The purged for-itself's self-conception is in an important sense non-egoistic. Each (purged) for-itself grasps itself under that universal and grasps its own freedom as indiscriminable from that of every other individual for-itself. While certainly for Sartre being-for-itself is *individuated* – the subject is not a self-less or impersonal consciousness; being-for-itself takes necessarily the reflexive form of an *ipseity*[21] – the subject who has emancipated herself fully from the aim of becoming *causa sui* is left with no purchase on their individuality relevant to the positing of value: "self-interest" has for them, at the transcendental level at which axiological reflection is here proceeding, no special claim to attention.[22] Thus no affirmation of my freedom in *opposition* to that of other for-itselfs makes sense. This explains also Sartre's repeated claim that in choosing for myself I choose for all men.[23]

What it is to pursue this task of affirming freedom in a universal form has yet to be determined, but two points need attention if affirmation of freedom is to be ethically meaningful.

No positive contentful account of freedom, on a par with Kant's identification of freedom with autonomy and hence with morality, is given by Sartre. Sartre's clearly stated view is that no analysis of or even conceptual approximation to freedom is possible: freedom has no inner constitution or essence which philosophical reflection might determine; not even freedom of will provides its correct conceptualization.[24] The blankness of Sartrean freedom fosters the suspicion that affirmation of the other's freedom is incapable of bearing practical implications, and that any claim to that effect will involve a surreptitious exchange of the ontological freedom of the for-itself, which is all that has been in question hitherto, for freedom in some more empirically determinate sense.[25] The point that needs to be made in response is that all

---

[21] *BN* 102–5.

[22] The plane of reflection here is "beyond egoism and altruism" (*BN* 626). See Sartre's repudiation of the theory of *amour propre* in *TE* 17–20.

[23] Whereby freedom is converted directly into responsibility; see *BN* 553–6, *EH* 23–5, 44–5, and *NE* 107, 248, 250, 493. Regarding the universality claim, see "Existentialism: A Clarification" (Sartre 2013), p. 89, *EH* 24, 43–5, *NE* 557, and "Kierkegaard: The Singular Universal" (*KSU*), pp. 424–5.

[24] *BN* 24–45, and Part 4, Chapter 1, Section I (*BN* 433–81).

[25] Sartre distinguishes freedom in such a sense, and makes clear that it is not what is at issue, at *BN* 483.

that is required for the ethical project to be launched is that we should know freedom negatively, in terms of its opposition to the mode of being of the in-itself: it is enough that we can recognize cases where it is negated. The contentlessness of Sartrean freedom is not just the source of its privileged status but also integral to its axiological role at this initial level of ethical thinking: the primary expression of the ethical is *resistance* to the temptation of bad faith, which entails resistance to incursions of the fundamental project in one's relation to others. Once this basis has been laid, the material and other factical dimensions of human reality can be brought into view and the concrete demands of freedom extrapolated.[26]

A second point concerns the accessibility of the other's freedom at the level of concrete interaction. Sartre takes a famously pessimistic view of the possibility of interpersonal fulfilment in his discussion of "concrete relations with others" in *Being and Nothingness*, where the dynamics of personal relationships are analyzed in terms of a fixed set of conflictual and self-stultifying strategies. This account of interpersonal desire is grounded in intersubjective awareness, which according to Sartre necessarily *alternates* between consciousness of my freedom and that of the other, and does so in such a way that not only can they not both be co-present to my conscious-ness, but each can be present only on the basis of a *negation* of the other. This structure intersects with the demands of the fundamental project to yield the projects of love, hate, indifference, and so on. Now, if the other's freedom is something that I must in any concrete context either seek to negate, or that I can affirm only at the expense of my own, then ethical action is no less impossible than the fundamental project. It is consequently vital that Sartre's thesis concerning the mutually repelling character of my freedom and that of the other has only limited scope. Sartre's primary purpose in the section in question is to counter Hegel's "ontological optimism," his claim that the supra-individual logic of interpersonality *necessitates*, independently of choice, accession to relations of mutual recognition. This leaves space, conceptually, for the possibility of mutual recognition of freedom on some other basis, and here Sartre is able to reinvoke his concept of purifying reflection: just as, in the intra-subjective context, in order to resist the temptation of bad faith, I am required, and able, to hold my transcendence

---

[26] This involves reworking critically the familiar categories of ethical theory. Sartre does this in the *Notebooks*: see, e.g., the treatment of rights, justice, and charity in *NE* 137–41.

and my facticity in equilibrium,[27] so similarly, in the intersubjective context, I am able to cognize the other's freedom as coexistent with my own. Interpersonal pathology, the "Hell of passions,"[28] may be the original but it is not the final form of intersubjectivity.[29]

The freedom of the other is thus a possible object of my will. The question then arises whether Sartre wishes also to conceive it in stronger terms, as either the fulfilment (as some sort of extension or deepening) of my freedom, or as in any sense a condition for it. Sartre's texts do affirm a deep interconnection of individuals' freedom,[30] but on the fundamental issue Sartre remains opposed to Hegel: the individual's freedom, like their self-consciousness, is ontologically independent of the other, not created or constituted by it,[31] and the prospective gains of reciprocal freedom, whatever they may be, are not part of the primary motivation for affirming freedom; the other's willing my freedom is not a condition of my *being* free. What is true is that the other's relation to my freedom – whether they too affirm it, or remain caught in the fundamental project – plays an essential role in determining how far I can get with the ethical task of *willing* freedom for its own sake, of *realizing* freedom as a universal value: the imperative of the converted subject is to render human reality transparent to freedom, to inhabit a world irradiated by it, and in that regard the freedom of each is indeed conditional on that of the other.[32] As will be seen shortly, the implications of this point are far-reaching.

What we have just seen is Sartre's core argument for the value of freedom, which he supplements and elaborates in several ways. Two of the most important are Sartre's introduction of the auxiliary motive of solidarity, and his notion of a shared project of unveiling being. The former urges us to as it were unite in light of our common human condition and in face of

---

[27] Facticity and transcendence "are and ought to be capable of a valid coordination" (*BN* 56). The intersubjective analogue of good faith is described at *NE* 468: a "perpetual tension" which takes account of both freedoms.

[28] *NE* 499.

[29] Sartre explains what it is for intersubjectivity to have a mutually recognitive character in *NE* 499–508; here he introduces the concept of authentic love. His later account of reciprocity, in *Critique of Dialectical Reason* (Sartre 1982), pp. 209–15, involves a change of view: Sartre now regards a mediating third element – roughly: materiality as it relates to some praxis – as a condition of mutual recognition.

[30] See *EH* 48–9, and *What is Literature?* (*WL*), ch. 1, concerning the interaction of writer and reader.

[31] *BN* 239.

[32] Dependence on the freedom of the other is emphasized by de Beauvoir in 2004, Part 2, and 1996: 67–72.

our common enemy – the fate we share of being condemned to exist teleologically in a reality indifferent to teleology, as if enduring a cosmic punishment, and to always feel the magnetic pull of the fundamental project, this ineradicable disposition inhabiting us like original sin.[33] The pathos of Sartre's vision is thus complex – tragic, adversarial, Augustinian, Promethean – and forms a vital component of his ethical outlook.[34]

The latter reworks a theme from Heidegger. Sartre affirms, as a subaltern end to that of freedom, that the for-itself must understand itself as committed to the project of "illuminating" – revealing, disclosing – being, and that this is necessarily a shared human endeavour. The project of illuminating being comprises cognition and praxis, is extended through history, and involves intersubjective norms; it presupposes a stance of epistemic generosity and implies a commitment to the value of truthfulness.[35]

DECISION: THE PROBLEM OF REALIZING FREEDOM IN ACTION

To affirm freedom as value – since this is in itself no merely cognitive act, value having the *exigent* character of a demand and not the given character of an object[36] – can have no other meaning than to *act* in ways that express (realize, embody) that value. The difficulty is to determine which acts satisfy this description. It is here that the problems of ethical life begin, and that Sartre diverges most sharply from Kant.

Kant supposes that the conditions for freedom-embodying action are (i) the conformity of its maxim to the formal conditions expressed by the categorical imperative, (ii) the motivational sufficiency of this conformity for the agent. A continuous logical transition from freedom, or pure practical reason, to situationally determinate moral judgements is secured according

[33] *NE* 479: "conversion consists in renouncing the category of appropriation, which can govern only those relations of the For-itself with things, in order to introduce into the internal relation of the Person the relation of solidarity, which will subsequently be modified into solidarity with others." Sartre explicates approvingly Kierkegaard's treatment of original sin in *KSU*; on what it encompasses, see *NE* 428.
[34] For a characteristic, purple passage, see the long note in *WL* 23–5.
[35] See in particular *Truth and Existence* (Sartre 1992b), esp. pp. 5–7, 45–8, 64–7. The theme of disclosure of being is emphasized by de Beauvoir in 1996, ch. 1. In the *Notebooks*, the unveiling of being, creation, and generosity or giving comprise a family of inter-related concepts: the for-itself grasps the necessity of reproducing its own gratuitous, quasi-creative relation to being in its relation to others, i.e., in generosity.
[36] *BN* 38.

to Kant by applying the formula(e) of the categorical imperative to whatever empirical content contingently presents itself, i.e., to the facts of inclination and circumstance considered in light of the actual laws of nature.

Sartre stands in line with those, beginning with Hegel, who believe that Kant's procedure is unable to yield determinate practical judgements. In his 1945 lecture *Existentialism is a Humanism*, Sartre recapitulates and endorses Kant's claims concerning the foundational role of freedom, the strictly universal character of moral judgement, the concept of self-legislation, and the ideal of a kingdom of ends,[37] but at the same time argues that the abstract formulae of Kant's categorical imperative fail to provide a sufficient basis for practical decision-making: nothing in them connects adequately with the complexity of a concrete historically conditioned situation.[38]

This is, as just noted, a familiar criticism of Kant. But Sartre also has other (and in his terms deeper) reasons for rejecting Kant's confinement of ethics to formal maxim-determination.

In the first instance, Sartre's attitude to Kant's ethics is critical: abstract moral rules exhibit a fixity and opacity alien to freedom, and in Kantian duty we relate ourselves to an Other, not to ourselves.[39] Again we see that Sartre's objection is not to the *objectivity* of ethics but to the mode in which we take up or "live" the ethical, and specifically to its *objectification* – which has the effect of undercutting the only possible source of its objectivity, viz. freedom. The expulsion of being-in-itself must be carried through with respect to morality itself, that is, morality must present itself and be apprehended in the correct, unmystified form; it must not degenerate into an inert social object, dissociated from the spontaneity of consciousness.[40]

Most importantly, Sartre considers that the good will of the Kantian agent encounters the following difficulty:

---

[37] *EH* 41–53. Sartre also takes over Kant's notion – in his account of the "fact of reason" – that awareness of a categorical imperative indexes the unconditional possibility of action in conformity with it, i.e. of (what Kant would call) transcendental freedom: see "Determinism and Freedom" (*DF*).

[38] *EH* 30–2, 46. Decision-making can therefore only be a matter of judgement, "like constructing a work of art" (*EH* 45–6). The universal validity that our actions lay claim to is, therefore, the Kantian "exemplary necessity" of beautiful objects.

[39] See *DF* 246, 252, and *NE* 469: duty is "a *thing*. Duty is the Other at the heart of my Will. It is the project of my will conceived of as the project of an Other."

[40] In so far as the primary condition of moral agency is an orientation not susceptible to discursive formulation, Sartre comes into contact with the tradition of virtue ethics. Of relevance here is Sartre's focus on generosity: see *NE* 9, 48, 129, 141, 197, 281, 375, 470.

If the city of ends remains a feeble abstraction, it is because it is not realizable without an objective modification of the historical situation. Kant, I believe, saw this very well, but sometimes he counted on a purely subjective transformation of the moral subject and at other times he despaired of ever meeting a good will on this earth ... [T]he purely formal intention of treating men as ends ... reveal[s] itself to be utterly futile in practice since the fundamental structures of our society are still oppressive. Such is the present paradox of ethics; if I am absorbed in treating a few chosen persons as absolute ends, for example, my wife, my son, my friends, the needy person I happen to come across, if I am bent upon fulfilling all my duties toward them, I shall spend my life doing so; I shall be led *to pass over in silence* the injustices of the age, the class struggle, colonialism, Anti-Semitism, etc., and, finally, *to take advantage of oppression in order to do good*. Moreover, the former will be found in person to person relationships and, more subtly, in my very intentions. The good that I try to do will be vitiated at the roots. It will be turned into radical evil.[41]

The Kantian might well retort that Sartre overshoots the mark: if ethics is presently paradoxical, then it is presently impossible, which is an absurdity; the sane conclusion is surely that, however resistant the social world may be to moral endeavour, we can at least strive to possess a good will. This however merely leads to the deeper issue contained in Sartre's remarks on Kant, indicated by Sartre's ominous reference to the presence of oppression "in my very intentions," and developed at great length in the posthumously published manuscripts from 1947–1948, *Notebooks for an Ethics*.

The post-conversion subject faces the task of targeting the freedom of the other across the medium of a world – the world interposes itself between subjects and constitutes the platform of human action; our interaction is not that of intelligible beings in a spirit-world. The problem is that the world of our facticity, which defines our situations and which my good intentions must traverse, is populated by entities which negate freedom. Earlier we said that reflective consciousness posits for itself a fictive mental substratum. In Sartre's full view these posited objects have, notwithstanding the fictiveness which they exhibit when considered transcendentally, *intersubjective reality* (Sartre gives the example: "I do everything possible to '*make Annie love me*', to

[41] *WL* 274–5. In *Saint Genet: Actor and Martyr*, Sartre writes: "The ethical 'problem' arises from the fact that Ethics is *for us* inevitable and at the same time impossible. Action must give itself norms in this climate of non-transcendable impossibility" (p. 186n). Adorno picks up the same theme when he asserts that the false life cannot be lived correctly. That this impossibility implies practical contradictions – seeking to treat man as an end, yet being unable to do so – Sartre spells out in *NE* 207.

'endow her with love for me'").[42] These intersubjectively real entities are moreover only the beginning of a social ontology replete with objects antagonistic to freedom, which Sartre in his later writings calls the "practico-inert" and which range from machine tools to language, ritual, and social identities ("the Jew" of anti-Semitism, etc.). What all of these items have in common is an abiding objectivity endowed with normative power that appears to transcend – even though it must have its source in – the consciousness of individuals. The importance for Sartre of the fact that the social world has an aspect of being-in-itself cannot be overstated. Sartre's *Critique of Dialectical Reason* represents perhaps the most intensive engagement in the history of philosophy with the transcendental problem of social ontology, that is, the question of how it is possible for a plurality of individuals to give rise to social *things*, trans-personal entities capable of reacting back on individual subjectivity. Whether or not Sartre solves the problem, the *Critique* succeeds at least in displaying the contradictory structure of intersubjective life, its combination of free subjectivity and nature-like objectivity, and in delineating the ways in which alienation is bound up with material scarcity and collective oppression.[43]

With this in view, it can be understood why Sartre considers naive Kant's view that the kingdom of ends can be approximated to, simply to the extent that each person has a good will. The problem is the translation of affirmation of freedom into concrete mundane facticity, and this cannot be secured by the mere existence of individual freedom-affirming wills, when the very

---

[42] *BN* 159.

[43] Though it should be clear from the foregoing why Sartre should have availed himself of certain Marxist concepts – alienation, exploitation, mystification, reification – it is less obvious, from what has been said so far, why any more substantial commitment to Marxism should have been taken out by him. The short answer is that, on the basis that (1) the "lack of being" in the for-itself, considered at the more concrete level of a human being, is in the first instance the material *need* of a living organism (a claim which departs from *Being and Nothingness* and signals a development in Sartre's thinking), and that (2) the fundamental terms in relations of oppression are social classes, Sartre believes that ethics leads into a broadly Marxist politics. The problem of human history and collective existence does not however originate ultimately for Sartre in material forces, any more than it does in the game-theoretic considerations, modelled in rational decision theory, which have driven so much political theory: its roots are once again metaphysical, lying ultimately (as for Schopenhauer) in the fact that being-for-itself is a totality which has been "detotalized," i.e. subjected to individuation. The "antinomic" structure of intersubjectivity, which sets a limit to Hegel's dialectic, is analyzed at *BN* 299–302 and again at *NE* 450–68.

conceptualizations that each must form of the other in order to formulate an intention towards them, and the means that they must adopt in order to execute their intention, are infected with being-in-itself, that is, negate the other's freedom. Since these accretions of being-in-itself are first and foremost the product of man's collective historical existence, ethics must develop to that higher plane:

> [T]he suppression of alienation has to be universal. Impossibility of being ethical *alone*. Whence the problem: History ↔ ethics. History implies ethics (without universal conversion, no sense or meaning to evolution or to revolutions). Ethics implies history (no morality is possible without systematic action in some situation).[44]

The difficulty that Sartre discovers in the task of ethics helps to explain why he did not directly publish an ethical sequel to *Being and Nothingness* – not because, as his critics would have it, he discovered its metaphysics to be ethically fruitless, but because the task of concrete ethical action in his estimation leads directly into a politics and theory of history, which he attempted to provide in his *Critique of Dialectical Reason*.[45] The metaphysics of *Being and Nothingness*, far from *precluding* ethical engagement with the world, motivate it so strongly and in such demanding terms that nothing less than a resolution of the problem of human history and collective existence will permit realization of man's ethical *telos*. This expansion of the borders of ethics beyond the pre-political individual puts Sartre in a recognizable tradition beginning with Rousseau and stretching up, via Schiller, Schelling, Hegel, and Marx, to Adorno.

ABBREVIATIONS

BN   *Being and Nothingness* (Sartre 1995)
DF   "Determinism and Freedom" (Sartre 1974)
EH   *Existentialism is a Humanism* (Sartre 2007)
KSU   "Kierkegaard: The Singular Universal" (Sartre 1983)
NE   *Notebooks for an Ethics* (Sartre 1992a)

---

[44] *NE* 471. See also *NE* 7, 9, 13, 141.
[45] The first volume of this work appeared in 1960, and the second, composed in 1958–1962, was published posthumously in 1985. It thus precedes Sartre's "second ethics," which may be regarded as an attempt to integrate the *Critique*'s theory of society and history with ethics. The reason for Sartre's non-publication of his second ethics is unclear.

TE   *The Transcendence of the Ego* (Sartre 2004b)
WL   *What is Literature?* (Sartre 1967)

BIBLIOGRAPHY

An asterisk denotes secondary literature especially suitable for further reading.

Anderson, Thomas C. 1979. *The Foundation and Structure of Sartrean Ethics.* Lawrence, KS: Regents Press of Kansas

Anderson, Thomas C. 1993. *Sartre's Two Ethics: From Authenticity to Integral Humanity.* LaSalle, IL: Open Court

Baiasu, Sorin 2011. *Kant and Sartre: Re-discovering Critical Ethics.* Basingstoke: Palgrave Macmillan*

Baldwin, Thomas 1986. "Sartre, *Existentialism and Humanism,*" *Royal Institute of Philosophy Lecture Series* 20: 287–307

Beauvoir, Simone de 1996. *The Ethics of Ambiguity,* trans. Bernard Frechtman. New York: Citadel Press [*Pour une morale de l'ambiguïté.* Paris: Gallimard, 1947]

Beauvoir, Simone de 2004. *Pyrrhus and Cineas,* in *Philosophical Writings,* ed. Margaret A. Simons with Marybeth Timmermann and Mary Beth Mader. Urbana, IL: University of Illinois Press, ch. 3, pp. 77–150 [*Pyrrhus et Cinéas.* Paris: Gallimard, 1944]

Bell, Linda 1989. *Sartre's Ethics of Authenticity.* Tuscaloosa, AL: University of Alabama Press

Danto, Arthur 1975. *Sartre.* London: Fontana

Detmer, David 1988. *Freedom as a Value: A Critique of the Ethical Theory of Jean-Paul Sartre.* LaSalle, IL: Open Court

Flynn, Thomas 1984. *Sartre and Marxist Existentialism: The Test Case of Collective Responsibility.* University of Chicago Press

Jeanson, Francis 1980. *Sartre and the Problem of Morality,* trans. Robert Stone. Bloomington, IN: Indiana University Press [*Le Problème moral et la pensée de Sartre.* Paris: Éditions du Myrte, 1947]

Lefebvre, Henri 2003. "Retrospections," in *Key Writings,* ed. Stuart Elden and Elizabeth Lebas. London: Athlone, pp. 6–13 [*L'Existentialisme.* Paris: Éditions Sagittaire, 1946, pp. 55–66]

MacIntyre, Alasdair 1981. *After Virtue: A Study in Moral Theory.* London: Duckworth

Marcel, Gabriel 1948. "Existence and Human Freedom," in *The Philosophy of Existence,* trans. Manya Harari. London: Harvill ["L'Existence et la liberté humaine chez Jean-Paul Sartre," in *Les Grands Appels de l'homme contemporain.* Paris: Éditions du Temps Présent, 1946]

McBride, William 1991. *Sartre's Political Theory.* Bloomington, IN: Indiana University Press

Plantinga, Alvin 1958. "An Existentialist's Ethics," *Review of Metaphysics* 12: 235–56

Poellner, Peter 2012. "Early Sartre on Freedom and Ethics," *European Journal of Philosophy* 23 (2): 221–47

Sartre, Jean-Paul 1963. *Saint Genet: Actor and Martyr,* trans. Bernard Frechtman. New York: Braziller [*Saint Genet, comédien et martyr.* Paris: Gallimard, 1952]

Sartre, Jean-Paul 1967. *What is Literature?,* trans. Bernard Frechtman. London: Methuen ["Qu'est-ce que la littérature?," in *Situations II.* Paris: Gallimard, 1948]

Sartre, Jean-Paul 1971. *Sketch for a Theory of the Emotions*, trans. Philip Mairet. London: Methuen [*Esquisse d'une théorie des émotions*. Paris: Hermann, 1939]

Sartre, Jean-Paul 1974. "Determinism and freedom," in *The Writings of Jean-Paul Sartre*, vol. 2: *Selected Prose*, ed. Michel Contat and Michel Rybalka, trans. Richard C. McCleary. Evanston, IL: Northwestern University Press, pp. 241–52 [from unpublished lecture notes, 1964]

Sartre, Jean-Paul 1982. *Critique of Dialectical Reason*, vol. 1: *Theory of Practical Ensembles*, trans. Alan Sheridan-Smith, ed. Jonathan Rée. London: Verso [*Critique de la raison dialectique. 1: Théorie des ensembles pratiques, précédé de Questions de méthode*. Paris: Gallimard, 1960]

Sartre, Jean-Paul 1983. "Kierkegaard: The Singular Universal," trans. John Matthews, in *Between Existentialism and Marxism*. London: Verso, pp. 141–69 ["L'Universel singulier," in *Situations IX*. Paris: Gallimard, 1972, pp. 152–90]

Sartre, Jean-Paul 1991. *Critique of Dialectical Reason*, vol. 2: *The Intelligibility of History*, ed. Arlette Elkaïm-Sartre, trans. Quentin Hoare. London: Verso [*Critique de la raison dialectique. 2: L'Intelligibilité de l'histoire*, ed. Arlette Elkaïm-Sartre. Paris: Gallimard, 1985]

Sartre, Jean-Paul 1992a. *Notebooks for an Ethics* (composed 1947–1948), trans. David Pellauer. University of Chicago Press [*Cahiers pour une morale*. Paris: Gallimard, 1983]

Sartre, Jean-Paul 1992b. *Truth and Existence* (composed 1948), trans. Adrian van den Hoven. University of Chicago Press [*Vérité et existence*, ed. Arlette Elkaïm-Sartre. Paris: Gallimard, 1989]

Sartre, Jean-Paul 1995. *Being and Nothingness: An Essay on Phenomenological Ontology*, trans. Hazel Barnes. London: Routledge [*L'Être et le néant. Essai d'ontologie phénoménologique*. Paris: Gallimard, 1943]

Sartre, Jean-Paul 2004a. *The Imaginary*, trans. Jonathan Webber. London: Routledge [*L'Imaginaire. Psychologie phénoménologique de l'imagination*. Paris: Gallimard, 1940]

Sartre, Jean-Paul 2004b. *The Transcendence of the Ego: A Sketch for a Phenomenological Description*, trans. Andrew Brown, introduction by Sarah Richmond. London: Routledge ["La Transcendance de l'égo. Esquisse d'une description phénoménologique," *Recherches philosophiques* 6 (1936–1937): 85–123]

Sartre, Jean-Paul 2007. *Existentialism is a Humanism* (lecture 1945), trans. Carol Macomber, ed. John Kulka. New Haven, CT: Yale University Press [*L'Existentialisme est un humanisme*. Paris: Éditions Nagel, 1946]

Sartre, Jean-Paul 2013. "Existentialism: A Clarification," trans. Richard C. McCleary, in Ronald Aronson and Adrian van den Hoven (eds.), *We Have Only This Life to Live: The Selected Essays of Jean-Paul Sartre, 1939–1975*. New York: NYRB, pp. 86–91 ["À Propos de l'existentialisme, mise au point," *Action* 17 (29 December 1944): 11]

Simont, Juliette 1992. "Sartrean Ethics," in Christina Howells (ed.), *The Cambridge Companion to Sartre*. Cambridge University Press, ch. 6, pp. 178–210

Stern, Alfred 1953. *Sartre: His Philosophy and Existential Psychoanalysis*. New York: Liberal Arts Press

Stone, Robert and Bowman, Elizabeth 1986. "Dialectical Ethics: A First Look at Sartre's Unpublished 1964 Rome Lecture Notes," *Social Text* 13–14: 195–215

Stone, Robert and Bowman, Elizabeth 1991. "Sartre's *Morality and History*: A First Look at the Notes for the Unpublished 1965 Cornell Lectures," in Ronald Aronson and Adrian van den Hoven (eds.), *Sartre Alive*. Detroit, MI: Wayne State University Press, ch. 2, pp. 53–82

49

French Ethical Philosophy since the 1960s

TODD MAY

A few years ago, while on sabbatical, I had the opportunity to sit in on an ethics course taught by Jeff McMahan and Derek Parfit. After class one day I mentioned to Parfit that my area of specialization was contemporary Continental thought. He asked me who, in my view, are the great ethical thinkers in the Continental tradition. Although in one sense the question is a straightforward one, applied to the Continental tradition it rings a bit false. As I explained, Continental philosophy rarely breaks down along thematic lines. If there was one thinker – at least in recent French thought – who would straightforwardly be classified as an ethical philosopher, it would be Emmanuel Levinas. However, there are inescapably normative, and indeed moral or ethical considerations, in the work of Jacques Derrida, Jean-Luc Nancy, Gilles Deleuze, Jean-François Lyotard, Michel Foucault, and even recent political thinkers like Jacques Rancière and Alain Badiou.

Recent French philosophy – in fact, most French philosophy, recent or not – consists less in specific philosophical contributions to particular areas of thought and more in the creation of larger perspectives. These perspectives are rarely far from normative considerations. After all, unlike in the US and the UK, philosophers are often at the center of public political debate. However, their ideas are embedded in philosophical perspectives that involve not only the specific normative considerations in play but a framework within which these considerations find their place. The reasons for this are many. However, a central one is that many recent French thinkers see their task not as one of contributing to an assumed trajectory of philosophical progress but instead as one of challenging the trajectory and its assumption of progress. It is the presupposed terms of thought that are often problematized in recent French philosophy, and this often for normative among other reasons.

Any thematic overview of recent French ethical thought, then, risks betraying the specificity of a thinker's perspective by grouping it with others.

In this chapter, I will run this risk in a specific way, by grouping thinkers according to at least one of their stated overriding ethical concerns.[1] An implication of this is that the categories of grouping are not mutually exclusive. Moreover, they are not all of the same type. The first two categories' center might be seen as conflicts between a transcendental and an immanent approach to ethics (although, as we shall see, that distinction is not straightforward), while the third involves the commitment to a specific ethical principle.

The categories are these: an ethics of the other, in which the major figures are Levinas, Derrida, Nancy, and to a lesser extent Lyotard; an ethics of immanence, whose major figure is Deleuze but in which we might situate certain aspects of Foucault; and an ethics of equality, which is presupposed in the work of Rancière and perhaps Badiou.

ETHICS OF THE OTHER

No discussion of an ethics of the other can commence without reference to Levinas' thought. In his two major works, *Totality and Infinity* (1969) and *Otherwise than Being, or Beyond Essence* (1997), Levinas lays out a thought of infinite responsibility to the other that has been deeply influential on Derrida and his deconstructionist allies and has left its mark on Lyotard's work.

Levinas may be seen as responding to Martin Heidegger's attempt to think Being. Such a project, Levinas argues, risks reducing the otherness of others to categories of the same, that is, not recognizing the alterity of others. That risk, in turn, runs the further risk of effacing the other in the name of the same – of denying the difference of the other from myself and therefore holding myself as the measure of all things, or at least all humanity. This denial is what Levinas calls *totality*, a term that would not be accidentally invoked by a Jewish thinker who was a prisoner of war in Germany during World War II and who lost family to the Holocaust. It is to be contrasted with the recognition of the infinite alterity of the other.

Levinas' claim, however, is not simply that thinking in terms of Being risks reducing the otherness of the other. It is more radical. He believes that each of us is partially constituted by the claim that the other has upon us. That is to say, our ontological wholeness is fractured by the call of the other, a call to

---

[1] I use the term *ethical* here to refer to what might be called either ethical or moral concerns in Anglo-American or analytic philosophy. With some thinkers, like Levinas, the ethical tilts toward what often goes under the name of the moral: that is, duties toward others. However, with other thinkers, e.g. Deleuze, the concern is more nearly ethical in the sense that it has to do with one's way of living.

which we can never adequately respond. As Levinas puts the point, "The consciousness is affected, then, before forming an image of what is coming to it, affected in spite of itself. In these traits we recognize a persecution; being called into question prior to questioning, responsibility over and beyond the logos of a response."[2]

This call, which is partially constitutive of who we are, is expressed in the face of the other. It is in the face of the other that we see written the call of conscience that is part of who we are. "The 'You shall not commit murder' which delineates the face in which the Other is produced submits my freedom to judgment."[3] The idea here should be a familiar one. It is very difficult to do violence to a face. When we imagine hitting someone in the face, it seems to violate a particular vulnerability embodied by a human face (and perhaps non-human faces, although Levinas is less sensitive to that point). Levinas' claim is that that sense of violation lies not simply in the other, but in a moral sensibility that is constitutive of who we are as subjects of experience.

Put this way, Levinas' view may seem to be akin to that of Adam Smith or David Hume in their treatment of sympathy. However, for Levinas it is not the likeness of the other but precisely its otherness that is the source of obligation. If it were the likeness of the other which is the ground of sympathy, that constituted my original moral relation to the other, then we would run the risk of totality. Subsuming the other would simply be a recognition of myself in the other. For Levinas, it is precisely the transcendence of the other to my categories, my inability to bring the other within my conceptual sphere, to which I am obligated. This creates a fracture in my own being, since I am partially constituted by an obligation that I can neither bring within the ambit of my understanding nor ever put to rest. I am never not obliged to the other, regardless of what I do to or for him or her. "Responsibility in fact is not a simple attribute of subjectivity, as if the latter already existed in itself, before the ethical relationship. Subjectivity is not for itself; it is, once again, initially for another."[4]

One might wonder what the role of moral discussion and discourse is, if ethics is in the end an inescapably elusive aspect of one's being. Levinas does not deny the role of discourse in ethics, but accords it a secondary place. He distinguishes the "said" from the "saying," and uses the word "justice" to refer to the aspects of morality that accord with the said. "Justice is necessary, that is, comparison, coexistence, contemporaneousness, assembling, order, thematization, the visibility of faces, and thus intentionality and the intellect,

---

[2] Levinas 1997: 102.   [3] Ibid., 303.   [4] Levinas 1985: 96.

the intelligibility of a system, and thence also a copresence on an equal footing as before a court of justice."[5] However, justice as a matter of the said is predicated on a more primordial relationship to the other that comes with the saying. And the saying, in turn, is founded on a yet more primordial relation to the other that is the fractured ground of one's subjectivity, a ground fractured by responsibility to the other.

Early in his career, Derrida sought to deconstruct Levinas' ethics in an essay entitled "Violence and Metaphysics."[6] Although deconstruction is often associated with the idea that the "metaphysics of presence" seeks to exclude an absence that is nevertheless constitutive of presence itself, in this essay Derrida moves in a complementary direction, seeking to show that one cannot embrace a "metaphysics of absence" (my phrase, not Derrida's) that excludes presence. However, as his career unfolds, Derrida moves closer to Levinas' view. He accords a greater place to the idea of a responsibility to the other that cannot ever be realized. This comes out in many places in his work, and is in accord with the general deconstructionist commitment to displaying at once the necessity and the impossibility of grasping what grounds our thought or our being, and doing so in a way that involves framing (while not entirely comprehending) an economy of presence and absence.

In his work *Of Hospitality* (2000), for example, Derrida argues at once for the necessity and impossibility of hospitality. On the one hand, in order for one to be hospitable, one has to have control over the resources that would realize or contribute to the well-being of another. If one has no control over them, then sharing them is hardly a gesture of hospitality. On the other hand, insofar as one retains control over the resources which one is sharing with the other, one is not really being hospitable. Hospitality requires a deeper vulnerability than the patronizing sharing of resources with another who ultimately remains in one's thrall. "[A]bsolute hospitality requires that I open up my home and that I give not only to the foreigner, but to the absolute, unknown, anonymous other, and that I *give place* to them, that I let them come, that I let them arrive, and take place in the place I offer them, without either asking of them reciprocity (entering into a pact) or even their names."[7]

In hospitality, then, the host is at once host and hostage in an unstable oscillation that cannot be reconciled to either pole. Hospitality, like gift-giving or forgiveness, is caught in an aporia that is at once obligatory and unrealizable. Like Levinas' ethics, Derrida's view expresses an unrealizable debt to the other, a relation to the other in which one can never be quits.

[5] Levinas 1997: 157. [6] Derrida 1978. [7] Derrida 2000: 25.

I should note, although I can do so only in passing, that some of the later work of Jean-François Lyotard is also oriented in a Levinasian direction, while that of Jean-Luc Nancy roots obligation to the other in a deconstructionist vein. Lyotard's treatment of ethics in *The Differend* (1988) is informed by a call of conscience that binds one without ground and which instills an obligation that cannot be realized, while Nancy's discussion of singularity and community in several of his works postulates an exposure to the other that is neither on the hither nor far side of subjectivity, an economy of openness that seeks to avoid both reduction to an autonomous subjectivity and effacement in an organic community (of which Nazism often provides his model).

This ethical stance is in one sense oriented toward transcendence and in another sense toward immanence. It is the transcendent in the sense that the other toward which one is obliged in Levinas – or the absolute hospitality of which Derrida speaks – is forever beyond one. It cannot be brought into one's sphere. However, this stance also involves a commitment to immanence in the sense that that beyondness is not outside of the subject for Levinas or the concept of hospitality for Derrida. It is precisely what is constitutive of the subject and of hospitality. We might say, then, that the ethical relationship for both of them is one of a transcendence within immanence, one which can be contrasted with the more purely immanent ethics of Deleuze.

ETHICS OF IMMANENCE

For Deleuze, there is a strict distinction to be drawn between morality and ethics. This distinction is not the traditional one between the question of what one's duties and obligations are and the question of how one should live. Morality, in Deleuze's eyes, requires transcendence, while ethics is a purely immanent affair. In this, he draws from Nietzsche's critique of morality. The duties prescribed by morality are exterior to life and inimical to it. They are ways of condemning life rather than developing its possibilities. In this particular sense, the ethics of the other embraced by Levinas, Derrida, and others would constitute a transcendent morality. Even though the responsibility for the other is grounded in an immanent sphere of self or concept, it is nevertheless a submission to an other by which one is always necessarily condemned. To be sure, it is not the other itself that condemns one, but one's inability to realize one's obligation to the other. Nevertheless, condemned one is, and in precisely the way that Nietzsche finds objectionable in Judeo-Christian morality.

The ethical question facing Deleuze is that of how to develop a purely immanent morality. His answer presupposes an entire ontological view, one which we can only gloss here. In doing so, we might adopt the broad framework of one of his philosophical heroes: Spinoza. For Spinoza, the cosmos is conceived immanently. There is only one substance. Attributes are that substance under different perspectives, and modes are expressions of that substance. For Deleuze, what appears in the world are actualizations of a virtual realm of pure difference. Being is difference which is expressed in actual beings in much the same way that, for Spinoza, modes are expressions of substance.

This description may sound to those familiar with Martin Heidegger's thought like the positing of ontological difference between Being and beings. There is, however, a crucial departure from Heidegger in Deleuze's thought. Being as difference is *not* to be thought separate from the actuality it expresses. While the virtual field of difference expresses itself in actual beings, it remains coiled within the beings in which that expression occurs. The actual, then, while distinct from the virtual, does not exist apart from it. (This is also a departure from Spinoza's thought. Near the end of his magnum opus *Difference and Repetition*, Deleuze writes, "All that Spinozism need to do for the univocal to become an object of pure affirmation was to make substance turn around the modes.")[8]

This departure grounds Deleuze's ethical view. If the actual does not exist apart from the virtual field of difference that it expresses, that means that there are further powers of expression that animate any particular thing. Or, to put the point another way, a particular actualization of a virtual field of difference is not the only way in which it might be actualized. There is always more that can be expressed than has been expressed in any particular actualization.

What else can be expressed is uncertain. Virtual fields of difference do not reveal themselves in their specificity. They are fields of difference rather than identity, so we cannot grasp the expressions they are capable of in advance. Deleuze says that one of the fundamental lessons of Spinoza's thought is that *"We do not even know of what a body is capable."*[9] Moreover, since the virtual exists within the actual, its possible expressions are partially constrained by the context of actuality in which it has expressed itself.

However, what Deleuze is committed to is the idea that a given is only one actualization of the power of the virtual differential field for expression. An

[8] Deleuze 1994: 304.   [9] Deleuze 1992: 226.

immanent ethics will hinge on the idea that there is more that can be expressed than has been expressed. Moreover, ethical well-being will lie in the ability to express, while ethical poverty will lie in the blocking of expression. Referring once again to Spinoza, goodness occurs when a body has its powers of expression increased, while badness occurs when its powers of expression, its ability to act, are diminished. Diminishing the power of a body to act, to express in new and different ways its virtuality, can happen in at least two ways. One would be in taking the actual to be all there is, that is, in refusing or neglecting to recognize the actual as merely one expression of the virtual. Another would be in the embrace of a transcendence or transcendent set of values that condemns existence, thereby discouraging or blocking expression.

In this immanent ethics, we can see the influence of Nietzsche, particularly his distinction between active and reactive forces. Active forces are expressive. Deleuze defines an active force as a "force which goes to the limit of its power."[10] By contrast reactive forces "separate active force from what it can do."[11] Deleuze's immanent ethics, then, is an ethics of expression rather than conformity. It is also an ethics of creation and novelty. To put it in the Spinozist terms cited above, Deleuze's ethics is that of asking of what a body is capable.

A NOTE ON DELEUZE AND FOUCAULT

There is a bond between Deleuze's view of ethics and the normative underpinnings of the genealogical thought of Michel Foucault. To speak of Foucault's normative commitments is always a dicey affair, since he was notably coy when asked what those commitments were. In *Discipline and Punish* (1977), for example, Foucault traces the rise of what he calls discipline – the set of practices and institutions that reinforce our self-understanding in terms of normalization, i.e. the normal and the abnormal. He shows how our practices of self-understanding, especially through epistemic areas like psychology, has helped produce us as beings who think of ourselves in relation to an ideal of normality. And he further argues that such self-understanding also helps produce us as efficient workers in a capitalist system, for instance by conforming our actions to what is considered to be normal in such a system. And, although his language is often critical, he nowhere states explicitly the normative commitments he holds that are contravened by disciplinary practices.

For my own part, I believe that Foucault had some implicit normative commitments that would bring him in close contact with the ethical

---

[10] Deleuze 1983: 59 [11] Ibid., 57

(although not the political) views of liberal political philosophers – commitments to autonomy and equality. In seeking to show how psychological epistemic commitments that appear to be natural – such as the distinction between the normal and the abnormal or, in the first volume of his *History of Sexuality* (1978–1986), considering sexual desire to be an important aspect of who we are – are actually the legacy of a recent and contingent history, he suggests that we can mold ourselves differently from how we have been made. Inasmuch as there is an implicit critique of these moldings, there seems to be a normative commitment to the idea that we should be able to mold ourselves differently. Furthermore, inasmuch as he is also implicitly critical of capitalist social and economic relationships, he would seem to be committed to some form of equality.

These more nearly liberal commitments aside, there are at least two important points of contact between Deleuze's ethical view and Foucault's. First, one of the reasons Foucault had for being reticent to state his own normative commitments was that he believed it was not his job to prescribe the good for others. As Deleuze once commented in a conversation with Foucault, "You were the first – in your books and in the practical sphere – to teach us something fundamental: the indignity of speaking for others."[12] (The reader may have noted that this is itself a normative commitment, one that has ties to conceptions of autonomy.) Second, both Deleuze and Foucault recognized the necessity of experimentation. They both thought that one cannot be sure of what might become of one's actions, and therefore that the creation of new forms of life could only happen by means of experimenting. For Deleuze this necessity lies in the character of the virtual, while for Foucault it lies in the fact of historical contingency. Nevertheless, taking both of these ideas – the indignity of speaking for others and the necessity of experimentation – one can see the affinity of Foucault's views to an immanent ethics that would foster expression rather than condemnation or conformity, experimentation rather than obligation.

ETHICS OF EQUALITY

The work of Jacques Rancière and Alain Badiou, perhaps the two most significant living thinkers in recent French philosophy, could hardly be categorized as moral or ethical. In fact, both of them criticize what Rancière characterized as "the ethical turn" in French thought. This turn is

---

[12] Foucault and Deleuze 1980: 209.

associated with Levinas' focus upon the vulnerability of the other and more generally on the responsibility toward vulnerability as it appears in discourses as disparate as reflections on Nazism and human rights discussions.[13]

However, if Rancière and Badiou reject an ethics of the other, they also reject Deleuze's ethics of immanence. The weakness of his approach lies in its rejection of conflict as reactive in the Nietzschean sense in favor of an embrace of creativity that appears more a-political. To grasp this, we might use an analogy from the politics of the 1960s. The conflict between leftist groups like the Students for a Democratic Society and the hippie movement saw the former accusing the latter of just dropping out rather than militating for change, while the latter accused the former of simply opposing the system without any vision of a better or more peaceful society. On this analogy, Rancière and Badiou would be the SDS members and Deleuze the hippie, albeit a Nietzschean one.

For both Rancière and Badiou, most social arrangements are both hierarchical and exclusive. In particular, they exclude certain groups of people – immigrants are the most commonly used example – from participation in the social and political order. Rancière refers to these groups as the "part with no part."[14] Badiou, by contrast, appeals to the mathematics of set theory and in doing so refers to the excluded groups as a "void" within the count.[15] This might lead one to think that the political project ought to be one of inclusivity, of incorporating the excluded groups into the political order. This would be a form of equality, i.e. recognizing the equality of the excluded groups.

However, Rancière's and Badiou's views are more complex than that. The task of incorporation might be seen as a liberal one: the political order has failed to offer equal participation to particular groups, and so must extend recognition to them. This would lay the burden of political change on the political system itself. Both Rancière and Badiou, however, focus not upon the political order but upon the excluded groups. As Rancière puts the point, "political activity is always a mode of expression that undoes the perceptible divisions of the police order [the existing hierarchical order – my note] by implementing a basically heterogeneous assumption, that of a part of those who have no part, an assumption that, at the end of the day, itself demonstrates the sheer contingency of the order, the equality of any speaking being with any other speaking being."[16]

---

[13] On the "ethical turn," see esp. Rancière 2009 and Badiou 2002.
[14] Rancière 2004: 9 and elsewhere.   [15] This term appears prominently in Badiou 2006.
[16] Rancière 2004: 30.

Rancière and Badiou are theorists of political action as a "mode of expression." They offer ways of conceiving what grassroots political change looks like when it is taken from the point of view of the excluded themselves. For Rancière, this point of view, when it is democratic in character – which, to his mind, is the only time in which it is truly political – operates on the presupposition of equality. This does not require that people engaged in political action reflectively consider themselves to be acting out of this presupposition. It is only required that the action itself reflects such a presupposition.

Although Badiou's considerations on this matter are more elusive, since they are embedded in a complex ontological framework, he insists that he too holds political action to occur out of the presupposition of equality, writing "equality *is* politics, such that, *a contrario*, any in-egalitarian statement, whatever it be, is anti-political."[17] On this score, Badiou criticizes Rancière for embracing a more spontaneist politics that cannot see through a vision of equality because, among other problems, it fails to recognize the necessity of militants to carry forward struggle through a "fidelity" to the event of political challenge.[18]

The embrace of equality as a presupposition of political change marks a distinctive normative position in recent French thought. It contrasts with an ethics of the other in two related ways. First, it considers matters from the point of view of the excluded themselves. Rancière and Badiou theorize not from the point of view of the dominant (e.g. the host) but from that of the dominated (the refugee). Second, because of this their views emphasize expression rather than obligation. They are less concerned with what is owed to the other than with action that challenges the vulnerability of their situation.

On the other hand, their view contrasts with Deleuze's ethics of immanence in being oppositional or conflictual rather than focusing on what Deleuze sometimes calls "lines of flight." In saying this, however, we must be careful not to reduce their views simply to oppositional ones. It is not that their politics commends an opposition to an exclusive political order in the name of equality. That would make the politics parasitical on the order it opposes. Rather, in acting out of the presupposition of equality, such political action necessarily winds up in conflict with an exclusive political order. It

---

[17] Badiou 2006: 347.
[18] See Badiou's article, "Rancière and Apolitics," in Badiou 2005. However, Jeff Love and I have argued, *contra* Badiou, that while Rancière's politics is egalitarian, Badiou's is universalist but not necessarily egalitarian. See Love and May 2008.

challenges the political order *in its very nature*, because it presupposes something rejected by that order: the equality of everyone in it.

EVALUATIVE CONSIDERATIONS

By way of conclusion, it would be worth outlining some evaluative reflections on the views presented here. These reflections are not intended to be conclusive. Quite the opposite, they are meant to raise issues associated with the positions in order to further rather than foreclose reflection upon them.

Levinas' view suggests an intriguing intersection with the current emphasis on emotions in morality. His claim that we are oriented toward others through a primal sense of responsibility rather than a set of rules can be a corrective to moral theories that seem to detach us from our pre-discursive relations with others. On the other hand, there are potential difficulties with his approach. One derives from the same anti-intellectualism that is its strength. Since our responsibility toward the other is rooted in a pre-discursive realm, indeed in our very being, it seems to resist rational reflection, or, as mentioned above, moral discourse. To be sure, Levinas does not neglect the role of the "said." However, he predicates it on the saying, and ultimately on the face of the other. Because of this predication, it is unclear how the said can offer critical reflection on any particular saying, or, conversely, how the saying is supposed to decide between two conflicting saids. Levinas might rejoin here that the face of the other should guide all saids, but that in turn raises the question of why the fact of our sense of responsibility toward the other should be taken as an ethical datum rather than a meta-ethical fact.

Derrida's view is a bit more puzzling. The inability for hospitality to be absolute grounds his deconstructive view of hospitality; but why should hospitality have to be absolute in order to be hospitality at all? Derrida's methodology here is one that is common to many of his writings. He shows that a term, taken to the limit, cannot sustain itself. It must appeal to its excluded opposite. But one might ask whether terms have to be taken to their limit in this way in order to function as the terms they are. This question leads to Derrida's reflections on language, most of which are rooted in his early writings and which set the stage for his later ethical and political reflections. It may be that the later reflections stand or fall with the plausibility of his view of semantics.

Deleuze's ethical view offers a vitality that often seems to go missing in the more sober moral approaches from which he takes his distance. Emphasizing as it does the role of creativity and novelty, and suggesting their potential emergence everywhere, his ethics turns us from the question of how to conform our lives to pre-given rules and toward the question of what we might make of ourselves. It encourages experimentation rather than conformity. However, the other side of this coin is that it offers no guidance for which kinds of experimentation might be enriching and which inimical or even egregious. It seems hard to justify any behavior or projects, individual or collective, solely on the basis of values of creativity and novelty. Not all creations are worthy ones, and if not, it may be difficult to avoid the return of the transcendent perspective of morality that Deleuze seeks to overcome. Alternatively, there may be a way of integrating a more nuanced moral perspective into the immanent view in which the values of creativity and novelty have their root. That would involve a re-thinking of some of the character of the virtual that Deleuze has introduced.

Rancière's and Badiou's embrace of equality are difficult to assess apart from the larger political views in which each finds its place. And, as we saw, their views are not entirely convergent. However, a common commitment of their thought is that equality is enacted through bottom-up rather than top-down political action. To paraphrase Martin Luther King, equality is not given; it is taken. Indeed, it is not even taken so much as it is created through the action itself. Seeing political action this way is promising, and reflects a number of contemporary political movements from the Arab Spring to Occupy. In fact, one might argue that most political change comes through pressure from below, and that in this sense Rancière's and Badiou's placement of equality in grassroots movements rather than in liberal institutional structures locates it in the right place.

However, one might also ask whether their views do not neglect the importance of institutional structures as guarantors of the equality that has been created or enacted. Might it be that equality must be thought not only at the level of action but also at that of institution in order that its appearance not be a passing phenomenon? And might this in turn require that an adequate political theory of equality be one that is not only bottom-up but also top-down? If this is right, then Rancière's and Badiou's embrace of equality must be supplemented in their political views with a thought of equality that is sustained, even if not offered, by a more top-down institutional structure.

BIBLIOGRAPHY

An asterisk denotes secondary literature especially suitable for further reading.

Badiou, Alain. 2002 *Ethics: An Essay on the Understanding of Evil*, trans. Peter Hallward. London: Verso Books

Badiou, Alain. 2005 *Metapolitics*, trans. Jason Barker. London: Verso

Badiou, Alain. 2006 *Being and Event*, trans. Oliver Feltham. New York: Continuum

Deleuze, Gilles. 1983 *Nietzsche and Philosophy*, trans. Janis Tomlinson. New York: Columbia University Press

Deleuze, Gilles. 1992 *Expressionism in Philosophy: Spinoza*, trans. Martin Joughin. Cambridge: Zone Books

Deleuze, Gilles. 1994 *Difference and Repetition*, trans. Paul Patton. New York: Columbia University Press

Derrida, Jacques. 1978 *Writing and Difference*, trans. Alan Bass. University of Chicago Press

Derrida, Jacques. 2000 *Of Hospitality*, trans. Rachel Bowlby. Stanford University Press

Foucault, Michel 1977. *Discipline and Punish: The Birth of the Prison*, trans. Alan Sheridan. New York: Pantheon.

Foucault, Michel 1978–1986. *The History of Sexuality*, trans. Robert Hurley. New York: Pantheon.

Foucault, Michel and Deleuze, Gilles. 1980 "Intellectuals and Power," in Foucault, Michel. *Language, Counter-Memory, Practice*, ed. Donald Bouchard. Ithaca, NY: Cornell University Press

Gutting, G. 2013 *Thinking the Impossible: French Philosophy since 1960*. Oxford University Press*

Levinas, Emmanuel. 1969 *Totality and Infinity: An Essay on Exteriority*, trans. Alphonso Lingis. Pittsburgh, PA: Duquesne University Press

Levinas, Emmanuel. 1985 *Ethics and Infinity: Conversations with Philippe Nemo*, trans. Richard Cohen. Pittsburgh, PA: Duquesne University Press

Levinas, Emmanuel. 1997 *Otherwise than Being, or Beyond Essence*, trans. Alphonso Lingis. Pittsburgh, PA: Duquesne University Press

Love, Jeff and May, Todd. 2008 "From Universality to Equality: Badiou's Critique of Rancière," *Symposium*, 12 (2) (Autumn): 51–69

Lyotard, Jean-François. 1988 *The Differend: Phrases in Dispute*, trans. Georges Van Den Abbeele. Minneapolis, MN: University of Minnesota Press.

Rancière, Jacques. 2004 *Disagreement*, trans. Julie Rose. Minneapolis, MN: University of Minnesota Press

Rancière, Jacques. 2009 *Aesthetics and its Discontents*, trans. Steve Corcoran. London: Polity Press

50

Wittgenstein's Ethics and Wittgensteinian Moral Philosophy

DAVID LEVY

Ludwig Wittgenstein (1889–1951) had no ethical theory. It is probably correct to say he had little or no specific moral philosophy either. Certainly, there was no ethical theory he endorsed in line with or as a consequence of his work in philosophical logic or language. Nonetheless, Wittgenstein was a man marked by a serious and personal concern with the ethical challenge posed by life. The evidence is in his diaries and letters. Those who knew him testify to the same. Indeed, these sources sketch a picture of Wittgenstein as striving to meet the demand of his own stringent ethical principles, especially with regard to being honest with himself and others about the conduct of his life.

FORMATIVE INFLUENCES

Wittgenstein's philosophical work in logic and language was shaped by his response to Gottlob Frege and formed by his study with Bertrand Russell. He was, however, for the most part ignorant of the history of philosophy and never made a systematic study of other philosophers. This was true for moral philosophy too. Wittgenstein's views of ethics and moral philosophy were not original. They developed under several cultural and intellectual influences. He had a schoolboy's interest in Schopenhauer that supplied a framework for his earliest recorded ethical reflections – especially his focus on the will – though he later shed much of this influence. While serving in the Austro-Hungarian Imperial Army during the First World War, Wittgenstein was devoted to Tolstoy's *The Gospel in Brief.* Tolstoy's book intensified Wittgenstein's prior orientation to a cultural Christianity familiar from his upbringing in the upper echelons of Viennese society. The images of spiritual and religious life to which Wittgenstein was drawn throughout his life were invariably Christian. Wittgenstein was in this and many respects culturally conservative. His Jewish ancestry was, by contrast, alien to him personally and to his thinking.

Identifying Wittgenstein as a practicing Christian or as a Christian adherent is a mistake, notwithstanding his attraction to the cultural inheritance of Christianity. While Wittgenstein often wished to yield to fate and accept his worldly powerlessness, he was not drawn to ideas of personal salvation received through divine grace. Instead, Wittgenstein conceived a person's life as a standing, personal demand to live a life of worth or character – upright and decent – rather than a life squandered. This idea was probably an influence of the work of Otto Weininger on the teenaged Wittgenstein. Weininger argued for a view of life in which individual character, broadly conceived, was of utmost importance. In later life, Wittgenstein continued to esteem the intellectual force of Weininger's views without endorsing them as a whole. The works of Kierkegaard were probably also familiar to Wittgenstein from his teenage years. Unlike Weininger's thought, the effect of Kierkegaard's thinking on Wittgenstein did not wane but deepened during Wittgenstein's life, especially in relation to how faith is exhibited in the conduct of life. Thus the formative influences on Wittgenstein's ethical views were predominantly religious and spiritual. These Wittgenstein translated into his own ethical focus on living a life of worth, a decent life.

TEXTS

Wittgenstein's writings on ethics are very few, with even fewer conceived for an audience of readers. Short remarks – none more than a page – are scattered among writings on other topics. Around a dozen pages in total, these were collected as mixed remarks for inclusion in *Culture and Value*, published posthumously.[1] *Tractatus Logico-Philosophicus*, the sole book published by Wittgenstein in his lifetime, contains three pages on ethics.[2] These pages are a selection from around a dozen pages written in 1916, printed in *Notebooks 1914–1916*.[3] Around another dozen pages are found in some of Wittgenstein's diaries from 1931 and 1937.[4] Records of Wittgenstein's remarks appear in several published personal records of conversations with

---

[1] Wittgenstein 1998. [2] Wittgenstein 1981.
[3] Wittgenstein 1979. For exegesis of Wittgenstein's extensive pre-*Tractatus* ethical writings see Levy 2007.
[4] Wittgenstein 2003.

Wittgenstein, but even adding these there are fewer than fifty pages of Wittgenstein's writings on ethics.

It is notable that Wittgenstein claimed that the point of his sole book – *Tractatus Logico-Philosophicus* – was ethical. Indeed he claimed that the book consisted of two parts, one written and the other unwritten. The unwritten part was the important one insofar as it defined the ethical by showing what remained unsaid in the written part.

The sole sustained work on ethics by Wittgenstein is the text he prepared in 1929 for a lecture he gave to The Heretics, an intellectual club in Cambridge. The Lecture on Ethics survives in several drafts, the longest being twenty-one handwritten pages.[5] In the lecture he claimed to speak personally and from the heart, a point he repeated in subsequent discussions of the lecture. There is every reason to suppose that the revised text of the lecture reflects Wittgenstein's considered view of the nature of ethics and moral philosophy, albeit constrained by the format of a public lecture of fixed length.

MANIFEST VIEW

Conjuring a view of ethics or a moral philosophy that one could attribute to Wittgenstein on a sound basis is not easy. The dearth of Wittgenstein's work on ethics is one obstacle. To this must be added a further, formidable obstacle. Wittgenstein maintained that talk of ethics was nonsensical and most of what was spoken by moralists was empty chatter. Ethics, Wittgenstein thought, was unsayable. Therefore, attributing views on ethics to Wittgenstein is an uncertain undertaking.

The *Tractatus*, being approved for publication by Wittgenstein, is a good starting point. Three terse pages with scattered supplementation, the view of ethics in the *Tractatus* revolves around three theses: the valuelessness of facts, unworldliness of the subject, and powerlessness of the will. The same theses are also focal in Wittgenstein's discussion of ethics in his wartime notebooks. The theses underwrite a view in which ethics is radically personal and independent of actions and worldly happenings.

The subject of the *Tractatus* is the logic of language, viz. the conditions under which signs or propositions are meaningful. The brief discussion of ethics in §6.4 addresses the subject of the book by asserting that there can be no ethical propositions, because all propositions are of equal value. Thus,

---

[5] Wittgenstein 2014.

without ethical propositions, ethics is unsayable, i.e. nonsense. And just this is the overt conclusion of the section, that ethics is not within meaningful language. The argument for this conclusion seems to depend on two claims. The first – central to the view of language in the *Tractatus* – is that when any meaningful proposition is understood it is understood by picturing a state of affairs that could be true or false, i.e. obtain or not. The second claim is that anything of genuine value must always have been and always will be of value. Value is thus eternal, not accidental or momentary. If courage is valuable, then it is always valuable regardless of circumstances or luck in how things turn out. If these two claims are accepted, then it is clear why there are no ethical propositions. Meaningful propositions picture states of affairs that could be false. An ethical proposition could never picture a state of affairs that could be false. For if it did, then it could picture something of value that was not of value at that time (because false), thereby contradicting the eternal nature of value.

The idea that we cannot speak of ethics as we speak of ordinary things is one that Wittgenstein kept long after the *Tractatus*. To put it another way, whatever conditions make ordinary language meaningful, they are not the conditions that would make ethical language meaningful. Wittgenstein sometimes elaborated this by indicating that ethics spoke of something "higher" than the ordinary happenings of people's lives. Sometimes this contrast was made out as between the natural and the supernatural or mystical. This in turn seems to have been underpinned by Wittgenstein's conviction that whatever did or did not happen in the world was itself of no value. Facts were valueless and there was no basis intrinsic to facts for separating those of putative value from the rest. So whether some facts came to obtain could not of itself be of ethical significance. This does not imply there is no value, only that it is not to be found in facts, states of affairs, or how things happen to be. And insofar as ordinary language speaks solely of the factual or natural – as Wittgenstein held – it cannot speak of value or the ethical.

Insisting that the factual happenings of the world are valueless can be understood as insisting that value is dependent on people creating value. That would not be an exceptional claim, but Wittgenstein makes it one by dividing moral subjects – i.e. people – from the ordinary world. People's bodies are obviously part of the world as more facts, e.g. they are constituted of physical stuff, spatially located, subject to causal law, etc. However, a person is not solely her body, she is also a subject, viz. an experiencing subject, with thoughts and attitudes. No doubt one is *dependent* on her body for the perspective in which her experiences appear, for example for what is in her field of view. Nonetheless, Wittgenstein claims people, as *subjects*, are not parts of the world. Persons are in this sense unworldly. They transcend the natural world of fact. The significance for ethics is direct because Wittgenstein also claims that it is subjects who are the sources of value or the ethical. Yet, since subjects are not part of the world and therefore not among the worldly facts, language cannot be used meaningfully to speak of the subject or of the relation between subject and value. The ethical remains thus unsayable.

It is a common thought that people are integral to value and ethics. Wittgenstein likely had a further reason for thinking that people were the source of value, by which he meant that the ethical (predicates) were carried or borne by individuals, i.e. it is people who are brave or cowardly. In the exercise of his will, a person is free. What a person wills is not something that just happens to him. His hopes, dreams, wishes, attitudes, and intentions are his own because he wills them into being or endorses them. If he did not do so, they would be inauthentic or insincere, because someone else's. So what a person wills is not an accident. Value too, for Wittgenstein, as noted above, is not accidental. Thus, what people will is a well-founded source of value, since neither is accidental, unlike happenings in the world. There is a potential problem with this picture. If my will changed the world – by my actions – then there would be something in the world that had not happened by chance, but by my willing, which is no accident. If my will is the source of value, then the effects of my action in the world could be happenings with value, in contrast to those that were mere chance. In which case, *some* facts would not be valueless, contradicting Wittgenstein's insistence on the value-lessness of facts.

Wittgenstein avoids this problem by allowing that the will is powerless to change the world. As he put it, it is always the gift of chance when what I will to happen does happen. I cannot necessitate its happening. This is easy to accept when my wish for an improbable event, like winning the lottery, does happen. My wishing did not make it so. It is harder to accept when what is willed is my own action. However, Wittgenstein observes that even in these cases, whether my action succeeds in its aim is contingent on no impediment arising. Even something as simple as raising my arm depends on my arm being unbound or its muscles undamaged, yet neither condition is mine alone to will, e.g. someone may restrain me. Thus even the simplest worldly happenings, such as the movement of my body, are a gift of chance. I cannot necessitate its happening, as I can my wishes or hopes or attitudes. We arrive at the conclusion that subjects are the source of value because what they will is not mere happening, but subjects are powerless in the world, so value and the ethical is still not in the world. Ethics is still unsayable.

Wittgenstein's conception of philosophy, which changed little during his life, was that philosophy cleared confusions arising from misunderstandings of language. If ethics is unsayable, then moral philosophy can have just one self-negating application: to clear confusion, by showing that language apparently about ethics is not.

Wittgenstein's view of ethics and moral philosophy in this general summary did not change, even as the underpinnings and details of his views of language, logic and philosophy did. Moral philosophy is used here to denote reflections on good and evil and the words related to them, such as courage, patience or vice. Ethics is used to mean systematic claims about the constitution of right conduct and value.

LATENT VIEW

The view of ethics found in the *Tractatus* is manifest, notwithstanding the gnomic exposition Wittgenstein gives. Wittgenstein's 1929 lecture on ethics,[6] a decade after the *Tractatus*, is superficially similar insofar as it also argues that the ethical is unsayable. Much of the lecture argues that language with an ethical or absolute sense is nonsense – so much so that many have thought that is its main point. However, *latent* in the lecture are clues about what motivates Wittgenstein's ethical view and his antipathy to ethical language.

Wittgenstein's motivation in the lecture is to isolate ethics from the realm of fact, as he did in the *Tractatus*. This is itself motivated by his demand that ethics be cut off from explanation. Wittgenstein, in his lecture, rejects anything that purports to explain ethical experiences or their descriptions in language. Wittgenstein insisted that someone misunderstood the nature of ethics if she thought it could be explained, described or analyzed. His principal purpose in his lecture is to warn his audience against the false hope that an analysis, description or explanation of ethics could make it less personally demanding.[7] Fundamentally, Wittgenstein conceives of ethics as a personal challenge that must not be evaded. The challenge of resisting vice, seeking worth and finding peace in one's life must be met solely by recourse to one's will and virtue. Seeking the authority of explanation or the control afforded by applying practical techniques like the logical analysis of

---

[6] Wittgenstein 2014.   [7] The purpose of the lecture is discussed in detail in Levy 2014.

language is, for Wittgenstein, seeking to evade the personal responsibility for the ethical content of one's life.

Explanations, Wittgenstein thought, occur with matters of fact by placing facts within the natural order of things. Language describes facts. Without language, there could not be explanations, including scientific explanations. If there is no ethical language, there can be no science of ethics. Individuals are then left with no possibility for speaking about ethics, except, as it were, in the first person, i.e. with no claim to general validity or import. Hence, to maintain focus on individual responsibility and authority, for Wittgenstein the ethical must remain unsayable in ordinary language.

Despite the undeniable importance that ethics had for Wittgenstein, it is striking that his philosophical work contains so little about ethics, especially within the prolific output of the last two decades of his life. There is, for example, no discussion of ethics in his late masterwork *Philosophical Investigations*.[8] It has been suggested that this apparent contrast is explained by supposing that, for Wittgenstein, philosophy itself was a kind of ethical endeavor. If philosophy were itself an ethical undertaking, perhaps Wittgenstein had no need for any additional ethical or moral philosophy. There is little doubt that Wittgenstein conceived philosophy as demanding many virtues, especially honesty. However, a better explanation for the dearth of ethics in the *Investigations* is that Wittgenstein's later philosophy of language allowed him to see that ethical language might be used for purposes other than describing or analyzing, such as for arresting someone's attention. This could be sufficient *moral philosophy* for Wittgenstein. His view of *ethics*, by contrast, eschewed philosophy's goal of systematizing general experience, thereby concentrating attention on the individual struggle to live a decent life.

WITTGENSTEIN'S INFLUENCE

Wittgensteinian moral philosophers have been little influenced by Wittgenstein's negligible moral philosophy or the remarks on ethics in the *Tractatus*. Instead these philosophers received their appellation by the possibilities they saw in Wittgenstein's philosophy of language for countering two trends prevailing in post-war moral philosophy. The first trend began with Jeremy Bentham but received a definitive expression in Henry Sidgwick's work.[9] Moral thinking, Sidgwick claimed, should be conceived as applying an

---

[8] Wittgenstein 2009.   [9] Sidgwick 1981.

impersonal method, like an expert technique or a science, to produce moral judgments about what to do and what is obligatory. The second trend emerged from G.E. Moore's shift in the focus of moral philosophy to the analysis of the logical form of moral judgments, not the content of moral judgments.[10] Both trends tended, in the view of the Wittgensteinians, to present a distorted picture of the phenomena that give us the very idea of morality and the experiences of someone who has felt herself subject to the claim of morality. An aspect of this distorted picture was the emphasis on judgment as the principal or exclusive exemplar of moral thought and response. Insisting that the constituents of moral judgments were always one of a few key concepts – e.g. ought, right, best, duty – exacerbated the distortion. By contrast, Wittgensteinian moral philosophers thought that many moral responses are neither expressions of nor analyzable as moral judgments about, e.g., what ought to be done or what duty requires.

The Wittgensteinians' animus was stoked by opposition to two ethical attitudes they believed the prevailing trends legitimated. The first attitude is that moral response or decision-making can yield to the application of a distinctively moral expertise or method. This attitude implies that morality can be *impersonal* insofar as personal responsibility for one's moral responses can be deferred to the authority of experts or an expert method. Indeed, a possible consequence of this attitude is that morality *should* be thus impersonal. But morality is personal, insisted Wittgensteinians, and an impersonal view leaches the seriousness from moral challenges, putting them on par with difficulties in engineering or accounting. The second objectionable attitude is taking the subject of morality, viz. good, as something mundane. This attitude takes many forms. Non-cognitivism, the view that moral judgments express attitudes rather than asserting possible truths, implies that good (and evil) are not real in the sense in which other things known cognitively are. For many non-cognitivists, statements about good are neither possibly true nor false; or, if they are so, it is in a sense (e.g. "quasi-true") distinguished from the ordinary by an essential link to personal dispositions. Good is thereby mundane because conventional, on the first, simpler view; or not a genuine impediment because limited to *actual* human dispositions on the second. In a similar vein, ethical naturalism, as the view that moral judgments are also judgments about what conduces to ends good for the kind of creature humans are, makes good mundane (or natural) in the sense that good is *self-serving* of broadly human ends. Against this,

---

[10] Moore 1993.

Wittgensteinian moral philosophers have been disposed to insist that good worthy of the name is not self-serving but transcendent, in a sense often understood through Plato, Simone Weil, or Judeo-Christian religious sensibility.

Certainly Wittgenstein would have been congenial to views of ethics with concomitant animosities and philosophical concerns toward prevailing trends in post-war moral philosophy. However, it is untenable to assert that his followers were carrying on his putative work in moral philosophy. Indeed, Wittgenstein would not likely have agreed that his conception of philosophy's aims – removing confusion, logical perspicuity or therapy – applied to the moral challenges arising in a human life.

WITTGENSTEINIAN MORAL PHILOSOPHY

Wittgenstein's *Philosophical Investigations* offered Wittgensteinian moral philosophers two principal resources with which to articulate a moral philosophy rival to that which predominated then and now. First, Wittgenstein's account of language emphasized that language is practical – viz. that it is used within human practices – with more purposes than judging, stating or describing. Admitting the plurality in the uses of language eases the pressure to analyze all moral responses as forms of judgment constituted from a limited set of general or abstract moral concepts, e.g. "ought." Moral language and expressions of moral response can instead take any form, using any language, for any purpose provided there is a practice in which language so used is intelligible as regarding moral matters. In this way, judgment is dethroned as the sovereign paradigm of moral thought and the supreme object of moral philosophical analysis. No doubt the sense of what is intelligible as moral will vary: Taking a moral approach could be understood as adopting "an attitude to a soul,"[11] or some concepts – such as pity, grief, love or remorse – might emerge as delimiting the contestable borders of what is intelligibly moral.

Wittgenstein's second resource lay in the philosophical conception of reality indicated in the *Investigations*. The conception is realist to the extent that the character of reality is independent of human agreements or conventions. For Wittgenstein, meaning in the linguistic sense was existent and real. There was a fact about whether some sounds made by some hominid at some time were meaningful. Facts about meaning were not facts of another kind, e.g. scientific

[11] Wittgenstein 2009: II.iv (Philosophy of Psychology – a Fragment §22).

facts about information transmission. Wittgenstein's realism about meaning was thus non-reducible and non-natural. However language is an integral part of the developed human species such that meaning is also dependent on actual human sensibilities, though not conventions. In short, Wittgenstein's picture of the reality of meaning made it independent of human agreements or purposes, yet not independent of actual human practices. The Wittgensteinian moral philosophers' insight was to see that Wittgenstein's account of the reality of meaning could also work for the reality of good. Realism about a transcendent moral good that was conditioned by, but not subservient to, human sensibilities undermined the motives for metamorphosing morality into something mundane or self-serving.

Taken together these resources were sufficient to dispute the prevailing moral philosophy with an alternative. The alternative indicated did not confront the impersonal attitude to ethics though, since Wittgenstein's picture of reality and practice did not provide an obvious role for the individual moral subject. Someone might yet hope to evade moral responsibility for her responses to moral challenges by deferring to the authority of prevailing practice. As it were, she would seek to follow the rules of the practice rather than making any assessment or interpretation of what the challenge demanded. She could have no personal investment in her response but simply do as the rules required. For the Wittgensteinians, the absence of a personal investment – at least of one's own authority – nullified the moral spirit of the response. Making morality personal required something of the individual.

A place for the individual was found in the observation that practices in Wittgenstein's sense were not static, but depended for their persistence and evolution on individual practitioners. Indeed, Wittgenstein simultaneously held that all practices were rule-governed and that every instance of following a rule was not fully determined by any representation of that rule. That meant that every time someone intended to follow a rule, she was also making a partial determination of the rule. Individuals followed rules, but they also extended them to cover new cases, or revised them, on their own *authority*. Determinations ultimately must be on one's own authority for rules are not self-determining nor is there an ultimate technique – e.g. rules for following rules – for determination. The dynamic character of rules and their dependence on individuals for ongoing determinations left the persistent possibility of irresolvable disputes. For rules governing a practice like chess, disagreements in determinations of the rules could mean that two people could no longer play chess together. For morality, with disputes about, e.g., pity, love or remorse, the import is in whether someone *can* interrelate with another person. The individual, in her determination of practice, in what she finds irresolvable in dispute, partially limits the practice by what she can tolerate, find intelligible, or respect. In short, she partially forms the extent to which we can live together – the very concern Plato advertised for philosophy.[12] Thus is morality made personal.

WITTGENSTEINIAN ANTI-THEORY

Inspired by Wittgenstein's philosophy, sharing something of his ethical outlook, Wittgensteinian moral philosophers offer a broad front with which to confront prevailing moral philosophy. For the most part, moral philosophers outside the Wittgensteinian tradition have responded with disinterest. There are several explanations. Wittgensteinian moral philosophy, like Wittgenstein's philosophy, is a philosophy that is anti-theory. It eschews the general and the picture of reasoning this implies by emphasizing the particular and the variety of our modes of engagement with it – any of which might be called moral. This is shown in an emphasis on examples; the limits to explanation; the importance of undeliberated responses; and on a limited relativism between cultures and individuals. Naturally this fails to engage ethical *theorists*. More, Wittgensteinian moral philosophy is anti-reductive and anti-non-cognitivist. So non-cognitivists are disengaged, while many cognitivists, being also reductivists, are similarly unresponsive. By denying the centrality of judgment, Wittgensteinian moral philosophy rejects meta-ethical theorizing. Similarly they reject normative ethical theorizing, by denying that some terms – e.g. right or good – are central. This leaves little common ground.

The difference between the groups is also one of attitude, perhaps even moral distance. By rejecting ethical theory and by making all language a possible vehicle for the expression of one's moral being, Wittgensteinian moral philosophy is never personally uncommitted morally. It is for this reason that some see philosophy itself as a *kind* of moral endeavor. If, by contrast, a philosopher believes that her theoretical commitments about ethics do not already imply personal moral commitments, she may not react well when told the contrary.

PEOPLE

The description of Wittgensteinian moral philosophers and moral philosophy above suggests a unity or a school with agreed tenets. This is a false picture. It

---

[12] Plato, *Euthyphro*, 7b6–7c10.

would be better to describe clusters of like-minded thinkers, carrying forward related and overlapping ideas, with differing emphases. If there were a school it would be the so-called "Swansea School" in Wales centered around Wittgenstein's friend Rush Rhees, at its height from 1951 until at least 1965. It comprised initially Rhees, Peter Winch, Roy Holland and J.R. Jones. Later members included D.Z. Phillips, H.O. Mounce, R.W. Beardsmore and Ilham Dilman. Members of the school influenced philosophers active later such as Raimond Gaita, Lars Hertzberg, David Cockburn and Cora Diamond. They in turn passed the baton to the next generation. The unrelated and original influence of Stanley Cavell is undeniably important as well as of sometime fellow travellers such as John McDowell, Alasdair MacIntyre and Sabina Lovibond.

BIBLIOGRAPHY

An asterisk denotes secondary literature especially suitable for further reading.

Crary, A., 2009, *Beyond Moral Judgment*. Cambridge, MA: Harvard University Press.*

Gaita, R., 2004, *Good and Evil: An Absolute Conception*, rev. 2nd edn. London: Routledge.*

Holland, R.F., 1980, *Against Empiricism: On Education, Epistemology and Value*. Oxford: Blackwell.*

Levy, D.K., 2007, "Wittgenstein's Early Writings on Ethics," in Wittgenstein 2007: 19–51.

Levy, D.K., 2014, "The Content of a Lecture on Ethics," in Wittgenstein 2014: 1–41.

Moore, G.E., 1993, *Principia Ethica*, 2nd edn. Cambridge University Press.

Phillips, D.Z., 1992, *Interventions in Ethics*. Basingstoke: Macmillan.*

Rhees, R., 1999, *Moral Questions*, ed. D.Z. Phillips. London: Palgrave Macmillan.*

Sidgwick, H., 1981, *The Methods of Ethics*. Indianapolis, IN: Hackett.

Wittgenstein, L., 1979, *Notebooks, 1914–1916*, 2nd edn, ed. G.H. von Wright and G.E.M. Anscombe. Oxford: Blackwell.

Wittgenstein, L., 1981, *Tractatus Logico-Philosophicus*, trans. C.K. Ogden. London: Routledge & Kegan Paul.

Wittgenstein, L., 1998, *Culture and Value: A Selection from the Posthumous Remains*, rev. 2nd edn with English translation, ed. G.H. von Wright, H. Nyman and A. Pichler, trans. P. Winch. Oxford: Blackwell.

Wittgenstein, L., 2003, *Ludwig Wittgenstein: Public and Private Occasions*, ed. J. Klagge and A. Nordmann. Lanham, MD: Rowman & Littlefield.

Wittgenstein, L., 2007, *Lecture on Ethics: Introduction, Interpretation and Complete Text*, ed. E. Zamuner, E.V.D. Lascio and D.K. Levy. Macerata: Quodlibet.

Wittgenstein, L., 2009, *Philosophical Investigations*, rev. 4th edn with English translation, ed. P.M.S. Hacker and J. Schulte, trans. G.E.M. Anscombe, P.M.S. Hacker and J. Schulte. Oxford: Wiley-Blackwell.

Wittgenstein, L., 2014, *Lecture on Ethics*, ed. E. Zamuner, E.V.D. Lascio and D.K. Levy. Oxford: Wiley-Blackwell.

51

Anti-Theory: Anscombe, Foot and Williams

SIMON ROBERTSON

'Anti-theory' in the context of ethics is a negative and methodological stance. It concerns how *not* to think about ethical matters – namely, in terms of *ethical theory*. This chapter traces its development across twentieth-century analytic ethics. Although it may overstate matters to claim that there has been an anti-theory 'school' as such, anti-theory leanings and styles of philosophizing are exhibited by some of the century's most influential ethical thinkers – notably, Elizabeth Anscombe, Philippa Foot and Bernard Williams, culminating in Williams' thoroughgoing anti-theory treatise *Ethics and the Limits of Philosophy*[1] (other possible luminaries include Iris Murdoch, Annette Baier, Charles Taylor and Alasdair MacIntyre). To many minds, anti-theory has had its heyday. However, it should be of more than merely historical interest. For not only have anti-theorists wrought significant changes to the moral-philosophical landscape, there is a growing sense that many of the deeper issues they exposed remain unresolved. As well as offering an overview of anti-theory's evolution, the chapter indicates some of those outstanding issues.

WHAT IS 'ANTI-THEORY'?

Four preliminary remarks. First, anti-theory is a skeptical outlook. But its skepticism need not be about *ethics* itself or *theory* per se. Indeed, anti-theorists typically agree that ethical issues are important, that there are ethical truths about which we can have knowledge, and that theories outside the ethical domain can play crucial roles in understanding ethical matters. Its critical focus, rather, is *ethical theory* – an approach to ethical enquiry that seeks a systematizing account of correct ethical thought and practice. Second, although a methodological and negative stance, anti-theory is motivated by *substantive* worries and a

[1] Williams 1985.

positive agenda. Anti-theorists are concerned with how ethical theories impede ethical understanding; and they believe that thinking about ethical matters in ways not distorted by inappropriate forms of theorizing will help us understand ethical life better. Third, their primary target is *substantive, first-order* ethical theory. Nonetheless, anti-theorists also engage critically with the conceptual frameworks via which these theories are articulated and the foundational assumptions they rest on. Fourth, there is unlikely to be a philosophically-neutral way to characterize 'theory' or 'anti-theory' in ethics. Any such characterization will reflect deeper substantive conceptions of what correct ethical thinking involves and what a theory in this domain can or should do; moreover, the distinction itself has become increasingly blurred in light of recent (e.g. virtue-based and particularist) views on these issues. Fortunately, for the purpose of sketching anti-theory's development we won't need a watertight definition. To help set up the basic contrast I'll first distinguish various conceptions of 'ethics' and 'ethical theory', and then outline some central motifs animating anti-theory.

In its broadest sense, the ethical sphere encompasses the whole domain of normative and evaluative thought as it bears on *how one should live* and what *a good life* involves. On a narrower conception, it concerns how relations between people should be *regulated*. Following Williams (1985: ch. 1, 1995e: 241) I'll here adopt the narrower view, though an important issue will be how the two connect. Modifying Williams' own account slightly (1985: 72–4), let's characterize an ethical *theory* thus:

> An ethical theory is an account of ethical thought and practice, which delivers (a) a *general test* for assessing the correctness of ethical claims, and/or (b) a *systematic* account of the basic ethical concepts and considerations via which ethical claims are appropriately assessed.

Theories that deliver (a) also deliver (b). We might call these theories 'rigorist', the most notable being standard consequentialist and Kantian theories. Some accounts deliver only (b), however, including various forms of deontological pluralism and virtue ethics for which ethical assessment is not amenable to a general codifiable test but instead requires the exercise of rational intuition or practical wisdom. It can be disputed whether these are 'theories'. Certainly, they lie at the less rigorist end of the theoretical spectrum. Nonetheless, they do bear some of the same theorizing hallmarks as rigorist theories. For that reason, there is a point to labeling them 'theories' of a 'looser' sort. Either way, thoroughgoing anti-theorists object to both (a) and (b).

The most rigorist ethical theories are those associated with a system of thought that many anti-theorists pejoratively label 'morality'. Morality, in this technical sense, is a specific form of ethical outlook structured through a particular notion of *obligation*. On most views, moral obligations have a special kind of *normative authority* and hence importance, because they are both *overriding* and *categorical*: they specify 'oughts', understood as conclusive requirements that override any competing reasons to act; and they are categorical in that you ought to do what the obligation specifies irrespective of whether doing so serves or conflicts with your own subjective desires, ends, interests, projects, evaluative commitments and the like. (For convenience I'll use Williams' term 'motive' [1981d] to cover all such elements amongst a person's motivational dispositions.) It follows that moral obligations are *universal* in scope, in the sense that no one falls outside their jurisdiction merely on grounds that doing what they specify conflicts with one's motives. Moral theories are 'structured through' this concept in several ways. The sphere of moral obligation is the sphere of morally right and wrong action (this chapter treats these interdefinably); and moral thought is directed towards establishing *whether* actions are morally obligatory (i.e. right, wrong, permissible, etc.). For those moral theories that deliver a general test, the test's primary role is to assess the correctness of claims about the moral status of actions. That in turn yields what many take to be the centerpiece of moral theory – a *criterion of right action*: a general criterion for testing and explaining, in an informative and comprehensive way, whether actions are morally right or wrong. Even looser moral theories are organized around an account of the substantive considerations that go into explaining whether you have a moral obligation. Both sorts of theories thereby treat obligation as central.

The primary target for anti-theorists has been obligation-centered moral theory, especially consequentialist and Kantian theories. Much of the following discussion therefore focuses on these, though as we will see some anti-theorists (notably Williams) cast their net wider. (To help keep matters clear, I'll use 'ethical theory' to denote any account satisfying either [a] or [b] in the above characterization, and use 'moral theory' when the express target is obligation-centered theories.) Anti-theorists' basic concern is that ethical (or at least moral) theories systemically distort ethical understanding.[2] This is not just an academic

---

[2] Anti-theory objections can be cast via different modalities: that ethical theory is *undesirable* (because inimical to ethical understanding, say), *unnecessary* (because sound ethical thinking can be achieved without it), or *impossible* (if its constitutive aims cannot be realized). In practice, though, it is often difficult to distinguish these sharply – depending on, say, whether the possibility of a theory is itself subject to avoiding relevantly undesirable features. But I'll leave it to the reader to consider these wider issues.

Anti-Theory: Anscombe, Foot and Williams

worry over how philosophers misconstrue an intellectual topic. It extends to how people quite generally, were they to think and live as those theories require, would misunderstand ethical life in ways that obstruct their living a good life. Why might ethical theories have such effects? The fuller story involves a range of themes interweaving in complex ways across different thinkers. But it will be useful to distinguish three types of objection:

Conceptual framework objections: there is something awry with the conceptual framework through which ethical theories are structured (be it particular concepts like obligation, or the drive to deliver a systematizing framework at all).

Foundational objections: the foundational presuppositions informing ethical theory rest on errors (e.g. that moral obligation possesses a special authority).

Substantive objections: ethical theories deprive us of the materials we need for living a good life (ethically or personally).

The remainder of the chapter maps the evolution of these worries. It starts by introducing some main themes from Anscombe's agenda-setting article 'Modern Moral Philosophy' (1958) and then traces the development of these ideas thematically.

SOWING THE SEEDS: ANSCOMBE VERSUS MODERN
MORAL PHILOSOPHY

The most provocative of the three theses with which Anscombe opens her indictment of modern moral philosophy is that the concepts of '*moral* obligation [. . .] and of what is *morally* right and wrong, and of the *moral* sense of "ought", ought to be jettisoned if this is psychologically possible; because they are survivals, or derivatives of survivals, from an earlier conception of ethics which no longer survives, and are only harmful without it' (1958: 1). The basic structure of her argument for this runs as follows. Obligation-centered moral theories represent a '*law* conception of ethics', in that the concept of obligation implies 'being bound or required as by a law' (1958: 6). Law conceptions were originally derived from theistic traditions positing an authoritative law-giver, i.e. God; and the concept of obligation is 'intelligible' or 'has reasonable sense' only within such a framework (1958: 5–6, 8). Modern secularized moral theories abandon a divine and hence authoritative law-giver. So, the concept of obligation, as deployed by secular moral theories, is no longer intelligible (1958: 2, 5–8,

13–14). Hence, secularized conceptions of moral obligation, and thus secular obligation-centered moral theories, should be jettisoned.

This combines conceptual framework and foundational objections: the concept of obligation through which modern morality operates is unintelligible; and normative claims couched via that concept lack authority. So, modern moral philosophy is in bad shape. One main root of the problem, Anscombe argues, is a key Humean assumption that had become dominant throughout secular moral theorizing: that there is a clear-cut 'fact–value' distinction, with the moral content of moral judgments lying wholly on the value side. This deprives moral thought of 'factual' content and, Anscombe believed, thereby robs it of an objective grounding that could explain either its normativity or its authority (1958: 2, 4, 6, 7–9, 18). The trouble, though, is that philosophers retain this talk of 'obligation'.

Although much of Anscombe's critique focuses on these meta-ethical issues, it is motivated in significant part by substantive concerns. In particular, she argues, moral theories are unable to prohibit actions that they themselves take to be wrong. Kantian and consequentialist theories, for instance, lack an account of how to correctly describe actions or the intentions behind them. This renders their tests for right and wrong action 'useless', since an action could pass the test under one description but fail it under another (1958: 2–3; see also Anscombe 1957). And that generates substantive errors: notably, a failure to prohibit actions that are viciously unjust (1958: 15–19).

SALVAGING MORALITY'S AUTHORITY?

Despite its objections, Anscombe's 'Modern Moral Philosophy' is far from exclusively critical. Probably its biggest legacy is the inspiration it provided for a revival in (mainly Aristotelian) virtue ethics as an alternative to obligation-centered theories.[3] Indeed, Anscombe outlines how each of the above objections

---

[3] On an orthodox 'straight' reading, Anscombe recommends a (secular, neo-Aristotelian) form of virtue ethics. An alternative reading, motivated by consideration of her own Christian faith alongside her criticisms of Aristotle, holds that the only legitimate ethical position is one sanctioned by a divine law-giver. Thus, even if she favors a form of virtue ethics, she remains skeptical about *all* secular ethical outlooks, obligation-centered and virtue-based. Either way, it took until the 1980s for virtue ethics to become systematically re-established as a distinctive, fully-fledged outlook in its own right (major contributors included Foot 1978b; MacIntyre 1981). This required further fuel via a range of additional misgivings about deontology and consequentialism, pushed most forcefully by Williams.

might be averted by reorienting ethical thought through virtue concepts (1958: 15–18).

On the one hand, conceptualizing ethical life via the virtues (like justice) might help discriminate right from wrong conduct (by ruling out grave injustices, say) and give us the descriptions under which we ought to act (though see Williams 1985: 10–11, 1995f: 190). At the same time, it may secure an objective grounding for ethical claims that makes their authority transparent. Virtue concepts are a species of (what are now often labeled) 'thick' ethical concept. In contrast to 'thin' concepts like *obligation, right* and *good*, they possess both 'factual' content that guides their correct application and 'evaluative' content that makes them action-guiding. Anscombe appealed to thick concepts to challenge the Humean assumption that there is a clear fact–value distinction, the thought being that their factual and evaluative contents cannot be wholly disentangled (similar themes were aired, more or less contemporaneously, by Foot [e.g. 1958] and Murdoch [1964]; see also Williams [1985: chs. 7–8]). This, in turn, might preserve ethical objectivity: judgments about justice, say, could at once be objectively true in virtue of the factual content regulating the application of the concept 'just' *and* carry with them an inseparable evaluative claim that inherits this objectivity.

Debates over this entanglement thesis persist today, as do disagreements about the objectivity it warrants. Anscombe hoped that, as well as securing evaluative objectivity, true 'virtue' judgments would straightforwardly entail more narrowly *normative* claims concerning what we ought or have reason to do – thus giving 'oughts' the authority they had been divested of by obligation-centered theories. Others were more skeptical, however. Williams, for instance, denies that evaluative claims uniformly entail reason claims (2001: 96). And, concerning thick concepts specifically, he remarks that, even if we apply such a concept correctly (qua factual content), and even if this implies that *we* think the person we apply it to has a reason to do as it recommends, whether the person does have that reason depends on whether *that* person '*has reason to use that concept*, to structure his or her experience in those terms'; but that, Williams urges, 'is a different, and larger, matter; all the work remains to be done' (Williams 1995b: 38). Foot (1972) raises a similar challenge (her specific target was Kantian moral theory, though the general worry may extend more widely). For although moral 'oughts' might look categorical by dint of having correct conditions of application that do not depend on one's motives, the same is true of many other 'oughts' that are *not* authoritative. Her example was 'oughts' derived from (frivolous, outdated, chauvinistic) norms of etiquette, as in 'women ought never to offer their hand when greeting a man before the man offers his'. It is therefore incumbent on theorists to justify the traditional assumption that moral 'oughts' possess a special authority lacking in other systems of norms – an assumption, Foot urged, that 'is more often repeated than explained' (1972: 309), but which, unless vindicated, leaves moral theorists 'relying on an illusion, as if trying to give the moral "ought" a magical force' (1972: 315).

There have subsequently been many responses to Foot's argument. Foot herself later recanted in favor of a more Anscombian approach that connects 'oughts' directly to 'virtue' (Foot 2001). Williams, however, doubted that the general challenge could be met. Despite his distaste for generalizations in ethics, he steadfastly defended a motive-based or 'internalist' interpretation of 'reason' claims, according to which you have a reason to perform a given action only if you have some motive which would be served by so acting (Williams 1981d, 1995b, 1995f, 2001). The further details are too wide-ranging to address here. But it is worth noting two implications for ethical theory.

First, Williams maintains that on any adequate account reasons for action should be capable of guiding the actions of the people they are reasons for. They must therefore be connected in the right ways to the things we care about, as embodied in our motives. If a theory's demands are too far removed from our deep-rooted commitments, we may have no reason to comply with them. Second, however, to ensure universality many theorists promote an outlook that is impartial with respect to individuals' subjective interests and/ or posit some special faculty (of pure practical reason or rational intuition, say) via which each person has the capacity to recognize the reason-giving force of ethical demands *whatever her motives*. Both approaches, Williams believes, are problematic. The first threatens to *alienate* us from the things we care about. The second represents a philosophical fantasy that not only offends against a naturalistically respectable picture of human psychology but, moreover, serves an *unrealistically* egalitarian and thereby unfair conception of moral responsibility and blame (1985: ch. 10, 1995b, 1995c). Both worries connect to more general tendencies within ethical (especially moral) theory to present an impartial outlook abstracted from the way people really are. The following offers a flavor of some core themes unifying Williams' anti-theory stance.

WILLIAMS' ANTI-REDUCTIVISM

The backdrop to his criticisms is an enduring commitment to the idea that an adequate picture of ethical life must be phenomenologically and psychologically realistic. It must take seriously deep-rooted aspects of how we experience ourselves and our relations to others, by recognizing that we are individuals with our own identity-grounding commitments and by giving due consideration to the roles these play in shaping our personal and interpersonal lives (Williams 1973d, 1981b, 1985: 88). However, he argues, ethical theories fail in these respects, owing significantly to their 'reductivist' ambitions. Indeed, it is these reductivist ambitions that make ethical theories *theories*. We can here separate two sets of explanatory ideals that make theories reductive.

First, theories in general seek an account of their subject matter that is explanatorily powerful, comprehensive and parsimonious – by explaining in an informative way as many of the relevant phenomena, but with as few basic concepts and substantive resources, as they can. Ethical theories, guided by similar aims, are likewise conceptually and substantively reductivist: they explain their subject matter (ethical thought and practice) via as few concepts (e.g. right, good, virtue) and as few types of substantive (e.g. right-making) considerations as possible. Ethical theories can be more or less reductivist. The most ambitious are rigorist. Kantian ethics and orthodox consequentialism, for instance, both deliver a *monistic* criterion of right action: they each provide a single principle that serves to assess the moral status of any action in any circumstance. Even looser theories exhibit reductivist propensities. Like rigorist theories, they organize ethical thought around a principal concept and tend to reduce ethical considerations to a few basic types specifiable in general terms. Both thereby systematize ethical thought into a relatively simple package.

However, Williams objects, moral philosophy's 'prevailing fault [. . .] is to impose on ethical life some immensely simple model, whether it be of the concepts that we actually use or of the moral rules by which we should be guided' (1985: 127). This is a fault because ethical life is complex – due both to the messiness of life itself and to the fact that our own ethical outlook is the contingent product of a range of traditions, each with its own conceptual repertoires and substantive ideals, fused together in ways that often pull in conflicting directions (Williams 1985: 16; see also McIntyre 1981). Yet by reducing their subject matter to a restricted set of substantive considerations explained through a minimal set of ethical concepts, theories either misinterpret features of ethical life they do acknowledge (e.g. by assessing qualitatively diverse features through a single concept or master-value) or else overlook aspects of ethical life that fail to fit their theoretical model. In either case, the simplified model they impose leaves a distorted picture of ethical thought and life. So why in the first place, Williams asks, is

there this 'expectation that [the truth about the ethical] should be simple?'
(1985: 17).

His answer revolves around a second theoretical ideal: consistency.
Much of ethical thought is predicated on the fact that people's interests
and needs often seem to *conflict*. And many theorists view conflicting ethical
claims – a set of claims that cannot be jointly satisfied – as a form of *logical
inconsistency*. A key assumption informing many ethical theories, then, is
that they must *resolve* such conflicts in order to preclude inconsistency. And
it looks easier to do that if the competing considerations can be compared
via a common conceptual and substantive currency – hence the drive to
systematize ethical thought into a parsimonious set of conceptual and
substantive materials.

The upshot, however, is that to preserve theoretical consistency ethical
theories are committed to eradicating the possibility of irresolvable inconsistencies – thereby producing a theoretical representation of ethical life
that *eliminates* the possibility of genuine (irresolvable) normative conflict.
This, Williams objects, fails to reflect the phenomenology: we do experience
ethical life as involving genuine conflict (1973b, 1981c). Ethical theories thereby
exemplify a '*rationalistic conception of rationality*': an ultimately 'administrative'
system that imposes onto the ethical sphere a simplistic conflict-resolution
model at odds with actual ethical experience (1985: 18, 197). Furthermore, the
model itself rests on dubious theoretical assumptions. First, it is far from
obvious that practical conflicts mark *logical* inconsistencies. Nor, therefore, is
it clear why we require a theoretical model that eliminates them. Second, the
reductivist enterprise generating this putative requirement rests on a further
'utterly baseless' 'assumption about rationality': that 'two considerations cannot be rationally weighed against each other unless there is a common
consideration in terms of which they can be compared' (1985: 17). And that
assumption typically results in one of two strategies: reducing the competing
considerations to a single evaluative currency, or invoking some standard or
method independent of the competing values to adjudicate between them.
Williams opposes both: he doubts there is just one basic value to which all
other values are reducible; and he doubts that some independent standard
could adequately represent and hence impartially evaluate all values not
reducible to it (1981c).

Thus, Williams believes, the theoretical assumptions underpinning ethical theory (qua explanatory unity and consistency) are unsustainable.
Furthermore, this reductivism has deleterious *substantive* effects, represented most starkly by rigorist moral theories.

A first set of concerns emerges from the point that a comprehensive criterion of right action, if it is to apply to each and every situation, must be highly general (Williams 1985: 116). But, experience shows, general ethical tests always generate deeply counterintuitive verdicts in some cases (1973d: 99) – verdicts contrary not just to common ethical opinion, but to psychologically and culturally deep-seated commitments we cannot easily discard. In addition, this generality requires that the criterion apply to each person. Moral theories therefore abstract from the particular commitments of particular persons, generating an outlook that is impartial across agents. However, Williams objects, this creates a clash between the impartial demands of a highly general theory and our concrete ethical commitments – a clash that 'impartial morality [. . .] must be required to win' (1981b: 14). Utilitarianism, for example, may require you to forego your commitment to justice or abandon someone you love if either commitment 'conflicts with what [you] are required to do as an impersonal utility-maximizer' (1981b: 14; 1973d). Similarly, to secure a moral law that obligates all persons irrespective of their subjective ends, Kant privileges an impartial moral perspective abstracted from these. This, however, removes from the moral sphere many of the materials Williams thinks we need to make sense of ethical life in the first place, including the emotional dispositions and other-directed desires through which actual people forge and sustain ethical relations (1981b; 1973c). His basic concern is that this drive towards impartiality, all in the name of providing a *general* theory, engenders an outlook that would produce ethically dis-integrated individuals: individuals who, because required to subordinate their deep-rooted ethical dispositions to an impartial standpoint, will become alienated from the very materials they need for ethical life.

A second but related worry is that moral theories present a distorting view of the relation between ethical life and the good life. Williams develops this in several places and in slightly different forms (1973d; 1981b, 1985: ch. 10; cp. Wolf 1982). But his basic concern is that, by prioritizing the moral-impartial standpoint, moral theories require us to systematically forego the non-moral goods that give our lives meaning – personal projects and excellences, friendships, emotional attachments, and so forth. This is one application of a more general objection that moral theories make ethical life too demanding. Utilitarianism, for instance, requires each person to promote the overall good impartially, since the good of one person is as valuable as the good of any other. Yet this would require you to sacrifice the personal projects constitutive of your own good whenever promoting the good of others will have better overall consequences – and, the worry goes, promoting others' good would almost always produce better consequences. Kantian theories are also susceptible to versions of the objection. For if moral requirements are requirements of pure practical reason that have priority over our non-moral ends, or if correct deliberation involves reflecting impartially by abstracting from our subjective ends, then those ends may ultimately become eclipsed by the demands of morality. On either theory, we could end up with an incessant and inescapable series of moral obligations, thus rendering it impermissible to pursue our own personal projects and depriving us of the very things that are 'a condition of [our] having any interest in being around in [the] world at all' (1981b: 14). Thus, Williams urges, morality is 'a particular variety of ethical thought [. . .] we would be better off without' (1985: 174).

THE CURRENT STATE OF PLAY

The moral-philosophical landscape has undergone significant change over the last thirty years, due in no small part to the concerns these criticisms exposed. We can separate three now-dominant approaches.

One response has been to defend consequentialist and neo-Kantian theories against the substantive objections raised by critics like Williams. Some concede that morality can be highly intrusive. But most seek to accommodate a wider range of ethical dispositions and personal goods, typically by denying that practical deliberation should be systematically structured via moral concepts or considerations, and by making moral obligation itself less pervasive or otherwise demanding (cp. Railton 1984; Brink 1986; Darwall 1987; Herman 1993; Hooker 1999). The adequacy of particular strategies depends on the details, of course. But it remains an important question whether these strategies address merely the symptoms rather than deeper causes – namely, the ambition to provide a reductivist theory.

The second and third trends mark a shift away from those rigorist aspirations. One residual worry with monistic theories is that, by delivering an explanatorily unified account, they sacrifice extensional adequacy. Deontological pluralists and virtue ethicists (typically taking inspiration from W.D. Ross and Aristotle, respectively) seek a substantively less unified account that stands a better chance of getting the right verdicts: first by incorporating a wider range of normative considerations into their account of rightness, second by arguing that the role these play is context-sensitive in ways that preclude reduction to a *codifiable* criterion or general test. Here the boundaries between theory and non-theory become blurred.[4] Although substantively pluralistic, both approaches are conceptually monistic: they each organize ethical thought around one basic concept, be it obligation or virtue. Contemporary virtue ethicists, often impressed by the worries Anscombe and Williams raise, maintain that part of the problem is moral theory's restrictive focus on *action* and *obligation*. They therefore seek a more holistic approach that reconceives ethical life as an ongoing process involving the cultivation of an ethically excellent (i.e. virtuous) character: someone disposed to do the right thing in the right circumstances, with the right intention and feelings.

Both forms of pluralism nonetheless face pressing issues. Many of these focus on the epistemologies they advance in light of denying that rightness is reducible to a codifiable test: epistemologies that appeal to either a form of intuitionism or practical wisdom. Williams raises characteristically antitheoretic worries for both. On the one hand, intuitionists typically reduce ethical disagreements to epistemic failures. This reflects the traditional theory-driven presumption that normative conflicts are always in principle amenable to determinate resolution. Moreover, absent an account of how intuition works, appealing to it fails to explain why our ethical judgments are correct – something Williams thinks we can and should explain without recourse to some special moral faculty (1985: 94, 1995d). On the other hand, virtue-based accounts need to explain why the cultivation of practical wisdom should be connected to (some particular set of) virtue-exemplifying character traits. This is a question not (just) about what the relevant virtues are, but about the *authority* a general theory of them could have: why, for instance, the model of an idealized agent whose character, projects, motives and abilities may be very different from our own is something *we* have reason to emulate (1985: ch. 3; 1995f).

That there are these different approaches indicates the extent to which antitheory has influenced recent moral philosophy. Contemporary debates,

---

[4] Ross' own pluralism retains strong reductivist proclivities that Williams (1985: 179–81) objects to, notably a desire to reduce right-making features to as few general types as possible. The more extreme forms of deontological particularism (e.g. Dancy 2003) deny that correct ethical thought rests on general, normatively invariant considerations at all; in that respect they exhibit strong anti-theory leanings. Contemporary virtue ethics likewise encompasses a spectrum of approaches more or less anti-theoretic in spirit – depending on, for instance, whether specific virtues are normatively invariant, how determinate facts about rightness are, and how systemically normative thought should be structured through the virtues (cp. McDowell 1979, Hursthouse 1996, Annas 2004).

however, tend to focus on the advantages and disadvantages of the competing theories – rather than on whether we should be seeking a theory in the first place. Here, then, it may be worth standing back and asking two simple questions (see Williams 1985: ch. 2; Dancy 2007: 773–4). First, what exactly is *the point* of an ethical theory? Second, *who* are ethical theories directed to, and why? It can be important to reflect on ethical matters and to reflect on how to do that, of course. But theories do more than this: they construct abstract models to explain the concepts, substantive considerations and perhaps methods via which ethical thought – *our* thought – *should* proceed. Yet what bearing can, or should, an abstract philosophical theory have on the lives of people quite generally? Do we – the people already inhabiting an ethical outlook – really need a *theory* to structure and systematize it for us? Yet if an ethical theory is not directed to the people whose lives it concerns, what is its point?

These are big questions that go to the heart of the relationship between ethical life and moral philosophy. But absent an adequate answer to them, perhaps Williams is right (1985: 17): 'A good deal of moral philosophy engages unblinkingly in this [theory-constructing] activity, for no obvious reason except that it has been going on for a long time.'

BIBLIOGRAPHY

An asterisk denotes secondary literature especially suitable for further reading.

Annas, J. 2004. 'Being Virtuous and Doing the Right Thing', *Proceedings and Addresses of the American Philosophical Association* 78: 61–75.

Anscombe, G.E.M. 1957. *Intention*. Oxford: Basil Blackwell.

Anscombe, G.E.M. 1958. 'Modern Moral Philosophy', *Philosophy* 33: 1–19.*

Brink, D. 1986. 'Utilitarian Morality and the Personal Point of View', *Journal of Philosophy* 83: 417–38.

Dancy, J. 2003. *Ethics Without Principles*. Oxford University Press.

Dancy, J. 2007. 'An Unprincipled Morality', in Russ Shafer-Landau (ed.), *Ethical Theory: An Anthology*. Oxford: Blackwell, pp. 771–4.

Darwall, S. 1987. 'Abolishing Morality', *Synthese* 87: 71–89.

Foot, P. 1958. 'Moral Arguments', *Mind* 67: 502–13. Reprinted in Foot 1978a: 96–109.

Foot, P. 1972. 'Morality as a System of Hypothetical Imperatives', *The Philosophical Review* 81: 305–16. Reprinted in Foot 1978a: 157–73.

Foot, P. 1978a. *Virtue and Vices*. Oxford University Press.

Foot, P. 1978b. 'Virtue and Vices', in Foot 1978a: 1–18.

Foot, P. 2001. *Natural Goodness*. Oxford University Press.

Herman, B. 1993. 'Integrity and Impartiality', in *The Practice of Moral Judgment*. Cambridge, MA: Harvard University Press, pp. 22–44.

Hooker, B. 1999. 'Rule-Consequentialism', in H. La Follette (ed.), *The Blackwell Guide to Ethical Theory*. Oxford: Blackwell, pp. 183–204.

Hursthouse, R. 1996. 'Normative Virtue Ethics', in R. Crisp (ed.), *How Should One Live?*. Oxford University Press, pp. 19–33.

MacIntyre, A. 1981. *After Virtue*. University of Notre Dame Press.

McDowell, J. 1979. 'Virtue and Reason', *The Monist* 62: 331–50.

Murdoch, I. 1964. 'The Idea of Perfection', *The Yale Review* 53: 342–80. Reprinted in I. Murdoch, *The Sovereignty of Good*. London: Routledge and Kegan Paul, 1970, pp. 1–45.

Railton, P. 1984. 'Alienation, Consequentialism, and the Demands of Morality', *Philosophy and Public Affairs* 13: 134–71.

Williams, B. 1973a. *Problems of the Self*. Cambridge University Press.

Williams, B. 1973b. 'Ethical Consistency', in Williams 1973a: 166–86.

Williams, B. 1973c. 'Morality and the Emotions', in Williams 1973a: 207–29.

Williams, B. 1973d. 'A Critique of Utilitarianism', in J.J.C. Smart and B. Williams, *Utilitarianism: For and Against*. Cambridge University Press, pp. 75–150.

Williams, B. 1981a. *Moral Luck*. Cambridge University Press.

Williams, B. 1981b. 'Persons, Character and Morality', in Williams 1981a: 1–19.

Williams, B. 1981c. 'Conflicts of Values', in Williams 1981a: 71–82.

Williams, B. 1981d. 'Internal and External Reasons', in Williams 1981a: 101–13.

Williams, B. 1985. *Ethics and the Limits of Philosophy*. London: Fontana Press.*

Williams, B. 1995a. *Making Sense of Humanity*. Cambridge University Press.

Williams, B. 1995b. 'Internal Reasons and the Obscurity of Blame', in Williams 1995a: 35–45.

Williams, B. 1995c. 'Nietzsche's Minimalist Moral Psychology', in Williams 1995a: 65–76.

Williams, B. 1995d. 'What Does Intuitionism Imply?' in Williams 1995a: 182–91.

Williams, B. 1995e. 'Moral Luck: A Postscript', in Williams 1995a: 241–7.

Williams, B. 1995f. 'Replies', in J.E.J. Altham and R. Harrison (eds.), *Mind, World, and Ethics*. Cambridge University Press, pp. 185–224.

Williams, B. 2001. 'Postscript: Some Further Notes on Internal and External Reasons', in Elijah Milgram (ed.), *Varieties of Practical Reasoning*. Cambridge, MA: MIT Press, pp. 91–7.

Wolf, S. 1982. 'Moral Saints', *The Journal of Philosophy* 79: 419–39.

52

Discourse Ethics

PETER NIESEN

"Discourse ethics" has become a generally accepted, though less than self-explanatory, label for a distinctive intersubjectivist approach in practical philosophy in general, and in moral philosophy in particular. It was first developed by Karl-Otto Apel and Jürgen Habermas from the 1970s onward; among its contemporary philosophical practitioners are Seyla Benhabib, Rainer Forst, and Cristina Lafont. In Anglo-American philosophy, the term "discourse ethics" has frequently been used *pars pro toto* for a complex conception of practical reason, a comprehensive theory encompassing discourse theories of law and democracy, of morality, and of the good life (e.g. Rawls 1995: 141). More often, it is understood in its narrower sense, as denoting that part of a systematic conception of discursive rationality that is concerned exclusively with claims to universal and categorical practical norms. Discourse ethics in the narrow sense is the philosophical study of morality, while the philosophical study of ethics (in the sense of conceptions of the good life) is another, parallel module within discourse theory as a whole.

In both its broad and its narrow sense, discourse ethics seeks to reformulate aspects of Kant's practical philosophy, drawing inspiration from the public use of reason and from the categorical imperative, especially its co-legislation formula. It follows Kant's lead in distinguishing a realm of morality proper from a realm of law and politics, but also in sharply profiling a narrow and strictly obligatory field of universal norms against the less stringent fields of the communal or personal values, of supererogation and virtue. Discourse theory parts company with Kantianism in practical philosophy not only in subjecting it to a linguistic and intersubjectivist turn, substituting omnilateral communicative exchanges for Kant's contemplative

I thank James Gledhill for perceptive comments on the penultimate version.

("monological") method of arriving at binding precepts, but also in embedding practical philosophy in a theory of social evolution.

Discourse ethics in both its generic and specific sense is perhaps best understood by focusing on its most influential formulation, that of Jürgen Habermas, in its revised version in and after *Between Facts and Norms* (1996a). In this work, Habermas continues and transforms the early modern program of "moral philosophy," leading up to Kant's *Metaphysics of Morals* and comprising politics, natural law, morality, and personal virtue. Habermas' discourse theory attempts to formulate a general account of various complementary normative orders, based on a single discourse principle (D). Practical normativity then is specified along two dimensions, along the lines of the types of reasoning employed (pragmatic, ethical, moral) and along the lines of the practical and institutional contexts in which these processes of reasoning take place (informal, legal, political). Discourse ethics in its core sense is then assigned the study of the moral use of reason in informal, non-coercive contexts of interaction. In what follows, I first delineate how the idea of a discourse theory is introduced in Habermas' *Theory of Communicative Action* (1984, 1987). I then turn to the distinction between moral and ethical discourses before commenting on the discourse principle (D) as neutral between various types of normativity. I finally turn to its instantiation in a theory of morality, i.e. as a discourse "ethics" in the narrow sense.

COMMUNICATIVE ACTION AND DISCOURSE

Philosophical ethics is sometimes exhorted to steer clear of controversial views in theoretical philosophy and social theory. In contrast, discourse ethics begins with a central question in sociology: How can people rely on their peers' cooperation under modern conditions? How can normative orders arise and be consolidated, built on nothing but the resources of modernity itself (Habermas 2009: 11)? In *The Theory of Communicative Action*, Habermas identifies "communicative" uses of language, both as "communicative action" and as "discourse," as practices apt to coordinate human interaction in non-arbitrary, uncoerced, rational and stable ways, drawing on ideas from Max Weber's theory of modernisation to analytic philosophy of language. Following John Searle's version of speech act theory, Habermas sees communicators as making various demands upon each other. If things go well, they can come to substantively agree on what to believe or do, based on a joint linguistic interpretation of what is at stake and a joint identification of their "illocutionary," i.e. action-inducing, commitments. Generalising

Searle's observation that whoever makes an assertion thereby commits to the truth of its content, Habermas identifies four commitments that any speaker undertakes in every act of meaningful communication. These are the four validity claims of propositional truth, practical rightness, personal sincerity or authenticity, and, as a formal precondition, linguistic intelligibility. The original insight of discourse ethics relates to the ways in which communicative use of language both presupposes and triggers reason-giving practices. On the one hand, communicators need to be aware of how validity claims can possibly be "redeemed." Generalising an insight from verificationist semantics, Habermas states that "[w]e understand a speech act when we know what makes it acceptable" in all four dimensions (1984: 297). In understanding a statement, demand, promise etc., we demonstrate an implicit knowledge as to what would have to be *argued* in order to entitle the speaker to perform it, and in order to move the audience to accept and comply with it (Cooke 1994). On the other hand, communicative action leads to practices of reason-giving precisely when it fails. Whenever a speaker's fourfold claim is rejected in either of its dimensions, the participants can "step out" of communicative action and exchange actual reasons in discourse. Discourses reflect the fact that, at any time, communicators have a "right to say no" to the claims that others cannot fail to raise in communicating (Günther 1992). Although they aim at agreement, discourses originate not in a search for consensus, but in the voiced dissent against the norms presupposed in everyday communicative practice as a matter of course. The technical term "discourse" signals that such reflexive processes must be suitably idealized, in abstracting away from the parochialisms of space, lack of information, lack of relevant participants, inequality of status, and the real-world pressure to generate results within a limited period of time.

Habermas holds on to the idea that the formal features both of communicative action and of discursive argumentation are empirically universal in the sense that no known culture and linguistic practice has done without the four validity claims, or failed to display reflexive practices of reasoning (1998: 43). Yet there are a number of features that link his theory of communication more closely to the modern life-world than to any other environment (Finlayson 2000, Heath 2014): firstly the sharp differentiation of the four validity claims from each other, distantly mirroring Weber's thesis of the differentiation of value spheres; secondly the semantic idea that only against the backdrop of their potential argumentative vindication can speech acts become fully plausible; finally, the idea that just as questions of truth can find a consensual and rational answer in discourse, so can claims to practical rightness. Emphasizing a theory-of-modernity reading of Habermas' discourse theory does not oblit-erate its claims to trans-cultural and trans-temporal correctness. The fact that autonomous, argument-based, "rational" normative orders can only arise under the social, cultural and epistemic conditions of modernity does not in itself devalue the trans-contextual appeal of their presuppositions. Also, despite the genealogical dependence of discourse theory in both the broad and narrow senses on a program in the philosophy of language, it is important not to overstate the relation between linguistic and practical normativity. Habermas does try to uncover a continuum between linguistic–pragmatic and social normativity, but he is not performing an "extraction of moral normativity from the normativity of language," based on an alleged obligation to provide reasons or, perhaps, to alternatively withdraw our claims (McMahon 2013: 1397, 1402). Although weakly normative, communicative action is not prescriptive in the sense of being morally mandated, nor does argumentative behavior in discourses count as a moral obligation (Habermas 1993: 33). *The Theory of Communicative Action* should not be read as a crypto-theory of morality, but as assembling a background of resources in social philosophy that universalist accounts of normativity can then tap into.

MORALITY AND ETHICS

While "practical rightness" had remained an unanalyzed basic notion in *The Theory of Communicative Action*, in later work Habermas introduced a distinc-tion between the pragmatic, the ethical, and the moral use of reason. The three dimensions or "discourses" of practical reason concern what is func-tional, good, or just, according to the "logic of the question at issue" (1993: 1–18; 1996a: 109). Pragmatic discourses concern what has traditionally been called "instrumental" or "means-ends rationality." They play out on the basis of agreed common goals, be they infrastructural projects such as erecting a bridge or political projects such as implementing a communal health policy. Within a cooperative scheme based upon pre-committed goals, pragmatic reason governs their efficient and effective technical realization. Means can be adequate or not, thus the pragmatic use is cognitive in principle. But from within the pragmatic use of reason, goals themselves cannot be questioned. Ethical discourses are teleological as well in that they are oriented toward goals, or more precisely the one goal of furthering the good life in a comprehensive sense, but they are free to question and change ends as well as means. However, even shared ethical goals and aspirations are based on collective identities and particular ways of life that often stand in conflict with other identities. They are relative to the "strong evaluations" (Taylor 1985) of a given person or community in that they do not transcend their individual or collective egocentrism. While ethical values typically derive from an historically entrenched ethos of sanity and normality, they likewise manifest themselves in freely chosen forms of existence, for instance in the processes of self-invention of modern romantic individualism. They comprise communal and political as well as existential concerns. Moral discourses, in contrast, are characterized by a formal criterion. They concern matters "of justice," i.e. matters that can be regulated impartially and in the general interest, and therefore exclusively process reasons that can be accepted jointly by all participants. In representing the perspectives of all, they must transcend the boundaries of community values and distill or generate universal norms. The moral use of reason parallels Kantian autonomy, i.e. the attempt to integrate my maxims with those of all others (Habermas 1993: 8). In addressing interpersonal conflicts based on what is acceptable to all, moral reasoning must pass a "threshold of reciprocity and generality" (Forst 2012: 67).

The distinction between the ethical and the moral use of reason has faced extensive criticism. Some criticisms are verbal, since they concern the translatability of a language of values into a language of norms, of a language of the good into a language of right. An ethical value that can be shown to be universally acceptable is, for discourse theorists, a moral value. Other criticisms are more material: Can moral arguments be sealed off from ethics, or are they crucially embedded in interpretations of our communal and personal values (McCarthy 1991: 191)? Is the moral realm drawn too narrowly in excluding matters of self-realization (Kettner 2002: 208)? Can the 'point' of morality be understood irrespective of structural conditions of the good life (Honneth 2009)? Finally, can the realm of morality be self-sufficient in the motivational dimension, so that entering into practices of moral reflection and complying with moral precepts does not need to rely on ethical convictions? While Habermas, drawing on Lawrence Kohlberg's theory of moral development, has stressed intrinsic motivational resources for moral discourse and moral action, he has at the same time presented the moral use of reason as a largely epistemic practice and emphasized the need for ethical and institutional back-up (1990: 207f). Forst has defended the more consistently Kantian claim that the distinction between morality and ethics is only compatible with a strongly "internalist" account of motivation (2012: 74–7). From the perspective of the moral use of reason, it seems hard to avoid the conclusion that reasoning towards the resolution of moral conflict may at the same time deliver excellent, though perhaps insufficiently specific, reasons to comply with the resulting norms in moral action.

Discourse ethics prioritizes the right (as determined by the moral use of reason) over the good (as determined by pragmatic and ethical uses), but in contrast to many liberal approaches in ethics does not link its distinction to questions of justified enforcement. Despite protestations to the contrary (Habermas 2009: 23f), there does exist a clear hierarchy between the three uses of reason or discourses. Once moral considerations are introduced, other uses of reason cannot remain oblivious to them. Moral arguments "trump" ethical arguments, just as ethical arguments are apt to suspend pragmatic considerations. Discursive ascent from pragmatic via ethical to moral normativity is not externally imposed by meta-discourses ensuring commensurability, but is based on "self-selective" processes internal to discursive exchanges as such (Habermas 1996b: 1534; Niesen 2011). It is also important to note that the authority to qualify arguments as ethical or moral is provisional and *a posteriori*. Only once all views and arguments are in will we be able to see whether a given claim concerns universal interests, or communal and existential values.

LAW, POLITICS, AND MORALITY

In *Between Facts and Norms* (1996a), Habermas gives his discourse theory its definitive form, starting again from the question of modern social order. The ordering principle is the distinction between the relatively independent spheres of law and democratic politics on the one hand, and morality and ethics on the other, as modernity's dual strategies of stabilizing normative expectations. Law and "rational" morality are seen as parallel and complementary developments, evolving simultaneously in the modern transition from integrated forms of societal ethos toward discursive forms of coordination. Both legal-institutional and informal modes of normative coordination, Habermas argues, are governed by one and the same overarching discourse principle (D). Principle (D) states:

> Just those action norms are valid to which all possibly involved persons could
> agree as participants in rational dialogues.
>
> (Habermas 1996a: 107, translation modified)

While Habermas had earlier introduced (D) as a principle of morality (1990: 66), he now insists that it is for law, democracy, morality, and ethics to flesh out the skeleton of (D) in their respective contexts. Although (D) is to reflect the "symmetrical relations of recognition built into communicatively structured forms of life in general" (1996a: 109), it cannot be applied in any immediate sense to either field. Habermas arrives at (D) by a process of elimination. In doing away with metaphysical, religious, and custom-based foundations, he insists that coupling normativity to general acceptability will generate the only conception of validity still feasible under the modern demands of a "post-conventional level of justification" (1996a: 107). It expresses neither less nor more than an unspecific "sense of impartiality of practical judgments" (ibid.). From a first-person perspective, (D) ensures that norms which do not stand up before my own use of reason cannot have any binding effect on me.

In specifying the *scope* of (D), Habermas uses the terms *Beteiligte* (those involved) and *Betroffene* (those affected) more or less interchangeably (1996a: 106–9). The three criteria of being subject to norms, being affected by them, and being recognized as a relevant authority on their validity appear as three different ways of picking out the same group. In applying (D) to moral questions, the difference between those who are subject to universal norms, and those who are affected by norm-governed behavior, is immaterial, at least as long as we disregard non-communicating beings.[1] As applied to law and democratic politics, (D) refers exclusively to all those subjected to its norms. As Habermas indicates in the political context of transnational migration, being affected in a causal way generates a claim to have one's interest considered in rational dialogues, but does not make the outcome of those dialogues dependent on one's agreement as a participant (1998: 231).

What counts as *rational dialogue* likewise varies significantly between democratic and legal discursive procedures and informal moral discourse. (D) does not in all circumstances require *deep* consensus. The notion of consent in rational dialogue does not entail agreement on the basis of shared or sharable reasons. In its interpretation as a principle of democracy, (D) even admits of political compromise between fairly placed negotiators (1996a: 110, 165f). In introducing non-ideal specifications of legal and democratic discursive procedures, discourse theory complements an independent, but often inefficacious morality. Once discourses are institutionalized in legal and political procedures, they are to channel and implement moral, ethical, and pragmatic uses of reason. It is important to see how this both empowers and limits moral discourses. All institutional procedures must allow, on some

---

[1] Discourse ethics cannot ascribe non-communicating beings equal status or equal obligations. In the case of non-communicating humans, this is to be compensated by their "advocatory" discursive inclusion. Direct moral duties vis-à-vis animals can be based on their voluntarist inclusion into a "horizon of our modes of human interaction" (Habermas 1993: 110f).

levels, the introduction of moral and ethical argument in order to qualify as discursive, and they must be structured such that moral arguments can win out against other types of argument. But not only do institutionalized discursive procedures aim to resolve conflict by coming to a decision, often taken by majority voting. They at the same time defeat the authority of informal moral or ethical discourses as bases of conflict resolution. Direct recourse to moral arguments in attempts to justify *coercive action* will short-circuit and subvert modernity's dual structuring of social order. An *"unmediated* moralisation of law and politics" would annihilate a distinction between law and morality established "for good, indeed moral, reasons" (Habermas 1998: 199).

THE DISCOURSE THEORY OF MORALITY:
UNIVERSALISM, FORMALISM, AND COGNITIVISM

Discourse theory's "principle of morality" is a specification of (D), introduced as "the principle of universalisation," hence (U). (U) states that

> A norm is valid when the foreseeable consequences and side effects of its general observance for the interests and value-orientations of each individual could be jointly accepted by all concerned without coercion.
>
> (Habermas 1998: 46; cf. 1990: 65)

Like the Categorical Imperative, (U) concerns action norms (maxims), but unlike Kant's principle, it does not claim to govern actions directly. Its function is to guide and constrain participants in practical discourses, as a "rule of argumentation." Note that the formulation of (U), by referring to interests and value-orientations, ensures morality's concern, beyond Kant, with both pragmatic and ethical goals, provided they prove omnilaterally acceptable.

Habermas presents (U) as embodying the universalist, formal, deontological, and, on the meta-ethical level, cognitivist features of discourse ethics (1990: 196). "Universality" refers to the general formulation of moral norms. They do not award privileges and contain no exceptions. With regard to formality, (U) instantiates the proceduralist practical epistemology introduced by (D). However, (U) is not to be misunderstood as a constructivist decision procedure directly capable of ruling out false norms and validating others. In contemporary versions of moral constructivism, including Rainer Forst's variant of discourse ethics, familiarity with a procedural criterion allows moral theorists faced with empirical controversy to infer what could

699

and what could not count as a satisfactory norm (Forst 2012: 20f). Habermas' avowed aim is the more modest one of clarifying the moral point of view, but, as we will see in the next two paragraphs, (U) can be read as having some substantive implications. As a presumption as to which norms would be validated by discourses under (U), Habermas has named basic or human rights, and fought off the interpretation that norms concerning distributive justice, benevolence, and solidarity would not qualify (1996a: 115; 1998: 43). To settle the validity of norms, it is necessary that *actual* discourses be conducted, yet interpreted under *idealizing* conditions. Only omnilateral participation would ensure that reasons are glossed from everyone's perspective, but since moral questions address all of "humanity or a presupposed republic of world citizens," such actual discourses will always remain parochial and must be conducted in a way that takes into account absent others (1996a: 108).

For Habermas, the deontological aspect of discourse ethics concerns the strict and unconditional character of moral norms (1990: 196). At the same time, (U) is a deontological principle in the sense that it does not propose to define the good independently from the right, nor define the right as maximizing the good (Rawls 1999: 22). Not only is it agnostic about what the good consists in; it imposes universal acceptability as a constraint on the pursuit of the good. However, (U) is not a deontological principle in a third familiar sense, defined by a disregard for consequences (Alexander and Moore 2012). (U) is exclusively concerned with consequences and side effects. A maxim such as *"fiat iustitia, pereat mundus"* ("Let there be justice, though the world perish") would hold no attraction in practical discourses under (U), given that it does not even pretend to accommodate people's interests. In including both intended and unintended consequences, (U) implicitly rejects the scholastic doctrine of double effect, according to which the anticipated, but non-intended, side effects of our actions can be discounted in the evaluation of moral maxims (MacIntyre 2011). Finally, attention to consequences induces a fallibilist feature into discourse ethics. Even well-supported norms can claim only *prima facie* validity since their support must rely on consolidated estimates of typical cases.

One much-debated issue is whether (U) is compatible with the prospect of utilitarian or other consequentialist moral norms winning out in practical discourses (Gunnarsson 2000: 109–19; Benhabib 1992: 35). Whether this prospect is understood as a *reductio*-type criticism or as illustrating the laudable neutrality of discourse ethics, a brief discussion can contribute to a better grasp of Habermas' position. Habermas appreciates utilitarian moral thought as a thoroughly modern competitor to Kantianism, and has criticized

Lawrence Kohlberg for ranking utilitarian moral views on a lower stage of moral development than Kantian ones (Habermas 1990: 172). Recall also that (D) only committed us to the "sense of impartiality of practical judgments," thereby allowing the validation of utilitarian action norms within discourse theory in general. Similarly, it seems that, under (U), people can agree freely and without coercion to a norm maximizing aggregate satisfaction, even if they, as a consequence, should lose out altogether, provided their interests were equally considered. However, earlier formulations of (U) and related materials suggest that discourse morality, as a precondition of rational acceptance, requires more than equal consideration of interests. It requires "the satisfaction of everyone's interest" or even the realization of "what is equally in the interest of all" (1990: 65; 1998: 13), thus putting strong indivi- dualist constraints on proposed norms. What finally makes a substantive, anti-utilitarian reading of (U) most plausible is that discourse ethics, display- ing a keen sense of the distinction between the rational demands of morality and supererogation, does not doubt utilitarianism's claim to universality, but questions the rationality of its precepts from a first-person point of view. If, for example, under generalized "lifeboat" conditions, there existed no way of resolving a conflict through generally acceptable norms ensuring the satisfac- tion of everyone's interests, the demands of morality would be suspended. "Enlightenment morality has done away with sacrifice" (Habermas 2005: 273). In contexts in which norms cannot guarantee the protection of everyone's interests, discourse morality has no authority.

Philosophical justifications of (U) and analogous principles have followed different strategies and have varied in strength. The one thing that authors have been able to agree on is that any justification of discourse ethics must be relative to an interlocutor's engagement in sincere reasoning, thereby per- mitting recourse to "unavoidable presuppositions" of such practices and the use of weak or strong transcendental arguments. Karl-Otto Apel has argued that whoever intentionally uses language in a meaningful way, but especially so in a scholarly or scientific context, accepts a principle like (U) as entailed by an "*a priori* of argumentation," as all attempts at meaningful denial must entangle them in "performative contradiction" (Apel 1980: 273). Rainer Forst has suggested a different transcendental justification, bypassing controversies in the philosophy of language, and emphasizing the dual character of justi- fication as accounting for validity and normativity. He has argued that a reflection on the nature of reasoning as owed to others gives us insight both into the correctness and into the binding character of the principle of morality. The autonomous character of morality ensures that a recursive justification of reason to itself will be convincing and, at the same time, normative for finite agents (Forst 2012: 58f). Habermas has pursued two justificatory strategies. One is an account of how rival, non-communicative processes of norm validation have withered away in modernity (1998: 39–41, 45). The other is a philosophical account that relies on "weakly transcendental" elements. Any derivation of (U), Habermas argues, must rest on a small number of implicit "rules of argumentation":

> (i) that nobody who could make a relevant contribution may be excluded; (ii) that all participants are granted an equal opportunity to make contributions; (iii) that the participants must mean what they say; (iv) that communication must be freed from external and internal coercion so that the "yes" or "no" stances that participants adopt on criticizable validity claims are motivated solely by the rational force of the better reasons. (1998: 44; cf. 1990: 89)

But these rules, unspecific for morality, by themselves will not yield (U), nor will they account for the moral "ought" conveyed (though not prescribed) by (U). *Contra* Apel, Habermas claims that a moral "ought" cannot be derived from the "so to speak transcendental constraint of unavoidable presuppositions of argumentation alone; rather it attaches ... to the norms *introduced* into discourse to which the reasons mobilized in deliberation refer" (1998: 45, original emphasis). This suggests that what confers validity upon the results of discourses are the substantive reasons for material norms. But the mere combination of non-specific rules of argumentation and substantive moral reasoning disregards the moral significance of one's participation in the discursive procedure itself, as sketched in (D). (U) must thus rest on (D), the rules of argumentation, and a further element, an understanding of what a moral norm is: an unconditional, general rule governing the distribution of goods, constrained by equal concern for all (Rehg 1994; 2011: 126). As we have seen, however, (D) itself has not been generally vindicated independently of its plausibility under modern conditions (Finlayson 2000).

The strongest case that can be made for (U), perhaps, is not that it may be without alternatives, but that only the self-legislative aspect of discursive validation is capable of conferring moral normativity on action norms. The central significance of the co-operative self-legislation of moral norms is brought out once we look at the cognitivist commitments of discourse meta-ethics. "Cognitivism" here should not be understood in a literal sense, as indicating that moral statements have truth values. In contrast to questions of empirical truth claims, which are "justification transcendent" in principle, the sense of "rightness" in moral questions just *is* the sense of "ideal warranted acceptability" (Habermas 2005: 248). Moral claims have to make up for their lack of objectivity by universal, maximally inclusive acceptability. This weak interpretation of cognitivism has come in for criticism from a moral realist variant of discourse theory, interpreting the "generalizable interests" clause in (U) as referring to objects for discovery, not construction (Lafont 1999: 315–60, Davis 1994). By introducing interests (and not, for example, participants' wishes) as the currency of morality in the formulation of (U), Habermas had suggested a potential basis for moral claims in empirical states of affairs. However, two reasons speak against a moral realist reading of discourse ethics. The first is the ontological argument that the interests in question are themselves open to construction, interpretation, and embedding in a meaningful practice. Unlike basic medical needs, say, they are not to be read off the objective circumstances of a situation, and depend on the world-disclosing features of participants' languages (Habermas 1993: 90). The second, and more important, reason is that a realist reading could only account for the correctness, not the normativity, i.e. the subjectively binding character, of whatever outcomes a practice under (U) yields. As a variant of Kantian ethics, discourse ethics insists that moral insight into the correctness of norms in itself represents an insight into being obligated towards others. Moral agents stand in need of an answer to the question of why the results of (U) are not just correct in the sense that non-compliance would be wrong and blameworthy, but why they should feel their normative pull and recognize themselves as obligated through them. In rejecting moral realism, Habermas denies that normativity could be derived from the existence of states of affairs in the world. Engaging in a process of a co-operative construction of generalizable interests, not from an observer's but from a participant's perspective, is ineliminably intertwined with the authoritative character any such construction would have (Habermas 2005: 268).

Finally, how does discourse ethics conceive of the action-guiding function of morality? We have seen that principle (U) restricts itself to the validation of norms, disregarding their employment in action, and especially in situations of moral conflict. Because moral norms are universal and categorically binding, discourse ethics is wholly opposed to gradualism or the balancing of moral norms, and especially so in cases of conflicting "ethical" or personal values. On the other hand, moral norms have been provisionally justified to apply in "normal" situations, in disregard of details, of unexpected constellations, of the non-standard claims of concrete individuals, and, perhaps most importantly, disregarding the fact that conflicting moral norms may simultaneously command our loyalty. Habermas' response lies in adopting, from

Klaus Günther (1993), a distinction between discourses of justification and discourses of application. Like Kant, Günther and Habermas believe that although obligations may seem to conflict, correct norms form a consistent and coherent system. Discourses of application are to resolve how one should act in a given, singular situation. They need to consider the morally salient features of the situation, including a concern for the embedded individual, in coming up with an answer as to which norm is most appropriate under the circumstances, i.e. which norm best does justice to all details of a complex situation. Outsourcing questions of application from justificatory discourses tempers the rigoristic consequences that deontological ethics of the Kantian type can evoke. It avoids the conclusion that various and incompatible obligations must leave us in situations of irresolvable and tragic conflict, and thus allows discourse ethics to uphold the categorical character of the moral "ought."

BIBLIOGRAPHY

An asterisk denotes secondary literature especially suitable for further reading.

Alexander, Larry and Michael Moore 2012. "Deontological Ethics," *Stanford Encyclopedia of Philosophy*: https://plato.stanford.edu/entries/ethics-deontological/

Apel, Karl-Otto 1980. *Towards a Transformation of Philosophy*, trans. G. Adey and D. Frisby. London: Routledge.

Benhabib, Seyla 1992. *Situating the Self*. Cambridge: Polity.

Cooke, Maeve 1994. *Language and Reason. A Study of Habermas' Pragmatics*. Cambridge, Mass.: MIT Press.

Davis, Felmon 1994. "Discourse Ethics and Ethical Realism. A Realist Re-Alignment of Discourse Ethics," *European Journal of Philosophy* 2, 125–42.

Finlayson, James Gordon 2000. "Modernity and Morality in Habermas's Discourse Ethics," *Inquiry* 43, 319–40.*

Forst, Rainer 2012. *The Right to Justification*, trans. Jeffrey Flynn. New York: Columbia University Press.

Gunnarsson, Logi 2000. *Making Moral Sense*. Cambridge University Press.

Günther, Klaus 1992. "Die Freiheit der Stellungnahme als politisches Grundrecht," *Archiv für Rechts- und Sozialphilosophie*, Beiheft (Supplementary Volume) 54, 58–73.

Günther, Klaus 1993. *The Sense of Appropriateness. Application Discourses in Morality and Law*, trans. John Farrell. Albany, NY: SUNY Press.

Habermas, Jürgen 1984. *The Theory of Communicative Action*, vol. 1. *Reason and the Rationalization of Society*, trans. Thomas A. McCarthy. Boston, Mass.: Beacon Press.

Habermas, Jürgen 1987. *The Theory of Communicative Action*, vol. 2. *Lifeworld and System: A Critique of Functionalist Reason*, trans. Thomas A. McCarthy. Boston, Mass.: Beacon Press.

Habermas, Jürgen 1990. *Moral Consciousness and Communicative Action*, trans. Christian Lenhardt. Cambridge, Mass.: MIT Press.

Habermas, Jürgen 1993. *Justification and Application*, trans. Ciaran P. Cronin. Cambridge, Mass.: MIT Press.

Habermas, Jürgen 1996a. *Between Facts and Norms*, trans. William Rehg. Cambridge, Mass.: MIT Press.

Habermas, Jürgen 1996b. "Reply to Symposium Participants, Benjamin N. Cardozo School of Law," *Cardozo Law Review* 17, 1477–1557.

Habermas, Jürgen 1998. *The Inclusion of the Other*, ed. Ciaran P. Cronin and Pablo De Greiff. Cambridge, Mass: MIT Press.

Habermas, Jürgen 2005. *Truth and Justification*, trans. Barbara Fultner. Cambridge, Mass.: MIT Press.

Habermas, Jürgen 2009. "Einleitung," in *Jürgen Habermas: Diskursethik. Philosophische Texte*, vol. 3. Frankfurt am Main: Suhrkamp, pp. 9–30.

Heath, Joseph 2014. "Rebooting Discourse Ethics," *Philosophy and Social Criticism* 40, 9, 829–66.

Honneth, Axel 2009. *Pathologies of Reason*, trans. James Ingram. New York: Columbia University Press.

Kettner, Matthias 2002. "The Disappearance of Discourse Ethics in Habermas' Between Facts and Norms," in René von Schomberg and Kenneth Baynes (eds.), *Discourse and Democracy*. Albany, NY: SUNY Press, pp. 201–18.

Lafont, Cristina 1999. *The Linguistic Turn in Hermeneutic Philosophy*, trans. José Medina. Cambridge, Mass.: MIT Press.

MacIntyre, Alison 2011. "Doctrine of Double Effect," *Stanford Encyclopedia of Philosophy*: https://plato.stanford.edu/entries/double-effect/

McCarthy, Thomas 1991. *Ideals and Illusions*. Cambridge, Mass.: MIT Press.

McMahon, Christopher 2013. "Discourse Ethics," in Hugh LaFollette (ed.), *International Encyclopedia of Ethics*. Oxford: Wiley-Blackwell, pp. 1396–1405.

Niesen, Peter 2011. "Legitimacy without Morality. Habermas and Maus on the Relationship between Law and Morality," in C. Ungureanu, C. Joerges and K. Günther (eds.), *Jürgen Habermas*, vol. 1, Avebury: Ashgate, pp. 123–46.

Rawls, John 1995. "Reply to Habermas," *Journal of Philosophy*, 92, 3, 132–80.

Rawls, John 1999. *A Theory of Justice*, revised edn. Oxford University Press.

Rehg, William 1994. *Insight and Solidarity. A Study in the Discourse Ethics of Jürgen Habermas*. Berkeley, Calif.: University of California Press.

Rehg, William 2011. "Discourse Ethics," in Barbara Fultner (ed.), *Jürgen Habermas: Key Concepts*. Durham: Acumen, pp. 115–39.

Taylor, Charles 1985. *Human Agency and Language. Philosophical Papers I*. Cambridge University Press.

53

Decision Theory

BEN EGGLESTON

Decision theory is important in the history of moral philosophy, and it is important in an unusual way. Many theories in the history of moral philosophy, such as utilitarianism and Kant's moral theory, are not only parts of that history but are also stand-alone moral theories in their own right. In fact, it is their prominence and influence as distinct moral theories that make them important parts of the history of moral philosophy. In contrast, decision theory is not a distinct moral theory. Instead, it is important in the history of moral philosophy in a different way: as a source of concepts and principles that play crucial roles in certain important moral theories. In short, although decision theory itself is not among the discrete parts of the history of moral philosophy, some of its elements are integral to several theories that are.

Before focusing on those elements specifically, it will be useful to briefly survey decision theory more generally. Decision theory is a field of thought that consists not of a single theory, but of many theories; it is a broad and variegated field, with its constituent theories having little in common other than being concerned with decision-making. But certain organizing distinctions are commonly made. One is the familiar descriptive/prescriptive distinction: some theories attempt to explain certain systematically or anecdotally observed patterns of decision-making, while other theories propose normative criteria for decision-making, such as principles for making certain kinds of decisions rationally. Another organizing distinction, independent of the descriptive/prescriptive one, hinges on the maker of the decision: there are theories that focus on the decisions of a single person, theories that focus on the decisions of several interacting people (as in game theory), and theories that focus on the decisions of groups constituted by multiple people (as in social choice theory). As discussed below, the elements of decision theory that are

I would like to thank Donald Bruckner, Dale Miller, Martin Peterson, and Ned McClennen for their comments on an earlier version of this chapter.

integral to major moral theories come mostly from prescriptive approaches to individual decision-making.

Given the breadth of the field of decision theory and the variety of the kinds of decision-making that fall within its ambit, one might wonder whether it claims moral theories as constituent theories as well. After all, most moral theories often focus on decision-making and the prescriptive half of decision theory would seem to accommodate them easily. The reality, however, is that moral philosophy is typically seen as separate from, rather than a department of, decision theory. Canonically moral concepts and principles such as fairness, justice, individual rights, and the golden rule are largely absent from decision theory (though some parts of social choice theory do attempt to address them). Instead, decision theory usually takes the pursuit of individual self-interest or well-being as its starting point; and even when it does not, it is principally concerned with non-moral aspects of decision-making, such as when and how a person's preferences can be represented in a mathematically convenient structure, how complex choices can sometimes be reduced to simpler ones, and what risks it is rational to take. The mostly non-moral character of decision theory is manifested in the elements of decision theory discussed in this chapter.

The organization of this chapter reflects the fact that elements of decision theory have been used in two main ways in the history of moral philosophy (or the history of ethics – different terms are, of course, used by different authors). First, moral theorists have drawn on elements of decision theory in order to more fully specify the contents of their moral principles. That is, they have drawn on elements of decision theory in order to articulate their principles of moral rightness and moral wrong-ness more explicitly, or to provide something like an algorithm that an agent can follow in order to act morally (by the lights of their theories) in a particular decision situation. Second, moral theorists have drawn on elements of decision theory in order to argue in support of their moral principles. In most cases, decision-theoretic reasoning has been used in combination with moral reasoning, but in some cases, decision-theoretic reasoning has been claimed to entail, by itself, substantive moral principles.[1]

---

[1] The plan of this chapter is but one of many possible ways of discussing decision theory and moral philosophy. For other approaches, see Dreier 2004 and the articles in *Ethical Theory and Moral Practice* vol. 13, no. 5 (November 2010), a special issue titled "Rational Choice and Ethics": Lumer 2010a, Narveson 2010, McClennen 2010, Verbeek 2010, Lumer 2010b, and Hansson 2010.

SPECIFYING THE CONTENTS OF MORAL PRINCIPLES

Moral theorists, as a group, have diverse aims and priorities in articulating their theories. Most of them, however, take the specification of a principle of rightness and wrongness to be a central task in their endeavors, and in this task most of them strive to make that principle highly determinate – i.e., providing specific guidance concerning how an agent should act in a large range of cases. Some moral theorists, especially consequentialist ones, find elements of decision theory to be helpful for this purpose.

Probably the most influential such element is the idea of expected utility. This is used primarily in the specification of consequentialist principles – in particular, in response to the fact that it is usually impossible for an agent to predict all of the consequences of all of her possible actions. For an illustration of how expected-utility theory can be used in such cases, suppose that there is an outbreak of a disease that a public-health doctor can treat with either a conventional antibiotic or an experimental antibiotic. It is known that the conventional antibiotic will result in partial eradication, and that the experimental antibiotic will result in either complete eradication or no change at all. Which option is better?

Expected-utility theory provides a way of answering this question, if two kinds of quantitative information can be established. First, probabilities need to be assigned to the possible outcomes. Given the description of the situation just provided, the conventional antibiotic obviously has a 100-percent probability of resulting in partial eradication. And let us also suppose that the experimental antibiotic has a 30-percent probability of resulting in complete eradication and a 70-percent probability of resulting in no change.

Second, the possible outcomes need to be assigned utilities that reflect their relative goodness. Obviously complete eradication is better than partial eradication, and partial eradication is better than no change. So, there is a goodness difference between the first outcome and the second, and a goodness difference between the second and the third. Expected-utility theory requires a comparison of the *magnitudes* of those goodness differences. So, let us suppose that complete eradication would be better than partial eradication *three times as much as* partial eradication would be better than no change. Then we can say that complete eradication, partial eradication, and no change have utilities of 5, 2, and 1. (Many other values, such as 27, 21, and 19, would work equally well. The absolute magnitudes do not matter; only the *relative* magnitudes of the *gaps* between the numbers matter.)

Given these pieces of quantitative information, expected-utility theory provides a way of ascertaining which option is better. The two options' expected utilities are to be computed, and the option with the higher expected utility is better. An option's expected utility is defined as the weighted average of the utilities of its possible outcomes, where the weights are the probabilities of the occurrences of the possible outcomes. Since the conventional antibiotic has a 100-percent probability of resulting in an outcome having a utility of 2, its expected utility is easy to compute:

$$100 \text{ percent} \times 2 = 2$$

And since the experimental antibiotic has a 30-percent probability of resulting in an outcome having a utility of 5 and a 70-percent probability of resulting in an outcome having a utility of 1, its expected utility can be computed as follows:

$$(30 \text{ percent} \times 5) + (70 \text{ percent} \times 1) = 1.5 + 0.7 = 2.2$$

Because the experimental antibiotic has the higher expected utility, it is the better option.

This sort of reasoning is invoked in several ways in the specification of consequentialist principles. J.J.C. Smart, articulating an act-utilitarian theory, writes that although expected-utility considerations do not affect whether an act is *right* (for that still depends on the act's actual consequences), having maximal expected utility is enough to make an act *rational*.[2] Some theorists, however, go farther, and make rightness itself depend on expected utility (or expected value, where value is understood to be broader than utility, as consequentialism is broader than utilitarianism). The best-known advocate of this maneuver is Frank Jackson, who formulates a "decision-theoretic consequentialism."[3]

Acts are not the only things whose effects interest consequentialists. Some consequentialists focus on the effects of various rules, motives, character traits, or institutions, and here, too, expected-utility reasoning provides a way of coping with unpredictability. For example, Brad Hooker begins his rule-consequentialist book by asking, "Shouldn't we try to live by the moral code whose communal acceptance would, as far as we can tell, have the best

---

[2] Smart 1961: 33–4. This material reappears in Smart 1973: 46–7. A similar position is suggested in Lyons 1965: 26–7.

[3] Jackson 1991: 463–4 (though the phrase "decision-theoretic consequentialism" is from the title of the article).

consequences?"[4] Because of the difficulty of identifying that code, Hooker writes that moral codes should be compared not in terms of the actual consequences of their communal acceptance, but in terms of the expected values of their communal acceptance.

We have seen how one element of decision theory – the idea of expected utility – is employed in the specification of the contents of moral principles. Although this is the element that is most illuminating to consider at length, other elements are also employed. For example, Smart suggests turning to decision theory for techniques for the assignment of probabilities to possible outcomes[5] and for deciding whether to comply with an onerous but generally beneficial rule.[6] Michael Slote suggests formulating act consequentialism as requiring only that the agent perform an act that is *good enough* rather than the *best* one – using the economist Herbert Simon's idea of "satisficing."[7] And there is an extensive literature debating the coherence of interpersonal comparisons of well-being.[8] In many ways, then, elements of decision theory are used in the specification of the contents of moral principles.

ARGUING IN SUPPORT OF MORAL PRINCIPLES

The other frequent use of elements of decision theory in moral philosophy is in the formulation of arguments in support of moral principles. Important examples of this kind of work are found not only in consequentialist theories, but in Kantian and Hobbesian ones as well.

Smart's Maximization Argument

One argument in support of act utilitarianism is the simple idea that if it is rational for one person to maximize his or her personal well-being, then it is equally justifiable, in the moral realm, for overall well-being to be maximized. This is true, according to this argument, even if maximizing overall well-being requires actions that decrease, rather than increase, certain persons' well-being. Smart makes this argument in the following passage:

---

[4] Hooker 2000: 1. All of the material from Hooker discussed in this paragraph is in Hooker 2000: 1–2, but also see Hooker 2000: 72–5.

[5] Smart 1961: 28–9; and Smart 1973: 40–1.

[6] Smart 1956: 351–2; Smart 1961: 43–4; and Smart 1973: 57–60. See also Gauthier 1965.

[7] The seminal works on this topic are Slote 1984 and Pettit 1984. See also Byron 2004.

[8] See, for example, Elster and Roemer 1991.

if it is rational for me to choose the pain of a visit to the dentist in order to prevent the pain of toothache, why is it not rational of me to choose a pain for Jones, similar to that of my visit to the dentist, if that is the only way in which I can prevent a pain, equal to that of my toothache, for Robinson?[9]

Smart offers this argument in response to a claim that John Rawls presents in his 1958 article "Justice as Fairness,"[10] and Rawls criticizes it in his *A Theory of Justice* (1971):

> This view of social cooperation [i.e., act utilitarianism] is the consequence of extending to society the principle of choice for one man, and then, to make this extension work, conflating all persons into one through the imaginative acts of the impartial sympathetic spectator. Utilitarianism does not take seriously the distinction between persons.[11]

This remains one of the most well-known objections to act utilitarianism, and its merits continue to be debated.[12]

Harsanyi's Hypothetical-Choice Argument

Another argument in support of act utilitarianism, one developed in the work of John C. Harsanyi, proceeds as follows.[13] If it would be rational for the people of some society to unanimously prefer that social decisions be made in accordance with a certain moral principle, then that fact would make that moral principle justified. (This is, of course, the intuition at the root of the social-contract tradition in moral and political philosophy.) Unfortunately, given the fact that persons' different positions in society cause it to be rational

---

[9] Smart 1961: 26; and Smart 1973: 37.   [10] Rawls 1958.   [11] Rawls 1971: 27.

[12] Probing discussions include Brink 1993 and Zwolinski 2008.

[13] This paragraph and the succeeding one are based on Harsanyi 1953; Harsanyi 1977: 48–51; and Harsanyi 1982: 44–8.

Harsanyi also formulated highly technical axiomatic arguments in support of act utilitarianism. See Harsanyi 1955; and Harsanyi 1977: 64–81. Although this approach attracted considerable attention from other decision theorists in the ensuing decades, it had a much smaller influence on the work of moral theorists. Harsanyi himself writes that it "yields a lesser amount of philosophically interesting information about the nature of morality" than the approach discussed in the text (Harsanyi 1982: 48). John Broome evaluates it more favorably; see Broome 1991: 58. For an overview and critical assessment of it, see Roemer 1996: 138–47. But for a largely favorable moral-theoretic reception, see Risse 2002.

Despite formulating these pioneering arguments in support of act utilitarianism, Harsanyi actually turned out to be a longtime advocate of rule utilitarianism, which he supported using decision-theoretic and other arguments. For what might be Harsanyi's last published work on this topic, see Harsanyi 1998.

for them to have divergent preferences, it seems hopeless to argue in favor of any moral principle in this way. But there are variations on this approach that might be fruitful. For example, if it would be rational for the people in some hypothetical choice situation to unanimously prefer that social decisions be made in accordance with a certain moral principle, and that hypothetical choice situation had moral force (despite being hypothetical), then that fact would also make that moral principle justified.[14]

Now (the argument continues), imagine a choice situation populated by people who are ignorant of their positions in society, so that each person must think impartially about how he or she would prefer for social decisions to be made. Surely this choice situation has moral force, despite being hypothetical; in fact, it gains its moral force from the very alteration that makes it hypothetical. Now, what would it be rational for the people in this choice situation to prefer? To answer this question, the argument invokes decision-theoretic reasoning. It claims that it would be rational for each person (1) to assume that he or she stood an equal probability of occupying each of the positions occupied by the people of that society, (2) to deduce that his or her expected utility would be maximized if social decisions were made in accordance with act utilitarianism, and (3) to prefer that social decisions be made in that way. Because of the moral force of the given choice situation (so the argument concludes), this preference entails that act utilitarianism is justified.

Although this argument has been criticized,[15] its basic strategy is ingenious. It starts with the obviously moral question of which moral principle is justified, and then argues that we would have an answer to this question if we could answer the non-moral question of what it would be rational for people in a certain choice situation to prefer. Finally, it invokes decision-theoretic reasoning to answer that non-moral question. In effect, it engages in just enough moral reasoning – the design of the choice situation – to enable the rest of the work to be done by non-moral reasoning. And the role of decision theory, of course, is to provide that non-moral reasoning.

Rawls's Hypothetical-Choice Argument

A similar argument is used by Rawls, in support of his Kantian theory of justice. Rawls follows Harsanyi in imagining a choice situation populated by

[14] A classic discussion of the general approach of invoking hypothetical situations in moral reasoning is Broad 1916.

[15] For a recent and accessible critique, see Roemer 2008.

people who are ignorant of their positions in society, so that each person must think impartially about how he or she would prefer for social decisions to be made. (Rawls calls his choice situation "the original position" and famously characterizes the persons' lack of information with the evocative metaphor of the "veil of ignorance.")[16] Then, in order to answer the question of what it would be rational for the people in this choice situation to prefer, Rawls again follows Harsanyi in drawing on a choice rule of decision theory. However, he departs from Harsanyi's path by denying that it would be rational for the people to employ the rule of maximizing expected utility. Instead, Rawls argues, it would be rational for the people to employ the maximin rule – the rule of choosing an option whose worst possible outcome is at least as good as the worst possible outcome of every other option. (As suggested by the name, the idea is to *maximize* the *minimum*. All of the options are compared solely in terms of their worst, or minimum, possible outcomes – their other possible outcomes do not matter.)[17] Rawls points out that if the people employ this rule, then they will reject the prospect of social decisions being made in accordance with act utilitarianism, since such a regime might cause the worst-off people in society to be worse off than it is necessary for the worst-off people to be. (After all, maximizing overall well-being does not necessarily maximize the well-being of the worst-off.)[18] Instead, the kind of regime recommended by the maximin rule is one governed by Rawls's conception of justice,[19] in which concern for the well-being of the worst-off people in society is explicitly built into the governing principle:

> All social primary goods – liberty and opportunity, income and wealth, and the bases of self-respect – are to be distributed equally unless an unequal distribution of any or all of these goods is *to the advantage of the least favored.*[20]

This is the "General Conception" of Rawls's theory of justice. In essence, it is the maximin decision rule restated as a principle of moral and political philosophy. Rawls further argues that the people would reason that "the long-run tendency" of this principle would require two kinds of strict equality – equality of political liberties and fair equality of opportunity – and would allow inequality only in the distribution of social and economic goods.[21] Consequently, the principles Rawls says the people would endorse are explicitly egalitarian in a way that the maximin rule is not. But the persons'

---

[16] Rawls 1971: 136–42.   [17] Rawls 1971: 154–5.   [18] Rawls 1971: 156, 158, 160, and 170–1.   [19] Rawls 1971: 152–7.   [20] Rawls 1971: 303, emphasis added.   [21] Rawls 1971: 152.

reasoning about what they would prefer is entirely guided by the maximin rule, not any moral or other independent commitment to equality.

Rawls's reliance on the maximin rule is generally seen as one of the more questionable parts of his theory. Rawls acknowledges that "Clearly the maximin rule is not, in general, a suitable guide for choices under uncertainty"[22] but defends the maximin rule as suitable when three conditions are satisfied: the basis for probability estimates is weak, the option selected by the maximin rule will lead to an acceptable outcome, and the options selected by other rules might lead to unacceptable outcomes.[23] (And he claims that these conditions are satisfied in the present case.)[24] Most moral theorists maintain that the general implausibility of the maximin rule (which Rawls acknowledges, as just mentioned) persists even when these conditions are satisfied, though some recent discussions of the maximin rule are more sympathetic.[25]

Gauthier and McClennen: Deriving Morality from Rationality

The last use of decision theory in moral philosophy to be considered here is found in the Hobbesian moral theory of David Gauthier and the closely aligned view of Edward F. McClennen.[26] One of the perennial questions of ethics concerns the seemingly irresolvable conflict between self-interest and morality – often encapsulated in the question "Why be moral?" It is a commonplace of discussions of this question that a person's interests are usually better served by complying with certain moral rules (such as rules requiring cooperation and the keeping of promises) than by breaking them. That is, it is usually rational to comply with certain moral rules. Gauthier and McClennen draw attention to the further, subtler truth that a person's interests are usually well served if she has a *disposition* to comply with certain moral rules, even if that disposition is so strong that it causes her to comply with moral rules in cases in which, all things considered, she would be better off breaking those rules. That is, it is usually rational to be disposed to comply with certain moral rules. Now, the next step in the argument is the novel one,

---

[22] Rawls 1971: 153.   [23] Rawls 1971: 154–5.   [24] Rawls 1971: 155–6.

[25] See Angner 2004 (which also provides a helpful overview of the previous debate over the maximin rule) and van Roojen 2008.

[26] For Gauthier, see Gauthier 1986: 182–7; Gauthier 1994: 701; and Gauthier 1998: 58, n. 5. For McClennen, see McClennen 1990: 157 and 209–13; and McClennen 1997: 231–3 and 241. Gauthier later revised his decision-theoretic views substantially; see Gauthier 2013: 606–9. The approach proposed there might, in time, turn out to be another important use of decision theory in moral philosophy.

from a decision-theoretic point of view. It is, in essence, the assertion of the principle that if some action is required by rules that it is rational for a person to be disposed to comply with, then that action is rational (for that person) – even if it makes the person worse off, all things considered. Given the earlier claim that it is rational to be disposed to comply with certain moral rules, it follows that the actions required by those moral rules are also rational, from a decision-theoretic point of view.

Two things are important to notice about this argument. First, the asserted decision-theoretic principle is highly unorthodox. Orthodox decision theory holds that an act is rational if and only if it maximally advances the person's interests: an act "inherits" its rationality (for a person) from its outcome's optimality (for a person). This is denied by the principle on which Gauthier and McClennen rely. That principle holds that an act inherits its rationality from the rationality of the rules that require it, and those rules inherit their rationality from the optimality of their outcomes. By analogy with the relationship between traditional (act) utilitarianism and rule utilitarianism, we can say that Gauthier's and McClennen's arguments aspire to nothing less than discrediting the traditional egoistic foundations of decision theory and re-founding the theory on the principle of rule egoism instead.[27]

The second thing it is important to notice about this argument is its extreme ambition: it is a genuine instance of attempting to derive morality from rationality. In the arguments for moral theories reviewed previously (those of Smart, Harsanyi, and Rawls), the premises include substantive moral claims as well as non-moral claims (such as decision-theoretic claims). But the argument suggested by the work of Gauthier and McClennen has no substantive moral claims among its premises. Instead, the argument purports to show that rather than needing to appeal to moral considerations in order to vindicate moral rules, we can just appeal to decision-theoretic rationality. Thus, the argument not only defends moral rules but also – and perhaps primarily – purports to give a deep and rigorous answer to the question "Why be moral?" It is thus one of the most ambitious uses of decision theory in the history of moral philosophy.

---

[27] This unorthodox conception of rationality is, of course, controversial. See, for example, MacIntosh 1988; Uzan-Milofsky 2009; and the articles in the symposium on Gauthier's *Morals by Agreement* in *Ethics* vol. 123, no. 4 (July 2013): Morris 2013, Gauthier 2013, MacIntosh 2013, Bratman 2013, Finkelstein 2013, and van Donselaar 2013.

BIBLIOGRAPHY

An asterisk denotes secondary literature especially suitable for further reading.

Angner, Erik 2004. "Revisiting Rawls: *A Theory of Justice* in the Light of Levi's Theory of Decision," *Theoria* 70: 3–21.

Bratman, Michael E. 2013. "The Interplay of Intention and Reason," *Ethics* 123: 657–72.

Brink, David 1993. "The Separateness of Persons, Distributive Norms, and Moral Theory," in R.G. Frey and Christopher W. Morris (eds.), *Value, Welfare, and Morality*, Cambridge University Press, pp. 252–89.

Broad, C.D. 1916. "On the Function of False Hypotheses in Ethics," *International Journal of Ethics* 26: 377–97.

Broome, John 1991. *Weighing Goods: Equality, Uncertainty and Time*. Oxford: Basil Blackwell.

Byron, Michael (ed.) 2004. *Satisficing and Maximizing: Moral Theorists on Practical Reason*. Cambridge University Press.

Dreier, James 2004. "Decision Theory and Morality," in Alfred R. Mele and Piers Rawling (eds.), *The Oxford Handbook of Rationality*, Oxford University Press, pp. 156–81.*

Elster, Jon and Roemer, John E. (eds.) 1991. *Interpersonal Comparisons of Well-Being*. Cambridge University Press.

Finkelstein, Claire 2013. "Pragmatic Rationality and Risk," *Ethics* 123: 673–99.

Gauthier, David 1965. "Rule-Utilitarianism and Randomization," *Analysis* 25: 68–9.

Gauthier, David 1986. *Morals by Agreement*. Oxford University Press.

Gauthier, David 1994. "Assure and Threaten," *Ethics* 104: 690–721.

Gauthier, David 1998. "Rethinking the Toxin Puzzle," in Jules L. Coleman and Christopher W. Morris (eds.), *Rational Commitment and Social Justice: Essays for Gregory Kavka*, Cambridge University Press, pp. 47–58.

Gauthier, David 2013. "Twenty-Five On," *Ethics* 123: 601–24.

Hansson, Sven Ove 2010. "The Harmful Influence of Decision Theory on Ethics," *Ethical Theory and Moral Practice* 13: 585–93.

Harsanyi, John C. 1953. "Cardinal Utility in Welfare Economics and in the Theory of Risk-Taking," *Journal of Political Economy* 61: 434–5.

Harsanyi, John C. 1955. "Cardinal Welfare, Individualistic Ethics, and Interpersonal Comparisons of Utility," *Journal of Political Economy* 63: 309–21.

Harsanyi, John C. 1977. *Rational Behaviour and Bargaining Equilibrium in Games and Social Situations*. Cambridge University Press.

Harsanyi, John C. 1982. "Morality and the Theory of Rational Behaviour," in Amartya Sen and Bernard Williams (eds.), *Utilitarianism and Beyond*, Cambridge University Press, pp. 39–62.

Harsanyi, John C. 1998. "A Preference-Based Theory of Well-Being and a Rule-Utilitarian Theory of Morality," in Werner Leinfellner and Eckehart Köhler (eds.), *Game Theory, Experience, Rationality: Foundations of Social Sciences, Economics and Ethics in Honor of John C. Harsanyi*, Dordrecht: Kluwer Academic Publishers, pp. 285–300.

Hooker, Brad 2000. *Ideal Code, Real World: A Rule-consequentialist Theory of Morality*. Oxford University Press.

Jackson, Frank 1991. "Decision-theoretic Consequentialism and the Nearest and Dearest Objection," *Ethics* 101: 461–82.

Lumer, Christoph 2010a. "Introduction: The Relevance of Rational Decision Theory for Ethics," *Ethical Theory and Moral Practice* 13: 485–96.

Lumer, Christoph 2010b. "Moral Desirability and Rational Decision," *Ethical Theory and Moral Practice* 13: 561–84.

Lyons, David 1965. *Forms and Limits of Utilitarianism*. Oxford University Press.

MacIntosh, Duncan 1988. "Libertarian Agency and Rational Morality: Action-Theoretical Objections to Gauthier's Dispositional Solution of the Compliance Problem," *The Southern Journal of Philosophy* 26: 499–525.

MacIntosh, Duncan 2013. "Assuring, Threatening, a Fully Maximizing Theory of Practical Rationality, and the Practical Duties of Agents," *Ethics* 123: 625–56.

McClennen, Edward F. 1990. *Rationality and Dynamic Choice: Foundational Explorations*. Cambridge University Press.

McClennen, Edward F. 1997. "Pragmatic Rationality and Rules," *Philosophy and Public Affairs* 26: 210–58.

McClennen, Edward F. 2010. "Rational Choice and Moral Theory," *Ethical Theory and Moral Practice* 13: 521–40.

Morris, Christopher W. 2013. "Introduction," *Ethics* 123: 595–600.

Narveson, Jan 2010. "The Relevance of Decision Theory to Ethical Theory," *Ethical Theory and Moral Practice* 13: 497–520.

Pettit, Philip 1984. "Satisficing Consequentialism," part II, *Proceedings of the Aristotelian Society* supplementary volume 58: 165–76.

Rawls, John 1958. "Justice as Fairness," *The Philosophical Review* 67: 164–94.

Rawls, John 1971. *A Theory of Justice*. Cambridge, MA: Harvard University Press.

Risse, Mathias 2002. "Harsanyi's 'Utilitarian Theorem' and Utilitarianism," *Noûs* 36: 550–77.

Roemer, John E. 1996. *Theories of Distributive Justice*. Cambridge, MA: Harvard University Press.

Roemer, John E. 2008. "Harsanyi's Impartial Observer Is *Not* a Utilitarian," in Marc Fleurbaey, Maurice Salles, and John A. Weymark (eds.), *Justice, Political Liberalism, and Utilitarianism: Themes from Harsanyi and Rawls*, Cambridge University Press, pp. 129–35.

Slote, Michael 1984. "Satisficing Consequentialism," part I, *Proceedings of the Aristotelian Society* supplementary volume 58: 139–63.

Smart, J.J.C. 1956. "Extreme and Restricted Utilitarianism," *The Philosophical Quarterly* 6: 344–54.

Smart, J.J.C. 1961. *An Outline of a System of Utilitarian Ethics*. Melbourne University Press.

Smart, J.J.C. 1973. "*An Outline of a System of Utilitarian Ethics*," in J.J.C. Smart and Bernard Williams, *Utilitarianism: For and Against*, Cambridge University Press, pp. 3–74.

Uzan-Milofsky, Marie 2009. "Shall We Be Resolute?" *Rationality and Society* 21: 337–57.

van Donselaar, Gijs 2013. "Sticks or Carrots? The Emergence of Self-Ownership," *Ethics* 123: 700–16.

van Roojen, Mark 2008. "Some Advantages of One Form of Argument for the Maximin Principle," *Acta Analytica* 23: 319–35.

Verbeek, Bruno 2010. "Rational Choice Virtues," *Ethical Theory and Moral Practice* 13: 541–59.

Zwolinski, Matt 2008. "The Separateness of Persons and Liberal Theory," *The Journal of Value Inquiry* 42: 147–65.

54

Rawls

KATRIN FLIKSCHUH

Rawls' political philosophy is widely seen as contractarian. Yet although the early Rawls describes his theory of justice in those terms, the later Rawls increasingly relies on 'constructivism' as an alternative summative statement of his position. Does constructivism *replace* contractualism or is it an elaboration of Rawls' distinctive contractualism method? Moreover, is constructivism a uniquely Kantian method of practical justification?

I am not persuaded that constructivism is uniquely Kantian. I think it more plausible to read Rawls' later constructivism as a development out of his earlier contractualism. This is not to say that there are no Kantian elements in Rawls' contractualist constructivism. To the contrary, Rawls' reading of Kant's ethics is essential to his formulation of both contractualism and constructivism. Indeed, Rawls' Kantianism mediates the development of his constructivism out of his contractualism. This, at any rate, is how I shall here interpret the relationship between contractualism, constructivism, Kant, and Rawls. There are numerous alternative ways in which to go about interpreting Rawlsian constructivism; given limited space I cannot engage in a discussion of comparative merits and demerits (Freeman 1990, Korsgaard 2008, O'Neill 1989, 2000). What follows is a partial and partisan interpretation: I am guided in my approach to Rawls by my sense of his *distance* from Kant. Though contentious, the reading here offered can serve as a useful contrast point to more dominant trends according to which Rawls' contractualist constructivism is fundamentally Kantian.

I shall proceed largely chronologically, beginning with Rawls' characterisation of his position as contractualist in *A Theory of Justice* (Rawls 1972), then moving to his article on 'Kantian Constructivism' (Rawls 1980), and finally to his outline of political constructivism in *Political Liberalism* (Rawls 1993). I shall ask what distinguishes contractualism from constructivism: methodologically, the latter's appeal to reasonableness over prudence seems important; normatively, constructivism is distinct from contractualism in its quest for social unity over mere cooperation. I shall ask what accounts for these differences, and shall suggest that one important source lies in Rawls' politicisation of Kant's ethics.

THE CONTRACTUALISM OF *A THEORY OF JUSTICE*

Rawls' Conception of the Social Contract Tradition

I shall use 'contractualism', 'contractarianism', and 'social contract theory' interchangeably, though I shall usually reserve the third of these terms for the history of social contract theorising. Traditional social contract theory offers a distinctive account of political obligation: it grounds the authority to rule in subjects' reciprocally agreed willingness to obey. Social contract theory construes subjects as the authors of their political subjection: the contract, willingly entered into, creates binding and enforceable obligations – though contract thinkers also typically specify the conditions that *unbind* contractees from these obligations. The index of *A Theory of Justice* contains four entries for 'social contract, traditional theory of'. There is no independent entry for 'contractualism', though there are over ten entries for 'social union'. The dearth of references to the social contract tradition is surprising in a 500-page disputation on social justice that claims to follow that tradition. However, if one takes into account entries for 'original position' and 'veil of ignorance' the number of entries is in line with what one would expect to find. Of the entries for traditional social contract theory, the first is frequently cited:

> My aim is to present a conception of justice which generalizes and carries to a higher level of abstraction the familiar theory of the social contract as found, say, in Locke, Rousseau, and Kant.　　　　　　　　(Rawls 1972: 11)

Rawls goes on to say that we are not to think of his contract theory as concerned with the problem of state foundation. The object of Rawlsian contractual agreement is principles of social justice for an already established civil society. The sense in which this is to employ contract theory at a 'higher level of abstraction' is clarified somewhat in the second entry on page 16:

> The merit of the contract terminology is that it conveys the idea that principles of justice may be conceived as principles that would be chosen by rational persons, and that in this way conceptions of justice may be explained and justified.　　　　　　　　(Rawls 1972: 16)

Traditional social contract theorists either presupposed independent criteria of justice (Locke) or took the content of justice to be a matter of positive law-making (Hobbes, Rousseau). Rawls, by contrast, employs the method of contractualist agreement to settle disputes over the shape and content of principles of justice. In so doing he transports contract thinking from the normative to the meta-normative level of justification (Milo 1995). But return to Rawls' list of classic contractarians: 'Locke, Rousseau, and Kant'. The omission of Hobbes is no less striking than is the inclusion of Kant. Pre-Rawls, any standard course on the history of political thought would have included Hobbes and excluded Kant. Kant invokes the idea of the contract in his political writings but it is another question how much work it does in Kant's account of political obligation. Hobbes is generally seen as the founding father of the idea of voluntary political obligation. Yet in a footnote to the cited passage on page 11 Rawls declares Kant's *Groundwork* to be 'definitive of the contract tradition', adding that, 'for all his greatness, Hobbes' *Leviathan* raises special problems' (Rawls 1972). Rawls does not elaborate on these special problems; he instead speaks of the 'contract view as primarily an ethical theory'. Hobbes appears to be excluded on these grounds. Rawls' casual exclusion of Hobbes' *Leviathan* and equally casual inclusion of Kant's *Groundwork of the Metaphysics of Morals* is responsible in no small measure for the ethicisation of modern liberal political morality.

Kantian Contractualism?

In what ways does the ethicisation of classic social contract theory manifest itself in *A Theory of Justice*? Methodologically, it does so in Rawls' deployment of what he calls Kant's 'categorical imperative procedure' in his construction of relevant circumstances of contractualist choice. Given their commitment to voluntarily incurred political obligation, contractualists standardly proceed by specifying a hypothetical choice situation. Ironically, this is clearest in Hobbes. Hobbes presents his readers with a binary choice: they can either remain in the state of nature or they can enter the civil condition. Hobbes supplies a number of supporting assumptions, including the assumption that choosers are rational maximisers of their own advantage who fear nothing so much as violent death. Being thus risk-aversive, they will 'choose' the civil condition. In Locke, too, the choice between the manifest inconveniences of the state of nature and the manifest conveniences of the civil condition ensures correctness in choice. Its 'rigging' of the initial choice situation is a frequent criticism of contractualism, including Rawls' contractualism (Dworkin 1975). Yet this is in fact the sort of reaction contractualists seek to elicit from their description of the hypothetical absence of state authority. At stake is not a preference-based choice between statehood or anarchy but subjects' reflective acknowledgement of the legitimacy of coercive political authority.

Although he shares his predecessors' voluntaristic rationale, Rawls' description of his hypothetical choice situation is more complex. Rawls does not offer a binary choice between 'state or no state', 'justice or no justice' – at issue is, rather, settlement on a set of principles for the regulation of the basic structure of society. Secondly, Rawls models circumstances of impartial choice. The question is not, 'which principles of justice do *you* prefer?' but rather 'which principles of justice do you judge *anyone* would prefer?' Rawls expects contractees to choose from the point of view of anyone; in this respect, his account comes closest to Rousseau's notion of collective social will formation. His evident debt to Rousseau notwithstanding, *A Theory of Justice* sketches a 'Kantian Interpretation of Justice as Fairness'. In the 'original position', representatives of persons find themselves behind a 'veil of ignorance' that deprives them of all personal information about themselves, though leaving them with information about their society's general level of socio-economic development. Rawls initially proceeds on the basis of what he calls 'standard economic rationality': he assumes that persons are mutually disinterested rational choosers who prefer more to fewer social primary goods. Like Hobbes, Rawls also assumes risk aversion. Once deprived of personal information about their particular socio-economic standing, representatives in the original position, mindful of the possibility that they may find themselves among the less advantaged, will choose principles designed to maximise the position of the worst off. The principal defence of Rawls' contractual choice is thus based on the assumption of prudential rationality. By contrast, the subsequent sketch of a Kantian interpretation of justice appeals to a notion of *morally* guided choice. Rawls once more alludes to the 'high point of contractarianism as found in Kant and Rousseau' (Rawls 1972: 252) – he now appears to have in mind the moralisation of contractualist prudence through an artificially enforced social point of view:

> The original position must be viewed as a procedural interpretation of Kant's conception of autonomy and the categorical imperative. The principles regulative of the kingdom of ends are those that would be chosen in this position, and the description of this situation enables us to explain the sense in which acting from these principles expresses our nature as free and equal rational persons. (Rawls 1972: 256)

On the Kantian interpretation, rational choice of principles from behind the veil of ignorance simulates Kantian autonomy – the capacity to choose only those principles of justice of which choosers judge that they could be rationally endorsed by anyone. Is the Kantian interpretation of justice as fairness a moral afterthought or is Kantian morality in fact much more deeply ingrained in the very composition of the original choice situation?

Turning to Rawls' published Kant Lectures in his *Lectures on the History of Moral Philosophy* (Rawls 2000) we see an interpretation of *Groundwork*'s categorical imperative that bears a striking resemblance to the decision procedure of the original position in *Theory of Justice*. Rawls once more characterises *Groundwork* as a quintessentially contractualist work. This characterisation is puzzling, given *Groundwork*'s preoccupation with the possibility of good willing. It is hard to see the interpersonal, contractual element within this essentially intrapersonal inquiry into the possibility of a morally good will. Yet Rawls takes the intrapersonal morality of Kantian good willing to have an interpersonal dimension: he assumes that a Kantian act of ethical *self*-legislation is simultaneously an act of universal law-giving – a giving of possible law to *others*. I can here draw attention only briefly to Rawls' exposition of what he calls the 'categorical imperative procedure'. Rawls claims that it constitutes the application of the more general moral law to the particulars of the human situation. The procedure has four stages: the agent's sincere adoption of a particular subjective maxim of action; his generalisation of that maxim as a possible 'precept' for everyone; the 'transformation' of that universal precept into a law of nature; the 'adjoinment' of this newly generated law of nature to the existing laws of nature (Rawls 2000: 168–9). Quoted out of context, these four steps are difficult to make sense of as a reading of *Groundwork II*. But the point here is the relevance of Rawls' reading of *Groundwork* to the decision procedure of *A Theory of Justice*. From that perspective, we can understand the obscure rendering of the categorical imperative as modelling the effects of moral decision-making on 'our social world'. From the perspective of Rawls' Kant Lectures, then, the decision-making procedure described by means of the original position and veil of ignorance in a *Theory of Justice* models a process of morally informed social reform: the reform of a largely unjust social world into a largely just social world by means of individual endorsement of principles of justice which each acknowledges as universally valid in the sense of being adoptable by all.

FROM CONTRACTUALISM TO CONSTRUCTIVISM

I suggested that Rawls' resort to Kant's categorical imperative has contributed to the ethicisation of liberal political morality. One may welcome this.

Why should the move away from Hobbesian prudential self-interest and towards Kantian impartiality not be desirable? The ethicisation of the motivational assumptions that typically inform contractarian choice situations imposes a heavy burden on citizens – one specifically ruled out by Kant in his *Doctrine of Right*. In Rawls, citizens are expected to act in a *conscientiously* impartial manner – they are to act *from* duties of justice, not merely in outward *conformity with* such duties. The later Rawls moves away from a contractualist conception of political morality that seeks to ensure limited and conditional social co-operation towards one that increasingly emphasizes the morally demanding ideal of a social union along the lines, broadly, of Kant's ethical ideal of a 'kingdom of ends'. In retrospect, Rawls' initial characterisation of his method as a higher-level contractualism represents a first step towards constructivism. We saw that, compared to classic social contract theory, Rawlsian contractees need to settle on principles of justice, not just make a binary choice for or against state entrance. Yet *A Theory of Justice* fails to expand on the reasons for this need. Rawls does discuss the difference between perfect and pure procedural justice; he mentions the conflict between equality and freedom and the fact that persons hold divergent conceptions of the good. Overall, however, the emphasis in *A Theory of Justice* is on the exposition and defence of justice as fairness as a substantive theory of social justice. By contrast, Rawls' publications since *A Theory of Justice* overwhelmingly engage with the issue of why the shape and content of principles of justice must themselves be the object of mutual agreement. Rawls' explication of his thesis of value pluralism is crucial to his methodological turn from contractualism towards constructivism. Mature liberal societies are characterised by radical value pluralism – i.e., by individuals' pursuit of divergent and even incommensurable conceptions of the good life. Value pluralism is a natural outcome of liberal toleration born out of the experience of religious wars and the Reformation; value pluralism is not antithetical to liberalism. Nonetheless, radical value pluralism requires renegotiation of an eroded social consensus: it is relative to this task that constructivism enters the picture.

Kantian Constructivism in Moral Theory

Ostensibly, 'Kantian Constructivism' is a mollifying response to the communitarian critique of *A Theory of Justice* (Sandel 1982). The communitarian attack on justice as fairness is an attack on Rawls' Kantianism. Rawls seeks to deflect the charge by clarifying his deeper methodological concerns. He ends up with a highly contextualised form of Kantianism, which he calls 'constructivism'. So what is Kantian constructivism and what motivates it? We know what motivates it: the absence of a social consensus on what counts as an adequate conception of the good life. We must renegotiate the basis of social consensus on alternative terms. The slogan of the 'priority of the right over the good' articulates the parameters of this renegotiation. We cannot simply presume a public comprehensive consensus on the morally good way of life but must seek to build (construct) a partial consensus focused on settling the question of 'right', or justice. Here we can rely on no antecedently assumed truth claims or higher-order moral values: value pluralism includes disagreement on issues of metaphysics. It follows that we must construct consensus on justice from starting points that avoid appeal to metaphysically contentious first principles. Instead of reliance on first principles, we must fall back on historically contingent building blocks, i.e. on values and principles that are latent in our shared social history and culture. One might assume that Kant, the moral metaphysician, would be the least likely partner of construction on those terms. Not so, says Rawls: the 'aprioristic' elements within Kantian moral reasoning have been over-emphasised. Crucial to Rawls' purposes is Kant's point of departure in a conception of practical reasoning rather than theoretical reasoning:

> What justifies a conception of justice is not its being true to an order antecedent and given to us, but its congruence with our deeper understanding of ourselves and our aspirations, and our realization that, given our history and the traditions embedded in our public life, it is the most reasonable doctrine for us. [. . .] Kantian constructivism holds that moral objectivity is to be understood in terms of a suitably constructed social point of view that all can accept. (Rawls 1980: 519)

Unlike rational intuitionism, which departs from antecedently assumed moral truths discoverable by theoretical reason, Kantian constructivism departs from a particular conception of the person as 'an element in a reasonable procedure of construction, the outcome of which determines the content of the first principles of justice' (Rawls 1980: 516). This is the conception of persons as free and equal: each has the capacity to form and pursue his own conception of the good and none wants to do so at the expense of others' ability to pursue their conception of the good. This conception to the person is familiar from *A Theory of Justice*. But Rawls now introduces the distinction between 'rational' and 'full' autonomy. He treats it as of a piece with Kant's distinction between instrumental and moral reasoning. The perceived relation between rational and full autonomy is obscure; however, Rawls suggests that full autonomy both *presupposes* and *constrains* rational autonomy – a formulation that foreshadows *Political Liberalism*'s concern over the 'strains of commitment'. If full autonomy represents the moral point of view as simulated by the veil of ignorance, and if rational autonomy represents persons' natural interest in their pursuit of their own conception of the good, to say that full autonomy presupposes rational autonomy is to say that the terms of morality need to acknowledge individual interests. To say that full autonomy constrains rational autonomy is to say that persons' pursuit of their individual interest must be consonant with the demands of morality. Again, as in *A Theory*, we have the attempted harmonisation of moral and prudential points of view.

According to 'Kantian Constructivism' the original position connects a certain view of the moral person with a corresponding conception of a well-ordered society. The original position mediates between these two conceptions, reconciling individual interests with the constraints of social justice. If we ask, 'what is constructed in Kantian constructivism?' the answer is, 'justice as fairness'. In contrast to *A Theory of Justice*, where representatives of persons choose preferred principles of justice from a specified list of alternative conceptions of justice, 'Kantian Constructivism' portrays erstwhile choosers as 'agents of construction' who renegotiate the basis of social consensus by way of reflecting on those social background conditions that would be most conducive to the pursuit by each of his or her own conception of the good.

From Kantian Constructivism to Political Liberalism

I suggested above that the shift from the contractualism of *A Theory of Justice* to 'Kantian Constructivism' represents an ethicisation of liberal political morality. I also said that the Kantianism of 'Kantian Constructivism' is highly contextualised. The ethicisation is evident in Rawls' introduction of the distinction between rational and full autonomy and in his greater concern to reconcile individuals' aspirations regarding their conception of the good life with the constraints of the social point of view. The 'Kantian Interpretation of Justice as Fairness' in *A Theory* already tells us that acting on the two principles of justice constitutes an 'expression of one's true self' (Rawls 1972: 255); it is to interpret the original position 'from the point of view of our noumenal selves' (Rawls 1972: 255). In 'Kantian Constructivism', we begin with rational autonomy and end with full autonomy: we find ourselves in a social union of sorts.

The contextualist character of Rawls' Kantianism is a function of Rawls' rejection of Kant's formalism. In his Kant Lectures Rawls assumes that the 'categorical imperative procedure' represents the application of abstract moral law to 'the human condition'; the 'categorical imperative procedure' is portrayed as responsive to human beings' 'true needs' (Rawls 2000: 174) – an attribution of particular substantive concerns to Kant's moral philosophy that probably foreshadows Rawls' conception of social primary goods in *A Theory of Justice*. Rawls' remarks on 'true human needs' reflect his acceptance of the Hegelian criticism, that Kant's categorical imperative without substantive content is an empty formalism. This Hegelian thought – mediated by Dewey – feeds into 'Kantian Constructivism'. Rawls emphasises the social nature of our moral learning from each other and the background social conditions, which make such learning possible so as to 'avoid some of the faults that Dewey found in Kant's view' (Rawls 1980: 554).

By the time of *Political Liberalism* (1993), yet more faults have been found with Kant's view. Rawls retreats from the idea of 'full autonomy'. He now concedes that Kantian autonomy depends on a particular metaphysics of the person. As such, Kantian constructivism is insufficiently free-standing. In outlining what he now calls 'political constructivism', Rawls juxtaposes the latter with both rational intuitionism and Kantian constructivism. Rational intuitionism departs from moral first principles and judgements that reflect commitment to 'an independent order of moral values'; it treats moral argument as a species of theoretical reasoning which relies on a 'sparse' conception of the person and a 'traditional' conception of truth or objectivity. Political constructivism shares with Kantian constructivism a commitment to the idea of moral principles as the outcome of a 'procedure of construction'. Both regard moral argument as a species of practical reason; both operate with 'complex' conceptions of the person; both substitute the idea of reasonableness for traditional truth claims. Yet in contrast to political constructivism, Kantian constructivism has a metaphysical conception of the person, given radical value pluralism that conception of personhood is incapable of eliciting general social consent. Secondly, the aims of Kantian constructivism are more ambitious than are those of political constructivism: Kantian constructivism aims at the 'unity of reason' in general, whereas political liberalism seeks merely to arrive at the unity of public reason within an otherwise radically pluralistic social world.

The principal difference between 'Kantian' and 'political' constructivism thus concerns matters of background conception. The constructivist procedure remains unchanged: the original position is still conceived as mediating between a conception of the person and the well-ordered society; the subjects of construction are still relevant principles of justice. Of the original position, Rawls says that it is not constructed but 'simply laid out':

Not everything is constructed; we must have some material, as it were, from which to begin. In a more literal sense, only the substantive principles specifying the content of political right and justice are constructed. The procedure itself is simply laid out using as starting points the basic conceptions of society and person, the principles of practical reason, and the public role of a political conception of justice. (Rawls 1993: 103–4)

When we compare 'Kantian constructivism' and 'political constructivism', the substantive outcome is more or less invariant: it is always endorsement of the two principles of justice as fairness. What varies is the description of relevant background conditions. Does this mean that, whether we start from either Kantian constructivism or political constructivism, the constructivist outcome will be the two principles of justice as fairness? This seems implausible: it seems more plausible to say that Rawls changes his mind about adequate background conditions. Political constructivism is then a corrective upon Kantian constructivism. And yet, in a sense, Rawls wants political constructivism to *encompass* the Kantian conception of the person. Indeed, not just the Kantian conception: the rational intuitionist, too, is to be accommodated. So although neither the Kantian nor the rational intuitionist's respective conceptions can supply the relevant material in 'laying out' the political constructivist's general conception of the person, the principles of justice that are to fall out of the constructivist procedure must be capable of endorsement from the Kantian and from a rational intuitionist perspective as instances of particular conceptions of the good. In contrast to the Kantian constructivist, the political constructivist must thus specify a conception of the person that is sufficiently general to encompass the Kantian and the rational intuitionist conceptions within it. That conception appears to be that of the citizen within a value pluralistic liberal society. Political constructivism operates with a conception of the citizen of mature liberal society as the relevant procedural conception of the person.

Rawls' concern in *Political Liberalism* to ensure an overlapping consensus on common principles of justice yields both a widening and a narrowing in the scope of his constructivist procedure. On the one hand, political constructivism works with a conception of the person that is sufficiently capacious to include a diverse range of privately held comprehensive conceptions of the good. On the other hand, in describing this conception of the person as citizen of a mature liberal society, Rawls falls back on membership criteria that drastically limit who can qualify as a partner in construction. Political constructivism becomes an enterprise strictly for co-citizens. It relies on a conception of public reasoning which, unlike Kant's account of practical reasoning, is indexed to a particular cultural and political context (O'Neill 1998).

CONTRACTUALIST CONSTRUCTIVISM: RAWLS
AND KANT

In the above, I have sketched Rawls' move from his higher-order contractualism to Kantian and then political constructivism in broad-brush strokes. My principal substantive claim has been that Rawls' contractualist constructivism aims at the renegotiation of a limited social consensus under conditions of radical value pluralism. Rawls' acknowledgement of the limits of a feasible social consensus under those conditions is modest and realistic. Yet in the course of his philosophical endeavour to secure limited consensus Rawls becomes ever more ambitious morally. Social consensus on principles of justice as fairness must be whole-hearted, not grudging and backed by the power of the sword as in Hobbes. The idea of a social union seems incongruous in the context of a political diagnosis that simultaneously emphasises radical value pluralism. Why this obsession with citizens' inner endorsement of the social point of view? As noted, it is Rousseau who springs to mind – and yet Rawls' use of Kant's ethics in the political context has ensured a close association in current philosophical perceptions between the Kantian kingdom of ends as an ethical ideal and the Rawlsian social union as a political ideal (Korsgaard 1996, Reath 2006, Flikschuh 2010).

Methodologically, too, Rawls' characterisation of his higher-order contractualism as a form of Kantianism has ensured a widespread general presumption towards constructivism as a distinctly Kantian method of philosophical justification. It is as if the constructivist method, which Rawls develops out of his interpretation of what he calls the categorical imperative procedure, were read back into Kant's position. Of course, there are Kantian elements in Rawls' constructivism: Kantian and Rawlsian philosophical justification share the avoidance of foundationalism and both assume the distinctness of practical reason from theoretical reason. Yet it is hard to think of Kant as mediating between a particular conception of the person and some specified social or ethical ideal. It is also hard to see Kant's ethical writings as fundamentally concerned with 'finding solutions to practical problems' (Korsgaard 2008). Kant's is a much more open-ended inquiry into the presuppositional grounds of humans' empirically evident capacity for morality: it seems forced to construe his as a *problem-solving* concern.

Kantian or otherwise, is constructivism a method of philosophical justification that could in principle be separated from Rawls' particular substantive concerns? Rawls himself makes no sustained claims to this effect. Nor did social contract thinkers think of the social contract as a general method of normative justification. Rawls-inspired constructivists often claim more general validity for constructivism as a method of normative justification (Milo 1995). At the same time, it remains genuinely difficult to specify what gets constructed from what in the constructivist procedure. We saw that the supposedly constructed fall-out of the Rawlsian procedure – his two principles of justice as fairness – remains remarkably constant throughout: what is constantly re-conceived is the 'material' used to 'lay out' the decision procedure itself. Oddly, the non-constructed elements in Rawls' procedure are the most often re-constructed: the question that seems to drive Rawls is less, 'what principles would the philosophical negotiation between a particular conception of the person and a particular conception of society yield?' but more, 'what conception of the person and of the well-ordered society is needed to yield principles of justice as fairness?' In that sense, Rawls' political constructivism continues to share social contract theories' limited concern: social contract theorists never doubted that the state was morally necessary – they just needed to find the right kind of description to convince others of this fact. Rawls too never doubts that the two principles of justice as fairness fit the mature liberal societies – he just needs to find the right kind of description to convince others of this fact.

BIBLIOGRAPHY

An asterisk denotes secondary literature especially suitable for further reading.

Dworkin, Ronald, 1975, 'The Original Position', in Norman Daniels (ed.), *Reading Rawls. Critical Studies of A Theory of Justice*, Oxford: Basil Blackwell, pp. 16–52.
Freeman, Samuel, 1990, 'Reason and Agreement in Social Contract Views', *Philosophy and Public Affairs* 19, 12–57.*
Korsgaard, Christine, 1996, *Creating the Kingdom of Ends*, Cambridge University Press.
Korsgaard, Christine, 2008, 'Realism and Constructivism in Twentieth Century Moral Philosophy', in her *The Constitution of Moral Agency*, Oxford University Press, pp. 302–26.
Milo, Ronald, 1995, 'Contractarian Constructivism', *Journal of Philosophy* 122, 181–204.*
O'Neill, Onora, 1989, *Constructions of Reason. Exploring Kant's Practical Philosophy*, Cambridge University Press.
O'Neill, Onora, 1998, 'Political Liberalism and Public Reason: A Critical Notice of John Rawls, *Political Liberalism*', *Philosophical Review* 106, 411–28.*
O'Neill, Onora, 2000, 'Kant's Justice and Kantian Justice', in her *Bounds of Justice*, Cambridge University Press.
Rawls, John, 1972, *A Theory of Justice*, Oxford University Press.
Rawls, John, 1980, 'Kantian Constructivism in Moral Theory: The Dewey Lectures 1980', *Journal of Philosophy* 77, 515–72.
Rawls, John, 1993, *Political Liberalism*, New York: Columbia University Press.

Rawls, John, 2000, *Lectures on the History of Moral Philosophy* (edited by Barbara Herman), Cambridge, MA: Harvard University Press.

Reath, Andrews, 2006, 'Legislating for a Realm of Ends: The Social Dimension of Autonomy', in his *Agency and Autonomy in Kant's Moral Theory*, Oxford University Press, pp. 173–92.

Sandel, Michael, 1982, *Liberalism and the Limits of Justice*, Cambridge University Press.

Index

CPSIA information can be obtained
at www.ICGtesting.com
Printed in the USA
BVHW052107070223
658071BV00011B/194